Case Histories
in International Politics

CASE HISTORIES
· · · · IN · · · ·
INTERNATIONAL
POLITICS

Kendall W. Stiles

Loyola University of Chicago

■ HarperCollins*CollegePublishers*

Acquisitions Editor: Leo A. W. Wiegman
Project Coordination: Ruttle, Shaw & Wetherill, Inc.
Text and Cover Design: Nancy Sabato
Map and Figure Design: Vantage Art, Inc.
Electronic Production Manager: Valerie A. Sawyer
Manufacturing Manager: Helene G. Landers
Electronic Page Makeup: RR Donnelley Barbados
Printer and Binder: RR Donnelley & Sons Company
Cover Printer: RR Donnelley & Sons Company

For permission to use copyrighted material, grateful acknowledgment is
made to the copyright holders on page 427, which is hereby made part of
this copyright page.

Case Histories in International Politics

Library of Congress Cataloging-in-Publication Data

Stiles, Kendall W.
    Case histories in international politics/Kendall Stiles.
        p. cm.
    Includes index.
    ISBN 0-06-501415-4
    1. World politics—1945—Case studies. 2. World politics—20th
century—Case studies. I. Title.
D843.S85 1995
327'.09'04—dc20   94-4750
                                                     CIP

98 99 00 01 02   9 8 7 6 5 4

CONTENTS

LIST OF MAPS

PREFACE

This text has a threefold purpose. First, it aims at providing important historical background to students of current events and international relations theory. Second, it will serve as a useful reference for teachers and students alike—particularly for those writing their first term paper. Finally, this book will make it easier for teachers to quickly incorporate case study teaching into their existing introductory international relations curriculum.

While we would like to think, as teachers, that our students are assiduously reading several major newspapers on a daily basis, and picking up reference books to fill in gaps, we all know this does not happen routinely. Students desperately need quick exposure to key developments in world history in order to begin to grasp the significance of the most basic concepts in the field of international relations. The cases in this text were chosen for their significance as watershed events and phenomena, a study of which should place any student in good stead to later on absorb more abstract theoretical material. In addition, the cases were chosen because they illustrate a particular concept in a particularly powerful way. The instructor will find the text organization "fits" a typical text outline, moving as it does through international relations concepts in order of complexity, and should mesh easily with most instructors' existing syllabi. Below is a more purely chronological outline for those who follow this approach. Instructors may find it more useful to simply rearrange the cases to suit themselves (for example, a segment on the Middle East can be nicely supplemented with cases 10, 18, 19, and 20, with additional insights in cases 3, 7, and 11.).

RECOMMENDED HISTORICAL SEQUENCING OF CASES

pre–1960	1	2	13	3						
1960–1973	4	14	20	11	6	8				
1973–1989	21	12	5	19	23	15	22	7	18	26	24
1989+	25	10	16	17	9					

The second purpose of the book, to serve as a ready reference for future study, is facilitated by a thorough index, a number of chronologies sprinkled through the cases, and an ample bibliography at the end of each case. Students' paper assignments might be tailor-made to take advantage of these resources. Faculty will find it convenient to have facts, figures and characters clearly presented for future reference as well.

Finally, the text presents historical cases in such a way that they can be incorporated into class discussion. Dilemmas, decisions, and problems facing policymakers and individuals are presented in order to prompt empathy and introspection on the part of the students. Specific questions are added to prompt discussion if all else fails. Instructors are encouraged to use these cases creatively, modeling on the Harvard Business School and Georgetown-based Pew case studies program, including perhaps simulations, writing assignments, and group projects centered on the text material.

In writing this text, I have received considerable help from colleagues Marc Simon and Roger Anderson, officials with Georgetown's Pew program, students of POLS 172 at Bowling Green State University and PLSC 257 at Loyola University Chicago, as well as direction from Lauren Silverman, Maria Hartwell, and Leo Wiegman at HarperCollins and numerous anonymous reviewers. Of course, I accept full responsibility for the contents of this text and I dedicate it to Kristen, Penelope, Renee, Alexander, and Christina, in the hope that they will watch and learn as history unfolds around them.

Kendall W. Stiles

PART

I

GREAT POWER
RELATIONS

German Nationalism

The nation-state is broadly assumed to be the central actor of international affairs. The nation-state is the conjunction of the legal unit known as the state and a societal grouping known as the nation. Where these come together in a coherent whole, one finds fulfilled the dream of self-determination. Creating a nation-state has therefore been the ambition of every nationalist. In reality, less than a quarter of the UN's members (Norway, Mexico, Iceland) fit this description, which explains why so many ethnic and national groups are dissatisfied.

Since the beginning of the eighteenth century, much blood has been spilt and many words have been written on the question of the status of Germany. Two world wars, a Holocaust, and a forty-five-year Cold War grew from recent attempts to impose a solution to the so-called "German Question." Germany's reunification in 1990 has left many observers wondering whether the issue has been resolved.

Germany exemplifies the problems inherent in the development of many nation-states. First, it is difficult to identify with any degree of exactness who is and who is not German. Over the years, language has been the most obvious common link. But the German language is shared by many people with different national loyalties. German-speaking Swiss have not felt any yearning to join any German federations, and speakers of Dutch or the Scandinavian languages, all Germanic, certainly do not consider themselves "German." To a certain extent, a person who calls himself German is, by definition, German. Bismarck saw Germans in geostrategic terms, in that he sought to annex territory that would increase Prussia's power. Hitler attempted to define Germans in racial terms, with horrific consequences. More recently, Germans have been forced to decide whether forty years of division has given those living under communism in East Germany a new identity and culture which makes them inherently different from capitalist West Germans.

Second, Germany shows how difficult it can be to determine what form of political organization a nation can or should have. From the very loose federation of princes of the Holy Roman Empire to the sprawling totalitarian monstrosity of Hitler's Third Reich to the modern Federal Republic, Germans have experimented with the gamut of political structures. The record shows that the formation of a federal, democratic, united Germany in October 1990 was far from inevitable, and may prove temporary.

Finally, Germany illustrates how national sovereignty is very much a problem that lies in other nations' hands. No nation has come into being without the consent of its international neighbors. Sovereignty is a privilege rather than an inherent right, and it must be granted by the existing community of states. This community's treatment of Germany over the years has been schizophrenic, to say the least. The same countries which hailed Germany's unification in 1871 and 1990 took part in its division in 1918 and 1945.

In this case study, we will first present an overview of the development of Germany in modern times. Then we will look at these three issues—national identity, government structure, and international reactions—in succession.

OVERVIEW OF GERMAN HISTORY

For centuries after the collapse of the Roman Empire, a large number of German-speaking princes and kings ruled domains in central Europe. They attempted to join into a federation at various junctures, and were known collectively as the Holy Roman Empire. This "empire" lasted until the Renaissance period when the nation-state emerged as an actor on the European stage. By the end of the eighteenth century, Prussia and Austria were the most powerful German-speaking kingdoms in central Europe (see Map 1.1).

Little thought had been given to a united, German-speaking nation until the invasion of Napoleon's armies (1796–1815) forced German states to have a collective response. After periods of neutrality, subjugation, and even alliance, German states joined to help defeat Napoleon. The Congress of Vienna awarded Austria and Prussia with new territory and created the Germanic Confederation—an international German organization complete with a parliamentary council of kings and princes (the Diet). Prussia stepped in to dominate the Diet and convinced German states in the north to join in a trade pact, or Zollverein. This promoted industrialization and economic growth during the nineteenth century, as well as a sense of political unity.

German national aspirations were expressed most forcefully in the democratic revolution of 1848. Inspired by attempts at democracy throughout Europe, German nationalists assembled in Frankfurt and Berlin demanded not only free elections and a parliament, but also began writing the constitution of a united German state. The conference foundered on the question of Austria's role, and there was strong disagreement on the nature of Germany's future government. Austria rejected the proposal to include only its German-speaking territories, since it wanted a dominant voice. Republicans, Marxists, and monarchists failed to find a suitable leader to champion their cause. Within months, the delegates' enthusiasm dissipated and the conference disbanded in failure, but not without securing reforms from Prussia's monarchy, including the creation of Germany's first popularly elected parliament, the Reichstag.

In 1862, Otto von Bismarck emerged as the dominant political voice in Prussia and set about to achieve Germanic unity through more traditional means. He had already concluded that the scattered and small German states were ripe for military conquest. As Bismarck put it: "Not by speeches and majority votes are the great questions of the day decided—that was the mistake of 1848 and 1849—but by blood and iron." Prussia first allied with Austria to seize territories claimed by Denmark, then in 1866 decisively defeated Austria's army, thereby securing complete Prussian control of northern German provinces. France, an uneasy bystander to this display of Prussian military prowess, found itself in a diplomatic wrangle with Prussia over the question of Spanish royal succession. The spat spilled over into war and in 1870 Prussia soundly defeated France's ill-prepared army, thereby allowing the German princes to proclaim the unification of the German Reich and to pledge their loyalty to Prussian ruler William I.

For the next twenty years, Bismarck reassured his European rivals that Germany was "sated" and had no further territorial ambitions. By 1890, the new kaiser, William II, was eager to make Germany a global power, however. After Bismarck's retirement, William II dramatically expanded the German navy and army and undertook imperial conquests in Africa. About 1900, liberal German nationalists cooperated with authoritarian romanticists and began to stir up xenophobic and chauvinistic feelings. (Note that these attitudes were prevalent throughout Europe at the time. See Hildebrand 1989, 236.) Germany, along with the rest of Europe, prepared diligently for a war which by 1910 seemed inevitable. She formed an alliance with Austria-Hungary against France and Russia and developed a strict plan for mobilization and deployment of troops against France.

The assassination of Austrian Archduke Ferdinand in Sarajevo in the summer of 1914 precipitated a chain of events over which political leaders seem to have had little control (see especially Tuchman 1962). By August, all of Europe was embroiled in a war that would prove the deadliest in history. The result was a bloody three-year stalemate ultimately broken by the Russian Revolution and the entry of the United States in the war in 1917. In October 1918, the kaiser was ousted in a democratic revolution, and Germany capitulated. The Treaty of Versailles severely punished Germany, leaving the blame for war on its doorstep. Germany's war machine was dismantled, the Bundesbank was required to pay heavy reparations, and portions of German territory were either carved up or occupied.

Europeans welcomed a new democratic federal government that was established at Weimar, with the Social Democratic party—a center-left party which favored social reform—at the helm. However, almost as soon as German nationalists learned of the humiliating treaty terms, conservative and fascist parties sprang up in Germany, including Adolf Hitler's fledgling National Socialist (Nazi) party in Bavaria. A traditional nationalist party—the Volkspartei—was created by former imperial supporters and became part of the ruling coalition government in the mid-1920s. The German economy, saddled with war reparations and heavy reconstruction costs, stagnated during the 1920s, and the Wall Street crash plunged it into deep depression in 1929. Radical parties on the right and the left flourished while none of the mainstream parties could solve the crisis. Violence in the streets spread as unemployment reached new highs. For several years the politicians in the Reichstag failed to organize a stable government and between 1930 and 1933 more and more Germans became disenchanted with democracy. In January 1933, figurehead President Paul von Hindenburg reluctantly asked the leader of the now-powerful Nazi party to join the Volkspartei in a coalition with Hitler as the nominal chancellor. Hitler immediately demanded of the Reichstag the power to rule by decree, which was granted out of desperation in March.

Hitler's dictatorship in Germany is well-known. Suffice it here to say that he applied his extreme conception of German nationalism in the eradication not only of Jews, Gypsies, and other minorities, but also of any Germans deemed inferior (viz., the handicapped and mentally ill). He imported Aryan bloodstock and attempted to build a race of supermen capable of controlling the world. Even his highest generals were shocked at the extent of his ambitions. Several attempts were made on his life, and during the mid-1930s, his ruthless government forced scores of Germany's scientists and artists to flee persecution.

Hitler methodically acted to reverse the most objectionable aspects of the Treaty of Versailles by rebuilding Germany's military, regaining control over lost territory, and refusing to pay war reparations. These actions, though illegal, met with little international resistance because British and French officials surmised that it might be wiser to grant Hitler what he demanded in the hopes that he could be sated, as was Bismarck. This effort to avoid confrontation by accommodating Hitler was called "appeasement."

Hitler further demanded the incorporation of all German-speaking peoples into the Third Reich—a policy which was at first glance consistent with the general goal of self-determination, but which would have resulted in a lopsided advantage for Germany in comparison to other continental powers. Hitler pressed his claims in Austria and Czechoslovakia, in particular. When Austria threatened to become an autonomous (rather than subservient) authoritarian state in early 1938, Hitler invaded and put his political allies in power. In Czechoslovakia, demands for autonomy by German-speaking Sudetens were rejected by Czech central authorities. Hitler mobilized his troops in preparation for an apparent invasion, prompting Neville Chamberlain of Britain to agree to Hitler's demands for Sudeten autonomy at a conference in Munich.

Hitler's racism justified in 1939 the invasion and annexation of non-German areas of Poland, Scandinavia, and much of Eastern Europe on the grounds that the German people required far more space in order to flourish. In 1941, it became clear that this so-called "Lebensraum" knew no limit as Hitler declared war on the Americans and Soviets. By 1942, Hitler had achieved dominance in all of Europe except Britain, and all of North Africa except for Egypt. Hitler's fortunes changed in the snows around Stalingrad in 1943. By 1944, with Axis armies in full retreat, Allied nations were planning postwar Europe. Perhaps the most important move made by Joseph Stalin, Winston Churchill, and Franklin Roosevelt was the decision at Yalta to permit two vast spheres of influence in Europe, roughly equivalent to the regions liberated by the Soviet armies in the East and the American and British and French armies in the West. Germany itself would be temporarily divided and administered by the two groups. With the end of the war in May 1945, Germany lost its independence and became a divided nation.

After Germany's capitulation, each occupying power began to apply its very different philosophies to governing the areas under their jurisdiction. The Soviets dismantled German industrial equipment and transported it to the Soviet Union as payment of war reparations. British and American occupiers began laying the groundwork for a liberal and independent democracy. By 1949, West Germany had a constitution (Basic Law) which promoted liberal democratic principles and human rights, while Communists in East Germany declared the nation a socialist state and outlawed rival parties. By 1950, both nations had become fully committed to the political goals of their sponsors.

Konrad Adenauer emerged as the leader of the Christian Democratic–led coalition government in 1949 and advocated a firm anti-Communist policy. Under Adenauer, the Federal Republic of Germany (FRG) (its official name) withheld diplomatic recognition of the German Democratic Republic (GDR)—East Germany—on the grounds that the division was illegitimate (the "Hallstein doctrine") and that Germans everywhere had a right to citizenship in the West (a policy which attracted many immigrants from East Germany from 1949 to 1961 and then again in the late 1980s). He brought West Germany into the North Atlantic Treaty Organization (NATO) and the European Community and made his country a model Western state. By the end of his chancellorship in the early 1960s, the Federal Republic was more prosperous and solidly democratic than nearly all its European neighbors.

Soviet officials were determined to make a prosperous socialist state of the Democratic Republic. Unfortunately, the rapid success of the West far exceeded the significant gains of the East, and its citizens could not resist the temptation to migrate. At two different junctures—1948 and 1953—Soviet and East German officials intervened with force to prevent the exodus, which by August 1961 had taken one out of six East Germans. The divided city of Berlin was an especially troublesome question, since many used it as an open doorway to the West. Finally, the decision was made not only to outlaw emigration, but to construct a physical barrier of wire and stone to the outside. The Berlin Wall—which encircled the western half of the city— long stood as a symbol of socialism's failure.

With the emigration problem solved, the Socialist Unity party government gradually responded to East Germans' demands for a higher standard of living. Soon, the GDR grew at remarkable rates and did in fact become the model of socialism, complete with heavy industry, guaranteed employment, cradle-to-grave security, and relatively high incomes. By the end of the 1960s, Ulbricht began to boast that the GDR's socialist industrialization was superior to the Soviet policies at home. He also criticized the Soviet foreign policy of détente (or relaxation of tensions) with the West. In 1971, he was ousted by Soviet-sponsored conspirators and replaced by Erich Honecker.

The political scene in the Federal Republic went into a period of flux after Adenauer's resignation until the Social-Democratic party of Germany (SPD) won elections in 1969 and organized a coalition government with Willy Brand as chancellor. Brand immediately initiated a series of actions aimed at improving relations with the East. In particular, he signed a new "Basic Treaty" with prodétente Honecker which reversed the Hallstein doctrine and extended diplomatic recognition. His opponents at home deplored the abandonment of the goal of unification, but applauded the reduction of Cold War tensions. Each Germany was permitted to fill a seat in the United Nations for the first time in 1973.

With this newfound recognition, both German governments began to move in a more independent political direction. West Germans were ambivalent about their role on the front line of the Cold War and largely rejected the renewal of tensions during the first Reagan term. Both Schmidt and later Helmut Kohl found it difficult to accommodate both public opinion and NATO demands. Likewise, East German officials found more to gain from working with the West Germans than with the Soviets in the early 1980s. Honecker attempted to instill in the Germans of the GDR a distinct "East German nationalism" that would discourage emigration by building pride in socialism. During this period, both Germanies signed a variety of treaties pledging economic and political cooperation. Both government leaders and opposition parties formulated joint statements concerning cooperation and the need for détente between the superpowers. The 1987 U.S.-Soviet Intermediate-range Nuclear Forces Treaty and the talks on reducing conventional forces in Europe were strongly supported by both the FGR and the GDR.

This much was already in place when, with the tacit approval of Mikhail Gorbachev in Moscow, all of Eastern Europe abandoned first strict emigration policies and then Communist control in 1989. What began as a small crack in the Iron Curtain at the Austria/Hungary border grew to a huge breach as East Europeans traveled West. From August to October, East German leaders faced increasingly militant crowds demanding free emigration and the dismantling of the Berlin Wall. Gorbachev, on October 7, suggested to Honecker that "life itself punishes those who delay" responding to historical forces, and Kohl promised substantial economic aid in exchange for free elections ("A Chronology of Events," 1990, 195). Finally, after a record-setting crowd of 500,000 demonstrated in East Berlin on November 8, Honecker opened the border to the West the next day. East Germany quickly experienced its first democratic elections, followed by diplomatic negotiations on a reunification timetable, and concluded by formal unification and relinquishing of Allied powers on October 3, 1990. Germany has occupied a single seat in the United Nations since 1991.

THE "GERMAN NATION"

Is German nationalism as coherent and aggressive as many outsiders believe? Recent studies indicate that it is a much more fragmented and limited phenomenon than many have claimed. In particular, it is important to understand that there exist three different nationalist forces in Germany, and that they rarely work as a united movement (Hughes 1988).

Since the early nineteenth century, many German intellectuals have yearned to create a country that would encompass all German speakers. As put in a famous poem by Ernst Moritz Arndt (1769–1860), typical of romantic German nationalism:

> What is the German's fatherland?
> Come, name for me this mighty land!
> As far as the German tongue resounds
> And from God in heaven song abounds:
> There it must be!
> That, noble German, belongs to thee!
> (Grass 1990, 77)

Romantic nationalists yearn for a German "Golden Age"—a mythical period roughly equivalent to the reign of Frederick the Great in Prussia (1740–86). Bismarck and William I made frequent references to this period in their efforts to garner public support for wars against Denmark, Austria, and France. Since World War I, romantic nationalists have continued to support a traditional, militaristic Germany based on Prussian traditions of hard work, discipline, and loyalty to the state. Contemporary Christian Democrats tend to lean in this general direction, and although Helmut Kohl's reunification of Germany was done in the name of democracy, traditionalists strongly endorsed the move. The recent ceremonial reburial of Frederick the Great in the former GDR exemplifies the symbolic activities of traditionalists today.

In southern Germany—Bavaria in particular—and among lower classes, nationalism has taken a more simple, xenophobic tone. Rather than taking pride in the real or imagined glory of a past Germany, xenophobes emphasize the dangers and threats of Germany's enemies. Xenophobia refers to the fear and loathing of things "foreign." In the years leading up to World War

I, William II exploited these sentiments in an effort to galvanize support for the coming war effort (Carr 1987). Hitler's philosophy stressed fear of aliens (Jews in particular), and mobilized violent demonstrations and murders of Jews called "pogroms." Today, neo-Nazi groups in Germany, organized as the Republican party, are looked upon as a nuisance, an embarrassment, and an ill omen. Since the reunification of Germany, Republican activities have increased and they have been joined in the political fight by new reactionary parties.

A third form of German nationalism has been a liberal democratic idealism based on Immanuel Kant and other Enlightenment philosophers. This philosophy led the 1848 revolution and dominated the Weimar Republic. The SPD and many German intellectuals have seen Germany as part of a wider Western culture, rather than as a separate entity following a "special path" (*Sonderweg*) (Hildebrand 1989, chap. 10). Modern German attachment to the European Community institutions and participation in the international economic system is consistent with this approach, although conservative German politicians have not always embraced the participatory democracy promoted by liberal nationalists.

At any given point in Germany's history, a mixture of these tendencies has resulted in a special form of behavior. Bismarck eagerly manipulated the mass media to intensify Germans' xenophobia in order to pursue traditional goals of the Prussian elite (Hughes 1988, 118). Hitler likewise combined xenophobia and traditionalism after the failure of the liberalism of the Weimar Republic. Hitler was unique, however, in his extreme emphasis on racist explanations of German superiority (Kershaw 1985). Certainly his crude and ruthless genetic engineering and genocide are looked upon with shame by everyday Germans today.

Many worry that German nationalism will reemerge as a destructive force (Bertram 1990). In order for this to happen, German democracy would need to be replaced by a more authoritarian structure, given the many checks on central authority and the strong popular commitment to a peaceful foreign policy in Germany today. Although the despair and resentment following the reunification of Germany has caused many in the former GDR to oppose the Kohl administration, there is little indication that even the most dissatisfied people want a return to authoritarianism of any shape. Flag-waving, saluting, jingoism, and attacks on foreigners, while practiced by a few, are far from the ordinary German's mind.

Some have wondered whether the official recognition of Polish control over formally German territory will resolve the desires of some to unite with their homelands. Some 15 million German speakers left Poland and other East European nations after World War II, although they still consider those regions home. On this subject, Kohl said:

> The truth is—and this should not be suppressed on a day such as this: the expulsion of the Germans from their native regions was a grave injustice. There was no justification, either moral or legal. Nor can we say decades later that it was legitimate . . . {Nonetheless} we . . . forego revenge and reprisal. This is our seri-

ous and heartfelt resolve in remembrance of the untold suffering that the past
. . . has inflicted on mankind. (Bundestag speech, June 21, 1990)

Such assurances are comforting, but it is also true that at least for another generation some people in Germany will long for their home across
the border (see Map 1.1).

THE GERMAN STATE

The German state has changed dramatically over the years both in dimension and governing arrangements (Table 1.1). As illustrated by the map and
table, the size of the German state spread from a loose confederation in the
early nineteenth century to a large empire covering much of central Europe.
At its zenith in 1942, German authority extended over all of Europe and
Scandinavia (excluding Britain, Italy, and the Balkans) and large parts of
Africa and the Soviet Union—territory which obviously extended far beyond those inhabited by German speakers. At the end of the war, Germany
had lost all political autonomy and was controlled by its occupiers. To a
large extent, Germany's borders have been decided by non-Germans. German unification in 1990 represents the first time the German people as a
whole were permitted a voice in determining their country's borders.

In addition to changing the country's territorial dimensions, German
governments have dramatically altered the regime style over the years.
These changes correlate with the three forms of nationalism discussed previously. In addition, the question of concentration of power in the center h~e
varied over the years.

The first unification of the German nation in 1871 was, as explained by
Carr, "the uneasy compromise between the forces of conservative federalism, the liberal unitary principle and the military might of Prussia. . . . The
Empire did not emanate from the will of the people" (Carr 1987, 119). It was
not until the Weimar Republic that the principle of popular sovereignty was
officially enshrined in the 1919 Constitution. In spite of liberals' attachment
to centralized democracy, the Laender retained much of their traditional authority over education, social policy, police, and church activity. The retention of the official title "Reich" acknowledged the tradition of centuries and
the desire on the part of the German people for national unity that are
bound up with the name Reich.

Hitler's concentration of power in Berlin is an exception to the tradition
of federalism in Germany, although the GDR's administrative structure
showed some similarities. As put in a recent government publication, "Germany always had a decentralized structure until its catastrophic experience
with centralism in the form of the National Socialist dictatorship from 1933
to 1945. The delegation of political authority to the regions is part of the
legacy of German constitutional history" (Reuter 1991, 1). What the article
omits is the tension between federal pressures rooted in traditional notions
of the sovereignty of principalities and duchies that made up the Reich, and

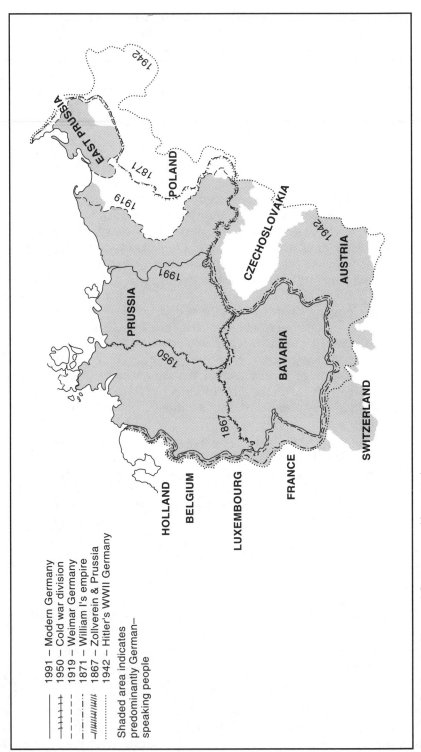

Key:
1991 – Modern Germany
1950 – Cold war division
1919 – Weimar Germany
1871 – William I's empire
1867 – Zollverein & Prussia
1942 – Hitler's WWII Germany

Shaded area indicates predominantly German–speaking people

Map 1.1 German territory and German-speaking peoples.
Source: William Carr, *A History of Germany, 1815–1985* (London: Edward Arnold, 1987).

It is interesting to note that although the Treaty of Versailles lays the blame for the war squarely on Germany's shoulders, several interesting alternatives have been offered. In particular, Tuchman (1962) argues that the war was essentially preventable, in that unwise and impetuous leaders blundered into conflict by allowing minor incidents to escalate into major crises. In a sense, Tuchman would blame all the European leaders collectively. On the other hand, Choucri and North (1975) present a statistical case for the argument that the war was inevitable and without villains because the long-term economic and demographic forces at work were beyond anyone's control. With so much growth and so few new outlets, confrontation was inevitable.

Containment of Germany was bought at a frightening price, and the formation of the League of Nations was motivated largely as an alternative to war. The Treaty of Versailles was punitive, but was quickly reinterpreted. At the Locarno Conference of 1925, Britain and France made it clear that Germany would be welcomed back as a full European power. French Prime Minister Aristide Briand and Britain's Chamberlain went out of their way in the late 1920s to accommodate Germany's legitimate demands and attempt to form economic and political ties that would bind Germany to the rest of Europe.

To a large extent, diplomacy succeeded, in that until Hitler arrived, German behavior was largely consistent with larger European goals. The Great Depression, the onslaught of fascism, and the militarism of Hitler obviously reversed this trend. However, rather than reacting forcefully, British and French officials maintained their accommodating stance vis-à-vis new, more daring, German demands. The remilitarization of the Saar, the renunciation of postwar reparations, the dramatic increase in military capability (German military spending nearly doubled each year between 1934 and 1939), and the annexation of Austria were met with little resistance. Not until Hitler attempted to annex the Sudetenland by force did Britain and France present forceful opposition. The Munich Conference was considered a major diplomatic achievement at the time, although Chamberlain quickly regretted his approval of Sudeten annexation. The invasion of Poland was the last straw and the war began—although somewhat hesitantly after Warsaw's fall. It took several months before Germany's armies directly confronted Allied forces, meeting little resistance.

Were British and French officials wrong to grant Hitler's government the retraction of certain objectionable features of the Versailles Treaty? One may perhaps question their motives—were they driven by fear of confrontation or did they seek greater respect for human rights? What started out as a sincere desire to integrate Germany in a new Europe (French officials already envisioned a version of the Common Market including Germany) became a desire to avoid war at all costs. This delay naturally provided Hitler time to build up Germany's war-fighting capability.

After the war, the Allied powers attempted to solve the German Question through partition and continued occupation. Integration of East and

West Germany into the alliance systems of the Soviet Union and United States was aimed not only at offsetting the power of the superpower rival, but also at keeping German power in check. The strategy worked for forty-five years, although at the expense of German freedom and self-determination. Where nineteenth-century Europeans generally favored German unification at the expense of European stability (perhaps unintentionally), the superpowers did not hesitate to sacrifice German integrity for the sake of the balance of power.

Germany's reunification was to a large extent a diplomatic achievement. As put by Kaiser, "German unification, brought about by a multitude of bilateral and multilateral negotiations and arrangements, represents one of the greatest triumphs of leadership and diplomatic professionalism in the postwar period" (Kaiser 1990/91, 179). George Bush quickly endorsed early proposals for unification by Helmut Kohl, although France and the Soviet Union expressed reservations. Events were propelled by the strong East German demands for reunification, and within three months of the Berlin Wall's collapse, the two Germanies had agreed on a diplomatic process to end partition in cooperation with the four World War II powers. The so-called "two-plus-four" talks centered on whether the Soviet proposals for German neutrality (or dual alliance membership) would be met, and what to do about foreign forces based in Germany. The solution arrived at ultimately granted the new Germany full sovereign rights to join whatever alliance it chose, but Germany agreed to a gradual repatriation of Soviet military located in the former GDR.

Thus far, the various approaches to the German Question—diplomacy, war, and partition—have failed to satisfy both the demands of the German people and the security needs of Germany's neighbors. Perhaps a strong, democratic, united Germany—which is tied inextricably to the world economy and European security arrangements—offers the best hope of achieving these otherwise irreconcilable objectives.

Questions to Consider

1. Germany's reunification obviously presents new problems—not only those internal to Germany, but also international. Will Germany's economy so dominate Europe that it will cause resentment and hostility?

2. Will a united Germany rediscover its chauvinistic past and begin to make new demands on its neighbors? Will a strengthened Germany remain loyal to Western security objectives, or will it chart a new foreign policy path?

3. How will Germany resolve its immigration problem? Will it continue to impose new restrictions? How will Germany deal with increasing discontent and unemployment in the East? Will a social revolution be the outcome?

References

Christoph Bertram. "The German Question." *Foreign Affairs* 69 #2 (Spring 1990): 45–62.

William Carr. *A History of Germany, 1815–1985* (London: Edward Arnold, 1987).

Nazli Choucri and Robert North. *Conflict Among Nations* (New York: W. H. Freeman, 1975).

"A Chronology of Events." *World Affairs* 152 #4 (Spring 1990): 195–197.

Carole Fink, Isabel Huill, and MacGregor Knox, eds. *German Nationalism and the European Response, 1890–1945* (Norman: University of Oklahoma Press, 1985).

Gunter Grass. *Two States—One Nation?* Trans. by Krishna Winston (New York: Harcourt Brace Jovanovich, 1990).

Klaus Hildebrand. *German Foreign Policy from Bismarck to Adenauer*. Trans. by Louise Willmot (London: Unwin Hyman, 1989).

Michael Hughes. *Nationalism and Society: Germany 1800–1945* (London: Edward Arnold, 1988).

Karl Kaiser. "Germany's Unification." *Foreign Affairs* 70 #1 (1990/91): 179–205.

Paul Kennedy. *The Rise and Fall of the Great Powers* (New York: Random House, 1987).

I. Kershaw. *The Nazi Dictatorship: Problems and Perspectives* (London: E. Arnold, 1985).

Thomas Kielinger. "Waking Up in the New Europe—With a Headache." *International Affairs* 66 #2 (April 1990): 249–263.

G. L. Mosse. *Masses and Man: Nationalist and Fascist Perceptions of Reality* (New York: H. Fertig, 1980).

Konrad Reuter. "Sixteen States, One Country: The Political Structure of the Federal Republic of Germany." *Inter Nationes*, Special Report (1991 manuscript).

Barbara Tuchman. *The Guns of August* (New York: Macmillan, 1962).

Henry Ashby Turner, Jr. *The Two Germanies Since 1945* (New Haven: Yale University Press, 1987).

Pearl Harbor

Intelligence is a word pregnant with intrigue and mystery. In fact, intelligence, as used in government circles, simply means the gathering and analysis of information on foreign policy problems. The vast majority of intelligence is gathered and analyzed the same way research papers are written—by informed observers using public documents. Some more unusual sources of intelligence include spying, electronic surveillance, and satellite reconnaissance. As technology has advanced, the significance of electronic information gathering has increased, typically at the expense of traditional spying. The case of Pearl Harbor shows what can happen when you rely too heavily on one particular type of information.

PROLOGUE

In the predawn hours of Sunday, December 7, 1941, a Japanese task force under the command of Vice Admiral Chuichi Nagumo bore down upon Oahu. His formidable armada centered around six aircraft carriers. Upon reaching a point some 220 miles north of the island, they launched two successive waves totaling 350 aircraft—40 torpedo bombers, 78 fighter aircraft, 103 high-level bombers, and 129 dive bombers. Their targets were the ships of Admiral Husband E. Kimmel's U.S. Pacific Fleet at moorings in Pearl Harbor. . . . Before a single shot had been fired, Commander Mitsuo Fuchida, leader of the air strike, knew that the Japanese had achieved total surprise, and so advised the flagship, Akagi, by the code word Tora! Tora! Tora! (Tiger! Tiger! Tiger!). At 0750 Fuchida signaled for the general attack. Approximately four hours later, his aircraft, the last to leave the scene, touched down on Akagi's flight deck. He and his men left behind a devastating sight. They had sunk, capsized, or damaged in varying degrees a total of eighteen warships—eight battleships, three light cruisers, three destroyers, and four auxiliary craft. The U.S. Navy's air arm had lost eighty-seven aircraft of all types. The Japanese had also destroyed 77 aircraft of [the Army's] Hawaiian

Air Force.... An additional 128 aircraft had been damaged.... Worst of all, 2,403 personnel of the Army, Navy, Marine Corps, and civilians had been killed, were listed as missing, or died later of wounds, while those wounded but not killed totaled 1,178. (Prange 1986, xxxi–xxxii)

The overwhelming reaction to the events at Pearl Harbor was shock and anger—shock that the United States could be so unprepared for such an attack and anger at those responsible—principally Imperial Japan. The unity and resolve that Pearl Harbor instilled in the American people carried them through four years of bloody conflict across the globe. Shortly before the war ended, however, probing questions arose concerning who in the U.S. government was responsible for the obvious lapses that made Pearl Harbor possible, if not likely. Before turning to these, a brief overview of the antecedents to the attack on Pearl Harbor is essential (Table 2.1).

PEARL HARBOR—THE CONTROVERSY

As early as 1944, with World War II nearly over, isolationists and Republicans in Congress and elsewhere began to openly question the origins of American involvement in the war. Roosevelt himself was mistrusted by many Americans who took his affable, confident demeanor to be a mask for an otherwise unscrupulous character. Roosevelt's desire to enter the war in support of Britain was well-known and his critics surmised that he had twisted and perhaps even precipitated events in such a way that the American people would ultimately come around to his side. To the cynic, Pearl Harbor was not only avoidable, it was contrived.

During the 1940 election campaign, Roosevelt promised to keep the country out of the war then raging in Europe and Asia. At the same time, though, he confided to his close advisors that he wished to quickly bring the American people around to supporting his quasi alliance with Britain after the election. In October 1940 he told Admiral James Richardson, commander of the Pacific Fleet (before being replaced by Admiral Husband Kimmel in January 1941), that he expected war to start with a Japanese "error" (Theobald 1954, 192). According to Bailey:

> Franklin Roosevelt repeatedly deceived the American people during the period before Pearl Harbor.... He was like the physician who must tell the patient lies for the patient's own good.... The country was overwhelmingly non-interventionist to the very day of Pearl Harbor, and an overt attempt to lead the people into war would have resulted in certain failure and an almost certain ousting of Roosevelt in 1940, with a consequent defeat of his ultimate aims. (Bailey 1948, 11–13, in Chamberlin 1965, 3)

Roosevelt quickly dropped his campaign promises after his third electoral victory. Even before his inauguration, Roosevelt responded to British pleas for military aid by pushing through Congress the lend-lease program, waiving the provisions of the Neutrality Act. Roosevelt secured congressional support in part by promising the United States would not be pulled

Table 2.1 PEARL HARBOR: A CHRONOLOGY

1931

Japan attacks Manchuria. U.S. Secretary of War Henry Stimson succeeds in pressing a policy of nonrecognition by the U.S.

1933

Japan leaves the League of Nations under protest, following imposition of sanctions.

1937

Japan launches war on China.

1935–1939

U.S. passes Neutrality Acts.

1939

July	U.S. cancels bilateral trade agreement with Japan.
September	Germany attacks Poland; France and Britain declare war—World War II begins.
November	Neutrality Act of 1939 commits U.S. to sell arms to belligerents only on a cash-and-carry basis.

1940

June	France falls to Germany.
September	Congress enacts draft by one vote. Germany, Italy, and Japan sign the Tripartite Pact, pledging mutual support in the event any of the three is attacked.
December	U.S. President Franklin Roosevelt receives urgent request for lend-lease aid from British Prime Minister Winston Churchill in violation of 1939 Neutrality Act.

1941

January	Congress approves lend-lease following Roosevelt's reiteration of formal neutrality. Pearl Harbor placed on high alert following rumors of Japanese attack.
March	U.S. Secretary of State Cordell Hull and Japanese Ambassador Kichisaburo Nomura negotiate in Washington over continued Japanese conquests in China and Japan's adherence to the Tripartite Pact.
July	Japanese Imperial Conference endorses policy of military conquest in the Pacific.
July 24	Japan moves into Indochina after pressuring the pro-Nazi Vichy government in France to relinquish colonial holdings.
July 26	U.S. government freezes Japanese assets and takes control of trade. Some argue that cutting off Japan from American oil and markets forced it to go to war.
August 6	Japan offers concessions of China issue in exchange for end to U.S. freeze on assets—U.S. rejects offer. Japan begins plans for attack on Pearl Harbor. They are ready by late October.
August 9–14	Roosevelt, Churchill meet in Newfoundland and issue Atlantic Charter which includes U.S. support for British and Chinese fight against Japan in the Pacific and rejection of Japanese domination of Manchuria.
August 17	U.S. warns Japan of a possible American resort to force to implement the Atlantic Charter.

(continued)

Table 2.1 *(continued)*

August–September	Japanese Prime Minister Fumimaro Konoye meets with Churchill.
September–October	U.S. destroyers attacked in the Atlantic—Roosevelt adopts shoot-on-sight policy against German U-boats.
September 6	Konoye offers proposal for summit with Roosevelt. U.S. Ambassador to Japan Joseph Grew warns Konoye government may fall if U.S. rejects offer.
October 2	U.S. rejects Konoye's proposals and defers summit meeting. Negotiations show no further progress from this point on.
October 16	Hideki Tojo, leader of the Japanese War Party, becomes prime minister when moderate Konoye cabinet falls.
November 3	Ambassador Grew warns that Japanese may be planning a secret attack, urges conciliation in Washington.
November 5	Army Chief of Staff George Marshall and Harold Stark, chief of naval operations, recommend to president that all support short of war with Japan should be given to China, but reiterate that Germany is the "most dangerous enemy." Roosevelt approves proposal.
November 7	U.S. rejects Japanese Imperial Conference's "Proposal A." Cordell Hull warns that Japan may be planning a secret attack in earlier cabinet meeting.
November 17	Congress passes amendments to Neutrality Act to allow convoy escorts into war zones by thin margin.
November 17	Special Japanese envoy Saburo Kurusu joins Nomura in Washington to begin negotiations (with secret Japanese deadline of November 30).
November 20	U.S. receives Japanese "Proposal B." U.S. again demands end to Japanese actions in the Pacific and China.
November 22-26	Hull weighs and rejects "modus vivendi" based on Proposal B in a ten-point note offering new proposals. Meanwhile, a Japanese carrier force leaves Japan for Hawaii under radio silence.
November 27	U.S. Army, Navy send secret war alerts to Pacific bases.
November 29–December 1	Japanese cabinet secretly rejects U.S. proposals, although response will not be conveyed until December 7.
December 2	Order to commence Pearl Harbor attack given to carrier groups: "Climb Mount Nitaka."
December 5–6	Japanese destroy codes in embassy, move troops south from Indochina.
December 6	Roosevelt sends urgent message of peace to Emperor Hirohito.
December 6	Roosevelt receives part of Japanese rejection of November 26 offer through code breaking: Roosevelt interprets it as a sign that war is imminent.
December 7	Cryptographers in Washington intercept Japanese instructions to ambassador in the U.S. to deliver declaration of war to Roosevelt by 1:00 p.m., Washington time. Message is not conveyed to Pearl Harbor prior to attack. Washington learns of Pearl Harbor attack at 7:55 a.m., Hawaii time, but Japanese legate fails to convey declaration of war until after the attack had already started.
December 8	Roosevelt delivers his "day of infamy" speech, after which Congress unanimously approves a declaration of war on Japan. Germany and Italy declare war within a week.

into war, although at the same time his closest advisor Harry Hopkins was secretly assuring Churchill that the country would stick with him come what may (Chamberlin 1965, 5). Roosevelt implemented lend-lease with enthusiasm, allowing not only the provision of weapons on credit but also protecting the delivery convoys to Britain with war ships. This led to attacks on U.S. vessels in the Atlantic in the fall and Roosevelt's order to retaliate and ultimately to shoot "enemy" ships on sight in October. As early as May, Roosevelt exaggerated the German threat, warning that the U.S. coasts were vulnerable to invasion in order to heighten public fears. The Atlantic Charter, signed in August, so fully committed the United States to cooperate with Britain that it amounted to an alliance.

Some have interpreted Roosevelt's actions as deliberately provocative of the Japanese, to the point of recklessness. The negotiations with Japan during 1941 involved little of the give-and-take typically associated with diplomacy. Japan, on its side, sought U.S. approval (or at least tolerance) of its conquest and annexation of much of China, with the possibility of U.S. support for a complete occupation of the country. For its part, the United States wanted to see Japan out of China (and later Indochina) as well as its abrogation of the Tripartite Pact—an alliance signed with Germany and Italy in September 1940. The United States also wanted assurances that Japan would no longer threaten the Philippines, a U.S. stronghold, and British and Dutch colonies in the South Pacific and Southeast Asia (these included Burma, Singapore, Malaya, Indonesia, Papua New Guinea, and Australia). Virtually every Japanese and U.S. proposal focused on these mutually exclusive demands.

What made American policy threatening, according to Roosevelt's critics, was the economic embargo on Japan, imposed gradually beginning with the refusal to renew a rather bland trade agreement in 1939 and culminating in the much more damaging July 26, 1941, sanctions which cut off vital oil exports (Theobald 1954, 193). This, according to revisionist critics, forced the Japanese to take the offensive in Asia in search of alternative sources of fuel and raw materials.

As the negotiations dragged on through 1941, the Japanese repeatedly urged American negotiators to open trade again, offering various, if minor, concessions on China. During the fall, the Japanese Ambassador Admiral Kichisaburo Nomura and special envoy Saburo Kurusu, following a number of unsuccessful talks, proposed a summit meeting between Roosevelt and Japanese Premier Prince Fumimaro Konoye. The preconditions imposed by the United States were unacceptable to Japan, however, and the meeting never took place. Revisionist historian Charles Beard asked: "Did the Japanese proposal offer an opportunity to effect a settlement in the Pacific and were the decisions [U.S. officials] made in relation to it actually 'looking' in the direction of peace?" (Beard 1965, 51). Both diplomatic intercepts and the ambassador to Japan Joseph Grew indicated that the Japanese were sincere and should be listened to. Grew advocated "constructive conciliation" and warned that failure to work with the Konoye government might lead to its downfall (Rauch 1965, 58).

The talks stalemated in spite of repeated attempts by the Japanese to keep them going. Even after the Konoye administration was replaced by the militaristic government of General Hideki Tojo, Tokyo put forward at least two more proposals for a temporary arrangement that would secure U.S. recognition of Japan's position in China and a removal of the economic sanctions in exchange for assurances of no further Japanese conquests or attacks in the Pacific. Secretary of State Cordell Hull dismissed these proposals perfunctorily, and in his final message of November 26, largely perceived as an ultimatum shrouded in veiled threats, left only the weakest hint of further concessions (Trefousse 1982, 35).

Not only did this diplomatic intransigence indicate a willingness (if not eagerness) to go to war over China and Southeast Asia, but the military deployments of 1941 seem to have been calculated to invite a surprise attack— the sort of attack Roosevelt had already indicated would be necessary to turn the American people around. In late 1940, Roosevelt ordered the Pacific Fleet to be docked in Pearl Harbor rather than in California in order to serve a deterrent function. Admiral Richardson opposed this plan on the grounds that it would leave the fleet too exposed and lost his job for it. Admiral Kimmel was more willing to support this forward basing in spite of the increased vulnerability it involved and he was given the command. Then, in the spring of 1941, Roosevelt ordered a sizable portion of the Pacific Fleet reassigned to duty in the Atlantic to fight German submarines, but this left the outpost even less defended than before. These moves could have only one purpose, according to Theobald: "The retention of the Fleet in Hawaii, especially after its reduction in strength in March 1941, could serve only one purpose, an invitation to a surprise Japanese attack" (Theobald 1954, 195).

In the days preceding Pearl Harbor, Washington officials failed to convey to officers in the field all they knew about the seriousness of diplomatic tensions with Japan. This lapse, while excused by Roosevelt's supporters, is consistent with the reckless policy of a war-bent Roosevelt. Intelligence reports indicating that November 30 was the deadline for diplomatic settlement set by Japan was not clearly conveyed to Hawaiian commanders, nor were the signs of December 3–7 showing the Japanese were in the final stages of breaking diplomatic relations and declaring war. Instead, the news was either kept in Washington or transmitted through the slowest of means, almost as if to insure that the island would be unprepared for an attack (Theobald 1954, 197). Some have even hinted that Roosevelt knew that the silent fleet was en route to Pearl before the fact (Coox 1990, 121).

In fact, the conspiracy theory seems to assume that Roosevelt had far more information and control over events than is logically conceivable. As pointed out by Morison,

> Even if one can believe that the late President of the United States was capable of so horrible a gambit, a little reflection would indicate that he could not possibly

have carried it off. He would have needed the connivance of Secretaries Hull, [Republicans] Stimson and Knox, Generals Marshall, Gerow . . . Admiral Stark, and many of their subordinates, too—all loyal and honorable men who would never have lent themselves to such monstrous deception. (Morison 1965, 94)

Not only would such a conspiracy have required the involvement of even the lowly radar men in Oahu who mistook the Japanese invasion force for a group of B-17s returning from California, it would have required all these individuals to knowingly put at risk the largest concentration of military power in the Pacific—hardly the sort of objective one would expect from those who would be expected to fight the war in the ensuing months and years (Kahn 1991/92, 149). Unless one goes so far as to opine that Roosevelt wanted us not only to be in the war, but to lose it as well. . . .

Likewise the point that the United States actually provoked a war with Japan through diplomatic confrontation is overblown. Although several diplomatic cables indicated a certain sincerity on the part of the Japanese negotiators, the overwhelming majority of their instructions were bellicose. As put by Feis:

[L]eaving Konoye to go on with his talks with the United States, the Army and Navy threw themselves at once into the plans for action [in August 1941]. The Operations Section of the Army began to get ready to capture Malaya, Java, Borneo, the Bismarck Archipelago, the Indies, and the Philippines; it was to be ready by the end of October. The Navy finished its war games. These included the surprise attack on Pearl Harbor and the American fleet there. At the end of the games the two general staffs conferred on the result and found it satisfactory. By the end of September these steps towards war—if diplomacy should fail—were well under way. . . . If Konoye was ready and able—as Grew thought—to give Roosevelt trustworthy and satisfactory promises of a new sort, he does not tell of them in his "Memoirs." Nor has any other record available to me disclosed them. He was a prisoner, willing or unwilling, of the terms precisely prescribed in conferences over which he presided. . . . It is unlikely that he could have got around them or that he would have in some desperate act discarded them. The whole of his political career speaks to the contrary. (Feis 1965, 39–41)

Once the Japanese war plans were in place, the country made ridiculous demands on Washington, tantamount to U.S. surrender in the Pacific (Rauch 1965, 62). War, to the Japanese planners, was the expected outcome. It is no surprise that talks therefore were allowed to fail—even the negotiators themselves were kept in the dark about these war plans lest it diminish their appearance of sincerity (Levite 1987, 52). If there was a conspiracy for war, it could be more easily found in the Imperial Conference than the Kitchen Cabinet.

To a certain extent, the Roosevelt and Truman administrations fueled the popularity of conspiracy theories of Pearl Harbor, in that the initial investigations so alarmed senior officials that they attempted to shift the blame to subordinates: "The administration created scapegoats who then attracted the attention of those who wished to discredit Roosevelt and his supporters" (Melosi 1977, 162). The eventual dismissal of Admiral Kimmel and Hawaiian sector Army commander General Walter Short created deep resentment among those who felt they had been left in the dark. Successive investigations in Hawaii, the White House, and Congress did little to clear up the confusion.

Looking elsewhere for an explanation to the lapse which made Pearl Harbor possible, one can cite a large number of instances of organizational failure and poor judgment on the part of both senior and midlevel officials. Perhaps the most direct comment in this regard is made at the conclusion of Wohlstetter's major work on the subject:

> The fact of surprise at Pearl Harbor has never been persuasively explained by accusing the participants, individually or in groups, of conspiracy or negligence or stupidity. What these examples illustrate is rather the very human tendency to pay attention to the signals that support current expectations about enemy behavior. If no one is listening for signals of an attack against a highly improbable target, then it is very difficult for the signals to be heard. (Wohlstetter 1962, 392)

In 1941, particularly after the January warning of a potential attack on Pearl Harbor turned out to be a false alarm, American military planners were preparing for a possible surprise attack in the South Pacific. Roosevelt was well aware of Japanese tendencies for dramatic gestures and had made sure that American commanders in the Philippines and around Indochina were alerted to the possibility of attack. This was the logical place for a Japanese attack, since a victory there would not only damage American capabilities, but more than likely bring territorial gains as well. Military planners in Washington doubted the Japanese ability to cross the Pacific and attack Hawaii—something Secretary of War Stimson later acknowledged publicly (Morison 1965, 70). Given this tendency to look to Asia, rather than Hawaii, war warnings tended to emphasize this region. Even the last war warning delivered on November 27 by the navy mentioned only "the Philippines, Thai or Kra peninsula, or possibly Borneo" as likely targets of Japanese aggression (Trefousse 1982, 173). As put by Prange:

> The human inclination to believe what one wants to believe, to see what one wants to see, no doubt played a part in the Pearl Harbor drama. . . . This lack of genuine, gut-level belief [in the threat of Japanese attack], as opposed to a cool, academic setting forth of theoretical possibilities, was the fundamental cause of the United States being caught flat-footed on December 7, 1941. All other sins of omission and commission were its sons and daughters. (Prange 1986, 525, 529)

Thus many signals pointing to Hawaii were either dismissed or ignored (more will be said about this later). More important, many important developments were simply never conveyed to the commanders stationed at Pearl Harbor. In an angry article written after the war, Admiral Kimmel listed the bits of information which were in the hands of Washington planners and intelligence officials but which were never transmitted to him: (1) details of intercepted diplomatic cables proving the deterioration of negotiations—especially Japan's rejection of Hull's ten-point note received on December 6 and 7; (2) information on Japan's strong efforts to secure detailed information on the facilities and ships at Pearl Harbor; and (3) specific deadlines announced by the Japanese, including the 1:00 p.m. Washington time deadline (7:00 a.m. Hawaii time) on December 7 when relations were severed. As he put it: "I cannot understand now—I have never understood—I may never understand—why I was deprived of the information available in the Navy Department in Washington on Saturday night and Sunday morning" (Kimmel 1965, 77). About the failure to transmit this information, Trefousse commented:

> Why this information was never forwarded to Pearl Harbor is a more serious question. If anybody should have known about Japanese interest in the anchorage of the Pacific Fleet, it was obviously Admiral Kimmel. Yet he neither received the messages nor any summary of them—a good example of the poor dissemination of intelligence information at the time. (Trefousse 1982, 47)

Washington planners were reluctant to communicate too much of the information drawn from the decoded signals in order to minimize security leaks. If the Japanese suspected their codes had been broken they would have immediately changed them. Furthermore, because intelligence was gathered separately by the army and the navy, interservice rivalry led to some delays in sharing crucial information (Clausen 1992). In addition, some communications were given higher priority for decoding based on assumptions about Japanese behavior. Thus the flood of cables from Tokyo to the Japanese embassy was handled expeditiously while the trickle of messages from the Hawaiian consulate was almost ignored, even though this was the channel through which the detailed schemas of the Pearl Harbor facilities were being transmitted (Levite 1987, 53). Finally, Washington commanders feared that sending too much information might devalue the importance of each item and lead to complacency. This was especially true of war warnings, which were sent with some regularity from January to December 1941 (Trefousse 1982, 71).

The ability to transmit vital information was further hampered by an apparent lack of anxiety in some circles in the Washington bureaucracy, culminating in the absence of several key individuals—not to mention whole departments—over the weekend of December 6 and 7. Secretary Stimson was unavailable and his Chief of Staff George Marshall was riding horses on Sunday morning in Washington (while it was still nighttime in Hawaii). They were not available to respond vigorously to the 1:00 p.m. deadline. Admiral Harold Stark, chief of naval operations, did not take the warning very seriously. As a result, the only response to the direct threat was sent to Hawaii at 12:18 p.m., Washington time, and was not received until after the bombs had started falling (Trefousse 1982, 69).

On November 27, two crucial messages were transmitted to commanders in Hawaii. They were the army and the navy's respective war warnings which called upon all American forces in the Pacific to go on extreme alert, as can be seen in the army's version:

> Negotiations with Japan appear to be terminated to all practical purposes with only the barest possibilities that the Japanese Government might come back and offer to continue. Japanese future action unpredictable but hostile action possible at any moment. If hostilities cannot, repeat cannot, be avoided the United States desires that Japan commit the first overt act. This policy should not, repeat not, be construed as restricting you to a course of action that might jeopardize your defense. Prior to hostile Japanese action you are directed to undertake such reconnaissance and other measures as you deem necessary but these measures should be carried out so as not, repeat not, to alarm civil population or disclose intent. (Trefousse 1982, 174)

While the warning seems unambiguous in retrospect, General Short and Admiral Kimmel complained later that the messages were confusing. They seemed to indicate that while alertness should be heightened, this should be done almost secretly, so as not alarm the locals. This is clearly not possible if by defensive measures the Washington commanders envisioned deployment of the fleet in the high seas. As a consequence, Kimmel and Short did little to change their ordinary routine over the next week. General Leonard Gerow, who received Short's rather bland response to the warning, failed to understand that he had not grasped the seriousness of the situation, and so the matter was dropped (Morison 1965, 70).

The importance of this failure of leadership and judgment is debatable. At no time did the Washington officials have any hard evidence that Japan intended to attack Pearl Harbor on December 7 (Levite 1987, 71). This was no accident. As put by Prange:

> We have seen how meticulously the Japanese perfected their planning; how diligently they trained their pilots and bombardiers; how they modified weapons to achieve maximum damage; how persistently they dredged up and utilized information about the U.S. Pacific Fleet. They balked at no hazard, ready to risk a wild leap to achieve their immediate ends. (Prange 1981, 736)

A useful analogy might be that a homeowner would take seriously a rumor of burglars in the neighborhood, but dismiss reports of terrorists driving tanks!

A point rarely made about war preparedness at Pearl Harbor is that the fleet may have been in even greater danger had it been alerted and deployed. After all, within ten minutes of the attack, all the navy's shipboard antiaircraft guns were manned and firing, but with little effect (Clausen 1992, 9). Had the fleet been at sea, it would have still been out-gunned and even more vulnerable to attack. Pearl Harbor provided the benefit of a shallow berth which, while not eliminating the risk of aerial torpedo attack, as the local commanders learned with chagrin, it did allow salvage of almost all the ships which were hit and even sunk, not to mention the rescue of the crews (Wallin 1968, 283). The most serious lapse was the air force, which left its planes wingtip to wingtip at every airfield on the island. Had it been airborne (in itself a departure from procedure), the Japanese planes might have been sighted and engaged sooner. At any rate, given the overwhelming military might brought to bear on the area by a committed Japanese force, Pearl Harbor was destined to be a bloodbath, warning or no.

The classic question remains, how much did Washington know and when did it know it? This refers to the intelligence capabilities of the U.S. government in 1941. The student should be reminded that such commonly available resources such as spy satellites, electronic eavesdropping devices, night-vision goggles, and aerial reconnaissance were either not available or of limited utility due to the primitive nature of the devices. Aerial reconnaissance, while in use during World War II, was of little value to a remote outpost such as Pearl Harbor, given the range and altitude capabilities of existing aircraft. Even radar, while available, was a novelty which even its operators did not understand. Given these technological constraints the means available for gathering intelligence on the Japanese consisted only of (1) public sources (newspapers, tourists), (2) diplomatic communications (ambassadors' analysis), (3) espionage (human intelligence), and (4) signals intelligence (intercepting coded radio messages).

By 1940, public sources from Japan were severely limited due to heavy censorship imposed by the government. Although reporters generally had a good idea of what was going on, they could not print it. What was worse, at the turn of the decade many of the most seasoned analysts were reassigned and replaced with far more inexperienced staff (Levite 1987, 46). With the economic sanctions imposed in July 1941, the many American traders, seamen, and investors who had previously kept in touch with Japan turned their attention elsewhere and were no longer available as a public intelligence source.

Ambassador Joseph Grew exerted considerable energies to not only acquire information on the Japanese government's intentions, but to convey his impressions and analysis to the secretary of state. He was the one who predicted the collapse of the Konoye administration and shared the Pearl Harbor attack rumor nearly a year before its occurrence. Unfortunately, because of his tendency to speculate without hard evidence, the Washington team discounted his opinions in favor of what they saw as its most important "hard intelligence": signals intercepts. That the government did not rely on espionage, as would be expected, is explained by the fact that:

> In sharp contrast to Great Britain, Germany, Japan, and the Soviet Union, which were investing, at the time, a lot of resources in espionage, the United States deliberately refrained from engaging in this type of intelligence activity due to moral, political, and budgetary considerations. (Levite 1987, 50)

The key element of U.S. intelligence on Japan came through the extensive message decoding operation known as MAGIC. Through it the army, under the direction of the Signals Intelligence Section (SIS), was able to intercept and translate almost all of Japanese diplomatic cables to the United

States and Hawaii from 1937 to 1941 (except for an eighteen-month period in 1939–40 when a newly introduced code had to be broken). In fact, the U.S. decoding efficiency was so high that American diplomats and senior officials often had copies of the cables before the Japanese delegates themselves. This obviously was a great asset to U.S. negotiators who knew precisely how much latitude the Japanese delegates were permitted by their home office. It also allowed Americans to follow the changing tone of the messages in order to gauge the increasing likelihood of war (Kahn 1991/92, 143).

Important interceptions obtained via MAGIC included: the announcement that the Imperial Conference had approved a strategy of aggression in the South Pacific in July 1941; a conciliatory message wedged between numerous belligerent ones on November 15, 1941; a self-imposed Japanese deadline of November 22 (later extended to November 29) for a settlement with the United States following which "things are automatically going to happen"; instructions to embassies to destroy documents and codes on December 3; the fourteen-part message rejecting Cordell Hull's ten-point note on December 6–7; and the December 7 announcement that relations would be severed at 1:00 p.m. Washington time (Trefousse 1982, 48). In addition, military planners in Washington were vaguely aware of messages to Japanese spies in Hawaii, also intercepted and interpreted through MAGIC. In addition, a controversial message over Tokyo radio known as the "winds execute" signal was detected by army intelligence on December 4 but never conveyed to Hawaiian commanders. This signal was a coded announcement that relations with the United States were being severed.

Although some have complained that these diplomatic communications were not relayed quickly enough to the commanders in Hawaii, the truth is they did not provide a consistent and coherent picture of Japanese plans in and of themselves. According to Wohlstetter, this was because of the overabundance of "noise":

> In short, we failed to anticipate Pearl Harbor not for want of the relevant materials, but because of a plethora of irrelevant ones. Much of the appearance of wanton neglect that emerged in various investigations of the disaster resulted from the unconscious suppression of vast congeries of signs pointing in every direction except Pearl Harbor. (Wohlstetter 1962, 388)

Because the diplomatic corps was not privy to the details of war plans, even this exhaustive source was not adequate. For its part, Navy intelligence was working on breaking the military codes. But due to the lack of staff, most of which were working in the Signal Corps (collecting communications) rather than cryptography, the navy was unable to crack the essential military codes and was forced to rely on mere traffic patterns to keep track of the Japanese fleet's deployment. By simply monitoring which ships were in radio communication at different times, it was possible to locate them with some precision. At various times, some ships went silent, but this was typically only when they were close to the mainland and captains could receive instructions by hand.

As of December 1941, the bulk of the Japanese fleet was detected moving south toward Indochina and Indonesia. That is, with the exception of one large carrier group which could not be located due to radio silence (Kahn 1991/92, 145). Intelligence analysts naturally assumed a repetition of the previous pattern and did not bother to alert Hawaii about this "lost fleet" (something which particularly annoyed Hawaiian commanders after the fact). In actual fact, the fleet was bound for Hawaii with lengthy and detailed orders which earlier had been hand-delivered in Japan. Thus the fleet was able to maintain radio silence in spite of their distance. Note that this situation also made diplomatic intervention to stop the fleet impossible without revealing its location and thereby causing a major incident.

The last line of intelligence gathering—on site in Hawaii—also proved inadequate. Navy radar operators on Oahu spotted a large blip on their screens early on the morning of December 7 indicating a large group of aircraft some 135 miles offshore. They were puzzled and a bit suspicious of this signal and called in to their base for clarification, only to be told that the blip was probably a group of army B-17s coming from the coast and to "forget it." No one bothered to check with the army to confirm the planes' estimated time of arrival. The radar operators, having already worked a half hour past quitting time, then shut off the machines and left (Trefousse 1982, 77).

To answer the question of how much the "U.S. government" knew is not the same as determining how much different individuals within the government were aware of. As we have already seen, intelligence details were shared grudgingly between the army and the navy, and the difficulty in processing the flood of signals forced the cryptography staff into a sort of intelligence triage, passing along only those messages they considered most vital. Many errors of judgment and cooperation were therefore made, although it is difficult to place blame on any one person.

Wohlstetter maintains that never before had the United States collected so much information on a potential belligerent, implying that it was within the capacity of the government, by pooling all of these facts and figures, to predict that an attack on Pearl Harbor on December 7 was likely (Wohlstetter 1962, 382). Kahn and Levite take exception to this conclusion, by arguing that even if all the information had been centralized, it would still have yielded an ambiguous and confusing picture (Kahn 1991/92; Levite 1987). As put by Levite:

> the United States was indeed poorly equipped, organized, and deployed to collect information regarding Japan's intentions and capabilities in general, and their preparations for attack on Pearl Harbor in particular. In fact, the overall picture is one in which the United States not only lacked systematic coverage of the Japanese military, but its sources were actually drying up in the period immediately preceding the Pearl Harbor attack. . . . It would seem that under the collection conditions prevailing prior to the Pearl Harbor attack, it would have taken an incredible stroke of luck for the United States to obtain concrete advance warning of Japan's intention to launch the attack. (Levite 1987, 60)

THE LESSONS OF "PEARL"

Because one cannot assume that intelligence gathering will ever yield the "smoking gun" proving an adversary's intent, the lesson of Pearl Harbor is not primarily to increase intelligence gathering efforts. These will always be inadequate in some way. Instead, the principal lessons of Pearl Harbor are first, intelligence, once gathered, should be centralized in order to allow analysts with a global perspective to assess the meaning of the material, and then disseminated as rapidly and widely through the government as security permits. Second, decision makers would do well to think creatively about an adversary's possible tactics and strategies. Rather than assume a particular chain of events is inevitable, assume it is merely "likely" and consider other, less probable scenarios.

Questions to Consider

1. To what extent has the U.S. government attempted to remedy the organization and attitudinal problems revealed by the Pearl Harbor disaster? Could it happen again?

2. Who or what is most to "blame" for Pearl Harbor? Roosevelt? Interservice rivalry? Tojo? Inept radar operators? Admiral Kimmel and General Short? Inadequate technology?

3. To what extent did the Pearl Harbor experience influence American military strategy in the postwar era? How has it affected nuclear strategy, for example?

References

Thomas A. Bailey. *The Man in the Street* (New York: Macmillan, 1948).

Charles A. Beard. "Appearance and Realities" in Waller, ed., *Pearl Harbor*, 48–56.

William Henry Chamberlin. "Roosevelt Maneuvers America into War" in Waller, ed., *Pearl Harbor*, 1–13.

Henry Clausen with Bruce Lee. *Pearl Harbor: Final Judgement* (New York: Crown Publishers, 1992).

Alvin D. Coox. "Repulsing the Pearl Harbor Revisionists: The State of Present Literature on the Debacle" in Hilary Conroy and Harry Way, eds., *Pearl Harbor Reexamined: Prologue to the Pacific War* (Honolulu: University of Hawaii Press, 1990), 119–126.

Herbert Feis. "The Road to Pearl Harbor" in Waller, ed., *Pearl Harbor*, 31–47.

A. A. Hoehling. *The Week Before Pearl Harbor* (New York: W. W. Norton, 1963).

Cordell Hull. *Memoirs of Cordell Hull*, 2 vols. (London: Hodder & Stoughton, 1948).

David Kahn. "The Intelligence Failure of Pearl Harbor." *Foreign Affairs* 70 #5 (Winter 1991/92): 138–152.

Husband Kimmel, "Admiral Kimmel's Story" in Waller, ed., *Pearl Harbor*, 72–79.

Ariel Levite. *Intelligence and Strategic Surprises* (New York: Columbia University Press, 1987).

Martin V. Melosi. *The Shadow of Pearl Harbor: Political Controversy over the Surprise Attack, 1941–1946* (College Station: Texas A&M University Press, 1977).

Elting E. Morison. "An Unanswerable Question" in Waller, ed., *Pearl Harbor,* 68–72.

Samuel E. Morison. "Who Was Responsible?" in Waller, ed. , *Pearl Harbor,* 94–98.

Gordon W. Prange. *At Dawn We Slept: The Untold Story of Pearl Harbor* (New York: McGraw-Hill, 1981).

Gordon W. Prange with Donald M. Goldstein and Katherine V. Dillon. *Pearl Harbor: The Verdict of History* (New York: McGraw-Hill, 1986).

Basil Rauch. "Principle in International Policy" in Waller, ed., *Pearl Harbor,* 57–68.

Robert A. Theobald. *The Final Secret of Pearl Harbor: The Washington Contribution to the Japanese Attack* (New York: Devin-Adair, 1954).

Hans Trefousse. *Pearl Harbor: The Continuing Controversy* (Malabar, FL: Krieger Pub, 1982).

George Waller, ed. *Pearl Harbor: Roosevelt and the Coming of the War* (New York, D.C. Heath, 1965).

Homer Norman Wallin, *Pearl Harbor: Why, How, Fleet Salvage, and Final Appraisal* (Naval History Division: Washington, DC, 1968).

Roberta Wohlstetter. *Pearl Harbor: Warning and Decision* (Stanford, CA: Stanford University Press, 1962).

Sino–Soviet–American Relations

As major powers seek security in international affairs, they have several options: increase their military capability beyond the level of any potential adversaries, declare neutrality, or align with other countries in order to combine their military strengths. The last option is the essense of the balance of power: as nations seek security by forming alliances, the international system will be composed of coalitions which balance each other. This is not to say that every state will remain in a given coalition, but that overall the arrangement of alliances will tend toward a stalemate. Advocates of the balance of power emphasize that this tendency toward balance is both inevitable and beneficial, since it prevents any one state from conquering the world. Opponents point out that the balance of power has failed to prevent world war in the past, and that it is at any rate based on the amoral principle that might makes right. This dynamic is aptly illustrated in the relations between the United States, the USSR, and the P.R.C. (People's Republic of China).

THE SUPERPOWER "TRIANGLE" AND STRATEGIC ALIGNMENTS

John Stoessinger recently opined:

> Machiavelli would have taken considerable pleasure in the dynamics of Sino-Soviet-American triangular relations in our time. During the 1950s, China and the Soviet Union were allies, and the United States feared the menace of a monolithic Sino-Soviet threat. In the 1960s, after the Cuban missile crisis had ushered in a detente between the Soviet Union and the United States, China began to fear

the specter of Soviet-American collusion. And in the 1970s, the Soviet leaders began to worry that the Chinese and Americans might be getting along too well. Each of the three powers has had its turn at being frozen out by the other two. (Stoessinger 1990, 257)

The tenuousness of superpower relations are symptomatic of the balance of power described earlier. To understand changes in relations between these countries, it is not enough to know the ins and outs of diplomatic language, protocol, and individual personalities. It is also not enough to understand the cultural heritage, historical habits, and ever-changing perceptions of world leaders. Instead, one should focus on how each nation has tried to increase its security by adjusting relations with a pair of enemies. This is the essence of the balance of power.

Little naturally links the United States, the Soviet Union, and China. In fact, it was not until the twentieth century that meaningful contacts developed between the three nations, at a time when they were each already major global powers. The historical circumstances that have forced these three nations to take on the burden of world leadership seem to have been largely beyond their control. Because of this, the response of these countries' leaders to these political choices can be more clearly attributed to strategic concerns rather than to habit, tradition, or heritage.

All three nations have viewed themselves as a model to the world. China's sense of cultural superiority was boundless until the twentieth century when the Western barbarians began to exact humiliating concessions for trade. The Russian empire has consistently viewed itself as a model of efficiency and sophistication, although its views of the West have been generally more sympathetic. The United States, with its feelings of "Manifest Destiny," has long considered its role as a model of democracy and scientific progress unquestioned. The Communist revolutions in Russia and China had the effect of accentuating ideological differences and feelings of uniqueness and superiority.

During the 1920s, the United States confronted both China and Russia militarily. At the turn of the century, the United States attempted to act as mediator of a dispute between Western powers intent on trade with China and anti-Western Boxers with their so-called "Open Door" policy, but in the end sided with the Westerners (Stoessinger 1990, 25). The United States refused to accept the October 1917 Bolshevik Revolution and joined an international force to overthrow the new regime in 1919. The Chinese were largely uninterested in Russia, although the Great Wall provided little consolation that the influence of the northern barbarians could be contained for long.

By the 1930s, however, relations between the three nations had grown generally warm. The Soviets provided support for both the Nationalist government in Beijing and the Communist party forces under Mao Zedong. In 1933, after the Soviet Union had demonstrated political and economic resilience through the Great Depression and America had not, the United States was more favorably disposed to working with the socialist behemoth on equal terms. The budding friendship was temporarily strained by Stalin's decision to sign a nonaggression pact with Hitler in 1939. Americans actively supported the beleaguered Chinese Nationalist government in its failed efforts to prevent the Japanese conquest of Manchuria (northern China). When Hitler invaded Russia in 1941 and the Japanese attacked Pearl Harbor a few months later, the three superpowers-to-be suddenly and quite unexpectedly found themselves on the same winning side in World War II.

The story of how these three World War II allies evolved into a great nuclear triangle is the great diplomatic saga of our time.

PART ONE—MAJOR INCIDENTS

Outbreak of the Cold War and Sino–American Tensions

Harry Truman addressed a joint session of Congress on March 12, 1947, and requested $400 million to support regimes in Greece and Turkey against Soviet-backed insurrections. Without naming the Soviet Union, Truman declared:

> It would be an unspeakable tragedy if these countries, which have struggled so long against overwhelming odds, should lose the victory for which they sacrificed so much. Collapse of free institutions and loss of independence would be disastrous not only for them but for the world. Discouragement and possibly failure would quickly be the lot of neighboring peoples striving to maintain their freedom and independence. (McCormick 1986, 59)

With that statement, all pretense of cordial postwar relations with the Soviet Union was dropped and the war time began in earnest. The 1945–1947 period had witnessed the "gradual disengagement" of the Soviet Union from its Cold War alliance with the United States (Ulam 1971, 102). Fueled by a persistent fear of invasion from Europe, Soviet leaders acted to consolidate control over Eastern European territories liberated by the Red Army in the closing months of the war. The response from the West was slow—the Truman administration held out a great deal of hope for the United Nations as a vehicle for postwar order.

Soviet attitudes toward the United Nations were disturbing. The "Baruch Plan" to bring all nuclear weapons under international control was rejected by the Soviets in 1946, as were countless resolutions in the Security Council where the Soviet veto prevented action. Americans deeply resented this frustration of a great cause and began to question Soviet commitment to peaceful coexistence. The fact that Stalin was in the process of an extraordinarily intense reindustrialization program at the time did little more to comfort the West.

Soviet forces and pro-Soviet leaders in East Germany became alarmed during 1948 at the collapse of the East German mark and the vulnerability of the economy generally. In response, Soviet forces were dispatched to seal off West Berlin from Western products and prevent travel by rail or road.

The United States then embarked on an eleven-month airlift which supplied so much food and other materials that prices for the goods fell below East Berlin levels. Such events confirmed the worst fears of Soviet intentions, and also demonstrated the importance of American leadership, technology, and boldness. One could have also learned from the Soviet decision not to shoot down the supply aircraft that there were clear limits to Soviet power and belligerence.

U.S. policy was heavily influenced by the thoughts of senior state department analyst George Kennan, who coined the phrase "containment." Kennan's call for diplomatic maneuvering to undermine the Soviet bloc imagined ways to pull apart the East European coalition through selective pressure, enticements, and determined resoluteness. This combined with the recommendation to act quickly to shore up collapsing pro-U.S. governments in Western Europe by providing massive economic aid and a strong military presence. In 1948 the Marshall Plan aid from the United States, which amounted to some $12 billion over five years, became available to West Europeans and in 1949 the United States helped to form the North Atlantic Treaty Organization (NATO), the military alliance aimed at preventing further Soviet expansion in Europe. The Allies moved quickly to restore German sovereignty and military might and redeployed thousands of American soldiers to the front. Soviets responded by organizing the Warsaw Pact and maintaining a large military force in the East European theater.

In September 1949, the Soviet Union detonated its first atomic weapon, thereby eliminating U.S. nuclear monopoly. The effect was primarily psychological, since the Soviets lacked the missiles to deliver quickly the weapon to a target. It was from this point, however, that the U.S.-Soviet nuclear arms race began.

The Chinese Revolution in 1949 culminated a fifteen-year Commmunist insurrection which had weathered assassinations, mass arrests, a "Long March" to regroup forces, and Japanese invasion. Mao Zedong received Soviet support, although he had sought American backing, and almost immediately turned to the Soviet Union once victory was complete. Soviets responded with large numbers of military, economic, and industrial advisors whose aim was the establishment of a large-scale industrial plant in China and inclusion of the Chinese Communist party in the Soviet-dominated Comintern—the umbrella organization of all Communist parties worldwide. Mao was quick to embrace Soviet support and formed what appeared to be a united front against imperialist capitalism. On the other hand, the United States denounced the revolution and preserved formal diplomatic ties with the exiled Nationalist government, now based on the island of Taiwan.

The formation of what appeared to be a united Communist bloc covering the entire Eurasian continent from Warsaw to Beijing gave U.S. containment strategy special urgency. The document designated NSC-68 took the original ideas of Kennan and tilted them toward a blatantly military strategy of direct confrontation (Gaddis and Diebel 1987, 6). The result was a readiness on the part of the United States to respond to Soviet "mischief" with proportional force. This primarily reactive policy led to the U.S. interventions in Korea, Vietnam, and Cuba over the next fifteen years.

The jury is still out on the question of who started the Cold War. As we can see, Soviet behavior in Eastern Europe can easily be interpreted as aggressive, especially when combined with its support for West European Communist parties which came close to taking power in the late 1940s. But, given Soviet apprehensions about the vulnerability of its western borders, her policies are easy to explain and even justify. From the Soviet perspective, U.S. attempts to shape the world through the UN, the Marshall Plan, and rearming Germany were no less threatening. After all, it was the United States which had delayed entry into the European theater by two years (Soviets expected an American landing by 1942); the Americans detonated an atomic weapon and in the process cut the Soviets out of the peace process in the Far East; and the Americans had participated in an invasion of the Soviet Union in order to reverse the Bolshevik Revolution.

Much like a family feud, the question of who started the conflict may be immaterial once the fight is on. It does, however, offer some interesting insights into the nature of the balance of power. One could easily argue that where two powers exist on the world stage without rival, they will tend to fear each other and therefore protect themselves against the other (Waltz 1979). Once this has begun, it is nearly impossible to distinguish "prudent preparations for potential conflict" on the one hand and "openly hostile actions" on the other. One cannot tell by looking at it whether a nuclear missile is "offensive" or "defensive" after all.

Cold War I: 1949–1965

With the stage set for an enduring three-way conflict between the United States, the Soviet Union, and China, all three nations were preparing for a possible outbreak of hostilities. On June 25, 1950, equipped with Soviet-made weapons and supported politically by China, North Korean forces cross the postwar dividing line of the 38th parallel to invade and ultimately annex U.S. ally South Korea. The United States called for multilateral action against the North Koreans, which was organized around the United Nations (the Soviet delegation was boycotting the Security Council to protest the continued occupation of the China seat by the Chinese Nationalists and so was not able to veto the proposal). American ships were already on their way and within days began pushing back North Korean forces which had already taken control of roughly seven-eighths of South Korean territory. General Douglas MacArthur led the counteroffensive and with the dramatic invasion at Inchon behind the front lines, succeeded in pushing back the invaders to the original frontier by late September. After MacArthur's demand for surrender went unheeded, the General Assembly authorized the landing of North Korea by the UN forces.

With the tables turned, the North Korean forces quickly fell back until the UN armies threatened to enter China, Korea's neighbor. In spite of Chinese threats not to approach the border, UN forces came within miles of China and prompted the Chinese 'volunteers' to enter the fray. Chinese intervention in the Korean War raised the very real possibility of full-scale world war in late 1950. MacArthur was sacked by President Truman precisely because he had ignored Truman's warnings to avoid accidental escalation. The front moved back into South Korean territory and eventually stabilized near the 38th parallel. Peace talks dragged as both sides hoped for a military breakthrough. An armistice was eventually signed on July 27, 1953, after 450,000 casualties on the South Korean side, of which 150,000 were Americans, and an estimated 2 million on the North Korean/Chinese side (Chai 1972, 86).

In the beginning of the Korean War, U.S. ships were maneuvered into the Formosa Straits between mainland China and Taiwan, in order to discourage would-be aggression by the People's Republic against the Nationalist government on the island. Throughout the 1950s and 1960s, both governments were adamant in their claims that the other side had no right to govern any part of China. The U.S. repeatedly acted to prevent aggression, but by so doing precipitated bellicose responses from Beijing. The U.S.-Taiwan Mutual Defense Assistance Agreement of 1951 confirmed China's fears that the United States sought domination of the entire Asian continent from this foothold (Camilleri 1980, 32). Combined with the formation of the Southeast Asia Treaty Organization (SEATO) which encircled China, Beijing had sufficient evidence to seek a preemptive strike to reassert its control over the region.

China began shelling some of the Taiwanese fortresses on the islands in the Formosa Straits in late 1954. In response, the United States demanded a cessation of hostilities, implicitly threatening U.S. intervention with atomic weapons. This U.S. policy of "brinkmanship" was used again in 1958 after Chinese shelling began again. The Chinese, meanwhile, were ambivalent. In 1956, China declared its interest in improved relations with the West in the context of the Third World Bandung Conference. The goal of disengaging the United States from the region had clearly failed, but concerns about precedents and appearances prevented a public capitulation on the issue. The result was simmering Sino-American hostility which was exacerbated by the United States entry into the Vietnam War in the mid-1960s.

During the 1950s, the U.S.-Soviet Cold War was in full swing. Although the Eisenhower administration offered tentative olive branches (his "Open Skies" proposal would have permitted free access by each nation's reconnaissance aircraft to the other's airspace), the dominance of confrontational rhetoric continued. John Foster Dulles, the U.S. secretary of state, strongly advocated a so-called "perimeter containment" strategy which led to the formation of numerous regional alliances (containment) in areas surrounding the Soviet Union. Minor skirmishes were to be treated as major tests of resolve. The enemy was seen as an insidious, pervasive, single-minded force bent on world domination. This perspective was codified in the 1957 "Eisenhower Doctrine" declaring U.S. support for any victim of "armed aggression from any country controlled by international Communism" (Spanier 1988, 101). We should note, that U.S. intervention stopped short of helping nations in the Soviet sphere, such as Hungary in 1956 where an anti-Soviet uprising was quelled with tanks.

The Soviets, on their side, viewed any American efforts at self-defense as inherently provocative. The rearmament of Germany beginning in 1950, the establishment of anti-Soviet alliances, the dramatic Korean War–era U.S. military buildup, and detonation of the hydrogen bomb in 1952 all seemed to convey that the United States was preparing to conquer the world. When combined with the economic aid provided to Western Europe in the context of European reconstruction and the isolation of the Soviet economy, Moscow had evidence that the United States also aimed at crippling the socialist world financially.

By 1960, Americans were close to panic following a chain of Soviet achievements: the Soviet detonation of a hydrogen bomb in 1953, the test of the first intercontinental ballistic missile in 1957, and the shocking success of the *Sputnik* satellite in 1957. Fidel Castro's successful revolution in Cuba in 1959 prompted the United States to intervene in what would be later called the "perfect failure"—the Bay of Pigs. A group of U.S.-backed Cuban exiles attempted an amphibious invasion to overthrow Castro's regime, only to be captured at great public embarrassment to the Kennedy administration (Higgins 1987). The downing of a U-2 reconnaissance aircraft in 1960 scuttled an important peace conference being planned at the time, and the Berlin Wall Crisis of 1961 severely tested the mettle of newly elected American President John F. Kennedy.

This is not to say that the entire period was a catastrophe. On the contrary, many felt that with the death of Joseph Stalin in 1953 his successor, Nikita Khrushchev, would bring a new warmth to U.S.-Soviet relations. A number of summits and agreements early on confirmed this hope. Khrushchev was the first Soviet leader to visit the United States when he attended a summit in 1959. Talks concerning the disposition of Germany continued throughout the decade, although with no resolution. American intervention to prevent the fall of Egypt's left-leaning Gamel Nasser during the 1956 war with Israel did much to convince Third World revolutionaries that the United States was capable of impartiality.

The culmination of these Cold War tensions was also the crucible for change. The Cuban Missile Crisis, which took place over a two-week period in October 1962, brought the two superpowers to the brink of full-scale nuclear confrontation. Kennedy estimated, at the height of the crisis, that the chances of all-out war were "between one out of three and even" (Allison 1971, 1). Ostensibly an attempt by the Soviet Union to offset the tremendous American advantage in nuclear weaponry, the deployment of Soviet medium-range nuclear missiles in Cuba was deemed provocative by the Kennedy administration and their removal became the object of a tense confrontation. Soviets demanded, after stonewalling for a week, U.S. assurance that Cuba would never again be attacked and that U.S. weapons deployed in Turkey would be dismantled. Kennedy placed a naval blockade around the island in an attempt to buy time and prevent completion of the missile project, only to find that by day thirteen the missiles were apparently operational. An American reconnaissance aircraft was shot down over Cuba and the United States prepared to implement plans for an all-out attack and invasion against Cuba. Only at the last moment did word come from Moscow, in the form of conflicting cables, that the Soviets would accept a settlement.

While the world breathed a sigh of relief, the immediacy of nuclear war led leaders on both sides of the Cold War to seek new arrangements and agreements to prevent this from happening again. From 1963 through 1979, the United States and the Soviets (later joined by the Chinese) entered a period of relative "détente" or relaxation of tensions. Although the Vietnam War marred this trend, the pattern is nonetheless visible (Stoessinger 1990, 207).

Détente I: 1963–1979

Kennedy and Khrushchev (soon to be replaced by Lyndon Johnson and Leonid Brezhnev) began almost as soon as the crisis was over to build bridges. The "hot line" was established in 1963 as a permanent communication link between the United States and the Soviet Union (although a Norwegian's plow once severed it!) and the problem of rapid communication in time of crisis was essentially solved. An above-ground nuclear Test Ban Treaty was also signed, ending the environmentally catastrophic practice of testing nuclear weapons in the atmosphere. As discussed in case #8, this was also the period of dramatic changes in the nuclear arms race. The Anti-Ballistic Missile Treaty and Strategic Arms Limitation Talks brought the previously unregulated arms race under at least nominal superpower control through mutually agreed on ceilings of deployment and development of certain types of nuclear weapons.

Perhaps the most significant development during this period, aside from the gradual rapprochement between East and West, was the severing of relations between erstwhile comrades in the Soviet Union and the People's Republic of China. While the Sino-Soviet alliance was clearly as much a marriage of convenience as an ideological alliance, the breakup was largely the result of differences in philosophy and priority. Mao's revolutionaries had long placed Third World liberation ahead of all other international objectives and did not hesitate to burn bridges with the United States in their efforts to liberate colonies and spread socialism. The Soviet Union, on the other hand, had learned that it was partly dependent on Western support and goodwill to succeed in the world and was more inclined to favor warmer relations. This difference in attitude became more pronounced after the Cuban Missile Crisis, when China found itself joined by more and more radical regimes in the Third World as decolonization went into full swing and as the Soviets mended fences with the West.

Another key factor in the rupture was China's resentment of the power exerted on its political and economic life by a Soviet Union intent on reproducing itself. Soviet economic advisors urged Chinese leaders to implement a full-scale industrialization program based on steel, machines, and other heavy industry. This plan collided with the largely agrarian context in which the Chinese Revolution had flourished. The Great Leap Forward, a program of intense modernization of the Chinese economy, was initiated as much to achieve economic objectives as to assert Chinese autonomy. Mao furthermore objected to the rather tentative Soviet reforms under Khrushchev which introduced more market-oriented policies. Chinese leaders felt that the Soviets had essentially sold out the revolution and that they alone held the torch of true socialism.

In 1962, Mao declared that the leaders of the Soviet Union were now "revisionists"—a withering attack from an ideological perspective which aimed at undermining Soviet leadership of international communism. In 1963, China condemned the Test Ban Treaty which would have excluded it from the ranks of the nuclear powers and in 1964 China tested its first atomic weapon as if to thumb its nose at what it saw as a U.S.-Soviet alliance forming against it (Yahuda 1982, 30). By the late 1960s, the Soviets and Chinese engaged in border skirmishes that threatened to escalate as the Soviets spoke of preemptive strikes against Chinese nuclear installations. Ultimately, it was the United States that intervened to defuse the conflict.

The Vietnam War created a new form of tension in what by the mid-1960s was clearly a three-way relationship. American support for the South Vietnamese government deeply troubled China, although its relations with the North Vietnamese were cool at best, stemming from Chinese claims on Vietnamese territory rejected by Hanoi. The Soviet Union, having supported Ho Chi Minh and the North Vietnamese revolution, was forced to provide support again throughout the Vietnam War. China was in the enviable position of watching its two enemies fight it out with each other. During this period of relative security, Mao undertook the Cultural Revolution to purify China's society of Western influences, although the result was the eradication of many of the nation's most accomplished intellectuals. The event so disgusted Western observers that six years later Zhou Enlai still felt obliged to explain it to Henry Kissinger on the occasion of his first visit (Kissinger 1979, 751).

The escalation from a handful of troops and advisors in 1964 to over 500,000 by 1969 was so gradual that it never, in and of itself, constituted a serious threat to global stability. It was not until the war began to wane, following Lyndon Johnson's decision in 1968 to begin troop withdrawals, that uncertainty entered into the process. Nixon's attacks on Cambodia, the "Vietnamization" of the war, through which poorly motivated South Vietnamese soldiers were given charge of the fighting, and the popular unrest at home and the on-again, off-again peace talks in Paris combined to give the closing years of the Vietnam War an unreal dimension which was eventually separated from the "real" world of superpower diplomacy. An illustration of this was the crucial invitation of Beijing to the United States to send a high-level representative in 1971. Henry Kissinger went to Pakistan and secretly on to China (absent on pretense of coming down with the flu!) where preparations were made for Nixon's historic trip. All of this took place against the backdrop of intensified American air attacks in North Vietnam and a secret U.S. invasion of Cambodia.

Nixon's visit to China came in late February 1972 and resulted in a rather ambiguously worded statement known as the Shanghai Communique. The statement pledged an effort toward normalization of relations and supported the notion of "One China," although it left unclear who should govern this entity—Communist Party in Beijing or the Kuomintang in Taiwan (Kissinger 1979, 1085). The visit to China was followed in May by the first-ever visit by an American president to Moscow, where the Strategic Arms Limitation Talks (SALT I) were accepted in principle. Each of these agreements came in spite of ongoing disputes between the superpowers over conflicts between China, India, and Pakistan; between North and South Vietnam (although the Paris Peace Accords ended U.S. involvement in the war in January 1973); between Israel and Arab nations (Anwar Sadat expelled Soviet advisors from Egypt in July 1972, five years after they supported his country during the Six-Day War); and in Cambodia and elsewhere.

The period of détente was perhaps best known for the general warming of relations between all Western nations and the East. Willy Brandt, chancellor of West Germany during the mid-1970s, established extensive ties with the Democratic Republic to the East. The Helsinki Accords were signed in 1975 and pledged all European nations, East and West, to safeguarding human rights and civil liberties. The United States under Jimmy Carter, continued these trends by deepening the arms control agreements made under SALT I and extending full diplomatic recognition to the P.R.C. now under the leadership of Deng Xiaoping in 1979. In short, there seemed to be every reason to hope that the United States had established an era of understanding and cooperation.

Cold War II: 1979–1985

The year 1980 will stand out as a critical turning point in the Cold War, since it was in January that the Soviet Union for the first time invaded a neutral country with its own troops. It would be another nine years before the troops were withdrawn, and during this period East-West relations would slip back into Cold War patterns.

Jimmy Carter declared, following the Afghanistan invasion, that "my opinion of the Russians has changed more drastically in the last week than in the previous two and a half years" (Stoessinger 1990, 232). It is still difficult to understand Soviet motives for the invasion, although the immediate cause was to shore up an embattled ally in a strategic region. The fall of the Shah in 1979 had led to the spread of radical Islamic fervor throughout the region and jeopardized Russia's long-term quest for a warm-water port, access to oil reserves, and proximity to Pakistan and India. Perhaps also the

Soviets estimated that the benefits of U.S. rapprochement were at a zenith and that things could only go downhill. The Soviets imposed martial law in Poland for much the same reason, it would seem, and with the election of Ronald Reagan as president in late 1980 détente was dead.

The Reagan administration took advantage of this situation to strengthen U.S. power at home and to improve ties with Beijing. Sino-American relations were never better. China imposed diplomatic sanctions against Moscow and joined the United States in its containment of Soviet expansionism (Stoessinger 1990, 106). Reagan expanded the arms buildup begun by Carter, even at the cost of an overwhelming fiscal deficit, and engaged in military involvement in Nicaragua, Lebanon, and Afghanistan. SALT II was left unratified and Reagan's aggressive rhetoric ("evil empire," "plan for Armageddon") alarmed Europeans without chasing away their support. Margaret Thatcher and Helmut Kohl, united in defiance of Soviet agression and against extraordinary public pressure, permitted the deployment of a new generation of medium-range nuclear missiles in Europe.

Reagan offered a few rather unrealistic arms controls proposals which resulted in a stalemate and ultimate Soviet walkout at the Strategic Arms Reduction Talks (START) and Intermediate-Range Nuclear Forces negotiations (INF). The Strategic Defense Initiative (SDI) was proposed in 1983 with the aim of enveloping the United States in a protective shield of high-tech weapons aimed at incoming Soviet missiles. He proposed repeatedly to abandon the research program in exchange for deep unilateral Soviet arms cuts.

It was not until the emergence of Mikhail Gorbachev on the world scene that Cold War II began to change course.

Détente II: 1985–1991

The story of the second wave of détente, culminating in the collapse of the Soviet Union itself, is likely familiar to the reader, and bears only a cursory review. Suffice it to say that Reagan embraced the new, youthful, and apparently open-minded Soviet leader with open arms. He noted that this was not a typical Communist, but was someone we could work with (Nathan and Oliver 1989, 483). A number of summits were arranged and by 1987 the INF Treaty, the first nuclear arms reduction agreement, was signed.

Strategic arms talks took much longer to resolve, with Gorbachev repeatedly asking the United States to abandon SDI in vain. It was not until the Soviet empire was crumbling during the Bush administration that a far-reaching strategic arms reduction treaty was signed. Before the ink was dry (prior to ratification by the Senate), a new, more profound agreement was signed with the new Russian Republic under the leadership of Boris Yeltsin. Other agreements with dramatic cuts in chemical weapons stockpiles and production bans, significant cuts in conventional (nonnuclear) weapons deployed across Europe, and an eventual U.S.-Soviet "alliance" against Iraq in the Gulf War of 1990–1991, demonstrated an entirely new era of U.S.-Soviet cooperation. With Soviets leaving Afghanistan and releasing control over all East European states in 1989, permitting the reunification of Germany in 1990, the Cold War was well and truly over. At this point, rehabilitation of the defeated erstwhile enemy is the pressing issue of peacetime, much as it was after the defeat of Nazi Germany and Imperial Japan in 1945.

What has become of the Chinese orientation to the Americans and Russians in the context? The well-known Tienanmen Square massacres of 1989 dealt a serious blow to the emerging democracy movement that had swept across China under Deng. The immediate result was the imposition of sanctions against China by the United States and Western Europe, although most of these were allowed to lapse by 1992. Relations between the Soviet Union and China improved significantly during the Gorbachev era. The Soviets supported a UN-mediated withdrawal of Soviet-backed Vietnam from China-backed Cambodia, culminating in free elections and the disarmament of the pro-China Khmer Rouge. A Sino-Soviet summit took place in 1989 (the first since 1956) where, according to one observer, "Russia wooed and China cooed" (Rourke 1990, 44). China became concerned about the closeness of U.S.-Soviet relations during the Gulf War, but stopped short of vetoing a critical UN resolution permitting armed intervention against Iraq.

Perhaps the only indication that serious differences persist in China's orientation toward the two superpowers was its decision to detonate a massive nuclear weapon in June 1992 and the September Bush decision to sell large numbers of fighter jets to Taiwan, thus violating a long-standing ban in the hopes of winning some votes. Bill Clinton threatened to cut off much U.S. trade with China in retaliation for its human rights abuses then reversed himself. It is simply too soon to tell how the "unipolar" world will look as China and Russia sort out the new international configuration.

PART II: THE BALANCE OF POWER TRIANGLE

As mentioned before, the balance of power theory assumes that major powers, in the pursuit of enhanced security and influence, will combine their forces with nations who share the same enemies. These alliances will shift over time as different nations develop greater capacity to wage war and thereby become a new threat. Overall, no single country will rise above the rest and every major power's essential identity will be preserved (or at least the basic number of major players will be stable).

Did this pattern of behavior show up in our case? First, it would be useful to discuss the nature of a three-way balance of power, usually referred to as tripolarity. There are four possible alliance patterns in a tripolar system, illustrated by the chart below. They include a very cordial "ménage à trois" in which all major powers are cooperating with each other, the "unit veto" system in which none of the players is cooperating, the intermediate stages of a "marriage" in which one player is positioned against the other two ("odd man out"), and the "romantic triangle" in which one player ("pivot")

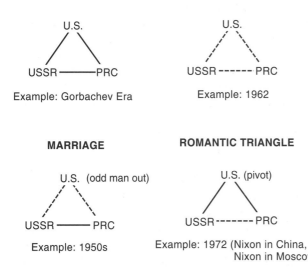

Figure 3.1 The tripolar system's possible configurations.
Source: Adapted from Lowell Dittmer, "The Strategic Triangle: A Critical Review," in *The Strategic Triangle* (New York: McGraw-Hill, 1987).

has good relations with each of the others, although they are antagonistic to each other (Dittmer 1987).

Figure 3.1 illustrates with examples the possible configurations of alliances in a tripolar system. In the case of the "marriage" and "romantic triangle" arrangements, numerous examples exist and deserve more attention. Segal and the contributors to his volume generally credit China with best understanding the nature of the "triangle" and with taking the most active role in changing its nature over time. After all, it was China that attempted to mend fences with the Eisenhower administration and ultimately invited Nixon to Beijing. And it was China that severed relations with the Soviets against Moscow's wishes (Segal 1982).

The United States also demonstrated some diplomatic sophistication beginning in the mid-1960s, particularly under the Nixon administration, when it abandoned twenty years of ideological principles in favor of an improved strategic position by warming up to China and working with the Soviets. One can hardly imagine two more unlikely individuals to meet with Chinese leaders in Beijing than Richard Nixon and Ronald Reagan, both passionate Cold Warriors from the outset!

Under Gorbachev, the Soviet Union maneuvered itself into something close to a pivot position of its own when it continued working closely with the Chinese during the Tienanmen Square period when U.S.-Chinese relations cooled significantly. This was a departure for the Soviets who tended to view the "China Factor" with some contempt—particularly in the presplit days when the Chinese were viewed as mere pupils.

Overall, by the 1960s, all superpowers were conscious of the tripolar dynamic in which they were enmeshed and made some effort to jockey for the best position—namely the "pivot" role. Barring this type of diplomatic success, each player at least attempted to avoid being locked in the least desirable position—that of "odd man out." For example, one can attribute China's eagerness to open diplomatic relations with the United States in the late 1960s to Beijing's perception of significantly improved U.S.-Soviet relations and the fear of being "left out"—even if their actions resulted in giving extraordinary influence to the United States. Gorbachev hoped that combining his good relations with the United States with improved ties to China could ultimately put him in the position of pivot, although this scenario never materialized.

The odd crisis, border dispute, military intervention, and the like simply set the stage for a rearrangement of the triangle. Gerald Segal and others have pointed out that communication between the superpowers has dramatically increased over time, with the result (perhaps unintended) that crises seem to be declining in intensity and frequency (Segal 1980, 3). This may have much to do with communication as a vehicle to clarify perceptions and avoid mistakes, key elements of the triangle according to Stoessinger (1990) and Gurtov and Hwang (1980). Summitry, the hot line, telecommunications, normalized relations, and the United Nations have all been new vehicles to improve communications, and crises have been more muted and cooperation more likely since their introduction.

This is not to say that realism is the only approach to explaining triangular relations. It is important to recall that for the first fifteen years at least, ideology was a key factor in explaining alignments and animosities. Had it not been for Mao's Communist ideology, China's alignment with the Soviet Union would likely not have happened, given the historical and structural tensions in the relationship. Likewise, had it not been for John Foster Dulles' intense dislike of socialism, he probably would have entertained the notion of normalizing relations with China rather than rebuffing their overtures. But by the mid-1960s, ideology took a backseat to power politics, with the result that American presidents often distinguished between "good" and "bad" Communists and Chinese ideologues were bending over backwards to explain why a revolutionary government could benefit from doing business with the most unabashedly capitalist nation in history. Even today, these ideological flip-flops are at the root of the political unrest in China and Russia, since they are fundamental to charting a future of economic and political freedom.

Questions to Consider

1. What does the future hold for this great power triangle? With the demise of the Soviet Union and the end of East-West antagonism in the European theater, do we now have China as the ultimate "odd man out" from here

on? Or can we expect to see a happy and peaceful "ménage à trois" for years to come?

2. To what extent were forces other than balancing power significant in determining alignment choices by the superpowers? Did ideology make a difference? What about perceptions? To what extent did bureaucratic process enter into the selection of policies?

3. To what extent were the needs of humanity served by the tripolar relationship? Were people safer? Better fed? Better educated? What does this teach us about politics and morality?

References

Graham Allison. *Essence of Decision: Explaining the Cuban Missile Crisis* (Boston: Little, Brown, 1971).

Joseph Camilleri. *Chinese Foreign Policy: The Maoist Era and Its Aftermath* (Seattle: University of Washington Press, 1980).

Winberg Chai. *The Foreign Relations of the People's Republic of China* (New York: Putnam, 1972).

Lowell Dittmer. "The Strategic Triangle: A Critical Review" in Kim Ilpong, ed., *The Strategic Triangle* (New York: McGraw-Hill, 1987).

John Lewis Gaddis and Terry L. Diebel, eds. *Containing the Soviet Union: A Critique of US Policy* (New York: Pergamon-Brasseys International Defense Publishers, 1987)

Melvin Gurtov and Byong-Moo Hwang. *China Under Threat* (Baltimore: Johns Hopkins Press, 1980).

Trumbull Higgins. *The Perfect Failure: Kennedy, Eisenhower and the CIA at the Bay of Pigs* (New York: Norton, 1987).

Henry Kissinger. *White House Years* (Boston: Little, Brown, 1979).

James M. McCormick, ed. *A Reader in American Foreign Policy* (Itasca, IL: Peacock, 1986).

James A. Nathan and James K. Oliver. *United States Foreign Policy and World Order*, 4th ed. (Glenview, IL: Scott, Foresman, 1989).

John T. Rourke. *Making Foreign Policy: United States, Soviet Union, China* (Pacific Grove, CA: Brooks/Cole, 1990).

Gerald Segal. *The Great Power Triangle* (New York: St. Martin's, 1980).

Gerald Segal, ed. *The China Factor: Peking and the Superpowers* (New York: Holmes & Meier, 1982).

John Spanier. *American Foreign Policy Since World War II*, 11th ed. (Washington, DC: Congressional Quarterly Press, 1988).

John G. Stoessinger. *Nations in Darkness: China, Russia, and America*, 5th ed. (New York: McGraw-Hill, 1990).

Adam B. Ulam. *The Rivals: America and Russia Since World War II* (New York: Viking Press, 1971).

Kenneth Waltz. *Theory of International Politics* (Reading, MA: Addison-Wesley, 1979).

Michael Yahuda. "China and the Great Power Triangle," in Gerald Segal, ed., *The China Factor: Peking and the Superpowers* (New York: Holmes & Meier, 1982).

Cuban Missile Crisis

When making a decision, we typically know in advance what we want. We consider the facts at hand, come up with a few alternative courses of action, imagine what might happen if we pick each one, and then choose the alternative that gets us what we wanted in the first place. This is the epitome of rationality. Anything other than this is not rational—not to say that it is necessarily wrong. We sometimes make choices based on habit or tradition, or we feel driven by our emotions. At the very least, our analysis of the situation and pursuit of alternatives is cursory at best. If you have ever worked on a committee, you know that groups rarely make decisions based on a careful calculation of costs and benefits—they typically go for the least common denominator. Imagine 3 million people trying to come to a decision and you will understand why rationality in foreign policy is a rare thing.

RATIONALITY AND THE CUBAN MISSILE CRISIS

Almost as soon as it was resolved, the October 1962 Cuban Missile Crisis became a focus of scholarly attention. It is seen by millions as a moment, suspended in time, when the earth's very survival hung in the balance. John F. Kennedy himself estimated the odds of nuclear holocaust at the peak of the crisis was "between one out of three and even" (Allison 1971, 1). Had he known the full extent of Soviet capabilities in Cuba, he would have put the odds even higher. Given the extreme danger and risk of the situation on the one hand, and its successful conclusion on the other, it is no surprise that this episode in world history has become a popular case study in conflict management and decision making. Considering how often trivial incidents have escalated into conflagration, it is heartening to find a case in which disaster is so elegantly avoided. Finally, another reason the Cuban Missile Crisis has received so much attention is because many of the key participants were young men with stories to tell. Memoirs, personal accounts, interviews, and symposia involving the participants have kept alive interest in this most critical event.

We will focus on what the Cuban Missile Crisis tells us about how policy is developed and carried out in a crisis. A crisis, as defined by Charles Hermann, is a problem which combines the elements of surprise, salience, and urgency (Hermann 1969). In other words, the problem springs into view with little warning, it directly threatens a high-security priority for the nation, and requires prompt action in order to avert catastrophe. Crises have been further defined as "coercive diplomacy" in which a nation seeks to blackmail an opponent into submission without the direct use of force (Craig and George 1990). Avoidance of bloodshed is the primary concern in such situations, although the risk of war is extremely great.

Hermann assumes that in a crisis situation, decisions are made at the top levels in a bewildering "pressure-cooker" setting in which other issues are set aside, facts are scarce, and anxiety is high. This can present an ideal opportunity for intensive and creative problem solving as the talents of the most powerful (and sometimes most competent) leaders in the country are riveted on a single task. On the other hand, because information is so scarce and time is so limited, a crisis may lead to flawed and even catastrophic miscalculations. The outcome depends on many factors, including the personalities and perceptions of those in power, the degree of planning for contingencies, the expectations of decision makers, and the organization of the decision-making unit. The key question in all of this is whether decision makers are able to specify their goals clearly, identify options and predict their respective outcomes, and choose the option that leads to an outcome most compatible with their objectives: the epitome of rationality.

Before determining whether the decisions made during the Cuban Missile Crisis were rational, it would be helpful to review the history of the event.

THE CUBAN MISSILE CRISIS

The Kennedy administration had faced serious tests in 1961, its first year in office. Just three months after inauguration day, the Bay of Pigs invasion, planned by the Eisenhower administration and executed poorly by the Kennedy administration, led to a disastrous and clumsy escapade in which U.S.-armed and funded Cuban exiles failed to invade Cuba and precipitate an anti-Castro revolution. The result was a further discrediting of U.S. policy in the Third World. The June 3–4 Vienna Summit between Khrushchev and Kennedy did not go as planned, and the Soviet leader came away with the impression that his young U.S. counterpart did not have the heart to stand firm in the face of diplomatic threats. The Soviets moved to take control of Berlin by erecting the Wall on August 12, 1961, and encountered no U.S. intervention to reverse the action. In early 1962, U.S.-USSR arms control talks went nowhere and the United States discovered that the Soviets had deployed significant military hardware in Cuba, making it a "bridgehead of Sino-Soviet imperialism and a base for Communist agitation" (Ferrell 1985, 362). To make matters worse, the U.S. economy was suffering and Republican opposition to Kennedy's apparent weakness meant midterm elections scheduled for November 1962 might bring very bad news to Democrats.

In this context, the Soviet Union began deploying medium-range nuclear missiles in early September 1962. Although denying it repeatedly through that month, Soviet officials placed forty-two such weapons, each "with a nuclear warhead twenty or thirty times more powerful than the Hiroshima bomb" (Sorenson 1965, 668). Soviet motives are as yet unclear, although it seems the goals of deterring an attack on Cuba and bolstering the apparent nuclear inferiority of the Soviet Union were central (Garthoff 1989, 23; Trachtenberg 1985, 163). Although U.S. officials suspected the buildup of Soviet weaponry in Cuba beyond what had been previously observed, it was not until Monday, October 15, when a lone U-2 spy plane brought back photographs of Soviet installations being erected in Cuba that they had their first evidence.

Early the next morning, John F. Kennedy was presented with the information by his national security adviser, McGeorge Bundy, who stressed the seriousness of the situation: the Soviets now had the capacity to attack more than half of the United States, including Washington, D.C., with only a few minutes' warning. The president was astonished by the report. As put by Robert Kennedy, U.S. attorney general at the time, ". . . the dominant feeling was one of shocked incredulity" (Kennedy 1969, 27). President Kennedy determined during that first meeting that some form of forceful response was incumbent on the administration, although Secretary of Defense Robert McNamara and others wondered out loud whether the placement of weapons close to the United States constituted, in and of itself, a mortal danger (note that whether a situation is a "crisis" can be highly subjective). By that evening, a group which came to be known as Ex Comm (Executive Committee of the National Security Council) had developed several options for the president: blockade or quarantine, surgical air strike/invasion, diplomatic overtures/negotiation, direct talks with Castro, and doing nothing (Sorenson 1965, 682). Robert Kennedy, groping for options, at one point threw out the possibility of placing nuclear missiles in Berlin (Schlesinger 1965, 735). Although certainly not mutually exclusive, these options rapidly narrowed to just two: air strike or blockade (Kennedy 1969, 34). It was ultimately determined that any air strike would have to be extensive and followed up with an amphibious invasion—thus the blockade option was by far the more modest of the two.

For nearly a week, the Ex Comm deliberated in order to develop a final plan that could receive unanimous approval. Each alternative proved deficient in some major way, but no other options could be imagined. The air strike posed by far the most serious difficulties—not only of execution but of justification. Robert Kennedy remembered stressing the moral imperative of not launching a surprise attack on Cuba—a "Pearl Harbor in reverse" (Kennedy 1969, 38), although recently declassified transcripts of the meeting indicate that he favored the air strike option in the beginning (Trachtenberg 1985, 167). President Kennedy rejected the military's contention that the Soviets would not respond to a U.S. air strike, arguing that such an action would simply expand the scope of the present crisis. The blockade, on its side, had the problem of failing to directly remove the missiles. A blockade was an act of war which would likely result in some reaction, the least of which was not the threat of the Soviets attempting to run the blockade. It could postpone real action while permitting the Soviets to finish installation of the missiles.

By Friday evening, October 20, Kennedy had made the tentative decision to impose a blockade, citing the advantage of giving Khrushchev more time to consider the implications of the situation (Sorenson 1965, 691). He readily acknowledged that "there isn't any good solution . . . but this one seems the least objectionable" (National Archives 1988, 7). The decision was made formal on October 22 when Kennedy spoke to the nation in a televised address. He announced the presence of the missiles, his intent to see them removed, and the means whereby this was to be accomplished—leaving plenty of room for further action in the future. He also alerted the nation to the risks involved in standing up to the Soviet actions:

> My fellow citizens: let no one doubt that this is a difficult and dangerous effort on which we have set out. No one can foresee precisely what course it will take or what costs or casualties will be incurred. . . . The path we have chosen for the present is full of hazards, as all paths are—but it is the one most consistent with our character and courage as a nation. . . . (National Archives 1988, 10).

Over the next four days, the situation worsened. Khrushchev, not anticipating Kennedy's response, was as bewildered as U.S. officials had been upon discovering the missiles. He ordered an acceleration of the construction efforts and waited until the last minute to stop ships on the verge of running the blockade (prompting Secretary of State Dean Rusk's famous exclamation, "We're eyeball to eyeball and I think the other fellow just blinked!"). Meetings were held at the Organization of American States (OAS) and the Security Council over the next week, where aerial photographs of the Cuban-based missiles were displayed and the bulk of diplomatic support came down on the side of the United States (Blight 1990, 17). Cryptic messages were relayed through direct and indirect channels (including several meetings between Bobby Kennedy and Soviet Ambassador Anatoly Dobrynin and a few especially crucial encounters between ABC reporter John Scali and Soviet delegate Alexander S. Fomin). Although the blockade held, there was no resolution of the crisis as it entered its second weekend on October 25.

The pivotal development of the crisis was a pair of contradictory messages transmitted on October 26 and 27, along with a back-channel communication from Alexander Fomin. In the first letter and the Fomin message, Khrushchev communicated a willingness to consider withdrawing the missiles if the United States would guarantee Cuban sovereignty. While this message was being translated and analyzed, a second letter arrived, one which added the demand that the United States withdraw Jupiter missiles based in Turkey. Our understanding at this point is that, rather than being overridden by the Politburo after having written the conciliatory first letter, Khrushchev wrote both letters with their full approval. The difference was a change in Soviet intelligence assessments regarding the imminence of an American air strike on Cuba (Garthoff 1989, 82). Furthermore, Fomin was acting on his own, according to recent interviews with senior Soviet officials, but he would have conveyed the results of his conversations to Khrushchev (Garthoff 1989, 80).

Further heightening tensions on "Black Saturday" (October 27, 1962) were reports of Major Rudolph Anderson, Jr., a U-2 pilot, having been shot down over Cuba. This, combined with otherwise minor events (a U-2 flight strayed over Soviet territory, Communist terrorists attacked U.S. oil firms in Venezuela, a Soviet vessel began moving toward the quarantine line), gave the clear impression that the crisis was escalating out of control. A sense of urgency gripped the Ex Comm members and they agreed that if a solution to the crisis were not reached by Monday, war would be the likely next step (Blight 1990, 18).

Special Assistant for National Security McGeorge Bundy and Special Adviser for Soviet Affairs Llewellyn Thompson developed the notion of ignoring the second letter and responding favorably to the first only. This so-called "Trollope Ploy" was at first dismissed by an increasingly pessimistic President Kennedy and Secretary McNamara. It was only after prolonged discussion that the option was eventually adopted, although with several contingencies in mind. In particular, the Joint Chiefs were preparing for large-scale air strikes and invasion, while Kennedy leaned heavily in favor of a tit-for-tat removal of missiles in Turkey and Cuba simultaneously (or at least tacitly).

What Khrushchev knew at this time, but Kennedy did not, was that the Soviet forces in Cuba were armed with short-range "tactical" nuclear weapons and had authority to use them without prior approval from Moscow (*Christian Science Monitor*, October 16, 1992, 13). Khrushchev also knew that the attack on the U-2 was not authorized by Moscow, but was initiated by local commanders who were following Castro's decision to defend the island unilaterally (Garthoff 1989, 91). This information naturally heightened Khrushchev's fears of accidental war.

Kennedy chose not to respond directly to the U-2 downing with the originally planned air strikes, but to transmit a favorable message to Khrushchev formally accepting the first letter's terms. He also dispatched Bobby Kennedy to Ambassador Dobrynin where the attorney general conveyed the president's acceptance, coupled with a threat (commitment to withdraw the missiles must occur within forty-eight hours) and a "sweetener" (eventual withdrawal of Jupiter missiles in Turkey) (Garthoff 1989,

88). By Sunday morning, October 28, a message was received from Khrushchev announcing his acceptance of the terms of the settlement.

Recent evidence indicates that Castro felt he was by far the greatest loser in this whole incident, in that the missiles, as well as a few nuclear-capable bombers, were removed from the island with little more than a verbal assurance that the United States would honor Cuban sovereignty. This must have seemed a very hollow pledge coming from a nation that had already invaded once, attempted Castro's assassination, and controlled a major naval base on the island itself (Guantanamo Bay). Although he exerted considerable effort to frustrate the deal (Garthoff, 1989, chap. 4), it was nonetheless consummated, and on November 19 President Kennedy officially announced the removal of the missiles and the end of the crisis.

ANALYSIS OF DECISION TO BLOCKADE CUBA

While it is clear that several critical decisions were made by a variety of individuals, the two decisions that are easiest to study are (1) Kennedy's decision to announce the presence of the missiles and impose a blockade on October 22, and (2) Kennedy's decision to formally accept the tentative favorable letter from Khrushchev while ignoring the harsher communication on October 27. Certainly, perhaps the most important decisions in the crisis are those which were taken in Moscow—to both deploy and later remove the missiles. The documents detailing how these decisions were made are incomplete at best.

To determine whether these two decisions of Kennedy's were "rational," we should try to identify his goals, assess the quality of the search for options and their possible outcomes, and check to see whether the final choice promised to achieve the original goals spoken of. To the extent that the decision-making process comes close to this ideal model, we can say that it was rational (Allison 1971, 33).

The decision to impose a blockade came about after roughly four days of intensive deliberations in the White House. Within twelve hours of learning about the missiles, Kennedy had assembled a collection of individuals chosen for their authority over certain key areas of foreign policy and/or for their expertise on a substantive matter. Thus we find the secretaries of state and defense (Dean Rusk and Robert McNamara), the director of the CIA (John McCone), the national security adviser (McGeorge Bundy), and the chairman of the Joint Chiefs (Maxwell Taylor). Douglas Dillon, secretary of the treasury, was also involved. Other experts and authorities included several other senior officials at The State and Defense Departments (George Ball, Alexis Johnson, Edward Martin, Roswell Gilpatrick, Paul Nitze, and Llewellyn Thompson—a Soviet expert). Others at the meeting were present primarily because of presidential trust or obligation: Robert Kennedy (attorney general), Theodore Sorenson (presidential counsel), Pierre Salinger (press secretary), and Lyndon Johnson (vice president). This so-called Ex

Comm met regularly, sometimes for ten hours at a time, although not all the members were always present. There was no automatic seniority in the group, although Bobby Kennedy and McNamara seemed to typically dominate the discussions while several members hardly participated.

The Ex Comm arrangement has been praised as an ideal form of decision making, in that the individuals were present, as Sorenson later put it, "on our own, representing the President and not individual departments" (Sorenson 1965, 679). Furthermore, as the days wore on, the group met in the absence of the president, split into smaller committees, and generally ignored protocol and rank in the process of fleshing out options and their implications. Bobby Kennedy commented, "It was a tremendously advantageous procedure that does not frequently occur within the executive branch of the government, where rank is often so important" (Kennedy 1969, 46). This represents a deliberate avoidance of what has been called "groupthink" by Irving Janis, in that there was little peer pressure to adopt dramatic and hard-line responses (Janis 1972). Furthermore, it minimized the significance of the "turf" battles for which bureaucrats are famous.

Perhaps the first decision was to determine whether the placement of missiles in Cuba was indeed a threat to the national security. Surprisingly, the question of the seriousness of the threat and its effect on U.S. overall strategic superiority did not even come up until the evening of October 16, and at the behest of McGeorge Bundy—not the president. McNamara made it clear that he felt the presence of missiles in Cuba was no threat at all, although the Joint Chiefs unanimously disagreed (White House 1985, 184). Unswayed by McNamara's comments, it appears that Kennedy reached the conclusion that the Soviet missiles were a threat almost immediately and without deliberation or reconsideration, although he continued to puzzle over the Soviets' motives for placing the missiles in Cuba (White House 1985, 190).

Once the problem was identified, the process of clarifying the goals and options began, although not necessarily in that order. Early on, Kennedy determined, with general approval, that the missiles in Cuba must be removed, but without force if at all possible. He was also deeply concerned about international public opinion—particularly in Latin America and at the UN. Kennedy was deeply concerned about whether Europeans would take seriously American alarm over the presence of nuclear missiles near U.S. territory, considering the obvious fact that such a situation already existed for Germany and many other North Atlantic Treaty Organization (NATO) allies (Sorenson 1965, 681). When the challenge later came from Khrushchev to trade Soviet missiles in Cuba for American missiles in Turkey, Kennedy agonized over how he could justify rejecting the offer and risk war over something others would see as a reasonable offer ("October 27, 1962," 58). By the end of the crisis, it becomes clear that avoidance of all-out nuclear war was the highest priority. Clearly a variety of goals coexisted, not all of which were complementary. For the time being, the immediate concern was to eliminate the missiles while at the same time minimizing the risk of escalation and total war.

McNamara was the first to clearly articulate three options for dealing with the crisis: (1) a "diplomatic" option involving public declarations, consultation with allies, UN resolutions, and other gestures aimed at condemning and publicizing the Soviet move; (2) a "middle course" of aggressive surveillance and interdiction (blockade) of new weapons bound for Cuba; and (3) a "military" option with several variants, ranging from air strikes on narrowly selected targets (missile launchers and installations) to a broad-ranging series of attacks on all Cuban military facilities to be followed by an amphibious invasion (White House 1985, 182). Other ideas were mentioned, including retaliatory measures, doing nothing at all, and somehow persuading Castro to expel the weapons (Sorenson 1965, 682). Beyond these general categories of action, specific implementation of each approach was discussed at length. Questions were raised: Should an air strike be preceded by a public announcement, or should it be a surprise (a "Pearl Harbor in reverse" as put by Bobby Kennedy)? Should diplomatic initiatives include a specific ultimatum and a deadline for withdrawal? Should an exchange of missiles in Turkey (which Kennedy had long urged be removed anyway) be offered up front to persuade the Soviets to quickly settle the problem? Should the nuclear arsenal be put on alert and forces mobilized? etc.

The transcripts and personal accounts indicate that discussion of these various questions was thorough and uninhibited, although certain voices and ideas clearly dominated. By the evening of October 16, the choices seemed to have been whittled down to two: blockade and diplomacy vs. air strikes and possible invasion. McNamara was the most systematic speaker in the group. At one point, when the president seemed to be leaning in favor of air strikes, which McNamara opposed, the secretary of defense suggested: "I think tonight we ought to put down on paper the alternative plans and the probable, possible consequences thereof in a way that State and Defense could agree on, even if we disagree and put in both views . . . [T]he consequences of these actions have not been thought through clearly" (White House 1985, 189). His suggestion was ultimately accepted as the group split into separate committees charged with drafting the pros and cons and implications of each of the various options (Kennedy 1969, 45). Heavy emphasis was placed on extrapolating the outcomes and implications of each action, including variations of the actions: What do we do when ships approach the blockade line? What about submarines? Where will the Soviets strike after our air strikes? (This question was perhaps the most urgent of all, especially since it was clear the Joint Chiefs' initial optimistic projection that there would likely be no Soviet response was soundly rejected by the president.) Can we count on the support of the OAS and NATO? Should we display evidence of the missiles along with our announcement of their presence? Note the following emotional exchange between Undersecretary of State Ball and McGeorge Bundy regarding the implications of an air strike:

BALL: This [surprise attack scenario] just frightens the hell out of me as to what's going beyond. . . .

BUNDY: . . . What goes beyond what?

BALL: What happens beyond that. You go in there with a surprise attack. You put out all the missiles. This isn't the end. This is the beginning. . . . (White House 1985, 194)

It was not until this process of deliberation, development of options, extrapolation of possible outcomes and assessment of risks, reactions, and secondary options had gone on for three days, culminating in a sort of "moot court" session in which advocates of the two major alternatives made their case and submitted to questioning, that the president decided in favor of the blockade option—primarily because it had the advantage of leaving more secondary choices available—not that it promised to end the crisis immediately. As put by CIA Director John McCone, the blockade option held out the promise of achievement of the objective at lowest possible cost. Gilpatrick, deputy secretary of defense, argued "essentially, Mr. President, this is a choice between limited action and unlimited action, and most of us think that it's better to start with limited action" (Sorenson 1965, 693–695). On Friday afternoon, the decision was finalized and preparations were made for a national address on Monday evening, October 22, to announce that the blockade was in place and lay out U.S. demands.

In reconsidering this decision-making ordeal, it seems that the participants self-consciously and painstakingly went out of their way to be as rational as possible. While the initial decision to define the situation as a crisis seems to have been fairly informal and unilateral on Kennedy's part, the following phases of the decision-making process, from determination of options and extrapolation of outcomes, to the final making of a choice, were very systematic and thorough. In particular, both the president's and Bobby Kennedy's penchant for challenging others' claims became a hallmark of the process. Nothing seems to have been assumed or taken for granted, although one can argue that the lack of information made perfect decision-making impossible anyway. Something that is difficult to determine from documents and memoirs is whether the president made the decision largely on his own or with the advice of a very small number of advisors, and that the Ex Comm exercise was primarily intended to subtly persuade other key officials to his side.

All told, I would argue that the decision-making process involved in this first stage was essentially rational. Perhaps a better term is "satisficing"—a concept developed by Herbert Simon and James March to describe a decision-making process which is rational to a point. Rather than exhausting all possible options to find the perfect outcome, satisficing involves identifying the first viable option which comes close enough to achieving the stated goals to satisfy the decision maker (March and Simon 1958). Thus, while the search may be systematic and goal-oriented, it may be abbreviated in the interest of time and the need for action.

We should note that formulating policy is often assumed to mean policy-making. In reality there may be a world of difference between the formulation of policy on the one hand (the creative process) and the implementation of policy on the other (the governing process). In the case of the Cuban Missile Crisis, bureaucratic operations impeded the precise fulfillment of President Kennedy's wishes. The management of the blockade was a particularly challenging experience for everyone involved. Because the blockade was intended as much as a political statement as a military operation, the Ex Comm determined to see to it that no accidental encounters occurred. After specifying the parameters of the blockade, the navy was left to manage it. However, on Tuesday, Kennedy decided to constrict the size of the quarantine area in order to permit Soviet ships more time to consider whether to run the blockade. Assuming that his orders had been carried out to the letter, he went on to other things. Various Soviet ships were hailed, stopped, and boarded over the course of the next three days, presumably along the new, tighter blockade line the president had ordered. In reality, according to Graham Allison, the blockade line was never moved. The navy was acting according to the guidelines in the Manual of Naval Regulations, in spite of the president's injunctions (Allison 1971, 130–131). Naval commanders operated under the assumption that a blockade was an act of war, not a subtle political gesture, and seemed prone to use force against noncompliant Soviet vessels. The implication of these anecdotes is that policy implementation may be more heavily governed by bureaucratic regulations and so-called "standard operating procedures" than the process of developing policy itself.

ANALYSIS OF RESPONSE TO SOVIET OFFERS

After several days of rancorous debate in the UN Security Council and a number of close calls on the high seas, the U.S. and Soviet administrations began exchanging genuine offers for settlement. Three messages in particular arrived at the White House between Friday evening, October 26, and Saturday morning, October 27. Considering the U-2 shoot-down which was reported late Saturday morning, one could say there were four messages, each containing serious ambiguities. The key question on this last day of the crisis was how the United States would respond to these various signals.

The messages that arrived on Friday included a lengthy, wandering letter from Khrushchev, presumably written by the man himself. Coming on the heels of rather reckless speculation about an imminent U.S. attack on the part of congressmen and reporters, it spoke of the dangers of nuclear war and the risks of approaching it too closely. He spoke of a knot, tied so tightly by the two competing countries that it could only be loosed by being cut—a reference to nuclear holocaust. Buried in this rhetoric was the "germ of a reasonable settlement: inasmuch as his missiles were there only to defend Cuba against invasion, he would withdraw the missiles under UN inspection if the U.S. agreed not to invade" (Sorenson 1965, 712). At roughly the same time this message was received and was being translated, Ambassador Alexander Fomin of the Soviet Embassy (KGB officer?) contacted John Scali of ABC to propose withdrawal of missiles and a pledge to never introduce them again, combined with an American promise to respect Cuba's sovereignty. After consulting with Dean Rusk, Scali took back the message to Fomin that the United States saw "real possibilities" in the proposal (Schlesinger 1965, 755). These messages combined provided tangible hope that a viable settlement could be achieved quickly.

On Saturday morning, the Soviet news agency TASS announced that the USSR would be willing to withdraw the missiles if the United States dismantled missiles in Turkey. There was profound confusion in Ex Comm about the fact that the message conflicted with the previous ones (although part of the explanation may come from the fact that Bobby Kennedy had communicated in private to Ambassador Dobrynin a tentative willingness to trade missiles in Turkey for missiles in Cuba—Welch and Blight 1987/88, 11). One should note that the idea may have come from a speech by Austrian Foreign Minister Bruno Kreisky and an editorial by Walter Lippman in the *Washington Post*. At any rate, the effect of the news was despondency in the White House. There was a growing sense of urgency, largely based on the impression that certain weapons would be operational in a short period of time (one week to one month) and that the situation had to be resolved before then. There was a more genuine fear that local commanders might be able to take it upon themselves to launch an attack with fully armed and operational weapons—beyond Moscow's control (Blight 1990, 71)—a notion that has turned out to have been true, given the presence of tactical nuclear weapons under local control in Cuba. Contingency plans by now consistently anticipated an air strike and invasion in the first half of the next week (Monday/Tuesday, October 29, 30).

It is clear from the transcript (although less clear from the memoirs) that President Kennedy was deeply shaken by the second Khrushchev letter. Note his response to the proposal:

> . . . We're going to be in an unsupportable position on this matter if this (the trade) becomes his proposal. In the first place, we last year tried to get the missiles out of [Turkey] because they're not militarily useful. . . . Number 2, . . . to any man at the United Nations or any other rational man it will look like a very fair trade. . . . I think you're going to find it very difficult to explain why we are going to take hostile military action in Cuba against these sites—what we've been thinking about. The thing that he's saying is, "If you'll get yours out of Turkey, we'll get ours out of Cuba." I think we've got a very tough one here. ("October 27, 1962," 36–37)

The president's advisers, arguing against the trade, pointed out that he would be undercutting a NATO ally and may undermine the entire alliance

("October 27, 1962," 45). This debate engendered a search for alternatives, although the pressure of time seems to have constricted the number of options considered. McNamara and others urged an emphasis first on immediate cessation of work on the missile sites (which had never ceased but had gone on round the clock) and issued some form of warning and implicit threat to the Soviets to remove the missiles within forty-eight hours. From that point, it seems to have been assumed that air strikes would have to begin by Tuesday at the latest.

The Ex Comm began drafting possible responses to Khrushchev's letters by midmorning on Saturday, one calling for an immediate stand down in Cuba without any specific promise to remove the Turkish missiles, but an open-ended promise to discuss the situation ("October 27, 1962," 49).

A more significant development came when the option of ignoring the second letter was pushed more heavily by McGeorge Bundy and particularly Llewellyn Thompson. The following is a pivotal exchange:

JFK: . . . we're going to have to take our weapons out of Turkey. I don't think there's any doubt he's not going to retreat now that he's made that public, Tommy—he's not going to take them out of Cuba if we. . . .

THOMPSON: I don't agree, Mr. President, I think there's still a chance that we can get this line [i.e., ignoring the first letter] going.

JFK: He'll back down?

THOMPSON: . . . The important thing to Khrushchev, it seems to me, is to be able to say "I saved Cuba, I stopped an invasion". . . . ("October 27, 1962," 59)

Kennedy was leaning toward accepting Thompson's recommendation and preparing a thank you note to Khrushchev for his first letter, without reference to Turkey, when a report arrived that the U-2 flight was downed. This brought an even deeper sense of gloom on the group and the growing realization that war may have become inevitable. The discussions focused on how limited the options were and how short the time was for action. So-called "Black Saturday" was at its darkest at this moment.

Even with the extreme pressure and sense of urgency and anxiety, the deliberations of Ex Comm continued to provide reasonable and rather innovative options for the president. McNamara and Taylor discussed whether continued surveillance was in order and decided to proceed after a one-day pause. There was extensive discussion about small-scale retaliatory action of simply striking the specific antiaircraft battery which committed the act itself versus a wider-ranging attack. President Kennedy continued to search for nonmilitary alternatives, although without any clear expectation of success. McNamara indicated an air strike could be postponed until Thursday, to give time for consultation with NATO allies—another attempt at delaying war.

It may have been the U-2 attack and the clear reality of war that moved discussions more quickly toward implementing the "Trollope Ploy" of accepting the first letter's offer and ignoring the second. Robert Kennedy was dispatched in the early evening to explain to Ambassador Dobrynin the content of the president's approval. At this meeting, Bobby Kennedy made it clear that the Jupiter missiles in Turkey would eventually be removed, although this was to be done privately, and without any direct link to the Cuban missile withdrawal. Meanwhile, Ex Comm discussions continued about such details as fixing specific targets for the air strikes and invasion and organizing a new government in Cuba. The news that Khrushchev had accepted the offer came on Sunday morning, October 27, and was a surprise to Kennedy.

Was the decision to use the Trollope Ploy a rational one? Something which rationality does not emphasize is the question not just of the immediate choice, but of the choices that will follow. The Trollope Ploy, while not guaranteeing much of anything except a pleasant exchange, offered something the other proposals did not: a second chance. Except for the very real, if largely conjectured, assumption that the missiles in Cuba would be operational within a matter of days (a possibility which may not have substantively altered the problem anyway, given the presence of operational missiles within the Soviet Union), delaying the attack while a response came to this letter kept the option of escalation in place. It seems the administration was already trying to develop yet more delaying tactics, given McNamara's indication at one point that any attack on Cuba should be delayed until Thursday after NATO consultation. Again, the prudent step seems to have been to expand options, even if in the short run the objectives were not realized.

In all of this, we can also see that on Black Saturday, more important to the Kennedy administration than removing the missiles from Cuba, was the avoidance of nuclear war—especially one that erupted from accidental escalation. Furthermore, the goal of retaining some control over the dynamic seems to have emerged as a primary objective somewhere in the midst of the crisis. Removing the missiles from Cuba seems to have moved to third on the list by the end of the crisis. Rationality does not account for rapid changes in the hierarchy of goals, such that from day to day the decision makers are seen striving for a different set of objectives in the midst of the self-same crisis. All in all, it would seem that the decisions were more than rational, in the sense that they transcended even the rather demanding conditions of pure rationality. They demonstrated flexibility, adaptability, and reflection.

CONCLUSION

I hope that you, the reader, have enough information to begin to draw your own conclusions about the Cuban Missile Crisis and rationality. We can see that rationality may not be enough for some decisions, in that circumstances and needs may change so rapidly that the best decision is to simply delay a final choice as long as possible. While this may be "rational," it is not entirely consistent with the clean, logical, "once-and-for-all" implications of rationality as described in the literature.

Questions to Consider

1. Were the Cuban Missile Crisis decision makers seized with "nonrational" compulsions? To what extent did habit, prejudice, emotion, or other nonrational elements enter into the decision-making process?

2. How did the social and group dynamics affect the decision-making process? Would these individuals have reached the same outcomes had they been alone?

3. To what extent did implementation shape the policy? Were decisions carried out once they were made?

References

Graham Allison. *Essence of Decision: Explaining the Cuban Missile Crisis* (Boston: Little, Brown, 1971).

James G. Blight. *The Shattered Crystal Ball: Fear and Learning in the Cuban Missile Crisis* (Savage, MD: Rowman & Littlefield, 1990).

Christian Science Monitor, Oct. 16, 1992, p 13.

Gordon Craig and Alexander George. *Force and Statecraft* (New York: Oxford University Press, 1990).

Robert Ferrell, ed. *The Twentieth Century: An Almanac* (New York: World Almanac Pubs, 1985).

Raymond L. Garthoff. *Refections on the Cuban Missile Crisis,* rev. ed. (Washington, D.C.: Brookings, 1989).

Charles F. Hermann. "International Crisis as a Situational Variable," in James N. Rosenau, ed., *International Politics and Foreign Policy* (New York: Free Press, 1969): 409–421.

Irving Janis. *Victims of Groupthink* (Boston: Houghton Mifflin, 1972).

Robert F. Kennedy. *Thirteen Days: A Memoir of the Cuban Missile Crisis* (New York: W. W. Norton, 1969).

James March and Herbert Simon. *Organizations* (New York: Wiley and Sons, 1958).

National Archives. *The Cuban Missile Crisis: President Kennedy's Address to the Nation,* October 22, 1962. (Washington, DC: Government Printing Office, 1988).

"October 27, 1962: Transcripts of the Meetings of the Ex Comm." *International Security* 12 #3 (Winter 1987/88): 30–92.

Arthur M. Schlesinger, Jr. *A Thousand Days: John F. Kennedy in the White House* (Greenwich, CT: Fawcett Pubs, 1965).

Theodore Sorenson. *Kennedy* (New York: Harper & Row, 1965).

Mark Trachtenberg. "The Influence of Nuclear Weapons in the Cuban Missile Crisis." *International Security* 10 #1 (Summer 1985): 135–163.

Mark Trachtenberg. Introduction to "White House Tapes and Minutes of the Cuban Missile Crisis." *International Security* 10 #1 (Summer 1985): 164–170.

David Welch and James Blight. "The Eleventh Hour of the Cuban Missile Crisis: An Introduction to the Ex Comm Transcripts." *International Security* 12 #3 (Winter 1987/88): 5–29.

"White House Tapes and Minutes of the Cuban Missile Crisis." *International Security* 10 #1 (Summer 1985): 171–203.

Military–Industrial Complex

Karl Marx opined that the basic building block of any society was neither ethnicity nor religion, but class. By class, he meant the relationship one had with the fundamental methods of production. Under feudalism, society was divided into nobility and peasants. In capitalism, it was those who owned the factories and land (bourgeoisie) eager to take advantage of workers (proletariat). This conflict is the essence of the Marxist class struggle which can only be resolved through socialist and ultimately Communist revolution. While the modern service economy bears little similarity to the mid-nineteenth-century industrial societies Marx described, many believe that these basic categories apply. Particularly where government weapons policy is concerned, a small elite seems to make all the decisions for essentially self-serving purposes. What is more interesting, the workers are being enlisted as foot soldiers for the bourgeoisie. . . .

THE IRON TRIANGLE

Washington insiders know that many national policies are developed, determined, and implemented by a rather narrow set of self-interested individuals. Although not necessarily as venal as 1992 presidential candidate Ross Perot's "alligator-shoed foreign lobbyists at Gucci Gulch," the policy-making elite tend to respond to special interests on a given topic—the more obtuse and complex, the more special interests are dominant. Many analysts have used the term "iron triangles" to describe one such cooperative network.

As put by Dye and Zeigler:

> Once the bureaucracy takes over an issue, three major power bases—the "iron triangles"—come together to decide its outcome: the executive agency administering the program; the congressional subcommittee charged with its oversight; and the most interested groups, generally those directly affected by the agency. The interest groups develop close relationships with the bureaucratic policy makers. And both the interest groups and the bureaucrats develop close relationships with the congressional subcommittees that oversee their activities. Agency-subcommittee-interest group relationships become established; even the individuals involved remain the same over fairly long periods of time, as senior members of Congress retain their subcommittee memberships. (Dye and Zeigler 1993, 283)

The military-industrial complex is a special and significant example of an iron triangle. Since the end of World War II, defense contractors, Pentagon procurement specialists (buyers), and congressional subcommittees charged with appropriating funds for weapons have come together in a you-scratch-my-back-I'll-scratch-yours arrangement that conforms rather neatly to the Marxist analysis of capitalist power in the American democracy (Adams 1982, 24–26).

This is not to say that the relationship between Congress, the Pentagon, and defense contractors has always been cordial. At various points, reform efforts have been instigated following disclosures of waste, fraud, and political intrigue in defense procurement. Such a reform effort was initiated in the mid-1980s, but it may be too soon to tell whether this movement has produced any tangible results.

In the final analysis, it will be up to the reader to determine whether the defense industry is the sort of capitalist villain Marx described, or whether it shows that democracy still works in spite of strong pressures.

DEPARTMENT OF DEFENSE–INDUSTRY COOPERATION

We will look at the military-industrial complex by considering each of the three relationships in the triangle sequentially. Following this, we will look at changes and pressures on this system that have developed in the last twenty years.

To begin, the relationship between the Department of Defense and defense contractors is special. On the surface, the defense department relies on contractors to manufacture the weapons they will use in war, while the defense contractors depend on the Pentagon for much of their business. The relationship goes beyond this simple exchange, however.

To begin, a great deal of valuable insider information and special expertise is exchanged between industry and defense contractors through the regular rotation of personnel. Because military officers can receive a retirement pension after only twenty years of service, those with experience in procurement and weapons purchasing often leave the Pentagon to work for contractors where they are well paid for their connections and background. In 1960, for example, 691 retired officers were working for defense contractors, while in 1968 that figure rose to 2,072 (Donovan 1970, 54). The benefits are obvious. As explained by Adams:

> The contractors obtain many benefits from the movement of personnel: information on current and future DoD and NASA plans, especially in research areas; access to key offices in Federal agencies, technical expertise for weapons development and marketing, skilled personnel with an intimate knowledge of both sides of contracting (Adams 1982, 79)

Understanding Pentagon intentions and procedures is naturally vital to defense contractor planning. To a certain extent, the bulk of defense contractor–Pentagon relations centers on contractors' efforts to secure as much information about future weapons and strategies as possible. Some of these efforts have become routine. Defense Science Boards bring together Pentagon and defense contractor officials "at the earliest possible stage, well before Congress or the general public are aware of" future programs (Adams 1982, 168). This effort to obtain information has been at the heart of some of the most serious fraud cases in the procurement process. Raytheon, creator of the Patriot missile, was charged with fraud in 1990 for illegally obtaining documents that gave it an unfair bidding advantage in 1983. The court ruled that a pattern of such behavior had existed from 1978 to 1985 (Donahue 1991, 28, 29).

Defense contractors are eager to have guidance through the bureaucratic maze of Pentagon procurement as well (Reppy 1983, 25). The specifications for the Amraam missile published in the late 1980s was 500,000 pages long (Huey and Perry 1991, 36). As put by Korb with regard to procurement in the 1980s,

> The laws and regulations governing acquisition were extremely cumbersome. For example, there are some 400 different regulatory requirements that are pegged to some 60 different dollar thresholds . . . [D]efense contractors were forced to spend more time dealing with inspectors and auditors than working on the project. DoD proudly proclaimed that it performed in excess of 10,000 audits of defense contractors per year. (Korb 1988, 36–37)

Not only do defense contractors struggle for information on the Pentagon (to the point that they will risk breaking the law to get it), but Defense Department planners in turn rely heavily on defense contractors for information about new weapons systems, testing results, etc., in their efforts to secure funding from Congress (Reppy 1983, 27). Defense contractors are happy to supply this information, because of their dependence on Pentagon representation and advocacy.

Table 5.1 THE TOP TEN DEFENSE CONTRACTORS (1989)

Company	Pentagon Contracts in millions ($129 billion total for 1989)	% of Total Sales	Major Weapons
McDonnell Douglas	$8,617	60	F-15 fighter; Tomahawk missile; AH-64 Apache attack helicopter
General Dynamics	$6,889	87	F-16 fighter; Trident II missiles; M-1 tank
General Electric	$5,771	16	Aegis radar; F-404 and F-110 engines
Raytheon	$3,761	55	Patriot, Hawk missiles
General Motors	$3,691	4	Amraam, Tow missiles; M-1 tank components; Mk-48 torpedo
Lockheed	$3,651	91	F-117A, F-22 stealth fighters; C-130 transport
United Technologies	$3,556	>20	F-100 and J-52 engines; Seahawk helicopter
Martin Marietta	$3,337	75	Hellfire missle; Lantirn night vision
Boeing	$2,868	20	AWACS aircraft; CH-47 Chinook helicopter
Grumman	$2,373	70	F-14 fighter; A-6, E-2C, and EA-6B aircraft

Source: "The Top 25 Contractors," Fortune (February 25, 1991): 68.

Many defense contractors not only sell to the Pentagon, but they have few alternatives. As can be seen in Table 5.1, six of the top ten defense contractors make a majority of their sales to the Pentagon. Lockheed sells more than nine-tenths of its products to the Department of Defense. The other 10 percent is sold to NASA, the Postal Service, and other government agencies. Even corporations which are primarily civilian-oriented such as General Motors and Boeing have grown especially eager to maintain and expand their government contracts as their civilian sales have faltered.

A list of normal business expenses would include such things as capital investments (buildings, factories), machinery, storage, research and development, market research, etc. Normally, these expenses and other "startup costs" are borne by the firm. They put pressure on executives to quickly turn a profit in order to begin paying off debts incurred in this beginning phase. If a new product fails, the business will be forced to either suffer losses, lay off workers, or both. Such is the life of the ordinary business.

For defense contractors, many of these risks are either shared with or borne entirely by the government. As a result, doing business with the Pentagon can be addictive. As put by Reppy,

> It is likely that the defense-oriented firms invest less in plant and equipment than other comparable firms. The contractual forms used by the DoD discourage capital investment by covering all allowable costs on cost-plus contracts and by

giving only a low weight to a firm's investment in new plant and equipment in negotiated profit rates. (Reppy 1983, 39)

A 1976 Department of Defense study concluded that defense contractors reinvested only 35 percent of their sales, while comparable commercial firms typically reinvested 63 percent. That the Pentagon routinely covers overhead expenses normally borne by the firms is a clear advantage to selling to the Pentagon. It isn't so clear that Marx would describe this as capitalist collusion.

Perhaps the most significant aspect of doing business with the Pentagon is its sharing of research and development costs. To begin, the Department of Defense covers much of the research and development costs for weapons construction, which put together make up the bulk of Research and Development expenditures for all American industry. Of the top defense contractors in the 1970s, over three-fourths of Grumman's Research and Development was covered by the Department of Defense, two-thirds for Northrop, roughly one-half for Lockheed and General Dynamics, and one-third for Rockwell (Adams 1982, 97). Overall, three-fourths of defense industry Research and Development is covered (Reppy 1983, 31).

Not only is the research related to officially approved programs partly covered, but the Defense Department provides seed money for promising proposals. As put by Cypher:

> Large arms contractors regularly bombard the Pentagon with "unsolicited proposals" (known in the trade as Independent Research & Development and Bid and Proposal Programs—IR&D/B&P). Thousands of such proposals pour into the Pentagon, and 7,000 or more are funded every year. (Cypher 1991, 11)

In some cases, the research and development component of the program is the key element. In the case of the Strategic Defense Initiative (SDI), a massive, high-tech antiballistic missile system, more than eighty percent of Department of Defense expenditure was devoted to Research and Development alone. As the technological component of weapons systems has grown, the Research and Development share of total costs has increased, roughly doubling from 1965 to 1985.

Another key dimension of Pentagon-contractor relations is the "follow-on imperative." The follow-on imperative is described in some detail in Kurth. As he explains, with specific reference to the aerospace industry:

> About the time a production line phases out of one major defense contract, it phases in production of a new one, usually within a year. Since new aerospace systems require a considerable period of development before production, the production line normally is awarded the contract for the new system about three years before production of the old one is scheduled to phase out. (Kurth 1989, 199)

For political reasons we will review later, the pressures to maintain a production line for these major industries are very strong. Few major firms lose successive bids as a result (Reppy 1983, 28). As a consequence, the survival rate of defense firms is very high. Lockheed, General Dynamics, McDonnell Douglas, Grumman, and other major contractors have been primary Department of Defense suppliers since before World War II.

This propensity to preserve a contractor seems to transcend inefficiency and even illegal behavior in the past. Following the Pentagon's decision to cancel General Dynamics' A-12 aircraft project due to cost overruns, the Department of Defense demanded the return of $1.9 billion originally advanced. General Dynamics appealed the demand on the grounds that this would bankrupt the firm, and Department of Defense relented, citing the need to "safeguard the nation's industrial base" (Cypher 1991, 10). Twenty-five of the nation's top defense contractors have already been convicted of procurement fraud, but are still obtaining new contracts.

Sometimes, follow-on contracts seem to be awarded as a sort of compensation for failure to win or preserve another program. In the 1960s, Rockwell was given the Apollo spacecraft contract shortly following the cancellation of the B-70. It was awarded the Space Shuttle contract after the B-1 was halted during the Carter administration (Kurth 1989, 204).

In addition to the exchange of information, covering overhead and Research and Development costs, and providing follow-on contracts, the Pentagon has almost guaranteed the profitability of defense contractors by tolerating inefficiency on a large scale. In 1969, Senator William Proxmire (D-Wisconsin) focused attention on the tendency for defense contractors to seriously underestimate total costs in their bids to the Pentagon. He lamented:

> What is so discouraging about both the past and the future is the cavalier way in which increases and overruns are shrugged off by the military. . . . What appalls us is the uncritical way in which these increases are accepted by the military. To be consistently wrong on these estimates of cost, as the military has been consistently wrong, should bring the entire system of contracting under detailed scrutiny. But there is not the slightest indication that this is being done by the military. In fact, when such questions are raised, we find the services far more defensive than they are eager to improve the system. (Proxmire 1971, 85–86)

Twenty years later, industry experts were repeating the refrain:

> Contractors are often rewarded for higher-than-planned costs with contributions to overhead, increased sales, and profits. And government managers are often rewarded for placing a higher priority on gaining congressional approval to begin a new weapon program (or to obtain additional funding for an ongoing program) than on controlling costs for existing programs. The acquisition cost problems of the 1970s and 1980s are not aberrations; they are the result of many government and industry participants reacting in perfect accord with the rewards and penalties that are inherent in the acquisition process. (Fox 1989, 155)

The net result of Pentagon tolerance of inefficiency seems to be significantly higher overall profit rates for defense contractors. When return on investment is used (as opposed to a percentage of sales), we find that defense

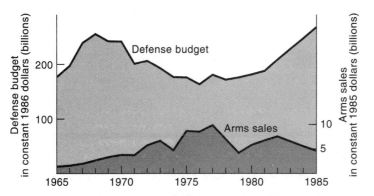

Figure 5.1 Defense budgets and U.S. arms sales to the Third World, 1965–1985.
Sources: Michael Brzoska and Thomas Ohlson, *Arms Transfers to the Third World* (New York: Oxford, 1987) and Leonard Sullivan, "The Defense Budget," in George Hudson and Joseph Kruzel, eds., *American Defense Annual*, 1985–86 (Lexington, MA: D.C. Heath, 1985): 53–76.

contractors earned roughly 30 percent higher profits than comparable commercial manufacturers as of 1980. A study commissioned by the navy in 1986 revealed that from 1977 to 1985 defense industry profits were not only above commercial firms (two and one-third times higher on average), but that during the recession years of 1982 and 1983 they were three and four times higher, respectively (Cypher 1991, 10).

The Department of Defense also arranges for the sale of weapons to foreign governments. As shown in Figure 5.1, foreign arms sales to Third World countries (roughly half of the total) have ebbed and flowed in inverse proportion to the size of the defense budget. Just as the follow-on imperative helps preserve production lines, Department of Defense–arranged arms sales make up for drops in new weapons purchases by the Pentagon.

As explained by Cypher:

> Through the Pentagon's Defense Security Assistance Agency, the U.S. government approves billions of dollars a year in foreign arms sales. In 1989, officially acknowledged arms sales totaled $15 billion . . . [In 1990], Deputy Secretary of State Lawrence Eagleburger sent a memorandum ordering [the State Department] to "get on board by helping open doors for U.S. defense vendors" (Cypher 1991, 11).

Rockwell and other defense contractors proudly trumpet their success in the area of foreign arms sales in their annual reports, with nary a reference to weapons proliferation or regional wars. Some have pointed out that when the Defense and State Departments criticize China and France for spreading weapons illegally, they are really trying to create new markets for U.S. defense contractors. Some analysts have even urged the expansion of overseas arms sales to save U.S. jobs (Bajusz and Louscher 1988). After the Gulf War, Bush approved a $21 billion sale of F-15 fighters, Apache helicopters, M-1 tanks, Patriot missiles, and rocket launchers to Saudi Arabia. "One congressional aide described the proposed sale as the 'defense relief act of 1990'" (Cypher 1991, 11).

In exchange for this consideration and support, the Defense Department is well rewarded. Each decade brings a new generation of increasingly sophisticated and impressive weapons with which to fight wars against increasingly weak adversaries. Defense industry officials are able to not only respond to Department of Defense concepts, but often stimulate new ideas about future weapons by showing research on what is possible. The SDI is an example of Department of Defense–driven research, while the Stealth technology was largely industry-driven.

In addition to these obvious benefits, each service competes for the fanciest new innovations in order to better encroach on the others' turf. Certain contractors have developed strong linkages with certain services (Grumman with the navy, Lockheed with the air force) on the presumption that their needs are so specialized that no other firms could satisfy them (Kurth 1989, 198). Past efforts by Pentagon officials to increase compatibility of weapons across services (persuading the air force to use the navy's F-15, for example) have not often been successful. The navy has refused to consider re-equipping air force jets for aircraft carriers, and the air force opposes sharing the A-10 "Warthog" attack aircraft with the army.

Just as the defense contractors welcome former Pentagon officials into their ranks, there is a limited degree of movement by defense contractor personnel to the Pentagon, usually as "seconded" staff on temporary assignment. Such cross-fertilization gives "useful insights into the contractors' way of doing business" (Adams 1982, 79).

Defense contractors maintain large Washington offices, which are a natural conduit for information, much of which gets passed on to Pentagon associates. Sometimes, the Department of Defense is able to get a better sense of what is happening on "the Hill" (in Congress) from industry lobbyists than through direct channels (Adams 1982, 131).

Overall, the incentives for both the Pentagon and defense contractors to maintain close relations are strong. The ties are also very intimate, to the point that at certain junctures it is difficult to know where the private sector leaves off and the public sector begins.

INDUSTRY–CONGRESS COOPERATION

Because almost all Department of Defense spending must be approved by Congress, defense contractors and Pentagon officials alike have learned to hone their lobbying skills and cultivate good relations with the ever-changing cast of characters on the Hill. Likewise, because many defense-related industries make up a crucial component of many congressmen's home district economies, politicians on the Hill have learned to look out for the interests of defense industries. Again, a symbiotic relationship has developed.

Candidate Bill Clinton learned the important electoral clout of defense industry workers during the Connecticut primary in 1992 where the future of the Seawolf submarine being built in New London was a key issue. Clinton had originally proposed scrapping it, but then changed his mind in favor of finishing one of the two units planned. There were simply too many jobs (and votes) at stake.

Defense-related employment currently hovers at around 7 million (6.4 percent of work force), up from 5 million in 1980 (4.7 percent of work force) (Cypher 1991, 9; Reppy 1983, 37). As we have seen during the 1991–1992 recession, dismantling (or "converting") the defense industry in an environment of slow civilian growth is nearly impossible without increasing unemployment. Even the closing of numerous military installations across the country has had a significant impact on many communities. The postclosure adjustment period has proven to be more difficult than previously imagined.

The concentration of defense-related jobs (and votes) has made an impact on the lobbying strategies of defense contractors. In California, for example, a half-million people work directly for the Department of Defense, and some $29 billion was spent on weapons contracts in 1985 alone. Some 70,000 jobs in the Silicon Valley area are directly connected to defense spending (Beers 1990, 30). In New York, over $11 billion was spent on defense contracts in 1985, of which nearly $4 billion went to Grumman alone. When presented with a choice between defense conversion and funding the Grumman F-14, Congressman George Hochbruechner (D-New York) went against his principles and chose Grumman. "We had to do this one, the F-14, because this is the bread-and-butter aircraft for Grumman. That's the one that makes the money" (Beers 1990, 66).

As if contractors' influence were not enough, defense contractors spend considerable sums on lobbying in Washington. In order to move specific bills forward, "[t]he Washington staff enlists the support of employees, shareholders, and the local communities dependent upon the economic well-being of their plants" (Adams 1982, 134). Defense contractors contributed well over $2 million to the Democratic members of the House and Senate Armed Services and defense-related Appropriations subcommittees in 1988 (Beers 1990, 67). Overall,

> The Washington office staff . . . weaves a network in Congress, starting with the Representatives and Senators on committees that are important to the company—Armed Services, Appropriations, Science and Technology—and from districts and states in which the company has plant locations. In general Washington staffers tend to visit and encourage friends, rather than try to sway opponents of a program. (Adams 1982, 131)

The promotion of defense industries and the military by some members of Congress borders on fawning. One former chairman of the House Armed Services Committee "claims he was never fortunate enough to serve in the military but he has managed to be captivated by the military leaders and serves them with undaunted loyalty. He has done more than most generals to advance the interests of the nation's military" (Donovan 1970, 47). Even after it was proved that McDonnell Douglas illegally obtained classified documents in order to unfairly secure the ATA (Stealth attack aircraft) contract in 1987, Senator Sam Nunn (D-Georgia) supported leaving it with the firm in order not to disrupt construction. Particularly under the Reagan administration, many congressmen bent over backwards to appear prodefense. As put by Korn and Daggett concerning congressional attitudes in 1988:

> Among the Democrats, the centrist stance is defined by support for the Midgetman missile and opposition to a ban on missile flight tests. The moderately liberal position is to oppose defense waste and mismanagement and to favor conventional arms. The very liberal position is to criticize the growth of military spending at the expense of social programs. Among Republicans, the major issue appears to be who is more vigorously in favor of SDI. (Korb and Daggett 1988, 60)

Such politicians often join one of the service associations and participate in numerous social activities sponsored by defense contractors and the Pentagon. "The major problem with contractor entertainment is that it reinforces the closed-circuit of policy-making in the 'iron triangle.' It contributes to shared perceptions of the present and expectations about the future, to the view that critics are the enemy of both industry and Government" (Adams 1982, 176). Richard Barnet has argued that there is no need to look for a conspiracy in the close relationship between the Congress, the Pentagon, and defense contractors. Its members have such common interests, backgrounds, and perspectives that they simply reinforce each other's natural tendencies (Barnet 1969).

THE REFORM MOVEMENT
AND THE PERSIAN GULF RENAISSANCE

If the situation described above seems as undemocratic as it is beyond remedy, it is important to temper this with a discussion of other developments in defense spending and procurement.

After the end of the Vietnam War, defense spending on new weapons declined by a third, and many firms struggled to survive (the General Dynamics operation in Fort Worth lost 23,000 workers in the early 1970s—Gansler 1980, 52). While foreign arms sales made up for much of this, the Carter administration's initial cost-cutting and program reduction placed the defense industry in a rather serious situation. Defense spending had declined not only in absolute terms, but also as a share of total government spending and as a share of the gross national product. Many deplored what was seen as a decline in American defense preparedness and a growing gap with advancing Soviet arsenals.

This all came to an end with the election of Ronald Reagan in 1980. Programs that had been canceled, such as the B-2 bomber and the MX missile, were resurrected and given unprecedented support. Several California firms reaped windfalls (Kurth 1989, 205) and new firms, such as TRW and Raytheon, became heavy hitters in this high-tech world of SDI. During the period 1981 to 1986, defense spending on new weapons increased by 75 percent and Research and Development grew by 86 percent in real terms (Sullivan 1985, 55).

On the heels of this growth came new pressures against inefficiency and fraud. As discouraging test results and alarming cost overruns came to the attention of Congress, a new mood of reform swept Capitol Hill. The Bradley fighting vehicle was a target in the early 1980s when tests showed that it could not float, as originally advertised, and that its "armor" could not stop much more than gunshots—a fact which led to its exploding in a ball of flame when hit with an antitank shell (Main 1991, 54). Other weapons, such as DIVAD, the Sergeant York, and the B-1B proved unable to carry out their assigned missions.

These reports, combined with stories of widespread fraud, resulted in a major reform movement in Congress and even at the White House. Commissions were formed, investigations launched, and hearings held. A new Defense Procurement Fraud Unit was set up, but soon proved to be mere window dressing and played little part in attacking corruption in the procurement process. The relationship between Congress, the Pentagon, and the defense contractors grew increasingly bitter as each shifted blame for the problems on each other (Korb 1988).

It is difficult to determine whether the reform movement has changed the military-industrial complex in any permanent way. The end of the Cold War and the relative decline in military budgets have certainly put the defense industry on notice that conversion is no longer desirable, but essential. Congress has cut SDI research in half in the 1990s and the Department of Defense has demonstrated a more aggressive attitude against waste by canceling the navy's A-12 attack aircraft project in 1990 (Huey and Perry 1991, 36) Over one-third of all procurement contracts are based on "fixed-price" calculations of parts and machinery, which aim at containing costs (Cypher 1991, 10). The result seems to be greater efforts at cost containment and experimentation with a team approach to management in such firms as McDonnell Douglas and Rockwell. The F-117A Stealth fighter was proudly delivered in record time and below cost in 1990 (Perry 1991, 48).

The opportunity to see the reform movement in its fullest may have been cut off by the war in the Gulf. Almost as soon as the bombs fell and the Stealth fighters and cruise missiles flew into Baghdad, criticism of the Department of Defense's penchant for high-tech weaponry melted away. As put by Senator John Warner, "I think you'll find the members of Congress voicing much less criticism with respect to high-tech weapons. The investment in these weapons systems has paid off" (Huey and Perry 1991, 34).

As put by Cypher:

The smooth transition from Cold War to global militarism highlights the extent to which military interests have developed their own momentum within the

United States. And while no one argues that the United States spearheaded the war against Iraq solely to benefit arms contractors, they may emerge as the biggest winners from the conflict. (Cypher 1991, 9)

THE FUTURE WITH CLINTON?

It is no exaggeration to say the military-industrial complex seems at a crucial juncture. As new arms control agreements with Russia and the former Soviet republics are signed and implemented, and as defense budgets continue to be pared down, defense contractors will find the triumph of the Persian Gulf War and its attendant good will ephemeral indeed. Bill Clinton's avowed support of economic development in areas hard hit by industrial change emphasizes the need for planning in the process of defense conversion. While not all defense contractors can go from building jets to building electric cars, there is good reason to think that much of the military-oriented technology of the past can be redirected toward successful commercial ventures.

There is as yet little clear sense of how this conversion will be accomplished and what role the federal government will play. The Congressional Defense Diversification Task Force has proposed legislation which calls for a firm-by-firm plan that will allow tax-free savings for firms undertaking conversion. In addition, the Clinton economic stimulus package for 1994 proposes funding for economic development for regions especially hard hit by cuts in defense spending. Some programs aimed at regional development have already been included in the 1994 defense budget, but it is too soon to tell what effect they will have, if any.

The defense conversion question is part of a larger issue of "industrial strategy." The question is: should the federal government target specific industries for enhanced growth and progress while allowing others to wither? For those who say that such activities are beyond the scope of government, we should point out that with an average of roughly $100 billion (in current dollars) going into the defense industry every year for the last forty-five years, this question is clearly moot. The key issue is how the government's experience in industrial development will be channeled in a post–Cold War environment (Borrus and Zysman 1992, 166).

Questions to Consider

1. To what extent does your community benefit from Pentagon spending? How does this spending affect you? What would be the consequence of a withdrawal of Pentagon monies from your community?

2. What is the moral implication of Pentagon spending as a vehicle for strengthening our economy? Is this good policy? Is it sound economics?

3. Was Marx right in his assessment of capitalist conflict? Does it apply to the defense industry, or is this an exception?

References

Gordon Adams. *The Politics of Defense Contracting: The Iron Triangle* (New Brunswick, NJ: Transaction Books, 1982).

William D. Bajusz and David J. Louscher. *Arms Sales and the U.S. Economy: The Impact of Restricting Military Exports* (Boulder, CO: Westview Press, 1988).

Nicole Ball and Milton Leitenberg, eds. *The Structure of the Defense Industry: An International Survey* (New York: St. Martin's Press, 1983).

Richard Barnet. *The Economy of Death* (New York: Atheneum, 1969).

David Beers. "Brother, Can You Spare $1.5 Trillion?" *Mother Jones* 15 #5 (July/August 1990): 28–33, 66–68.

Michael Borrus and John Zysman. "Industrial Competitiveness and National Security," in Graham Allison and Gregory Treverton, eds., *Rethinking America's Security: Beyond Cold War to New World Order* (New York: Norton, 1992), 136–175.

Michael Brzoska and Thomas Ohlson. *Arms Transfers to the Third World, 1971–85* (New York: Oxford University Press, 1987).

James M. Cypher. "The War Dividend." *Dollars & Sense* #166 (May 1991): 9–11, 21.

Jim Donahue. "The Patriots at Raytheon." *Multinational Monitor* 12 #3 (March 1991): 26–29.

James A. Donovan. *Militarism, U.S.A.* (New York: Charles Scribner's Sons, 1970).

Thomas R. Dye and Harmon Zeigler. *The Irony of Democracy: An Uncommon Introduction to American Politics* (Belmont, CA: Wadsworth, 1993).

J. Ronald Fox. "Obstacles to Improving the Defense Acquisition Process," in Joseph Kruzel, ed. *American Defense Annual, 1989–1990* (Lexington, MA: D.C. Heath, 1989): 145–160.

Jacques S. Gansler. *The Defense Industry* (Cambridge, MA: MIT Press, 1980).

John Huey and Nancy J. Perry. "The Future of Arms." *Fortune* (February 25, 1991): 34–36.

Lawrence Korb. "The Department of Defense, Defense Industry and Procurement: Fatal Misconception," in Herbert L. Sawyer, ed., *Business in the Contemporary World* (New York: University Press of America, 1988): 35–42.

Lawrence Korb and Stephen Daggett. "The Defense Budget and Strategic Planning," in Joseph Kruzel, ed., *American Defense Annual, 1988–1989* (Lexington, MA: D. C. Heath, 1988): 43–65.

James R. Kurth. "The Military-Industrial Complex Revisited," in Joseph Kruzel, ed., *American Defense Annual, 1989–1990* (Lexington, MA: D. C. Heath 1989): 195–216.

Jeremy Main. "FMC Profile." *Fortune* (February 25, 1991): 50–56.

Nancy Perry. "Lockheed Profile." *Fortune* (February 25, 1991): 47–48.

William Proxmire. "The Costs of Military Spending," in Kenneth S. Davis, ed., *Arms, Industry and America* (New York: H. W. Wilson Co., 1971): 82–89.

Judith Reppy. "The United States," in Nicole Ball and Milton Leitenberg, *The Structure of the Defense Industry: An International Survey* (New York: St. Martin's Press, 1983): 21–49.

Leonard Sullivan. "The Defense Budget" in George Hudson and Joseph Kruzel, eds., *American Defense Annual, 1985–1986* (Lexington, MA: D. C. Heath, 1985): 53–75.

Vietnam Homefront

Until several major powers became democratic, public opinion was important only to the extent that soldiers were willing to fight and citizens were willing to pay taxes without excessive pressure from the state. By the turn of the century, however, it was widely accepted that public opinion was crucial, even to nondemocratic governments. One can distinguish between fundamental and short-term public attitudes. Nationalism, a sense of duty toward the state, a feeling of community with compatriots, and confidence in the rightness of the national course tend not to vary significantly from month to month or year to year. These represent what could be called the "national character." On the other hand, public opinion polls demonstrate that the national mood and opinions about specific policies change dramatically from month to month—even minute-by-minute during a crisis. A successful leader will distinguish between these two and learn how to use them to his advantage. An unsuccessful one will kick against the pricks of mass opinion at his peril.

War in a democracy is a hazardous endeavor for any politician seeking reelection. Although a democratic nation united in battle is an awesome force, democracies are uniquely prone to discouragement when wartime sacrifices seem to outweigh promised benefits. In such a situation, politicians have been forced to break off an unpopular fight in order to save their political skin. Many argue that this is precisely what took place in the Vietnam era in the United States. Still today, Americans experience a sense of deep personal ambivalence with regard to Vietnam. We ask ourselves: Could we have won the war? Was our cause just? Who is to blame for our failure? These doubts and questions were at the root of the public opposition to the war which in turn contributed to the fall of two presidents and a dramatic change in our foreign policy priorities. As put by former Deputy Secretary of Defense George Ball:

We have never recovered from the anger and divisiveness of the latter 1960s, and I find increasing evidence of the baleful mark left by our Vietnam experience on almost all aspects of American life. . . . (Ball 1982, 467)

In order to better understand both how public opinion was formed during the war and how this opinion may or may not have affected policy, we should briefly review the key events of the Vietnam War itself. The reader should understand that U.S. involvement in Vietnam's civil war goes back at least to World War II, and began in earnest in 1954 when the French colonists withdrew from Vietnam after their defeat at Dien Bien Phu. Ho Chi Minh, leader of the Viet Cong Communist guerrillas since 1941, became the leader of the provisional North Vietnamese government in Hanoi, while a succession of largely unpopular governments emerged in Saigon with U.S. support. The rest of the story can most quickly be told with this simple chronology (Table 6.1).

PUBLIC OPINION AND VIETNAM

The American public generally favors presidents who deal decisively with foreign policy crises, even when their efforts fail. In the case of Vietnam, public support was not only strong, but sustained until 1968. Following the Tet Offensive, the domestic consensus on the rightness of the U.S. war effort in Vietnam took a palpable shift, with a direct consequence on the way the White House fought the war. In order to better understand this shift, we need to look at the chain of events that preceded and followed it.

TONKIN GULF AND RALLY–ROUND–THE–FLAG

The Kennedy administration came to office with a call to sacrifice in the fight against communism. Kennedy referred to a "New Frontier" of progress and leadership. In response to the *Sputnik* shock, the "missile gap" scare, the fall of Cuba, and other deeply troubling events, the country seemed to be on a war footing. Although Kennedy met a setback in the failed invasion of Cuba at the Bay of Pigs, he captured the country's imagination with his firm stand against Moscow over the Cuban missiles (Kattenburg 1980, 210). Thus, for reasons of national pride, compassion for the citizens of "captive nations," as well as out of simple fear, the American public was well-disposed in the early 1960s to a crusade on distant shores (Levy 1991, 16). Thus, although Vietnam had not yet entered the public consciousness, Kennedy and Vice President Lyndon Johnson could feel assured of its latent support.

After Kennedy's assassination in November 1963, Johnson came to power in the White House. His attitude was far less patient than Kennedy's, who had tolerated the overthrow of South Vietnam's leader Ngo Dinh Diem after refusing to support this unpopular president. Johnson was more eager to score victories on the battlefield, where the Communist Vietcong insurgents, funded and supplied by North Vietnam, were making significant progress. Looking for a popular rationale for deploying more troops to the

Table 6.1 THE VIETNAM WAR: A CHRONOLOGY[a]

1955

January	U.S. begins training South Vietnamese army.
July	Soviet Union and China begin providing aid to North Vietnam.
October	Ngo Dinh Diem becomes president.

1956

Diem begins crackdown of Communist sympathizers (Vietminh).

1957

May	Diem and Eisenhower meet in Washington.
October	North Vietnamese government helps organize guerrilla army (Vietcong) in South Vietnam.

1959

May	Ho Chi Minh Trail, running through Laos and Cambodia from Hanoi into South Vietnam, becomes an operational supply route for matériel for Vietcong.
July	First Americans die in Vietnam fighting.

1960

April	Universal military conscription imposed in North Vietnam.
November	Unsuccessful coup attempt against Diem amid growing protests over regime in South Vietnam.
December	Civil war erupts in Laos with Soviets supplying rebels.

1961

May	Geneva Conference on Laos leads to creation of neutral government.
	Lyndon Johnson returns from visit to South Vietnam with recommendation for more aid to Diem regime.
October	Maxwell Taylor and Walt Rostow recommend covert military aid after visit with Diem—Kennedy opts for more financial support.

1962

February	U.S. organizes formal military support in South Vietnam, increases number of advisers from 700 to 12,000.

1963

January	Vietcong score victories in battles with South Vietnamese army; army unrest increases in the South.
May/June	Buddhist demonstrators shot, commit suicide by self-immolation.
August	U.S. urges Diem to change repressive policies, warns of coup attempt.
November	General Duong Van Minh overthrows Diem in coup, Diem is assassinated.
December	U.S. advisors number 15,000; U.S. aid in 1963 equals $500 million.

1964

January	General Nguyen Khanh seizes power in Saigon.

(continued)

Table 6.1 *(continued)*

June	Robert McNamara, Dean Rusk encourage more support; military plans bombing raid against North Vietnam.
August	Tonkin Gulf incident involving purported North Vietnamese attacks on U.S. intelligence ships off the coast leads to passage of Tonkin Gulf Resolution, giving Lyndon Johnson significant powers to respond.
Autumn	Johnson rejects retaliatory bombing following Vietcong raids against U.S. installations.

1965

February	Operations Flaming Dart and Rolling Thunder begin systematic bombing of North Vietnam.
	General Khanh removed by Phan Huy Quat in Saigon.
March	First Marines land at Da Nang airfield.
June	Nguyen Cao Ky new prime minister with Nguyan Van Thieu as president.
July	In light of defeats for South Vietnamese army, Johnson authorizes deployment of forty-four more battalions.
December	Johnson suspends bombing campaign over Christmas to induce North Vietnamese to negotiate.
	U.S. troop strength reaches 200,000.

1966

January	Bombing of North Vietnam resumes.
Spring	Battles of Hue and Da Nang give South Vietnam/U.S. forces major victories.
December	U.S. troop strength reaches 400,000.

1967

Spring	Johnson secretly corresponds with North Vietnamese on peace options; North Vietnamese demand halt to bombing prior to negotiations.
August	McNamara testifies before Congress that bombing campaign is ineffective.
October	Massive antiwar protest at the Pentagon.
November	General William Westmoreland exudes confidence during trip to U.S.
December	U.S. troop strength reaches 500,000.

1968

January	Tet offensive involving Vietcong and North Vietnamese attacks on South Vietnamese cities is repulsed, but demonstrates strength of North Vietnamese forces to surprised American audience.
March	Johnson decides to halt escalation, announces he will not run for reelection.
April	Paris peace talks begin between U.S. and North Vietnam.
July	Democratic Convention in Chicago the scene of antiwar demonstrations.
October	Johnson halts bombing.
December	Troop strength peaks at roughly 540,000.

1969

January	South Vietnamese included in Paris peace talks.

Table 6.1 *(continued)*

March	President Richard Nixon begins secret bombing of Cambodia.
June	Thieu and Nixon announce withdrawal of 25,000 U.S. troops under the rubrique of "Vietnamization."
October	Massive antiwar demonstration in Washington.
November	Mylai massacre revealed.
December	U.S. troop strength down to 480,000.

1970

April	Nixon reveals covert attacks against Cambodia.
May	Four students killed in antiwar protest at Kent State University.
Autumn	Nixon explores simultaneous withdrawal with North Vietnamese.
December	Troop strength down to 280,000.

1971

March	Lieutenant William Calley convicted of murder in connection with Mylai.
June	Pentagon Papers published, leading to investigation of Daniel Ellsberg.
December	Troop strength down to 140,000.

1972

January	Nixon reveals secret talks between Kissinger and North Vietnamese (since February 1970).
March	North Vietnamese army attacks across frontier.
April	Nixon approves bombing of Hanoi.
August	Paris negotiations continue in spite of South Vietnamese resistance.
October	U.S.–North Vietnamese reach accord, Thieu opposes.
December	After collapse of talks, bombing raids resume.

1973

January	Peace accords signed in Paris.
March	Last U.S. troops leave South Vietnam.
August	Congress forces administration to halt bombing of Cambodia.
November	Over Nixon's veto, Congress passes War Powers Act.

1974

January	War initiated again.

1975

January	Final North Vietnamese push begins.
March	Hue falls.
April	Saigon falls; South Vietnam ceases to exist.

[a]Karnow (1983) provides the best chronology available (pages 670–686).

region, he seized upon an incident in the Gulf of Tonkin. Two U.S. patrol boats exchanged fire with North Vietnamese warships in close proximity to the coast, prompting an outcry from the White House which was echoed on Capitol Hill. Johnson asked Senator William Fulbright to shepherd a resolution giving Johnson broad powers to retaliate immediately and in the future. This so-called "Tonkin Gulf Resolution" passed on August 7, 1964, by a vote of eighty-eight to two.

As pointed out by Herring,

> From a domestic political standpoint, Johnson's handling of the Tonkin Gulf incident was masterly. His firm but restrained response to the alleged North Vietnamese attacks won broad popular support, his rating in the Louis Harris poll skyrocketed from 42 to 72 percent overnight. He effectively neutralized [hawkish Republican presidential hopeful Barry] Goldwater on Vietnam, a fact which contributed to his overwhelming electoral victory in November. (Herring 1986, 122)

As explained by Kattenburg, this support was largely naive, since the American public did not fully understand the nature of the war that was now underway.

> [T]he American people wanted to believe [the New Frontier rhetoric], and believe they did. When the number of U.S. military men increased from under 1,000 to about 15,000 in Vietnam in a little over six months, few people realized that the New Frontier had in effect started the process of extending U.S. borders to those of Indochina with Thailand. (Kattenburg 1980, 209)

Lyndon Johnson won an overwhelming victory against Goldwater in 1964, campaigning as the peace candidate (a position which he would reverse shortly after the election—Kattenburg 1980, 251). Support for the war was at 65 percent by late 1965, and when news of the bombing campaigns was received, public opinion was supportive (Mueller 1973, 119). This "spike" in public support is an illustration of the "rally-round-the-flag" phenomenon whereby large segments of the public express support for the president's policies in any crisis situation, regardless of the substance of the policies. Leslie Gelb argues that in spite of the emergence in 1965 of an antiwar movement, "the widespread belief that South Vietnam should not be lost to communism generated and sustained that war" (Gelb 1976, 103). This said, it should be pointed out that letters opposing the bombing campaign poured into Capitol Hill offices following the announcement (Herring 1986, 133). Overall, the signals sent by the public in the early stages of the war were somewhat contradictory and confusing. Political leaders could and did read into them what they wanted.

GROWING SKEPTICISM

During the years 1966 and 1967 Johnson's policy of escalation was in full swing. By the end of the year, nearly half a million troops were deployed and nearly 10,000 had fallen in combat. Sustained bombing of the North, coupled with CIA covert operations, complemented the marines in the field. Vietnam was very much on the minds of Americans, to the point that it was viewed as the single most significant issue of the day by 1967. However, as the fight wore on, at three different levels the American people began to question the rightness of the war.

The first to defect was a group of already disenchanted individuals who later came to form the core of the antiwar movement across college campuses. Although more will be said about the peace movement later, suffice it to say that by 1965 it consisted of pacifists, leftists, and radicals, but included a growing number of housewives, moderate academics, and various celebrities. By mid-1965, antiwar groups could muster crowds of 15,000 and more (Levy 1991, 126). In November 1965, a major march in Washington, aimed at being respectable with major mainstream figures, nonetheless deteriorated into a circus of sorts. It was not until the Fulbright hearings of early 1966 that dignified opposition could be articulated.

Of much greater significance to Johnson than antiwar demonstrations was the defection of several high-level policy advisors and congressmen, who had previously supported the policy of escalation. Senator Fulbright began hearings on the war in the spring of 1966 with Senate Majority Leader Mike Mansfield's tacit support (Herring 1986, 172). At the hearings, the Senate Foreign Relations Committee questioned senior officials as well as prominent outsiders to the administration in order to make the point that there was no clear objective or plan of action in the war. In August 1967, Secretary of Defense Robert McNamara gave the committee much ammunition by stating that the intensive bombing campaign in the North was not only failing to achieve its objective of halting the supply of matériel to the South, but would likely never succeed.

A group of senior unofficial advisers to Johnson, including such respected figures as former Secretary of State Dean Acheson, advised him privately in mid-1967 and publicly thereafter, that the war could not be won and that he should look for a way out. The newly appointed Secretary of Defense Clark Clifford consistently encouraged Johnson to begin troop withdrawals and a general program of "Vietnamization"—turning over the prosecution of the war to local South Vietnamese forces (Karnow 1983, 559–562).

It is important to note that most of these defections were by individuals who were firmly committed to U.S. leadership in the fight against communism. It wasn't that they opposed the New Frontier, it was simply that they felt Vietnam, with its largely illegitimate government, ill-defined battle fronts, and ambiguous context, ought not be the test case (Gelb 1976, 111).

Overall, as documented by Holsti and Rosenau (Table 6.2), elite opinion in the United States shifted dramatically against the war. One can see in the table, that not only did 38 percent of the elites in the country begin by favoring the war and end by opposing it, but only 16 percent consistently supported the war effort. If one adds the "ambivalent supporters" whose enthu-

Table 6.2   CLASSIFICATION OF ATTITUDES ON VIETNAM

	Toward the end of US involvement			
When the war first became an issue	I tended to favor a complete military victory	I tended to feel in-between these two	Not sure	I tended to favor a complete withdrawal
I tended to favor a complete military victory	SUPPORTERS (n = 363, 15.9%)	AMBIVALENT SUPPORTERS (n = 346,15.2%)		CONVERTED CRITICS (n = 867, 38.0%)
I tended to feel in-between these two	CONVERTED SUPPORTERS (n = 128, 5.6%)	AMBIVALENTS (n = 128,15.6%)		
Not sure				
I tended to favor a complete withdrawal		AMBIVALENT CRITICS (n = 63, 2.8%)		CRITICS (n = 378, 16.6%)

Source: Ole Holstiand James Rosenau, *American Leadership in World Affairs* (Boston: Allen & Unwin, 1984).

siasm for the war clearly wanes to the "critics," "converted critics," and "ambivalent critics," one finds that three-fourths of the elites in the country were either critical or tending to be more critical of the war at its end than at its outset (Holsti and Rosenau 1984, 33). This kind of pressure from individuals that have tended to play an active role in politics was overwhelming for Johnson.

The third level of disenchantment with the war came from the "general" public—that poorly organized mass of opinion which pollsters constantly seek to measure and plot. Although there is much uncertainty about the nature of public opinion prior to 1968, it seems that

> the U.S. public perception changed slowly after 1965 from an initial and fairly general understanding that external aggression was being resisted by the South Vietnamese, to a largely unexpressed image of Vietnamese, both southern and northern, resisting the imposition by U.S. means of a type of U.S.-made order upon Vietnam. (Kattenburg 1980, 244)

The press played some role in all of this, since as early as 1963 it was reporting on the confusing nature of the war. Stanley Karnow criticized the corrupt regime of the Diem family in the mainstream magazine the *Saturday Evening Post* (Levy 1991, 52) and visual reports from televised news media brought home the brutal and ugly nature of this conflict. The question of a "credibility gap" between official military projections and the apparently conflicting reality of televised reports became the focal point of the debate on the war by 1968. Ultimately, the Tet Offensive tipped the balance ever so slightly against the war (see Figure 6.1 on public opinion).

Casualties   Poll

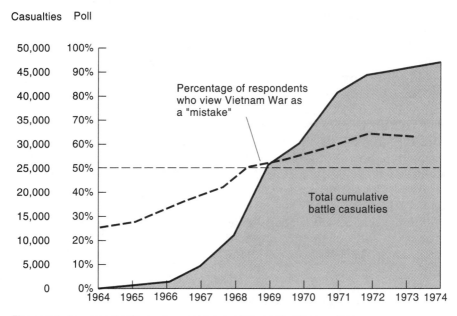

Figure 6.1 Americans' attitudes toward Vietnam War and battle casualties.
Sources: Various issues of Gallup Poll annual editions.

TET SHOCK AND JOHNSON'S "RESIGNATION"

During the January 1968 lunar new year celebrations (called Tet) in Vietnam, the Vietcong and North Vietnamese army took advantage of a general lull in the fighting to launch an all-out offensive on every conceivable target in South Vietnam. The so-called "Tet Offensive" involved Vietcong and, North Vietnamese Army (NVA) troops as far south as Saigon, outside the U.S. embassy complex there. Cities, airfields, and fuel depots were all targeted by the most visible and dramatic military operation of the war.

All of this was covered in painful detail and was exaggerated to melodrama by the American media (Levy 1991, 145). Although the military engagement was clearly won by U.S.-led troops, the psychological effect of the event was to shock the American public into a realization that this war was far from over. Walter Cronkite, "the most trusted person in America," said on February 27, 1968, following an analysis of Tet, that it seemed "more certain than ever that the bloody experience of Vietnam is to end in a stalemate" (Karnow 1983, 547). Shortly thereafter, Martin Luther King declared his opposition to the war. A majority of Americans for the first time agreed that our involvement in Vietnam was "a mistake," although there was no consensus on how we should extricate ourselves from it (roughly half of those who opposed current policy felt the United States should escalate in order to finish the job, while roughly half felt we should simply withdraw— Karnow 1983, 546). By 1968 the U.S. public seemed to reach the consensus that preserving South Vietnam was not vital to our national interest (Kattenburg 1980, 244).

On the purely political front, the Tet Offensive coincided with the beginning of the 1964 presidential campaign. While it was assumed that Johnson would be the party's nominee, he had failed to file as a candidate in time for the New Hampshire primary in March. A relatively unknown senator named Eugene McCarthy, running on an antiwar platform, inundated the state with an army of clean-cut young college students and managed to secure just 300 votes less than write-in candidate Johnson in what was seen as the political upset of the decade. While one should take care not to assume all those who voted for McCarthy were doves (three out of five in fact believed the U.S. should escalate the effort in Vietnam—Kearns 1976, 354), the event galvanized opposition to Johnson within the Democratic party. Within a week, Senator Robert Kennedy announced his candidacy for the presidency and declared his opposition to the war as the key issue of the race (Karnow 1983, 559). As put by Roche:

> The defection of Robert Kennedy was a decisive event in the anti-war saga. At last the anti-war forces had a senior, legitimate political figure who could not be written off as a Hanoi stooge or some species of eccentric. (Roche 1976, 131)

Lyndon Johnson had suddenly become what he feared most—the "war candidate." Furthermore, his visceral antipathy toward Robert Kennedy knew no bounds. He was haunted by him in his dreams (Kearns 1976, 264). He immediately set out to draft a full-blown peace proposal, to be announced before the next round of primary elections in April. Finally, on March 31, Johnson announced a halt to the bombing of North Vietnam, a beginning of troop withdrawals, and his own decision not to run for reelection. The Tet Offensive, while failing to topple the South Vietnamese government, succeeded in felling a president.

During this stage, it is clear that Johnson was heavily influenced by public opinion. As stated by adviser William Bundy:

> My own impression—for what it is worth—is that the thrust of professional civilian advice would probably have been toward the most limited possible force increases, but that the change in bombing policy was greatly influenced—particularly in Secretary Clifford's actions and recommendations—by a sense of the progressively eroding domestic political support that was so dramatically evident to us all during the month of March. (Schandler 1977, 329)

The combination of elite and mass opinion (as expressed most concretely in New Hampshire) had a significant impact on the president's decision. What is less clear is the impact, if any, the by-now large antiwar/peace movement was having.

THE PEACE MOVEMENT

The antiwar demonstrations of the 1960s and 1970s were among the most dramatic outpouring of public sentiment on a foreign policy issue in U.S. history. Roughly half a million gathered in Washington for the Vietnam Moratorium in October 1969. During the student protests following the Kent State/Cambodia incidents, 450 college campuses across the country were closed (Levy 1991, 155–159). In fact, the peace movement was strong among veterans of the war and even soldiers in Vietnam itself. Desertions rose to some 500,000 over the course of the war, and toward its end, many officers were reluctant to assign dangerous missions because of numerous incidents of "fragging" (assassination by another soldier) (Kattenburg 1980, 284). It is estimated that nearly 10 million of the 27 million draft-eligible men either deserted, fled to another country, or obtained legal deferments to avoid service.

In general terms, the resistance of the youth of the country to the war effort went far to debilitate its prosecution, but did not in and of itself alter government policy. In fact, Herring concludes:

> Anti-war protests did not turn the American people against the war, as some critics have argued. . . . Public opinion polls make abundantly clear, moreover, that a majority of Americans found the anti-war movement, particularly its radical and 'hippie' elements, more obnoxious than the war itself. In a perverse sort of way, the protest may even have strengthened support for a war that was not in itself popular. (Herring 1986, 173)

And, according to Gelb:

> Passionate opposition and intellectual arguments, in the end, counted for very little and changed few minds. The argument that finally prevailed at the end of the Johnson Administration was the weight of dead Americans. (Gelb 1976, 112)

The antiwar movement was never centralized. It consisted of a wide variety of interests organized primarily at the local level at certain major universities and cities. The San Francisco Bay area, with the University of California at Berkeley as the focal point, was early on a key hub of the movement. The principal elements of the movement were pacifist, radical, and anarchist in the early stages. Even these early leaders disagreed over methods and aims. It seems in retrospect that the only thing they shared was a disgust with the war. This problem would come back to haunt the more moderate elements of the movement in later years, because it became apparent that antiwar activists were successful only to the extent that they focused exclusively on Vietnam (Levy 1991, 48).

Some of the important figures and bodies associated with the antiwar movement were the Students for a Democratic Society (which later spawned a small terrorist group known as the Weathermen), the National Mobilization Committee to End the War, the Vietnam Moratorium Committee, and the National Peace Action Coalition. Important leaders included Tom Hayden, Jerry Rubin, Abby Hoffman, David Dellinger, and later Daniel Ellsberg, Dr. Benjamin Spock, Jane Fonda, Joan Baez, Bella Abzug, and even Tony Randall (Kattenburg 1980, 274). As further evidence of the disparate interests at work in the peace movement, the individuals listed above had very different, even contradictory, interests. For example, when an effort was made to organize a massive antiwar demonstration in front of the Pentagon in October 1967, many were content to sing folk songs and sign petitions, while others in the group physically assaulted the military police (Levy 1991, 136).

This split became especially pronounced during the 1968 election campaign when a large number of activists joined forces with Eugene McCarthy and Robert Kennedy to work for gradual change. In the meantime, anarchists and radicals who called for an overthrow of the political system itself through civil disobedience and even violence, became more active (Brown 1976, 122). The contrast was vividly displayed during the tumultuous 1968 Democratic Convention in Chicago.

On the floor of the convention, for those delegates whose credentials were approved, the fight, while acrimonious, was relatively formal. For the better part of a day, the convention delegates debated inclusion of an antiwar plank in the party platform, which was quickly countered by a plank supporting administration policy. When the vote was finally tallied, it demonstrated a profound split—1,568 in favor, 1,041 against the proadministration policy (Levy 1991, 149). The absence of Robert Kennedy, shot in California in June, meant that antiadministration forces were unprepared to counter the nomination of Vice President Hubert Humphrey, who reluctantly advocated the administration's positions (Karnow 1983, 568).

Outside the convention hall, a large number of antiwar protesters had assembled in order to confront, before a live television audience, the aggressive Chicago police force. As put by Shils:

> Hippies, pacifists, socialists, propagandists for a North Vietnamese and Vietcong victory came together and challenged the Chicago police. The provocation was deliberate and successful. The police responded as they were desired to respond, and the television services showed the entire country what the establishment was like—heavy-handed, monstrous, brutal, and incompetent. (Shils 1976, 57)

In a famous moment, the crowd, recognizing the cameras were rolling, began chanting "the whole world is watching!" Viewers at home were generally repulsed by both sides of this confrontation, and it generated little sympathy for the antiwar movement.

The Nixon administration continued the policy of rapid troop withdrawal begun by Johnson in April 1968, and the peace movement lost some momentum. The urgency of changing government policy dissipated, and the movement returned to its more radical roots as moderates lost interest. The revelations in April 1971 that the administration had escalated the war by launching large-scale bombing raids in Cambodia and Laos, however, stirred a new enthusiasm for protest. Almost no campus was prowar by this point (Shils Lake 1976, 56). Unrest broke out, most notably at Kent State University where National Guardsmen, under the direction of Governor James Rhodes, fired into an unruly crowd with live bullets, killing four students. As mentioned earlier, the outrage that followed the incident paralyzed the educational system of the country. For the first time, the public's sympathy was with the demonstrators (Kattenburg 1980, 278).

Did the peace movement change policy? Lyndon Johnson never appreciated the message the activists conveyed, and he always felt unable to communicate with them. They did not seem to understand the feelings of self-sacrifice, devotion to country, and dread of communism that were so much a part of his generation's world. Likewise, Johnson feared the freedom, tolerance, and moral outrage spoken of by the students and activists.

> Divided in values and assumptions, they went their different ways, the peace movement to the streets, Johnson to the refuge of his adamant convictions. Perhaps for the first time in his life, he could not even fathom the position of the other side. No longer the mediator, he had become a righteous if ineffective advocate of his own inflexibility. (Kearns 1976, 343)

Even leaders of the antiwar movement recognize that they achieved few of their goals regarding changing public policy (although this may be a function of unrealistic expectations). Activist Sam Brown gave a postmortem of the movement after the war, and found that the split in leadership and excessive reliance on the college community (rather than a larger population of workers, professionals, and minorities) hindered the movement's ability to grow. Furthermore, litigation aimed at defending Daniel Ellsberg and the militant "Chicago Seven" cost the movement 2 million which could have gone toward organizing efforts (Brown 1976, 124). This said, the antiwar movement set a precedent that was followed in the early 1980s by the nuclear freeze movement, as well as protests against each military intervention since then.

THE NIXON ERA AND CONGRESSIONAL REASSERTION

Richard Nixon at one point claimed to have a "secret plan" to end the war in Vietnam. Just as Johnson had misled the public in the 1964 election, Nixon's claims were deceptive. There was no "secret plan"—only a plan to escalate the violence while pursuing confidential contacts with the North Vietnamese (Levy 1991, 152). In fact, Nixon ended up dropping even more bombs on Indochina than had Johnson (Roche 1976, 135).

The reality that the war was not ending soon prompted an intensification of general opposition to the war. "Lou Harris observed that 'a literal race was on between successive Nixon announcements of further troop withdrawals and a growing public appetite for faster and faster removal of troops from Vietnam" (Levy 1991, 161). Twenty-six percent of respondents felt that troop withdrawals were progressing too slowly in late 1969. In May 1971 that figure was up to 45 percent and in November it had reached 53 percent. This increase in opposition paralleled the cumulative casualty figures and mounting financial costs of the war as well. The publication in mid-1971 of the Pentagon Papers, a collection of classified documents related to prosecuting the war, revealed a pattern of deception and secret escalation on the part of successive administrations (*New York Times* 1971, xi). When combined with the Cambodia revelations and the Mylai massacre of Vietnamese civilians by Lieutenant William Calley's unit, the result was a new public consensus—this time in favor of rapid withdrawal regardless of the implications for South Vietnamese sovereignty (Kattenberg 1980, 258).

Nixon's general plan of "peace with honor" finally came to fruition shortly after the 1972 election with the Paris Agreement of January 1973. By then the public felt no remorse over the "loss" of Vietnam—only relief at the end of the conflict. As Saigon fell in mid-1975, then-President Gerald Ford did nothing to prevent it.

Congress had grown increasingly restive, adopting a variety of tactics to limit presidential prerogative. Following the Fulbright hearings in 1966–67, several other committees followed suit—taking testimony from witnesses, traveling to Vietnam on fact-finding missions, and ultimately issuing antiwar resolutions aimed at curtailing the length and scope of the war. The Tonkin Gulf Resolution was repealed in late 1971, although an effort to prevent further military operations pending a formal declaration of war was defeated. Following a string of resolutions calling for withdrawal by a given deadline, Congress passed a bill banning all further military operations in Vietnam in 1973 (after the troops had already been withdrawn). In an effort to prevent future unilateral executive military interventions, Congress passed the War Powers Act over President Nixon's veto. The net result of congressional reassertion was a collapse of much of the power which had accreted to the White House over the period following World War II. The question of presidential war powers is still one of the most hotly debated constitutional questions of our time (note Senate debate on the Gulf War in 1991).

CONCLUSIONS: CAN THE PUBLIC SHAPE FOREIGN POLICY?

The experience of Vietnam can teach several lessons for those wondering about the role of public opinion in foreign policy. However, it also leaves at least as many questions unanswered.

On the one hand, the Vietnam experience demonstrates the limited impact of street activism in influencing national policy. To a certain extent, this is easily explained, because those who resort to mass demonstrations tend to be those who lack institutional power. That a large number of college students, many of whom could not even vote, failed to alter national policy through protest marches is therefore not surprising. Instead, the Vietnam experience demonstrates the significance of elite opinion in shaping national policy as well as the potential role of "mass opinion" in at least limiting the options a president might otherwise choose. The attentiveness with which successive presidents studied public opinion, as well as their considerable efforts to shape it (including deception, obfuscation, and misrepresentation) are testament to the significance politicians attach to this amorphous social entity.

However, because the Vietnam War created a moral conflict in the American public, opposition was never unambiguous. Those who favored continuing the war generally deplored its cost, while those who had come to favor withdrawal often regretted the loss of face and prestige this would cause. Congressional ambivalence through most of the war reflected this tension and prevented it from taking control. Interestingly enough, one can argue that even congressional assertion as expressed in the War Powers Act did more to legitimate presidential assertiveness than limit it, particularly since the act has done little to hinder presidential freedom since 1973.

Questions to Consider

1. What was the relationship between the peace movement and society in general? Between the peace movement and the White House? How much influence did it really have over policy and shaping alternatives?

2. To what extent did Nixon and Johnson misjudge fundamental American attitudes? What are the apparent limits to patriotism in the United States?

3. What are the lessons of Vietnam in terms of the role of public opinion? How did this shape later military operations (Grenada, Nicaragua, Panama, Persian Gulf, Somalia . . .)?

References

George Ball. *The Past Has Another Pattern* (New York: W. W. Norton, 1982).
Sam Brown. "The Defeat of the Antiwar Movement," in Lake, ed., *The Vietnam Legacy*, 120–127.
Leslie Gelb. "Dissenting on Consensus," in Lake, ed., *The Vietnam Legacy*, 102–119.
David Halberstam. *The Best and the Brightest* (New York: Fawcett Crest, 1972).
George C. Herring. *America's Longest War: The United States and Vietnam, 1950–1975*, 2nd ed. (Philadelphia: Temple University Press, 1986).
Ole R. Holsti and James N. Rosenau. *American Leadership in World Affairs: Vietnam and the Breakdown of Consensus* (Boston: Allen & Unwin, 1984).

Stanley Karnow. *Vietnam: A History* (New York: Viking Press, 1983).

Paul Kattenburg, *The Vietnam Trauma in American Foreign Policy, 1945–1975* (New Brunswick, NJ: Transaction Books, 1980).

Doris Kearns. *Lyndon Johnson and the American Dream* (New York: New American Library, 1976).

Irving Kristol. "Consensus and Dissent in U.S. Foreign Policy," in Lake, ed., *The Vietnam Legacy*, 80–101.

Anthony Lake, ed. *The Vietnam Legacy: The War, American Society and the Future of American Foreign Policy* (New York: New York University Press, 1976).

David W. Levy. *The Debate Over Vietnam* (Baltimore: Johns Hopkins University Press, 1991).

John Mueller. *War, Presidents, and Public Opinion* (New York: John Wiley & Sons, 1973).

New York Times. *The Pentagon Papers* (New York: New York Times Co., 1971).

John P. Roche. "The Impact of Dissent on Foreign Policy: Past and Future," in Lake, ed., *The Vietnam Legacy*, 128–138.

Herbert Y. Schandler. *The Unmaking of a President: Lyndon Johnson and Vietnam* (Princeton NJ: Princeton University Press, 1977).

Edward Shils. "American Society and the War in Indochina," in Lake, ed., *The Vietnam Legacy*, 40–65.

Iran-Contra Scandal: The Tower Commission Report

No decision is truly final until it is acted upon. While this may seem a truism at the personal level, this bedeviling statement can be an overwhelming question at the governmental level. Franklin Roosevelt used to joke that try-ing to change navy policy was like hitting a big pillow—no matter how hard you swing, it stays the same. This illustrates the most common dysfunction of bureaucracies—inertia, or the tendency to perpetuate past behavior. While frustrating in itself, this is not so disconcerting as the tendency for some bureaucracies to become politicized, or to adopt policies independent of the executive. While we will never know all the details, the Iran-Contra scandal seems to illustrate government running amok.

On December 1, 1986, President Ronald Reagan appointed a commis-sion to conduct an independent inquiry on the recently revealed arms-for-hostages swaps in the Middle East. Former Senator John Tower, former Sec-retary of State Edmund Muskie, and former National Security Adviser Brent Scowcroft were tasked with "getting the facts out" and promptly issuing a report including their recommendations for future government decision making. Given the thoroughness of the report, and its nature as a public document, I decided that it should form the central basis for this case study. Uncharacteristically, then, we will look at lengthy excerpts from this single source in our review of the Iran-Contra scandal. Following this presentation, we will consider some of the more recent findings and analysis as well as discuss the implications of the events.

EXCERPTS FROM THE TOWER COMMISSION (PRESIDENT'S SPECIAL REVIEW BOARD) REPORT ON THE IRAN–CONTRA SCANDAL, FEBRUARY 26, 1987*

Background

The Shah of Iran was overthrown on January 16, 1979, ending an intimate, twenty-five year relationship between the United States and Iran. Mutual hostility and tension characterized U.S. relations with the regime of the Ayatollah Khomeini, which, after some months, succeeded the Shah's rule. On November 4, 1979, radical Iranian elements seized the U.S. embassy in Tehran and held its staff hostage. The United States responded by blocking the transfer of all property of the Iranian government, imposing a trade embargo, freezing all other Iranian assets, and breaking diplomatic relations. In addition, the United States imposed an embargo on all arms shipments to Iran, including arms that had been purchased under the Shah but not yet delivered.

On January 19, 1981, many of these restrictions were lifted, as part of the agreement that led to the release of the embassy staff. However, this did not extend to the embargo on arms transfers. Iraq had attacked Iran on September 22, 1980. The United States had adopted a policy of neutrality and refused to ship arms to either side. The result was a continuation of the arms embargo against Iran.

The Reagan Administration had adopted a tough line against terrorism. In particular, the United States adamantly opposed making any concessions to terrorists in exchange for the release of hostages—whether by paying ransom, releasing prisoners, changing policies, or otherwise. Sometime in July of 1982, the United States became aware of evidence suggesting that Iran was supporting terrorist groups, including groups engaged in hostage-taking. On January 20, 1984, the Secretary of State designated Iran a sponsor of international terrorism. Thereafter, the United States actively pressured its allies not to ship arms to Iran, both because of its sponsorship of international terrorism and its continuation of the war with Iraq.

Arms-for-Hostages

By early 1984, Robert McFarlane, the National Security Advisor, and members of the NSC staff, had become concerned about future U.S. policy toward Iran. They feared that the death of Khomeini would touch off a succession struggle which would hold important consequences for U.S. interests. They believed that the United States lacked a strategy and capability for dealing with this prospect. ... [I]n early 1985 the U.S. intelligence community began to believe that serious factional fighting could break out in Iran even before Khomeini died. This change in the community's assessment provided a second opportunity for a policy review.

[NSC staff members Howard] Teicher, and to a lesser extent [Donald] Fortier, worked closely with CIA officials to prepare an update of a previous Special National Intelligence Estimate on Iran. Dated May 20, 1985, the update portrayed the Soviets as well positioned to take advantage of chaos inside Iran. The United

*Material in brackets—[]—has been added by the author.

States, by contrast, was unlikely to be able directly to influence events. Our European and other allies could, however, provide a valuable presence to help protect Western interests. The update concluded that the degree to which these allies can fill a military gap for Iran will be a critical measure of the West's ability to blunt Soviet influence.

[Following this analysis, Robert McFarlane and CIA Director William Casey endorse limited arms transfers to Iran while Secretary of State George Shultz and Secretary of Defense Caspar Weinberger vehemently oppose this.]

While the NSC staff was seeking a reexamination of U.S. policy toward Iran, several staff members were growing ever more concerned about the hostage issue. . . . Frustration at the lack of progress in freeing the hostages in Beirut grew perceptibly within the U.S. government, especially in the face of pleas to the President for action by the families of the hostages. In the summer of 1985, a vehicle appeared that offered the prospect of progress both on the release of the hostages and a strategic opening to Iran.

Israel had long-standing interests in a relationship with Iran and in promoting its arms export industry. Arms sales to Iran could further both objectives. It also offered a means of strengthening Iran against Israel's old adversary, Iraq. Much of Israel's military equipment came originally from the United States, however. For both legal and political reasons, Israel felt a need for U.S. approval of, or at least acquiescence in, any arms sales to Iran. In addition, elements in Israel undoubtedly wanted the United States involved for its own sake so as to distance the United States from the Arab world and ultimately to establish Israel as the only real strategic partner of the United States in the region.

Iran badly wanted what Israel could provide. The United States had been the primary source of arms for the Shah, but U.S. shipments to Iran were now barred by the embargo. Iran desperately wanted U.S.-origin TOW and HAWK missiles, in order to counter Iraq's chief areas of superiority—armor and air forces. Since Israel had these weapons in its inventory, it was an alternative source of supply. Israel was more than willing to provide these weapons to Iran, but only if the United States approved the transfer and would agree to replace the weapons.

Iranian interest in these weapons was widely known among those connected with the arms trade. These included Manucher Ghorbanifar, an Iranian businessman living in France, and Adolph Schwimmer and Yaacov Nimrodi, private Israeli arms dealers with contacts throughout the Middle East including Israel. Since September, 1984, Mr. Schwimmer had also been a consultant to then-Prime Minister of Israel Shimon Peres. In a series of meetings beginning in January 1985, these men had discussed using arms sales to obtain the release of U.S. citizens held hostage in Beirut and to open a strategic dialogue with Iran. Some of those meetings included Amiran Nir . . . an advisor to Prime Minister Peres on counterterrorism. Also involved was Saudi businessman Adnan Khashoggi, a man well-connected in the Middle East and enjoying a special relationship with key Israeli officials. All these men subsequently played a role in the brokering of the arms deals that later did occur. . . .

On the 4th or 5th of May, 1985, Michael Ledeen, an NSC staff consultant, with the knowledge of Mr. McFarlane, went to Israel and met with Prime Minister Peres. Mr. Ledeen told the Board that he asked about the state of Israeli intelligence on Iran and whether Israel would be willing to share its intelligence with the United States. Two months later, the United States received the first of three separate requests regarding Iran from the Israeli government. . . .

On July 3, 1985, David Kimche, the Director General of the Israeli Foreign Ministry, met at the White House with Mr. McFarlane. . . . Mr. Kimche asked the position of the U.S. government toward engaging in a political discourse with Iranian officials . . . [T]hese Iranian officials had conveyed to Israel their interest in a discourse with the United States. Contact was to be handled through an intermediary (later disclosed to be Mr. Ghorbanifar) who was represented as having good connections to Iranian officials. . . .

[T]he Iranians understood that they would have to demonstrate their bona fides and that the Iranians believed they could influence Hizballah to release the hostages in Beirut . . . [U]ltimately the Iranians would need something to show for the dialogue, and . . . this would "probably" be weapons. . . .

On July 13, 1985, Mr. McFarlane apparently received a second request, this time brought by an emissary directly from Israeli Prime Minister Peres. The emissary was Mr. Schwimmer, who delivered the request to Mr. McFarlane through Mr. Ledeen. The emissary carried word of a recent meeting with Mr. Ghorbanifar and another Iranian in which the Iranians had said that others inside Iran were interested in more extensive relations with the West, and particularly, the United States. The Iranians reportedly said that their contacts in Iran could achieve the release of the seven Americans held in Lebanon but in exchange sought 100 TOW missiles from Israel. This was to be part of a larger purpose of opening a private dialogue on U.S./Iranian relations. The emissary asked for a prompt response. . . .

[The next day] Mr. McFarlane cabled this proposal to Secretary Shultz, who was traveling in Asia. Mr. McFarlane recommended a tentative show of interest in a dialogue but with no commitment to the arms exchange. He asked for Secretary Shultz's guidance and indicated he would abide fully by the Secretary's decision. By return cable on the same day, Secretary Shultz agreed to a tentative show of interest without commitment. He said this was consistent with U.S. policy of maintaining contact with people who might eventually provide information or help in freeing hostages. . . .

White House Chief of Staff Donald Regan . . . and Mr. McFarlane met with the President on this issue in the hospital a few days after the President's cancer operation [on the 13th]. Mr. Regan [claimed] that the matter was discussed for 20 to 25 minutes, with the President asking quite a few questions. He recalled the President then saying yes, go ahead. Open it up. [President Reagan did not later recall this meeting.]

[What occurred in August 1985 was described differently by the principals:]

Mr. McFarlane said that Mr. Kimche made a special proposal that 100 TOWs to Iran would establish good faith and result in the release of all the hostages. Mr. McFarlane told the Board that he discussed this proposal with the President several times and, on at least one occasion, with all the full members of the NSC. Within days after the meeting, the President communicated his decision to Mr. McFarlane by telephone. He said the President decided that, if Israel chose to transfer arms to Iran, in modest amounts not enough to change the military balance and not including major weapon systems, then it could buy replacements from the United States. Mr. McFarlane said that the President also indicated that the United States was interested in a political meeting with the Iranians. Mr. McFarlane said he reminded the President of the opposition expressed by Secretary Shultz and Secretary Weinberger, but that the President said he wanted to go ahead—that he, the President, would take all the heat for that.

Secretary Shultz [claimed] that on August 6, 1985, during one of his regularly scheduled meetings with the President, he discussed with the President a proposal for the transfer of 100 TOW missiles from Israel. The Iranians were for their part to produce the release of four or more hostages. Secretary Shultz [stated] that he opposed the arms sales at the meeting with the President. He said that Mr. McFarlane was present at this meeting. Secretary Shultz did not recall a telephone call from Mr. McFarlane regarding a decision by the President.

Secretary Weinberger recalled a meeting with the President at his residence after the President's return from the hospital. He [claimed] that he argued forcefully against arms transfers to Iran, as did George Shultz. He said he thought that the President agreed that the idea should not be pursued.

Mr. Regan also recalled an August meeting with the President [and] that the President expressed concern with any one-for-one swap of arms for hostages and indicated we should go slow on this but develop the contact. Mr. Regan [claimed] that in early September, Mr. McFarlane informed the President that Israel had sold arms to the Iranians and hoped to get some hostages out. Mr. Regan stated that the President was upset at the news and that Mr. McFarlane explained that the Israelis had simply taken it upon themselves to do this. Mr. Regan said that after some discussion, the President decided to leave it alone.

. . . The President said he did not recall authorizing the August shipment in advance. He noted that very possibly, the transfer was brought to him as already completed. . . . The President stated that he had been surprised that the Israelis had shipped arms to Iran, and that this fact caused the President to conclude that he had not approved the transfer in advance. . . . [In Reagan's words: "I don't remember—period."]

On August 30, 1985, Israel delivered 100 TOWs to Iran. A subsequent delivery of 408 more TOWs occurred on September 14, 1985. On September 15, 1985, Reverend Benjamin Weir was released by his captors. . . .

In a message to VADM [John] Poindexter on November 20, 1985, LtCol [Oliver] North described the following plan. The Israelis were to deliver 80 HAWK missiles to a staging area in a third country {two days hence}. These were to be loaded aboard three chartered aircraft, which would take off at two hour intervals for Tabriz, Iran. Once launch of the first aircraft had been confirmed by Mr. Ghorbanifar, directions would be given to release the five U.S. citizens held hostage in Beirut. No aircraft was to land in Tabriz until all the hostages had been delivered to the U.S. embassy in Beirut. Israel would deliver forty additional HAWKs at a later time. The Iranians would commit to seeing that there were no further hostages seized.

In contrast to the August TOW shipment, the United States became directly involved in the November transfer of the HAWK missiles. Sometime [in mid-November], while Mr. McFarlane was in Geneva for the November summit, Mr. Rabin called Mr. McFarlane to say that a problem had arisen. Mr. McFarlane referred the matter to LtCol North.

North signed a letter for Mr. McFarlane dated November 19, 1985, requesting Richard Secord, a retired U.S. Air Force general officer, to proceed to a foreign country, to arrange for the transfer of sensitive material being shipped from Israel. That day Mr. Secord made arrangements for transshipment of the Israeli HAWKs.

But late in the day on November 21, these arrangements began to fall apart. The foreign government denied landing clearance to the aircraft bringing the

HAWKs from Israel. LtCol North contacted Duane Clarridge of the CIA for assistance in obtaining the required landing clearance. When the CIA's efforts failed, LtCol North asked Mr. Clarridge to find a reliable commercial carrier to substitute for the Israeli flight. Mr. Clarridge put Mr. Secord in contact with a carrier that was a CIA proprietary.

The plan went awry again {the next day}, when Mr. Schwimmer allowed the lease to expire on the three aircraft they had chartered to take the HAWKs to Tabriz. Mr. Secord was able to provide an aircraft for this leg of the journey, however. The CIA arranged for overflight rights over a third country. On November 25 the aircraft left a European country. Delivery was three days late, however, and the aircraft carried only 18 HAWKs. Contrary to LtCol North's description of this plan, the aircraft delivered the HAWKs before the release of any hostages. In fact, no hostages were ever released as a result of this delivery.

Not only were just 18 of the initial shipment of HAWKs delivered, the HAWKs did not meet Iranian military requirements. In addition, they bore Israeli markings. [They were later returned after much diplomatic embarrassment.]

On November 30, 1985, Mr. McFarlane resigned as National Security Advisor. VADM Poindexter was named National Security Advisor on December 4. That same day, LtCol North raised with VADM Poindexter a new proposal for an arms-for-hostages deal. It involved the transfer of 3,300 Israeli TOWs and 50 Israeli HAWKs in exchange for the release of all the hostages. . . .

The proposal was considered at a meeting with the President [three days later] in the White House residence. The President, Secretary Shultz, Secretary Weinberger, Mr. Regan, Mr. McMahon, Mr. McFarlane, and VADM Poindexter attended. . . .

[Weinberger and Shultz remembered objecting to the plan, but Reagan finally approved sending McFarlane (no longer national security advisor) to London to confer with Iranians. The result of the trip was a conference between McFarlane and Ghorbanifar, where McFarlane's proposal to stop sending arms to Iran met with stern opposition from Ghorbanifar, which resulted in a temporary suspension of his role as intermediary.]

. . . [O]n December 9, LtCol North submitted to VADM Poindexter a memorandum proposing direct U.S. deliveries of arms to Iran in exchange for release of the hostages, using Mr. Secord to control Mr. Ghorbanifar and the delivery operation. . . . [This was later specified as an Israeli-mediated exchange via Mr. Nir.]

On January 7, 1986, this proposal was discussed with the President at a meeting, probably held in the Oval Office, attended by the Vice President, Secretary Shultz, Secretary Weinberger, Attorney General Edwin Meese, Director Casey, Mr. Regan, and VADM Poindexter. Although the President apparently did not make a decision at this meeting, several of the participants recall leaving the meeting persuaded that he supported the proposal. . . .

A draft Covert Action Finding had already been signed by the President the day before the meeting on January 6, 1986. . . . On January 17, a second Finding was submitted to the President. It was identical to the January 6 Finding but with the addition of the words and third parties to the first sentence. . . . [Reagan signed this Finding.]

Although the draft Finding was virtually identical to that signed by the President . . . , the cover memorandum [by VADM Poindexter] signaled a major change in the Iran initiative. Rather than accepting the arrangement suggested by Mr. Nir, the memorandum proposed that the CIA purchase 4000 TOWs from DoD and, after receiving payment, transfer them directly to Iran. Israel would still make the necessary arrangements for the transaction.

This was an important change. The United States became a direct supplier of arms to Iran. . . . That day, President Reagan wrote in his diary: I agreed to sell TOWs to Iran. . . .

In the months that followed the signing of the January 17th Finding, LtCol North forwarded to VADM Poindexter a number of operational plans for achieving the release of all the hostages. Each plan involved a direct link between the release of hostages and the sale of arms. LtCol North, with the knowledge of VADM Poindexter and the support of selected individuals at CIA, directly managed a network of private individuals in carrying out these plans. None of these plans, however, achieved their common objective—the release of all the hostages. . . .

. . . VADM Poindexter and LtCol North met with Clair George, Deputy Director of Operations at CIA, Stanley Sporkin, CIA General Counsel and one of the primary authors of the January 17 Finding, the Chief of the Near East Division with the Operations Directorate at CIA. They began planning the execution of the plan. Because of an NSC request for clearance of Mr. Ghorbanifar, on January 11, 1986, the CIA had administered a polygraph test to Mr. Ghorbanifar during a visit to Washington. Although he failed the test, and despite unsatisfactory results of the program to date, Mr. Ghorbanifar continued to serve as an intermediary. A CIA official recalls Director Casey concurring in this decision.

On January 24, LtCol North sent to VADM Poindexter a lengthy memorandum containing a notional timeline for Operation Recovery. The complex plan was to commence [that day] and conclude February 25. It called for the United States to provide intelligence data to Iran. Thereafter, Mr. Ghorbanifar was to transfer funds for the purchase of 1000 TOWs to an Israeli account at Credit Suisse Bank in Geneva, Switzerland. It provided that these funds would be transferred to a CIA account in that bank; and that the CIA would then wire the $6 million to a U.S. Department of Defense account in the United States. The 1000 TOWs would then be transferred from the DoD to the CIA.

Mr. Secord and his associates, rather than the CIA, had the more substantial operational role. He would arrange for the shipment of the TOWs to Eliat, Israel. From there, an Israeli 707, flown by a crew provided by Mr. Secord, would deliver the TOWs to Bandar Abbas, Iran. . . . The plan anticipated that the next day (February 9) all U.S. citizens held hostage in Beirut would be released to the U.S. embassy there. Thereafter, 3000 more TOWs would be delivered. The plan anticipated that Khomeini would step down on February 11, 1986, the fifth anniversary of the founding of the Islamic Republic. . . .

On February 18, the first 500 TOWs were delivered to Bandar Abbas. . . . On February 24–27, LtCol North, a CIA official, Mr. Secord, Mr. Nir and Mr. Albert Hakim (a business associate of Mr. Secord) held a series of meetings in Frankfurt, Germany with Mr. Ghorbanifar and other Iranians to review the details of the operation. On February 27, the second 500 TOWs were delivered to Bandar Abbas. Although a hostage release and a later meeting between senior U.S. and Iranian officials had been agreed upon at the Frankfurt meeting, the plan fell through. No hostages were released and the meeting failed to materialize until much later. . . .

Preparation for a meeting between Mr. McFarlane and senior Iranian officials began shortly after LtCol North's return from Frankfurt. . . .

Lt Col North, [retired CIA officer George] Cave, and a CIA official met with Mr. Ghorbanifar in Paris on March 8, 1986. LtCol North reported on this conversation to Mr. McFarlane on March 10. He said he told Mr. Ghorbanifar that the United States remained interested in a meeting with senior officials as long as the hostages were released during or before the meeting. . . . He said Mr. Ghorbanifar responded by presenting a list of 240 different types of spare parts, in various quantities, needed by Iran for its HAWK missile units. He also emphasized the importance of an advance meeting in Tehran to prepare for the meeting with Mr. McFarlane. This advance meeting would establish the agenda and who should participate from the Iranian side. . . .

[Plans were made for an April 1986 meeting, arms sales and hostage release that did not materialize.]

On May 6, 1986, LtCol North and Mr. Cave met with Mr. Ghorbanifar in London. Mr. Ghorbanifar promised a meeting with senior Iranian officials but asked that the U.S. delegation bring all the HAWK spare parts with them. . . . [North apparently agreed to bring one-quarter of the order.]

On May 22, 1986, LtCol North submitted the final operational plan for the trip to VADM Poindexter. It provided that the McFarlane delegation would arrive in Tehran [three days later]. The next day . . . , the hostages would be released. One hour later, an Israeli 707 carrying the balance of the spare parts would leave Tel Aviv for Tehran.

On May 17, LtCol North strongly urged that VADM Poindexter include Secretary Shultz and Secretary Weinberger along with Director Casey in a quiet meeting with the President and Mr. McFarlane to review the proposed trip. VADM Poindexter responded, 'I don't want a meeting with RR, Shultz and Weinberger.'

LtCol North noted in a message to VADM Poindexter on May 19 that CIA was providing comms, beacons, and documentation for the party. All other logistics had been arranged through Mr. Secord or affiliates. Mr. McFarlane, along with LtCol North, Mr. Cave, and a CIA official, left the United States on May 23. . . .

[Forty-eight hours later] the delegation arrived in Tehran. Without the prior knowledge of Mr. McFarlane, the aircraft carried one pallet of HAWK spare parts. The delegation was not met by any senior Iranian officials. No hostages were released. Because of this, a second plane carrying the rest of the HAWK spare parts was ordered not to come to Tehran. Two days of talks proved fruitless. The Iranians initially raised demands for additional concessions, but later appeared to abandon them. Mr. McFarlane demanded the prior release of all hostages and the Iranians insisted on the immediate delivery of all HAWK spare parts. On May 27, Mr. McFarlane demanded the release of the hostages by 6:30 A.M. the next day. When no hostages were released, Mr. McFarlane and his party departed, but not before the pallet of HAWK spare parts had been removed from their aircraft by the Iranians.

In a report to VADM Poindexter on May 16, Mr. McFarlane stated: 'The incompetence of the Iranian government to do business requires a rethinking on our part of why there have been so many frustrating failures to deliver on their part. . . .'

[Following the failed trip, Mr. Nir and Mr. Ghorbanifar, anxious not to see the U.S.–Iranian link severed, were apparently instrumental in the release of Father Lawrence Jenco on July 26, 1986.]

In a memorandum to VADM Poindexter dated July 29, 1986, LtCol North recommended that the President approve the immediate shipment of the rest of the HAWK spare parts and a follow-up meeting with the Iranians in Europe. . . . The President approved this proposal [the next day]. Additional spare parts were delivered to Tehran on August 3.

From the start, U.S. officials had stressed to Mr. Ghorbanifar that Iran must use its influence to discourage further acts of terrorism directed against the United States and its citizens. Whether as a result of those efforts or for some other reason, from June 9, 1985, until September 9, 1986, no U.S. citizen was seized in Lebanon. But on September 9, 1986, terrorists seized Frank Reed, a U.S. educator at the Lebanese International School. Two more U.S. citizens, Joseph Cicippio and Edward Tracey, were taken hostage on September 12 and October 21.

The McFarlane mission to Tehran marked the high-water mark of U.S. efforts to deal with Iran through Mr. Ghorbanifar. For a year he had been at the center of the relationship. That year had been marked by great confusion, broken promises, and increasing frustration on the U.S. side. LtCol North and other U.S. officials apparently blamed these problems more on Mr. Ghorbanifar than on Iran. The release of Rev. Jenco did little to mitigate their unhappiness.

Sometime in July 1986, an Iranian living in London proposed to Mr. Hakim a second Iranian channel. On July 25, Mr. Cave went to London to discuss this possibility. On August 26, 1986, Mr. Secord and Mr. Hakim met with the second channel and other Iranians in London. The Iranians said they were aware of the McFarlane visit, the Israeli connection, and Mr. Ghorbanifar. They referred to Ghorbanifar as a crook. . . . [T]he President was briefed about the second channel on September 9, 1986. . . .

On October 5–7, 1986, LtCol North, Mr. Cave, and Mr. Secord met with the second channel in Frankfurt, Germany. They carried a Bible for the Iranians inscribed by the President on October 3. During the meeting, LtCol North misrepresented his access to the President and attributed to the President things the President never said. . . .

At the October 5–7 meeting, LtCol North laid out a seven-step proposal for the provision of weapons and other items in exchange for Iranian influence to secure the release of all remaining U.S. hostages, the body of William Buckley, a debrief by his captors, and the release of John Pattis, a United States citizen whom Iranians had arrested on spying charges several months earlier. The Iranians presented a six-point counter-proposal that, in part, promised the release of one hostage following the receipt of additional HAWK parts and a timetable for future delivery of intelligence information. The Iranians made clear that they could not secure the release of all the hostages. Mr. Cave recalls that the Iranians proposed exchanging 500 TOWs for the release of two hostages. He stated that the U.S. side agreed. . . .

At a meeting [a week later] between representatives of the State Department and the second channel . . . , the Iranians said that both sides had agreed to [a modified] nine-point agenda . . . Secretary Shultz [claims] that he informed the President the next day. He said that the President was 'stricken' and could not believe that anything like this had been discussed. . . .

Because of a delay in the transfer of funds the TOWs actually delivered to Iran on October 29, 1986, were Israeli TOWs. The 500 U.S. TOWs were provided to Israel as replacements on November 7.

On November 2, hostage David Jacobsen was released. The next day, a pro-Syrian Beirut magazine published the story of the McFarlane mission. On November 4, Majlis Speaker Rafsanjani publicly announced the mission." [At this point, the arms-for-hostages operation was suspended.]

Contra Diversion

Early in 1986, the need to find funds for the support of the Contras was desperate. At the same time, the idea of diverting funds from the arms sales to Iran surfaced. . . .

In January, 1986, the President requested $100 million in military aid to the Contras. The request revived the often bitter Congressional debate over whether the United States should support the Contras. The obligational authority for the $27 million in humanitarian aid to the Contras approved by the Congress in 1985 would expire on March 31, 1986. LtCol North, who had primary responsibility for matters relating to the Contras, became increasingly concerned. While anticipating Congressional approval of the President's January 1 request, LtCol North feared the Contras would run out of funds before then. On April 22, 1986, he wrote Mr. Fortier: [T]he picture is dismal unless a new source of 'bridge' funding can be identified. . . . We need to explore this problem urgently or there won't be a force to help when Congress finally acts.

It is unclear who first suggested the idea of diverting funds from the arms sales to Iran to support the Contras. The evidence suggests that the idea surfaced early in 1986. . . .

[North told Meese] that $3 to $4 million was diverted to the support of the Contras after the February shipment of TOW missiles and that more (though how much LtCol North was not sure) was diverted after the May shipment of HAWK parts. . . .

It is unclear whether LtCol North ever sought or received prior approval of any diversion of funds to the support of the Contras. LtCol North prepared in early April an unsigned memorandum entitled 'Release of American Hostages in Beirut,' which sought Presidential approval for what became Mr. McFarlane's May trip to Tehran. In that memo, LtCol North stated that $12 million in 'residual' funds from the transaction would "be used to purchase critically needed supplies for the Nicaraguan Democratic Resistance Forces." No evidence has emerged to suggest that this memorandum was ever placed before VADM Poindexter, the President, or any other U.S. official.

As a general matter, LtCol North kept VADM Poindexter exhaustively informed about his activities with respect to the Iran initiative . . . [Poindexter told Meese] Ollie had given him enough hints that he knew what was going on, but he didn't want to look further into it. But that he in fact did generally know that money had gone to the Contras as a result of the Iran shipment.

Inquiry into the arms sales to Iran and the possible diversion of funds to the Contras disclosed evidence of substantial NSC staff involvement in a related area; private support for the Contras during the period that support from the U.S. government was either banned or restricted by Congress.

There are similarities in the two cases. Indeed, the NSC staff's role in support for the Contras set the stage for its subsequent role in the Iran initiative. In both, LtCol North, with the acquiescence of the National Security Advisor, was deeply involved in the operational details of a covert program. He relied heavily on private U.S. citizens and foreigners to carry out key operational tasks. Some of the same individuals were involved in both. When Israeli plans for the November HAWK shipment began to unravel, LtCol North turned to the Contra support operation. This network, under the direction of Mr. Secord, undertook increasing responsibility for the Iran initiative. Neither program was subjected to inter-agency overview. In neither case was Congress informed. In the case of Contra support, Congress may have been actively misled.

These two operations also differ in several key aspects. While Iran policy was the subject of strong disagreement within the Executive Branch, the President's emphatic support for the Contras provoked an often bitter debate with the Congress. The result was an intense political struggle between the President and the Congress over how to define U.S. policy toward Nicaragua. Congress sought to restrict the President's ability to implement his policy. What emerged was a highly ambiguous legal environment.

On December 21, 1982, Congress passed the first 'Boland amendment' prohibiting the Department of Defense and the Central Intelligence Agency from spending funds to overthrow Nicaragua or provoke conflict between Nicaragua and Honduras. The following year, $24 million was authorized for the Contras. On October 3, 1984, Congress cut off all funding for the Contras and prohibited DoD, CIA, and any other agency or entity 'involved in intelligence activities' from directly or indirectly supporting military operations in Nicaragua.

The 1984 prohibition was subject to conflicting interpretation. On the one hand, several of its Congressional supporters believed that the legislation covered the activities of the NSC staff. On the other hand, it appears that LtCol North and VADM Poindexter received legal advice from the President's Intelligence Oversight Board that the restrictions on lethal assistance to the Contras did not cover the NSC staff. . . .

[P]rivate contributions for the Contras were eventually funnelled into 'Project Democracy,' a term apparently used by LtCol North to describe a network of secret bank accounts and individuals involved in Contra resupply and other activities. In a message to VADM Poindexter dated July 15, 1986, LtCol North described 'Project Democracy' assets as worth over $4.5 million. They included six aircraft, warehouses, supplies, maintenance facilities, ships, boats, leased houses, vehicles, ordnance, munitions, communications equipment, and a 6520-foot runway. The runway was in fact a secret airfield in Costa Rica. LtCol North indicated in a memorandum dated September 30, 1986, that the airfield was used for direct resupply of the Contras from July 1985 to February 1986, and thereafter as a primary abort base for damaged aircraft. . . .

The CIA Headquarters instructed its field stations to 'cease and desist' with action which can be construed to be providing any type of support either direct or indirect to the various entities with whom we dealt under the program. The Chief of the CIA Central American Task Force added that in other respects the interagency process in Central America was in disarray in October 1984 and that 'it was Ollie North who then moved into that void and was the focal point for the Administration on Central American policy until fall 1985.'

As early as April 1985, LtCol North maintained detailed records of expenditures for Contra military equipment, supplies, and operations. . . .

Evidence suggests that at least by November 1985 LtCol North had assumed a direct operational role, coordinating logistical arrangements to ship privately purchased arms to the Contras. . . .

In 1986, North established a private secure communications network. North received 15 encryption devices from the National Security Agency from January to March 1986, provided in support of his counter-terrorist activities. One was provided to Mr. Secord and another, through a private citizen, to a CIA field officer posted in Central America. Through this mechanism, North coordinated the resupply of the Contras with military equipment apparently purchased with funds provided by the network of private benefactors. . . . At least nine arms shipments were coordinated through this channel from March through June, 1986.

CONCLUSION

The Tower Commission was unable to secure testimony from North and Poindexter, although its findings were generally corroborated by the testimony the two presented before Congress later in 1987. The Contra supply network was clearly a fact and their participation led to criminal convictions for North, Poindexter, and a number of other senior officials (although most of these were later overturned or set aside). Although Reagan has never been charged, George Bush was unable to entirely extricate himself from the scandal, a fact which may have contributed to his failure to secure reelection in 1992. Bush did succeed in pardoning most of the key Iran-Contra participants, however, and with the end of Special Prosecutor Lawrence Walsh's investigation, the Iran-Contra scandal seems to be over.

Questions remain. Did Reagan know about the Contra diversion? Ollie North clearly thinks so ("President Reagan knew everything" he declares in his memoirs, although with only circumstantial evidence—North 1991, 12). Reagan denied it in writing his memoirs, however, and the Republicans on the Select Committee on Iran-Contra warmly endorsed this conclusion (Inouye and Hamilton 1988, 439). Perhaps the best explanation for the amazing notion that the president was not aware that his national security adviser had sanctioned such an operation was that (1) Poindexter made a point of withholding specific knowledge from the president (as well as avoiding the details himself) and (2) Reagan's short attention span. Poindexter testified before Congress that he had intentionally protected the president from specific knowledge of the plan in order to give him "plausible deniability" were it to be revealed. Reagan, on the other hand, was not only forgetful, but tended to blot out of his mind information shortly after it was presented—as if he could somehow rewind his memory and erase it. This may explain his perpetual state of contentment.

Perhaps more pressing: How could such an operation have gone forward in the first place? Several explanations have been offered. First, all of the principals (McFarlane, Poindexter, North, Secord, etc.) were military men with a keen sense of loyalty. Perhaps better put, they sought to anticipate the wishes of their commander in chief. A parallel is found in the story of King Henry II who simply let it be known that he wished cleric Thomas à Becket somehow eliminated and his knights rushed to carry out the unstated order (Wroe 1991, 115). Reagan had made it abundantly clear that he was willing to twist U.S. policy to both secure the release of the hostages as well as maintain the Contras' fighting strength. Poindexter, North, and McFarlane simply put this wish into action.

Another plausible explanation relates to a level of corruption in the Reagan administration that was borne of its arrogance and contempt for the democratic process. A landslide electoral victory in 1984 was seen as a vindication of the president's policies. Congress was seen as a temperamental obstructionist out of step with the nation. In such circumstances, constitutional technicalities should be put aside, so the thinking went, in favor of a more pure form of democracy. Noam Chomsky refers to the "Fifth Freedom" for the U.S.—the freedom to exploit the Third World for its own ends (Chomsky 1988, 1). In a sense, the mood of the time in the White House tied together this disregard for justice, both substantive and procedural, in favor of expediency.

Still others deny that there was any wrongdoing in the Reagan administration and that the whole exercise was simply a Democratic witch-hunt aimed at discrediting an otherwise successful president. Republican apologists such as Elliot Abrams deplored the transformation of a policy dispute into a criminal proceeding (Abrams 1993). Certainly, considering the contribution the Iran-Contra scandal has made to the tarnishing of Reagan's "Teflon" image, there may be justification for this lament. Nonetheless, the bipartisan nature of the congressional inquiry indicates that the problem may be better understood as an institutional power struggle over the nature of presidential powers and congressional oversight. This particular dispute is far from resolved.

Finally, one can argue that the Iran-Contra scandal is the story of the absence of guidance—from the president, from Congress, from the Constitution—and the victory of improvisation. Certainly the National Security Agency was never intended to engage in operations of this type. A combination of gung-ho military men, an absentee president, and a fickle Congress which forgot to specifically include the NSC in its 1984 prohibitions on aid to the Contras created an opening for bureaucratic entrepreneurship. Although one can doubt the coexistence of these conditions in the future, what is remarkable about the attitudes of the participants in the process is precisely how unremarkable it all seemed to them.

Questions to Consider

1. What are the implications of these developments?

2. Did the administration achieve its objectives in Iran and Nicaragua? What does this tell us about covert operations?

3. Was Reagan truly ignorant of what took place, was he lying, or does it matter anyway? What does this experience say about accountability?

4. What alternatives were available to an administration eager to free the hostages and support the Contras without securing congressional support? Were these goals mutually exclusive?

References

Elliott Abrams. *Undue Process: A Story of How Political Differences Are Turned into Crimes* (New York: The Free Press, 1993).

Noam Chomsky. *The Culture of Terrorism* (Boston: South End Press, 1988).

Daniel Inouye and Lee Hamilton. *Report of the Congressional Committees Investigating the Iran-Contra Affair, With the Minority View.* Abridged edition edited by Joel Brinkley and Stephen Engelberg (New York: Times Books, 1988).

Oliver North. *Under Fire: An American Story* (New York: HarperCollins, 1991).

United States, President's Special Review Board. *Report of the President's Special Review Board* (Washington, DC: Government Printing Office, 1987).

Ann Wroe. *Lives, Lies and the Iran-Contra Affair* (London: I. B. Taurus & Co., 1991).

CASE 8

SALT I and Its Aftermath

This case study is intended to illustrate the concept of arms control. Arms control is any effort by nations to negotiate future levels of weapons. It can involve expenditure limits, restrictions on testing, ceilings on deployment, and/or prohibitions on new types of weapons. Arms control need not result in arms reduction, meaning that arms control may in fact lead to an overall increase in the amount of weapons in existence. In general, arms control agreements demonstrate that nations are aware that an open-ended arms race is inherently dangerous and needs to be channeled by political leaders.

Imagine you are a basketball coach who has just been handed a secret serum guaranteed to add six inches to the height of your players. Furthermore, the drug cannot be detected by testing methods currently in use by your league. However, you have heard rumors that your rival school's coach has acquired a drug, also undetectable, that will allow his players to jump six inches higher. To further complicate matters, you know your drug is very expensive and suspect his is too. You receive an invitation to "do lunch" with your rival coach to talk about drug policy in your conference. Do you accept the invitation, and if so, do you offer to cut a deal to outlaw both drugs? Perhaps we should add that if you fail to win the championship this year, you will be lynched by a mob of angry alumni. . . .

This situation is at the heart of arms control. In the case of the Soviet Union and the United States at the end of the 1960s, it was clear that each side had the capability to inflict overwhelming pain on the other. What was more serious, it seemed that new technologies, procurement programs, and deployment patterns created a very real risk that nuclear war might break out either by accident or impulse. In order to minimize the risk of accidental or precipitous nuclear attack, as early as 1962 the nations entered into agreements on such things as enhanced capital-to-capital communication (the "hot line"), increased security of nuclear arsenals (the nonproliferation agreement and sharing of fail-safe technology), and capping overall nuclear arsenals (the Strategic Arms Limitation Talks, or SALT I and SALT II). But each side was eager not to foreclose future opportunities to gain some advantage.

Were the SALT negotiations a useful step in lessening tensions between the superpowers, or did they simply become yet another contentious issue? Did they lead to the results the negotiators hoped for, and were these expectations mutually compatible? How did the SALT experience prepare each side for the dramatic arms control and disarmament breakthroughs of the 1990s?

An arms control agreement may be stabilizing or destabilizing, but much depends on the sincerity of each side's desire to control an arms race. If each wants to dupe the other into thinking it has slowed its rate of arms procurement in order to cheat and thus gain unilateral advantage, no agreement of any type will stabilize the relationship. On the other hand, if each party is sincere, certain types of weapons should be encouraged or at least tolerated in agreement if it is to prove stabilizing:

> A stable strategic weapon should be capable of delayed response; it should be invulnerable; and it should be unambiguously deprived of what is called a first-strike, or damage-limiting, capability. Put differently, it should not be able to disarm some portion of the other side's forces, or diminish them appreciably. Measured by these standards, the least-stable element of America's triad is the Minuteman [ICBM] force. (Newhouse 1989, 20)

Against this standard should one judge the SALT negotiations of the 1970s. But before proceeding, some definitions are in order. There were three ways nuclear weapons could be delivered to a target in 1970: intercontinental ballistic missiles, based on land (ICBMs); submarine-launched ballistic missiles (SLBMs); and strategic bombers carrying traditional gravity bombs (and later cruise missiles capable of hugging the ground and evading radar). By 1970, the United States had begun changing the traditional nature of a nuclear-capable missile by placing multiple warheads (the nuclear device itself) in the nose cone of the missile, and further refining this development by inventing a booster and guidance system that would allow the operator to aim each warhead (also known as a reentry vehicle) at a different target (see Figure 8.1). This innovation, called "multiple, independently targeted re-entry vehicles" (MIRV), dramatically changed the nature of offensive nuclear weapons by increasing the number of targets which could be knocked out by the launch of a single missile. The larger the missile, the larger the "throw-weight," the larger the payload it could deliver, the more MIRVed warheads it could carry. As of 1970, only the United States was close to deploying MIRVed missiles, but the Soviets were far ahead in throw-weight.

Nuclear defenses, particularly popular in the Soviet Union, included standard anti-aircraft guns, since these could be used to knock out bombers, as well as a variety of missiles capable of intercepting incoming ballistic mis-

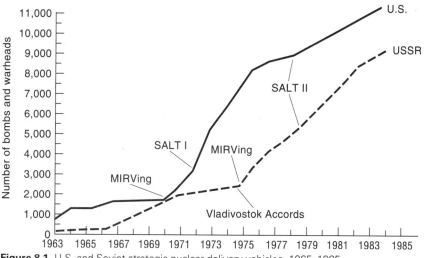

Figure 8.1 U.S. and Soviet strategic nuclear delivery vehicles, 1965–1985.
Sources: David Barash, *The Arms Race and Nuclear War* (Belmont, CA: Wadsworth,1987) and Thomas W. Wolfe, *The SALT Experience* (Cambridge: Ballinger, 1979).

siles, much like the Patriot missile of Gulf War fame. The Soviet anti-ballistic missile (ABM) defenses seemed to U.S. planners to increase the likelihood that Moscow would survive an American nuclear attack with enough operational missiles to devastate the United States (second-strike capability), which in turn prompted the Americans to push for MIRVing, to overwhelm these defenses, and deployment of American ABMs. It was this dynamic that ultimately led to the beginning of arms negotiations in 1971.

ANTECEDENTS TO SALT I

The Johnson administration saw the military balance in the mid-1960s as extremely volatile. On the one hand, the United States was in a generally anti-military mood. Secretary of State Robert McNamara had concluded that the United States had too many nuclear missiles and was pressing for a ceiling of roughly 1,000 ICBMs for the foreseeable future, contrary to a Republican proposal to double the Minuteman ICBM force. His conclusion was based on the fact that the United States needed only 400 missiles to devastate the Soviet Union, and with 900 ICBMs to the Soviet Union's 250, the United States could easily survive a nuclear attack with the capacity to deliver a crushing blow to the USSR. Given the rising costs of the Vietnam War, ceilings on missile procurement also made good financial sense (Newhouse 1989, 57). The United States was also concerned about the wisdom of ABM systems as well, since their effectiveness in battle was suspect, they would cost inordinate sums to be deployed around every major city and missile installation, and they might provoke the Soviets to building even more missiles.

While this attitude made sense in the context of a steady Soviet force, it no longer worked when the Soviets began building new missiles and ABM systems at an impressive rate after 1965. By 1966, the Soviets were moving quickly to enlarge their ICBM force and deploy an ABM system around Moscow, while the Johnson administration's buildup was leveling off (Labrie 1979, 4). Between 1964 and 1969, Soviet nuclear forces tripled while American forces increased by half. After 1969, American forces remained level (delivery vehicles only) while the Soviets' doubled, achieving numerical parity in 1972. Assuming reasonable accuracy for Soviet weapons, this force size virtually nullified the solid second-strike capability that was the foundation of McNamara's strategy (Payne 1980, 13). There were even indications as early as 1967 that some Soviet planners were anticipating the day when the USSR could so disable the United States with a first strike that no retaliation could be mounted (Payne 1980, 15).

Two alternatives presented themselves at this point: mounting a massive U.S. buildup or negotiating with the Soviets over the possibility of agreeing on a freeze of nuclear weapons at current levels. In January 1967, President Johnson proposed such a freeze on offensive and defensive systems at current levels to Soviet Premier Aleksey Kosygin. The responses were tepid at best. From the Soviet perspective, the proposal seemed to freeze their forces into inferiority and therefore had little appeal. In June 1967, at the Glassboro, New Jersey, summit, the appeal was made again, this time with Robert McNamara issuing warnings about the implications of continued ABM deployment in the Soviet Union. He painted a dark picture of the escalation that would result from the move, which would necessitate deployment of an American ABM as well as a dramatic increase in the offensive nuclear arsenals (he withheld information on the MIRVing program then being tested) (Newhouse 1989, 95).

While the speech made little impression on Kosygin, the U.S. announcements of MIRVing and deployment of the Sentinel ABM system in late 1967 seem to have had a profound effect. Beginning in January 1968, the Soviet Union began working toward serious arms control negotiations aimed particularly at controlling American ABMs (Newhouse 1989, 102). By June 1968, the Politburo had issued a lengthy document, provided to the United Nations, which committed the nation to a wide range of both improbable and potentially significant arms control and disarmament objectives. Among the more interesting was a proposal to limit the total number of nuclear delivery vehicles (ICBMs, SLBMs, and bombers). The gesture convinced them to commence strategic arms negotiations, which were announced formally at the signing of the Non-Proliferation Treaty (NPT) on July 1, 1968. The NPT was likely an important ingredient to Soviet cooperation, since it prohibited always-threatening Germany from acquiring nuclear weapons (Payne 1980, 16).

The talks were scheduled to begin in the fall of 1968, but the day before that announcement was to be made, Moscow sent tanks into Prague, Czechoslovakia, prompting a U.S. protest which included shelving the talks. The Soviets were eager to begin again the SALT process in order to rehabilitate their image, but were unable to make progress with the Johnson administration. The Nixon administration, victorious in the November elections, undertook a thorough review of the SALT concept and waited until November 1969 (Wolfe 1979, 3).

Factors that contributed to reaching agreement to beginning the negotiations were manifold. First and foremost was the attainment in 1969 of effective nuclear parity by the Soviet Union (see Figure 8.1). As put by Payne:

> The most important reason for the Soviet agreement to begin the SALT negotiations in 1969 was the Soviet Union's attainment of strategic parity with the United States. By mid-1969 the Soviet Union was close to attaining this goal and by mid-1970 had virtually as many strategic nuclear missiles as the United States. This was recognized in both countries as a fundamental factor. President Nixon said in retrospect: "The approaching strategic parity provided an opportunity to achieve an overall agreement that would yield no unilateral advantage and could contribute to a more stable strategic environment." A Soviet commentator described 1968 as "one of those rare moments in history when both sides are ready to admit equality in the broadest sense and to look on it as a starting point for achieving agreement on limiting and eventually reducing armaments," and urged political leaders "not to let this chance slip away." (Payne 1980, 18, 19)

Secondary factors included improvements in satellite reconnaissance which by the late 1960s made verification of a nuclear agreement possible without resort to on-site inspection (Newhouse 1989, 70). The Nixon administration hoped to use the talks to link U.S. acceptance of Soviet parity with Soviet agreement to cooperate on a number of international "hot spots" such as the Middle East and Vietnam (Labrie 1979, 8). On purely military terms, the United States hoped it could avoid the next round of arms racing, including a new Soviet MIRV threat and a U.S. ABM buildup (Newhouse 1989, 21). Finally, the hope was that by accomplishing all of these goals, the international system would enter into a more stable and predictable, if not necessarily fair, period. Failure to enter into an agreement carried the very real threat of an uncontrolled and volatile arms buildup in which each side would be forced to develop large numbers of first-strike weapons (Pfaltzgraff 1973, 17).

OBJECTIVES, TRADE-OFFS, AND OUTCOMES OF SALT I

The SALT negotiations began on November 17, 1969, in Helsinki, Finland, under an extraordinary media glare. The talks went on until May 26, 1972, when the ABM Treaty and an "Interim Agreement" on strategic arms were signed in Moscow. The location of the negotiations alternated between Helsinki and Vienna, cities chosen for their relative neutrality and experienced hosts. The U.S. delegation was led by Gerard Smith, head of the Arms Control and Disarmament Agency, although by January 1971 the negotiating process was largely controlled by Henry Kissinger, Nixon's national security adviser. On the Soviet side, the Politburo remained actively engaged behind its negotiator, Vladimir Semenov.

The principal objectives have already been outlined, but it is interesting to note that early on, the Nixon administration chose to ignore possible linkages between the SALT negotiations and other international problems (Bowie 1973, 128). For their part, the Soviets quickly rejected a tentative U.S. proposal to ban MIRVs and MIRV testing. Thus the talks focused on ABM systems and numerical limits on missiles (Newhouse 1989, 181).

In general terms, the United States sought firm, binding, specific agreements which could be verified, while the Soviets were more attracted to broad statements of intent which allowed maximum flexibility of implementation (Wolfe 1979, 9):

> Initially, the U.S. suggested possible approaches involving both numerical and qualitative limitations on strategic offensive and defensive systems, including MIRVs. We also put forward an alternative comprehensive approach which would not constrain MIRVs, but would involve reductions in offensive forces in order to maintain stability even in the face of qualitative improvements. The Soviet Union, for its part, submitted a general proposal which diverged from ours in many respects, including a major difference on the definition of strategic systems. (Bowie 1973, 135)

This difference of approach later led to significant difficulties, particularly when definitions (of "heavy missiles," for example) were central to the agreement.

The principal subjects of discussion in the early stages of SALT I were the ABM systems each nation would be permitted, and the possible limitation of total delivery vehicles of nuclear warheads. The two sides reached early agreement on the notion that any ABM system should be well short of countrywide. Thus, the options of a national capital area (NCA) defense with or without deployment of ABMs to protect missile installations emerged as the most promising. The U.S. negotiators presented several ABM proposals in quick succession (which may have contributed to Soviet confusion and overconfidence—Newhouse 1989, 191). Meanwhile, the Soviets were adamant about their most contentious demand—conclusion of an initial ABM agreement without specific commitments to offensive missile limits (Labrie 1979, 12).

During 1970, the talks stalemated. As put by participant Newhouse, "At best, it was an impasse. At worst, SALT was having a perverse effect, planting doubts and uncertainties instead of promoting some understanding on each side of the other's position. Suspicion and mistrust were being fed, not dissipated" (Newhouse 1989, 195).

In early 1971, several developments broke the deadlock at SALT. First, Henry Kissinger met secretly in Washington and in Moscow with Soviet Ambassador A. F. Dobrynin and Politburo members to work out a compromise for SALT. This so-called "back-channel" negotiation produced a tentative settlement in May 1971. The key element involved acceptance on the Soviets' part of a temporary offensive missile ceiling, in combination with an ABM treaty, which would be renegotiated shortly after the conclusion of the first round of talks. In addition to the Soviets accepting a temporary offensive missile agreement, the United States accepted an unequal ceiling for the Soviet Union (Newhouse 1989, 204). As put by Henry Kissinger:

> This is why at crucial moments in these negotiations there had been direct contacts between the President and Soviet leaders which led by mutual agreement to breakthroughs—the first on May 20 of 1971, in which there was an agreement that broke the deadlock that had developed between the Soviet insistence that an agreement cover antiballistic missile systems only and our view that an agreement involved as well the offensive weapons. The compromise was that the initial treaty would deal with ABMs and that this would be accompanied by a freeze on certain categories of offensive weapons. (Kissinger 1979, 33)

This agreement was facilitated by the elevation of Leonid Brezhnev, a committed arms control supporter, to supreme party chief in March (Payne 1980, 75).

Critics of SALT focus on the way Kissinger operated. SALT delegation head, Gerard Smith, has challenged the wisdom of one American taking on the entire Soviet establishment in face-to-face talks. The result, he points out, was a largely out-maneuvered and often disoriented Kissinger. Kissinger was so distrustful of his colleagues that he refused to use American interpreters to go over the Russian drafts of the agreement (Smith 1980, 223, 407). The episode did much to undermine the delegation's confidence as well. "I thought the whole episode a sad reflection on the state of affairs in the Administration. Kissinger and the President went the Soviets one better. At least in the Soviet Union, the whole Politburo was consulted, on several occasions. The bulk of the American national security leadership was never consulted. It was informed after the fact" (Smith 1980, 234). As a result, several concessions made or implied in the May 1971 agreement were later rescinded or modified.

The unequal missile ceiling anticipated by this May 1971 agreement has since led to much contention in U.S. circles. The most celebrated opposition came from Senator Henry Jackson, who was able to place a condition on eventual Senate ratification of the treaty, insisting that any future agreement provide for equal ceilings. In fact, the unequal ceilings could be justified on several grounds. First, the Soviets agreed to exclude "forward based systems"—nuclear missiles located in Europe but under American control. Second, U.S. targeting and MIRV technology gave its missiles much more punch in comparison to the less accurate, single-warhead Soviet missiles. Third, U.S. submarine-launched missiles were much harder to detect, given their quieter drive mechanisms, and the fact that they also enjoyed the MIRVing and targeting advantages of their ground-based counterparts. Finally, the U.S. bomber fleet was much larger than the Soviets' with the result that the United States had a much larger number of more accurate warheads and bombs, even if it had fewer missiles (Barash 1987, 223).

While the May 1971 statement set the stage for the conclusion of negotiations over the next year, many points were left unresolved. On the ABM front, the Soviets ultimately moved in the direction of U.S. support for missile defense systems and, after considering a number of alternatives, settled on a one-plus-one arrangement which would allow a missile defense system and an NCA arrangement, each limited to 100 missiles (Newhouse 1989, 232). In addition, both sides agreed to ban "exotic" ABM systems, such as space-based missiles.

The offensive missile ceilings were far more complex, in that there was little in the arsenals of the two nations that was directly comparable. Small, MIRVed missiles seemed to the Soviets a greater threat than their large, single-warhead missiles, although American negotiators were quick to point out that the Soviet missiles, with their larger throw-weight (capacity to lift larger warheads), could carry a very large number of MIRVed missiles in the near future (see Figure 8.2). American efforts to limit the size of Soviet missiles ended in an agreement in principle to a cap of 313 "heavy missiles," although the United States was forced to define "heavy missile" without Soviet concurrence (Nitze et al. 1979, 12). The Soviets also accepted in principle the U.S. proposal to limit enlargement of existing silos, although the expanded dimensions would still accommodate the newest generation of heavy missiles.

The final agreement on offensive land-based missiles provided for a ceiling of 1,054 ICBMs for the United States—equal to its existing inventory—and 1,618 for the Soviet Union—slightly more than it controlled at the time. Both limits provided for continued modernization and improvement of the missiles, meaning that MIRVing would be unimpeded. The Soviets agreed to destroy 210 obsolete missiles to make way for newer ones, while the United States destroyed only 54.

In the final stages of the talks, the question of submarine-based missiles reached center stage. Particularly at the final round during the Moscow summit, a number of proposals and counterproposals were reviewed. The Soviets were eager to achieve a very high ceiling on total submarines, since it was in the process of manufacturing many more each year. The Soviets sought and obtained a limit of 62 submarines (or six additional) versus 44 for the United States (or three additional). The number of SLBMs controlled by the Soviets in 1972 was a subject of debate until the final hours of the talks—the Soviets claimed a high number of 768 while U.S. intelligence estimates pegged the number at 640. Nixon and Brezhnev agreed on 740 as the benchmark, to which the Soviets could add 210 additional SLBMs (Labrie 1979, 13). This compared with 710 SLBMs from a baseline of 656 for the United States.

Perhaps the most interesting feature of the agreements signed in May 1972, from an international law perspective, was the establishment of a Standing Consultative Commission to interpret the treaty (Wolfe 1979, 11). In fact, the commission has been approached several times for clarification of the agreement. Furthermore, the agreements provided an opt-out

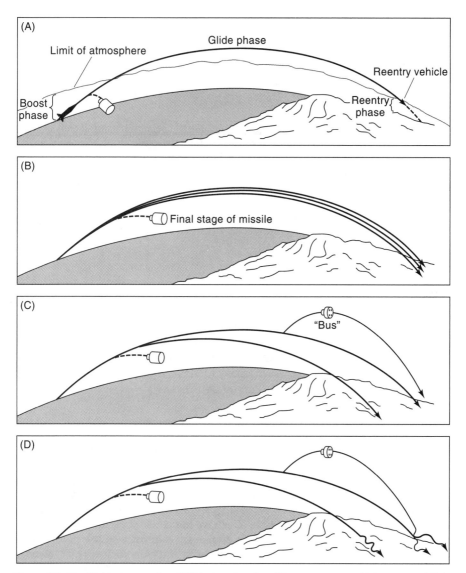

Figure 8.2 The flight phases of an ICBM, also showing different reentry vehicle patterns (A) A single-warhead missile with one RV. (B) A MRVed missile, with three RVs, which are not independently targeted. (C) A MIRVed missile, carrying three RVs, each of which is aimed at a different target. The "bus" delivers the first RV to target 1, reorients itself to permit the second RV to go to target 2, and so on. (D) A MARVed missile, carrying three RVs that are independently targeted and also maneuver prior to reaching their target.
Source: David Barash, *The Arms Race and Nuclear War* (Belmont, CA: Wadsworth 1987).

clause—made explicit in the case of the ABM and implied by the five-year duration of the Interim Agreement.

The various assessments of SALT I are largely a reflection of expectations (Van Cleave 1973, 327). The administration sought a means to control the accelerating pace of Soviet arms acquisition. Both Kissinger and Secretary of State William Rogers agree that the threat of a spiraling arms race was very high in 1969 and that threat was largely abated (Rogers 1979, 68–69). As put by Kissinger:

> [T]he question to ask in assessing the freeze is not what situation it perpetuates but what situation it prevents. The question is where we would be without the freeze. And if you project the existing building programs of the Soviet Union into the future, as against the absence of building programs over the period of the freeze in either of the categories that are being frozen, you will get a more correct clue to why we believe that here is a good agreement and why we believe that it has made a significant contribution to arresting the arms race. The weapons are frozen, as we pointed out, in categories in which we have no ongoing programs. (Kissinger 1979, 34)

Although he objected to the way the agreement was reached, Smith concurred the SALT I Treaty was an honest beginning to an ongoing process of arms control (Smith 1980, 34).

Critics on the left pointed out how SALT provided for considerable increases in nuclear weapons on both sides, either through MIRVing old missiles or building new ones. As can be seen by Figure 8.3, which shows warhead and bomb counts, SALT I seems to have done more to propel the warhead race than slow it down. As put by Bowie:

> In practice, neither side has suspended its weapons programs. Throughout the period of the SALT the Soviet Union has continued to install SS-9s and other missiles at a rapid rate, to build Polaris-type submarines at the rate of eight per year, to test multiple warheads and improved ABMs, and to dig nearly one hundred new silos. The United States has likewise gone forward with missiles equipped with MIRVs for the modified Polaris submarines and for Minuteman ICBMs, and with the revised ABM Safeguard systems. . . . There is no evidence that the weapons actions by either side have impeded the SALT. Indeed, it can be argued that unilateral suspension of planned improvements would remove one of the motives for Soviet agreement to restrictions in the SALT. (Bowie 1973, 136)

Some feared that such a weak agreement would actually exacerbate the arms race by encouraging development of new technologies that could fit in existing missiles. Defense Department officials campaigned vigorously in 1972 and 1973 for new generations of submarine and land-based weapons, as well as the B-1 bomber program, justifying them as legal, if not essential, under SALT (Labrie 1979, 82). Furthermore, MIRVing programs and other innovations were viewed as potential bargaining chips in future negotiations, much as the ill-conceived ABM system proved to be in the SALT I process (Newhouse 1989, 78).

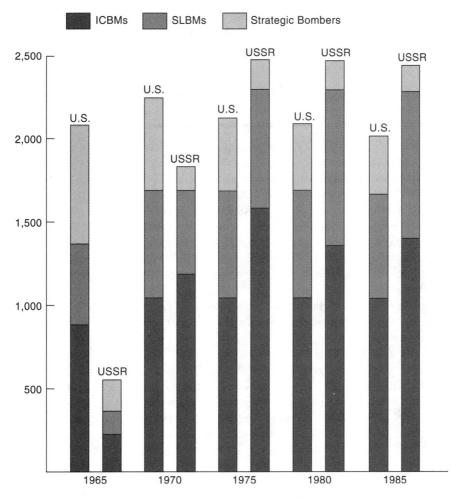

Figure 8.3 Number of bombs and warheads,1963–1985.
Source: David Barash, *The Arms Race and Nuclear War* (Belmont, CA: Wadsworth 1987).

Critics on the right expressed strong concern about the headroom issue, as was already pointed out, as well as the question of verification. They objected to exclusive reliance on "national means" of checking Soviet compliance (satellite photography) on the grounds that the USSR had every reason to cheat in spite of promises. Given their throw-weight advantage, existing ABM systems, and incipient MIRVing, conservatives stressed the Soviets had the capacity to achieve first-strike capability by the end of the decade (Labrie 1979, 153).

On the other hand, claims of success in SALT are certainly justified. It achieved a degree of confidence and predictability which failure to negotiate would have made impossible (Wolfe 1979, 14). Parity was acknowledged and enshrined, mutual deterrence legitimated, and uncontrolled arms acquisition and improvement discouraged. From the Soviet perspective, the

SALT elevated their status as nothing else could in 1972, while excluding China. Furthermore, it consolidated the power within the Soviet Union of Brezhnev and supporters of détente (Payne 1980, 77).

MANEUVERING IN SALT II

Much has been written about the ill-fated SALT II process, which began six months after SALT I was signed and ended with Jimmy Carter's withdrawal of the signed treaty from Senate consideration after the Soviet invasion of Afghanistan in 1980. Although the failure of SALT II is interesting in itself, we will limit ourselves to a more general overview of the SALT II process and its implications for arms control and disarmament in the 1990s.

The Soviet Union approached the SALT II negotiations with greater confidence and perhaps more stubbornness than during SALT I. The Soviets were convinced that the "correlation of forces" was moving in their favor, meaning that when all dimensions of power were taken together—military, diplomatic, economic, moral, ideological—the Soviet Union was on the verge of overtaking the United States (Wolfe 1979, 95). In such a situation, concessions are generally counterproductive and patience is by far the greatest virtue.

The talks stalemated rather quickly, primarily because of Watergate and Richard Nixon's resignation in 1973–1974. But the talks would not have progressed far in any case, since the questions of headroom, Euro-missiles, MIRVing, bombers, etc., had already delayed coming to agreement by the mid-1975 deadline. The prospect of a permanent offensive missile treaty was dim at best (Barash 1987, 227). In particular, on the MIRVing question, the Soviets were particularly emboldened by their successful tests of 1973 and their plans for deployment in 1974–1975. Some Soviet planners imagined the possibility of deploying as many as 15,000 independently targeted warheads, given the throw-weight of their land-based missiles (Wolfe 1979, 98).

Other new developments undermined the prospects for an early conclusion of SALT II: the development of the cruise missile and the Soviet Backfire bomber and the emergence of Ronald Reagan as a force in the Republican party. While for very different reasons, both challenged previous assumptions. The cruise missile, while in existence during SALT I, was not included in the discussions. Whether to include them or the medium-range Backfire bomber was a troublesome issue, largely because of questions about whether their limited range but forward deployment classified them as "strategic" weapons The cruise missile complicated negotiations doubly, since its capacity to evade radar detection made it an ideal first-strike, and therefore destabilizing, weapon (Barash 1987, 227).

The Republican party was torn apart by a split between the moderate, pro-SALT wing and the conservative wing dominated by Reagan and such groups as the alarmist Committee on the Present Danger. The strong showing of Reagan during the 1976 Republican primary elections undermined then-President Gerald Ford's efforts at détente with Moscow. The split ultimately damaged the administration's political viability and allowed the election of a political newcomer, Jimmy Carter, in November.

In spite of these obstacles, a significant agreement in principle was reached at Vladivostok in 1974. This agreement became the foundation of the eventual SALT II of 1978 and therefore deserves special consideration. Early in the SALT II process, in response to the Jackson Amendment concerning strategic parity, the Nixon administration proposed ceilings on all strategic weapons, including bombers. Given U.S. numerical superiority in strategic bombers, this move alone went far to achieve the target of overall strategic parity (Nitze et al. 1979, 12).

The question of MIRVing was addressed next, with the United States proposing an overall throw-weight ceiling, and the Soviets countering with a limit on the total number of MIRVed missiles. Given the small size of U.S. missiles, a throw-weight ceiling would have given it the opportunity to build a much larger number of individual, MIRVed missiles. The Soviet counterproposal preserved its advantage in throw-weight (Wolfe 1979, 100–102).

It was clear by mid-1974 that a permanent offensive weapon agreement was beyond reach, and so both sides focused on achieving another interim settlement, this one to last until 1985. An additional agreement was achieved in late 1974 when the Soviets dropped their demand that American-controlled Euro-missiles be included in the accord. Cruise missiles and the Backfire bomber were also excluded from the framework agreement. From these concessions, a general agreement was relatively easy.

The Vladivostok Agreement signed by President Ford and Secretary Brezhnev provided for an overall ceiling of 2,400 delivery vehicles, with each bomber counted as one delivery vehicle. This figure provided for a small increase for the U.S. (+258) and a slight reduction of Soviet forces (–99). The treaty made a modest effort to constrict MIRVing by providing a sublimit of 1,320 MIRVed missiles or cruise-missile-carrying bombers. This limit was much higher than the 1,000 ceiling originally proposed by the Soviets. Perhaps the most interesting feature of the treaty was the "freedom to mix" provision, which meant that each nation could choose its nuclear emphasis. For example, the United States or USSR could deploy more land-based missiles or bombers, so long as it reduced its sea-based missiles by the same number (Barash 1987, 225). Other provisions of the Interim Agreement (SALT I) were extended (Wolfe 1979, 174). In addition to the offensive weapons agreement, the Vladivostok Summit produced a refinement of the ABM Treaty, cutting the number of ABM systems allowed to only one.

Supporters of the agreements noted the virtue of unambiguous ceilings on overall strategic weapons. Opponents on the left were quick to emphasize the high level of this ceiling, which provided for a continued arms race, both quantitative and qualitative (Barash 1987, 225). Critics on the right charged that the throw-weight imbalance canceled out the numerical parity, and inadequate verification provisions made considerable cheating possible.

The Carter administration entered the fray in 1977 with optimistic proposals which were treated with disdain by the Soviets. Quickly the talks returned to the cautious give-and-take that had become the pattern for SALT. The ultimate SALT II agreement signed in 1979 bore close resemblance to the Vladivostok Accords of 1974. They provided for a slightly lower overall ceiling (2,250) and included cruise missiles. While allowing "freedom to mix" in principle, SALT II included a number of sublimits on MIRVed weapons (of the 1,320 total, no more than 820 MIRVed ICBMs and 1,200 total MIRVed ICBMs and SLBMs) (Panofsky 1979, 820).

The debate over SALT II echoed previous debates, with the complicating factor that although the Vietnam War was finally over, Soviet adventurism in the Third World was on the rise. The situation was further complicated by Carter's rather weak influence over the Senate and his ambivalence about Soviet human rights violations. By the time the Senate was about to formally consider the treaty for ratification—a doubtful prospect at best—the Soviets had invaded Afghanistan, prompting Carter to withdraw the treaty in order to both sanction the Soviets and avoid a defeat in the Senate (Barash 1987, 228).

IMPLICATIONS OF THE SALT PROCESS

The SALT experience shows clearly that arms control is quite different from disarmament. Throughout the SALT process, arms acquisition continued at a rapid pace, particularly in terms of warhead accumulation. In only a few instances were older missiles retired—something which may well have been done without an agreement. The objective of SALT was clearly not a reduction in the number of weapons, but a change in the arms race dynamic. SALT was intended primarily as an effort by the United States to prevent the Soviets from developing first-strike capability by rapidly improving their arsenal at a time when the United States was unwilling to invest in continued improvements.

It was not until the United States launched a costly and risky arms buildup in the early 1980s that genuine disarmament became possible. With the collapse of the Soviet economy in the mid-1980s and the emergence of Mikhail Gorbachev, the United States found a willing negotiating partner at a time when its arsenal was clearly excessive. Just as the Sentinel ABM system provoked the Soviets to enter into negotiations, the Star Wars program (an alleged violation of the ABM Treaty) prompted them to renew the suspended START (Strategic Arms Reduction Talks) process. Disarmament treaties came in rapid succession in the late 1980s: the Intermediate-Range Nuclear Forces Treaty (INF) in 1987, the Conventional Forces in Europe (CFE) Treaty in 1990, the first START agreement in 1991, followed by a second START agreement in 1992 (signed before the Senate had completed review of the first treaty, and later ratified by the Ukraine and Belarus).

Whether the lessons of SALT bear any relation to the successes of START is an open question. Some have argued that arms control is possible only when it is no longer necessary. Presidents George Bush and Bill Clinton announced unilateral arms cuts that exceeded those negotiated in 1992 and 1993. Mikhail Gorbachev induced U.S. participation in arms talks by imposing a unilateral ban on weapons testing for eighteen months in 1986. All of this implies that when political conditions are ripe, arms control is simply one of many symptoms of warmer relations. On the other hand, when tensions are high, arms control cannot be expected to solve the problem, in and of itself.

Questions to Consider

1. What factors seem to have precipitated arms control negotiations? To what extent did they steer the content of the talks thereafter?

2. To what extent did expectations contribute to the decision to engage in arms control talks? Were these expectations fulfilled?

3. How did domestic debate affect the progress of arms control? Is it possible for world leaders to remain unaffected by such things?

References

David P. Barash. *The Arms Race and Nuclear War* (Belmont, CA: Wadsworth Publishing Co., 1987).

Robert R. Bowie. "The Bargaining Aspects of Arms Control: The SALT Experience," in Kintner and Pfaltzgraff, eds. SALT, 127–140.

William Kintner and Robert Pfaltzgraff, eds. SALT: *Implications for Arms Control in the 1970s* (Pittsburgh, PA: University of Pittsburgh Press, 1973).

Henry Kissinger, *White House Years* (Boston: Little, Brown, 1979).

Roger P. Labrie, ed. *The SALT Handbook: Key Documents and Issues, 1972–1979* (Washington, DC: AEI, 1979).

John Newhouse. *Cold Dawn: The Story of SALT* (New York: Pergamon-Brassey, 1989).

Paul H. Nitze, James Dougherty, and Francis Kane. *The Fateful Ends and Shades of SALT: Past . . . Present . . . and Yet to Come* (New York, Crane, Russak & Co., 1979).

W.K.H. Panofsky. *Arms Control and SALT II* (Seattle, WA: University of Washington Press, 1979).

Samuel B. Payne, Jr. *The Soviet Union and SALT* (Cambridge, MA: MIT Press, 1980).

Robert L. Pfaltzgraff, Jr. "The Rationale for Superpower Arms Control," in Kintner and Pfaltzgraff, eds. *SALT,* 3–20.

Gerard Smith. *Doubletalk: The Story of the First Strategic Arms Limitation Talks* (New York: Doubleday, 1980).

William R. Van Cleave. "Implications of Success or Failure of SALT," in Kintner Pfaltzgraff, eds., *SALT,* 313–336.

Thomas W. Wolfe. *The SALT Experience* (Cambridge, MA: Ballinger, 1979).

U.S. Role After the Cold War

"National interest" is an incredibly elastic concept—capable of stretching to encompass any potential foreign threats for which an overzealous internationalist wants to prepare. On the other hand, it can shrink to cover only life-threatening dangers on your doorstep. Because of the concept's malleability, it might be best to dismiss it as a mere rhetorical flourish. Beneath the rhetoric, however, is a fundamental question of what really matters in American foreign policy, and drawing the line between vital interests and peripheral preoccupations is the great question of our time.

THE "GREAT DEBATE"

Americans have not always accepted the U.S. role as leader of the free world. Prior to the entry of the United States into World War I, for example, the bulk of opinion makers in the country agreed that the U.S. should remain aloof from European troubles. After the war, United States membership in the League of Nations and establishment of a standing army were rejected by Congress. Meanwhile, the White House and State Department had grown attached to American leadership and repeatedly advanced its necessity. At the heart of this debate was the question of whether American idealism—its quest for peace and justice—should push the country into a leadership role in world affairs (exporting idealism, as it were), or whether it should avoid all "entangling alliances" (to use George Washington's phrase). This debate was ultimately resolved with Pearl Harbor.

Today, we face a renewal of this debate. As a consequence of the collapse of the Berlin Wall, the dismantling of the Warsaw Pact, and the dissolution of the Soviet Union, much of the U.S. foreign policy establishment now finds itself without a clear purpose. The question of what to do in the next century has gripped policy analysts in a dramatic way. Such publications as *Foreign Affairs, Foreign Policy, National Interest, National Review,* and the *Atlantic Monthly,* to name a few (See also Kegley and Wittkopf 1992; Schmergel 1991; Lynn-Jones 1991; Lynn-Jones and Miller 1992), have recently been almost entirely devoted to a single question: What should be the guiding principles of U.S. foreign policy in this new era? In this case study, we will review the major points of this debate by organizing the various proposals into three general categories: the "national interest" approach, the "hegemonic imperative" school, and the "multilateralist" position.

NATIONAL INTEREST

The "national interest" position, often espoused by politicians seeking the votes of unemployed steel or textile workers, aims at defining national interest in narrow terms. John F. Kennedy's pledge on behalf of the American public in 1961 to "bear any burden" in the cause of freedom rings hollow to these analysts who see a declining U.S. economy, an urban and even suburban social infrastructure in shambles, where problems of the outside world seem trivial at best. To the McGovern Democrats' call of "Come Home America" many neoconservatives are adding the refrain "America First." As put by Charles Krauthammer, "[T]he internationalist consensus is under renewed assault. The assault this time comes not only from the usual pockets of post-Vietnam liberal isolationism (e.g., the churches) but from a resurgence of 1930s-style conservative isolationism" (Krauthammer 1990/91, 23).

Republican Patrick Buchanan and Democrat Tom Harkin made "America First" a prominent campaign theme during the 1992 presidential election, and numerous analysts have written extensively about the need for relative retrenchment in U.S. foreign policy. Alan Tonelson argued that the Bush administration's attachment to Cold War activism was misguided and neglected the simple fact that U.S. power must be founded on a strong domestic society and economy. "The contrast between American victories in the cold war and the Gulf war, and growing domestic social and economic decay shows that the traditional benchmarks for evaluating United States foreign policy are sorely inadequate" (Tonelson 1992, 145). William Pfaff argued that, as the world system becomes more complex and unpredictable, U.S. capability will be based as much on inner strength and resistance to instability abroad as on the ability to project power beyond our borders (Pfaff 1990/91). Paul Kennedy and Arthur Taylor, in testimony on Capitol Hill, argued that the only way to stop the decline of U.S. strength is by redirecting resources from international commitments to domestic retooling and rein-vigoration (U.S. Congress 1990).

Most national interest authors emphasize the need for the United States to withdraw from nonessential international obligations. The *Atlantic Monthly* July 1991 cover story criticized the failures of internationalism which, in the authors' view, was out of step with the American public and had led to wasting billions on problems of only remote importance to the U.S. citizenry (Tonelson 1991). They urged a renewed emphasis on programs which directly benefit the United States, although they did not dismiss all international activities. "An interest-based foreign policy would tend to rule out economic initiatives deemed necessary for the international system's health if those initiatives wound up siphoning more wealth out of this country than they brought in" (Tonelson 1991, 38).

In the tradition of avoiding "entangling alliances" (Hendrickson 1992), the new national interest would exclude international commitments which involve long-term and open-ended obligations, on the grounds that these would limit U.S. flexibility and self-reliance. Such analysts see no further need for our involvement in NATO given the dissolution of the Warsaw Pact, as well as our maintenance of military bases across the world, and call for a large-scale withdrawal of troops. They furthermore question the merits of an overwhelming nuclear missile deterrent in the face of the collapse and democratization of our principal nuclear adversary, the Soviet Union, and call for unilateral disarmament (Krasner 1989).

Some emphasize the need for reducing oil dependency and import dependency generally, while others focus on the need to control foreign investment flows into the country in order to preserve U.S. control of critical resources, industries, and even symbolic entities such as Rockefeller Plaza and the Seattle Mariners. Protectionism, investment controls, export promotion, and maintaining an undervalued currency are among the international economic policies consistent with this approach.

Analysts who accept the national interest approach emphasize the primacy of American sovereignty. However, liberals and conservatives disagree on what in America needs fixing. Liberal neo-isolationists stress repairing urban decay, alleviating poverty, fighting racism, and rebuilding schools. Neoconservatives, on the other hand, seek reductions in government regulations, handouts to the poor, and a reversal of the decline of "family values." Conservatives therefore dismiss liberal isolationism as merely a ploy "to spend the maximum amount of money on social programs at home and the minimum abroad" (Kristol 1990, 20).

While the national interest approach seems particularly appealing during tough economic times, the Bush administration and liberal internationalists outside government argued strongly against it. Such retrenchment, so the logic goes, will take us down the well-worn path toward isolation, xenophobia, and ultimately the collapse of modern world order. Richard Nixon has argued that the choice between domestic resurgence and international activism is a false one. "We do not face a choice between dealing with domestic problems and playing an international role. Our challenge is to do both by setting realistic goals and by managing our limited resources" (Nixon 1992, 277–278). Anti-isolationists argue that even a limited retrenchment from international obligations, whether collective or unilateral, could lead to an increase in America's insecurity as renegade states, reactionary dictatorships, and protectionism abroad flourish and undermine U.S. interests.

HEGEMONIC IMPERATIVE

Many feel that the United States is still, both by duty and by right, the leader of the free world. With the collapse of the Soviet Union, we no longer need to worry about an overwhelming threat to our security. But with that collapse goes much of the order and stability of the international system and the risk of new, unforeseen dangers (Gaddis 1987 and 1991). As pointed out by chairman of the Joint Chiefs Colin Powell, none of the troop deployments of the Bush administration (Panama, Persian Gulf, Somalia) were anticipated at the time of his inauguration—a fact that reinforces the need for the country to be prepared for threats to peace, no matter how remote they may seem beforehand (U.S. Congress 1992, 367).

Many of these authors argue that the United States has the capability to lead and only lacks the will. Joseph Nye, an antideclinist, disagrees with President Bush's lament that the United States lacks not the will but the wallet by saying that the reverse is true: in terms of what we can afford as a nation, we are far too tight-fisted in dealing with global problems (Nye 1990). Richard Cooper argued before Congress that the United States must not shrink from global responsibilities for fear of what it will cost (U.S. Congress 1990). Alexander Haig echoes the sentiment, pointing out that it is up to the executive to promote a domestic consensus about the need for American leadership abroad, and then to act on that consensus (Haig 1991).

There is a further sense from many authors that the United States has the right not only to lead, but to act unilaterally. Although they pay some lip service to multilateral institutions, they imply that the United States has the best ideas, the strongest institutions, and the natural gifts required to create world order. Charles Krauthammer points out "American preeminence is based on the fact that it is the only country with the military, diplomatic, political and economic assets to be a decisive player in any conflict in whatever part of the world it chooses to involve itself" (Krauthammer 1990/91, 24). Coupled with this assumption of preeminence comes a disdain for the cumbersome mechanisms of the United Nations and the assumption that the UN will never have effective enforcement powers. This tone has been criticized by many critics as vain "triumphalism."

For others, the U.S. leadership role is merely an extension of old Cold War attitudes and behaviors as if the Soviet Union never collapsed. Richard Lugar declared "Americans must demonstrate staying power and the ability to master and prolong the peace" (Lugar 1992). Many call for maintaining alliances, defense spending, and nuclear weapon arsenals at roughly constant levels in anticipation of future conflicts.

In their exuberance, some have gone so far as to declare the end of international conflict. With the end of the Cold War, so the thinking goes, we find ourselves at the conclusion of the grand struggle between liberalism and authoritarianism—the "end of history" itself (Fukuyama 1989). Given this situation, we may find ourselves well and truly in an age without the threat of global war. Naturally, some have steered clear of such dramatic predictions and contented themselves with pointing out the unique nature of America's position in the world, with a call for continued leadership and international engagement (Huntington 1989).

The "errors of endism" are probably obvious enough, but bear repetition here. Sanders has warned that attachment to a "unipolar myth" will quickly lead to frustration by those who ignore the reality of the diffusion of power in the last few years. This frustration with America not always getting its way may in turn lead to nationalist retrenchment, with equally serious consequences (Sanders 1991).

More subtle are the debates among would-be supporters of U.S. hegemony concerning the goals of U.S. leadership. On the one side are those who feel that U.S. internationalism should be firmly rooted in American idealism and that the nation should devote its energies to supporting and sustaining democracy and human rights. For example, candidate Bill Clinton argued for, among other things: sanctions against China for its repression of students in 1989, support for Somalis, Kurds, and Bosnians fighting against authoritarian enemies, and admission of Haitian refugees into the United States on humanitarian grounds (See also DLC 1991).

On the other hand, many feel that the United States need not be a crusader. Our international engagement should be based on a sort of expanded self-interest. A stable world order is good for America, since it minimizes surprises, allows for methodical planning, and usually results in economic prosperity. The object of U.S. foreign policy should be to discourage instability by supporting the status quo, particularly where existing regimes are already pro-United States. Krauthammer and others stress the fact that the great enemy is no longer an organized opposition but rather disorder itself. They emphasize the need to contain this "chaotic sphere" in international relations by controlling the spread of weapons, intervening in civil wars before they spread, maintaining existing troop deployments in order to respond more rapidly to crises, and otherwise taking on the burden of enforcing international law—unilaterally if necessary (Krauthammer 1990/91; Gaddis 1991). Note however that nowhere in this discussion is there any mention of U.S. compliance with international law if such compliance undermined our own interests.

We have already discussed the neo-isolationist critique of this traditional approach to U.S. foreign policy. We will now turn to the multilateralist response.

MULTILATERALISM

The differences between the multilateralist and hegemonic approach are rather subtle, but nonetheless profound. To begin, most multilateralists are skeptical of the argument that the United States has either the capability or the prerogative to lead the world. Foremost among their concerns is the fact that the world is no longer bipolar and will never be unipolar. At best, the world is tripolar, with Germany, Japan, and the United States at three opposite poles (Tarnoff 1990). With the end of the Cold War, raw military might has become largely obsolete. We live in an age of economics. As pointed out by Fred Bergsten, "the central task in shaping a new American foreign policy is to set priorities and select central themes. Those choices must derive from America's national interests, which have shifted sharply in the direction of economics" (Bergsten 1992, 4).

Given the primacy of economic concerns over security issues, these analysts go on to point out that America has declined relative to other powers. Bergsten goes so far as to paint a scenario in which, given 4 percent annual gross national product growth for Japan, 2 percent for the United States, and a modest appreciation of the yen relative to the dollar, the total Japanese gross national product could surpass that of the United States by 2002 (Bergsten 1992, 6). Japan has already passed the United States as the world's largest creditor nation and holder of the largest trade surplus, while the United States has struggled with a huge trade deficit and has become the world's leading debtor. A future United Europe could leapfrog the United States with the largest market, the largest gross product, and other substantial assets, including ready-made links to the emerging markets of the former Soviet bloc. The end result would be a much higher degree of parity between the three major economic powers (Aho and Stokes 1990/91). This economic parity has already led to increased tensions among major trading partners and heightened fears of trade wars and other departures from liberalism. U.S.-Japanese trade relations have been more often than not characterized by tension and even suspicion in the 1980s, and fears of Europe withdrawing on itself once the unification process is complete seem well-founded (Cohen 1991).

The economic issue has led many to urge a collaborative U.S. policy based on close cooperation between the United States, Japan, and Europe (via Germany) (U.S. Congress 1990). Such a tripartite arrangement will go the farthest to promote open markets, liberal monetary policy, and free investment activities (Tarnoff 1990). They emphasize the need to work through multilateral institutions, such as the General Agreement on Tariffs and Trade (GATT) and the International Monetary Fund (IMF), as well as create yet more, stronger rules and enforcement mechanisms to preserve open markets (Aho and Stokes 1990/91). They assume a failure to continue expanding free trade will lead quickly to a rapid retreat into protectionism.

This urge to "go multilateral" stems not only from an acceptance of the United States' decline into parity (or at least the rise of Europe and Japan) but from a hope that security concerns will continue to remain back-burner issues in the future. Some have pointed out that democracies do not go to war with each other, concluding like the "endists" that the threat of global conflict is virtually over (Jervis 1992). War has not only become less likely because of the nature of states, but it has become less profitable and therefore less attractive to rational actors interested in maximizing gains over losses (Kaysen 1991). The implication of these developments is that we have reached a point when collective security may finally be a feasible method for dealing with all international conflict—a solution which would eliminate the need for American unilateralism. Russett and Sutterlin feel that now is the time to give the UN the authority and capability to intervene actively in conflict situations in order not only to "keep" the peace but also to "make" it. The success of the UN in the Persian Gulf War:

> can enhance the United Nations' ability not just to restore the status quo as it existed prior to a breach of the peace, but also to change the parameters of the global order to something more favorable than existed under the prior status quo. In this it may even go beyond the vision of the U.N. founders. (Russett and Sutterlin 1991, p. 82)

Although it is assumed that the UN will continue to be supportive of U.S. goals of promoting democracy, spreading free trade, and enforcing international law, there is an implicit acknowledgment that in the future the United States must accept that it will not always get its way. Former U.S. envoy to the UN Daniel Patrick Moynihan deplores the fact that the United States has a bad habit of giving lip service to the letter of international law without complying with its spirit. We sign the Optional Clause of the World Court, thereby showing our support for rendering its decisions binding, then deny their validity on technical grounds when they go against us. We draw up a UN Charter which pledges our support for establishing a UN-commanded standing military force, then refuse to allow U.S. troops to participate in peacekeeping operations. It is time, so the multilateralists say, to play by all the rules, not just those we like (Chace 1992).

It may seem rather ironic that multilateralists, while accepting the fact of American decline, believe that American idealism can now be adopted as the global standard. There is the hope that, given the core values of fairness and tolerance, a weaker United States will actually live more closely to its own rhetoric. On the down side, multilateralists fear that American decline and increased great power parity create an urgent need to institutionalize idealism quickly. Failure to do so may lead to a collapse of the precarious consensus we now enjoy.

Critics of multilateralism come from many corners. Neo-isolationists fear that multilateralism will become yet another way to "sell the farm" to foreign interests. Yielding to international pressures does not come naturally to most Americans, particularly those who deny any automatic or inevitable international role for the United States. They deny the need for continued international involvement as a prerequisite for national renewal, and see multilateral institutions as an impediment to national strength, not a help.

Unilateralists deny the inevitability of U.S. decline and feel that multi-lateralism, although acceptable when applied to other nations, should not be U.S. policy. They point to the economic troubles experienced by Europe and Japan in the second half of 1992 as evidence that there is nothing inevitable about their ascendance. They further point to the paralysis of the European Community in the face of full-scale civil war in Yugoslavia as evidence that we should not expect international leadership from Brussels or Berlin. The UN has been incapable of enforcing international law, and international economic institutions have more often than not provided a cover for unfair trading practices by our economic rivals, so the logic goes. Thus, although the unilateralists share the multilateralists' internationalism, they emphasize leadership. Furthermore, they share with the neo-isolationists the position that the United States should never voluntarily submit to international law if this law is dysfunctional and runs contrary to our interests (however defined . . .).

CONCLUSIONS

If you, the reader, are still a bit uncertain about where you stand on the question, do not be dismayed. Although the initial positions taken by many authors are fairly explicit, even the experts have begun to hedge a bit in recent months. Secretary of State James Baker, a unilateralist at heart, emphasized the need for the United States to share both burdens and powers with our allies via multilateral institutions (U.S. Congress 1992). Joseph Nye likewise seems to straddle the fence on whether the United States should take control of global institutions or be more of a team player (U.S. Congress 1990). Even military analysts who seem most readily inclined to accept uni-lateralism have given lip service to the UN.

On the other hand, some neo-isolationists are quick to acknowledge that there might be a role for some U.S. troops overseas (as a trip wire, perhaps) and caution against the dangers of a too-rapid demobilization (Hyland 1990; Brzezinski 1991). They will accept that although weapons manufacturing is no longer essential, maintenance of production lines, jobs, and even technological research may continue to have a place in a peacetime economy. Even the threat of protectionism is seen by many as merely a bargaining strategy to persuade other nations to open their markets and embrace true free trade.

There are thus few purists in the real world of U.S. foreign policy. Even the Clinton administration has left open many options for the future. The campaign emphasized support for multilateral institutions and democratic ideals, without specifying at what point the United States would be willing to go against the international community to protect its interests. While in office, Clinton has been forced to address real limitations on U.S. power, re-tracting his plans to use force in Yugoslavia, reversing his support of Haitian refugees, withdrawing his reservations about the North American Free Trade Agreement (NAFTA), and waffling on the question of future U.S. leadership. Even within the State Department, there is high-level disagreement on whether the United States should be more of a supportive team player or leader (policy analyst Peter Tarnoff was reprimanded by Secretary of State Warren Christopher for taking the former position). It is simply too soon to tell whether the Clinton administration will forge ahead with a bold vision of a new U.S. role or move step-by-step and crisis-to-crisis.

Questions to Consider

1. If you were adviser to President Clinton, what would you recommend?

2. What basic values can you identify in relation to each of the perspectives on post–Cold War U.S. policy? With which values do you find yourself most comfortable and why?

3. Can one make a "rational" decision about such issues when so much is tied up in values, perceptions, beliefs, and assumptions? Or are these part of rationality itself?

References

Michael Aho and Bruce Stokes. "The Year the World Economy Turned." *Foreign Affairs* 70 #1 (1990/91): 160–178.

Fred Bergsten. "The Primacy of Economics." *Foreign Policy* 87 (Summer 1992): 3–24.

Zbigniew Brzezinski. "Selective Global Commitment." *Foreign Affairs* 70 #4 (Fall 1991): 1–20.

James Chace. *The Consequences of the Peace: The New Internationalism and American Foreign Policy* (New York: Oxford University Press, 1992).

Stephen D. Cohen. "United States-Japanese Trade Relations." *Current History* (April 1991): 152–155; 184–187.

Democratic Leadership Council. *The New American Choice: Opportunity, Reponsibility, Community*. Resolutions Adopted at the DLC Convention, Cleveland, Ohio, 1991.

Francis Fukuyama. "The End of History?" *National Interest* 16 (Summer 1989): 3–18.

John Lewis Gaddis. *The Long Peace: Inquiries into the History of the Cold War* (New York: Oxford University Press, 1987).

John Lewis Gaddis. "Toward the Post–Cold War World." *Foreign Affairs* 70 #2 (Spring 1991): 102–122.

Alexander Haig. "The Challenges to American Leadership," in Schmergel, ed., *U.S. Foreign Policy in the 1990s*, 34–46.

David Hendrickson. "The Renovation of American Foreign Policy." *Foreign Affairs* 71 #2 (Spring 1992): 48–63.

Samuel Huntington. "No Exit: The Errors of Endism." *National Interest* 17 (Fall 1989): 3–11.

William Hyland. "America's New Course." *Foreign Affairs* 69 #2 (Spring 1990): 1–12.

Robert Jervis. "The Future of World Politics: Will It Resemble the Past?" in Lynn-Jones and Miller, eds., *America's Changing Strategy*, 3–37.

Carl Kaysen. "Is War Obsolete? A Review Essay," in Lynn-Jones, ed., *The Cold War and After*, 81–103.

Charles Kegley and Eugene Wittkopf, eds. *The Future of American Foreign Policy* (New York: St. Martin's Press, 1992).

Stephen Krasner. "Realist Praxis: Neo-isolationism and Structural Change," *Journal of International Affairs* 43 #1 (1989): 143–160.

Charles Krauthammer. "The Unipolar Moment." *Foreign Affairs* 70 #1 (1990/91): 23–33.

Irving Kristol. "Defining Our National Interest." *National Interest* (Fall 1990): 16–25.

Richard Lugar. "The Republican Course." *Foreign Policy* # 86 (Spring 1992): 86–98.

Sean Lynn-Jones. ed. *The Cold War and After: Prospects for Peace* (Cambridge, MA: MIT Press, 1991).

Sean Lynn-Jones and Steven Miller, eds. *America's Changing Strategy in a Changing World* (Cambridge, MA: MIT Press, 1992).

Richard Nixon. *Seize the Moment: America's Challenge in a One-Superpower World* (New York: Simon & Schuster, 1992).

Joseph Nye. *Bound to Lead: The Changing Nature of American Power* (New York: Basic Books, 1990).

William Pfaff. "Redefining World Power." *Foreign Affairs* 70 #1 (1990/91): 34–48.

Bruce Russett and James Sutterlin. "The U.N. in a New World Order." *Foreign Affairs* 70 #2 (Spring 1991): 69–83.

Jerry Sanders. "Retreat from World Order: The Perils of Triumphalism." *World Policy Journal* 8 #2 (Spring 1991): 227–250.

Greg Schmergel, ed. *U.S. Foreign Policy in the 1990s* (New York: St. Martin's, 1991).

Peter Tarnoff. "America's New Special Relationships." *Foreign Affairs* 69 #3 (Summer 1990): 67–80.

Alan Tonelson. "Prudence or Inertia? The Bush Administration's Foreign Policy." *Current History* 91 #564 (April 1992): 145–150.

Alan Tonelson. "What Is the National Interest?" *The Atlantic Monthly* (July 1991): 35–52.

U.S. Congress, House. *The Future of U.S. Foreign Policy in the Post–Cold War Era.* Hearings before the Committee on Foreign Affairs, 102nd Congress, 2nd Session, 1992.

U.S. Congress, House. *U.S. Power in a Changing World.* Special Report 28-802 prepared for the Committee on Foreign Affairs, 101st Congress, 2nd Session, 1990.

Persian Gulf War

CAPABILITY AND INFLUENCE

Central to the debate over the best definition of power is how a nation's power capabilities are converted into actual influence. A nation is often described as "powerful" when it has a large military establishment, sizable natural resources, and a large and well-educated population, among other things. These features are more properly described as "capabilities" and they may or may not translate into "influence," in terms of changing or preserving the international system. A 2-million-man army and several thousand nuclear warheads did not bring American victory in the Vietnam conflict, and many feared that the overwhelming advantage of the U.S.-led coalition in the Persian Gulf would likewise be for naught. Control of oil was an advantage for Iraq, but, paradoxically, control of oil consumption turned out to be a more significant asset for the United States and the West.

Resources are certainly vital to a nation's power for many reasons. As pointed out by Rothgeb, they provide (1) the impression of power (which may be enough in and of itself to bring about compliance with your wishes), (2) expanded vehicles for influencing others (bribery, boycotts, invasions, etc.), and (3) resistance to others' efforts at influencing your own policies (oil stockpiles protect against embargoes, for example) (Rothgeb 1993, 192).

This is not to say that capability is sufficient to generate influence. Much depends on how this power is utilized in day-to-day, dynamic situations. If military threats are not credible or are poorly communicated, they will probably not deter undesired action. If a nation's capabilities are exaggerated, the country may enjoy a false sense of security until a crisis unravels everything.

In this case study, we will pay especially close attention to the way power is used in a crisis where stakes are high and "all necessary means" are brought to bear. The number of players in the Gulf War was quite large, and their interests and power varied dramatically. To what can we attribute

George Bush's success in assembling an anti-Iraq coalition involving countries in Western Europe, the Middle East, and many other regions? How significant was the UN's involvement? Could this have occurred in different circumstances?

ANTECEDENTS TO THE WAR

On August 2, 1990, the Iraqi army, fourth-largest in the world, led by over 4,000 tanks, poured across the Kuwaiti border to overrun a nation roughly the size of Connecticut. Moral outrage, fear of what might happen next, and a desire to test the post–Cold War environment led to an overwhelming military defeat for Iraq and the liberation of Kuwait. One might ask, given this ultimate outcome, why did Saddam Hussein do it? In order to answer this question, one must understand both the circumstances of the invasion as well as the character of the Iraqi regime and its leader.

A longtime member of the Baathist political movement, Saddam Hussein began his career as a torturer for the short-lived Baathist regime that governed Iraq from 1958 to 1963. Upon their return to power in 1968, the party rewarded Hussein's loyalty and energy with the position of deputy chairman of the Revolutionary Command Council, where he set about insuring that the party would never again be victimized by factional infighting as it had in 1963. Within a few years, he emerged as the de facto leader of the state and, with the wealth he derived from oil following the 1973 price hike, covered himself with riches and power. He assumed the presidency in 1979 and immediately purged the upper ranks of the party, often carrying out the executions personally and with great publicity (Miller and Mylroie 1990, 45).

The legacy of Hussein's rule is well-known. Several villages populated by ethnic Kurds in the northern regions of Iraq were attacked with chemical weapons at several points during the 1980s on the grounds that they sought a separate statehood. The Shi'a Muslim majority of Iraq (as opposed to the minority Sunni to which Hussein belonged) was a frequent target of Saddam's internal attacks because of their support for the radical Ayatollah Khomeini in neighboring Iran. During the Iran-Iraq War (1980–1988), Hussein was accused of aggression because his tanks crossed the border into Iran and his Scud missiles fell on Iranian urban centers (although the World Court was unable to determine who actually "started" the war).

Throughout his reign, Hussein frequently attacked Israeli "Zionism" as a racist threat to Arab unity, although his own attachment to the Arab cause seems to have been more contrived than genuine. His relations with Kuwait, Syria, and Saudi Arabia were always tense, and he often threatened to take matters into his own hands when unable to negotiate on his terms. Organization of Petroleum Exporting Countries' (OPEC) matters were especially problematic, given Iraq's dependence on oil exports and the tendency of smaller OPEC members to undercut the organization through overproduction. At various OPEC summits, Hussein challenged the Arab nations to display greater solidarity and anti-Israeli unity. Iraq's $70 billion war debt, accumulated during the Iran-Iraq war, created an especially urgent financial problem for the country, and prompted demands for debt forgiveness (Kono 1990, 37), particularly from Kuwait, to whom Iraq owed billions.

In order to understand more fully why Iraq was willing to invade a neighboring Arab country in spite of pan-Arabism, we need to look at Kuwait's image in the Arab world. Kuwait had a reputation for arrogance borne of its record-breaking wealth. Many Arabs resented the Kuwaiti practice of hiring other Arabs for the most menial jobs they were not willing to do themselves, and then denying them any political or civil rights. It was widely believed that Kuwaitis were siphoning oil from the Rumaila oil field under Iraqi territory (*New York Times*, September 3, 1990, A7). And Kuwait regularly exceeded its OPEC-imposed production quota in order to reap unfair profits at OPEC's expense. All this Saddam Hussein knew full well. He knew that millions of Arabs in the streets of cities from Morocco to Pakistan would delight in the humiliation of Kuwait, and that these throngs would put pressure on their governments to support Iraq in this apparently noble quest—especially if the call was issued with religious imagery and symbols.

Iraq has had territorial claims against Kuwait for decades, and especially since 1932 when the current borders were established following the carving up of the Ottoman Empire by the British and French. When Kuwait gained its independence in 1961, the Iraqi government once again explicitly stated its perpetual claim on Kuwaiti territory (Miller and Mylroie 1990, 197). In particular, Iraq felt it needed definitive control of the Euphrates River estuary and the Kuwaiti islands of Bubiyan and Warbah, critical choke points controlling access to Basra and Umm Qasr, the country's only ports.

In spite of all this, the two nations were actually on the same side during the Iran-Iraq War, although Kuwait adopted an officially neutral position. Kuwait shipped Iraq millions of dollars in aid and suffered through numerous terrorist attacks from Iranians. Its tankers were reflagged and protected by American ships in 1987, a move that preserved the flow of roughly 1.5 million barrels per day from Kuwait. Paradoxically, Kuwait had even joined Iraq in strident anti-Israeli rhetoric during the early 1980s. This rather ambivalent and mixed relationship between Iraq and Kuwait may help to explain the shock Kuwaitis and others felt at the savagery of Hussein's surprise attack. There were as many reasons against an attack as there were in favor.

One can see Iraq's policies in 1990 in terms of balance of power politics (Sayigh, 1991,) and in terms of anti-Zionism. As Egypt was neutralized by the Camp David Accords, Saudi Arabia and the Gulf States tilted ever more to the West, the Soviet Union was unwilling to support radical regimes, and Iran moved toward a moderate position, Hussein saw himself as the last of the militant anti-Israeli Arab states. In addition, Iraq had the largest military in the region and was challenged only by Israel, Iran and Syria. The desire to lead the anti-Zionist elements in the Middle East (including the masses in Jor-

Desert Shield had begun. The immediate goal of establishing a "trip wire" force that would deter an attack against Saudi Arabia was soon expanded. The U.S. force size was rapidly increased to serve a full-scale combat role in the event of an Iraqi attack. By the end of September, some 250,000 troops from twenty eight countries had amassed in the region.

The UN Security Council was busy throughout this early period, passing a dozen resolutions ranging from a sweeping condemnation of the Iraqi "breach of the peace," demanding a restoration of the situation to the pre–August 1, 1990, conditions (Resolution 660), and setting up extensive economic and diplomatic sanctions in the hope they would force Iraq to leave Kuwait (Resolution 661). These sanctions were to be enforced by the U.S.-led coalition through sea power (Resolution 665). Ultimately, in a dramatic show of unity, the foreign ministers of the Security Council members approved Resolution 678 on November 29, 1990, which authorized nations to enforce all preceding sanctions "by all necessary means"—a clear signal that military intervention had the UN's blessing. Resolution 678 was in a sense a sign of the failure of diplomatic efforts by James Baker of the United States, Tariq Aziz of Iraq, and Eduard Schevardnadze of the USSR to reach a settlement on the Kuwaiti problem.

In the early weeks of the crisis, a central issue was the treatment of foreign nationals trapped in Kuwait at the time of the invasion. Several thousand Westerners were residing in Kuwait in August 1990, and were captured by Hussein's forces during the invasion. They were relocated throughout Iraqi territory, in particular at sensitive military installations, in order to dissuade a surprise attack from the West (*New York Times*, August 10, 1990, A1) and to force a U.S. withdrawal from the region (*New York Times*, August 20, 1990, A1). Called "guests" by Hussein, these hostages represented an unnerving twist in what was becoming a very different sort of war. The taking of civilian hostages by a government at war was a clear departure from the 1948 Geneva Convention and gave a strong indication that Iraq did not intend to be bound by international treaty commitments. In a gesture of supposed "goodwill," the hostages were permitted to leave the country in time for Christmas (*New York Times*, December 8, 1990, A6). In the meantime, the Iraqi government cut off all food and water to the embassies of coalition members in Kuwait, leaving hundreds of diplomats stranded. American diplomatic personnel staged a heroic last stand in spite of rapidly deteriorating conditions and the departure of other diplomatic teams. Ultimately, they were withdrawn, and by the new year all Westerners wishing to leave Kuwait were gone.

Until November 1990, many efforts were made by U.S. diplomats to identify common ground between Kuwait and Iraq in an effort to avert war. These efforts revolved around pressure on Iraq through economic sanctions, pressure on Kuwait to accept the possibility of future concessions, and pressure on other powers to support the U.S. decisions. Economic sanctions held surprisingly well throughout the period, although some leaks at the Iraq-Jordan border were noted. According to Tucker, "those sanctions were almost completely successful in stopping Iraqi oil exports, and Iraqi imports were reduced by 90 percent. Iraq's GNP fell almost immediately by 40 percent. In their severity, these economic sanctions were unprecedented in modern history" (Tucker and Hendrickson 1992, 101). In spite of these costly penalties, Iraq's position hardened during the period. Not only did Iraq not withdraw from Kuwait, but it officially annexed it and moved to terrorize the local inhabitants and suppress any hint of rebellion.

Other diplomatic efforts centered on both consolidating an anti-Iraq military coalition and planning for an eventual postcrisis political realignment in the Gulf. President Bush, drawing on his extensive personal contacts with European leaders, was able to blunt reservations expressed by French and Soviet diplomats. By late August, the Western powers, Japan, and the Soviet Union were essentially speaking with one voice. Germany and Japan were pressed to provide substantial financial support to the exercise—a move which placed the Japanese government in a very awkward position at home. Tokyo's initial offer of $1 billion was judged inadequate by Washington, but the next offer of $4 billion for the U.S. and regional allies was barely accepted in Japan's parliament. Ultimately, the Japanese provided even more, although a constitutional provision prevented the government from deploying troops in the Gulf region (the so-called Peace Constitution, largely inspired by U.S. occupation forces in the 1940s, prohibits such deployments). In Germany, a similar clause in the Basic Law limited the government's options to financial support and endorsement of NATO's role in the crisis. Countries contributing troops to the coalition included Britain, France, Canada, Saudi Arabia and Egypt—twenty eight nations all together.

The Soviets, unwilling to join the coalition itself, were especially active in seeking a compromise between the parties in the crisis. Foreign Minister Eduard Schevardnadze, special envoy Yevgeny Primakov, and Primakov's aide Serge Kiripitchenko undertook their own shuttle diplomacy. On September 5, one month after the invasion, Iraqi Foreign Minister Tariq Aziz visited with Soviet President Mikhail Gorbachev to determine whether there was any possibility of diplomatic movement in Iraq. Instead of new flexibility, the Soviets heard old demands that Israel withdraw from Palestinian occupied territories in exchange for Iraqi withdrawal from Kuwait (*Middle East Insight*, December 1990, 11–17). Soviets indicated a willingness to consider new political arrangements in the Gulf region after Iraqi withdrawal, which included acknowledging Iraq's prewar demands. Up to the day before the beginning of the ground offensive, Soviet emissaries were pressing for a deal which would prevent war. In the end, Iraqi leaders went so far as to promise to withdraw from Kuwait and release all prisoners of war. Because it included demands for ending sanctions before the withdrawal was complete and did not stipulate Iraqi reparations to Kuwait, it was rejected by the United States and replaced with tougher demands the next day, in spite of Soviet objections. When these were finally rejected by Hussein, the ground offensive began (*New York Times*, February 23, 1991, A1).

One can question Iraqi and U.S. sincerity during these diplomatic exchanges. It seems clear that Iraq was only interested in dividing the coalition by appealing to Arab unity and anti-Israeli sentiments in the Middle East.

One can also see Soviet diplomatic efforts as a vehicle for Hussein to under-mine coalition unity. "Although the American-led coalition had the capabil-ity to do as it threatened, the Iraqi government apparently believed that it possessed the military muscle needed to neutralize any moves by the coali-tion. Thus, Iraq largely ignored the American threats made in the fall of 1990 and the winter of 1991" (Rothgeb 1993, 101).

American demands, which were more modest in the early weeks of the crisis, became more and more inflexible as the U.S. military presence grew. Bob Woodward of the *Washington Post* has argued that the decision to rely entirely on military force was made as early as late October and that all diplomatic moves from that point were largely posturing and rhetoric (Woodward 1991). On November 6, a few days after the midterm election, George Bush announced his decision to essentially double U.S. troop strength in the Gulf, from roughly 250,000 to over 500,000—half of Amer-ica's active-duty combat forces (Stork and Wenger 1991, 12). This decision, as fate would have it, soon revealed itself to be irreversible—and perhaps this was the intention of the president. It became clear that sustaining a mili-tary force of 500,000 in the harshest climate on earth, where merely provid-ing water took extraordinary measures, could not last very long. When com-bined with the coming of the summer months, where temperatures would rise to 120°F, the prospects were even more dim. In addition, placement of these forces in Saudi Arabia presented a political dilemma for the local Arab leaders, since it sent a clear message to all that the United States had gained control of the situation and that all talk of an Arab-led alliance was mere rhetoric. Finally, the systematic destruction of Kuwait by Iraqi forces and re-ports of atrocities put extraordinary pressure on the coalition to use these forces to put an end to it all (*New York Times,* December 16, 1990, A1).

At home, the debate over whether to permit sanctions to do the job of getting Iraq out of Kuwait without resort to war was raging. The debate in the Senate in early January was heated and passionate. At issue was a reso-lution supporting the UN's "all necessary means" language (while stopping short of a declaration of war). For some, like Republican minority leader Bob Dole, support of the president's foreign policy program was reason enough to vote for the resolution. Others, like Democrat Al Gore, felt the chances of Iraqi withdrawal without war were slim and that the resolution merited their vote. Forty-five Democrats and two Republicans voted against it, pri-marily on the grounds that sanctions had not been given enough time, al-though they were often quick to add that military intervention should not be ruled out entirely.

For the nation as a whole, most citizens expressed a willingness to sup-port their president, although lingering doubts about the justice and neces-sity of the war were frequently voiced. Former National Security Advisor Zbigniew Brzezinski, no pacifist, joined others in support for continued re-liance on sanctions (Brzezinski 1990; Elliott et al. 1990). Neo-isolationists, such as Patrick Buchanan, joined with pacifists and radicals in academia in calling for a withdrawal of U.S. forces from the Middle East. Stories of the army placing a rush order for 16,000 body bags in December alarmed many friends and relatives of Gulf War soldiers, and confirmed fears of a blood-bath. In the final analysis, the Senate vote reflected the ambivalent attitudes of the nation at large, and George Bush took "a divided nation into battle," to quote Representative Ron Dellums (*New York Times,* January 13, 1991, A1).

Thus it was, with a UN-imposed deadline for Iraqi compliance with all UN resolutions of January 15, 1991, that the region was poised for war. It was estimated at the time that some 550,000 troops were in place on the Iraqi side, although more recent figures put the total at closer to only 380,000 (Tucker and Hendrickson 1992, 75). Five thousand Soviet-made tanks, several hundred Scud missiles (thought to be carrying chemical or nuclear weapons), 600 combat aircraft, and some 2,000 artillery pieces rounded out the Iraqi army's resources in the region (Stork and Wenger 1991, 24). It was generally assumed that the Republican Guard troops, deployed deep inside Kuwait, were the greater threat, and that their sand dune defenses would make for tough slogging after the initial thrust into the country.

On the U.S./coalition side, one could count at least 470,000 ground troops from fifteen countries mostly deployed just south of the Kuwaiti border. These troops were armed with roughly 6,500 tanks and supported by 2,200 combat aircraft—including the new Stealth fighter and Patriot missiles. In addition, some 50,000 Marines were stationed offshore in the Gulf itself, preparing for a possible amphibious invasion. In the Gulf and the Mediterranean, the United States and Britain deployed 6 aircraft carriers, along with over 25 additional attack craft, which were loaded with a total of over 700 nuclear bombs and missiles (Stork and Wenger 1991, 25). The stage was set for the "mother of all battles," as put by Saddam Hussein.

THE AIR WAR PHASE—JANUARY 17–FEBRUARY 23, 1991

Those who watched the events unfold on television will long remember the beginning of the air war on Baghdad early in the morning of January 17 (3:00 a.m. local time). Memories of anxious foreign correspondents—CNN's Bernard Shaw, Peter Arnett, and Wolf Blitzer, NBC's Arthur Kent—are burned into the national consciousness from watching hour upon hour of special reports. It was a moment of collective action which is rare in contemporary society. As put in a dramatic *New York Times* essay, "Suddenly, in public places where cacophony is the norm, there was an unusual silence, eerie rather than giddy. Grand Central Terminal in Manhattan—where even whispers can take on an echoing, high-decibel intensity—was quiet" (*New York Times,* January 17, 1991, A1). President Bush appeared on the screen in his "warrior mode" and declared the beginning of the attack as well as its purpose, making frequent references to the U.S. invasion on D day 1944: "The liberation of Kuwait has begun."

The tactic in the air war was fairly simple: destroy all targets that could conceivably support the Iraqi war effort. As a result, not only such things as radar installations, military airfields, and bunkers, but also electrical power plants, highways, water treatment facilities, and commercial airports were on the list of targets. Within less than a week of bombing, Baghdad had no water or electricity (*New York Times,* January 20, 1991 A1). Early attacks were carried out primarily by Tomahawk cruise missiles and Stealth fighters launched from ships offshore, and which could hug the ground and pass below radar. Although Iraq eventually responded with antiaircraft artillery, the defense of Baghdad was anemic at best, and after the first few hours, Iraqi air defenses were essentially "blind" (*New York Times,* January 17, 1991, A1). It was estimated that over 150 targets in Iraq were hit after the first night of bombing, although many later revisions on these and other estimates brought these figures down over the course of the war.

Iraq responded the next day with Scud attacks on Israel, a move aimed at widening the war and undermining Arab support for the United States. In an unprecedented show of restraint, Israel refrained from retaliating against Iraqi targets. U.S. bombers attempted to destroy Iraqi Scud launchers with only partial success over the course of the war. Of more remarkable note was the ability of U.S. and Israeli troops to fend off Scud attacks with the Patriot antimissile system, which seemed to consistently knock down incoming missiles (again kill estimates were revised downward after the war).

By January 20, U.S. forces had achieved air superiority. Iraq's radar installations were inoperative, and many Iraqi combat aircraft were fleeing into Iran. The A-10 Thunderbolt II "Warthog" was now brought in for its slow, low-level flying abilities and the operations moved toward destroying the Republican Guard and other ground troops in Kuwait (*New York Times,* January 20, 1991, A1). The successes did not come entirely without costs, though, in that the Scud attacks continued to threaten Israel and the viability of the coalition. Also, several aircraft were shot down and seven American prisoners captured by Iraq were paraded before television cameras and forced to make anti-American statements. But these sacrifices fell far short of what many feared, and by the end of the first week, the war began to take on a surrealistic feeling. Emphasis on technical details of missile targeting led some to describe this as the "Nintendo War" (Florman 1991). Daily reports of targets destroyed and images from cameras mounted on missile nose cones seemed like so many graphics from a video game (see Map 10.1).

It is interesting to note that during this phase, as well as before, the United States felt compelled to turn a blind eye to the other problems in the world. Syria invaded Lebanon in the fall, ending a bloody civil war with martial law, with little criticism from Washington. On January 20, Soviet commandos stormed a building controlled by Latvian independence forces in an unsuccessful attempt to quell the growing movement toward separation. In all of this, the need to keep the coalition together prevented the president from responding.

Scud attacks continued to rattle the nerves of Israelis, although the repeated donning of gas masks proved unnecessary, given the fact that none of the warheads contained chemical weapons. Twenty-seven U.S. soldiers

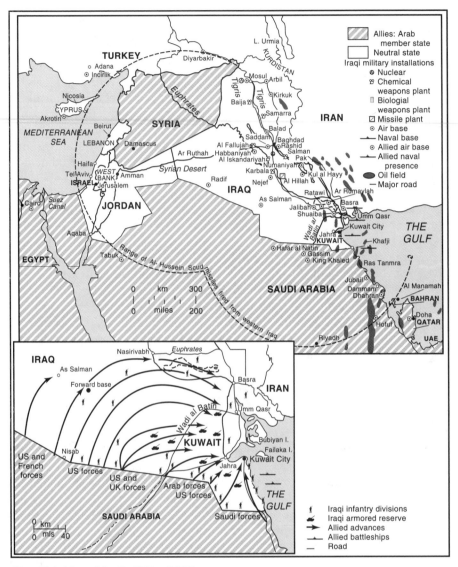

Map 10.1 Map of the Gulf War (1991).
Source: Michael Dockrill, *Atlas of Twentieth Century World History* (New York: HarperPerennial, 1991), 114–115.

were killed when a random Scud fell on a barracks in Riyadh, Saudi Arabia. This incident caused the single largest loss of U.S. life.

On January 26, Hussein's forces opened valves on numerous Kuwaiti oil wells and spilled millions of gallons of crude oil into the Gulf, clogging desalination plants in Saudi Arabia and devastating the natural surroundings. While the act may have made an amphibious invasion less convenient, it seemed to have no discernible military purpose (*New York Times,* January 26, 1991, A1). One can only conclude that it was a gesture of spite and defiance. Only hours before the ground offensive, Iraqi troops set fire to many of the oil wells they had previously opened, as well as to numerous ponds filled with petroleum. Over 150 wells were aflame by the time of the invasion, and continued to burn throughout the war and for months afterwards.

Throughout the air war period, reports of the effects on Iraq were sketchy at best and propagandized at worst. U.S. military spokesmen routinely underestimated civilian casualties. They were defensive when clear evidence was presented that several hundred were killed in a bomb shelter, accusing the Iraqi government of deliberately planting civilians in a known military target area (*New York Times*, February 14, 1991, A1). Estimates of Iraqi civilian casualties vary, but the general consensus is that 7,000 were killed as a direct result of the bombing (Hooglund 1991, 4). Troop losses during this phase of the war seem to have numbered around 75,000. The condition of Iraqi soldiers captured and of refugees coming into Jordan gave visible evidence of widespread disease and malnutrition in the Iraqi capital and on the front lines. Neither side wanted to admit at the time that the situation in Iraq was near the breaking point—Hussein feared loss of morale and Americans feared overconfidence in the troops. But it was clear by the end of the air war that the outcome of the war was no longer in doubt. This may explain Iraq's willingness to make diplomatic concessions and Bush's eagerness to press the war to its conclusion.

THE GROUND WAR PHASE—FEBRUARY 24–FEBRUARY 28, 1991

In the middle of February, new deadlines were set, new ultimata laid down, and new battle plans set in motion. On February 24 (4:00 a.m. local time), U.S.-led troops and tanks stormed southern Iraq and Kuwait in a dramatic sweep from the west through miles of barren desert (see Map 10.1). In what was dubbed the "Hail Mary" operation—an allusion to a last-ditch pass by a football quarterback into a crowd of receivers in the end zone—US General Norman Schwartzkopf ordered the deployment of troops originally massed on the Kuwaiti border to positions stretching 150 miles westward along the Saudi-Iraq border. Marine forces were kept in the waters off Kuwait City, thus forcing the Iraqis to maintain a strong presence and leave their rear relatively unguarded. With French forces unfurling a protective cover in the extreme left flank of the operation, U.S. and British divisions stormed into the desert, performing a pivoting maneuver at and around Kuwait, thereby completely isolating Iraqi troops stationed in the area. The tank battle that ensued was extremely lopsided, in that only American tanks were equipped with targeting systems which allowed them to fire while moving at full speed and through dust and smoke. "We're meeting the enemy, and we're not having any trouble destroying him" said the military spokesman on Tuesday after thirty-six hours of fighting (*New York Times*, February 26, 1991, A1).

Within forty-eight hours, nearly all of southern Iraq and most of Kuwait were in coalition hands, and Iraqi soldiers were surrendering by the battalion. The Iraqi news agency announced the country's decision to withdraw immediately from Kuwait, although this was considered insufficient since the statement was not made by Hussein himself. In effect, this declaration gave tacit approval to what would become one of the saddest retreats in modern history. Tens of thousands of fleeing Iraqi troops lined the road leading northward out of Kuwait City, many of them with Kuwaiti hostages. Coalition jets targeted the troops as if they were still part of the fighting.

The movement created a column twenty-five to thirty miles long, three or four abreast in places, and except for a few surface-to-air missiles, they were defenseless against the F-15, F-111, and F-16 fighter-bombers that came at them, wave after wave, along with navy planes. In the wind and the driving rain, "it was close to Armageddon," an air force officer said (*New York Times*, February 27, 1991, A1).

In the waning hours of the campaign, Soviet and Iraqi delegates pressed the United Nations for a cease-fire to no avail. The allied attack penetrated deep into Kuwait City, where the Republican Guard crumbled after a vain but fierce battle. The most serious problem for American commanders was the disposition of prisoners of war, who numbered nearly 100,000 by war's end, and burying the Iraqi dead, estimated at 20,000 (Hooglund 1991, 4). After 100 hours of fighting on the ground, and the expulsion of Iraqi forces from Kuwait, President Bush officially announced a cessation of hostilities on February 28, 1991.

WINNING THE PEACE

A wide range of problems fell upon coalition governments with the end of the war, and most of these have yet to be resolved, two years later. Saddam Hussein's forces destroyed oil tanks and set 500 oil wells on fire, leading to an oil spill of some 6 million barrels (twenty times that of the 1989 *Exxon Valdez* accident) and a smoke plume spreading to Kashmir, 1,500 miles away (Canby 1991, 2). Iraqi forces moved to suppress uprisings in Kurdistan and in Shiite dominated cities in the south. The Kuwaiti regime took far longer to reestablish itself than expected, and encountered determined opposition from forces favoring a liberalization of the regime. Finally, the question of Iraqi weapons and general compliance with UN resolutions dealing with war reparations and boundary guarantees are yet to be finally resolved.

The environmental catastrophe following the Gulf War served not only to destroy the region's wildlife, but also the Kuwaiti regime's credibility. Countless delays, largely the result of bureaucratic incompetence in Kuwait, prevented the speedy extinguishing of the 500 wells. It took a total of fifteen months to finally put out all the fires—but at least five months of this time were largely wasted. The regime has struggled with the question of restoring its stature ever since, the most recent development being the formation of a strong anti-monarchy movement in the parliament, a move which may be throttled by a regime still unsure of its tolerance for dissent.

As it turned out, the environmental impact of the oil spill and fires could have been far more serious. For example, five times more animals died in the *Exxon Valdez* incident. Nearly half of the oil spilled simply evaporated as it floated down the Gulf. Also, desalination plants were protected and oil recovery efforts netted roughly 20,000 barrels each day (Canby 1991, 25). The contaminated air in Kuwait City itself was dangerous in many ways, and numerous cases of smoke inhalation and bronchitis have occurred throughout the Gulf, but the air above Kuwait had sulphur dioxide concentrations that fell within tolerable limits, according to U.S. health standards.

U.S. troops left the region by May, although the humanitarian crisis in northern Iraq following the displacement of thousands of Kurds reached epidemic proportions shortly after the end of the war. Some 300,000 Kurds were killed by Iraqi troops, both before and after the war, through systematic razing of Kurdish villages. As put by Tucker, "The Shi'a and Kurdish peoples within Iraq, who mistook the president's call to overthrow Saddam Hussein as a pledge of support and protection and who rose up in response, were then left alone to suffer the might of Saddam Hussein's fury" (Tucker and Hendrickson 1992, 194). Ultimately, in order to protect and provide for these people, a zone of Iraq north of the 36th parallel (roughly 20,000 square miles) was declared a sanctuary by the UN and patrolled by peacekeeping forces (*New York Times*, May 19, 1991, A8). There is little prospect of any change in this arrangement so long as Hussein remains in power. This is not to say that the UN will always intervene in such cases, but rather that the Kurdish situation is extreme (Mayall 1991, 421).

To the south, Shiite Moslems rebelled against Hussein and were suppressed, not only immediately after the war but throughout 1991. It was not until the summer of 1992 that the UN acted to impose a no-fly zone over the southern regions of Iraq (south of the 32nd parallel). This has had the effect of eliminating the more wanton aspects of Iraqi reprisals, but it also has led to a more permanent role for U.S. pilots tasked with enforcing the rule.

The destruction of Iraqi weapons precipitated several violent and nearly disastrous encounters between Iraqi officials and UN inspectors through 1992. Given the task of destroying all Iraqi weapons of "mass destruction" by the Security Council, the UN inspectors went where angels fear to tread—into Iraqi nuclear weapons laboratories and other extremely sensitive sites. In July 1992 a team of inspectors sought access to the Agriculture Ministry building in Baghdad in pursuit of documents relating to Iraq's nuclear weapons program, and were denied entry. After a two week standoff, punctuated by increasingly strident threats by the West, the government finally relented, but not before it had ample opportunity to remove documents, if there were any (*New York Times*, July 25, 1991, A1).

All told, the situation in Iraq is not far from what George Bush hoped, in that Saddam Hussein, while still in power, is seriously constrained and no longer represents a threat to the region (Talbott 1992, 49). The situation for Kurds and Shiites is far from settled, and the inability to resolve their condition will probably dog the region for years to come. The environmental situation has essentially been addressed and should not be a permanent problem. In addition, the plodding and halting progress of Middle East Peace negotiations provide some hint of a long-term resolution of Middle East issues not directly related to the Gulf War (*Christian Science Monitor*, October 30, 1992, 1). Finally, oil continues to flow virtually uninterrupted.

Perhaps the most significant question, in the context of the discussion of power, is whether the resort to war was necessary, or rather a sign of weakness on the part of the United States. Many have argued that the U.S. instructions to Iraqi representative April Glaspie were simply too ambiguous to be effective in deterring an Iraqi attack against Kuwait prior to the war. An issue during the 1992 presidential race (the so-called Iraq-gate question) also stressed the significance of U.S. aid to Iraq prior to the invasion and the degree to which these funds were channeled into military hardware. Independent congressional inquiries have determined that this was probably not the case, and the Bush administration has vehemently denied it. Also, whether U.S. funds were diverted is a moot point, since provision of aid freed up the Iraqi budget for other activities.

One might argue that the fact Saddam Hussein chose to intervene is sufficient evidence that the United Sates failed to give clear signals of its intent. But this assumes Hussein was rational and risk-averse. Throughout the Gulf War, even after it was clear that the United States was indeed serious about its intentions to remove Iraq from Kuwait, Hussein made almost no effort to extricate himself from the situation. While he took measures to protect himself and his family, he did little else. It appears that he relished his role as underdog and welcomed the possibility of defeat. This posture was also a strategy aimed at preserving his own power. Charles Tripp wrote in December 1990:

> The importance, as far as Saddam Hussein is concerned, of maintaining a determined and decisive image cannot be overstressed. To vacillate is dangerous because it suggests to those who have hitherto supported him that he is losing his touch. The fear will arise that others will act upon this signal, seizing their opportunity to attempt the overthrow of Saddam Hussein and his patronage network. (Tripp 1990, 9)

In such a situation, the United States was in the unenviable position of making the situation worse by doing and saying the sort of things that would normally cause the adversary to shrink and reverse course. With each ratcheting up of the rhetoric in Washington, and with each new troop deployment, the United States was making Hussein more intransigent and Iraq's withdrawal from Kuwait less likely. Although the use of brute force ultimately achieved the overall goal, it also created new problems, such as protecting the Kurds, which will require considerable energy and resources to contain. Given this, one can conclude that the use of force was in fact the consequence of failed diplomacy and misread history. And given the fact that as many people died per day during the Gulf War as during World War I, one cannot help but wonder whether it was all worth it.

Questions to Consider

1. Was the Gulf War a legitimate and/or moral use of American power? What did international observers (UN, press, foreign governments) say about this?

2. To what extent was resorting to military force a sign of weakness or strength?

3. Did the Gulf War achieve the political objectives of the Bush administration? To what extent were international and domestic public opinion a deciding factor in how Bush prosecuted the war?

4. Does the Gulf War case help you to decide when military force should and should not be used? Are there causes worth fighting for?

References

Zbigniew Brzezinski. "Patience in the Persian Gulf, Not War." *Washington Post,* October 7, 1990.

Thomas Y. Canby. "After the Storm." *National Geographic* (August 1991): 2–35.

Christian Science Monitor, October 30, 1992 , p. 1

Paul Davis and John Arquilla. *Deterring or Coercing Opponents in Crisis: Lessons from the War with Saddam Hussein* (Santa Monica, CA: RAND, 1991).

Kimberly Elliott, Gary Hufbauer, and Jeffrey Schott. "The Big Squeeze: Why the Sanctions on Iraq Will Work." *Washington Post* (December 9, 1990).

Samuel Florman. "Engineers and the Nintendo War." *Technology Review* 94 #5 (July 1991): 62.

Jochen Hippler. "Iraq's Military Power: The German Connection." *Middle East Report* (January–February 1991): 27–31.

Eric Hooglund. "The Other Face of War." *Middle East Report* (July–August 1991): 3–13.

Tom Kono. "The Economics Behind the Invasion." *Middle East Insight* 7 #4 (December 1990: 36–41).

James Mayall. "Non-intervention, Self-determination, and the New World Order." *International Affairs* 67 #3 (1991): 421–429.

Middle East Insight, December 1990: 11–17.

Judith Miller and Laurie Mylroie. *Saddam Hussein and the Crisis in the Gulf* (New York: Random House, 1990).

New York Times, July 25, 1990, A1.

New York Times, August 10, 1990, A1.

New York Times, August 12, 1990, A1.

New York Times, August 20, 1990, A1.

New York Times, September 3, 1990, A7.

New York Times, December 8, 1990, A6.

New York Times, December 16, 1990, A1.

New York Times, January 13, 1991, A1.

New York Times, January 17, 1991, A1.

New York Times, January 20, 1991, A1.

New York Times, January 26, 1991, A1.

New York Times, February 14, 1991, A1.

New York Times, February 23, 1991, A1.

New York Times, February 26, 1991, A1.

New York Times, February 27, 1991, A1.

New York Times, March 1, 1991, A11.

New York Times, March 21, 1991, A17.

New York Times, May 19, 1991, A8.

New York Times, July 25, 1991, A1.

New York Times, September 25, 1991, A18.

R. K. Ramazani. "U.S. Gulf Policy: Regional Security and the Dangers of Impatience." *Middle East Insight* 7 #4 (December 1990): 18–21.

John G. Rothgeb, Jr. *Defining Power: Influence and Force in the Contemporary International System* (New York: St. Martin's Press, 1993).

Yezid Sayigh. "The Gulf Crisis: Why the Arab Regional Order Failed." *International Affairs* 67 #3 (1991): 487–507.

Joe Stork and Martha Wenger. "From Rapid Deployment to Massive Deployment." *Middle East Report* (January–February 1991): 22–26.

Strobe Talbott. "Iraq: It Could Be Even Worse." *Time* (September 28, 1992): 49.

Charles Tripp. "The Gulf Crisis and the Politics of Iraq." *Middle East Insight* (December 1990): 4–10.

Robert W. Tucker and David C. Hendrickson. *The Imperial Temptation: The New World Order and America's Purpose* (New York: Council on Foreign Relations, 1992).

Robert Woodward. *The Commanders* (New York: Simon & Schuster, 1991).

United Nations
and the Use of Force

For those who feel international relations should be governed by something other than "might makes right," international law has a strong appeal. But this does not resolve the question of enforcement: once you decide what may and may not be allowed, how can you make countries comply? At the turn of this century, the answer came: bring a united, global force to bear against the lawbreaker until it ceases the offending policy. This concept was named "collective security" and still animates the United Nations Security Council.

MIGHT VS. RIGHT

During the Gulf War (see previous case), observers were given the impression that the whole world had united in righteous indignation against a criminal state. Diplomacy was portrayed more as a "plea-bargaining" exercise rather than a negotiation among equals. Saddam Hussein was given ample opportunity to repent and make restitution, but failed to do so, and therefore suffered the consequences.

This image is a far cry from many other wars fought over the years. Carl von Clausewitz, a nineteenth-century German military writer, argued that war is merely diplomacy by other means (Vasquez 1990, 298). Clausewitz's contemporaries, German Chancellor Otto von Bismarck and his European counterparts, agreed that there was no reason a nation should hesitate to attack a rival, as long as the fight could be won. Such callous cynicism is characteristic of the "realist" approach in world politics.

153

What George Bush and the other coalition partners were trying to convey was a sense of legality and rightness to their cause. And the United Nations went far to legitimate the operation, while it stopped short of actually commanding the troops. This cuts at the heart of the debate on collective security. Should nations be held accountable when their actions violate another nation's legal rights, and how should the international community respond? The answer will go far to determine what type of future we will see in world politics. Should the superpowers withdraw from the unilateral use of force and yield instead to a multilateral approach, or should nations always rely on themselves for defense and security? Should the UN become an international law enforcement agency, complete with global police/military forces, international tribunal, prosecuting attorneys, and penitentiaries? Or would such a change bring more rather than less instability?

EVOLVING ROLE OF COLLECTIVE SECURITY

As was mentioned in the conceptual overview, the United Nations has been at the center of this debate. After the League of Nations failed to prevent the Japanese invasion of Manchuria, the Italian war in Ethiopia, and the outbreak of World War II, world leaders wanted to try to create an organization with the same philosophical roots but with much stronger enforcement powers. The anti-Fascist alliance during World War II was seen as the first successful effort at collective security, and the alliance became formally known as the "United Nations" (Riggs and Plano 1988, 15). Franklin Roosevelt envisioned a political future where gone would be "the system of unilateral actions, exclusive alliances and spheres of influence and balances of power and all the other expedients which have been tried for centuries and have always failed" (Kaufmann and Shrijver 1990, 57).

The UN Charter provides for two forms of enforcement against outlaw states: negotiated settlement of disputes (Chapter VI) and collective security, including sanctions (Chapter VII). The power to both identify and deal with a breach of international peace was vested in the Security Council. Article 42 states that ". . . the Security Council . . . may take such action by air, sea, or land forces as may be necessary to maintain or restore international peace and security." Such legal "teeth" were expected to give the UN real power to prevent and stop all conflict. However, as succinctly pointed out by Weiss and Chopra, "the onset of the Cold War and victory by Mao Tsetung over the Chinese Nationalists prevented the kind of unanimity among the five permanent members upon which the logic of the Charter was based" (Weiss and Chopra 1992, 4).

The Security Council is an organ of the UN that deserves more detailed description. The council consists of fifteen members, five of which are permanent. When the charter was signed, it provided that any of the five permanent members (United States, USSR, United Kingdom, France, and China) could halt any action by simply voting no. This is what is meant by the "veto." The other ten members of the Security Council are determined by election and geographical distribution. A certain number of seats are earmarked for each region (two for Latin America, three for Africa, for example) and filled by members of those regions electing representatives for two-year staggered terms. As a result, each year ten Security Council members from the previous year are joined by five new ones. A resolution passes the Security Council if approved by at least nine members and not opposed by any of the "Perm-5" (five permanent members).

Given the extreme hostility of certain Perm-5 nations towards others, the concept of collective security became the first casualty of the Cold War. Although the Korean War was initially sponsored by the United Nations in 1950, this sponsorship was the result of a diplomatic fluke. After the Chinese Revolution in 1949, the United States refused to recognize the government of Mao Tse-tung (for thirty years!) and with its veto blocked the People's Republic's accession to the China seat on the Security Council. The Soviets, in a diplomatic pique and in order to demonstrate socialist solidarity, boycotted the Security Council meetings for a month. It just so happened that it was during this moment that North Korea crossed the 38th parallel and came dangerously close to overrunning South Korea. American troops were already on their way to support South Korea when the UN addressed the issue and voted to sponsor a collective security action. Even with UN involvement, the United States continued to lead the action and provided well over 90 percent of the foreign troops. The UN became almost entirely marginalized after the Soviets ended their boycott and began vetoing efforts to maintain the support, and the action was transferred to the General Assembly for safekeeping. President Harry Truman acted alone in removing General Douglas MacArthur in 1951. The UN was not involved in the peace negotiations in any substantive way, and in every other respect the operation was merely a unilateral American conflict (Riggs and Plano 1988, 130).

In what ways did the Korean operation violate the principle of collective security? Although it did represent a legally authorized action by the Security Council and was an international effort to reverse a clear case of aggression, it lacked the legitimacy implied by the concept. The opposition of a major power (in this case both the Soviet Union as well as numerous Third World nations) undermined the assumption of unanimity we mentioned before. U.S. domination of the operation, both in terms of command and composition of troops, challenges the legal fact that the operation was multilateral. In a resolution passed on July 7, 1950, the Security Council essentially relinquished control of the operation to the United States. Multilateralism assumes no single nation can dominate the operation without the active consent of the other participants. Thus, although the operation was based to a large extent on legal provisions of the charter, it violated the spirit of multilateralism and collective security.

The end of superpower unanimity resulted in increased tensions and hostility worldwide, and the ever greater need for efforts to resolve these conflicts. The UN struggled for many years to find a role in maintaining and creating peace, but was largely frustrated. The Soviet Union adopted the position described as "Mr. Nyet," which included the following:

- A rejection of any form of supranational decision making in favor of the dogma of absolute national sovereignty.

- Frequent use of the veto in the Security Council.

- Opposing a broad interpretation of the powers of the Secretary-General.

- The refusal to pay its share of the costs of peacekeeping operations.

- Arms control initiatives projected to discredit Western policies.

- Support for radical Third World positions in the General Assembly combined with refusal to implement them. (Kaufmann and Schrijver 1990, 90)

U.S. attitudes towards the UN were somewhat less strident, but it was clear by the time John Foster Dulles became secretary of state and began to direct U.S. policy on the basis of a rigid anti-Communist ideology that multilateralism and the UN would never be the centerpiece of American foreign policy.

PEACEKEEPING

In these circumstances, many "middle powers" such as Austria, Norway, Canada, and the Netherlands began to search for an alternative to what had become gridlock in the Security Council. Trygve Lie, the first UN secretary-general, proposed the formation of standing UN police forces to patrol areas where competing territorial claims had not been resolved (Luard 1979, 24) and in fact developed the idea of "observer missions" to simply monitor development in "hot spots." Lester Pearson, soon to be prime minister of Canada, urged Secretary-General Dag Hammarskjöld, Lie's successor, to find a role for the UN independent of the superpowers (Harrelson 1989, 77). The concept of a sort of "referee for the world" emerged and was embraced by the secretary-general (Gordenker 1967). The secretary-general saw his role as that of a mediator and honest broker with a duty to anticipate conflicts and intervene personally before they escalated to violence. Furthermore, he felt that the charter provided the authority to dispatch troops in a trouble spot to keep the peace once a cease-fire has been accepted. As currently defined in UN documents, peacekeeping is "an operation involving military personnel, but without enforcement powers, undertaken by the United Nations to help maintain or restore international peace and security in areas of conflict" (UN 1990, 4).

In 1956, the UN took its first action as a peacekeeper. After Egypt declared sole ownership of the internationally managed Suez Canal and several months of failed negotiations, Britain, France, and Israel mounted a joint military operation to reclaim control of the canal on October 19, 1956. Dag Hammarskjöld called for a cease-fire, which was supported by both the United States and USSR, although France and Britain vetoed efforts to pass a Security Council resolution condemning the invasion. The General Assembly took up the issue, in keeping with the 1950 Uniting for Peace resolution granting that authority to the assembly in the event the Security Council is deadlocked, and passed resolutions calling for a cease-fire, withdrawal of foreign troops, and introduction of a peacekeeping force to monitor the situation and prevent new hostilities. On November 7 a cease-fire was signed and the United Nations Emergency Force (UNEF I) was deployed progressively into the Sinai Peninsula between Egyptian and Israeli troops.

As explained in a UN document:

> The creation of UNEF . . . represented a significant innovation within the United Nations Organization. It was not a peace-enforcement operation, as envisaged in Article 42 of the Charter, but a peacekeeping operation to be carried out with the consent and the cooperation of the parties to the conflict. It was armed, but units were to use their weapons only in self-defense and even then with restraint. Its main functions were to supervise the withdrawal of the three occupying forces and, after the withdrawal was completed, to act as a buffer between the Egyptian and Israeli forces and to provide impartial supervision of the cease-fire. (UN 1979, 79)

Peacekeeping troops were only deployed into territory where the government was willing to accept them, and their costs were paid by the parties to the conflict and other UN members (although several nations routinely refused to pay if they voted against the operation, even after the World Court ruled that it was part of their UN mandatory obligations). In the case of UNEF, for example, when the political situation deteriorated in the Middle East again in 1967, its troops were withdrawn prior to the outbreak of hostilities at the request of the Egyptian president. Shortly after the so-called Yom Kippur War (or Ramadan War) in 1973, UNEF II was organized and deployed until 1979, when the Camp David Accords settled the question of the Sinai Peninsula and there was no longer a need to monitor developments.

The UN's experience with peacekeeping is long and checkered. Throughout the period until 1987, the UN was forced to address only those conflicts that were not vital to the superpowers or other permanent members of the Security Council. As a result, many major and important conflicts came and went with minimal UN involvement, such as the Vietnam War, the Hungary and Czechoslovakia invasions by the Soviet Union, and the Falklands War between Britain and Argentina. Even wars where the superpowers had not firmly taken sides, such as the Iran-Iraq War, raged on for

Table 11.1 UN PEACEKEEPING MISSIONS, 1956–1993

Operation	Location	Duration	Peak Troop Strength	Purpose/Function
UNEF I	Sinai	11/56–6/67	3,378	Establish buffer zone between Egyptian and Israeli forces
ONUC	Congo	6/60–6/64	19,828	Preserve Congo independence and prevent/stop civil war
UNFICYP	Cyprus	3/64+	6,411	Monitor cease-fire between Turkish and Greek/Cypriot forces
UNEF II	Sinai	10/73–7/79	6,973	See UNEF I
UNDOF	Golan Heights	6/74+	1,450	Monitor buffer zone between Israel and Syria
UNIFIL	Lebanon	3/78+	7,000	Monitor Israeli troop withdrawal and movement to promote Lebanese independence
UNIIMOG	Iran-Iraq	8/88–2/91	399	Monitor cease-fire and troop withdrawal
UNTAG	Namibia, Angola	4/89–3/90	7,993	Monitor Namibian independence
ONUCA	Central America	8/89–7/92	1,098	Monitor implementation of regional peace accords
UNIKOM	Iraq, Kuwait	4/91+	1,440	Monitor zone between Iraq and Kuwait
UNTAC (UNAMIC)	Cambodia	3/92+) (11/91–3/92	15,000+	Monitor cease-fire and disarmament; support UN transitional administration
UNPROFOR	Former Yugoslavia	2/92+	14,000	Promote peace, humanitarian assistance in the former Yugoslavia
UNISOM	Somalia	4/92+	21,000	Humanitarian assistance, police patrol, formation of new government

Source: Adapted from Thomas Weiss and Janet Chopra, United Nations Peacekeeping, ACUNS Reports and Papers 1992-1, 1992.

years before the UN could intervene. Table 11.1 lists UN operations that could clearly be called "peacekeeping" rather than merely "observation missions."

There has been a total of twenty-nine UN peacekeeping operations, including observer missions and humanitarian activities, to date. Several deserve more attention as examples of how UN operations address the opportunities and obstacles they encounter. Perhaps the most famous cases of peacekeeping involve the Congo and the Middle East.

The Congo (now Zaire) declared independence on July 5, 1960, in the midst of a hasty and poorly planned withdrawal by the former colonial power Belgium. Patrice Lumumba, the elected leader of the country, was unable to control his troops, who mutinied against the few Belgian forces remaining in the Congo. Belgium sought permission to intervene in order to protect Belgian nationals and property, but were rebuffed by Lumumba. Belgian paratroopers landed in the capital of Leopoldville and other cities across the Congo in order to restore order. Moïse Tshombe, a Lumumba opponent, declared the independence of his region, Katanga. Any semblance of order and self-determination was rapidly evaporating.

The UN Security Council determined on July 14 that Belgian troops must leave the country and created ONUC (French acronym for UN Operation in the Congo) with over 14,000 troops. However, as the troops (primarily from African nations) began to arrive, the situation deteriorated further. The president of the country, Kasavubu, dismissed Lumumba and sought the support of Tshombe, who proved unreliable. The United States distanced itself from Lumumba as well, and ultimately supported a coup attempt by military commander Mobutu Sese Seko. At one point in 1961, there were three separate governments in the Congo, each one rejecting the other, and numerous Belgian troops and private mercenaries operating throughout the country. ONUC and Tshombe forces clashed in late 1961, much to the consternation of Belgium and France, who had begun to support his secessionist movement for Katanga. The United States and the Soviets by now supported opposing sides in the capital city, and it seemed there was no hope for establishing a stable government (Bennett 1991, 154).

In this setting, Dag Hammarskjöld flew to the Congo to meet with Tshombe to secure his support for a united government. On the way there, his plane crashed (it was not known until late 1992 that it had in fact been shot down). U-Thant, his successor, was given a broad mandate to vigorously prosecute the war against any opponents of ONUC, particularly in Katanga. By early 1963, all military opposition had ceased, and ONUC forces withdrew in mid-1964. The government of Mobutu began after a successful coup in 1965, and he continues to govern what has become the laughingstock of Africa—a "cleptocracy" (government by theft) (Young and Turner 1985).

With regard to the UN's role, there are mixed messages from ONUC. On the one hand, the UN succeeded in its immediate goal of preserving some form of political stability in the heart of Africa, and in promoting self-determination for the Congolese people (Lefever 1965). On the other hand, the operation seriously jeopardized the organization's fiscal and legal viability. The Soviets and French determined in the early stages of the operation that they would no longer provide funding to continue it, even though this ran the danger of costing them their voting rights. At $400 million (above and beyond the expenses borne by participating nations), ONUC's expenses exceeded those of the rest of the UN combined and was easily the most expensive operation up to that point (Bennett 1991, 92). The principal lesson of ONUC was to never again allow the General Assembly to spearhead a peacekeeping operation, but rather to retain Security Council control, in spite of the potential for superpower stalemate.

In the Middle East, the UN has been actively engaged, sometimes in spite of itself, since Israel's declaration of independence in 1948 (and even before). Much of the material on the Arab-Israeli conflict is discussed elsewhere in the text, but it is important here to review the role of peacekeepers in the Middle East. It is important to understand that for most of Israel's history, all of its Arab neighbors have considered its very existence illegal and immoral. Israeli settlers had for years encountered determined opposition from Palestinian and other Arab populations, manifesting itself in numerous armed clashes. The decision by the General Assembly in 1948 to partition Palestine was rejected at the time, and was never implemented (although it remains a legal touchstone in Middle East peace talks). Instead, Israel declared its control of the entire Palestinian area in 1948, following which several Arab neighbors declared war. Following the withdrawal of troops and the securing of new territory by Israel, Jordan, and Egypt, the UN Truce Supervision Organization was deployed in 1948 to serve as a liaison between parties. This force of 500 is still present.

Over the years, the UN established peacekeeping groups at various points along the Israeli border: in the Sinai (UNEF I and II), the Golan Heights (UNDOF), and Lebanon (UNIFIL). In each case, UN troops were deployed to supervise and monitor a withdrawal of Israeli forces from a particular region following a serious battle. For example, in 1978 Palestine Liberation Organization (PLO) commandos based in southern Lebanon claimed responsibility for an attack against targets in northern Israel, near the Lebanese border. In retaliation against this and previous incidents, Israel invaded the country in order to take control of PLO staging camps and civilian installations. A week later, the Security Council responded to Lebanon's protest by calling upon Israel to withdraw immediately and establish UNIFIL for a six-month period. UNIFIL was never able to restore Lebanese sovereignty over the entire region and conceded a strip of land along the border to Israeli-supported troops. PLO installations operated with little impediment and as a consequence, Israel invaded again in 1982, through the UNIFIL forces which posed little obstacle. In the words of the UN: "This invasion changed UNIFIL's situation drastically. For three years, UNIFIL in its entirety remained behind the Israeli lines, with its role limited to providing protection and humanitarian assistance to the local population. . . " (UN 1992).

Over time, Lebanon's capital of Beirut became a devastated city, with opposing militias and governments vying for control of certain neighborhoods. Shortly before the Gulf War, in 1990, Syria gained control of the bulk of Lebanon and established a stable government. Israel, in 1994, retains a substantial foothold in the country and UNIFIL has yet to fulfill its full mission. In addition, UNIFIL has been a financial millstone around the UN's neck, given the fact that the United States, the Soviet Union, and the parties to the dispute themselves have never provided consistent support. UNIFIL was continually in jeopardy as each six-month renewal was the target of intense debate. As of 1991, total unpaid contributions to UNIFIL equaled almost two year's worth of costs. Given the tasks which UNIFIL has been relegated, this general lack of support seems almost forgivable.

As you can see, the UN peacekeeping forces have been ill-equipped to solve international disputes. This objective has clearly been in the minds of

UN leaders, but the difference between a cease-fire and a settlement has proven substantial. Obstacles such as financial difficulties, superpower opposition, the intractable nature of many regional conflicts, and the practical difficulties of mounting an effective peacekeeping operation have led to a certain amount of despondence over the chances of using the UN to resolve conflict (Haas, 1983). Not until the 1980s was the UN able to compile a record of performance that has given observers some optimism.

RESURGENCE OF UN ENFORCEMENT ROLE

In 1987, Mikhail Gorbachev officially announced in an editorial in Pravda, the official Soviet newspaper, that the Soviet Union would cease its obstructionist behavior in the UN and seek accommodation and compromise on the Security Council. As mentioned in the material on the General Assembly, the mood at the UN immediately changed. Combined with a greater tolerance for multilateralism on the part of the United States and a tempering of rhetoric in the Third World, the Soviet action went far to restore some of the lost effectiveness at the organization.

This was never more apparent than when the Security Council became directly involved in enforcing the end of the Iran-Iraq War and the withdrawal of Soviet troops from Afghanistan, where they had fought the mojahedin resistance for ten years. Although it was impressive to see the Soviet Union approve the use of UN troops, the UN force proved ineffective in bringing a settlement to what became a chaotic situation as the Soviet-supported Afghan government held off an increasingly divided resistance movement backed by the US and Pakistan (Tessitore and Woolfson 1991, 44). The collapse of the Soviet Union in 1991 and the eventual success of the Afghan resistance made much of the UN's work irrelevant, but at least a precedent was set for involving the UN in matters directly affecting the superpowers.

The active role of the UN in supervising peaceful elections in Nicaragua in mid-1990 was further evidence of superpower tolerance of UN involvement in vital problems. For nearly a decade, the United States had funded opposition guerrillas (named Contras) in and around Nicaragua in an effort to overthrow the Soviet-backed Sandinista government (see case #7). After repeated efforts by the countries of the region, led by Mexico and Venezuela, a general settlement was finally reached on the withdrawal of superpower support to the Nicaraguan combatants as well as other players in the area. In connection with this, a UN monitoring group was deployed in November 1989 to monitor compliance with the agreement, and a team was sent to supervise the elections in Nicaragua, where a conservative, pro-U.S. coalition won the presidency. Both developments received support from the United States and the Soviet Union, testifying to the new spirit of cooperation that had developed.

Three more areas are worthy of note because they put the UN in new situations, using new enforcement tools: the Gulf War, Yugoslavia, and

Cambodia. In the case of the Gulf War, ample detail is provided in case #10. Suffice it here to say that the UN was drawing on some rarely used provisions of the charter and reinterpreting still others. Article 4 (2) prohibits the use of force by UN members for the settlement of disputes. However, Chapter VI provides for economic and diplomatic sanctions and Chapter VII anticipated their enforcement. Only in the case of South Africa and Rhodesia were widespread mandatory economic sanctions put in place prior to the actions against Iraq following its invasion of Kuwait on August 2, 1990. Within a week, the Security Council had approved mandatory sanctions on Iraq, and by August 25 it had approved the use of force in enforcing these sanctions. The instrument to be used was the military force of the nations patrolling the waters near Iraq, not the UN itself. By late September, these mandatory sanctions were expanded to cover all transportation flows in and out of Iraq and were applied to nations who were not members of the UN, like Switzerland (Kaufmann et al. 1991, 13).

In all this enforcement activity, the UN was broadening its interpretation of Article 4 (2) without explicitly invoking provision under Articles 41 and 42 calling for direct UN control. When the Security Council passed Resolution 678 in November, it went still further by authorizing the use of force to implement all UN resolutions relating to Iraq, although it did not organize a UN-commanded force. Instead, it merely gave its blessing to those armies already assembled in Kuwait's behalf. Only a loose interpretation of Article 51 offers a legal underpinning for the UN's action (it provides for nations taking actions in self-defense or organizing an alliance for defensive purposes) (Kaufmann et al. 1991, 25). In legal terms, this simply means that the UN relinquished control of the enforcement of sanctions and authorized a self-existing military coalition to act to protect an ally. Although far from mere balance of power politics, it is clear that this is also far from strict collective security as envisioned by the UN's founders.

The situation in Yugoslavia has proved far more resistant to solution than the problem in the Gulf (see case #16). The problem in Yugoslavia has defied description in traditional diplomatic terms. When the violence broke out in 1991 the parties to the dispute were not entirely nation-states, and thus lacked diplomatic standing in the UN. Bosnia had such little control over its territory that its diplomatic standing was only hypothetical, while Serbia's voting rights were rescinded. Today, the role of outside actors in the situation in Bosnia is extremely complex, in that the Serbian government seems to not only be supplying material to the ethnic Serb fighters in Bosnia, but also commanding the troops' movements. Although European Union negotiators have been involved from the outset, there has yet to be a settlement. The only area of consensus in the Security Council is on the need to provide humanitarian relief to besieged cities such as the capital of Bosnia, Sarajevo, but even this raises serious questions since Serb troops until March 1994 blocked most of the access routes and have threatened relief planes.

Perhaps the most interesting question the Yugoslav problem raises is the extent to which the UN can act when there is a lack of resolve on the part of the permanent members of the Security Council. None of the Perm-5 are interested in taking risks in this situation, and this tentativeness seems to come across in the wording and tone of UN resolutions. Another question that will be addressed as the months go on is whether an international war crimes tribunal can be assembled while the fighting continues. It is essential to have the accused in custody before a meaningful trial can take place (see case #13), but a symbolic trial may have the effect of lessening the "ethnic cleansing" operations, for fear of future prosecution and punishment.

The Cambodian situation is also unique in that for the first time the UN has taken full responsibility for governing a nation. As a result of the Paris Accords of 1990, the UN has been plunged into the center of a most complex situation. To begin, at least four major parties have an immediate stake in the country and some legitimate claim on government: Prince Norodom Sihanouk and his supporters (backed by the United States), the radical Khmer Rouge (backed by China), the more mainstream Khmer People's National Liberation Front which is headed by Sihanouk's son Son San (backed by China as well), and the sitting government of Hun Sen (backed by Vietnam and the Soviet Union). All of the opposition parties formed a government-in-exile in Thailand and have occupied the Cambodia seat at the UN, although they strongly disagree over the future of the country and possible power-sharing arrangements.

For several years, coinciding with the decision by Vietnam to withdraw from Cambodia and the Soviet withdrawal of support to Vietnam, the parties to the Cambodian disputes have held periodic discussions. Not only did the Cambodians themselves meet, but the Perm-5 and other Asian observers held concurrent meetings in Paris to work out a compromise coalition government that gave all the players a share of power. Naturally, the United States and Soviets opposed the Khmer, while the Chinese balked at a major role for Prince Sihanouk. After several false starts, the Australians proposed a UN-dominated transitional government that would disarm the factions and supervise elections after a one-year-cooling-off period. This became the core of the arrangement ultimately accepted by the various parties (Tessitore and Woolfson 1991, 55).

UNTAC was deployed in March 1992 with a total of nearly 22,000 personnel, including several police contingents, public administrators, military forces, and technical advisors (UN Chronicle, June 1992, 10). The central effort of UNTAC has been disarming the various factions on the ground, an effort that had come up against serious resistance by Khmer Rouge guerrillas. Prince Sihanouk has been approved as the nominal head of the new Cambodian regime, buttressed by numerous UN officials serving at high levels throughout the government, but has yet to establish a strong degree of central authority over the entire nation (and may never accomplish this). At any rate, the charter has once again been interpreted loosely in response to a consensus by the Perm-5 to remedy a serious problem. In May 1993, elections were held in spite of a Khmer boycott. More than four-fifths of eligible Cambodians braved sniper fire and threats of civil war to go to the polls. The result was a fair election with a centrist government under the loose leadership of Prince Sihanouk in power. As of this writing (March 1994), the Khmer Rouge are still engaged in guerilla warfare, however.

In Somalia, a UN operation begun officially in April 1992 was dramatically strengthened by the deployment of marines in December. Since then, the UN/U.S. operation has taken a very aggressive policy in bringing food supplies to Mogadishu, the capital, and later small towns in the countryside. The action has been so strong that some Somalis have turned their weapons away from each other and against the UN peacekeepers, who in turn have resorted to air attacks and search-and-destroy missions. While the withdrawal in March 1994 of US troops has put an end to large-scale UN involvement, the experience in Somalia represents a new plateau in UN military intervention.

With increasing frequency, the UN is being called upon to resolve the burning crisis of the day. Whether it involves the provision of relief aid in warlord dominated Somalia, or the protection of Bosnians against Serb ethnic cleansing, or the elimination of weapons of mass destruction in Iraq, the UN is at center stage, and is being asked to carry out actions that stretch the charter in new and intriguing ways.

WHITHER THE UN: PEACEKEEPER OR PEACEMAKER?

In the case study on the General Assembly, we will consider the complaints of many UN critics who saw the institution as merely a talk shop, or even a threat to the peace. Recent discussion of the future of the Security Council and collective security has been far more ambitious. Not only have the Soviets pledged to do more to promote the organization and its principles, but the United States has made a number of concrete proposals that will result in substantial increases in UN powers. In his September 21, 1992, address to the General Assembly, George Bush spoke warmly of an expanded enforcement role for the UN, although he stopped short of committing U.S. troops to the effort as called for in the charter (*Christian Science Monitor*, September 23, 1992, 1). He has discussed the possibility of providing U.S. bases to train and U.S. air transport to move UN troops during operations. Candidate Bill Clinton hinted during the presidential debates in October 1992 that such moves were minimally satisfactory, although he also had reservations about placing American soldiers in harm's way.

In July 1992, in response to a request by the Security Council to review UN peacekeeping, Secretary-General Boutros Boutros-Ghali published "An Agenda for Peace," a comprehensive statement of his vision for a revitalized United Nations. In it he calls for more substantial UN capabilities to intervene in international crises and conflicts as well as greater specialization in the type of forces at the organization's disposal. Among the list of new UN powers, he included the establishment of a standing UN force, as described in Chapter VII of the charter, greater power for the secretary-general to order troops into a conflict zone, "peacemaking" authority to restore order against the will of belligerents, "nation-building" capability to reconfigure a nation's police and security forces, and preventive intervention of UN troops prior to the actual outbreak of hostilities. He hoped these forces would be financed through a "Peace Endowment Fund" established through assessments, voluntary contributions, interest payments on arrears, and possible taxation (Tessitore and Woolfson 1993, 282).

While the Security Council has been reluctant to grant the UN these new powers, its actions over the past two years have included many items from the list. UN operations in Yugoslavia are described elsewhere in the text. In Somalia, following unsuccessful peacekeeping efforts aimed primarily at providing humanitarian assistance to starving refugees, the United States led a dramatically stepped-up role with large-scale intervention in late 1992 followed by a significant expansion of the UN presence. Tactics in Somalia have included not only traditional peacekeeping and humanitarian assistance, but also search-and-destroy missions in order to arrest warlord Mohammed Farah Aidid, all with the aim of creating a stable government amid the ruins of clan violence. And in Cambodia, the UN has gone far to build a nation by monitoring and protecting elections, disarming many Khmer Rouge guerrillas, and overseeing the return of Prince Norodom Sihanouk and the establishment of a democatic government.

Because Western powers have not increased funding for UN peacekeeping, the organization has faced a financial crisis since 1991. In addition, they have opposed giving the UN standing forces under the secretary-general's command. The track record of UN successes has been severely tarnished by setbacks in Yugoslavia, Somalia, and most recently in Haiti where ousted President Bertrand Aristide has been unable to assume his post in spite of a negotiated settlement with the military commanders on the island. On the other side, Third World governments fear an expansion of UN intervention would provide the West with yet another avenue to exert power (Iraq, not surprisingly, has led the way in voicing this concern!) (Wurst 1992, 10).

Are there institutional arrangements which can lessen the risk of these negatives? Many have proposed the expansion of the Security Council to include more representative nations, including such genuine powers as Germany and Japan, as well as key Third World players such as India and Brazil, on a permanent basis. Others have considered doing away with the veto, or perhaps modifying it in some way, in order to prevent a superpower conspiracy, but this proposal will more than likely itself be vetoed by those who hold this power. For that matter, such a move may undermine the essential support these great powers give to the organization and lead to the marginalization of the institution as it was in the early 1980s (Kaufmann et al. 1991, 130).

The immediate question of expanding the role and powers of peacekeeping forces has been addressed (MacKinley 1989). Some have argued that peacekeepers cannot fulfill the types of roles they will most likely play in the future without some offensive capability and authority. In the case of Cambodia, for example, the inability of peacekeepers to persuade the

Khmer Rouge to voluntarily lay down their arms runs the risk of scuttling the entire arrangement. In such a situation, UN forces should actively pursue those who are clearly trying to undermine the legitimate arrangement (Weiss and Chopra 1992, 23).

In this connection, an immediate solution to the problem of demilitarizing the American and Russian economies would be to place a large number of their currently active-duty forces and bases under the auspices of the UN, as called for in Article 43, with the proviso that they could be returned to exclusive national service at a later date. Such a move could solve both the problem of overextended military, since an arrangement could be made to share costs of training and providing for these troops, as well as the problem of uncertainty and weakness in UN enforcement powers. It seems the biggest obstacle to such a move is the psychological attachment many in both Russia and the United States still have to unilateralism and national autonomy—the heart of the problem.

Questions to Consider

1. Is "collective security" the best description of what the UN is engaged in? To what extent is this merely "great power policing"?

2. How could UN operations be improved? What obligation do UN members have to support and direct peacekeepers?

3. What are the rights of nations where peacekeepers operate? How might these be violated?

References

A. LeRoy Bennett. *International Organization: Principles and Issues*. 5th ed. (Englewood Cliffs, NJ: Prentice-Hall, 1991).

Christian Science Monitor, September 23, 1992, p 1.

Grenville Clark and Louis B. Sohn. *World Peace Through World Law* (Cambridge: Harvard University Press, 1958).

Leon Gordenker. *The UN Secretary-General and the Maintenance of Peace* (New York: Columbia University Press, 1967).

Ernst Haas. "Regime Decay: Conflict Management and International Organizations, 1945–1981." *International Organization* 32 #2 (Spring 1983).

Max Harrelson. *Fires All Around the Horizon: The UN's Uphill Battle to Preserve the Peace* (New York: Preager, 1989).

Johan Kaufmann, Dick Leurdijk, and Nico Schrijver. "The World in Turmoil: Testing the UN's Capacity." *ACUNS Reports and Papers 1991–94*, 1991.

Johan Kaufmann and Nico Schrijver, "Changing Global Needs: Expanding Roles for the United Nations System." *ACUNS Reports and Papers 1990–95*, 1990.

Ernest Lefever. *Crisis in the Congo: A United Nations Force in Action* (Washington, DC: Brookings Institution, 1965).

Evan Luard. *The United Nations: How It Works and What It Does* (New York: St. Martin's, 1979).

John MacKinley. *The Peacekeepers: An Assessment of Peacekeeping Operations at the Arab-Israeli Interface* (London: Unwin Hyman, 1989).

Robert Riggs and Jack Plano. *The United Nations: International Organization and World Politics* (Chicago: Dorsey Press, 1988).

John Tessitore and Susan Woolfson. *Issues Before the 48th General Assembly of the United Nations* (New York: University Press of America, 1993).

John Tessitore and Susan Woolfson. *Issues Before the 46th General Assembly of the United Nations* (Lexington, MA: Lexington Books, 1991).

United Nations. *The Blue Helmets: A Review of United Nations Peace-Keeping* (New York, UNDPI, 1990).

United Nations. *Everyone's United Nations*, 9th ed. (New York: UNDPI, 1979).

United Nations. "United Nations Peace-Keeping Operations: Information Notes." *UNDPI*, January 17, 1992.

UN Chronicle, June 1992, p 55.

John A. Vasquez. *Classics of International Relations*. 2nd ed. (Englewood Cliffs, NJ: Prentice-Hall, 1990).

Thomas Weiss and Jarat Chopra. "United Nations Peacekeeping: An ACUNS Teaching Text." *ACUNS Reports and Papers 1992–1*, 1992.

Jim Wurst. "A Man, A Plan, Now What?" *Bulletin of the Atomic Scientists* 48 #7 (September 1992): 9–11.

Crawford Young and Thomas Turner. *The Rise and Decline of the Zairian State* (Madison, WI: University of Wisconsin Press, 1985).

General Assembly of the United Nations

An international organization is any formal association of nation-states. It can range from a regional alliance (North Atlantic Treaty Organization) to a functional agency (International Monetary Fund) to a universal, multipurpose organization (UN). International organizations have a legal character in that they are based on a treaty and charter which stipulate membership conditions, privileges, and duties. In this way they differ from many transnational organizations which are more informal and need not include nation-states as members.

The United Nations was conceived during World War II as an alternative to power politics. The lofty phrases of the preamble to the UN Charter declared that the founding nations were "determined to save succeeding generations from the scourge of war." In addition, the United Nations was charged with reaffirming "faith in fundamental human rights . . . and to promote social progress and better standards of life in larger freedom." In all of its activities, the UN was expected to follow basic democratic principles of "one nation-one vote" with the General Assembly at the heart of it all.

Such a wide-ranging mandate has naturally been impossible to fulfill, and many UN observers and participants have learned over the years to modify their expectations and images of the United Nations. Most agree that the UN should somehow remain "above politics" and provide a higher standard of international conduct, although no one knows for sure how this is to be done. Others argue that the UN should simply promote those principles most important to the great powers: stability and order. Still others feel that the UN is in a unique position to stand as an advocate of the underprivileged—a global social worker as it were. Finally, many argue that the UN works best when it restricts its activity to those few things which facilitate diplomacy: providing facilities for negotiations, translating speeches, improving communication, etc. No one expected the UN to become a powerful "world government," although a few have since imagined how this could come about (Clark and Sohn 1958).

Which of these perspectives best describes the actual behavior of the General Assembly of the United Nations? Has the character of the UN changed so much over the years that each perspective has been accurate at certain times? Such questions can only be answered by looking at the evolving roles and activities of the General Assembly over its nearly half-century of operation.

EVOLUTION OF THE GENERAL ASSEMBLY'S ROLE

Charter Provisions

The General Assembly was assumed to be the key legitimating organ of the United Nations, providing as it does a legal voice for all of its members on an equal basis. The General Assembly shares authority to debate international crises and conflicts with the Security Council, but has sole authority "in the economic, social, cultural, educational and health fields, and assisting in the realization of human rights. . . " [Article 13 (1.b)]. The General Assembly controls the UN budget and supervises the activities of all UN specialized agencies as well as the Secretariat and meets annually to review international developments and all UN activities. In this way, the General Assembly is the key organ of the United Nations.

The General Assembly was given so much authority because the earlier League of Nations Assembly was a key player, and also because the great powers expected most UN members to be cooperative (Riggs and Plano 1988, 17). When one considers that the pro-U.S. bloc which emerged during the early years of the Cold War outnumbered the pro-Soviet bloc by roughly six to one, it is easy to understand why the West promoted the General Assembly.

In spite of this apparent power, the General Assembly is still largely an advisory body. Its decisions are not automatic, but have to be approved or carried out by the Security Council in most cases. The General Assembly's "resolutions" are not "legislation" in the traditional sense of the word. All members of the United Nations retain their sovereign rights and could choose to violate international agreements. This is not to say that such violations would be without consequence, but in an anarchic world, retribution is typically sui generis.

In spite of this institutional and legal weakness, the General Assembly's role in the UN system is pivotal, particularly as it gives legal standing to all else that happens in the UN as a whole. Whether the General Assembly has moved beyond the role of mere housekeeper or international conscience will be addressed in the next section.

U.S. Dominance: 1945–1960

Perhaps the simplest way to summarize the character of U.S. dominance in the General Assembly in the first fifteen years is to show the degree of agreement between U.S. votes and General Assembly majorities. From 1945 to 1960, the US voted with the majority roughly 70 percent of the time. It was not until 1965 that the United States voted against the majority more often than not (Riggs and Plano 1988, 61; Rowe 1969). While raw numbers hint at an interesting story, it is important to recount the history more carefully before drawing a conclusion.

For the first fifteen years of the UN, the United States could count on a solid majority of Western and sympathetic Third World states to support its initiatives. Although the Security Council was sometimes a frustrating forum, given the Soviet veto, the General Assembly was accommodating. A key moment arrived in 1950 when the Soviet Union used its veto to block continuation of UN support for the Korean War effort. The United States decided to shift the forum handling Korea to the General Assembly and proposed the Uniting for Peace resolution. This resolution expanded the charter and empowered the General Assembly to fill the collective security role of the Security Council if it "fails to exercise its primary responsibility . . . in any case where there appears to be a threat to the peace, breach of the peace, or act of aggression." The resolution passed by a wide margin. The World Court later reaffirmed the legality of the resolution in response to a Soviet challenge (van den Haag and Conrad 1987, 64).

Another seminal achievement of the early General Assembly was the acceptance of the Universal Declaration of Human Rights, a document shaped substantially by the U.S. delegate, Eleanor Roosevelt. Nations pledged to provide freedom of expression, access to government, social rights, and freedom of thought, thus codifying what up to then had merely been moral norms.

The United Nations of the first fifteen years was a fairly demure and decorous place. As put by John Conrad:

> The 51 original member states were mostly European or American, all of them with well-established diplomatic traditions and experience in the conduct of foreign affairs. . . . Discourse in the General Assembly was usually temperate and reasoned, even when the vast differences between Western republicanism and Eastern Marxism led to confrontations. (van den Haag and Conrad 1987, 65)

A key problem the United States and USSR managed to resolve in 1955 was the admission of states which had already taken sides in the Cold War. Until then, the Soviets and Americans had blocked new admissions in order not to allow the other side more supporters. By 1955, the number of such countries was ten—evenly split between the two superpowers—so they were admitted en masse.

Third World Dominance: 1960–1981

Beginning with the admission of Pakistan in 1947, the General Assembly became the first stop for newly independent nations seeking international recognition. Beginning in 1960, the British and French began a systematic and often hasty retreat from empire by relinquishing control over dozens of former colonies. In 1960 alone, nearly twenty new nations took their seats in the General Assembly, thereby nearly doubling its original size. By the 1980s, Third World and Soviet bloc nations would outnumber Western states nearly five to one. Figure 12.1 shows this growth.

This dramatic shift in the UN majority brought with it a change in the agenda of the United Nations. "The balmy days of 1945–60 now seem a distant shore. Then, the United States could command the U.N.'s agenda; nowadays the tendency is to think of the U.N. as a Venus fly-trap, to be approached warily or, better, not at all. . . " (Franck 1985, 246). This shift also brought a crisis of legitimacy to the UN, in that for the first time states that formed a majority in the General Assembly were incapable, both financially and politically, of carrying out the resolutions they passed.

Several items emerged on the General Assembly agenda which dominated this period. First and foremost was the question of economic development and redistribution of wealth. Most Third World nations were led in these early years by individuals and political parties who favored massive state intervention in the local economy. Such Third World activists as Nehru of India, Kenyatta of Kenya, Nasser of Egypt, and Castro of Cuba all promoted the role of the state in building a new, postcolonial society and economy. In this context, these leaders favored a strong role for the governments of wealthy countries in promoting international development. Debate over establishing the Special UN Fund for Economic Development (SUNFED) during the 1950s began to shape the issue, such that when the majority shifted in the 1960s, Third World leaders were poised to take the initiative.

In the early 1960s, the General Assembly authorized and supported a special conference on development and trade (UNCTAD) which first met in 1964 and again every three to four years after that. A well-respected economist from Argentina named Raul Prebisch framed an ambitious proposal calling for a dramatically expanded role for developed countries in Third World development. What became known as the New International Economic Order (NIEO) program was based on increased aid for developing nations, trade concessions by wealthy nations, supports for commodity prices on tropical products exported by developing countries, and expanded sharing of technical and scientific information. Given the tendency of developing nations to pay proportionally more for developed country imports than they could earn on their exports, protection was seen as a logical solution to balance the equation. "Infant industry" protection was promoted by Prebisch and others as a logical justification for postponing free trade until newly established

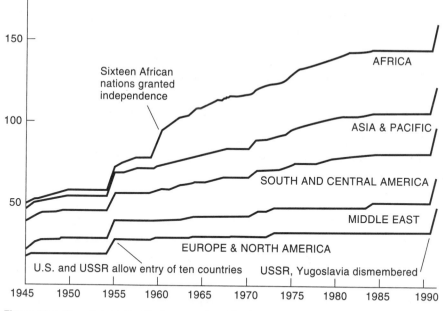

Figure 12.1 Growth in United Nations membership since 1945.
Source: Adapted from A. LeRoy Bennett, *International Organizations* (Englewood Cliffs, NJ: Prentice Hall, 1988).

firms in developing nations, most of which were heavily subsidized by the state, could become competitive (Prebisch 1959). All of this was generally resisted by the developed world, but the Third World nations were able to force the UN to place these items on the agenda of the General Assembly and hold the first UNCTAD meetings in spite of this. Some developed nations accepted the Third World argument that the crime of colonialism required some sort of compensation to the poor nations of the world and therefore became advocates of greater aid and support (Rothstein 1979).

At the first UNCTAD meetings in 1964, the Group of Seventy-Seven (G-77) developing nations became a bargaining coalition against the now-outnumbered developed nations and pressed for adoption of each of the planks on the NIEO agenda. Largely successful, the G-77 pressed on their offensive and expanded UNCTAD. The high point of Third World influence came shortly after the OPEC oil price hikes of 1973 when many industrialized nations paid greater respect to Third World demands, partly out of fear. With the election of a series of left-leaning governments in Germany, Britain, and the United States, Third World leaders had a sympathetic audience for the latter half of the 1970s. Former West German Chancellor Willy Brandt, along with former leaders of France, Canada, and other European powers, authored a study in 1980 calling for wholesale reform in the way the international economy was governed, providing for a greater role for developing countries in shaping rules, setting policy, and establishing new institutions (Brandt 1980).

The results of the NIEO program were relatively meager. Although foreign aid did increase, both in bilateral and multilateral terms, only a few northern European nations reached the goal of providing 0.7% of their gross national product for development. The World Bank significantly increased its lending and the International Monetary Fund began to lend resources on a more lenient standard. However, if one takes into account the problem of Third World debt, the legacy of aid in the 1970s was a net transfer of resources from the developing nations back to the industrialized nations in the 1980s. In other areas, such as trade, the results were more substantial. The liberally oriented General Agreement on Tariffs and Trade was amended to explicitly provide concessional trade arrangements for Third World members. In a few cases, developed countries participated in establishing a system of "buffer stocks" whereby surpluses of commodities were stockpiled during plentiful harvests in order to prevent a collapse in prices. Although these buffer stocks were designed to release the product in lean years, in practice they tended to simply grow in order to ratchet the commodity prices still higher. Overall, then, the NIEO program has left a very mixed legacy, one which would be almost entirely reversed in the 1980s.

In addition to the question of economic justice, the problem of self-determination and racial justice dominated UN deliberations. These problems crystallized around the question of Palestinian rights and apartheid. The Palestinian question gripped the General Assembly almost since its creation, in that the disposition of the former British mandate over Palestine was laid squarely in the hands of the UN. The first Arab-Israeli war in 1948 forced thousands of Palestinians from their homes and prompted General Assembly calls for the preservation of Palestinian rights. The UN Relief and Works Agency for Palestine Refugees (UNRWA) was created and continues to provide humanitarian and development assistance for Palestinians in the Middle East. In 1968, the General Assembly created a special committee to investigate allegations of Israeli abuse of Palestinian rights—a move made primarily to embarrass Tel Aviv and Washington (UN 1979, 80). Each year, the General Assembly, under the leadership of Arab nations, intensified the pressure on Israel by expanding recognition of Palestinian rights. In 1974 the Palestine Liberation Organization (PLO) was permitted a seat as an observer at the General Assembly and in 1975 the famous "zionism is racism" resolution passed with a slim majority, a vote which prompted the Israeli delegate, Chaim Herzog, to rise, condemn the resolution, and rip it in two (Franck 1985, 206).

In the case of South Africa, the General Assembly took the lead, under the influence of the nearly fifty newly independent African states, in condemning apartheid, the program of racial segregation practiced in the country. As the majorities of developing nations grew, the tone of the attacks became progressively harsher. In 1962 a Special Committee Against Apartheid was established by the assembly which, according to a recent survey, was the source of most of the resolutions condemning South Africa. In the two decades that followed the Assembly took even more drastic actions against apartheid. Among these actions were the adoption of a resolution expressing solidarity with the opponents of apartheid, the adoption of an International Convention on the Suppression and Punishment of the Crime of Apartheid, and . . . the many endorsements of "armed struggle" against apartheid. (Tessitore and Woolfson 1991, 29)

Not only did these concerns shape the General Assembly agenda, but they had a major effect on the activities and mandates of the many agencies affiliated with the UN. As put by Williams, "[M]ost of the organizations of the United Nations, even those whose primary function according to their constitution was technical and regulatory, became to some extent arenas for debate, or sometimes confrontation, between the market economy North and the less developed South" (Williams 1987, 8). UNCTAD, United Nations Economic and Social Council (UNESCO), the UN Development Program, and other specialized agencies became more concerned about the slow pace of development and assessing blame for this than anything else, much to the dismay of many industrialized nations.

By the end of this period, a shift in the politics of the General Assembly brought about the beginning of the most disheartening phase of UN history. With the end of the 1970s came a new impatience on the part of developed nations for Third World rhetoric. Election victories for Margaret Thatcher in Britain, Ronald Reagan in the United States, and Helmut Kohl in Germany brought a new conservative zeal in the West which vehemently rejected the socialist/redistributive solutions offered by the G-77.

Perhaps more important, the Third World coalition began to fracture during this period, even as it was achieving its greatest successes. OPEC nations found they had less and less in common with the Third World colleagues and Latin American debtors had more urgent business than reforming global capitalism. African and Asian "basket cases" such as Sudan and Bangladesh were forced to rely on Western humanitarian assistance and were not inclined to alienate them with antagonistic rhetoric. This left only a small number of the original G-77 (which ultimately expanded to over one hundred) in a position to press the NIEO agenda. The net result was a substantial loss of influence of the General Assembly in world affairs as Western powers ignored it and Third World nations struggled to regain the initiative.

The Disenfranchised General Assembly: 1982–1989

A popular roadside billboard that sprang up in many parts of the Midwest in the late 1970s declared "The U.S. Out of the U.N. and the U.N. Out of the U.S.!" Even as late as 1987, an important book written by two UN experts could ask "The U.N.: In or Out?" of American readers (van den Haag and Conrad 1987). UN ambassador in the 1970s Daniel Patrick Moynihan declared the UN a "dangerous place" and Jeanne Kirkpatrick, Reagan's representative in the General Assembly, staunchly defended the administration's right to ignore UN and World Court condemnation of armed intervention in Grenada, Libya, and Nicaragua (Henkin et al. 1991). Many experts had come to the conclusion that the UN was not only failing to achieve minimal goals of promoting peace and prosperity, but was actually increasing tension and undermining economic growth (Franck 1985). Clearly the UN had fallen out of favor among U.S. leaders and had little prestige in the American public at large.

Criticisms of the UN focused on two principal issues: politicization and bureaucracy. These problems prompted the United States to seriously reconsider its attachment to the UN in general and to several specialized agencies in particular. This reassessment culminated in the temporary suspension of membership in the International Labor Organization in the late 1970s and in the more permanent withdrawal of both the United States and Britain from UNESCO.

UNESCO was charged with a broad mandate and relatively little specific guidance in its early years. Over time, the UNESCO governing bodies became heavily involved in the philosophical debates over north-south relations, human rights, Palestine, and apartheid. Socialist states were successful in pushing the organization to specifically promote programs and activities tilted toward their interests, such as preserving monuments to socialist revolutions in Third World countries. In addition, a variety of projects involving archeology in and around Jerusalem were colored with heavy anti-Israel rhetoric. More recently, UNESCO became the focal point for the highly contentious New World Informations and Communications Order (NWICO) program proposed by developing nations to increase their control over international media, among other things.

UNESCO was accused of mismanagement, waste, and corruption. With a staff of over 1,300 and a budget over $600 million at the beginning of the 1980s, UNESCO was clearly one of the largest and best funded UN specialized agencies. Because it "has always been the most 'political' of the UN agencies," it is not surprising to find monies being spent on highly controversial projects, such as studies on nuclear disarmament and a code of conduct on transnational corporations—activities far outside its already broad mandate (Williams 1987, 62, 63). In addition, the director-general who led the agency throughout this tumultuous period, Amadou M'Bow, was accused of nepotism and graft—charges which seem to have been well-founded (Franck 1985, 265).

In 1983, the U.S. Senate cut American contributions to the UN by $500 million over four years, although the final version simply froze future funding at 1983 levels. The Reagan administration began a policy of withholding U.S. allotments to the UN, resulting in roughly $600 million in arrears by the late 1980s. In 1984 the United States formally withdrew from UNESCO, citing politicization and mismanagement (Franck 1985, 264).

Although total U.S. withdrawal from the UN was never seriously considered, the loss of nearly 20 percent of its operating budget amounted to largely the same thing, and put the UN in a serious financial crisis. The General Assembly was forced to take a long, hard look at its behavior which led to a gradual reassessment of priorities and practices. The combative tone of U.S. and British delegates, combined with resorting to the use of the financial weapon, proved a potent attack against an already fractured Third World coalition. But it would take the end of U.S.-Soviet political rivalry to bring this unhappy period in General Assembly marginalization to an end.

The Empowered General Assembly: 1989+

The growing cooperation between Russia and the United States culminated in a series of dramatic agreements and a significant change in UN politics for the 1990s. As was seen in the previous chapter, both the Soviet Union and the United States began, starting in 1987, to search for consensus rather than force the other into the embarrassing use of the veto. This same tone permeated the General Assembly beginning around 1988.

To begin, several long-standing international problems came closer to resolution in the late 1980s, which led to a lessening of tensions in the United Nations. The South African government significantly relaxed many of its harshest apartheid policies beginning in the mid-1980s, culminating in the release of African National Congress leader Nelson Mandela in early 1990. Mandela spoke to an exuberant General Assembly in the summer of that year and went far to healing decades-old wounds. This is not to say that the General Assembly has forgotten about apartheid—in fact it passed a number of resolutions calling for an acceleration in its demise (*UN Chronicle*, March 1991, 75).

Yasir Arafat spoke before a General Assembly convened in Geneva to announce his renunciation of terrorism and the declaration of the independence of Palestine—a move which earned him much higher standing in both U.S. and international diplomatic circles. Some sixty nations recognized Palestine's independence, and Palestinians have met with Israeli leaders face-to-face to discuss the future of the West Bank and Gaza Strip. Such conciliation on both sides has gone far to defuse the issue and eliminate the perceived need for harsh rhetoric. This movement toward more level-headed cooperation was epitomized by the repeal of the "zionism is racism" resolution on December 16, 1991—an unprecedented step in General Assembly experience (*The Economist*, December 21, 1991, 42–44).

The end of the Cold War has naturally eliminated the tendency for the north-south debate to take on an East-West aspect, in that the Soviet Union no longer has any interest in advocating the claims of national liberation movements in the Third World, as was the case in the past. In 1989 the United States and the Soviet Union cosponsored a resolution calling for eventual global nuclear disarmament, the type of resolution normally passed by an overwhelming majority in the General Assembly against either Soviet or American opposition. In fact, the collapse of socialism and the rise of market-oriented democracies have left only a half-dozen ardent advocates of global economic restructuring in the General Assembly. This has naturally done much to alter the tone of General Assembly debates (*UN Chronicle,* December 1991, 41–45). A recent resolution on economic development actually endorsed the promotion of "entrepreneurship"—clearly a "dirty word" in the days of the NIEO! More than half of all resolutions passed in the 1990s have been accepted unanimously.

The promotion of human rights, environmental protection, resolution (rather than mere control) of international disputes, and other global problems now take precedence over merely ideological debates in the General Assembly. Emphasis on practical solutions has helped promote a settlement of the Namibian question and the independence of this former South African protectorate, an end to the civil wars in Central America and Cambodia, and a resolution of the Afghanistan and Iran-Iraq conflicts.

This is not to say that serious and even fundamental differences do not persist. Roughly half of the world's inhabitants are mired in poverty (Kempton 1991). The "Earth Summit" held in mid-1992 demonstrated that Third World expectations and perceptions of global environmental problems are still far removed from developed-country attitudes. While human rights, including democratic civil rights, are taken for granted in the West, these are still very precarious and tentative elsewhere. The use of force by Western powers in the promotion of international law does not often please Third World audiences who fear a United States without checks on its power. China could yet lead a coalition of cautious Third World diplomats who would like to see more fairness and balance in the distribution of power and resources worldwide.

For now, the UN is on a high plateau and is poised to grow dramatically in stature and presence. In 1988 the UN peacekeepers were collectively awarded the Nobel Peace Prize and the UN was largely credited for the dramatic victory in the Persian Gulf. On the other hand, famine in Africa, instability and bloodshed in central Europe, and continued international economic stagnation are problems which, if not quickly solved, may come back to haunt the General Assembly for years to come.

FUTURE DIRECTIONS FOR THE GENERAL ASSEMBLY

As mentioned before, the UN is poised on the threshold of new opportunities, which will likely require a change in its identity and purpose. Should the UN become more than a global forum and the conscience of the world? Can it undertake more ambitious assignments and a more vigorous role?

Given the centrality of sovereignty in the UN Charter, it is unlikely that the organization will become a "world government." To do so, member states would be required to relinquish control over many essential elements of governance, such as their military forces, social policies, and civil rights policies. If the UN were to be a world government, it would require implementation powers which it currently lacks. The capacity to enter a nation with a substantial police force, a centralized system of international courts with full authority to interpret and apply the law, and some form of international incarceration are essential features. Although some have envisioned how such an institution could be constructed on the current UN foundation (Clark and Sohn 1958), such a change would immediately run into serious and determined opposition from the vast majority of member states. Alternatively, an invigorated UN with an enhanced role in not only peacekeeping but "peacemaking" might be a more feasible solution. The discussion of this alternative was addressed in the previous chapter, so suffice it here to say that this could involve granting larger access for the UN to national military forces for use in restoring peace to areas of instability. The most likely situation for such a role would be the Balkans, where the UN peacekeepers receive additional authority from the Security Council each day as new obstacles are placed in the path of their mission to provide assistance to civilians caught in the war. The General Assembly can play a pivotal role in such a reform by buttressing Security Council actions and providing incentives to member states to carry them out.

Perhaps more realistically, the UN General Assembly could move beyond the role of "talk shop" by fostering a more businesslike environment. The current trend toward pragmatism and consensus is precisely the direction this course would take. The next step could involve developing more rational procedures for drafting and debating resolutions, a streamlined administrative arm at the UN, and a more efficient use of resources. For example, efforts could be made to limit the number of documents requiring translation into all six of the organization's official languages, which currently takes the largest single part of the Secretariat's budget and staff allocation.

For the General Assembly to be taken more seriously, it is also essential that the role of the major powers of the world be expanded. Some connection between power and influence should be institutionalized—for example through the means of extraordinary majorities and weighted voting, whereby the consent of these major powers would be necessary for certain resolutions to pass. This could eliminate the problem of the General Assembly majority passing resolutions which it cannot implement by virtue of the poverty and weakness of the nations constituting a majority. Such institutional arrangements have been in place in many of the UN's specialized agencies with solid results.

There are those who would say that it is not essential for the UN to become more efficient or effective, since its role has always been circumscribed by the charter. Perhaps "talk shop" is the wrong phrase, but many advocate a UN that speaks "above politics" on behalf of the weak and oppressed of the earth. Some defended the "politicization" of the UN on the grounds that developing nations had no other outlet for their frustrations and no other forum where their voice could always be heard (van den Haag and Conrad 1987, 220). One could even conceive of a sort of "people's parliament" in which not governments but political movements would be represented and given the opportunity to address the world community directly. The alternative Earth Summit involving native peoples and other social groups that had not been invited to the political summit itself illustrates this viewpoint.

Questions to Consider

1. At this point, would you say we are better off with the UN than without it? Has it lived up to the charter or its original billing? Has it at least achieved what it set out to do on a case-by-case basis?

2. How can one go about evaluating such a novel institution? Are there precedents?

3. What should be the U.S. role in the UN?

References

A. LeRoy Bennett. *International Organizations: Principles and Issues*. 4th ed. (Englewood Cliffs, NJ: Prentice-Hall, 1988).

Willy Brandt, et al. *North-South: A Programme for Survival* (Cambridge, MA: MIT Press, 1980).

Grenville Clark and Louis Sohn. *World Peace Through World Law* (Cambridge, MA: Harvard University Press, 1958).

The Economist. (December 21, 1991): 42–44.

Thomas Franck. *Nation Against Nation: What Happened to the U.N. Dream and What the U.S. Can Do About It* (New York: Oxford University Press, 1985).

Louis Henkin et al. *Right vs. Might: International Law and the Use of Force*. 2nd ed. (New York: Council on Foreign Relations, 1991).

Murray Kempton. "The Back of the Bus." *New York Review of Books* 38 #18 (November 7, 1991): 52.

Raul Prebisch. "Commercial Policy in the Underdeveloped Countries." *American Economic Review* 49 (May 1959): 251–273.

Robert E. Riggs and Jack C. Plano. *The United Nations: International Organization and World Politics* (Chicago, IL: Dorsey Press, 1988).

Robert L. Rothstein. *Global Bargaining: UNCTAD and the Quest for a New International Economic Order* (Princeton, NJ: Princeton University Press, 1979).

Edward T. Rowe. "Changing Patterns in the Voting Success of Member States in the United Nations General Assembly: 1945–1966." *International Organization* 23 (Spring 1969): 231–253.

John Tessitore and Susan Woolfson, eds. *Issues Before the 45th General Assembly of the United Nations* (Lexington, MA: Lexington Books/UNA-USA, 1991).

UN Chronicle. (March 1991): 75.

UN Chronicle. (December 1991): 40–45

United Nations. *Everyone's United Nations: A Handbook on the United Nations* (New York: UN, 1979).

Ernest van den Haag and John P. Conrad. *The U.N.: In or Out?* (New York: Plenum Press, 1987).

Douglas Williams. *The Specialized Agencies and the United Nations: The System in Crisis* (New York: St. Martin's Press, 1987).

Nuremberg Trials

International law is a collection of principles, rules, and procedures that are designed to govern international affairs—particularly relations between nation-states. International law is derived from a wide variety of sources: treaties, conventions, protocols, traditions, scholarly writings, customs, habits, etc. Although international law aims at creating the sort of order in international society that exists in domestic society, it lacks a central element: centralized enforcement. Because there is no world government, international law can only be applied by the consent of members of the international community. Historically, international citizens have been reluctant to take the risks required to enforce international law militarily, so wars come and go as always. An important exception to this rule was the disposition of Nazi war criminals in 1945.

How should the world community respond to the systematic slaughter of 6 million Jews, 2 million Soviet prisoners of war, thousands of handicapped persons, and still more Gypsies, Poles, and other ethnics? How do civilized nations respond to one regime's ruthless plan for global domination? How does one punish behavior that was never before imagined?

These questions faced American, British, French, and Soviet military and diplomatic leaders in the waning months of World War II and ultimately led to the war crimes trials at Nuremberg. Looking back, we can ask ourselves: On what basis were the leaders of a nation judged as criminals? Were these charges and the ensuing judgments justified? Have these actions and decisions set any precedent for the bloody acts of scores of other countries in dozens of other wars since that time? Are we a more civilized world thanks to Nuremberg?

ORGANIZING THE TRIAL

Early on, the behavior of Hitler's Germany in World War II was described as criminal. Statements by Roosevelt, Churchill, and later Stalin condemned the aggressive acts of a ruthless dictator, the mistreatment of prisoners of war, and the systematic slaughter of millions (although the full extent of the atrocities did not become clear until concentration camps were liberated and documents examined). Clearly, this was no gentleman's war, and the objectives of the Allied forces quickly escalated far beyond a simple return to the status quo. Nothing less than the eradication of Nazi institutions and ideology would suffice to avenge the atrocities and restore world order.

In this context, it is understandable that radical measures were conceived regarding the planned treatment of the leaders of the Nazi regime after the war. Churchill and much of British government favored the summary execution of Nazi leaders upon their capture by Allied troops. Henry Morgenthau, the U.S. Secretary of the Treasury, strongly advocated the execution of Nazi leaders, the deportation of former SS officers, the total deindustrialization of Germany, and even contemplated arresting children of senior officials in an effort to purge the society of all real and potential Nazi influence (Smith 1981, 40). Soviet leaders advocated a purge of all senior and midlevel Nazis (roughly 50,000 in all).

It was not until Henry Stimson, the powerful U.S. Secretary of War, began promoting the notion of a public legal proceeding that a number of individuals in Washington began planning for such an event. From the start, the idea of a trial was highly controversial, since it necessitated breaking new diplomatic, military, and legal ground. Questions raised included: Which laws had the Nazis broken? Which individuals are truly responsible? Who should gather documents and on what basis? What forum should be used for this trial? How can the procedure be anything but a "high-class lynching"?

In late 1944, Stimson used a proposal developed by a midlevel officer, Murray Bernays, to flesh out his idea and gather support from other cabinet officers. He found the road very hard, in that even the Joint Chiefs of Staff were skeptical of his proposal. Once the questions listed above began to be raised, however, the proposal was nearly dropped. "After six weeks in which the plan had repeatedly been examined, debated, and revised, only to be challenged once more, not a single government department had formally approved it" (Smith 1981, 112).

As was common in wartime planning, policy decisions were often swept up by events on the battlefield. In January 1945, reports from Belgium described a slaughter of eighty American prisoners of war by Nazi guards apparently acting under specific orders. The act so directly violated the 1924 Geneva Convention on the treatment of prisoners of war that Roosevelt was prompted to formally endorse the idea of a war crimes trial. By March, American officials were speaking in favor of a wide-reaching war crimes trial and ultimately managed to persuade British and Russian diplomats.

The key sticking points until the finalization of the plan in June were questions over the notion of a conspiracy to commit aggressive war and the prosecution of organizations themselves. Both were new ideas to the Europeans, since conspiracy trials are uniquely American inventions. The definition of "aggressive war" was not only weak at the time, but continues to be elusive to this day. Finally, the guilt of an entire organization was never attempted at even the domestic level, and there were serious questions about whether this was possible or appropriate. After all, not all members of an organization are of equal culpability should the organization become involved in criminal activity. And besides, only individuals can be accused of crimes, not social institutions. These questions were ultimately left unresolved and it would be up to the judges at Nuremberg to determine the merits of the charges separately.

The organization of the trial was based on the four-part alliance which defeated Germany. American, British, Soviet, and French judges were named, along with an alternate for each one. They heard all the documentary, film, and oral testimony about the crimes of twenty-two men chosen for their prominence, breadth of experience in different aspects of the Nazi regime, and direct participation in war crimes. Prosecutors from each of the countries gathered documents, interrogated witnesses and defendants, and undertook cross-examination at the appropriate time. Each defendant was allowed a German defense attorney of his choosing, and all materials were made available in German and English, with the hearings being simultaneously translated into English, French, German, and Russian (a first for IBM!).

The defendants in the Nuremberg Trials were each notorious in their own right, although as it would become clear during the course of the proceedings, they differed dramatically in their degree of participation and control over the commission of atrocities and war crimes. Hermann Goering and Rudolf Hess were perhaps the closest to Hitler himself, although Goering's influence had waned and Hess was profoundly schizophrenic. Other prominent organizers of Nazi rule gathered at Nuremberg included Ernst Kaltenbrunner (SS), Hans Frank (governor-general of Poland), Arthur Seyss-Inquart (Anschluss organizer), Alfred Rosenberg (theoretician/East Europe commander), Martin Bormann (Haas aide),Wilhelm Frick (Cabinet Minister), Julius Streicher (prominent anti-Semite), Baldur von Schirach (Hitler Youth leader), Konstantin von Neurath (member of the "secret cabinet"), Albert Speer (production/labor organizer), Fritz Saukel (labor), and Hans Fritzsche (propagandist). To complete the list, leaders of the military (Admiral Karl Doenitz, Admiral Erich Raeder, General Alfred Jodl, Field Marshall Wilhelm Keitel), the economy (Walter Funk, Hjalmar Schacht), and the formal government (Franz von Papen) were assembled.

Each of the defendants was charged with one or more counts of either (1) conspiracy to commit aggressive war, (2) crimes against peace, (3) war crimes (traditional), and (4) crimes against humanity (see Smith 1977, chap. 1). Count 3—traditional war crimes—was the easiest to establish, in that clear treaty provisions already existed. The Hague Convention of 1907 and Geneva Convention of 1924 clearly prohibit harsh treatment of prisoners of war, the use of chemical and bacteriological weapons, and deliberate attacks on defenseless noncombatants. Of the eighteen charged with traditional war crimes, only two (Hess and Fritzsche) were acquitted. The German high command, the Nazi party organization, and other supporting organizations had left behind an unambiguous paper trail demonstrating the planning and perpetration of abuses of rules of war as codified in these treaties. German leaders often went to great lengths to conceal their actions by burning the bodies of their victims and inventing gross lies to explain away deaths—acutely aware that "the world would hold the Wehrmacht (German military) responsible for such outrages and killings," as put by a senior aid to Jodl (Conot 1983, 189). Amazingly, even as they attempted to hide the facts of these atrocities, they carefully preserved a record on film and on paper!

The other counts raised serious problems of "post facto" prosecution. As put in the final judgment at Nuremberg: "It was urged on behalf of the defendants that a fundamental principle of all law—international and domestic—is that there can be no punishment of crime without a preexisting law. . . " (Falk et al. 1971, 97).

To be sure, the notion of a crime against humanity, while intuitively appealing, had never been mentioned or discussed prior to Nuremberg. The concept was put forward originally by the Soviet judge, General I. T. Nikitchenko, as a way to punish the Nazis for the Holocaust. Given the doctrine of soverign immunity, which allows a government to treat its own citizens in any way it pleases, there could not be any traditional international law against Germans killing Jewish Germans. "Crimes against humanity" was a device to make such prosecution possible. Given the fact that the law did not exist in 1939, the defense charged that new laws were being invented and applied retroactively to their clients.

To justify this charge, lawyers for the prosecution argued that even though it had not been codified on paper, in 1939 an international moral consensus against genocide (the deliberate slaughter of a race of people) existed. As put by Robert Jackson, the American prosecutor:

> It is true, of course, that we have no judicial precedent for [these charges]. But International Law is more than a scholarly collection of abstract and immutable principles. It is an outgrowth of treaties and agreements between nations and of accepted customs. . . . The real complaining party at your bar is Civilization. (Falk et al. 1971, 84, 7)

Sir Hartley Shawcross, the British prosecutor, put it more directly:

> The rights of humanitarian intervention on behalf of the rights of man, trampled upon by a state in a manner shocking the sense of mankind, has long been considered to form part of the recognized law of nations. . . . If murder, rapine, and robbery are indictable under the ordinary municipal laws of our countries, shall those who differ from the common criminal only by the extent and systematic nature of their offenses escape accusation? (Conot 1983, 180)

The judges at Nuremberg determined during the course of the trial that Nazi atrocities were so far beyond what could be considered civilized behavior, even in time of war, that they upheld the charge of "crime against humanity." Documents evidencing the desperate speed with which extermination camps carried out the "Final Solution" to exterminate all European Jews clearly pointed to a complete abandonment of any pretense of humanity in the waning years of the war.

The crime of conspiring to commit aggressive war involved at least four different legal problems:

> It was submitted that ex post facto punishment is abhorrent to the law of all civilized nations, that no sovereign power had made aggressive war a crime at the time the alleged criminal acts were committed, that no statute had defined aggressive war, that no penalty had been fixed for its commission, and no court had been created to try and punish offenders. (Falk et al. 1971, 97)

The Kellogg-Briand Pact of 1928 was a lofty pledge by the world's major powers to never resort to war. The signatories (which included Germany) declared "in the names of their respective peoples that they condemn recourse to war for the solution of international controversies, and renounce it as an instrument of national policy in their relations with one another" (Falk et al. 1971, 46). It was determined by the judges at Nuremberg that this treaty by itself was sufficient to show that international law prohibited the initiation of war (although very narrow provisions existed in which preemptive war was permissible). Through the course of their deliberations, they settled on the fact that Germany planned its attacks far in advance, that the Nazis attacked neutral nations, and that they did so without regard for international law. Hitler himself offered the most telling comment when he said, with regard to his plan to attack France via neutral Belgium and Holland: "Breach of the neutrality of Holland and Belgium is meaningless. No one will question it when we have won" (Conot 1983, 191).

The existence of a conspiracy was all-important to the Americans. Collusion and organized crime were not considered separate offenses in Europe and so the French judges in particular had great difficulty with this concept, as well as with the notion of charging whole organizations with crimes. As it happened, however, the charge of conspiracy could be proven thanks again to the meticulous record keeping of the Third Reich. At several meetings, the attendance at which was recorded, Hitler, Goering, and others explained plans to annex first Austria, then Czechoslovakia, and later to invade Poland. Plans to breach the Moscow Pact and attack the Soviet Union in 1941 were clearly articulated at a number of secret gatherings, along with the program to exterminate all Jews in Europe (the Final Solution). The guilt of an individual defendant could have easily been determined by his presence at such meetings, but the judges showed leniency if the defendant later acted to delay or scale back the implementation of the plans.

The question of whether the Nuremberg Tribunal had the authority to prosecute heads of state for war crimes was and still is a tricky legal problem. After all, the court derived its authority from the military occupation forces and was not directly connected to the United Nations or the International Court of Justice. To a large extent, it could be said that this was merely a complicated way for victorious nations to seal their success. On the other hand, this position of power permitted the Allies to treat their prisoners with far more harshness than they in fact used. Under the circumstances, the Allies who organized the trial felt they were offering the accused far more respect and compassion and fairness than they deserved. The alternatives of a "show trial," summary executions, and wide-scale purge were rejected on the grounds that none of these gave the criminals any opportunity to defend themselves. They would have made the process entirely political and idiosyncratic (Russians made it clear they looked forward to executing any apparent war criminal who fell into their hands while the French favored greater leniency).

As put by Robert Jackson,

> If these men are the first war leaders of a defeated nation to be prosecuted in the name of the law, they are also the first to be given a chance to plead for their own lives in the name of the law. Realistically, the Charter of this Tribunal, which gives them a hearing, is also the source of their only hope. . . . Despite the fact that public opinion already condemns their acts, we agree that here they must be given a presumption of innocence, and we accept the burden of proving criminal acts and the responsibility of these defendants for their commission. (Falk et al. 1971, 82)

It is clear, in retrospect, that although one might quibble about the impartiality of a tribunal of victors judging the actions of a vanquished government, and one might ask whether the full array of legal protections accorded under any given country's legal system was offered to the Nuremberg defendants, nonetheless, the accused did in fact receive relatively fair treatment. The judges were clearly disposed to give each defendant the benefit of the doubt, and often ruled against prosecution's requests—particularly in the area of granting defendants' rights of reply. During the trial, each defendant was permitted not only to have defense of his own choosing, but to call witnesses (the vast majority of which were German themselves—and often senior aides to the defendants during the war), review documents, and speak on their own behalf at several junctures. It was possible to appeal sentences (although none of these efforts were successful). Whatever bias emerged during the trial tended to be in the direction of social status—the judges showed a marked penchant to give intellectuals and professionals leniency—rather than in political views. As put in a *New York Times* editorial written at the conclusion of the trial, "In short, the international tribunal had meted out what it was supposed to mete out—stern and exact justice, but justice, not vengeance" (Conot 1983, 435).

COURTROOM DRAMA

The trial itself was largely tedious and disorganized, involving primarily a rambling discussion of documents (many of which were read out loud in their entirety) and enumeration of countless minor incidents, obscure characters, and secret meetings. During the waning weeks of the trial, as the warm and humid Bavarian sun beat down on the poorly insulated courtroom, the judges themselves had great difficulty staying awake! On the other hand, graphic films of concentration camp victims, angry confrontations between prosecutors and defendants during cross-examination, and the coldly frank discussion of mutilation, crematoriums, and experimentation on human specimens could not help but keep the attention of the international audience.

The trial opened on November 20, 1945, after eight months of gathering documents, interrogating defendants and witnesses, and registering the charges. The judges of the tribunal were Francis Biddle and John Parker of the United States, Lord Geoffrey Lawrence and Norman Birkett of the United Kingdom, I. T. Nikitchenko and A. F. Volvchov of the USSR, and Donnedieu de Vabres and Robert Falco of France. The dominant voices on the tribunal were Birkett and Nikitchenko, involved in drafting the charter of the court. Donnedieu de Vabres spoke consistently for leniency in sentencing and Lawrence did much to promote orderliness and efficiency during the proceedings.

The first three months of the trial consisted of a detailed account of the crimes committed by the defendants and the broader Nazi regime in general. The prosecution used 5,000 different documents which had been translated from German, in order to show the planning and execution of the Nazi leadership's goal of world domination, starting with the subversion of the Weimar Republic in 1931, and the famous Reischtag fire which propelled the Nazis into full control of a police state (an event which was later proven to be the fault of Goering himself). The establishment of a system of state-sponsored terrorism, the placing of the economy on a war footing, and the beginnings of abuses against Jews came next.

From then on, the narrative became somewhat haphazard, in that prosecutors took advantage of the availability of witnesses when convenient. In the process, they attempted to prove that a wide array of German institutions and agencies were implicated in the atrocities. For example, the Reichsbank (central bank of Germany) laundered the considerable amount of jewelry, watches, and even gold teeth through its official accounts during the heyday of Jewish exterminations after 1942. The Hitler Youth organization was so effective in shaping the next generation that Hitler was known to tell regime opponents that he cared little for their complaints since he already "had" their children. The army's blind obedience made the invasion of Germany's neutral neighbors possible, and the Gestapo and SS repression prevented internal uprisings. Even the industrial system was intertwined with atrocities, since millions of prisoners of war and Jews were put to work in weapons-making factories and other programs. All of this was laid out in painful detail through testimony, documentary films, and written records.

By mid-March 1946, it was the turn of the defense to present its case. As put by Conot:

> Since in the minds of the defense as well as of the prosecution, there was little doubt that the essence of the Nazi regime's criminality had been proved, the task of the individual accused in attempting to show his innocence or mitigate his guilt was to disassociate himself from the group, to demonstrate that he had not participated in the alleged 'common plan' and had not been involved in violations of international law or crimes against humanity. (Conot 1983, 330)

Nearly all the defendants took the stand during the trial, which gave rise to the most interesting dramatic moments. Goering was first. After he articulated his basic position that he was in fact heavily involved in all of the Third Reich's highest bodies, he went on to explain that, according to international law, his actions were not criminal. In a heated cross-examination by Jackson, Goering pointed out that bombing campaigns by the Luftwaffe, which were categorized as part of his war crimes, were no worse than Allied attacks on Dresden and other German cities, and that most charges against him were ex post facto. Jackson was disarmed by Goering's able self-defense (Conot 1983, 338). Even Jackson's sympathetic biographer acknowledged that Goering had the upper hand (Gerhart 1958, 394). The judges permitted Goering considerable latitude to give speeches while explaining his answers, according to observers. While this infuriated Jackson, it did not especially help the witness either, in that Jackson was able to argue a strong case on the major charges. Goering was found guilty on all four counts and sentenced to death. He avoided the noose only by taking a cyanide capsule.

Few defendants had the arrogance of Goering, and some were apologetic and remorseful, but most waffled about their prominence and responsibility. Keitel admitted his guilt from the stand: "I cannot make white out of black." Schirach and Frank also admitted complicity, with the latter exclaiming, "A thousand years will pass and still this guilt of Germany will not have been erased!" In his final statement, Saukel said, "In all humility and reverence, I bow before the victims and the fallen of all nations, and before the misfortune and suffering of my own people, with whom I alone must measure my fate." Many Nuremberg defendants excused their behavior on the grounds that they were either ignorant of the regime's worst offenses, or were not senior enough to have set policy, or else that they were simply "doing their job." Jodl, the stern military man, said, "As for the ethical code of my action, I must say that it was obedience." Rosenberg weakly rationalized his participation in the Holocaust by pointing out that the Jewish Talmud itself says Gentiles are inferior, and therefore it is no crime to treat Jews as inferiors. The capacity for Nazi self-justification was so great that it has prompted numerous psychological studies of complicity in institutionalized violence (note the famous Milgram experiments in which college students willingly administered apparently lethal levels of electric shock to their peers because a scientist in a lab coat told them to).

In many cases, the documentary evidence was overwhelming, establishing attendance at key meetings and certain knowledge and authorization of many atrocities. Where documents were not enough, it was usually possible to bring German eyewitnesses to testify against their former superiors.

Ribbentrop's secretary, Margaret Blank, inadvertently gave the prosecution vital evidence of his close ties to Hitler even though she had been called as a defense witness! The commander at Auschwitz testified that Kaltenbrunner, contrary to his own testimony, was fully aware of the large-scale gassing that occurred at the extermination camp.

In general terms, the prosecution was assisted by the relatively weak performance by the defense attorneys. The effort on the part of the judges to allow defendants leeway in answering questions and utilizing and translating documents made the task of the prosecution more difficult nonetheless. Out of a total of seventy-four individual charges, there were twenty-two acquittals—a surprisingly high failure rate, considering the defendants were carefully selected for their obvious culpability. The general consensus on the part of most observers—German and Allied—was that the trial gave all parties ample opportunity to present their cases in the best possible light. Jackson offered in summation: "Of one thing we may be sure, the future will never have to ask, with misgiving, what the Nazis could have said in their favor. The fact is that the testimony of the defendants has removed any doubt of their guilt" (Conot 1983, 469).

THE JUDGMENT

The eight justices met during most of the month of September 1946, immediately after the conclusion of the trial, and quickly handed down sixteen convictions. The justices were unanimous in their decisions on the guilt of Goering, Ribbentrop, Kaltenbrunner, and Streicher, and only briefly debated the convictions of Keitel, Jodl, Rosenberg, Frank, Frick, Saukel, and Seyss-Inquart. On the grounds that each of these individuals had an active and direct role in the planning and execution of Nazi war crimes, they were each sentenced to be hanged.

Regarding the other defendants, the judges debated vigorously. Three were sentenced to life in prison: Hess, Funk, and Raeder. Because Funk and Raeder were judged to be outside of the inner circle of Hitler's advisers and Hess was clearly only marginally competent, they were spared the gallows. The moderate sentences of Doenitz (ten years), Speer (twenty years), Neurath (fifteen years), and Schirach (twenty years) were not so much because of guilt on specific charges, but rather due to extenuating circumstances and compromises among judges. Bradley Smith argues that the personal background of the defendants had much to do with their sentences, since professional types were consistently treated more kindly that the uneducated ruffians in the group (Smith 1977, 305).

Three defendants were acquitted largely due to a fluke of rules. Early on, the judges determined that unless a defendant was convicted by a clear majority (three countries against one), then that individual should be acquitted. In the case of von Papen, the Russians called for the death penalty, as they had throughout the proceedings concerning nearly all the defendants, and the French called for a light sentence on principle. The British and American judges were unconvinced by the evidence and called for acquittal. Thus, although the French and Russian judges disagreed about the nature of the penalty, their agreement on the need for conviction led to Papen's acquittal by producing a 2–2 stalemate. After considerable discussion, it was decided to go back to the previous convictions of Fritzsche and Schacht and acquit because of the remarkable similarities in the roles of all three men.

The charges against certain Nazi and German organizations were upheld; however, rather than urging the prosecution of any member of these groups, the judges instructed future prosecutors to ascertain on a case-by-case basis the individual culpability of each member. The result was a cumbersome and ultimately short-lived legal process which resulted in only a few hundred prison sentences over the next two years. The immediacy of the Cold War pushed World War II business to the back burner everywhere but in Israel, where holocaust war crimes trials continue to this day.

On October 16, 1945, the defendants sentenced to death were hanged outside the courtroom (with the exceptions of Goering and Bormann who had already died), with their bodies later cremated and their ashes scattered near Munich. Thus the birthplace of Nazism became its grave.

IMPLICATIONS OF THE NUREMBERG TRIALS

The Nuremberg Trials offer a significant and rich example of international law in all of its aspects: as a general body of values and principles, as a set of codified treaties, and as a feature of domestic law. In addition, these trials allow us to see both the development and application of international law—a rare opportunity. Finally, the Nuremberg Trials offer a legacy that continues very much alive today, as illustrated by George Bush's call for prosecution of Saddam Hussein on war crimes charges in 1991.

A crucial problem becomes clear when considering the Nuremberg Trials—that is the dilemma of applying law which is not yet codified in treaty form. German defendants and later critics have argued that the law applied at Nuremberg was ex post facto, especially insofar as crimes against peace and humanity are concerned. The linking of the concept of aggressive war with the unenforceable Kellogg-Briand Pact created further difficulties. There was nothing in existing international law (as of 1939) which expressly forbad a head of state from launching any sort of war under penalty of death. On the contrary, given the heritage of colonialism with all its bloody dimensions, the many minor and major wars which had taken place throughout the nineteenth and early twentieth centuries, and the escalation in weaponry and tactics, it could easily have been inferred that the type of war Germany contemplated was perfectly legal according to existing legal codes and customs.

So why was there such an effort to prosecute the Nazi leadership? As Jackson and others put it, there was a consensus among those holding the power at the time to establish a new standard for international behavior. This could be done most quickly by establishing a judicial precedent at Nuremberg—in spite of the absence of formally codified laws (see Harris 1954, 491). This reflects a view of international law as a sort of global common law—an ad hoc collection of rules and judgments that are handed down to future generations for their own interpretation. While this view is certainly convenient, the general trend since World War II has been the codification of explicit declarations—worded generally—as a precursor to more specific and binding treaties. Thus the Universal Declaration on Human Rights of 1949 has served as a backdrop for the more recent Declaration on the Rights of the Child, which in turn will permit more forceful agreements on child labor laws and health standards. Perhaps the most significant result of the Nuremberg proceedings was not the convictions themselves, but the articulation of general principles.

Since the trial, several new treaties have in fact been drafted which articulate specific crimes related to the Nazi actions. The Geneva Convention was updated in 1949 to cover a wider array of acts against prisoners of war and noncombatants. In 1950 The United Nations established the International Law Commission which has as its mission the codification of existing rules and principles. An important first step was the drafting of the Genocide Convention in 1949, which prohibits any attempt to destroy a "national, ethical, racial or religious group" and clearly makes all individuals involved in such crimes responsible and punishable "whether they are constitutionally responsible rulers, public officials or private individuals" (Articles II and IV) (see Woetzel 1960).

The so-called Nuremberg Principles were accepted by the United Nations in 1950 and offer the legal justification for the actions of the tribunal. For example, Principles I and II state:

> Any person who commits an act which constitutes a crime under international law is responsible therefor and liable to punishment. The fact that internal law does not impose a penalty for an act which constitutes a crime under international law does not relieve the person who committed the act from responsibility under international law.

This notion of personal responsibility has also been written into domestic laws, including the Constitution (Basic Law) of Germany and the field manuals of the U.S. Army. The principles further specify that all accused have a right to a fair trial and list specific crimes which warrant prosecution: crimes against peace, war crimes, and crimes against humanity. These were and are applied in the Tokyo War Crimes Trials, the Adolf Eichmann trial of 1961, and may yet serve as the basis for trials against those guilty of "ethnic cleansing" and other atrocities in the conflict in the Balkans.

To what extent have the Nuremberg Principles and other new treaties affected international affairs and the conduct of war in particular? While a complete answer is impossible here, it is interesting to note that to begin with the debate over acts committed during wartime is a common theme in the press today. During the Vietnam War, it became clear by the late 1960s that a large number of atrocities were being committed both deliberately and inadvertently as a result of U.S. military operations. The "carpet bombing" missions involving hundreds of B-52 bombers saturating large sections of North Vietnam with heavy bomb payloads resulted in thousands of civilian casualties throughout the war. More directly, several U.S. officers were accused of and formally charged with violations of military law as a result of large-scale attacks on unarmed civilians.

Mylai and Son My were two villages attacked by American forces at the height of the war. In these cases, villagers were rounded up and shot in a particularly brutal way by American servicemen under orders to maximize their "body count" of Vietnamese casualties. It is clear from the testimony delivered at the court-martials of those involved, including Lieutenant William Calley, that many prisoners of war were killed and many villages razed in order to improve body count statistics, and these actions were tolerated and even implicitly encouraged by commanders. Lieutenant Calley seems to have played the role of scapegoat for a system that had become fundamentally corrupted (Falk et al. 1971, 226).

Bertrand Russell conducted a mock tribunal to judge American war crimes in 1967, complete with witnesses, documentation, and cross-examination. Although the exercise was primarily a media event, the record he gathered is impressive and serves to impeach the policymakers at all levels of the U.S. government.

Few war crimes trials have been undertaken outside the World War II context, and no other war crimes trials have been sponsored by an international tribunal. An important and simple explanation for this is the difficulty involved in bringing would-be war criminals to trial. Unless the government is brought down around his ears, most heads of state are able to protect themselves against foreigners attempting to capture them. The government of Iran under the Ayatollah Khomeini petitioned the U.S. government to transfer the Shah Mohammed Reza Pahlavi in 1979 with no success. The United States launched the invasion of Panama in 1989 in order to capture Manuel Noriega—hardly a war criminal. Calls for Saddam Hussein's prosecution are rather empty gestures given his stronghold on what remains of the Iraqi government and society. So long as the government of a belligerent stands, war crimes trials are meaningless.

Perhaps more seriously, war criminals who win are unlikely to be prosecuted. Not only will the victors still have the protection of their government, but they will have a hand in deciding the parameters of war crimes themselves. The Russians, during the Nuremberg Trials, were careful to prevent the judgment from encompassing their own misdeeds during the war. As the saying goes, "If the traitors are victorious, none dare call it treachery."

Terrorism is an instance of a quasi-military action against primarily civilian targets. Although the acts of terrorists are not explicitly covered under existing international law, they are clearly violations of the domestic law in places where they occur. The Reagan administration prosecuted terrorists it caught if they had been involved in attacks on American citizens through domestic U.S. courts. In some cases, bringing the terrorists into custody has involved some very flamboyant military and diplomatic maneuvers, such as the current contest between the United States, the United Kingdom, and Libya over the release of individuals held in Libya and wanted for the downing of Pan Am flight 103 over Lockerbie, Scotland, in 1988. The United Nations is currently drafting an international code to more clearly define international crimes and terrorism as well as mechanisms for prosecution, including the possible establishment of a permanent international criminal court.

A dilemma yet to be resolved in international law is the definition of the concept of aggression. Although numerous resolutions have been put forward, they have invariably offended certain key UN players. For example, the mere launching of an attack across a border cannot be considered aggression according to Israel, since Israelis have rather frequently carried out attacks on neighboring territory because of a fear of imminent attack. Although the UN has passed a resolution condemning nuclear weapons as well as preparation for nuclear war, the United States opposes such measures on the grounds that nuclear deterrence can bring peace. Most revolutionary states oppose the prohibition of infiltration and indirect intervention on the grounds that this is a necessary step in the fight against oppressive capitalist regimes. To arrive at a definition of aggression which does not offend one or another nation is probably impossible, given the tendency for countries to be aggressive toward each other.

Overall, the Nuremberg Trials served many important purposes although they clearly fell short of their ambitious goal of preventing future war crimes. Without the trial, much of the information we now have about the Holocaust would have remained unorganized. Without the trial, German leaders would have likely been shot summarily, and treated very differently depending on the country that captured them. The trials prevented the martyrdom of Nazi leaders, as well as a popular uprising against the occupation forces. The trials went far to help Germany establish firm anti-Nazi laws and constitutional government. The elevation of what were perhaps subconscious moral principles to the level of international law has also served an important moral purpose, if not a panacea for all the world's evils. As put by Harris: "It has become a test of faith that the victors now live by the rules of law they used to condemn and punish the leaders of Hitler's Germany" (Harris 1954, 560).

It is conceivable that the prosecution of German heads of state engaged in wartime policies will prompt future belligerents to decide not to sue for peace on the chance that they too could be charged with war crimes after the war is over. Although this scenario is possible, it is not likely, given the rarity of total victories in modern warfare. Certainly even oppressive regimes such as those in Iraq, Iran, Libya, South Africa, and Syria seem to be capable of negotiating settlements to wars in which atrocities were committed.

It is easy to be cynical about the effects of the Nuremberg Trials. As put by Conot, "While many of the principles of Nuremberg have been incorporated into international law, practices have changed little" (Conot 1983, 520).

Although certainly the victimization of the Kurds, Afghans, Vietnamese, Cambodians, and many others in recent years may lead one to be discouraged about the future, a new backdrop has been drawn behind each of these situations. Never again will governments behave thus in ignorance of international standards. With each new atrocity, guilty leaders will feel the weight of global condemnation. And perhaps we will never know whether some lives have been spared by the decision of some hesitant despot to refrain from killing.

Questions to Consider

1. Were the Nuremberg Trials really a legal undertaking, or merely window dressing for what was essentially the spoils of victory? How can such trials be governed purely by law?

2. To what extent is the Nuremberg experience a precedent? In law? In morality? In social interaction? How could the Nuremberg Principles be applied in Yugoslavia? In Somalia? In Los Angeles?

References

Robert E Conot. *Justice at Nuremberg* (New York: Harper & Row, 1983).

Richard Falk, Gabriel Kolko, and Robert Jay Lifton, eds. *Crimes of War: A Legal, Political-Documentary, and Psychological Inquiry into the Responsibility of Leaders, Citizens, and Soldiers for Criminal Acts in Wars* (New York: Random House, 1971).

Eugene C. Gerhart. *America's Advocate: Robert H. Jackson* (New York: Bobbs-Merrill Co., 1958).

Whitney R. Harris. *Tyranny on Trial: The Evidence at Nuremberg* (Dallas: Southern Methodist University, 1954).

Bradley F. Smith. *Reaching Judgement at Nuremberg* (New York: Basic Book, 1977).

Bradley F. Smith. *The Road to Nuremberg* (New York: Basic Books, 1981).

Robert K. Woetzel. *The Nuremberg Trials in International Law* (New York: Praeger, 1960).

PART

2

CONFLICT IN THE PERIPHERY

CASE 14

Decolonization in Africa

Since 1960, over 100 states have secured membership in the United Nations, thus fulfilling the nationalist dreams of billions of people. Perhaps the most dramatic example of this is the decolonization of Africa. Statehood means membership in an elite club which brings with it such perks as diplomatic recognition and the opportunity to join countless international organizations, declare war, attend state dinners, etc. By definition, a state is any government with control over a territory and population, but inclusion in the club of nations is the legal capstone to self-determination. As we consider the African decolonization, we should consider whether statehood was a means to an end or an end in and of itself.

In the space of less than ten years at the end of the nineteenth century, the great powers of Europe took control of nearly 90 percent of the African continent. In the 1960s, thirty-one African states (out of a present total of fifty-one) gained membership in the United Nations as independent, sovereign states. The story of this colossal transfer of power from the weakest to the greatest and back again is one of the great sagas of twentieth-century history. The problem of establishing political authority and identity following decolonization in Africa is far from resolved.

Although many have written about decolonization in Africa, as a whole, such an approach tends to distort a process that was as varied as the geography and as diverse as the cultures involved. Algeria and Angola's bloody wars of independence bear little similarity to the relatively peaceful changing of the guard in Tanganyika, Kenya, and Nigeria. UN intervention ended the injustice of South African–supported apartheid in Namibia, quite unlike the difficult and costly UN activities in the Belgian Congo. To lump together all African nations is a great injustice, and so every effort will be made to highlight differences across the continent, after briefly reviewing the international context of decolonization.

THE CONTEXT OF AFRICAN DECOLONIZATION

Europeans have been in control of parts of Africa since antiquity, but the modern phase of European colonialism began in the Age of Discovery, when various African ports were first used and then claimed by various seafaring European states. Throughout the age of early imperialism (eighteenth century) Europeans contented themselves with strengthening their foothold on coastal areas of the continent through a variety of treaties (typically imposed upon local chieftains). It was not until the late nineteenth century that the inland expanses of Africa came under direct European control as a result of the "scramble for Africa"—a period of intense European rivalry for control over raw materials and potential markets. Belgian King Leopold II decided to claim a vast expanse of central Africa as a Belgian possession in the 1870s, setting off a contest over control of Africa's interior. France and Britain nearly went to war over the Sahara and Germany used subterfuge to assert its claims in East Africa (Hargreaves 1988, 26). By 1900, Europeans had laid claim to nearly all of Africa (except for parts of the Sahara, Liberia, and Ethiopia), and white Afrikaaners and British South Africans were heading toward a bloody fight called the Boer Wars. The scramble for Africa was over. The consolidation of colonial rule was underway.

In general terms, Portuguese, Belgian, French, and, to a lesser extent, German colonialists undertook a policy of "assimilation" of their colonies into the political life of the mother country. This led to efforts to dismantle and destroy local ethnic identities and cultures. The British, on the other hand, allowed for some local autonomy by ruling indirectly through local chiefs. Both policies failed to win over native peoples to European ways and by the 1920s African nationalism was becoming more and more pronounced (Oliver and Crowder 1981, 193).

The two world wars led to deep introspection among European imperialists. The League of Nations and the United Nations organizations instituted a system of caretakership whereby colonial rule would be legitimate only as a vehicle for eventual independence (Bennett 1991, 351, 356). In order to prevent unrest, and to make the colonies more profitable and self-reliant, administrators began to undertake economic development projects in many colonies during the 1930s (Hargreaves 1988, 42). The Great Depression had the effect of both slowing down these efforts, given the lack of funds in the mother country, and of demonstrating to the native populations the potential weakness of their continental masters. The collapse of many European powers during World War II further galvanized nationalist aspirations. Finally, the eye-opening experiences of many Africans who served their colonial masters at war brought home their lack of opportunities at home and exacerbated the feelings of injustice that were already growing (Oliver and Page 1988, 191).

Shortly after the war, African nationalist parties began to spring up across the continent for different reasons and with different purposes. A few prominent individuals set in place a sort of hero worship, while elsewhere independence movements were based more on ideology (Hargreaves, 1988, 68). At the same time, unrest boiled over into anticolonial violence. In the early 1950s, the Mau Mau in Kenya and the Arabs in Algeria attacked their white patrons with reckless abandon. The result of these actions was rather extreme: on the one hand, a weakening of imperial resolve, as in Egypt, Ghana, and Sudan, where independence was achieved early on; on the other hand, a strengthening of the military instrument, as in Kenya, Algeria, and Angola where imperialists brutalized native peoples. In South Africa, white nationalists introduced a virulent form of antiblack racism known as apartheid and attempted to enforce it beyond their borders. Egypt, under Nasser, became a model for radical pan-Arab anticolonialists. A key factor in predicting the type of imperial response to nationalist pressures was the size of the white European community in the colony and their attachment to their dominance. The larger and more determined the white population, the more difficult the transition.

The influence of the United States and the USSR during the early years of decolonization was mixed. While on the one hand the Soviet Union tended to promote anti-imperialist movements, its resources were quite limited and it was not a key player in most cases. While the United States weighed carefully the concerns of its imperialist allies, it tended as often as not to undermine colonialism with its support of certain independence movements. During the Suez Crisis of 1956, for example, both the Soviets and the Americans joined in persuading the British, French, and Israeli forces that occupied Nasser's canal to withdraw or face serious consequences. It was not until the 1970s that Africa became a serious Cold War battlefield. Unstable countries like Angola and Ethiopia were made far more violent as a result of the American and Soviet arms that flowed to the warring factions.

Rather than attempt any further generalizations, we will now look at three specific cases of decolonization in Africa. These cases—Algeria, Tanzania, and Zaire—were chosen primarily because they illustrate differences in how African states achieved independence. For an overview of African decolonization, see Map 14.1.

CASES IN AFRICAN DECOLONIZATION

Algeria: Civil War in Two Countries

Algeria is a region of northern Africa originally inhabited by a variety of rulers and tribes with little connection to each other. It was largely by virtue of the French decision in 1830 to conquer, populate, and ultimately annex the territory to France that the nation of Algeria gained a political identity. As late as 1936, only eighteen years before the start of the war of independence, prominent Algerian Arab Ferhat Abbas declared, "I will not die for an Algerian nation, because it does not exist. I have not found it" (Horne 1987, 40).

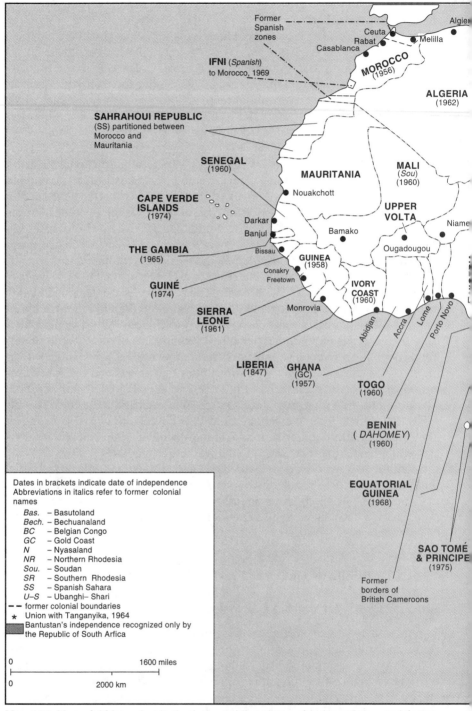

Map 14.1 Map of African decolonization providing dates of independence and former colonial names.

Source: John Hargreaves, *Decolonization in Africa* (New York: Longman, 1988).

dan and elsewhere) and the opportunity to position Iraq as the primary challenger to Israel may have been an important factor in the decision to invade.

Throughout the 1980s, the United States had a rather ambivalent position vis à vis Iraq and Kuwait. Although it tilted toward Iraq in its war with Iran, the United States shipped relatively few weapons. There is evidence, as determined by UN inspection teams who arrived after the Gulf war, that the United States played a part in Iraq's nuclear weapons program. Also, some U.S. grain credits offered to Hussein seem to have been diverted for military purchases. In addition, the United States sold Iraq $240 million worth of military equipment in 1987 and 1988 (Hippler 1991, 28–29). It should be emphasized, however, that 53 percent of Iraqi weapons purchases in the 1980s were of Soviet origin, and most of the military's foreign training took place in the Soviet Union (a fact which caused no small amount of second-guessing in Moscow after the war, when the poor performance of these weapons was amply demonstrated—*New York Times*, March 1, 1991, A11).

In the months leading up to the invasion, the U.S. position was especially mixed—a problem that dogged George Bush during his 1992 presidential re-election campaign. U.S. envoy to Iraq, April Glaspie, was accused of telling Saddam Hussein in June that territorial disputes between Arab neighbors were a strictly regional matter, hinting that the United States would stand on the sidelines. Although this has been denied (*New York Times*, March 21, 1991, A17), rumors persisted through 1992. In testimony on Iraq's human rights record in April, U.S. State Department officials downplayed abuses and applauded the improvements they saw. According to a CIA official, the United States knew as early as January 1990 that Iraq was prepared to attack Kuwait (*New York Times*, September 25, 1991, A18). It was not until Iraq spoke openly in July 1990 of military action against both Kuwait and the United Arab Emirates, following failed attempts to negotiate for lower oil production, that the United States clearly signaled its willingness to intervene by deploying combat ships to the Gulf (*New York Times*, July 25, 1990, A1).

In spite of this, the United States claimed to have been entirely surprised by Iraq's invasion of Kuwait—an observation which demonstrates a serious lapse of military and diplomatic intelligence (Davis and Arquilla, 1991). Likewise, Saddam seems to have been taken off guard by the vigorous U.S. response, which shows a profound lack of communication. When the invasion occurred, the president consulted his top military advisers to determine whether this constituted a real threat to the United States. The need for U.S. intervention was never self-evident because of the ambiguous nature of American interests in the region (*New York Times*, August 12, 1990, A1).

THE DIPLOMATIC PHASE—AUGUST 2–JANUARY 16, 1990

Within a week of the invasion of Kuwait, as Iraqi forces began to mass on the Saudi Arabian border to the south, the United States deployed the 82nd Airborne upon request (perhaps contrived) of the Saudi ruler. Operation

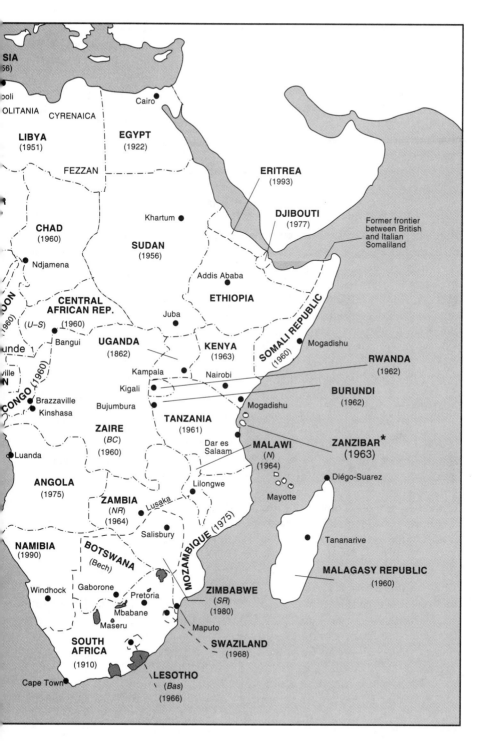

SIA
56)

poli
OLITANIA   CYRENAICA

Cairo

LIBYA
(1951)

EGYPT
(1922)

FEZZAN

ERITREA
(1993)

Khartum

DJIBOUTI
(1977)

Former frontier
between British
and Italian
Somaliland

CHAD
(1960)

SUDAN
(1956)

Ndjamena

Addis Ababa

ETHIOPIA

**CENTRAL
AFRICAN REP.**
(U–S)   (1960)

Juba

ON
960)

Bangui

UGANDA
(1862)

KENYA
(1963)

SOMALI REPUBLIC
(1960)

Mogadishu

unde

ville
N

CONGO (1960)

Brazzaville
Kinshasa

Kampala

Kigali

Bujumbura

Nairobi

RWANDA
(1962)

BURUNDI
(1962)

Mogadishu

TANZANIA
(1961)

ZAIRE
(BC)
(1960)

Luanda

Dar es
Salaam

MALAWI
(N)
(1964)

ZANZIBAR*
(1963)

Diégo-Suarez

ANGOLA
(1975)

ZAMBIA
(NR)
(1964)

Lusaka

Lilongwe

Mayotte

MOZAMBIQUE (1975)

Salisbury

Tananarive

NAMIBIA
(1990)

BOTSWANA
(Bech)

Windhoek

Gaborone

Pretoria

MALAGASY REPUBLIC
(1960)

ZIMBABWE
(SR)
(1980)

Mbabane
Maseru

Maputo

SWAZILAND
(1968)

**SOUTH
AFRICA**
(1910)

Cape Town

LESOTHO
(Bas)
(1966)

For the first 100 years of French involvement in Algeria, the region was dominated by the 1.5 million so-called "*pieds noirs*" of French, Spanish, and Italian descent. Europeans from across the Mediterranean flocked to this country of warm sun and relatively fertile soil. Major cities grew with strong links to Europe, but with a clear identity. The *pieds noirs* felt themselves inferior in many ways to their continental brothers, but were also fiercely proud of their dominance in this new region. They were nonetheless dependent on the "metropole" to repress periodic unrest in the overwhelming majority of 9 million Arabs who lived in Algeria.

Various programs instituted by Paris aimed at industrializing and modernizing Algeria were not without substantial success. Attempts at liberalizing the political system in order to extend more civil rights to Arabs met with tenacious resistance by the *pieds noirs*. By the beginning of World War II, the best Arabs could hope for was participation in a rump assembly especially designated for them, while the white population enjoyed direct representation in Paris and almost complete dominance over political structures in Algeria, where colonial officers continued the century-old system of direct control. This situation did not change in any appreciable way throughout the period of French dominance in Algeria. What was worse, from the perspective of the Arab nationalist, was that when Arabs were permitted a role in government, they were almost always handpicked yes-men ("Beni-Oui-Oui") who would parrot the *pieds noirs'* party line (Tlemcani 1986, 43).

At the end of World War II, during V-E day celebrations in fact, Algerian Arabs revolted. At the town of Sétif, a massive spontaneous uprising resulted in the death of over 100 *pieds noir's*—particularly individuals who represented the French government. While this was shocking in and of itself, the official reaction to the events was extremely violent, culminating in the deaths of between 15,000 and 40,000 Muslims. While the action eliminated any resistance for a decade, the emotional and political impact on Algeria was irreversible. From that point, the prospect of a moderate solution to the Algerian question was virtually impossible.

In response to Setif, a variety of incipient Algerian independence movements began to organize themselves underground. The Movement for the Triumph of Democratic Freedoms (MTLD), later renamed the Algerian Nationalist Movement (MNA)—all acronyms are based on the French version—under Messali Hadj began developing a program for revolutionary independence, while moderate Ferhat Abbas organized the Democratic Union for the Algerian Manifesto (UDMA) in order to bring about democratic reforms in Algeria under the auspices of French governance. A combination of strong personalities, imprisonments, financial difficulties, and ideological and tactical disputes led to the eventual splitting of the MTLD into a more moderate faction and a radical National Liberation Front (FLN) wing which would later grow to encompass all Algerian nationalist movements (in 1955, Ferhat Abbas himself joined the FLN) (Tlemcani 1986, 59). In 1954, the first deliberate attempt to organize armed resistance came about with a group known as the Revolutionary Committee of Unity and Action (CRUA) which included those who would become the core of Algeria's revolution: Balkacem Krim, Ahmed Ben Bella, and Hocine Ait Ahmed. Unlike other African revolutionary groups, however, Algeria's FLN lacked consistent leadership centered around a particular individual. One can attribute this to the efficiency of the French police which managed to imprison most FLN leaders.

The Algerian Revolution began "officially" on November 1, 1954, when the CRUA mounted a series of attacks on urban *pieds noirs* targets across Algeria. Simultaneous to the attacks was a declaration calling for full independence for Algeria, full civil rights for all inhabitants of Algeria, and international endorsement of the declaration. The CRUA and FLN would never waiver in their demands as the revolution dragged on, a strategy which, according to Horne, ultimately led to their overwhelming success in the face of French growing ambivalence (Horne 1987, 145).

For the next three years, the French progressively, after a very weak beginning, reasserted control over Algeria. Various French leaders in Algeria attempted reforms, but without success—only the military approach seemed to reap benefits. The violence of the war was particularly appalling, as Algerian rebels resorted to terrorism, mutilation, and eventually reprisals against Arab collaborators in their effort to galvanize support. By 1957, FLN strength was so great that its leadership called for direct confrontation with the French in the capital city of Algiers. The "Battle of Algiers" was in fact a fairly brief campaign of bomb attacks and general strikes which were suppressed by an increasingly organized French military, led by paratroopers and counterinsurgency teams. Their techniques included wide-scale use of "bleus"—Algerian collaborators, including former FLN members—and torture, the use of which ultimately led to a backlash among French liberals at home. In 1957, the military approach almost eliminated the FLN's leadership. In addition, internal dissent in the FLN reached a crisis point (Horne 1987, 128).

This is not to say the FLN was failing entirely. On the international front, the FLN was gaining in reputation, support, and experience. The Non-Aligned movement had publicly embraced the FLN and the United Nations had added Algerian independence to its agenda. Egypt's Nasser was, slowly but surely, beginning to provide logistical and diplomatic support, and even such prominent Western politicians as John F. Kennedy had endorsed Algerian independence. All of this culminated in the declaration of the provisional government of the Republic of Algeria by FLN leaders in exile, under Ferhat Abbas.

Beginning in 1958, relations between whites in Paris and Algiers would prove to have far more significance for Algeria's future than battles between paratroopers and the FLN. A massive revolt of *pieds noirs* in Algiers brought down the governor-general responsible to Paris and led to a temporary military government. This began a chain of events which led to the abandonment for a time of constitutional democracy. When Charles de Gaulle returned to power in May, he governed by decree for six months, after which the constitution for the French Fifth Republic was approved by the National Assembly.

De Gaulle was troubled by the international and domestic disapproval the Algerian Revolution had heaped on the French government. While trying to maintain good relations with the *pieds noirs,* he took many steps to end the conflict. He dispatched a new military commander to replace the dangerous Massu and Salan and encouraged an end to the war first by military means. He also initiated peace talks beginning with a first meeting in Melun, France, in June 1960. The talks proffered no solution as the FLN stuck with its initial demands from 1956–1957. Two major revolts, first of civilian *pieds noirs* against the military in 1960 and later of the military against Paris in 1961, rocked Algiers. In each case de Gaulle was able to restore order by appealing directly to the rebels in televised addresses. All of this unrest, as well as a nearly successful assassination attempt on de Gaulle himself, combined with ever-increasing international pressure (the UN endorsed Algerian self-determination in December 1960), culminated in the decision by de Gaulle to sue for a settlement in Algeria on the FLN's terms (Horne 1987, 465). The peace accords signed on March 18, 1962, called for a referendum on independence and a cease-fire in Algeria. Although the white backlash was substantial, by June the *pieds noirs* had signed a truce with the FLN. On July 1 the referendum yielded a 6 million to 16,000 majority in favor of independence and on July 3, 1962, Charles de Gaulle recognized Algerian sovereignty. Beginning in August, nearly 1.5 million *pieds noirs* left Algeria—only 30,000 stayed behind.

The Algerian Revolution was one of the most wrenching experiences for France and one of the bloodiest wars of independence in Africa. By the end of the war, the French government had experienced the fall of one constitution, a succession of military coup attempts, and civilian unrest on a large scale. European deaths amounted to 18,000 French soldiers and 10,000 *pieds noirs,* while roughly 300,000 Arabs were killed (of which nearly 100,000 died at the hands of FLN vigilantes). While the French recovered from the experience and went on to a prosperous period of European prominence, the Algerians were forced to transplant an entire government-in-exile, complete with internal dissent and personal rivalries (Tlemcani 1986, 84). Although Algeria has had the trappings of democracy, it has yet to develop a healthy two-party system with tolerance for opposition movements. Algeria's economy, thanks in large part to its oil reserves and aggressive government intervention, has been vibrant, if largely one dimensional. Given a recent rise in Muslim fundamentalism, Algeria's political stability is now in question, however.

Tanzania: Nyerere's Statesmanlike Revolution

Tanzanian and Algerian independence are a study in contrasts. Tanzania never had a large expatriate community, the British government never intended to create a transplant white government, and it had little interest in defending its state with force. Where the Algerian Revolution lacked a single leader, Julius Nyerere was from the beginning an important focal point in Tanzanian independence. Where the Arab Algerians were continually excluded from government, Africans were courted actively by the British and even controlled the government in the waning days of the colony. The international community, while somewhat interested in Algeria, took an active and direct role in Tanzania.

Tanzania was, like Algeria, composed of a variety of chieftains and kingdoms which had little in common until the first Europeans arrived in the sixteenth century. Portuguese were followed by French and British as well as travelers from the Middle East. The first major attraction to the region was its people—as a commodity. Slave trade lasted until the mid-nineteenth century, when British interests intervened to halt the practice in favor of free trade which redounded to British advantage. By the 1850s, the British were entrenched on the island kingdom of Zanzibar, off the coast of Africa, and British, German, French, and even American companies had operations in so-called Tanganyika on the mainland. Never a particularly lucrative colony, no single power sought control of the area until the scramble for Africa, when in 1885 the Germans presented other European leaders a variety of dubious and often laughable "treaties" with local rulers (who were often illiterate) as evidence of their supremacy in the region. Germany was able to play off tensions between France and Britain in their move.

Germany governed what is now Tanzania until after World War I, during which time it attempted to consolidate its authority. Germany was never able to pacify the region, however, and throughout its rule uprisings were common. In 1905 the Maji Maji rebellion prompted Germans, fearful that it would spread to better-organized tribes, to slaughter the rebels with machine guns.

In World War I the Germans lost the colony to Britain, which was granted legal stewardship over the area through a League of Nations mandate. This meant that the British were expected to provide annual reports on the state of the people in the colony, particularly with regard to social progress. The League took no action to shape British policy, however. By 1926, the British had instituted a sophisticated system of local rule involving tribal leaders and government appointees dispersed throughout the country. The British also instituted somewhat broader educational opportunities for Africans, although the number of college graduates never rose beyond a few hundred until the 1960s.

British governors in Tanganyika tended to be fairly enlightened in their efforts to give Africans a voice in government. Donald Cameron approved the formation of the Tanganyika African Association (TAA) in 1929—an organization which would later create the independence-minded Tanganyika African National Union (TANU) under Julius Nyerere. Richard Trumbull, governor during the late 1960s, played a crucial part in the nation's independence by treating Nyerere as a spokesman for Tanzanians and deferring to him on numerous matters of national policy. The British governors helped instill a sense of national unity for Africans by recognizing African-led national organizations (Hatch 1972, 91).

The period before and after World War II was a painful one for Tanzania, in that it felt the effects of the Great Depression, Nazi Germany made claims on the territory, and border skirmishes were common. Educational opportunities dried up, production was reemphasized, and Britain rejected out of hand a UN proposal to grant the colony independence by 1975 (Taylor 1963, 82).

It was in this context that, beginning in 1950, the TAA was transformed into a political movement to press the governor for reforms—political, social, and economic. In 1953, Nyerere, an educated son of a lesser chieftain, was elected to lead the TAA. He called for the creation of TANU as a free-standing political party. Nyerere consistently favored reform of the Tanganyikan political system rather than its overthrow and was generally successful in calming the voices of militants. He was convinced that only by working through the British legal system could genuine independence be achieved. TANU was endorsed by various UN officials who visited the country and grew to be the focal point of disaffected Africans throughout the country. This was reinforced by a decision to exclude whites and Asians from the organization at the outset. In a short time, TANU was a force to be reckoned with for then-governor Edward Twining (who generally favored limiting power for blacks). Within TANU, each regional office had considerable autonomy and there was little effort to indoctrinate the masses (Yeager 1982, 19).

By 1957, with the independence of Ghana and the nearing of the end of governor Twining's term of office, the die was cast. In a series of elections, Nyerere's TANU party fielded candidates (against the wishes of many radical TANU members who favored boycotts—see Taylor 1963, 163) and posted impressive victories. The party benefited from an absence of serious opposition and the gradual incorporation of many nonblack TANU supporters. In October 1958, elections were held for a new multiracial assembly in which all the seats were up for grabs, regardless of race (previously the seats had been split evenly between Europeans, Asians, and blacks). TANU won every seat in this new legislature and Nyerere became its leader (Hatch 1972, 123). The speed of independence was greatly accelerated by the cooperation of the newly appointed governor Turnbull who pushed forward scheduled election dates, including the election in August 1960 which resulted in Nyerere forming his own cabinet. The governor was then responsible for foreign policy only. The biggest problem facing Tanganyika's African leaders seems to have been arrogance on the part of many elected officials and apathy on the part of the electorate, who had already come to expect the huge electoral victories (Hatch 1972, 128). On December 9, 1961, under the sympathetic eye of governor Turnbull, the Union Jack was lowered and the Tanganyikan flag was raised for the first time.

Militants and unionists dogged the early years of Nyerere's regime, which had become a one-party state quite against his wishes. Maintaining the populist character of the TANU party prompted strict guidelines on membership by Nyerere and eventually the enunciation of a socialist doctrine that would serve as a model for African Marxists. An important development—which is largely separate from TANU-led politics—was the decision to form a federation with politically unstable Zanzibar off the coast at the sheik's request (Yeager 1982, 23). In 1964 the two nations merged as Tanzania, with Zanzibar retaining substantial autonomy through the 1970s.

Zaire: The Congo in Turmoil

Zaire, known originally as the Belgian Congo, is in the heart of what Stanley and Livingstone called "darkest Africa." For many years it served as a private hunting reserve for the flamboyant Belgian King Leopold II. In 1879, he determined to secure European recognition of Belgium's control of the region. "Probably it was Leopold, more than any other single statesmen, who created the 'atmosphere' of scramble" (Oliver and Page 1989, 161).

Belgian rule over the Congo epitomized the worst of colonialism. The entire country was converted into a vast resource extraction operation. Railways were built at the cost of hundreds of lives, plantations flourished through slave labor, and eventually great mining companies operated with reckless abandon in the Katanga region in the southeast. All this was directed by a 10,000-strong Belgian colonial administration and a sizeable expatriate community which eventually reached 100,000 shortly before independence. Although some Belgian officials embraced the "white man's burden" of Kipling fame with paternalistic authority ("control to serve" was one administrator's slogan), the result was not only the pillaging of the country, but a reduction in the size of the native population (Young 1965, 60).

The Congo consisted of numerous regional groupings, ethnic identities, and social classes. Educated Africans in the capital sought civil rights equal to the Europeans. The mining region of Katanga felt confident of its capacity to govern itself and sought independence. Other regions, particularly the northeast, were remote, poorly organized, and easily cut off from the capital. All of these factors became extremely important in the years following independence.

Although sporadic violence against Belgian rule was common throughout the century, it was not until well after World War II that anything approximating an independence movement became evident. Interestingly enough, Belgians were quick to address African grievances, in the hope of reaching a quick solution based on association of whites and blacks (Young 1965, 40). When African demands became more coherent in the mid-1950s, Belgians quickly abandoned these dreams in order to avoid a revolution. Elections were held in 1957 even though no African political parties had been formed. Even with the election of a self-governing body in 1959, no truly national Congolese parties existed. Spontaneous riots in the capital of Leopoldville (now Kinshasa) precipitated what can only be described as a helter-skelter independence process, culminating in national elections in early 1960 and Belgian withdrawal in June. To a large extent, nothing approximating a state was in place with the granting of independence. This failure to prepare for self-rule led to five of the most turbulent years of recent African history.

The first leader of the Congo was Patrice Lumumba, a native of the northeastern region who had embraced a form of pan-African Marxism only a few years before independence. As the leader of the Chamber of Deputies, he was empowered to organize a government, although the high degree of splintering in the Parliament led to formation of a weak coalition government. Lumumba was never especially secure in his position, particularly since the capital was located in an area dominated by his political rivals. Joseph Kasavubu, long a prominent African in the Congo, became president of the country with rather uncertain powers of appointment and censure. Given Kasavubu's political rivalry with Lumumba, the struggle over these powers would prove the undoing of the country's constitution.

Within less than a week of independence, Congolese troops rebelled against their Belgian officers who had remained in transition. Within a short time, groups of angry soldiers began brutally harassing Belgian expatriates in an effort to humiliate them (Young 1965, 321). This prompted the Belgian government to request direct military intervention in order to protect its nationals. While this action was not opposed by Lumumba, it led to a severance of diplomatic ties between the two nations. The mineral-rich province of Katanga declared independence under the leadership of Moise Tshombe. Belgian troops openly supported Tshombe's government and encouraged the recruitment of foreign mercenaries, much to the chagrin of Lumumba who contacted Nikita Khrushchev after breaking with Brussels. By this point 80,000 Belgians had fled and most of the country was in disarray.

It was in this context that Lumumba petitioned the United Nations to intervene in support of his country's territorial integrity and unity. Secretary-General Dag Hammarskjöld strongly endorsed UN intervention and used his powers of persuasion to obtain Security Council approval for the deployment of peacekeepers (Franck 1985, 124). Within two weeks of independence, UN troops were deployed into the Congo under the auspices of UN Operation in the Congo (ONUC) with the task of restoring public safety and political stability. In the beginning, UN forces refrained from taking sides in the Katanga rebellion and merely acted to prevent bloodshed. As the crisis wore on, the UN found this position increasingly untenable. In fact, Hammarskjöld was prone to interpreting ONUC's mandate very broadly and by the end of the crisis the UN troops were actively engaging secessionist forces.

In September 1960, Kasavubu revoked Lumumba's authority as prime minster and appointed Joseph Ileo. Meanwhile, Lumumba revoked Kasavubu's authority, while himself under house arrest (Young 1965, 328). The legal wrangle that ensued was finally resolved when Mobutu Sese Seko, a military commander, suspended the constitution in a coup d'état. The Parliament was suspended and Ileo left in his position on an interim basis. Lumumba's forces organized a rival Congolese government based in the north-east around the person of Antoine Gizenga. When the Kisai region in central Congo declared its independence in mid-1960, the country could count four different governments. This chaotic state of affairs continued for roughly a year, while the UN struggled over which government to support.

Congo's politics began to find some coherence in August 1961 when the leaders of the major rival governments (Tshombe excepted) settled on a compromise candidate for prime minister. Cyrille Adoula, former minster of interior under Kasavubu, received unanimous approval. The initial effort at reunification of the country was centered on the Gizenga regime. Lumumba was assassinated in February and Gizenga himself was finally arrested in January 1962 and, with Kisai's forced and bloody reentry into the Leopoldville-centered regime, the country was left with only one outstanding conflict (Young 1965, 338).

The role of the UN dramatically expanded during 1962 and 1963 as officials on the ground engaged in frequent, if largely fruitless, negotiations with the Tshombe regime. The Security Council approved Hammarskjöld's request for expanded authority and ONUC went on the offensive against the Katanga rebels. Operation "Rumpunch" in August netted hundreds of foreign mercenaries who were deported (O'Brien 1962, 220). Tshombe sued for peace, only to break yet another truce once his forces had regrouped. During the middle of these difficult times, Hammarskjöld himself intervened in the negotiations by flying to meet with Tshombe. His plane was shot down by Katangan forces and crashed into a mountain (at the time it was thought the crash was accidental).

Finally, Tshombe accepted the terms for reintegration into the Congo proposed by Adoula, but later violated the agreement. The new secretary-general, U Thant, proposed still other terms, which were again accepted—and broken. It wasn't until UN forces were successful in capturing key military and government installations in Katanga that Tshombe finally called off the rebellion in January 1963 (Young 1965, 343). ONUC was withdrawn as quickly as possible thereafter.

The Congo continued to experience profound political instability for many years. Constitutional government was abandoned following another coup d'état by Mobutu in 1965 which set in place the most corrupt African regime in modern history. Under the newly renamed Zaire, Mobutu undertook a systematic pillaging and self-aggrandizement which defies description. Analysts have been forced to place the regime in an entirely new category of political phenomenon: the "cleptocracy" (Callaghy 1984).

COLONIALISM AND INDEPENDENCE

If few generalizations can be drawn from these cases, it is by design. It is difficult to predict how an independence movement will come into being, how it will make its demands on the established colonial administration, and what will be the outcome. In the case of Algeria and the Congo, overzealousness to retain and/or relinquish the colony proved disastrous to a future of constitutional democracy. In the case of Tanzania, the presence of one man played an extraordinarily important role—an accident of history, perhaps. It is difficult to explain the ingredients necessary for successful separation from a mother country.

An important issue for all newly independent countries is how to establish both administrative services and political legitimacy, in order to develop a relationship of trust and responsibility with the society at large. Where democratic institutions were already in place, in Tanzania, this process was greatly facilitated. Where unifying ideologies existed, as in Algeria, success was more likely. But where the idea of nationhood was a largely artificial construct, as in the Congo (and perhaps in all African states), the task was made more difficult. At this point, in many African nations, legitimacy—the belief that the government has a right to govern—is seriously in question. From Zaire, where Mobutu remains in power after nearly three decades of dictatorship, to Somalia, where at the time of writing there simply is no government, the average citizen wonders whether they have central government or simply an aristocratic elite that enjoys international recognition.

Questions to Consider

1. Why was statehood an important goal for the Algerians, Tanzanians, and Zairians? What did they hope to accomplish by achieving this goal? Did statehood bring peace or prosperity to the people of Algeria, Tanzania, and Zaire?

2. Who really wanted statehood? Who benefited most from its achievement? Were there secessionist tendencies in the new states? Did the subnational groups achieve statehood?

3. What role did diplomacy play in the quest for statehood? Did international organizations, diplomatic conferences, or great powers intervene to grant recognition at crucial times?

References

A. LeRoy Bennett. *International Organizations: Principles & Issues* (Englewood Cliffs, NJ: Prentice Hall, 1991).

Thomas Callaghy. *The State-Society Struggle: Zaire in Comparative Perspective* (New York: Columbia University Press, 1984).

Thomas M. Franck. *Nation Against Nation: What Happened to the U.N. Dream and What the U.S. Can Do About It* (New York: Oxford University Press, 1985).

John D. Hargreaves. *Decolonization in Africa* (New York; Longman, 1988).

John Hatch. *Tanzania: A Profile* (New York: Praeger, 1972).

Alistair Horne. *A Savage War of Peace: Algeria 1954–1962.* Rev. ed. (New York: Penguin Books, 1987).

Arslan Humbaraci. *Algeria: A Revolution That Failed: A Political History Since 1954* (New York: Praeger, 1966).

Conor C. O'Brien. *To Katanga and Back: A UN Case History* (New York: Simon and Schuster, 1962).

Ronald Oliver and Michael Crowder, eds. *The Cambridge Encyclopedia of Africa* (New York: Cambridge University Press, 1981).

Ronald Oliver and J. D. Page. *A Short History of Africa* (New York: Facts on File, 1988).

J. Clagett Taylor. *The Political Development of Tanganyika* (Stanford, CA: Stanford University Press, 1963).

Rachid Tlemcani. *State and Revolution in Algeria* (Boulder, CO: Westview Press, 1986).

Ridger Yeager. *Tanzania: An African Experiment* (Boulder, CO: Westview Press, 1982).

Crawford Young. *Politics in the Congo: Decolonization and Independence* (Princeton, NJ: Princeton University Press, 1965).

CASE 15

South Africa and Apartheid

"Inalienable rights," a notion fundamental to the American system, declares that people enjoy certain privileges simply by virtue of being human, and no government has the right to take them away. Where these rights came from matters little, although the fact that they are "inalienable" means that they came before governments were ever established. When we speak of "human rights" in international affairs, it is generally to these inalienable ones we are referring. They include not only the familiar freedom of speech, freedom from slavery and discrimination, and the right to participate in public life, but also rights with unique importance on the global level: self-determination, prohibition against genocide, the right to peace. Over time, a consensus has developed on these and still other economic and social rights, such that countries who routinely and wantonly violate them have been found more and more often the object of international censure. South Africans understand this better than most.

> Either the white man dominates or the black man takes over. I say that the non-European will not accept leadership—if he has a choice. The only way the Europeans can maintain supremacy is by domination. . . . And the only way they can maintain domination is by withholding the vote from the non-Europeans. (Dr. Daniel F. Malan, South African Prime Minister, 1948–1954)

> We, the people of South Africa, declare for all our country and the world to know that South Africa belongs to all who live in it, black and white, and that no government can justly claim authority unless it is based on the will of all the people . . . that only a democratic state based on the will of all the people can secure their birthright without distinction of colour, race, sex or belief. . . . (Freedom Charter of the African National Congress, 1955)

The reader will find in these two quotes the essence of the struggle in South Africa. Unlike the civil rights movement in the United States, South Africa pitted a minority in power against an overwhelming but largely powerless majority. That minority controlled the bulk of the wealth, schools, businesses, and property of the country against the will of the majority. Moreover, that minority became more and more determined, during the middle part of this century, to maintain not only their power, but their exclusive right to citizenship in an ever more narrowly defined state.

There are many misconceptions about the nature of apartheid, the policy of separation of the races in South Africa. Furthermore, there is much ignorance about the origins and basis for this national policy. Although the history which follows is extremely brief, hopefully it will begin to orient the student toward this vital and burning issue of international politics.

ORIGINS OF SOUTH AFRICA—1652–1912

Beginning in the days of Magellan, the Cape of Good Hope was recognized as a useful weigh station for travelers between Europe and India. The Dutch first decided in 1652 to establish a permanent claim and settlement here under the leadership of Jan van Riebeeck. He almost immediately set about establishing a viable farming colony populated by "freeburghers" (pioneer farmers) which extended into the neighboring territory. Native black tribes opposed this encroachment, prompting van Riebeeck to assert white superiority by force. Within fifty years, black slaves from other African territories were imported to expand the farming capacity of the colony (they are the ancestors of modern-day "coloureds" in South Africa). "Thus he persuaded the company to take the four decisions that shaped South Africa: to found the colony, to settle freeburghers, to establish superiority over the local tribes and to import slaves" (Lapping 1986, 4).

By the end of the eighteenth century, the Dutch were unable to control overseas territories, then under attack by Napoleon's France, so the British first protected and then purchased the Cape Colony in 1815, dispatching a colonial administration to govern the settlement (see Map 15.1). The British introduced "pass laws" for the first time, obliging the nomadic African Khoikhoi to carry a written "pass" proving their association with a particular Dutch settler. The British presence was resented from the start by the now-independent Dutch settlers, or Boer ("farmer"), particularly when these foreign administrators began issuing legal judgments in favor of native African tribesmen. In 1815, while carrying out an arrest order against several Boers, a British detachment was attacked. The offending Boers were arrested and later hanged at Slachter's Nek—the event serving as a symbol of British authoritarianism (Lapping 1986, 10).

British officialdom became ever more ubiquitous as English-speaking missionaries attempted to establish schools for both Afrikaner (descendants of Dutch settlers) and black children. Ultimately, the Boers decided that they

Map 15.1 The Homelands.
Source: Anthony Lemon, *Apartheid in Transition* (Boulder, CO: Westview Press, 1987).

could no longer tolerate such imposition of British culture and power and so embarked on one of the great migrations of people in history: the Great Trek. In 1837, some 6,000 Afrikaners began moving both eastward along the coast and 800 miles northward into largely unpopulated wilderness to found a new homeland for themselves. The principal concentrations came in the area south of the current city of Johannesburg in the Orange Free State, and along the coast around modern-day Durban in Natal province. By 1854, some 10,000 Afrikaners and an equal number of coloured and black servants had migrated from Cape Colony toward what would become the heart of South Africa.

White South African propaganda maintains that the Boers arrived in an unpopulated territory where blacks later migrated (in part drawn by the prosperity of the whites) (Republic 1973, 10). In fact, there is not only ample archaeological evidence of a substantial African presence before the Great Trek, but the Zulu nation under Shaka Zulu had already advanced far into the same territory, resulting in several bloody skirmishes with the advancing Boers. The most famous involved trekker Piet Retief who, after being tricked by a Zulu interpreter, was cornered along with his pioneers by several thousands Zulu warriors on December 15, 1838. By virtue of their position against a mountain pass, the Boers were able to protect their rear and face the Zulus with overwhelming firepower. While 3,000 Zulus were killed, not a single Boer perished. Many Afrikaners attribute the Boers' success to a covenant with God entered into the day before offering Afrikaner devotion and piety in exchange for victory (they also promised to build a church, which was later converted to a stable) (Lapping 1986, 16).

The Boers eeked out a living for the first years after their trek, but in 1867 mineral discoveries began to rapidly alter the character of their nation. Diamonds found in Kimberly, in the Northern Cape, overwhelmed the underequipped British authorities, who quickly moved in en masse to administer the territory. Famous explorers, financiers, and speculators from across the empire converged on the area and made easy fortunes. Cecil Rhodes became one of the richest men in the world by purchasing numerous apparently dry wells from impatient excavators—the holes in fact contained billions of dollars worth of diamonds.

Within ten years, the British government, with Afrikaner urging, established race-based laws to govern the ownership of diamond mines. As put by Brown: "The momentous step in the development of apartheid occurred in 1867 when diamonds were discovered along the Orange and Vaal rivers. . . . [I]n 1875 the right to own and operate a diamond concession was permitted only to whites" (Brown 1981, 59). Thus from 1875 the blacks of South Africa were effectively excluded from profiting from the most promising opportunity to come to the African continent until oil strikes in Libya. In addition to this deprivation, blacks were relegated to the status of mere laborer. The same was true when it came to gold mining after it was begun around Johannesburg in 1880.

A radical interpretation does not seem out of place at this juncture:

> Whenever superior races settle on lands where lower races can be profitably used for manual labour in agriculture, mining and domestic work, the latter do not tend to die out, but to form a servile class. This is the case, not only in tropical countries where white men cannot form real colonies, working and rearing families with safety and efficiency, and where hard manual work, if done at all, must be done by "coloured men," but even in countries where white men can settle, as in part of South Africa and of the southern portion of the United States. (Hobson 1965, 258, in Magubane 1979, 8)

As further explained by Magubane:

> South Africa is not a plural society; it is a society with a dual labor market: a primary (white) market of relatively secure, well-paid jobs, and a secondary (black) market of insecure, filthy, low-paid jobs. African workers are confined to a marginal, yet indispensable, role by fraud, violence, and a system of institutionalized racism that protects 'the white masters of the world'. (Magubane 1979, 17)

As the end of the century neared, the struggle for control of gold and diamonds in the heart of South Africa continued to intensify. While the British were able to establish clear control in the Kimberly area, Afrikaners held out in the Orange Free State and further to the north in the Transvaal where the plucky Boer Paul Kruger retained control in 1899 after three abortive British seizures. In 1899 a new British governor, Alfred Milner, embarked on a systematic, all-out effort to dislodge the independent Afrikaners from the Transvaal and elsewhere in the north by deploying a large British army into the region. The "Boer War," which lasted nearly three years, caused tens of thousands of casualties. In particular, the British introduced the practice of "concentration camps" by capturing thousands of women and children and interring them in tent cities across the region, where disease and malnutrition took some 26,000 civilian lives. In the countryside, the British practiced a "scorched earth" policy in order to deprive the Boer guerrillas of sustenance from the land (Lapping 1986, 31).

After the Boers finally surrendered in 1902, the British moved to consolidate their gains by inviting more British settlers into the country and establishing a united federal state with the consent of the Afrikaners in the Transvaal and the Orange Free State (a form of expansive home rule tantamount to independence was offered as an inducement). A new generation of Afrikaner politicians, led by Jan Smuts and Louis Botha, embraced the British offers and in 1910 the Union of South Africa was proclaimed as a part of the British Empire.

ESTABLISHMENT AND CONSOLIDATION
OF APARTHEID—1910–1965

Part of the deal done with the Afrikaners involved British concessions on social policy. A series of race-related laws guaranteeing Afrikaner superiority was implemented in the 1910s. Before discussing the details of these and other laws, we will look at the philosophy and social norms that undergird apartheid.

The Afrikaners held that their presence in South Africa was more than merely a coincidence of human migration—rather it was the product of divine intervention on behalf of the white race as a whole. Dr. Daniel Malan, prime Minster in the 1950s and former Dutch Reformed church minister, declared

> We hold this nationhood as our due, for it was given us by the architect of the universe. His aim was the formation of a new nation. The last hundred years have witnessed a miracle behind which must lie a divine plan. Afrikanerdon is not the work of men but the creation of God. . . . Not because we Afrikaners are tremendously good people, but because God, the Disposer of the lot of the nations, has a future task for our People (Lapping 1986, 66).

From this perspective, local tribulations represent the punishments of a just and loving God working for their betterment. Their separate development from the Africans is required not only for economic reasons, but for the sake of preserving the white race. By the 1940s, it was difficult to distinguish Afrikaners' talk of their destiny from the anti-Jewish rhetoric of the Nazis in Germany. Malan "made the attempt with as ambitious—or ridiculous—a claim as any politician has ever made: that God's destiny for the Afrikaner people, the reason he had chosen them, punished them, saved them, was to preserve the white race" (Lapping 1986, 71).

This religious rhetoric was not always part of the white propaganda. It was not until the latter part of the nineteenth century that Dutch Reformed church ministers began to reach out to the poor Afrikaners by stressing their uniqueness in world history. Paul Kruger spoke often of God's concern for the Afrikaner as a way of galvanizing support for their efforts at independence. After the defeat of the Boer War, much of Afrikaner history was embellished with such interpretations as a way of building national morale. As put by a UNESCO-sponsored study:

> The Europeans were in a minority in the country; their more advanced scientific and technical skills, coupled with their religious beliefs, their practice of slavery, and the fact that farms were large and scattered, meant that the Boers (farmers) felt that they needed to stress their authority. This need, they believed, had to be based on the idea that they were superior to other peoples. And so, out of what was considered necessity plus self-esteem—a characteristic not unknown elsewhere—the mythology of racial superiority was born. (Brown 1981, 58)

For many years after apartheid had been largely established, the South African government justified the policy not just on religious, but also on human rights, grounds:

> A policy designed to avoid group conflicts cannot be said to run counter to civilized conceptions of human rights, dignities and freedoms, irrespective of race, colour or creed. On the contrary, the Government's fundamental aim with self-determination for all the country's peoples is the elimination of the domination of one group by another. . . . The principle of self-determination to which the Government is committed, leaves the way open for each population group eventually to make its own choice regarding its political future. (Brown 1981, 74)

The clear implication is that the creation of homeland reservations—nominally independent territories designated for and populated by blacks—offers the moral equivalent of self-determination. Conversely, a policy of integration was rejected on the grounds that it would lead to the blending and blurring of ethnic and racial differences—the ultimate form of "cultural genocide." Only by separating the races and providing political and economic rights within one's homeland can each race achieve true self-determination:

> The integration model is totally unacceptable to almost the entire white nation. This is a fact that cannot be wished away; nor the fact that they wield the political and economic power and are numerically the second strongest nation in South Africa. The South African political party which advocates political integration based on the concept of merit, obtains scarcely three percent of the vote in the general election. For all practical purposes this is an overwhelming rejection of the concept of integration. (Brown 1981, 73)

To the extent that either the religious or human rights arguments are accepted, there can be little room for negotiation or compromise.

Shortly after the consolidation of the republic, the Transvaal and Orange Free State enacted a number of restrictive racial policies. In particular, new pass laws forced blacks, coloureds, and a growing Indian immigrant population to carry identification cards at all times. Failure to produce the pass when confronted by a policeman typically resulted in incarceration. Such controls on physical movement combined with continued restrictions on property ownership and very severe limitations on non-white suffrage prompted protests and petitions by certain educated blacks, four of whom formed the African National Congress (ANC) in 1912. It is important to note that these Africans asked little more than a retention of certain rights they had been granted prior to 1910 as British subjects. They failed to get a hearing with the king when they traveled to London in 1913 under the leadership of Sol Plaatje. In the meantime, the Native Lands Act, which the ANC had warned against in London, passed, thereby creating a system of reservations for blacks—some 7.3 percent of South Africa's poorest land was designated for the more than 60 percent of the population that was black. Rather than alienate the newly pacified Afrikaners, the monarchy and Parliament in London refused to reverse the policy. When World War I broke out, these ANC leaders pledged the support of Africans for the British war effort in the hopes of obtaining rights on the basis of being veterans and loyal subjects, along with their white neighbors, even though they knew this would alienate the generally pro-German Boers.

An important parallel development occurred in the Indian community where Mohandas Gandhi—the advocate of nonviolent resistance and future leader of India—organized a series of demonstrations against pass laws and property restrictions. Although for a time he was successful in securing a softening of pass law enforcement, the effort was fairly short-lived (Lapping 1986, 49).

In the 1920s and 1930s, relations between Africans, Afrikaners, and the English deteriorated substantially. Black worker strikes in 1918, born of frustration with the failure of the ANC accommodation, led to massive arrests. The ANC was shaken by the reversal and for the next twenty years would drift. Meanwhile, the Afrikaner workers protested and struck over the limited promotions some black mine workers received (some whites were passed over by British managers) and in 1922 Prime Minister Smuts ordered troops to quell the disturbance—some 200 Afrikaner miners were killed in the ensuing action. The event led to electoral victory for pro-Afrikaner militants in 1924, which in turn led to strengthened white worker rights and the eventual removal of the limited black electoral franchise by 1936.

Black workers began to adopt an increasingly militant style in the 1940s and by 1944 Anton Lembede had organized the Youth League, loosely affiliated with the ANC, and began training what would become the next generation of ANC leadership: Nelson Mandela, Walter Sisulu, and Oliver Tambo

(Lapping 1986, 82). They adopted a more consciously problack, anti-capitalist philosophy and urged direct action against the white government.

A variety of conservative Afrikaner politicians felt that their time had finally come in the 1930s. They seized on the misery of the depression with its attendant anti-British and anti-Jew fearfulness and the symbolism surrounding the centennial of the Great Trek to catapult themselves into power in the 1948 elections—the first which produced an all-Afrikaner cabinet.

The importance of the 1948 election cannot be exaggerated. At the same time the United States was working to desegregate the military, schools, and all public facilities, the Afrikaner government in South Africa embarked on a program to introduce and intensify racial separation. In 1950, Prime Minister Malan appointed Dr. Hendrik F. Verwoerd minister of native affairs. Verwoerd, in this position and later as prime minister until his assassination in 1966, was the single most important architect of apartheid (Lapping 1986, 106).

Verwoerd's legislative strategy displayed a systematic approach to separation of the races. The Population Registration Act set about classifying every resident of South Africa by race. It then "empowered the government to mark off areas for residence, occupation and trade by the different races and then to move each race into its own area, by force if necessary" (Lapping 1986, 105). Some 100,000 disputed their racial classification, which was based on "appearance, general acceptance and repute" (Omond 1985, 22). This basic classification has been refined and clarified over the years, although as recently as 1985 nearly 800 people had their racial classification legally changed. The Prohibition of Mixed Marriages Act ensured racial purity in mainstream family relations while the Immorality Amendment Act of 1957 outlawed any intercourse whatever between individuals of different races.

Verwoerd was famous for his promotion of the status and symbolic powers of the various black tribal leaders across South Africa. He promoted himself as the great "Bantu" (Native African) chief of chiefs and joined the tribal leaders in elaborate ceremonies reaffirming their legitimacy as rulers of black nations. The South African government began emphasizing differences between the various black tribes:

> In a nutshell, the inescapable feature of the South African situation is that South Africa is a country of many nations: Four million whites of European origin, four million Xhosa, four million Zulu, two million Tswana, two million Sotho and so on. Each group is a minority—there is in fact no single majority group. (Republic 1973, 29)

Verwoerd hoped to accomplish the dual purpose of undermining black solidarity and creating a vast network of black supporters of the white Pretoria regime. In this context, the Bantu Authorities Act of 1951 designated specific homelands for each of a dozen African tribes residing in South Africa. Regardless of where members of these various tribes happened to be living at the time, the government expected that they would migrate to these areas and away from white cities: "The Bantu in the cities are not distinct from the Bantu in the Native Reserves.... Their roots are in the Native Reserves. The opportunities for them to enjoy rights, whether they be social or political rights, are available in their home areas" (Lapping 1986, 113). In these territories the black leaders were permitted control of certain governmental functions (subsidized often to the tune of 75 percent of their budgets by Pretoria) and "tribal citizens" could exercise their right to vote. South African citizenship was, however, denied. In the late 1960s, a few of these homelands were granted independence by the Pretoria government (Transkei in 1976, Bophuthatswana in 1977, Venda in 1979, and Ciskei in 1981) although this did little to change their government, other than reinforce the separate legal status of homelands residents. As put by one of Verwoerd's successors in a speech before Parliament:

> If our policy is taken to its logical conclusion as far as the black people are concerned, there will not be one black man with South African citizenship.... Every black man in South Africa will eventually be accommodated in some independent new state in this honourable way and there will no longer be a moral obligation on this parliament to accommodate these people politically. (Omond 1985, 102)

In this context, Verwoerd argued that education was to be strictly controlled and segregated:

> Native education should be controlled in such a way that it should be in accord with the policy of the state.... If the native in South Africa today in any kind of school in existence is being taught to expect that he will live his adult life under a policy of equal rights, he is making a big mistake.... There is no place for him in the European community above the level of certain forms of labour. (Omond 1985, 80)

Lemon has pointed out that South Africa is one of the only countries where the educational system for a majority of its citizens is specifically designed to restrict, rather than create, opportunity by limiting them to a homeland-specific training (Lemon 1987, 52). This was later extended to the university level.

In these homelands, medical services, agrarian support, infrastructural development, and the like were severely limited. The total welfare support for all blacks in the homelands was less than half that provided to the minority white who were at any rate relatively affluent and protected by private forms of insurance (Omond 1985, 67). There was roughly one doctor per 500 Europeans, but only one per 10,000 blacks in 1960. Education spending for each student in the homelands was roughly 8 percent that for whites. Most of the land was arid and unproductive, especially since much of it included the Kalahari Desert. In general terms, living conditions were deplorable. Hence the need for the government to adopt very aggressive measures to ensure that as many Africans as possible relocate to their respective homelands.

In spite of the deep concerns over unproductive lands in the Bantu regions expressed in the essentially pro-apartheid Tomlinson Commission Report of 1951, Verwoerd pressed forward with relocating blacks from white neighborhoods in Johannesburg and Pretoria. Over a five-year period, many thousands of blacks were moved out of white neighborhoods. In the 1960s, thousands of blacks who were unwilling to migrate voluntarily were simply rounded up, transported to their assigned homelands (officially known as "Bantustans"), and dropped on the side of the road—sometimes in a desert miles from a village. The elderly and infirm were specifically targeted for removal. As put by one of Verwoerd's successors in 1967:

> It is accepted government policy that the Bantu are only temporarily resident in the European areas of the Republic for as long as they offer their labour there. As soon as they become, for one reason or another, no longer fit to work or superfluous in the labour market, they are expected to return to their country of origin or the territory of the national unit where they fit ethnically. (Lapping 1986, 154)

By 1980, roughly half of black Africans were residing in the Bantustans—the end result of thirty years' governmental effort (Lemon 1987, 199). It has been estimated that as many as 3.5 million people have been relocated in connection with the Native Lands Act through the 1980s, with another 1.8 million vulnerable to future expulsion (Omond 1985, 114).

At the same time as the government worked to deport as many blacks as possible from the more restricted territory of white South Africa, actions were taken to remove other nonwhites from white neighborhoods in major cities. "Townships" near Johannesburg, Port Elizabeth, and other towns were created in the 1950s in order to eliminate so-called "black spots" (integrated neighborhoods). A variety of laws, including further restricted property rights, intensified pass laws, and the Separate Amenities Act of 1953 which prohibited multiracial use of public facilities, were passed and enforced with great vigor. Once these townships were formed, blacks who were productive laborers were "encouraged" to migrate in much the same way the less productive were encouraged to migrate to the homelands and Bantustans. For example, Sophiatown—a Johannesburg neighborhood of 58,000—was entirely emptied over a five-year period in the 1950s—first through inducements, then by intimidation, finally with force (Lapping 1986, 119).

All of this has created a large and growing migrant worker population in South Africa. The mere relocation of workers has done little to spur the relocation of the workplace. In 1970, some 1 million blacks were forced to migrate to work. That figure had increased to 1.4 million by 1982 (Lemon 1987, 199). Such an imposed life-style has wreaked havoc on the black family:

> From the standpoint of the homelands and their people, the economic and social disadvantages of the migrant labour system are overwhelming. Socially, the break-up of family life and impediments to normal sexual relationships affect

some of the most basic human needs . . . illegitimacy, bigamy, prostitution, homosexuality, drunkenness, violence and the breakdown of parental authority [are] direct effects of the system, whilst venereal disease, tuberculosis, malnutrition and beriberi are some of the indirect results of the lifestyle of migrant laborers. Men are degraded by a system which deprives them of a family role, whilst women are left behind feeling lonely and helpless, anxiously waiting for letters and money from their husbands. (Lemon 1987, 200)

In addition to this deprivation, the migration pattern resulted in an indirect subsidy to white areas by the homelands. Some 80 percent of migrant workers' incomes has been spent in white neighborhoods. Migrant workers were paid less than comparable white labor on the grounds that black workers did not need to pay for family housing. And although blacks continually increased their skills over the course of their careers, promotions were forbidden, thus allowing the owners to utilize more and more efficient labor without paying the price. Finally, the Native Labour Act of 1953 prevented blacks from organizing labor unions since it declared that no black could be classified as an "employee" (Omond 1985, 90).

All of these policies were more easily enforced by virtue of strengthened pass laws, expanded police powers, and increasing support by the tribal leaders benefiting from the homelands policy. Throughout the period, government officials and tribal leaders (with the possible exception of KwaZulu leader Mangosuthu Buthelezi) repeated the "big lie" that blacks welcomed the privilege of living in their homelands and did so voluntarily.

Not all blacks accepted the new order passively or sought to take advantage of it for their own aggrandizement. The ANC attracted an increasingly diverse assortment of followers—coloureds, Indians, Communists, academics—with a leadership under growing pressure to radicalize the movement. Albert Luthuli, ANC leader in the 1950s, was cautious about such demands and worked to keep the ANC legal and able to work with the government. In 1952, the ANC initiated what was expected to be a series of peaceful demonstrations and civil disobedience gestures as part of this moderate approach. The campaign degenerated into a series of melees between police and passersby untrained in nonviolent techniques. The government cracked down on ANC leaders, restricting their travel to their own neighborhoods. Although the ANC consequently lost face with the government, its membership grew from a mere 7,000 to 100,000 (Lapping 1986, 119).

In 1955, through the efforts of new ANC members working as messengers and organizers, and in spite of warnings of police intervention, the organization held a momentous Congress of the People to protest apartheid laws and draft a plan of action. The "Freedom Charter" was the result of the Congress's desire for a democratic, multiracial South Africa. In addition to these civil rights, the Freedom Charter called for land reform, labor rights, and redistribution of wealth to "the people as a whole." This represented the most radical and united statement by blacks in South Africa's history and became a rallying cry for all opponents of apartheid. Beyond South Africa's borders, nations began to take notice. The government of India repeatedly raised the question of apartheid at the United Nations until condemnation of this social system by this international body became one of the strongest bonds of Third World solidarity.

The government, dismayed at the apparent power of the ANC as an alternative political order, responded ferociously. The leaders of the ANC were declared traitors to the state and were imprisoned. As a direct consequence, the world's attention was drawn even more sharply to the plight of blacks in South Africa. Sympathetic newspaper accounts flowed from Pretoria even as contributions from across the world flowed into the ANC's accounts. A lengthy and bitter trial ensued before the glaring eye of international public opinion. The government's prosecutor bungled the charges of treason and Communist sympathies, instead creating ideal opportunities for the ANC leaders to make their own case publicly, clearly, and eloquently. Nelson Mandela presented himself the indignant lawyer and future leader of the ANC with this scathing attack on the legitimacy of the proceedings:

> Firstly, I challenge it because I fear that I will not be given a fair and proper trial. Secondly, I consider myself neither legally nor morally bound to obey laws made by a parliament in which I have no representation. In a political trial such as this one, which involves a clash of the aspirations of the African people and those of whites, the country's courts, as presently constituted, cannot be impartial and fair. In such cases, whites are interested parties. To have a white judicial officer presiding, however high his esteem, and however strong his sense of fairness and justice, is to make whites judges in their own case. . . . The Universal Declaration of Human Rights provides that all men are equal before the law, and are entitled without any discrimination to equal protection of the law. In May 1951, Dr. D. F. Malan, then Prime Minster, told the Union parliament that this provision of the Declaration applies in this country. . . . But the real truth is that there is in fact no equality before the law whatsoever as far as our people are concerned, and statements to the contrary are definitely incorrect and misleading. . . . The white man makes all the laws, he drags us before his courts and accuses us, and he sits in judgement over us. . . . I feel oppressed by the atmosphere of white domination that lurks all around in this courtroom. Somehow this atmosphere calls to mind the inhuman injustices caused to my people outside this courtroom by this same white domination. (Mandela 1990, 134)

In the end, all of the accused were acquitted, primarily because of prosecutorial incompetence.

Having failed to achieve its goal through the use of laws then on the books, the government, now under Verwoerd himself, adopted new laws. The ANC was included among a number of outlaw organizations under the 1960 Unlawful Organization Act. By 1963 such prominent ANC leaders as Walter Sisulu, Nelson Mandela, Robert Sobukwe, and Oliver Tambo were imprisoned or forced into exile, along with some 14,000 other blacks who had demonstrated in Sharpeville and participated in a number of bombings and sabotage under the rubric of "Umkonto" we Swezwe (Spear of the Nation)—an underground vigilante group. These leaders would not see freedom for a quarter century.

The 1960 Sharpeville Massacre was a case of police impatience. The Pan-African Congress, a black organization with somewhat more radical objectives than the ANC, organized a demonstration of 5,000 in what was thought to be a model township. However, unemployment, dissatisfaction with the pass laws, and forced migration had created a spirit of intense hostility with the white government. The marchers surrounded a police station where they waited for the better part of the day until a scuffle broke out, the crowd surged forward, and the police began shooting into the throng. Nearly 100 blacks were killed—most of them in the back—in the ensuing chaos. Luthuli called for a day of work stoppage and peaceful protest which the government in turn repressed by arresting 18,000 strikers across the country. New laws permitted the government to detain suspects indefinitely with a judge's approval and to detain for interrogation anyone the police wanted. The Public Safety Act allowed the government to declare a state of emergency and thereby suspend most of the few remaining civil rights in specific areas for limited but renewable periods of time (Omond 1985, 158). By 1963, South Africa was reviled in international circles as the worst human rights violators on the planet.

STALEMATE—1965–1988

The period 1965 to 1988 can be described as a stalemate between the galvanized but largely leaderless black community and the increasingly ambivalent white government unable to maintain both social domination and economic prosperity. The inflexible apartheid of the Verwoerd era was inherently unstable in that at the same time it protected the white population from association with blacks, it deprived the nation of its most important asset: black labor and intellect. At best, black Africans were learning to manipulate the system to their own ends—hardly the basis for legitimate government (Lambley 1980, 125). Even more serious was the impact of increasingly strict international economic and diplomatic sanctions on the vitality of the South African economy. These objective conditions ultimately forced the white government to reverse most of apartheid's structures during the 1980s and begin the process of democratizing the country in the 1990s.

A leaderless black community drifted for much of the 1960s until new philosophies and organizational structures began to emerge. Steve Biko, a black medical student, having failed to convince the white leaders of multiracial student organizations of a need for greater black participation and influence, worked to form an all-black student group known as the South African Student Organization (SASO) in 1968. Based on a firm belief that blacks in South Africa were part of a global struggle against oppression, and feeling that whites could never understand or represent their interests, SASO declared its manifesto in 1971:

SASO is a Black Student Organization working for the liberation of the Black man first from psychological oppression by themselves through inferiority complex and secondly from physical oppression occurring out of living in a White racist society . . . SASO believes: . . . That . . . because of the privileges accorded to them by legislation and because of their continual maintenance of an oppressive regime Whites have defined themselves as part of the problem. . . . That in all matters relating to the struggle towards realizing our aspirations, Whites must be excluded. . . . That this attitude not be interpreted by Blacks to imply "anti-Whitism" but merely a more positive way of attaining a normal situation in South Africa. (Fatton 1986, 70)

Steve Biko put it even more eloquently:

Black Consciousness is an attitude of mind and a way of life. . . . Its essence is the realization by the black man of the need to rally together with his brothers around the cause of their oppression—the blackness of their skin—and to operate as a group to rid themselves of the shackles that bind them to perpetual servitude. It is based on a self-examination which has ultimately led them to believe that by seeking to run away from themselves and emulate the white man, they are insulting the intelligence of whoever created them black. This philosophy of Black Consciousness therefore expresses group pride and the determination of the black to rise and attain the envisaged self. . . . (Fatton 1986, 78)

In the context of the spread of this Black Consciousness movement, black students across South Africa protested their forced education in Afrikans in the 1970s. In Soweto, an overcrowded township near Johannesburg where many black intellectuals resided, feelings were particularly strong and spilled over as large demonstrations. Over the course of several days in June 1976 these protests swelled to involve tens of thousands. Police fired into the crowd, which then went on a rampage through neighboring black and white areas for several days. In the end, nearly 600 black protesters were killed and 3,000 wounded. The police incarcerated and beat numerous individuals, not the least of whom was Steve Biko himself, who died following police beatings. As explained by Lapping, "Steve Biko's death may have been no worse than several dozen others. It was merely the one that attracted world attention and can therefore be described in most detail. Biko was never found guilty of any crime, never arrested for inciting violence, never accused of it" (Lapping 1986, 160).

Government repression intensified even as leaders of the National Party, which governed South Africa for most of the post-War era, began reconsidering the long-term viability of apartheid. Executions increased from roughly 50 each year in the mid-1970s to 125 per year in 1977–1980 (Omond 1985, 144). Outdoor meetings were banned selectively at first and then outright in 1983. Declarations of states of emergency became more common and travel restrictions intensified. The border with by-now radical black African neighboring states became a virtual war zone, complete with intensive patrols, periodic incursions against ANC members in exile, and strictly enforced prohibitions against foreign aid to what had by 1978 become an openly militarized outlaw ANC.

Meanwhile, the new prime minister, P. W. Botha, began seriously considering relaxing apartheid as early as 1979 in the face of growing opposition in the South African business community. Business leaders pointed out that the economy would thrive best if the work force—largely black—were stable and content (which the 100 strikes in 1979 steadily increasing to 1,000 strikes in 1989 proved was not the case—ILO 1990, 31), and if blacks could become affluent enough to provide a market for goods made in South Africa (St. Jorre 1986, 63). Foreign firms operating on the pro–civil rights "Sullivan principles" were proving that a policy of racial equality in the workplace could increase productivity and profitability.

The hope that traditional tribal leaders could somehow undermine black support for the ANC proved entirely baseless. Even the practice of recruiting blacks to serve in the police force and township government backfired, in that this simply made them targets of black hatred rather than legitimate representatives to their communities. Much of the black-on-black violence that occurred in the 1980s stemmed from tensions among blacks over loyalty to the state. Some form of democratic participation was clearly in the offing, even as the police, soon to be joined by the military, intensified their enforcement of old apartheid laws.

In the early 1980s, several regulations were passed which had the effect of loosening some of the more "purely irritating" aspects of apartheid, including the laws against interracial marriage. This led to an increase in the number of blacks admitted to white universities, a relaxation of restrictions on black job advancement, and somewhat more permissive pass laws (Omond 1985, 47, 85). In 1983 a new constitution came into effect which provided for two new non-white assemblies—one for Indians and one for coloureds. The government hoped that even if its chances of gaining support from blacks (who were still legally attached to their homelands rather than to Pretoria) were remote, it might secure the backing of other racial groups in an effort to legitimate white rule. Indians and coloureds stayed away from the polls in large numbers (only 10 to 15 percent of those eligible voted). Reverend Allan Boesak of the newly formed United Democratic Front, a loose coalition of moderate antiapartheid organizations, warned prospective Indian voters in 1983:

> Working within the system for whatever reason contaminates you. It wears down your defenses. It whets your appetite for power. . . . And what you call 'compromise' for the sake of politics is in fact selling out your principles, your ideals and the future of your children. . . . (Lapping 1986, 171)

Likewise, the other moves toward relaxation of apartheid did little if anything to satisfy blacks. The ANC continued to grow in popularity and strength, subsuming the Black Consciousness movement in 1984 and winning the support of moderate black leaders (Brewer 1986, 274). By 1984 the black opposition was clearly divided into the staunchly antiapartheid ANC and the more conservative accommodationist tribal leaders, including especially the Inkatha party under Buthelezi (who had entirely sold out, however).

saw themselves plunged into a protracted and ugly struggle for power between these major factions. It is also widely believed that the government
actively instigated and bankrolled Inkatha fighters in order to provoke anti-
ANC fighting (*Europa Yearbook 1993*, 2453).
in order to provoke anti-ANC fighting (*Europa Yearbook 1993*, 2453).

White South Africans were divided to the breaking point over the pace
and direction of reform. Racist Afrikaners broke with the National party to
form the Conservative party which soon became the major opposition in
Parliament and also resurrected an old vigilante organization—the
Afrikaner Resistance movement. Conservative party leader Andries Treurnicht defiantly declared:

> People who think that Mr. Botha's 'crossing of the Rubicon' and his abdication
> of white government mean the end of the Afrikaner and broader white national-
> ism are making a big mistake. We will not allow the Oppenheimers and
> American pressure groups to create a potpourri of people or to establish a non-
> racial economic empire upon the ruins of a white Christian culture and civiliza-
> tion. A people is only conquered when it has destroyed its own spirit. We are
> not prepared to consider national suicide . . . no one will silence the awakening
> white nation. The battle for the return of our political self-determination has
> only just begun. (Treurnicht 1986, 100)

Liberal white politicians increasingly coalesced around a collection of antiapartheid parties—particularly after the state of emergency began in 1985.
This culminated in the formation of the National Democratic movement in
1987. Botha's political support was thus being threatened from both the left
and the right until in 1989 he felt compelled to resign his post. The National
party under his successor F. W. de Klerk won less than half of the popular
vote that year, although it retained a majority of seats in Parliament.

In Sharpeville in 1984, black residents protested proposed rent and bus
fare increases by targeting the many black administrators in the area. Violence spread rapidly as many collaborators were subjected to the "necklace"
(a tire, doused in gasoline, placed around the victim's neck and set alight).
Unable to control the unrest, the government declared a state of emergency
(particularly around Port Elizabeth) in July 1985 (Lemon 1987, 339). Eight
thousand were arrested within the first year and over 750 killed by police
and army forces. The police quickly gained a reputation for brutality by
beating and electrocuting detainees on their way to prison. Children were
specifically targeted during this period—many of them shot in the back
while fleeing the soldiers. Children incarcerated under the state emergency
were, like their adult counterparts, subjected to torture, beating, terror, and
often death (Lawyers 1986, 6–8). Efforts by children to receive medical treatment at hospitals were frustrated by the police practice of arresting any in-
jured admitees—thus many died without treatment after being shot during
a demonstration. Likewise, attempts by physicians to reveal the extent of
prison violence were halted by official cover-ups. The state of emergency
was extended several times until it began to be lifted piecemeal in 1989 and

1990. Thirty more antiapartheid groups were banned, including the United Democratic Front, and some 50,000 individuals were detained from 1985 to 1988.

The Botha government worked simultaneously and feverishly to dismantle apartheid, hoping to not only placate the uncontrollable black demonstrators but also to lessen the ever-increasing international sanctions and business opposition, while stopping well short of granting Mandela's demand of legalization of the ANC and democratic elections (St. Jorre 1986, 81). As it turned out, nothing short of the complete elimination of apartheid would satisfy these various communities.

International sanctions intensified during the mid-1980s, including disinvestment by numerous foreign firms operating in the country. By the end of the decade, some $12 billion in foreign investments had been withdrawn or sold to local investors (in soft local currency of no use in repaying mounting foreign debts). International banks, bending to pressure from such institutional depositors as shareholders and universities, city governments and pensions, began imposing conditions of political reform on debt rescheduling. By 1989, the net effect of these sanctions was that the South African economy, according to local independent estimates, was some 15 percent smaller than it should have otherwise been. The World Bank downgraded South Africa's economic status from "upper middle income" to "lower middle income" (ILO 1990, 9). To express their dismay, in 1985 ninety-one South African business leaders took out an ad in the country's largest newspaper, calling for "the granting of full South African citizenship to all our people" and still others met with Walter Sisulu, leader-in-exile of the banned ANC, at his headquarters in Zambia to discuss dismantling apartheid (Mann 1988, 81).

DISMANTLING APARTHEID—1989+

Following P. W. Botha's resignation in 1989, the new government of F. W. de Klerk moved aggressively to dismantle the most disturbing and fundamental aspects of apartheid, in spite of growing white violence and continuing black violence. The French call this a "fuite en avant" ("forward retreat") whereby a desperate government makes itself radical for its own survival. In the case of the de Klerk government, the tactic thus far seems to have worked.

Between 1989 and 1991, the legislative keystones of apartheid were one by one removed: the Group Areas Act, the Separate Amenities Act, the Population Registration Act, and various provisions barring peaceful political assembly and organization. The state of emergency was lifted throughout much of the country (although continuing unrest may well have justified retaining the provision in certain areas), and police powers were circumscribed. Perhaps most dramatic of all: Nelson Mandela was released from prison in February 1990, shortly after Walter Sisulu was released and less than a year before Oliver Tambo, president of the ANC, returned to South Africa after a thirty-year exile. By 1992 the ANC enjoyed a full complement of leadership and unfettered rights to assemble, demonstrate, travel overseas, and eventually negotiate with the government as legitimate representatives of the bulk of blacks in South Africa. As put by Payne:

> By removing most of apartheid's legal underpinnings by June 1991, with the notable exception of black voting rights, South Africa had made a major and largely unanticipated first step toward creating a relatively egalitarian and nonracial society. The overwhelming white support in the March 1992 referendum for de Klerk's reforms underscored the commitment to change. Dismantling the more intractable social and economic components of a legal system of racial domination into which all South Africans had been socialized for almost half a century was clearly a more Herculean endeavor. Nonetheless, the vast majority of South Africans had embraced a hopeful but uncertain future. (Payne 1992, 149)

The political processes at work in South Africa today are centered on the Convention for a Democratic South Africa (CODESA), a constitutional convention bringing together nearly all black and most white parties and the homelands governments. While some black and white parties have rejected the legitimacy of the exercise, it has the full backing of the government, the Inkatha party, and the ANC. A referendum of white voters in February 1992 revealed that an overwhelming majority supported the CODESA efforts to establish a fully democratic government in South Africa. The result went far to marginalize white conservatives, who felt compelled to join the process. The funerals of Afrikaner nationalist Andries Treurnicht and black Communist leader Chris Hani in April 1993 were a study in contrasts, with tens of thousands mourning Hani and only a few hundred turning out for Treurnicht.

Events in September and October 1993 dramatically changed the prospects for a peaceful transition to democracy for South Africa. On the one hand, the CODESA process reached its conclusion with the drafting of a federal-style constitution which was expected to be ratified by the white-controlled Parliament. Prior to that, a "super cabinet" consisting of representatives of each party involved in CODESA was proposed, accepted by Parliament, and organized to control the National party's cabinet during the transition (*New York Times*, September 24, 1993, A1). The so-called Transitional Executive Council (TEC) will have the power to override de Klerk's government in order to assure fairness in the national elections set for April 27, 1994. These remarkable steps forward resulted in an end to the sweeping economic and diplomatic boycotts imposed on South Africa by the United Nations, the Organization for African Unity, the Commonwealth, and the European Community, not to mention the United States as well. Loans and investments are expected to flow freely into South Africa to take advantage of the end of sanctions (*Christian Science Monitor*, October 1, 1993, 8). As recognition for their achievement, Nelson Mandela and Frederik de Klerk were awarded the Nobel Peace Prize in mid-October.

These historic achievements may not, however, be the beginning of South Africa's healing, but instead could mark an intensified and broader conflict. The ANC-Inkatha rivalry intensified as black-on-black violence has resulted in an average of ten deaths each day. A short-lived show of solidarity by Mandela and Buthelezi collapsed into mutual recriminations as Buthelezi pulled his Inkatha Freedom party out of CODESA. He demands virtual autonomy for the KwaZulu region he governs—something Mandela has been unwilling to grant. Blacks in Buthelezi's native KwaZulu Natal province are split in their support of the ANC and Inkatha, and many view Buthelezi's efforts as a last-ditch attempt to retain some degree of power.

This message is also being sent loudly by white conservatives who have felt their meager influence slipping away. Although only able to muster 5 percent of the vote in a national popularity polls, Afrikaners engaged in secret talks with Mandela and de Klerk in which they demanded control over territory constituting 16 percent of South Africa's total (*Christian Science Monitor*, September 27, 1993, 2). When Mandela publicly rejected the Afrikaners' demand for "self-determination," they pulled out of the negotiations and subsequently joined forces with Buthelezi to form the "Freedom Alliance" (*Christian Science Monitor*, October 13, 1993, 2). Both Mandela and de Klerk recognize the danger inherent in a coalition of these disaffected parties, and are torn between the need to include the maximum number of participants in the transition process and the need to proceed with the elections as scheduled. Failure on either score will likely result in widespread violence—the choice may be between which option would be the most bloody.

At the time of writing (early April 1994), the candidates were hard at work, with de Klerk campaigning in black townships and Mandela speaking to groups of white businessmen in an effort to broaden their respective political bases. Polls still showed an overwhelming advantage to Mandela, however.

The key issue as the election approached was the extent of participation by populations living in the soon-to-be-dissolved homelands. Leaders in Ciskei, Bophuthatswana and elsewhere announced in March, 1994, their determination to prevent the April elections in their homelands, only to find their respective police forces, intellectual elites, and civil servants, rising up in protest. In each case, unrest grew so intense that the South African police, under the direction of the TEC, took control of the homeland to guarantee safe and fair elections (*New York Times*, March 23, 1994, A1).

The key holdout was Buthelezi and his KwaZulu homeland. Unlike other homeland leaders, Buthelezi was strongly supported by the Zulu ethnic group in his determination to prevent elections. As Pretoria moved against other regions, Zulus took up arms against ANC and government targets. Dozens died in violent clashes in Johannesburg in late March, and unrest spread in the streets of Durban and other KwaZulu cities. The TEC ordered additional troops into the area, but the Independent Electoral Commission feared in early April that it would be impossible to hold fair elections without risking whole-sale civil war. Elections in Kwazulu-Natal were held only after a last-minute agreement with Buthelezi (*Chicago Sun Times,* April 6, 1994, 26).

The achievements of Mandela and de Klerk certainly merit the recognition they have received, but it is clear that perilous dangers still face them. How the South African leadership and people will move through this historic transition is as yet uncertain.

Questions to Consider

1. To what extent has nonviolence succeeded where violence has not? Have Mahatma Gandhi's theories been validated by the South Africa experience?

2. How have human rights been perceived by various groups in South Africa? How have South Africans responded to international standards of human rights?

3. To what extent has the international community succeeded in changing the human rights policies of the South African government? Does this strengthen the case for economic sanctions?

References

John D. Brewer. *After Soweto: An Unfinished Journey* (Oxford: Clarendon Press, 1986).

Godfrey N. Brown. *Apartheid: A Teacher's Guide* (New York: UNESCO, 1981).

Chicago Sun Times, April 6, 1994, 26.

Christian Science Monitor, September 27, 1993, 2

Christian Science Monitor, October 1, 1993, 8

Christian Science Monitor, October 13, 1993, 2

Europa Yearbook 1993 (London: Europa Publishers, 1993).

Robert Fatton Jr. *Black Consciousness in South Africa: The Dialectics of Ideological Resistance to White Supremacy* (Albany: SUNY Press, 1986).

J. A. Hobson. *Imperialism* (Ann Arbor: University of Michigan Press, 1965).

International Labor Organization. *Special Report of the Director-General on the Application of the Declaration Concerning Action Against Apartheid in South Africa and Namibia* (Geneva: ILO, 1990).

Peter Lambley. *The Psychology of Apartheid* (Athens: University of Georgia press, 1980).

Brian Lapping. *Apartheid: A History* (New York: George Braziller, 1986).

Lawyers Committee for Human Rights. *The War Against Children: South Africa's Youngest Victims* (New York: Lawyers Committee, 1986).

Anthony Lemon. *Apartheid in Transition* (Boulder, CO: Westview Press, 1987).

Bernard Makhosezwe Magubane. *The Political Economy of Race and Class in South Africa* (New York: Monthly Review Press, 1979).

Nelson Mandela. *The Struggle Is My Life* (New York: Pathfinder, 1990).

Michael Mann. "The Giant Stirs: South African Business in the Age of Reform," in Philip Krankel, Noam Pines, and Mark Swilling, eds., *State Resistance and Change in South Africa* (London: Croom Helm, 1988), 52–86.

New York Times, September 24, 1993, A1.

New York Times, March 23, 1994, A1.

Roger Omond. *The Apartheid Handbook* (London: Penguin, 1985).

Richard J. Payne. *The Third World and South Africa: Post-Apartheid Challenges* (Westport, CT: Greenwood Press, 1992).

Republic of South Africa. *Progress Through Separate Development: South Africa in Peaceful Transition* (New York: Information Service of South Africa, 1973).

John de St. Jorre. "White South Africa Circles the Wagons," in Mark A. Uhlig, ed., *Apartheid in Crisis* (New York: Vintage Books, 1986), 61–84.

Andries P. Treurnicht. "Conservative Party Congress Speech," in Mark A. Uhlig, ed., *Apartheid in Crisis* (New York: Vintage Books, 1986), 100–102.

C A S E   1 6

Yugoslavia's Collapse

Anarchy is perhaps the most essential concept of international relations. Simply put, it describes the international system, lacking a central political authority capable of imposing order. At the global level, such a state of affairs has existed at least since the days of the medieval Holy Roman Empire, if not the Roman Empire itself. Although the term anarchy connotes chaos and violence, we can see in the chapters on international law and organization that this need not be the case. Only when anarchy prevails at the local level do we often find bloodshed and mayhem, as in the case of Yugoslavia.

In collecting evidence for a future war crimes trial in Yugoslavia, the U.S. State Department has certified the following accounts:

July 24, 1992: 200–300 [Muslim] men [were imprisoned in] a single room estimated to be about 80 square meters [about 1,000 square feet] in size, with a small alcove in the right rear corner. The room had a single window high up in the front wall above a large sheet metal garage-type door with a smaller opening in it. Prisoners received little water or food. The temperature in the room was stifling, the conditions nearly unbearable. On July 24, the prisoners in the room were given some water, but in the words of one of the witnesses, 'they put something in the water' and the men 'became crazy.' Then something was shot through the window which produced smoke and gas. The prisoners began screaming and pounding on the doors; some began to hallucinate and fight each other. Others managed to force a hole in the sheet metal of a door and started to escape the room, but were then killed by guards standing outside.

After the disturbances in the room had gone on for some time, the soldiers opened fire with large machine guns. The bullets came right through the sheet metal doors. Those near the door were killed first.... An estimated 150 men were killed or wounded. On the following day, July 25, soldiers came into the room and chose about 20 of the surviving prisoners, took them outside, lined them up against an outside wall of the room, and shot them. (U.S. State Dept. Dispatch November 16, 1992, 826)

Sept 24, 1992: Muslims from Kamenica reportedly killed more than 60 Serb civilians and soldiers in Serbian villages near Milici on September 24–26. An American freelance writer reported that he saw the bodies of mutilated and tortured Serbs from the villages of Rogosija and Nedeljiste at the St. Paul and Peter Serbian Orthodox Church in Vlasenica after the Lids on about 10 of the coffins were removed by soldiers for viewing: 'Some bodies were burned to a charcoal, others had fingers cut off on their right hand which the Orthodox use to bless themselves, some were circumcised as a final affront [contrary to Orthodox teaching], some had their eyes gouged out, gaping knife wounds everywhere, and heads were battered beyond recognition, arms and legs broken and severed'. (U.S. State Dept. Dispatch November 16, 1992, 825)

May 21, 1992: A former employee of the Zvornik medical center reported that he was required to remain on duty in the center from April 8 until his dismissal on May 26. He said that the need for more hospital space for wounded Serbian soldiers eventually led to the mass murder of Muslim patients on May 21. At about 1 pm that day, he watched as 36 remaining Muslim adult patients were forced outside and shot to death on hospital grounds. Shortly thereafter, uniformed and non-uniformed Serbian soldiers moved through the pediatric center breaking the necks and bones of the 27 remaining Muslim children, the only children left as patients in the hospital. Two soldiers forced him to watch for about 15 minutes, during which time about 10 or 15 of the children were slaughtered. Some were infants. The oldest were about 5 years old. The witness said that a Serbian surgeon, who also stood by helplessly, later went insane. (U.S. State Dept. Dispatch November 16, 1992, 828)

One cannot read this without being both moved and disgusted. Questions beg to be answered: How could this happen? How could people justify this bloodshed in their minds? Was the civil war in Yugoslavia inevitable—a product of international anarchy? Or is it a unique aberration in history? And more importantly, can the international community do anything to restore some order and peace?

Lest the reader assume that all combatants in the Yugoslav civil war are without conscience, the following moment is instructive:

One of the victims of an earlier reported rape of 40 young women from Brezovo Polje [by Serbian soldiers] told a reporter in late August that her Serbian abductor had told her, 'We have orders to rape the girls. I am ashamed to be a Serb. Everything that is going on is a war crime' (U.S. State Dept. Dispatch November 16, 1992, 831)

HISTORY TO 1918

To a certain extent, the history of ethnic relations in Yugoslavia has seen little disruption: increasingly mobilized linguistic and religious communities find themselves overwhelmed by a foreign invader; the communities either collaborate or resist; the invader becomes increasingly unable to maintain control on the fringe territory; a new invader unseats the previous power, giving the local community the opportunity to develop a new political arrangement (*Economist*, August 23, 1992, 36.) In the process, differences between the communities are exaggerated and rivalries based on the different experiences emerge.

The earliest Balkan peoples arrived near the dawn of man, but were organized only at the family, clan, or tribe level. It was not until the early Middle Ages that these nations became a force to be reckoned with. Bulgaria reached its zenith during the tenth century, Croatia in the eleventh, and Bosnia and Serbia were each independent kingdoms of some note in the fourteenth century. Although these moments of glory may seem quaint episodes from the perspective of modern times, these glory days soon became imbedded in the concept of "rightful heritage" which continues today: "In the nineteenth century the national leaders, looking back on this period, tended to consider the maximum extension of their medieval kingdoms as the natural historical boundaries for their nations" (Jelavich 1983 I, 27).

By the fifteenth century, however, the Balkans was the battleground of empires, much like Poland to the north. Contact with numerous powerful empires left its imprint on Balkan society and spirit (see Map 16.1). "In each region the population represented a fusion of original inhabitants with subsequent invaders, an amalgamation achieved through military conquest by a stronger group, the absorption of one people by another owing to the weight of numbers, or the acceptance of another language because of the cultural attraction offered by a more advanced civilization" (Jelavich 1983 I, 27).

The Ottoman Empire, a relic of the great Muslim nation established by the prophet Mohammed, advanced into the Balkans and beyond in the fifteenth century, and defeated the Serbs and their allies in 1444 at the battle of Varna (still cited as a dark day in Serbian history). By the year 1500 the Muslims had established firm control over the Balkan peoples, pressuring them to embrace Islam and submit to the "Porte" or central government. The Ottoman hold continued through the seventeenth century, when Russian and Hapsburg (a central European dynasty embracing a wide variety of nationalities) armies threatened the Balkan territories. Christian dissent, of both the Orthodox and Catholic varieties, was exacerbated by these competing external forces, and in the eighteenth century the Porte began to lose its authority in Croatia, Slavonia, and other fringe territories.

Some of the Ottoman domain was simply seized and controlled by Russia and the Hapsburgs. In other cases, such as Montenegro, the hostility of both the terrain and the people prevented any effective administration. In still others, such as Serbia, local Muslim strongmen emerged, exercising dictatorial powers without sanction from the Porte.

In the case of Croatia, the Hapsburgs, while dominant, permitted the surviving Catholic elites to exercise considerable discretion and power over the domain. Orthodox Serbs remained organized, thanks largely to geogra-

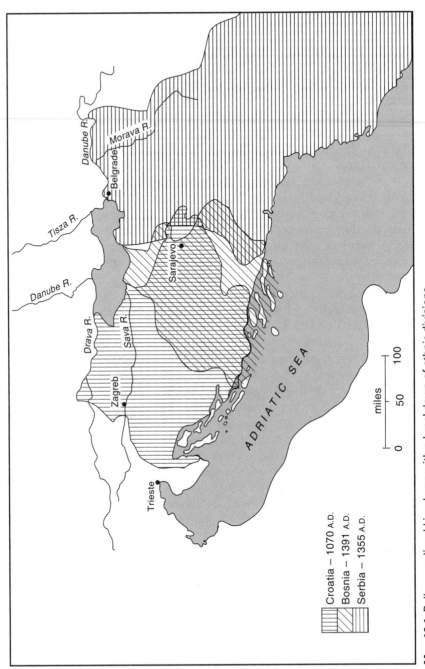

Map 16.1 Balkan medieval kingdoms with a breakdown of ethnic divisions.

Source: Adapted from Barbara Delavich, *History of the Balkans: 18th and 19th Centuries* (New York: Cambridge University Press, 1983).

phy and the tenacity of the Orthodox church hierarchy. In Bosnia, most of the elites converted to Islam, but only one-third of the general population did so, leaving the Orthodox as the largest group.

During the second half of the eighteenth century, war raged across the region, particularly in Bosnia and in Serbia, where local Serbs rebelled against despotic Muslim leaders with Porte endorsement. By 1806, the Serbs, successful on the battlefield and far from the Porte's power, established an independent kingdom. Although the Ottomans were able to reassert some control, the Porte gave the Serbs considerable autonomy—a condition that would continue to some degree until World War I (Jelavich 1983 I, 196).

The Croats of the Hapsburg Empire were nominally subject to the Hungarian crown. Croats repeatedly sought greater autonomy and status within the empire, demanding control of newly acquired territories to the south and east. An emerging Croat intelligentsia began to assert national ideals in the late seventeenth century and by 1830 were caught up in the nationalist spirit of Europe. They demanded the right to educate their children in Croat (not Latin) and claimed the status of freemen in relation to Hungary. They resented Hapsburg attempts at "divide and rule" (Cohen 1992, 369). The unrest boiled over into full-fledged rebellion in 1848, during the Hapsburg Revolution, and Hungary, Zagreb, and Vienna went to war. Because Croatia fought against Hungary on the side of Vienna, it expected to gain more autonomy when Budapest fell. In fact, little changed and Croatia rebelled again in 1871. While this disturbance was quelled, Croatia was granted additional powers (Jelavich 1983 I, 206).

Shortly after Croatia attempted to secure autonomy from the Hapsburgs in general and Hungary in particular, Bosnia and Serbia were in revolt against the Ottomans. The conflict was exacerbated by the active involvement of Russia, the Hapsburgs, and other continental powers, eager to bring stability and their presence to a volatile and strategic region. The Treaty of San Stefano (1877), a largely Russian creation, provided for an independent Serbia and Montenegro as well as an overwhelming Bulgaria under Russian occupation. The Congress of Berlin in 1878 was called by the other European powers to counter this Russian power play, and led to both a much smaller Bulgaria and Bosnia-Herzegovina's inclusion in the Hapsburg Empire (Jelavich 1983 I, 358). The problem of Macedonia was finessed by simply leaving it under Ottoman control—the last major bastion of Muslim power (see Map 16.2). Macedonia would prove to be a persistent bone of contention between Serbia (and Yugoslavia), Bulgaria, and Greece for the next century—and is still a major diplomatic concern today (Stravianos 1963, 95).

The late nineteenth century brought with it an increasing sense of frustration, borne of the mitigated success of each group. Increasingly Balkan peoples understood that they could achieve more by joining together, but the years of conquest and division had left profound animosities. Serbs considered Bosnia and Macedonia their rightful heritage, based largely on medieval and ethnic considerations. Croats felt largely the same way about

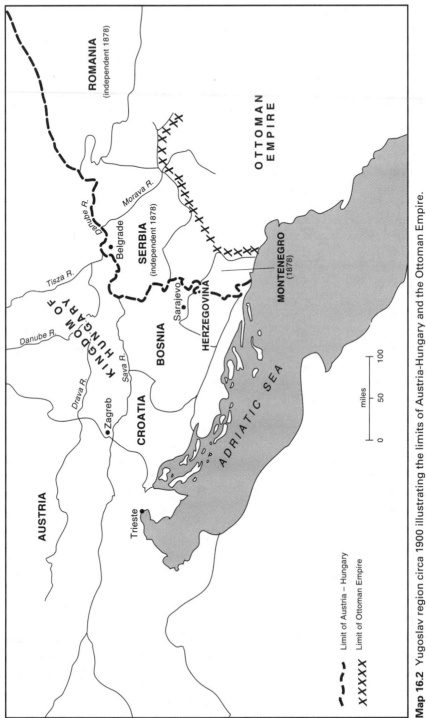

Map 16.2 Yugoslav region circa 1900 illustrating the limits of Austria-Hungary and the Ottoman Empire.

Source: Barbara Jelavich, *History of the Balkans: 18th and 19th Centuries; 20th Century* (New York: Cambridge University Press, 1983), vols. 1 and 2.

Bosnia. The Muslim population of Bosnia was never considered "authentic" by Serbs or Croats, coming as it did as a product of Ottoman imperialism (Djilas and Mousavizadeh 1992, 26). Not only were these antagonisms ethnically based, but it soon became clear that there were concrete balance-of-power considerations that made suspicion and apprehension rational attitudes. None of the Balkan states had the capacity to insure its own safety, and any alliance between neighbors could tip the balance against a lone state. Hence the combination of competing experiences with outside powers, perceptions of national heritage, religion, language, and security concerns combined to prevent a lasting bond between the nations (Armour 1992, 11).

The great power game of continental Europe was being played with gusto by the turn of the century. Austria wanted to strengthen its southern borders and so decided to annex Bosnia outright, for which it received Russia's tacit blessing. This move naturally enraged Serb leaders who felt betrayed by their erstwhile sponsors (Stravianos 1963, 110). At about the same time, the traditional leadership in the Ottoman Empire was overthrown by the "Young Turk" revolt. These young colonels were determined to bring a sense of national unity to all the empire's colonies. The Balkan States saw this as a concrete threat to their hard-earned independence and for the first time organized a strong alliance. The alliance was so confident that in 1912 they launched an attack against Turkish forces and succeeded in pushing them virtually off the continent.

Ironically, it was as a result of their success that the most tragic episode of Balkan relations began. The question of territorial compensation aroused intense disagreement, since each nation felt its military victories had earned them more spoils of war than they were slated to receive. In particular, Russia's demand that a new Albanian state be formed from the former Ottoman territories angered Serbia, since it anticipated direct control over the area. Serbia sought an extra piece of Montenegro and Macedonia as compensation, which in turn infuriated the Bulgarians and Montenegrins. War broke out. Serbian and Greek forces overwhelmed the Bulgarian army. Serbia then proceeded to annex most of Macedonia outright. The Treaty of Bucharest (1913) was signed in an effort to show that the problem was resolved, but it simply "papered over cracks for the time being. The period between the Balkan Wars and World War I was but a breathing spell during which Balkan states jockeyed for position. . . . From the Balkan point of view, World War I was essentially a continuation of the Balkan Wars" (Stavrianos 1963, 113).

World War I, made almost inevitable by a hair-trigger alliance network, long-standing grievances, gross imbalances of power, and the end of colonial opportunities, was sparked by a gunman in Sarajevo, a member of a Serbian nationalist group, who shot the Austrian archduke Ferdinand in July 1914. Austria declared war on Serbia, Serbia allied with Russia, Russia declared war on Austria, Austria allied with Germany, and so on. Four years and 16 million dead later, the war ended.

As the defeated Hapsburg and Ottoman Empires were dismantled, many new nation-states were formed. Even before the war ended, Croats and Slovenes were organizing a postwar united Yugoslavia which could become the strongest nation in the Balkans and aspire to great power status in Europe. A Yugoslav Committee was formed and it prepared a draft constitution providing for Serbian participation. When the proposal was forwarded to the Serbian monarchy, it was accepted almost immediately. "Thus the organization of the Yugoslav state was primarily the work of national committees, and the initiative came from the Hapsburg South Slavs" (Jelavich 1983 II, 147). The proposal had to be validated in London, where the territory was formally mapped. On December 1, 1918, the Kingdom of the Serbs, Croats, and Slovenes was officially proclaimed (Cohen 1992, 369).

1918 TO 1980

The first attempt at Yugoslav federation failed after ten years, when the largely nationality based parliament demanded more autonomy for the various regions than the central government in Belgrade was willing to concede (see Map 16.3). Serbs in Belgrade hoped to instill a sense of national unity, but these efforts only exacerbated tensions (Cohen 1992, 370). "The basic problem of the state was that, despite the hopes of some intellectuals and political leaders before 1914, a Yugoslav nationality did not come into existence" (Jelavich 1983 II, 151).

The principal rivalry was between Croats and Serbians, since the smaller ethnic groups were able to bargain for concessions from the Serbs in exchange for support. Questions of language use, representation in the government, and self-rule became extremely intense in the late 1920s, and in 1929, following violent demonstrations in Zagreb, the king dismantled parliamentary institutions and imposed a dictatorship on the country. He was assassinated in 1934. His successor brought back some of the democratic structures, only to see his country overwhelmed by German Nazi forces in 1941.

The wartime experience of Yugoslavia has often been cited as a cause of the present antagonism. Much of this is because the Catholic Croatian region was treated very differently from the Orthodox Serbian areas. Croatia was granted independence and membership in the various Axis-led international organizations. This diplomatic status and newfound autonomy, after years of failed attempts, was greeted warmly by many Croats. "A wave of enthusiasm pervaded Zagreb at this time, not unlike that which had swept through the town in 1918 when the ties with Hungary were severed" (Jelavich 1983, II 264). The Catholic hierarchy gave firm instructions to the clergy to serve the new rulers. In the words of the Zagreb archbishop: "These are events . . . which fulfill the long dreamed of and desired ideal of our people. . . . Respond readily to my call to join in the noble task of work-

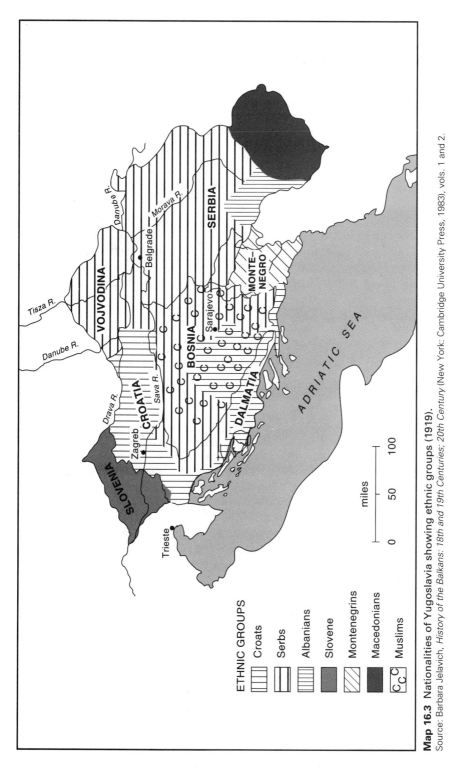

Map 16.3 Nationalities of Yugoslavia showing ethnic groups (1919).

Source: Barbara Jelavich, *History of the Balkans: 18th and 19th Centuries; 20th Century* (New York: Cambridge University Press, 1983), vols. 1 and 2.

244 CONFLICT IN THE PERIPHERY

ing for the safety and well-being of the Independent State of Croatia" (Maclean 1957, 88). The clergy worked with the fascist regime to force thousands of Orthodox Serbs to convert to Catholicism.

Croatia slipped into the fascist mode, and the new leadership worked closely with Italy. Moderate elements retired from the scene as the Ustasa movement, a fascist Croatian group based in Italy, undertook a systematic and egregious rule of terror. Serbs residing in Croatia were the primary target and they "suffered greatly at the hands of the Croatian fascists . . . " (Cohen 1992, 371). According to the current Bosnian Serb leader, some 700,000 Serbs were killed from 1941 to 1945 at Croatian Catholic and Muslim hands (Karadzic 1992, 50). These atrocities left deeply bitter memories among Serbs.

Meanwhile, Josip Broz Tito, leader of the outlawed Communist party, organized a highly effective resistance movement in the mountains around Serbia and Bosnia. Because Yugoslavia's collapse had been swift, Germany never completely occupied the country and there were many peasants with weapons ready to take to the mountains, as their forefathers had done so many times before. Another substantial resistance movement, the Chetniks, was formed, but because its aims were to restore the monarchy, the two rarely collaborated. By the end of the war the Chetniks were found to have worked with the Nazis (Jelavich 1983, II 267).

By the end of the war, tensions were extremely high between the various groups. Partisans regularly rounded up and shot Croatian fascists. One incident reveals the depth of animosity:

> As the Ustase were being led off to execution, a peasant woman rushed into the middle of them and began scratching and hitting at them, screaming all the time. The Partisans had difficulty pulling her off them. Then the shots rang out and she again rushed forward, this time among the corpses, dancing in the blood. "A-ah!" she gasped, dripping with sweat and blood. It seemed the Ustase had slaughtered all her sons. (Maclean 1957, 156)

Fearful of such reprisals, one particularly large group of Ustase surrendered to the British in the closing days of the war, only to be sent back to the Partisans. Reports indicate that between 40,000 and 100,000 of them were killed within days (Jelavich 1983 II, 272).

Tito organized a government among the Partisans, although a royal government-in-exile in London had the support of the United States and Britain. To consolidate his political support in Yugoslavia, Tito declared Macedonia, previously a province of Serbia, a full-fledged republic in the future Yugoslavia, a status which did and still does profoundly disturb Greece to the south and Bulgaria to the east. Tito received Soviet support and recognition and moved early after the war to join the emerging Soviet bloc as a socialist state. An ill-fated USSR-inspired attempt at a Balkan federation failed by 1948, which contributed in part to the eventual separation of Yugoslavia and the Soviet Union.

Tito embarked on a unique and solitary path toward socialism based on decentralized worker organizations, tolerance of nationalities, and intense socialist propaganda campaigns (Jelavich 1983 II, 388). Tito hoped that socialist solidarity and idealism, combined with dynamic economic growth and prosperity, would lead to a pan-Yugoslav nationalism. He put this nationalism into practice by leading the Non-Aligned movement and working with the West at various junctures.

Tito's nationalism in international affairs was undercut by continual tension over the division of the political spoils among the national republics at home. In 1967, 1971, 1981, and throughout Yugoslav history, ethnic tensions remained. As put by Jelavich:

> With the loosening of the central bonds, more authority was transferred to the capitals of the republics, the majority of which had been, and still were, strongholds of fervent nationalist sentiments. When disputes arose over economic or political questions, the local leaders tended to dust off the old flags and symbols and return with enthusiasm to the battles of the past. . . . (Jelavich 1983 II, 388)

Tito felt compelled in 1971 to use force to suppress first Croatian and later Kosovo Albanian demands for greater autonomy and more national rights. Through it all, he appealed to the people's socialist solidarity to overcome these political disputes. In the final analysis, however, Marxism failed as an integrative force in Yugoslavia (Braun 1983, 37). Tito died in 1980 without a clear successor. As would be seen in the 1990s, not only did Tito not have a successor, but with the removal of the Communist state "all that remained was the nation, and the ideology of nationalism" (Hayden 1992, 43).

AFTER TITO

The decade of the 1980s was one of economic hardship and lack of central leadership in Yugoslavia, which together accentuated nationalist demands in Croatia. The League of Yugoslav Communists failed to maintain cohesion, even though after forty years there were many party officials, military commanders, and government agents who were firmly entrenched in the federal bureaucracy (Cohen 1992, 370).

By 1987, Slobodan Milosevic emerged as a Serbian leader resentful that Croatians and others had encroached on Serb influence in Belgrade:

> Through his brash articulation of Serbia's political discontent, and particularly his populist mobilization of Serbian ethnic consciousness at mass rallies—sometimes referred to as 'street democracy'—Milosevic challenged the oligarchic Titoist style of managing the 'national question' and also provoked a sharp nationalist backlash from Yugoslavia's other republics and ethnic groups. (Cohen 1992, 371)

The winds of democracy swept through Yugoslavia following the tumultuous fall of 1989. Between April and December 1990, each republic held elections. In Slovenia, Croatia, Bosnia, and Macedonia, new democratic parties were elected, while former Communists were returned to power in Serbia, Montenegro, and Vojvodina.

Although the elections of 1990 were an impressive exercise in regime transition, the results left the country even more politically fragmented than it had been during the last days of Communist rule. Thus, whether born-again Communists or non-Communists, both the newly elected political authorities and the bulk of the opposition forces in all regions of Yugoslavia were committed to programs of regional and ethnic nationalism that seriously challenged the power of the federal system (Cohen 1992, 371).

Milosevic, following an undemocratic election, spearheaded efforts to preserve the federation with Serbia at the center, finding considerable support among the federal power elite. He proposed a "modern federation" which would preserve the size of the military and the predominance of the Communist party. In the meantime, he supported efforts by Serbs residing outside of Serbia to exercise self-determination, while maintaining their potential rights to citizenship in Serbia proper.

This question of ethnic rights for minorities came to a head later in 1990 when the Croatian assembly approved a constitution which failed to specifically mention protection of the rights of Serbs living in Croatia. This move was repeated across the nation. As put by Hayden:

> The solution found in the various Yugoslav republics was the creation of systems of a constitutional and legal structure that guarantees privileges to the members of one nation over those of any other residents in a particular state. (Hayden 1992, 41)

Serbians living in Krajina, a Croatian city where Serbs are in the majority, began demonstrating against Croatian authority and seized control of government bureaus and facilities. In early 1991 the Croatian government moved to suppress the unrest.

WARFARE IN SLOVENIA AND CROATIA

During the first part of 1991, Slovenia and Croatia moved toward outright independence by directly challenging the legitimacy of the shared federal presidency. In March, when the Croatian delegate was scheduled to take his seat at the head of the table, the Serbian delegation protested and in May vetoed it altogether (*New York Times,* May 19, 1991, A1).

While attempts were made to preserve the federal structure, irreconcilable demands and fast progress toward independence and diplomatic recognition in Slovenia and Croatia frustrated the efforts (*New York Times,* June 7, 1991, A5). When the Croatian and Slovene parliaments approved independence resolutions on June 26, the Bush administration announced its "regret" for such "unilateral action," implicitly endorsing Belgrade repression (Cohen 1992, 373). On June 28, Yugoslav tanks battled Slovene troops that had taken control of border posts. Slovenia defeated the incursion and held firm to independence in spite of Belgrade concessions. European Community officials offered to mediate the dispute and by early July managed to sketch out terms of a settlement. In August, however, it became clear that many of the soldiers in the field had no loyalty to the Belgrade government. Yugoslav army units were "out of control" (*New York Times*, August 30, 1991, A3).

In Croatia, violence erupted in Zagreb and quickly spread across the region inhabited by Serbs. Serb fighters used Croatian civilians as human shields when attacking Croatian outposts (*New York Times*, July 31, 1991, A1). Conversely, Serbian soldiers with Croatian relatives agonized over orders to shoot (*New York Times*, October 1, 1991, A1). The fighting intensified over the fall and continued through most of 1992. Vukovar was described as a "wasteland" in November after eighty-six days of shelling and aerial bombardment (*New York Times*, November 21, 1992, A1). By December, the actions lost most of their strategic content and took on the form of vendettas. Reports of unconfirmed atrocities became commonplace by early 1992. By the end of initial phase of hostilities in March, some 10,000 were dead and 500,000 homeless.

The Western response was tepid at best. In spite of Germany's insistence, the European Community did not officially extend diplomatic recognition until January 1992 and the United States waited until the spring. These delays hampered attempts to treat the problem as an international, rather than civil, conflict. Some have argued that this inaction helped intensify the fighting (Mastnak 1992, 11).

Over the course of several months, beginning in November, the UN Security Council deliberated a proposal to send a group of peacekeeping forces to monitor a future cease-fire in Croatia. This force, originally pegged at 10,000, was ultimately increased to 14,000 and was deployed strategically not only in the Serb-inhabited zones of Croatia ("pink zones"), but also in Belgrade and Sarajevo. Wanting to assure himself that the UN troops would not be in serious danger, the new Secretary-General Boutros Boutros-Ghali waited until a cease-fire held for several days. This did not happen until March, following Croatian, Serbian, and eventually Serb-Croatian support (although in the case of Serbs living in Croatia, supporters of the peacekeeping operation had to force out an intransigent leadership—*New York Times*, February 22, 1992, A1). The troops' arrival on March 16 marked the end of civil war in Croatia for the time being.

WARFARE IN BOSNIA

No sooner did peacekeepers arrive in Croatia than a full-scale war broke out in Bosnia-Herzegovina. The scale of atrocities approaches World War II proportions, prompting the coining of a new phrase in international discourse: "ethnic cleansing."

Bosnian leaders declared their independence from the rest of Yugoslavia in October 1991 and scheduled a referendum for early March 1992. Ethnic Serbs, which make up roughly one-third of the Bosnian population, protested by boycotting the vote. On March 1 the country overwhelmingly approved independence. Within a month, Serb irregulars were fighting in the streets of Bosnia with the support of the local leader, Radovan Karadzic. During a large proindependence rally in Sarajevo in early April, Serb sharpshooters fired into the crowd, killing dozens. They then fled into the mountains to begin organizing a large guerrilla force. Serbian leaders in Bosnia immediately received considerable support from the Serbian government, which by late April had declared itself, along with Montenegro, Vojvodina, and a reluctant Kosovo, a rump Yugoslav federation.

The international community acted swiftly in granting recognition to Bosnia (Cohen 1992, 374). Discussion of deploying peacekeepers began almost immediately, and Boutros Boutros-Ghali was forced to slow things down by pointing out that the level of violence in Bosnia posed a grave danger to any future deployment. He also rejected a call from Bosnian Muslim President Alija Izetbegovic for an "intervention force" on the ground that this would require "many tens of thousands" of soldiers—far beyond the UN's capacity (*UN Chronicle,* September 1992, 8).

The scale of destruction in Bosnia far exceeded that of Croatia. The artillery barrage against Sarajevo continued virtually uninterrupted for the next year, with as many as 3,000 shells falling on the city in a single day. Serbs moved quickly to gain control of Bosnian territory and by summer had seized nearly three-fourths of the territory. The refugee population grew at the rate of 30,000 per day in the early months of the war.

After some hesitation to take sides, the UN Security Council began in May to condemn not just the war and its associated atrocities, but specifically Serbia and the Serbs of Bosnia. The United States and European Community imposed economic and diplomatic sanctions against Serbia and Montenegro in April, expanding them in May. On May 30, 1992, the Security Council placed blame for the violence squarely on Serbia and called for sanctions on the basis of Chapter VII of the UN Charter (*New York Times,* May 31, 1992, A1). In September Yugoslavia's UN membership was revoked, in spite of serious legal questions ("Current Development" 1992, 832).

The focus of UN efforts in Bosnia was the provision of humanitarian assistance to the besieged Muslims in Sarajevo and other towns and villages that were cut off from food and fuel supplies. The Sarajevo airport, overrun by Serb gunmen, was eventually opened thanks to Security Council intervention and much diplomatic activity, including a personal visit by François Mitterand, president of France (*New York Times,* June 29, 1992, A1). Serbs continued to block access to more remote villages on the grounds that even humanitarian assistance had significant military implications, prompting the Security Council to pass a resolution in late June allowing military escorts for humanitarian aid convoys. The Security Council later approved the use of "all necessary means"—a phrase taken from the Gulf War—to ensure that aid reached its destination (*Economist,* August 15, 1992, 37–38). Although direct confrontation was avoided, in March 1993 the rather innovative tactic of airdrops brought significant amounts of food. Perhaps the most heroic figure in the war has been General Phillippe Morillon, commander of UN forces in eastern Bosnia, who has made the saving of Srebreniza his personal quest. Entering the Muslim enclave in spite of shelling and inadequate food, he defied the Serbian troops to attack the helpless city. Even this effort has largely failed, however, since many Muslims were eager to abandon the city (against Bosnian Muslims military leaders' hopes) and the secretary-general was growing weary of Morillon's grandstanding (*New York Times,* April 8, 1993, A5).

Eventually, the UN became actively involved in evacuating Muslims from such cities as Srebreniza and Gorazde. Such intervention raised disturbing questions about UN complicity with Serbian ethnic cleansing, the practice of deliberate depopulation of Muslim-dominated regions. Ethnic cleansing not only involved the forced removal of thousands but also mass executions and even large-scale rape aimed at diluting Muslim ethnic identity (*New York Times,* May 22, 1992, A1). Soundly condemned by the Security Council, the General Assembly, and the Human Rights Commission, reports of not only ethnic cleansing but also death camps prompted charges of "war crimes" and the ultimate approval in September of the creation of a war crimes tribunal along the lines of the Nuremberg precedent (see case #13). In a conference held in London in August, 1992 Acting Secretary of State Lawrence Eagleburger warned Serb delegates:

> [W]e should, here at this conference, place squarely before the people of Serbia the choice they must make between joining a democratic and prosperous Europe or joining their leaders in the opprobrium, isolation, and defeat which will be theirs if they continue on their present march of folly. (U.S. State Dept. Dispatch Supplement September 1992, 1)

Lest the narrative appear too one-sided, it is important to present other developments that took place during the first months of the war. To begin, we should know that Croats and Muslims were guilty of atrocities and ethnic cleansing on their part as well. For example, in early June, Bosnian Muslims and Croats residing in Bosnia were reported to have rounded up whole villages and killed the inhabitants. Radovan Karadzic, the Bosnian Serbs leader, is convinced that Muslims have been working for years to dominate the country through means of population control:

> The Bosnian Muslims want, ultimately, to dominate, relying on a very high birthrate. They even wanted to move some Turks from Germany to Bosnia to help build their Islamic society. Since such a strategy of domination would be at the expense of Bosnian Serbs, we have resisted it by protecting our own villages. . . . We have not been fighting to gain territory. We have been fighting for the principle that there will be three autonomous communities in Bosnia-Herzegovina in order that no one of the three dominates the other. . . . We are

fighting to protect ourselves from becoming vulnerable to the same kind of genocide that coalition waged upon us in World War II when 700,000 Serbs were killed. Today, Serbs would be 60 percent of the population of Bosnia if this genocide had not been committed. We will never again be history's fools. (Karadzic 1992, 50)

In addition, it is important to understand that there are numerous Serbs who oppose violence. In late May, tens of thousands demonstrated in the streets of Belgrade against Slobodan Milosevic and called for his resignation. In the village of Gorazde, an ethnically mixed community, Serb residents are angry with Karadzic's policy of "ethnic cleansing." When asked about his remarks that Serbs and Muslims are inherently hostile, they responded: "Remarks like that are simply stupid . . . Serbs and Muslims have lived in the same valleys, used the same roads, worked in the same places, and intermarried throughout history. Now Karadzic wants to tear us apart" (*New York Times*, March 9, 1993, A5).

Parliamentary leader Milan Panic, a longtime resident of the United States, pressed for a liberal solution to the Yugoslav problem and even ran a strong campaign for president until his defeat and eventual ouster in the fall. He portrayed the situation this way:

I look at all this a little like a family feud. One family happens to be mine, the Serbs. They happen to live across the river in Bosnia. But they are my family, they are Serbs. To ask Serbs from one side of the river not to help Serbs on the other side is not fair. . . . Now I'm not saying send the army. But we need to help each other, to protect each other. (Panic 1992, 49)

The struggle in Yugoslavia is far from a simple one, since it involves the mutually exclusive principles of territorial integrity and self-determination for a multiethnic state (Woodward 1992, 54). When past experience is overlaid on such a Gordian knot, it is no surprise that there is virtue and blame for all.

As the war has dragged on, the United States and the UN more generally have struggled with ways to deal with the problem without becoming involved in an unpopular and costly land war. In October 1992 a no-fly zone of little military significance was established over Bosnia, although as of mid-April 1993 efforts to enforce it were stalled. At last count there were some 500 violations of the ban. A naval embargo has been maintained with somewhat greater success, and citizens of Serbia have seen inflation skyrocket and living standards deteriorate. Such measures and their effects have appeared to have no effect on policy, however.

The principal diplomatic effort in 1993 has focused on the so-called "Vance-Owen" Plan, drafted by UN envoys Cyrus Vance of the United States and Lord David Owen of the United Kingdom. The plan calls for "cantonization" of Bosnia into ten ethnically based provinces (even though the London meetings explicitly excluded such an approach): three provinces would be Muslim-dominated, one Serb-dominated, and five provinces would have shared power between Muslims and either Croats or Serbs. Sarajevo itself would be an "open city" (see Map 16.4). Negotiations that

Visions of Peace vs. Bosnia's Reality

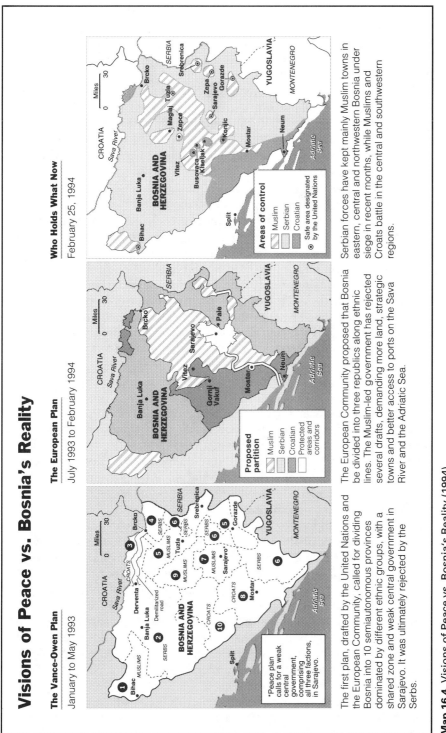

The Vance-Owen Plan
January to May 1993

The European Plan
July 1993 to February 1994

Who Holds What Now
February 25, 1994

The first plan, drafted by the United Nations and the European Community, called for dividing Bosnia into 10 semiautonomous provinces dominated by different ethnic groups, with a shared zone and weak central government in Sarajevo. It was ultimately rejected by the Serbs.

*Peace plan calls for a weak central government, comprising all three factions, in Sarajevo.

The European Community proposed that Bosnia be divided into three republics along ethnic lines. The Muslim-led government has rejected several drafts, demanding more land, strategic towns and better access to ports on the Sava River and the Adriatic Sea.

Serbian forces have kept mainly Muslim towns in eastern, central and northwestern Bosnia under siege in recent months, while Muslims and Croats battle in the central and southwestern regions.

Map 16.4 Visions of Peace vs. Bosnia's Reality (1994).
Source: The New York Times, February 25, 1994.

had been ongoing since the London meetings in August became more urgent and intense in January 1993 when the proposal was formally tabled. Both Izetbegovic and Karadzic attended the talks (though they never spoke to each other), and hopes rose for a breakthrough (*New York Times,* January 4, 1993, A5).

The initial responses were mixed: Milosevic of Serbia expressed his opposition to the plan, while Karadzic tentatively accepted the idea. Izetbegovic of Bosnia also tentatively accepted the plan as the best way to save his people, if not the country (*New York Times,* March 15, 1993, A3). It was not until April 3, 1993, when the rump Bosnian Serb Parliament rejected the plan, that it was destined for failure.

The latest proposal centers on legal endorsement of Serb and Croat advances on the battlefield with the partition of the country into three regions. This distasteful and perhaps even immoral approach follows several unsuccessful attempts by the Clinton administration to forge a Western alliance against Serbia. Clinton proposed in succession tougher sanctions on Serbia, a lifting of the ban on military sales to Bosnia, imposition of a no-fly zone around Bosnia, and finally preservation of six "safe-havens" around towns still controlled by Muslims. Each of these proposals was in its turn criticized and ultimately abandoned by the other European Community and Security Council nations as too costly and dangerous. The last proposal for partition simply represents an acceptance of the preeminence of brute force over the rule of law in Yugoslavia.

As of mid-November, even this proposal has been rejected by both Muslims and Serbs. The propsect of a peaceful settlement, or even a clear military victory by any side, is dim at best. *"Necemo rat, necemo mir"* (no war, no peace) is the Serbo-Croatian phrase often used to sum up the stalemate as it moves into yet another winter (*New York Times,* October 10, 1993, A1). The negotiations have been described as "in a shambles," "a diplomatic vacuum," and "swept under the rug" (*Washington Post,* November 2, 1993, A12). There is no leadership from either the Europeans or the United States as both parties seek risk-minimizing strategies.

A breakthrough in the conflict occurred as a direct consequence of one of the worst atrocities of the war. Early in February, 1994, Serb artillery struck an outdoor market in Sarajevo, killing 60 Muslim civilians. The event provoked an immediate and firm response in the West. For the first time, NATO leaders managed to muster a consensus in favor of military strikes against Serb positions. The alliance set a deadline, with Security Council concurrence, of February 20, for removal of all Serb heavy weapons from the area around Sarajevo. Failure to remove the artillery would result in air strikes. Shortly after the threat was delivered, Serb forces set about removing the weapons, but only after Russia intervened with NATO on their behalf. Russia not only persuaded the West to delay air strikes as long as possible, but also deployed its own peacekeepers in Serb-populated areas (the peacekeepers, widely known to favor the Serb position, were greeted as heroes) (*New York Times,* February 23, 1994, A4). The weapons were ultimately removed, and Sarajevo began to taste a semblance of peace for the first time in nearly two years. At the time of writing (early April 1994), the city was making plans for reconstruction efforts and enjoying a glut of food and fuel.

The February breakthrough set the stage for another, potentially more significant development. In March, 1994, after months of fighting, Muslims and Croats signed accords which ended their mutual hostilities and laid the foundation of a federation between the two nations (*New York Times,* March 19, 1994, A6). The move not only ended an important dimension of the war in Bosnia, but led to a military alliance which strenghtened the Muslim's capacity to fight Serb troops. Washington officials hoped the changed balance of power would induce Serb diplomats to sue for peace.

In fact, the prospect of an impending end to the fighting seems to have prompted Serbs to step up their efforts to claim as much territory as quickly as possible. This was apparent in their attacks on the U.N.-declared safe haven of Gorazde, where Serb artillery and tanks came close to taking the city in early April. The situation prompted the first-ever air strikes by NATO forces on April 10, 1994. Although the situation is still uncertain, it appears that, in the final analysis, the events of February, 1994 marked the beginning of the end of the conflict in Bosnia.

WHITHER YUGOSLAVIA?

It is clear that, although the means may exist in the UN Charter provisions, there is no political will to undertake a large-scale, Gulf War–style intervention in Bosnia. It is further becoming clear that the final resolution of this situation will include a de facto recognition of Serbian control of territory now under its occupation. Furthermore, it seems just as likely that another war will begin when the Bosnian war ends—this time in the Albanian-dominated Kosovo. Such a scenario would likely lead to the participation of Albania, Greece, Bulgaria, and perhaps the great powers in what could be a protracted and bloody period. As early as 1992 reports were being received concerning anti-Albanian ethnic cleansing in this currently Serbian territory.

Jacques Attali, head of the European Bank for Reconstruction and Development, is philosophical about the violence in Bosnia. "From the expulsion of the Muslims in 1492 to the concentration camps of the Second World War, the greatest European vice has been that of racial repression" (Attali 1992, 39). As put by Robert Hayden, advisor to the London Conference:

> The 'totalitarian disease' of national socialism has been seen as an aberration from the modern ideology because of its transformation of the principles of individualism, which implies the struggle of all against all, into a philosophy of inherent racial conflict and extermination. . . . Ominously, almost all of the multinational politics of mitteleuropa have seen tendencies toward fascism among their dominant nations. This was made clear during World War II in Croatia, Hungary, Romania and Slovakia, as well as Germany. All of these regions had

major concentrations of minority nations but majority populations yearning to create nation-states. (Hayden 1992, 45,46)

Hayden goes on to look more carefully at what current Croatian President Franjo Tudjman has said about the nation:

> Nations . . . grow up in a natural manner . . . as a result of the development of all those material and spiritual forces that in a given area shape the national being of individual nations on the basis of blood, linguistic and cultural kinship. . . . Every nation, no matter what its size or character, has the natural and historic right to its sovereignty and its place in the human community, just as the individual has in society. . . . Only a free and sovereign nation, like a fully developed and free human being, can give its full contribution to the world. (Hayden 1992, 42)

This conception of the nation as a unitary entity has disturbing implications for international relations. It implies that minority groups are impurities that must be eliminated from the homogeneous nation-state either through "territorial truncation . . . or the expulsion of the disloyal minorities." As put recently by Karadzic:

> Let us help all people to get where they want, no matter whether we Serbs love some territory or not. We need to settle this issue of peoples and border once and for all so that there won't be cause for war again in the Balkans. . . . The peace process initiated in London cannot achieve success because it was too one-sided against the Serbs, as we are to blame for everything. There are 11 million Serbs. We are about to stand up and say to the rest of the world, "that is enough. Get your hands out. We want to make our own state, and we don't need you since you are not interested in our survival." (Karadzic 1992, 51)

Such a negation of tolerance and international law raises the very real possibility that the "New World Order" could make life for all "solitary, poor, nasty, brutish and short"—the very definition of anarchy.

Questions to Consider

1. How does one judge the merits of a nation's demand for self-determination? At what point does such a demand become the concern of the international community, and what criteria does it have to grant or deny it?

2. In the case of Serbs residing outside of Serbia, what claims should the Serbian government itself have? Should they treat them as Israel treats the Jews of the world or West Germany treated the Germans outside their lands: as latent citizens? Or should they be viewed as completely alien in the same way the U.S. government deals with British citizens in spite of obvious ethnic connections?

3. Once these decisions are made, what sort of enforcement is appropriate? Should Serbs take matters into their own hands if the international community denies them their rights? Should Croatians and Bosnian Muslims

take up arms to protect what might be, after all, unjustified dominion over foreigners?

4. On a personal level, how do you feel when Americans are taken hostage abroad, even if they have lived overseas most of their lives? Conversely, do you feel the government of Mexico should look out for their own across the Rio Grande? Does the United States have the right to have only one or two official languages when the population is so heterogeneous? And should the UN have any involvement in these matters?

References

Ian Armour. "Nationalism vs. Yugoslavia." *History Today* 42 (October 1992): 11–13.

Jaques Attali. "Europe's Descent into Tribalism." *New Perspectives Quarterly* 9 #4 (Fall 1992): 38–40.

Aurel Braun. *Small-State Security in the Balkans* (Totowa, NJ: Barnes & Noble Books, 1983).

Leonard J. Cohen. "The Disintegration of Yugoslavia." *Current History* 91 #568 (November 1992): 369–375.

"Current Development—UN Membership of the 'New' Yugoslavia." *American Journal of International Law* 86 #4 (October 1992): 830–833.

Aleska Djilas and Nader Mousavizadeh. "The Nation that Wasn't." *New Republic* (September 21, 1992): 25–31.

The Economist, August 23, 1992.

The Economist, August 15, 1992.

Robert Hayden. "Yugoslavia: Where Self-determination Meets Ethnic Cleansing." *New Perspectives Quarterly* 9 #4 (Fall 1992): 41–46.

Barbara Jelavich. *History of the Balkans—Vol 1: Eighteenth and Nineteenth Centuries; Vol 2: Twentieth Century* (New York: Cambridge University Press, 1983).

Radovan Karadzic. "Salvation Is a Serbian State—Interview." *New Perspectives Quarterly* 9 #4 (Fall 1992): 50–51.

Fitzrog Maclean, *The Heretic: The Life and Times of Josip Broz Tito.* (New York: Harper, 1957)

Tomas Mastnak. "Is the Nation-State Really Obsolete?" *Times Literary Supplement* (August 7, 1992): 11.

New York Times, May 19, 1991, A1.

New York Times, June 7, 1991, A5.

New York Times, July 31, 1991, A1.

New York Times, August 30, 1991, A3.

New York Times, October 1, 1991, A1.

New York Times, February 22, 1992, A1.

New York Times, May 22, 1992, A1.

New York Times, May 31, 1992, A1.

New York Times, June 29, 1992, A1.

New York Times, November 21, 1992, A1.

New York Times, January 4, 1993, A5.

New York Times, March 9, 1993, A1.

New York Times, March 15, 1993, A3.

New York Times, April 8, 1993, A1.

New York Times, October 10, 1993, A1.

New York Times, February 23, 1994, A4.

New York Times, March 19, 1994, A6.

Milan Panic. "The Future Is Forgetting—Interview." *New Perspectives Quarterly* 9 #4 (Fall 1992): 47–50.

L. S. Stravianos. *The Balkans: 1815–1914* (New York: Holt, Rinehart, and Winston, 1963).

Susan Woodward. "The Yugoslav Wars." *Brookings Review* 10 #4 (Fall 1992): 54.

U.N. Chronicle, September 1992, 8.

U.S. State Department, *Dispatch,* November 16, 1992.

U.S. State Department, *Dispatch, Supplement,* September 1992.

Washington Post, November 2, 1993, A12.

Nationalism
in the Caucasus

The nation is an essential building block to international society. A nation is a group based on language, culture, religion, race, ethnicity, or other factors which lead its members to agree on their common identity. The only sure way to identify nationalities is to ask people to categorize themselves, since every other method may well be irrelevant. Nationalism is the expression of a group's national pride and/or desire for self-determination—the political autonomy of a given nation. There is a fine line between healthy nationalism, commonly called patriotism, which motivates a community to make sacrifices for the good of the group, and chauvinism, xenophobia, ethnocentrism, racism, or any other sentiment that places one's own nation above others and engenders hatred and even war.

Imagine a United States in which only 52 percent of the population is white English speakers. Imagine that the scores of Native American tribes and nations that existed when the Pilgrims landed on Plymouth Rock were still as strong as ever and each had their own state government with senators in Washington. Now imagine that these states retained their own official language, deep-seated customs, and mutual rivalries rooted in centuries-old relationships. The State of Nez Perce might be at war with the Sioux Republic, the Comanche and Apache governments might be sponsoring terrorism against the Caucasian Union. They could align themselves with the Freed Slaves Province. Only economic dependence on the whites, laced with police repression and "anglification," keep the country together. Now imagine the government in Washington collapsing. . . .

This scenario is a useful (if a bit bizarre) way for an American audience to begin thinking about the nationalities problem in the former Soviet Union. Roughly one-third of the citizens of the USSR were involuntarily brought under Russian control in the last 200 years, after centuries of political autonomy and unique cultural development. If such names as Uzbeks, Tajiks, Latvians, Ossetians, and Azeris seem strange and even quaint to the Western observer, they are full of meaning and import to the people themselves. Our ignorance does in no way diminish the historical weight they hold.

It is impossible in a chapter this brief to portray in detail the character and history of these various nationalities. This can only be accomplished by thorough study. Already, one hears serious conversations among American students on the civil rights of Russian emigres living in Latvia, the disposition of Nagorno-Karabakh in the Caucasus, and whether the Ukraine will ratify the START nuclear weapons treaty. It is hoped that this chapter will help students put these developments and the many more to come in political and historical context.

RUSSIAN EXPANSIONISM

Much like the United States, the Soviet Union grew largely by conquering weaker neighbors. Russia's expansion also came through great power rivalry in which small states were passed around as war prizes. As put by Seweryn Bialer, "The internal empire (together with its external empire in Eastern Europe) makes the Soviet Union and Russia the world's largest and last colonial . . . power" (Bialer 1986, 32).

Map 17.1 gives a general view of Russian expansion. The Russian state itself was not fully consolidated until the 1470s when Ivan the Great expelled the Mongol invaders originally led by Genghis Khan in 1230. Three powerful nations occupied what is now European Russia at the time: the Kiev kingdom, roughly corresponding to modern Ukraine; the Novogorod Republic which spread over the Baltic States, Finland, and most of northern European Russia; and Muskovy in and around Moscow. By 1570, under Ivan the Terrible, Muskovy had pacified both of these rival kingdoms and was pushing southward and eastward, toward the Black Sea and the Pacific. By the time of Peter the Great (1682–1725), the borders of the Russian state corresponded roughly with the present Russian Republic, complete with a variety of foreign nationalities, nomadic peoples in Siberia, discontented Ukrainians, Asiatic peoples, and chauvinistic Russians who wanted to eliminate these ethnic differences.

At the end of the eighteenth century, the Russian Empire was fighting successful wars against Sweden for control of Finland, against France for control of Poland and Moldavia, and against Turkey for the Caucasus. Although periodic setbacks, such as the defeat in the Crimean War of

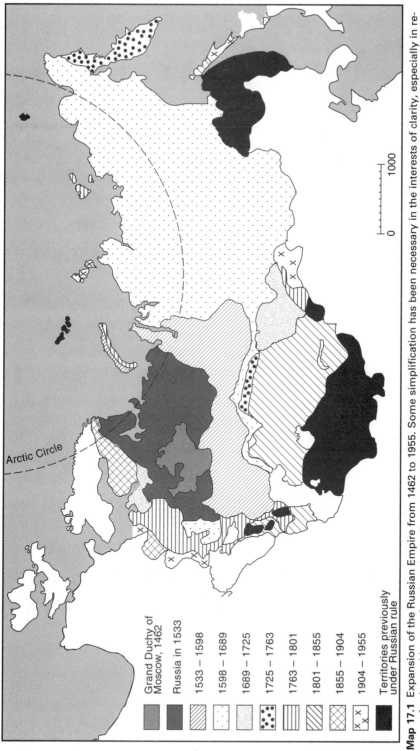

Map 17.1 Expansion of the Russian Empire from 1462 to 1955. Some simplification has been necessary in the interests of clarity, especially in respect of gains and losses of territory in the European areas.

Source: Leslie Symon, ed., *The Soviet Union: A Systematic Geography* (Totowa, NJ: Barnes & Noble Books, 1983).

Grand Duchy of
Moscow, 1462

Russia in 1533

1533 – 1598

1598 – 1689

1689 – 1725

1725 – 1763

1763 – 1801

1801 – 1855

1855 – 1904

1904 – 1955

Territories previously
under Russian rule

Arctic Circle

1000

0

1854–1856, prevented complete control of newly acquired areas for some time, by the late 1800s, the western frontier of Russia penetrated deep into Europe (*Cambridge Encyclopedia*, 1982, 458–462).

In the 1860s, the serfs were freed and the central Asian peoples (Kazakhs, Turkmens, Kirgiz, Tadzhiks, Uzbeks, etc.) were conquered. By the beginning of World War I, the frontiers of the Russian Empire approximated the Soviet Union's familiar silhouette. While these would be cut off, following the defeat of the newly declared USSR in 1918, through the liberation of Finland and the Baltic States, the end of World War II would see the reincorporation of these republics (save Finland) in the Soviet territory. With the signing of the Warsaw Treaty in 1955 and the close cooperation between the USSR, the People's Republic of China, North Vietnam, and Mongolia, the sphere of Soviet dominance spread from Berlin to Vladivostok (via the Arctic Circle) in the north, and from Sofia to Hanoi in the south. With a de facto empire covering roughly one-fourth of the world's surface and incorporating nearly one-third of its inhabitants, the Soviet state stood as the greatest power in human history.

One could interpret the history of the Soviet Union since the mid-1950s as the saga of a collapsing empire, but this would be too simplistic. Although the Sino-Soviet split in the early 1960s deprived Moscow of two-thirds the Soviet bloc's population, and India, Yugoslavia, and Albania placed themselves beyond its control, the USSR was still the second largest power in the world, complete with thousands of nuclear warheads and a military presence in over a dozen countries. With the ascent of Mikhail Gorbachev in 1985 the nation was clearly a superpower, although the Soviet Union was struggling under mountains of debt, a defense burden which absorbed one-fourth of the nation's stagnant economy, and a demoralized and divisive citizenry (see Map 17.2 for Soviet ethnic diversity).

SOVIET POLICIES TOWARD NATIONALITIES

In Eastern Europe, the priority for the Soviet Union was to promote loyalty, stability, and Moscow-centered socialism. While government leaders were encouraged to promote the "socialist man"—an idealized patriot imbued with egalitarianism and a healthy work ethic—there was little emphasis on Russification (the process of assimilating foreign culture into Russian). This orientation was perhaps most evident in the German Democratic Republic, where the only distinction between it and the Federal Republic was socialism itself (see case #1).

The Soviet Union periodically intervened to quell nationalist unrest on the basis of the Brezhnev Doctrine (Hungary 1956, Czechoslovakia 1968, Poland 1981), but it did so primarily if it threatened the cohesiveness of the Soviet military and economic bloc, not because it was nationalist per se. The Soviet Union set in place international agreements which were entirely lop-

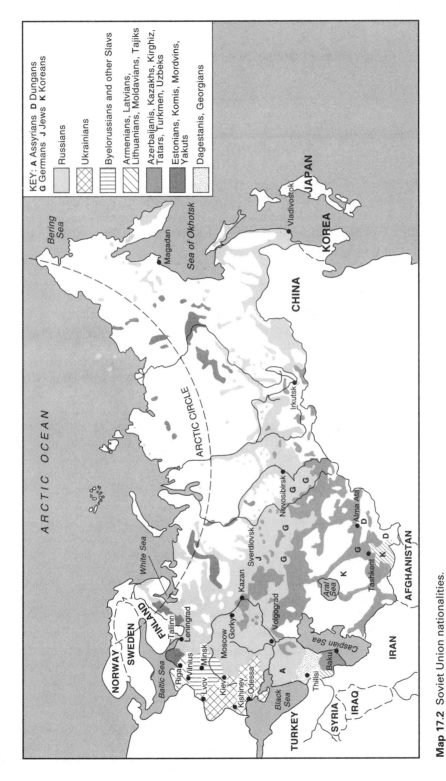

Map 17.2 Soviet Union nationalities.

Source: *The Cambridge Encyclopedia of Russia and the Soviet Union* (Cambridge: Cambridge University Press, 1982).

sided in Moscow's favor. This was particularly the case with regard to the Warsaw Treaty which provided for the basing of thirty-one Soviet divisions in East Germany, Poland, Czechoslovakia, and Hungary. As put by Carrere d'Encausse:

> ... although [the USSR] does not dominate the continent and the world, it dominates Eastern Europe and cannot allow any retreat there. And in order not to retreat, it has to take root, to anchor itself in this family that it has established, evidence of its power today and its expansion tomorrow. (Carrère d'Encausse 1987, 302)

Even the most pliant Soviet satellite, Bulgaria, retained its cultural and linguistic identity throughout the Cold War era. And the more rebellious socialist states in the region—Yugoslavia, Albania, and Rumania—developed an entirely independent political culture and social structure, often much harsher than the Soviets themselves.

The story was very different where nationalities within the Soviet Union were concerned. The repression of ethnic minorities under the czars is legendary, the result of which was the virtual elimination of half of the empire's 200 distinct languages and nationalities. In 1917, although originally promising greater tolerance of national differences (a promise which helped to get the support of peasants during the Revolution), Lenin spoke of "fusion" of various cultures (Nahaylo and Swoboda 1990, 221). Many ethnic groups were granted nominal self-government through a complex system of republics and autonomous regions, although cultural diversity was generally discouraged. Perhaps the most notorious enforcer was Stalin, who in the 1930s undertook radical agrarian reforms, destroying the social fabric of numerous towns and villages where tens of millions of national minorities resided. Beginning in 1934, Stalin imposed a harsh program of Russification on most ethnic groups in the country, particularly in the area of Russian language instruction—a symbol of assimilation. During the war, Stalin relocated seven whole nations, including the Jews of western Russia and German expatriate communities, on the grounds that they were a threat to national security. It was not until the Khrushchev era that Moscow authorities began to acknowledge the distinct nationalities in the country (*Cambridge Encyclopedia*, 1982, 304).

The major national groups have long been granted a separate political identity—although not an authentic national voice—through the vehicle of the Union Republics, of which there were fifteen. These large governing units were distinguished by ethnic/national groups and were represented in the "Nationalities" chamber of the Supreme Soviet (national parliament). The Union Republics were also joined by and partitioned into a variety of smaller national units, each described by the word "autonomous" (although the term was meaningless in the Communist party-dominated political world of the Soviet Union). The Russian Federated Union Republic incorporated thirty-one of these distinct national units. Each republic is accountable to the center, and each smaller federal division (autonomous republics, autonomous regions, etc.) is accountable to the republic in which it is located. In actual fact, these various regions have been used primarily as an administrative expedient for implementing economic plans developed in Moscow. Few republics or regions were satisfied with the little influence they were permitted, and even cautious reformers long called for greater participation in national decision making.

The hostility between the various nationalities largely focused on the question of power within these political units. The federal system of the Soviet Union provided extensive legal rights with extremely limited actual powers. Although the constitution provides for each republic to enter into foreign relations, only the Ukraine and Byelorussia had anything amounting to a foreign policy (they were each granted a seat at the United Nations as an inducement to Stalin to sign the charter). Even such large republics as Kazakhstan had no diplomatic corps. Each republic also had the nominal right to secede from the Union at any time, although in practice this proved illusory. When the Baltic States pressed for independence in 1989, Gorbachev was forced to clarify the steps required for secession, which to no one's surprise proved to be far more cumbersome than those states could manage.

Moscow's hold on the various national republics was superficially firm, but never entirely secure. By the 1980s, several prominent non-Russian writers and artists began openly challenging the right of Moscow to promote Russian culture and language, although it was not until the Gorbachev era that nationalist movements began to form in a systematic way. Even under Gorbachev, in spite of glasnost (political openness), many national liberation leaders were held in prison for their traitorous calls for independence. In 1985, minor nationalist unrest in the Baltic States, the Ukraine, and other nations was suppressed aggressively by Moscow (Nahaylo and Swoboda 1990, 229). Demands for linguistic freedom and restoration of national languages were made with greater frequency but either were ignored or berated. During 1986, widespread protests in Kazakhstan were barely contained, Byelorussian and Ukrainian writers openly protested Russification, and people in the Baltic States began protesting water pollution resulting from mismanagement by Moscow bureaucrats in the first step toward demands for autonomy. By mid-1987, nationalism was the central issue in many regions and its appeal was "spreading like a virus," in the words of the head of the KGB. Even American observers such as Patrick Buchanan feared that Gorbachev's tolerance of nationalist movements could lead to unhinging the Soviet Union and warned "he is today fairly inviting upon himself the same fate Nikita Khrushchev suffered a quarter century ago" (Lefever and Lugt 1989, 89).

THE COLLAPSE OF SOVIET POWER

The pace of events since 1987 has been dizzying. This is evident in the chronology we have provided of key events relating to the collapse of the Soviet Union and the ensuing ethnic resurgence (see Table 17.1). The issue of

Table 17.1   SOVIET COLLAPSE: A CHRONOLOGY

1987

April	Mikhail Gorbachev visits Czechoslovakia and suggests making political reforms.
May	Mikhail Gorbachev encourages Warsaw Treaty Organization members to share their ideas frankly.
June 14	Several thousand protest in Latvia.
July	Bulgaria announces political reforms.
July 29	Several hundred Crimean Tatars protest in Moscow.
August 23	Baltic States stage large protests against the Moscow-Ribbentrop Pact, which had resulted in Soviet annexation of the region.
October 17	Protests in Armenia focus on pollution and transfer of Armenian-inhabited Nagorno-Karabakh, located within neighboring Azerbaijan, to Armenia proper.
November 1	Byelorussian patriotic movement holds its first national meeting.

1988

January	Estonian nationalists publish demands for autonomy.
February 21	After Moscow refuses to grant transfer of Nagorno-Karabakh, Armenians begin series of massive demonstrations, culminating in a nationwide strike and a rally which included 700,000 (more than one-fourth of the country's population!)
February 27	Azeris attack Armenians living in Azerbaijan, killing twenty-six. Refugees from both regions begin to flow across the border.
April 13	Nationalist union formed in Estonia, pressing demands for political and economic autonomy.
May	Solidarity carries out strikes against Polish economic programs.
May 22	Economic reformer Karoly Grosz appointed head of Socialist Worker's party in Hungary.
June	Asian republics express concerns over territorial borders—hint at tensions.
June 13	Estonians replace official language and flag; 150,000 join meeting to assert national rights on June 16.
June 21	Ukrainians try but are forbidden to establish nationalist union. Large demonstrations follow.
June 28	Gorbachev announces reform of parliamentary bodies to provide broader participation.
July 13	Armenians in Nagorno-Karabakh vote for secession from Azerbaijan following violent police action by Soviet forces.
August	Soviet police stop demonstrations in Byelorussia, Leningrad, and the Ukraine, while Baltics press demands.
August	Yegor Ligachev, Gorbachev rival, publicly criticizes perestroika and market reforms.
October 28	Czechoslovak police break up large antigovernment protest.
November 16	Estonia declares its sovereignty and assumes the right to supersede Moscow authority.
November 30	Two million Lithuanians sign petition granting official status to Lithuanian language and flag.

| December 8 | Gorbachev announces unilateral withdrawal of 5,000 troops from Eastern Europe. |
| December 8 | Massive earthquake hits Armenian capital. |

1989

January	Numerous antigovernment demonstrations repressed in Czechoslovakia.
January 12	Hungary legalizes opposition parties.
February 3	Demonstrations in Tashkent (Uzbek Republic) over language, religious and economic rights.
February 7	Poland's military government initiates power-sharing talks with Solidarity (free labor union) with Moscow's blessing.
February 18	Following similar actions by the Abkhaz minority in Georgia, Georgians protest treatment of their compatriots in the Abkhaz Republic.
March 26	First free elections in USSR result in overwhelming defeat for many Communist party candidates. Andrei Sakharov and Boris Yeltsin are elected.
March–April	Hungary dismantles border fences with Austria.
May 24	Ethnic Turks killed during protests against government in Bulgaria.
June 6	Polish Communist party rejected in parliamentary elections.
June 8	Uzbeks clash with Meskhetian minority. Seventy killed in spite of Soviet intervention. Meshkhetians, who had been removed from Georgia in World War II and placed in Uzbekistan, are eventually airlifted to Russia.
June 26	Widespread rioting in Kazakhstan and Tadzhikistan targets police.
July 7	Warsaw Treaty Organization declares the "right of each to develop independently its own political line."
July	Violent clashes occur between Georgians and Abkhazians and between Tadzhiks and Kirgizians over border and minority questions.
July 29	Bolstered by Estonians securing of greater economic rights from Moscow, Latvians declare sovereignty.
August	East German government reaffirms its socialist identity in numerous speeches.
August 19	Tadeusz Mazowiecki named prime minister in Poland following Solidarity victory at the polls.
August 19	500,000 demonstrate as emerging Popular Front in Azerbaijan forces government to make reforms.
August 29	Violent clashes between Azeris and Armenians continue despite larger Soviet troop strength. Nagorno-Karabakh the target of an Azeri blockade.
September	Widespread demonstrations erupt across East Germany.
September 8	Ukrainian nationalist movement (Rukh) holds first conference.
September 9	Hungary allows East Germans to go to Austria via Hungary. 60,000 East Germans flee.
October	East Germans seek asylum in various embassies in Berlin; government refuses exit permits.
October 9	Hungarian Communist party is dissolved.
October 17	Erich Honecker resigns as leader of East Germany. New leader promises reforms.
October 22	Following months of growing assertiveness, Russian nationalists form the United Popular Front.

(continued)

Table 17.1 *(continued)*

October 25	Ukrainian nationalists pass laws granting official status to Ukrainian language and flag.
November 4	Crowd of 500,000 marches in Berlin, demanding democratic reforms.
November 8	New government comes to power in East Germany.
November 9	Berlin Wall opens. East Germans emigrate at the rate of 2,000 per week.
November 10	Bulgarian secretary-general resigns. "Palace Coup" takes the place of genuine reform.
November 17	Peaceful demonstration in Prague, Czechoslovakia, brutally suppressed—more demonstrations follow.
November 28	Czech opposition calls for nationwide strike in spite of resignation of entire government.
December 7	Lithuanian Parliament removes Communist party powers.
December 17	Protests over ill-treatment of Hungarian minorities in Rumania turn anti-government.
December 21	Progovernment rally for Nicolae Ceauşescu erupted into a melee, with government troops firing into huge crowds.
December 22	Ceauşescu captured while open warfare rages on. Military switches sides to newly formed government. Crowds seize television station. Ion Iliescu carries National Salvation Front banner.
December 25	Ceauşescu executed by military tribunal.
December 29	Vaclav Havel and Alexander Dubcek take over government in peaceful transition in Czechoslovakia. The "Velvet Revolution" is over.

1990

January	Rumanian strongman Ion Iliescu organizes antidemocratic protests and plans to field candidates for upcoming elections (breaking his pledge to remain above politics).
January 29	Polish Communist party dissolves.
March 18	Elections in East Germany bring Christian Democrats to power on a platform of early reunification.
March 28	Hungarian elections result in overwhelming defeat for Communist party, the nation becoming the "only true multiparty democracy in Eastern Europe."
April 21	In response to Slovak demands and resentment over Czech dominance, the country's name is changed to the "Czech and Slovak Federal Republic".
May	Lech Walesa begins to assert power over the Polish prime minister, demanding accelerated removal of Communist party officials still in government. This resulted in a split in the Solidarity movement.
May	Yugoslav Communist party, failing to satisfy nationalist demands with its own dissolution, loses elections in Slovenia and Croatia, and will continue to suffer setbacks in Bosnia (November) and Macedonia (December).
May 21	National Salvation Front wins elections in Rumania under leadership of strongman Ion Iliescu.
June 13	Civic Forum, the Czech democratic umbrella group, forms government in parliament.
June 14	Weak opposition movement attacked with massive force in Rumania—coal miners let loose on students.

July	Gorbachev and West German Chancellor Helmut Kohl agree on drastic cuts of Soviet forces in East Germany, the remaining troops to be maintained by the Germans.
August 1	Following months of negotiation, Bulgarian democratic leaders form new government after slim electoral victory.
September 12	"Two-plus-Four" negotiations result in treaty by Germanies and World War II victors on reunification.
October 3	Germany reunited.
December	Communists retain control in Serbia, Yugoslavia's largest republic. Slovenes vote for independence in referendum.
December 23	Lech Walesa defeats Prime Minister Mazowiecki in presidential campaign.

1991

January 11	Soviet "Black Berets" crush Lithuanian activists and seize control of key government agencies.
February	Czech Civic Forum splits into two wings.
February	Russian conservatives call for Gorbachev to declare martial law. Yeltsin calls for his resignation. Mass protests in Moscow echo conflicting demands.
March 18	Massive referendum on Soviet unity shows victory for retaining current structure, although city dwellers remain opposed.
April 1	Warsaw Treaty Organization dissolved.
April 1	Georgians vote overwhelmingly for independence.
April 25	Gorbachev's resignation rejected by party leaders. Yeltsin agrees on crisis management proposal.
May	Violence in Caucasus continues despite Soviet troops.
June 14	Boris Yeltsin is elected president of the Russian Republic in open elections.
June 26	Croatia and Slovenia formally declare independence from Yugoslavia.
July	Rumanian democratic organizations hold nationalist convention in spite of threats by Iliescu regime.
July 27	Soviet Communist party abandons socialism.
August 19	Gorbachev removed from power in right-wing coup.
August 20	Thousands gather in standoff with troops uncertain of their loyalties. Soviet tanks surrounding the Russian Parliament building defect to Boris Yeltsin.
August 21	Crowds of up to 200,000 gather across the Soviet Union to protest the coup. Defections of soldiers now widespread.
August 22	Coup organizers flee as Gorbachev is brought back to Moscow. Yeltsin seen as new leader of USSR.
August 24	Gorbachev cabinet resigns. Gorbachev himself resigns as Communist party General Secretary. Communist party disbanded by Yeltsin, who takes on broad powers over central government as president of Russian Republic.
August 25	Byelorussia and Ukraine declare independence.
August 26	Russian leaders warn seceding republics they will protect Russian nationals.
August 27	Moldavia declares independence. New union formed by Russia, Kazakhstan, and Kirghizia, later joined by Ukraine.
September 1	Uzbekistan and Kirghizia declare independence.

(continued)

Table 17.1 (continued)

September 1	Baltic Republics extended full diplomatic recognition by Moscow, European Community, and United States.
September 3	Gorbachev endorses radical restructuring of Soviet Union as loose federation of sovereign states.
September 10	Tadzhikistan declares independence.
September 18	Yugoslav army under control of Serbia launches attack on Zagreb in Croatia.
September 18	Demonstrators in Georgia protest authoritarian policies of Zviad Gamsakhurdia.
October 7	Serbian leadership launches offensive against Croatia.
October 28	Turkmenistan declares independence as former Soviet republics forge closer ties outside of USSR framework.
November	Croatian City of Dubrovnik under siege by Serb-dominated Yugoslav army. City of Vokuvar destroyed.
November 12	Vaclav Havel promotes Czech and Slovak unity in spite of growing opposition to perceived Czech dominance in Slovakia.
December 1	Russian Republic takes over finances of USSR.
December 4	Ukrainians vote overwhelmingly for independence.
December 14	Central Asian Republics join Slavic states in forming the Commonwealth of Independent States. The move is made official on December 21.
December 23	Germany extends diplomatic recognition to Croatia and Slovenia. Presses European Community to do likewise.
December 25	Gorbachev resigns as president of the Soviet Union. He transfers to Boris Yeltsin the command of the Soviet nuclear and conventional arsenal.
December 31	The Soviet Union ceases to exist. It is temporarily replaced by a loose confederation of twelve independent states corresponding to the former Soviet Republics (minus the Baltic States). The Russian Federation takes over the seat of the former Soviet Union at the United Nations.

Sources: Nahaylo and Swoboda 1990; de Nevers 1990; Tismaneanu 1992; *New York Times; Washington Post; Current History.*

nationalism in the Soviet Union and Eastern Europe was suddenly forced upon the West. Beginning with open unrest and ethnic war in the Caucasus, moving through the collapse of the Berlin Wall, to the dismantling of the Soviet Union itself after the August 1991 coup attempt, Europe and the Soviet Union were radically transformed in less than three years. With each new headline of ethnic unrest one point is underscored: nationalism has the power to move history. It has proved more resilient than czarist pogroms, tougher than international socialism, impervious to international law, and unimpressed by economic sanctions and even natural disasters.

THE CASE OF THE CAUCASUS

Rather than attempt to discuss all the national problems in the former Soviet Union, we will focus on one dramatic situation that will serve to illustrate the general problem of nationalism in the former Soviet Union—the Caucasus. A brief overview of the nations in the region will be followed by a more detailed description of conflicts in the area.

As can be seen on Map 17.3 of the Transcaucasus region, there are no less than twenty-three distinct languages (not including dozens of dialects and languages, such as Ukrainian and Byelorussian, spoken by immigrants to the region) spoken in this area which is the size of Missouri. While this alone defies the imagination, even more significant is the fact that the Caucasus acts as the junction between at least three worlds: the Islamic world of Turkey and Persia, the Christian world of the Mediterranean, and the Orthodox Slavic world of Russia and the Ukraine. Wedged between these powerful influences, the people of the Caucasus have survived.

The Armenians are perhaps the most unfortunate people in the region in that they have suffered both political dispossession and genocide in this century alone. Armenia's history extends to Roman times when it was a powerful kingdom stretching from the Caucasus to Syria and Lebanon. It became a province of the Roman Empire in 55 B.C. Following the collapse of Rome, Armenia developed as a composite kingdom that spread from the Mediterranean to the Caspian and covered much of modern-day Turkey and Azerbaijan. Armenians played a dominant role in the Byzantine Empire and even organized a colony on the Mediterranean. In the seventeenth century, Armenia was carved up by the Ottoman and Persian Empires and did not regain its sovereignty until 1991. Russians conquered Armenia in the early years of the eighteenth century, but struggled with Turkish and Iranian armies to control it. Perhaps the most tragic episode in Armenian history was the slaughter of Armenians living in eastern Turkey in 1915. This came about during World War I when Turks and Russians fought for control of the area. Fearing the possibility of an Armenian fifth column, the Turkish government killed or starved 1.5 million Armenians (Katz 1975, 146). By 1920 the Soviet Union consolidated its dominance over Armenia, although the territory was always more free than other Soviet republics. In spite of a purge of zealous nationalists in the 1930s, Armenians continued to press for ethnic rights from both Russians and Turks across the border.

Armenians have had their own language and writing since the fourth century A.D. and maintain strong ties to Armenians throughout the world (*Cambridge Encyclopedia*, 1982, 64). Only two-thirds of the 1.5 million Soviet Armenians live in Armenia, although another 20 percent live elsewhere in the Caucasus region. The Armenian-controlled enclave of Nagorno-Karabakh is entirely surrounded by Azerbaijan, and has been the focus of recent violence. Armenia's religion, known as Gregorian Christianity (Armenian Apostolic—a unique brand, separate from the Orthodox and Roman churches) has been a firm, stable element in Armenian society for centuries. "[T]he memory of the long history of the Armenian church as well as the more recent experience of genocide are of major significance to Armenian identity"(Karklins 1986, 200). Even Soviet attempts to purge the church in the Stalinist era failed, although younger people today rarely participate actively in church services.

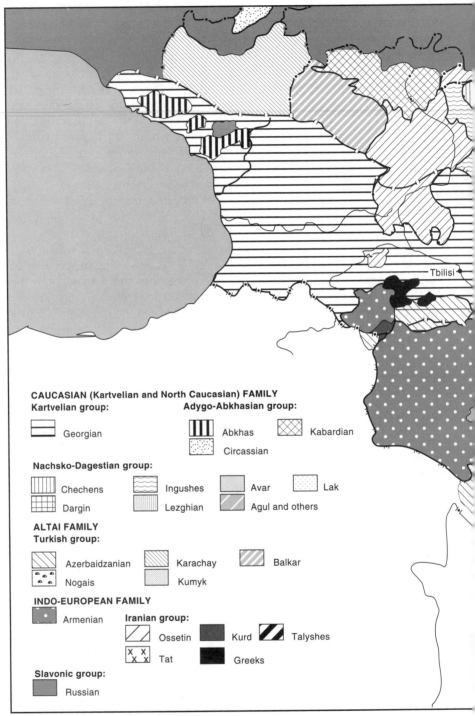

Map 17.3 Linguistic groups of the Caucasus.

Source: Viktor Kozlov, *The Peoples of the Soviet Union* (Bloomington, IN: Indiana University Press, 1988).

Baku

Given the experience with Turkey, and the implicit alliance between Turkey and Azerbaijan, animosity between the groups has been intense. Nationalist feelings are rarely suppressed in Armenia. Animosity toward Georgians (an otherwise remarkably similar nation) is high, stemming from the perception that Stalin, a Georgian himself, showed marked favoritism to that republic over Armenia. There is evidence of a seige mentality in Armenia, particularly given the presence of numerous Muslim and non-Armenian peoples in the territory of the republic itself. Nonetheless, Armenians are generally confident that their legendary cunning will allow them to prevail.

The 5.5 million Azeris are a Muslim people which were dominated for many centuries by Turkish overlords, although the cultural, religious, and linguistic influence of Persia (Iran) were somewhat more substantial. For centuries, until the late 1800s, Azeris saw themselves closely linked to the Persian culture and Shiite religion, rather than to Turkey, Russia, or Sunni Muslims in Arabia (Katz 1975, 205). It was not until the emergence of oil drilling and the development of Baku as an industrial city that Azeris began to lean toward Turkey and wean themselves from Iranian influence. When combined with a strong dose of Marxist socialism, Azeri nationalism was a potent force. In fact, Baku led the way in the promotion of Muslim Marxism and achieved independence for a brief period after World War I. Russian troops secured Azeri cooperation with brute force by 1920 and adopted a policy of cultural assimilation.

The traditional nature of Azeri society is revealed in the extremely high rate of marriage within the ethnic group, compared with Armenians' tendency to marry outside the nationality, and their low migration rates. Roughly 85 percent of Soviet Azeris live in Azerbaijan, and the rest live in an Azeri enclave in Armenia. Although Baku is rather cosmopolitan, the social norms of the countryside are substantially traditional, based on the tenets of Islam (Katz 1975, 205). Generally thought of as a taciturn, self-reliant nation, Azeris feel a strong kinship to Turkey, as well as to the 4 million Azeris in northern Iran. Azeris also worry about their relatively low standard of living, in spite of their oil reserves.

Georgians (who call themselves Kartlians) are thought of as the swaggering, successful people of the Caucasus. They are fiercely proud of their favorite son, Josef Stalin, and still feel authoritarianism has more advantages than democracy. Georgians have been particularly opposed to de-stalinization over the years, engaging in anti-Khrushchev demonstrations in the 1950s, for example. Georgians trace their political genealogy to the sixth century B.C., when scattered tribes organized the first Caucasian kingdom. Georgia, like Armenia, became a Roman outpost and ultimately an extension of Christian Byzantium, although it adopted the more traditional Orthodox religion. For a few centuries, Georgia came under Persian domination, although by the eleventh century it reasserted its identity and grew to be the dominant kingdom in the region for 100 years. Georgia became the target of only partially successful attempts at annexation, first by the Mongols of Genghis Khan, then by the Ottoman Turks, then by Safavi Iran (Katz 1975, 164). Throughout, Georgia retained much of its identity and some of its autonomy. It was not until the beginning of the nineteenth century that Georgia finally fell under foreign (Russian) domination.

Georgians became closely integrated with Russian society, taking advantage of its culture and educational opportunities. At the turn of the century, Georgian Mensheviks played a pivotal role in the Revolution, but were partially excluded from the successful Bolshevik coup d'état. After the Caucasus were ceded to Turkey, Georgia, along with Azerbaijan, declared independence—a status recognized in a peace treaty with the new Soviet Union in 1920. In 1921, however, the Red Army overran Georgia and later annexed it. Georgia eventually became an autonomous republic along with Azerbaijan and Armenia, when the republic of Transcaucasia was divided in 1936. Georgia generally benefited from a hands-off approach by the Moscow authorities—a policy owed in part to the influence of Stalin and other top Communist party officials native to Georgia. As Georgians became more accustomed to a hands-off attitude from Moscow, a thriving black market developed. It was Eduard Schevardnadze who, in the 1970s, ushered in a period of severe austerity in compliance with Moscow directives.

Georgian cultural life is quite similar to Armenia's in many respects. Georgians are famous for their liturgical music and filmmaking and take pride in their contributions to Soviet life. Thought of as the "California of the USSR," Georgia has been a very attractive retreat and a target of substantial immigration. Georgian pride borders on arrogance, and there is a common saying that "in Georgia, every peasant is a prince" (Katz 1975, 183). This attitude often expresses itself in a contempt for proper procedures and rules; the black market thrives in Tbilisi. In the end, Georgians may have an overdeveloped sense of pride, as found in their tendency to romanticize even the saddest periods of their history.

Georgia also includes other linguistic and ethnic groups, including some 95,000 Abkhazians who seek control of their own "autonomous republic" within Georgia where they are still in a minority. Even in the early 1970s, the Abkhaz nationalist groups were becoming militant, and in 1989, anti-Georgian violence erupted, leaving eighteen dead (Nahaylo and Swoboda 1990, 325). Today, Ossetians, Ajarians, and others are clamoring for more independence and different boundaries.

UNREST IN THE TRANSCAUCASUS

As pointed out earlier, much of the ethnic unrest in the former Soviet Union centers on the question of which nationality will have real power in these various federal units established by the USSR. One could dismiss this as merely a "turf" dispute, but, given the long-standing historical roots of these issues, even such seemingly minor problems take on enormous import for local groups. Especially where several ethnic groups are in competition for control of a region, tensions have been very high. The most crucial problem in the Caucasus is the question of who will control and populate the enclave regions of Nagorno-Kharabakh and Nakhichevan.

Nagorno-Karabakh is an area almost entirely populated by Armenians, but which is located in the republic of Azerbaijan. Given the legal authority of the Azeris over this region, there has been understandable resentment among Armenians for decades. As early as 1955, leaders of the Armenian Republic called upon Khrushchev to annex both Nagorno-Karabakh and Azeri-inhabited Nakhichevan to Armenian territory—a demand which was tabled at the time (Nahaylo and Swoboda 1990, 117). In 1965, 100,000 Armenians, rather than commemorate the fiftieth anniversary of Turkish genocide as planned, began demonstrating for annexation of the territories, much to the embarrassment of Moscow dignitaries. A letter to Brezhnev in 1977 from a prominent Armenian writer demanding action on the matter received no response.

In late 1987, delegates from Nagorno-Karabakh made several trips to Moscow, in which for the first time they were given indications that their demands for union with Armenia might finally be met. Local authorities in the enclave began preparations for the transfer and spoke highly of Gorbachev's insight and vision. Azeri leaders disputed the claim and warned the enclave residents to stop their activities. By now, Moscow was at the center of a major dispute it had wanted to postpone. Faced with the defiant mood in Nagorno-Karabakh, as well as the implication of accepting a transfer (three times as many Armenians lived in other parts of Azerbaijan and some 160,000 Azeris lived in Armenia), Moscow rejected the demand and confirmed Azerbaijan's authority over the enclave (Nahaylo and Swoboda 1990, 285). Almost immediately, unrest broke out among Armenians across Azerbaijan and Nagorno-Karabakh, with rumors of ethnic attacks and casualties. By the end of February 1988 close to a million people had demonstrated in various parts of the region and over thirty people were dead. The region was temporarily placed under the direct control of Moscow and refugees poured from the area to safe havens in their respective republics.

In March of 1988, Moscow sent mixed signals to the inhabitants of Nagorno-Karabakh, offering aid and a listening ear one day, and condemning defiance the next. The situation died down during the spring of 1988, and in June the leaders of the two regions showed remarkable unity when they spoke at the Nineteenth Communist Party Congress and both criticized the failure of Moscow to anticipate and intervene in the situation. Anti-Moscow demonstrations following the inconclusive party conference resulted in troops being deployed to Yerevan, the capital of Armenia. On July 18, Gorbachev and the cabinet ruled definitively on retaining Azeri control of Nagorno-Karabakh, but this only led to a shouting match with the Armenian representative, who declared that Armenian nationalism was far from dead. By the end of the year, as if to prove him right, the all-Armenian National movement was formed on a platform of radically increasing its autonomy from Moscow, although stopping short of independence (Nahaylo and Swoboda 1990, 341).

The devastating earthquake in the Armenian capital on December 8, 1988, caused very extensive damage and killed thousands, most of whom were crushed in their flimsy state-built brick homes. Gorbachev cut short a visit to New York to deal with the problem, and used the occasion to increase Soviet repression. In January, Moscow again asserted direct control of Nagorno-Karabakh in the name of stability, and rounded up a number of Armenian agitators in the region (Nahaylo and Swoboda 1990, 317). This action did little to endear the once popular Gorbachev in the hearts of Armenians. Azeris were incensed by this heavy intervention and began to organize a nationalist movement, the Azerbaijan Popular Front. Most of 1989 nonetheless passed relatively quietly, as the Berlin Wall fell down.

Meanwhile, tentative proindependence demonstrations in Georgia grew increasingly strident, culminating in a massive rally on April 9, 1989. Because the demonstrations were blatantly proindependence in their tone, authorities (with apparent approval from Moscow) intervened with troops armed with sharpened spades and, allegedly, chemical weapons. The result was twenty civilian casualties and, ironically, a declaration of full Georgian independence two years later on that same date (Olcott 1991, 337).

In late 1989, the Popular Front demanded the return of Nagorno-Karabakh from Moscow's control. During the summer, Azeris had succeeded in surrounding the enclave and had thereby cut off its flow of support from Armenia. The situation was very serious. In addition, Azeri leader's sought greater control over their nation's oil wealth which they said was being siphoned off to Moscow. Moscow relented and returned full control of the Nagorno-Karabakh region to Azerbaijan—an event which precipitated a new wave of demonstrations and protests. By now the homespun Popular Front of Azerbaijan had grown in influence over the Moscow-appointed party leaders in Baku, and had galvanized the Azeri population to respond to Armenian demonstrations with counterdemonstrations of their own. In spite of the Popular Front's desire to keep the demonstrations peaceful, attacks on Armenians living in Baku increased and led to the imposition of martial law by Moscow. When the Soviet tanks rolled in, nearly 100 civilians were killed in the violence (Olcott 1991, 341).

The declaration of martial law brought some stability to the region. Soviet troops moved progressively through Nagorno-Karabakh and the surrounding Armenian-dominated villages and by the summer of 1991 established some semblance of peace—at the price of goodwill and freedom (*Washington Post*, May 8, 1991, A32). A peace agreement between the parties was violated, however, and both sides prepared for what was expected to be the final struggle following the collapse of the Soviet Union in December 1991. By the beginning of 1992, Armenians controlled most of Nagorno-Karabakh itself, although their contacts with Armenia proper were severed.

In April 1992, violence escalated and adopted a far more systematic and mechanized character. Armenians secured control of the entire region of

Nagorno-Karabakh by mid-May, including a corridor linking it to Armenia itself, and launched an offensive against the Azeri-populated Nakhichevan adjacent to Armenia. Azeris forced the discredited Baku government to hold elections which resulted in the elevation of the Popular Front, led by Abulfez Elchibey, to power in early June. The Popular Front, elected on a nationalist platform, immediately launched a large-scale counteroffensive in Nagorno-Karabakh with tanks and helicopters (*Washington Post*, June 23, 1992, A3). Turkey considered intervening on the side of Azerbaijan until talks between the Turkish president and Boris Yeltsin delayed the prospect of third-party intervention. The UN decided in May to send a fact-finding mission. By then, the war had already resulted in 3,000 dead and some 300,000 refugees. Warring factions signed a tentative peace treaty on May 26, 1993, raising the hopes of many but failing to resolve the status of Nagorno-Karabakh (*New York Times*, May 27, 1993, A6). However, as the winter of 1993–1994 set in, Armenians in the enclave had resumed fighting, pushing into regions of Azerbaijan and precipitating a new round of refugee flights (*Christian Science Monitor*, November 1, 1993, 3).

The most recent development in the Caucasus is a new outbreak of the civil war over Abkhazian independence from Georgia, where Georgian troops intervened in August 1992 and became embroiled in large-scale fighting. No sooner had a drive for independence by Georgian Ossetians (to reunite with Ossetians in Russia) been resolved temporarily through agreement between Russia and Georgia to create a joint peacekeeping force in the region, that the violence in Abkhazia broke out. Eduard Schevardnadze returned to Georgia after the collapse of the Soviet Union and the military's ouster of Zviad Gamsakhurdia in December 1991 to lead a provisional government and ultimately win election to the presidency. He is, as he put it, "at a loss" with regard to this situation, which continues to escalate thanks to participation by numerous irregular forces, including former Soviet troops left over in Georgia. Russians seemed to be providing increasing support to the guerrillas as well as irregular forces north of the Caucasus, and Schevardnadze made it clear that he was willing to fight to preserve Georgian rights in the Abkhaz—a region where Abkhazians constitute only 17 percent of the population (*Christian Science Monitor*, October 22, 1992, 7).

His pledge was put to the test in the fall of 1993 when he was faced with two major uprisings at the same time. While fighting in Abkhaz showed signs of waning with the signing in late July of a cease-fire and mutual disarmament agreement between Abkhaz and Georgian forces, Zviad Gamsakhurdia returned in September with numerous loyalists to attempt to retake power from Schevardnadze by force. As he launched his offensive, Abkhaz rebels renewed fighting for their own independence. Despite an impressive last stand in the Abkhaz capital of Sukhumi, the outgunned Georgian troops, led personally by Schevardnadze, were forced to abandon the territory on September 27. Gamsakhurdia's forces pressed eastward from their base near the border of Abkhazia and took control of vital rail and road links between the Georgian capital Tbilisi and the Black Sea (*London Times*, October 18, 1993, 12). Faced with the prospect of the total collapse of his government and country, Schevardnadze reversed himself and called upon the Russian Federation for support, agreeing in addition to joining its Commonwealth of Independent States. While this may have been a bitter pill for him to swallow, the action had the desired effect. Russian soldiers took up defensive positions along the road and rail links, freeing up Georgian militiamen to engage the rebels head-on (*Christian Science Monitor*, November 1, 1993, 3). On November 7, Georgians recaptured Gamsakhurdia's last stronghold and Schevardnadze declared an end to the rebellion (*New York Times*, November 8, 1993, A6). Georgia now faces the task of recovering Abkhaz, making new arrangements with south Ossetians and other separatists, and rebuilding an economy which is devastated—perhaps beyond repair.

CONCLUSION?

Perhaps it will seem a bit unsettling to leave our discussion of nationalist problems in the Transcaucasus here, but history rarely ends neatly. Indeed, one may well ask whether we are witnessing the end of one historical phase or the beginning of a new one. Will we one day look back on the current troubles in the Transcaucasus and say "That's where it all began!"?

There is no way at present to predict where these and many other situations involving emerging nationalities will lead. As of late 1993, major ethnic disturbances were taking place in Ossetia, Abkhazia, Tadzhikistan, Moldova, Eastern Germany, Armenia, Azerbaijan, the Ukraine, Dagestan, the former Yugoslavia, and among Gagausz, Tatar, and German minorities scattered throughout the former USSR. This does not include simmering disputes between many other nations which could easily flare up at any moment (*New York Times*, May 24, 1992, 10).

Questions to Consider

1. Should every national group be provided statehood? Is there a limit to self-determination?

2. Is it appropriate for nations to take up arms to settle territorial disputes inherited from imperial regimes? What are the best methods for addressing such questions?

3. What role should international agencies play in these disputes? What does international law say about territorial acquisition?

4. How can these problems be forestalled? What will it take to prevent civil war, secessionism, irridentism, and local wars over ethnicity from starting in the first place?

References

Seweryn Bialer. *The Soviet Paradox: External Expansion, Internal Decline* (New York: Alfred A. Knopf, 1986).

The Cambridge Encyclopedia of Russia and the Soviet Union (Cambridge: Cambridge University Press, 1982).

Helene Carrère d'Encausse. *Big Brother: The Soviet Union and Soviet Europe,* trans. by George Holoch (New York: Holmes & Meier, 1987).

Christian Science Monitor, October 22, 1992, 7

Christian Science Monitor, November 1, 1993, 3

Renée de Nevers. *The Soviet Union and Eastern Europe: The End of an Era* (London: International Institute for Strategic Studies, 1990).

John Hiden and Patrick Salmon. *The Baltic Nations and Europe: Estonia, Latvia and Lithuania in the Twentieth Century* (New York: Longman, 1991).

Rasma Karklins. *Ethnic Relations in the USSR: The Perspective From Below* (Boston: Allen & Unwin, 1986)

Zev Katz, ed. *Handbook of Major Soviet Nationalities* (New York: The Free Press, 1975).

Viktor Kozlov. *The Peoples of the Soviet Union* (Bloomington, IN: Indiana University Press, 1988).

Ernest Lefever and Vander Lugt, eds. *Perestroika: How New Is Gorbachev's New Thinking?* (Washington, DC: Ethics and Public Policy Center, 1989).

London Times, October 18, 1993, 12.

Bohdan Nahaylo and Victor Swoboda. *Soviet Disunion: A History of the Nationalities Problem in the USSR* (New York: Free Press, 1990).

New York Times, May 24, 1992, A1.

New York Times, May 27, 1993, A6.

New York Times, November 8, 1993, A6.

Martha Brill Olcott. "The Slide into Disunion." *Current History* 90 #558 (October 1991): 338–344.

Leslie Symon, ed. *The Soviet Union: A Systematic Geography* (Totowa, NJ: Barnes & Noble Books, 1983).

Vladimir Tismaneanu. *Reinventing Politics: Eastern Europe from Stalin to Havel* (New York: The Free Press, 1992).

United States Department of State. *Atlas of United States Foreign Relations,* 2nd ed. (Washington, DC: Government Printing Office, 1985).

Washington Post, May 8, 1991, A32.

Washington Post, June 23, 1992, A3.

Middle East Arms Race

An arms race is the competitive escalation in hardware and technology that often takes place between two rival nations. Arms races have proven extremely difficult to identify in fact, and even more difficult to explain. The simple search for security is not enough to predict that two nations will continually increase their military capabilities, since there are costs to such activities. Likewise, there is no clear understanding of what will be the result of an arms race—it does not always lead to war as was commonly assumed. The greatest arms race in history—the nuclear weapons competition between the United States and USSR—led to exhaustion, not bloodshed.

The Middle East has been described as the ideal proving ground for modern weaponry since countries in the region are in a constant state of war. Particularly since the oil price increases of the early 1970s, Arabs, Persians, and Jews alike have competed with each other for the latest in battle-ready weaponry. Not content with arms available on the open market or through bilateral agreements, several Middle Eastern countries have taken to producing their own. Since the mid-1970s, Israel, Iraq, and possibly other nations in the region have undertaken nuclear programs, which raises the fear that the next Arab-Israeli war will lead to holocaust (Jabber 1981, 25).

BACKGROUND TO 1973

Without going into great detail, suffice it to say that in 1948, following British and American encouragement, a large group of refugees from Hitler's Holocaust proclaimed a Jewish state along the Mediterranean coast in biblical Judea and Galilee. The native Palestinian Arabs were joined by most of the then-independent Arab states in a fight against this new entity.

For several months, war raged in the area and the Israeli forces gained what would prove to be a stronghold through military conquest. Palestinians began a long struggle to regain their territory and identity.

To a large extent, the problems of the Middle East revolve around this central historical moment (see Map 18.1). Wars in 1956, 1967, and 1973 have pitted Israel against Egypt, Syria, Iraq, Jordan, and other Arab neighbors bent on eradicating the Jewish presence. Israeli incursions into Lebanon in the 1970s and 1980s stemmed from Palestinian attacks across the border. Jordanian attacks against Palestinians in 1970 were precipitated by frustration in Amman over Palestinian provocation of Israeli attacks in the West Bank. The half-decade-long *intifadah* (uprising) by Palestinians in the West Bank against Israeli occupation forces is merely the latest form this ongoing Arab-Israeli conflict has taken.

However, it would be a mistake to neglect the frequent conflicts that have arisen outside of this Israeli nexus. Most recently, the Iraqi invasion of Kuwait is a vivid example of inter-Arab conflict, which also includes wars in Yemen on the Arabian Peninsula, border clashes between Libya and Egypt (as well as most of Libya's neighbors), and Iraq's war against Iran following the fall of the shah. When internal conflicts in Syria, Iraq, Saudi Arabia, Jordan, Egypt, and other Middle Eastern countries are considered, the number of Arab and Persian dead from non-Israeli hands far outnumbers those casualties of the anti-Zionist struggle.

The complexity of Middle East conflicts is bewildering, and helps to explain the fact that explaining and predicting not only an arms race but even war itself is a treacherous undertaking. To begin, we will focus particularly on the Arab-Israeli conflict, however, and will later address inter-Arab and Arab-Persian disputes.

Given its 1948 experience of facing a virtually united Arab coalition arrayed against it, Israel has taken an expansive view of its adversaries.

> Despite the lack, at present, of any form of integrated command set-up, Israel sees the combined forces of Syria, Jordan and Iraq, as forming one single front stretching from Mount Hermon to the Red Sea and threatening the whole eastern border of Israel (Duncan 1984, 109).

This perception of the Arab threat has prompted Israel to undertake several parallel strategies. First, Israel has endeavored to keep its military spending and arsenals as large as possible, even at the risk of jeopardizing national economic health. Figures 18.1 and 18.2 show the extraordinary efforts to invest in military hardware by Israel during the 1960s and 1970s—particularly following the 1973 war when Israel was caught relatively unprepared for the Egyptian attack along the Suez. These expenditures dropped off in the late 1970s (see Figure 18.3).

Second, Israel has perfected the "preemptive strike" strategy to compensate for its small size compared to the combined strength of its Arab neighbors. In 1956 and 1967, Israel interpreted the bellicose rhetoric of its neighbors as a warning of war. In the 1950s, Egyptian leader Gamel Nasser had taken a radical approach in his relations with the West, evidenced by his ef-

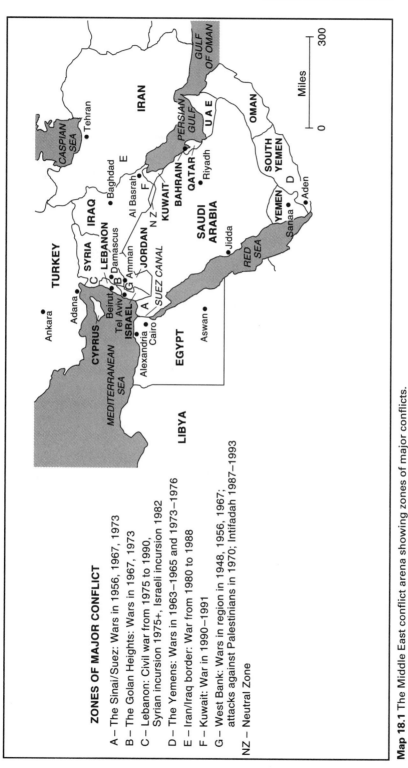

ZONES OF MAJOR CONFLICT

A – The Sinai/Suez: Wars in 1956, 1967, 1973

B – The Golan Heights: Wars in 1967, 1973

C – Lebanon: Civil war from 1975 to 1990,
Syrian incursion 1975+, Israeli incursion 1982

D – The Yemens: Wars in 1963–1965 and 1973–1976

E – Iran/Iraq border: War from 1980 to 1988

F – Kuwait: War in 1990–1991

G – West Bank: Wars in region in 1948, 1956, 1967;
attacks against Palestinians in 1970; Intifadah 1987–1993

NZ – Neutral Zone

Map 18.1 The Middle East conflict arena showing zones of major conflicts.

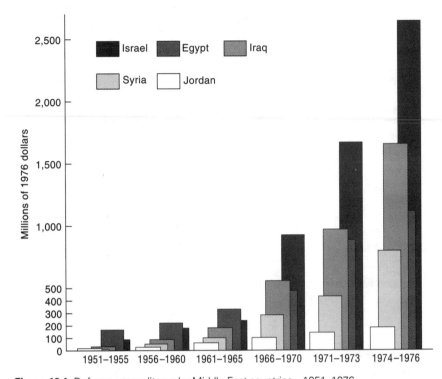

Figure 18.1 Defense expenditures by Middle East countries—1951–1976.
Source: Paul Jabber, *Not by War Alone: Security and Arms Control in the Middle East* (Berkeley: University of California Press, 1981).

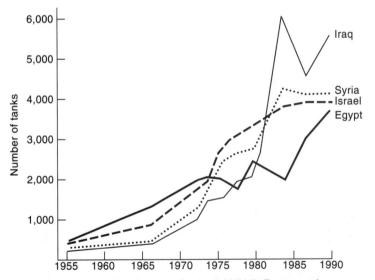

Figure 18.2 Arsenal of battle tanks of selected Middle East countries.
Sources: Paul Jabber *1981 and the Military Balance* (London: International Institute for Strategic Studies, various years).

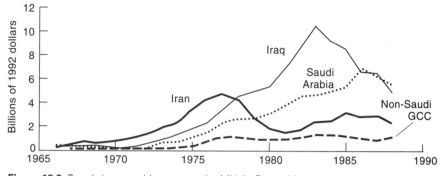

Figure 18.3 Trends in arms shipments to the Middle East, 1965–1988, as measured by the value of imported military goods and services, Persian Gulf theater.
Source: Congressional Budget Office based on data from the Arms Control and Disarmament Agency.

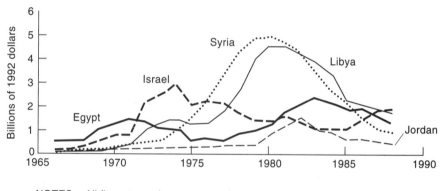

NOTES: All figures are three-year moving averages.
Scale of the bottom graph is 50 percent smaller than scale of the top graph.
GCC = Gulf Cooperation Council.

Figure 18.4 Trends in arms shipments to the Middle East, 1965–1988, as measured by the value of imported military goods and services, Arab-Israeli theater.
Source: Congressional Budget Office based on data from the Arms Control and Disarmament Agency.

forts to nationalize the Suez Canal and his policy of forming a joint military command with Syria and Saudi Arabia. As Nasser made his move to nationalize the canal, Israel, in conjunction with French and British forces, invaded the Sinai and took possession of the canal zone, only to withdraw because of American and Soviet pressure (McFadden 1987, 39). In 1967, Nasser again gave clear signals of his intent to attack Israel when he called for the removal of UN peacekeeping troops deployed in the Sinai following the 1956 war, and Israel again attacked first. This time, its forces overran the Sinai, the West Bank, and the Golan Heights within three days and remained there until the 1980s (McFadden 1987, 40). The policy of preemptive strike allowed Israel to prevail in spite of numerical disadvantage.

A third policy in Israel is the development of a highly integrated military structure. In a region where the military typically is divided in its political loyalties, the Israeli Defense Force (IDF) is more typical of Western military organizations. In a region where these divided loyalties are played out in competing command structures (where paramilitary internal security forces are often better equipped than the military itself), the IDF command is centralized and its tactics and strategies clearly integrated. The shrewd use of air support for mechanized advances and the speed of interservice communication has been pivotal to Israel's success in the battlefield (Levin and Halevy 1983).

AFTERMATH OF THE 1973 WAR

The 1973 Yom Kippur (Ramadan) War is known in Israel as the "near thing." Israeli forces were taken by surprise when Egyptian and Syrian forces joined in a coordinated attack on two fronts. Israel was able to regain its composure and pushed back Syrian troops in the Golan and broke through Egyptian ranks in the Suez region. Within two weeks a cease-fire line extended beyond the original 1967 limits of Israeli advance. In spite of this remarkable success, Israelis have been experiencing a crisis of confidence. Part of this stems from the fact that Israeli intelligence failed to warn of the attack. In addition, the level of Israeli casualties was staggering. In 1956, Israeli battle deaths numbered in the dozens. In 1967, they were well below 1,000. In the 1973 war, they approached 3,000 (given Israel's small population, this was equivalent to 200,000 casualties for the United States—Jabber 1981, 21). Finally, it demonstrated that Israel misjudged the size of military defenses that would deter an attack.

Part of Israel's failure, such as it was, was the result of its own success. Following the 1967 war, Palestinians and Egyptians alike began organizing for a future showdown. The Palestine Liberation Organization (PLO) adopted a policy of systematic terrorism which forced Israel to pay closer attention to internal security. Israeli troops engaged in repeated attacks against Palestinian bases and towns in the West Bank (precipitating Jordanian attacks against the inconvenient PLO forces on its soil). Egyptians, fearful of Israeli forces massed on their border a mere sixty miles from Cairo, began bombarding the Sinai in the "War of Attrition," which forced Israel to retaliate in kind. As Israel launched air strikes against Egyptian artillery, sometimes coming within miles of Cairo itself, Egypt appealed to the Soviet Union for better air defenses and other hardware. Egypt also reorganized its military strategy, taking a page from the IDF book by integrating its command structure and learning the doctrine of the preemptive strike. As Egypt began to feel confident in its newfound capabilities it decided to launch the attack. Thus, one can argue that Israel's success in 1967 sowed the seeds for its much more difficult challenge in 1973.

Other elements in the Arab-Israeli equation began to change as a result of the 1973 war. To begin, a superpower policy of restraining arms exports to the region began to crumble. Over the years, the United States, France, Britain, and even the Soviet Union had entered into tacit and even explicit agreements to limit the amount and quality of weapons bound for the Mid-

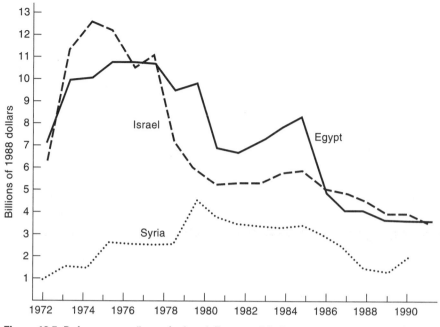

Figure 18.5 Defense expenditures for Israel, Egypt, and Syria.
Sources: Various issues of SIPRI Yearbook.

dle East. In the 1950s, for example, the United States, France, and Britain kept a formal agreement to severely limit arms sales in the Middle East, no small thing given France and Britain's colonial presence in the region. From 1967 to 1972, the United States and the USSR promised each other they would limit sales of older weapons and stop shipments of state-of-the-art arms altogether (Power 1991, 15). As a result, most weapons in the Middle East prior to 1973 were at least ten years old and were generally under-equipped when it came to payloads, guidance systems, and electronics generally (Mottale 1986, 42). As put by Smoler:

> With the Soviets and the United States as reasonably prudent arms suppliers, the regional balance of power was admirably polyvalent: local powers were generally unable to attempt the conquest of weak neighbors without producing coalitions to defend the status quo. (Smoler 1991, 350)

To illustrate the point, when Iraq decided to join the fight in 1973 by sending 600 tanks, they had no way to transport them to the Golan except under their own power (a trip of some 400 miles across mountainous desert). Half of the tanks never made it, and of the 300 that saw action, 111 were destroyed (Wagner 1983, 68).

Following the Yom Kippur/Ramadan War, however, great power inhibitions were cast aside. As can be seen in Figures 18.3, and 18.4, Israel and Iran began importing considerably more military hardware, including state-of-the-art F-15 fighters from the United States. Israel also invested heavily in a ballistic missile program labeled "Jericho." This missile program coincided

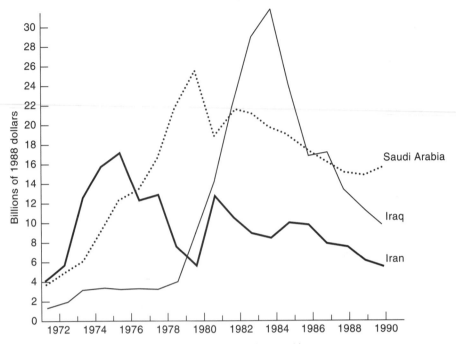

Figure 18.6 Defense expenditures for Saudi Arabia, Iraq, and Iran.
Sources: Various issues of SIPRI Yearbook.

with the acquisition of two nuclear facilities from Europe which together gave Israel the capacity to develop nuclear warheads (Jabber 1981, 28). More will be said later about nuclear escalation in the Middle East.

At the same time, the Soviet Union responded favorably to appeals for more and better weapons from Egypt, Syria, Libya, Iraq, and other nations. Iraq began its own nuclear weapons program in 1976 (Feldman 1984, 117). Partly in response to this increased Soviet activity, the United States provided considerable weaponry to the shah of Iran (Smoler 1991, 351).

Farther from the Israeli front, Arab nations were either at war or anticipating it. After Nasser came to power in Egypt, he created considerable disquiet in the conservative monarchies of Jordan and Saudi Arabia (Dawisha 1984, 3). On the other hand, Syria, fearful of Iraq's growing power, which itself was precipitated by U.S. support for Iran and Israel, sought to increase its defenses (Rabinovich 1984, 38) and solidify its Soviet ties, which in turn affected its balance with Israel. U.S. support for Iran and its consequences for Iraqi buildup in turn caused anxiety in Riyadh and a Saudi weapons program (Smoler 1991, 351). Thus, even assuming stable diplomatic relations, one can see that outside involvement accelerates arms acquisitions.

Throughout this period, alliance relationships were constantly shifting, such that allies one year were often enemies the next. An example is Egypt, which shifted from the radical bloc with Syria and Iraq to an alliance (along with Syria) with conservative Saudi Arabia in the early 1970s. In the late 1970s, Egypt withdrew into a narrow regional bloc and signed a peace treaty with Israel (Taylor 1982, 122–124). Certainly the sudden transfer of control of U.S. weapons from a conservative monarchy to a radical Shiite regime in one blow (the fall of the shah in 1979) is enough to further illustrate the point that Middle East arms races seldom end up the way they started.

The common link between the arms sales of these superpowers is the sudden increase of wealth (in hard currency no less) experienced by Iran, Iraq, Saudi Arabia, Libya, and the Gulf states following the dramatic oil price hikes of 1973–1980. While this is discussed in some detail in case #21, it is worthwhile to mention that Saudi Arabia, for example, took in some $181 billion from 1973 to 1978 that it would otherwise not have seen, while Iran earned $118 billion (Mottale 1986, 40). Such wealth can go far toward building a modern defense. By the early 1980s, the Saudi air force, which in 1973 had only 95 antiquated aircraft, boasted nearly 300 combat aircraft with F-15s and an AWAC from the United States on the way, putting it on a par with Germany.

Unfortunately, the oil wealth that came to the Middle East had none of the progressive and integrative power that industrialization and modernity have brought to the West. As put by Mottale, oil wealth simply intensified "military conquest, holy wars, and the Bedouin-military tradition, Iran's imperial past and the military hegemony of the Ottoman Empire in the Middle East until the early twentieth century" (Mottale 1986, 34).

A final impetus for great power exports to the Middle East in the 1970s stems from the needs of the military-industrial complex (see case study #5). As the Vietnam War faded away in the mid-1970s, many defense contractors in the United States were deprived of the steady flow of weapons contracts from the Pentagon. In order to preserve production levels, the Department of Defense helped coordinate foreign arms sales, the bulk of which went to the Middle East. In addition, American and Soviet defense planners were eager for new proving grounds for their increasingly sophisticated weapons systems, and the Middle East offered just the opportunity they sought (Jabber 1981, 14).

Thus an arms race took place in the Middle East during the 1970s, elevating not only the size of the military establishments across the region, but also their quality and their international linkages.

THE 1980s AND THE MIDDLE EAST ARMS RACE

When the United States sponsored the Camp David Peace Accords between Israel and Egypt in 1978, it made a long-term commitment to maintaining a balance of power in the Middle East. When combined with its growing support for Saudi Arabia (made all the more important by the declaration of the Carter Doctrine in 1980 pledging U.S. commitment to continued oil flows from the Persian Gulf) and its relationship with Iraq, Kuwait, and other Middle Eastern powers, the United States was the dominant factor in the arms buildup in the region (Peterson 1986, 126). The Camp David Accords obligated the United States not only to continued aid to Israel (to the tune of well over 10 percent of Israel's gross national product), but to a proportional level of support (roughly 90 percent of Israel's aid levels) to Egypt. Thus, in a very real way, the United States is a direct party to a continuous, if controlled, arms race between Israel and Egypt.

U.S. support for Israel and Egypt further complicates the overlapping Middle East tensions already described. As put recently by Frenkel:

> This is the way it works: the United States, for example, supplies arms to Israel. Afterward, to create 'balance,' the Americans rush off to supply weapons to Egypt too. The arming of Israel scares Syria, and the supplying of Egypt frightens Libya, and both dash off to arm themselves with Soviet weapons. Soviet weapons in Syria scare Turkey and Jordan, and they waste no time in obtaining Western arms; they also frighten Iraq, who buys from both West and East. Iraqi arms set off alarms in Iran, which quickly sells a great load of oil to get money to buy from everybody. Naturally, the Iran-Iraq arms spree makes the Saudis, the Kuwaitis and the rest of the Gulf Emirates very nervous, and they in turn purchase Western weapons. This of course frightens the East-leaning states in the Southern Arabian peninsula and eastern Africa. The Soviets, and the Chinese too, are only too pleased to help. (Frenkel 1991, 40)

In the early 1980s, tensions in Lebanon and Iran exploded. Syria had invaded parts of Lebanon in 1975, much to the dismay of most Arab states as well as Israel and prompting Israel to make plans for an invasion of the southern section of the country. As Palestinian camps in southern Lebanon became increasingly threatening, Israel invaded in 1982 and occupied roughly one-third of the country (to the outskirts of Beirut) before Western powers convinced her to halt the advance and begin withdrawals.

Israeli troops remained in parts of southern Lebanon throughout the decade, however, and the Southern Lebanese Army, supported by Israel, continued to operate in the area. Atrocities against Palestinian refugees trapped by the Israeli advance prompted a reconsideration in the United States of support for Israel. The Palestinian uprising which began in 1987 led Israel to adopt an even harsher policy toward Arabs in the West Bank and an accelerated settlement effort. When combined with Israeli problems in Gaza and deprivation of the civil rights of Arabs within Israel itself, Israeli policies caused policymakers in the Reagan administration to soften U.S. support publicly while maintaining relatively constant financial support. It was not until the Bush administration came to power that the United States began to engage the PLO in direct negotiations and openly criticize the more inflexible Israeli policies vis à vis the West Bank.

In the Sinai, Israeli disengagement was completed in April 1982 and peaceful relations between Egypt and Israel survived the assassination of peacemaker Anwar Sadat. Egypt has proven to be an important interlocutor for Israel in the Arab world, particularly with the conservative monarchies, although Egypt has paid a diplomatic price in its relations with more radical states such as Iraq and Libya.

In the Persian Gulf, Saddam Hussein decided to take advantage of Iranian chaos following the fall of the shah in 1979 to seize control of important shared waterways and stifle growing Islamic militancy in the southern regions of the country. The Iran-Iraq War, begun with a successful offensive in 1980, dragged on throughout the decade. In 1982, Iran mounted a strong counteroffensive, although at the cost of hundreds of thousands of young lives. By 1984, with Iran unable to press its advantage with inroads into Iraq, the war reached a deadly stalemate. Seeking to cut off Iran's oil revenues, Iraq began attacking tankers in the Gulf and Iran retaliated. Kuwait asked the United States to provide military support (at the same time as it asked the Soviets as well) and by 1987 the United States had a sizeable military presence in the Persian Gulf. Saudi Arabia, fearful of the implications of a virulent fundamentalist presence in the region, tacitly supported Iraq's efforts, as did the United States (Smoler 1991, 351). Saudi and Western support were short-lived, however; they ended with Iraq's surprise invasion of Kuwait in 1990, two years after a truce was declared with Iran.

Through all this, efforts to increase and improve arsenals continued, albeit at a slower pace. Iraqi arms imports alone during the 1980s came to between $80 and $105 billion, of which as much as half was purchased on credit (Smoler 1991, 347). In 1981, following the increase in the price of oil to $40 per barrel of "Arabian light" crude oil (up from the roughly $1.50/barrel levels of pre-1973), when Saudi Arabia earned over $100 billion in just one year, the price began to fall until by 1986 it had collapsed to less than $10 a barrel. Saudi oil earnings fell to roughly $30 billion per year in the 1980s. As can be seen in Figure 18.6, the result was a general dropping off of military expenditures for all Middle Eastern countries in the latter half of the 1980s, although the expenditures stayed relatively high in gross national product terms. One can note in this parallel downward trend a similarity with superpower behavior. Such downward movement need not be encouraging, since it only reflects the year-to-year changes in expenditure and says little about the accumulated stockpiles of weapons, which are quite large (see Figure 18.2).

The lack of resources forced several Middle Eastern countries to focus on qualitative improvements in their arsenals and more creative deployment options. Saudi Arabia has benefited from U.S. support in the form of state-of-the-art aircraft and early warning systems. It has chosen to deploy these weapons at Tabuk, a new base located in the northwest region of the country, which puts Israel in easy striking distance of Saudi Arabia (Dawisha 1984, 23). Iraq worked to improve the Soviet Scud missiles by lowering the payload and increasing the range, to the point that it could strike directly at Israel, as evidenced by the rather clumsy attacks on Tel Aviv in 1991. Israel's Jericho program has now provided it with between 50 and 100 ballistic missiles with a range of some 900 miles, within reach of Riyadh, Tripoli, and all of the Near East. The Dimona nuclear facility in Israel is rumored to have produced as many as 200 nuclear warheads, which is consistent with ballistic missile programs underway. In fact, some have argued that the Jericho missiles are simply too expensive to be loaded with conventional warheads, since many cheap alternatives exist (Jabber 1981, 30).

It may well be that any future efforts to control the flow of foreign arms to the Middle East will have little impact on the regional arms race, since arsenals and domestic production facilities in many countries are already more than adequate to carry on a protracted war. Nonetheless, the Gulf War has left the region in a new condition, which deserves some comment.

THE POSTWAR MIDDLE EAST

The hopes for Middle East peace since the Persian Gulf War have largely been frustrated. What is more troublesome is evidence that yet another round of a Middle East arms race is underway. Absent Iraq's counterweight, Iran has engaged in active shopping in the apparent hope of laying claim to dominance in the Gulf. The contraband weapons market in the former Soviet Union has been active and available, and Iran is reported to have there acquired new submarines, aircraft, missiles, ammunition, and possibly even nuclear warheads (from Kazakhstan).

The United States has readily jumped into the Middle East arms market, recalling its post-Vietnam enthusiasm. Saudi Arabia obtained a sizeable grant of military aid from the United States immediately following the Gulf War (of the $22 billion originally proposed, the aid will more than likely be in the $10–$12 billion range). Saudi Arabia furthermore has bought and deployed some 120 Chinese-made DF-3 ballistic missiles in the past five years. These missiles have a 1,600-mile range with a 4,400 pound conventional warhead (SIPRI 1991, 325). Egypt obtained 46 fully equipped F-16 fighters from the United States in 1991 and Israel has been given more Patriot missiles to protect against now-dismantled Scuds, as well as support for its own antimissile missile program (Morrison 1991, 850).

In the final analysis, it would seem that the Middle East arms race, with its superpower participation and overlapping conflicts, is off and running again. Given past experience, it is likely that the only winners will be the arms manufacturers themselves. Certainly the superpowers have generally been disappointed in their efforts to steer Middle East politics. As put by Mottale:

> To a large extent the relative inability of the superpowers to control or influence appreciably the recipients of the arms transfers is due primarily to the internal configurations of power within those states and in their relations with one another and their neighbors. (Mottale 1986, 57)

It is clear that any effort at peacemaking in the Middle East is doomed without considerable effort on the arms control side. However, arms control rarely has been possible in an atmosphere of tension and mistrust. Perhaps only another Anwar Sadat, willing to break with allies in order to embrace a foe, can change the course of conflict in the Middle East.

Questions to Consider

1. If the Middle East illustrates a typical arms race, what seems to accelerate it or slow it down? To what extent do relations within the region determine how many weapons a country will acquire?

2. What role do outsiders play in Middle East arms acquisition? Should this relationship be regulated somehow? What methods would you envision?

3. To what extent is an arms race a bad thing? What negative consequences are clearly the result of the arms race itself, or merely coincidental?

References

Congress of the United States, Congressional Budget Office. *Limiting Conventional Arms Exports to the Middle East* (Washington: Government Printing Office, 1992).

Adeed Dawisha. "Saudi Arabia's Search for Security," in Tripp, ed., *Regional Security*, 1–36.

Andrew Duncan. "The Military Threat to Israel," in Tripp, ed., *Regional Security*, 106–115

Shai Feldman. "A Nuclear Middle East," in Tripp, ed., *Regional Security*, 116–124.

Shlomo Frenkel. "The Pushers: How the Great Powers Arm the Middle East." *New Outlook* #9/10 (September/October 1991): 38–42.

Richard A. Gabriel, ed. *Fighting Armies: Antagonists in the Middle East—A Combat Assessment* (Westport, CT: Greenwood Press, 1983).

Paul Jabber. *Not by War Alone: Security and Arms Control in the Middle East* (Berkeley, CA: University of California Press, 1981).

Marlin Levin and David Halevy. "Israel," in Gabriel, ed., *Fighting Armies*, 3–26.

John H. McFadden. "The Strategic Arena," in Bernard Reich, *The Powers in the Middle East: The Ultimate Strategic Arena* (New York: Praeger, 1987), 3–52.

David C. Morrison. "Still Open for Business." *National Journal* 23 #15 (April 13, 1991): 850–854.

Morris Mehrdad Mottale. *The Arms Buildup in the Persian Gulf* (New York: University Press of America, 1986).

J. E. Peterson. *Defending Arabia* (New York: St. Martin's, 1986).

Jonathan Power. "When Will They Ever Learn?" *World Press Review*, 38 #4 (April 1991): 14–15.

Itamar Rabinovich. "The Foreign Policy of Syria: Goals, Capabilities, Constraints and Options," in Tripp, ed., *Regional Security*, 1984, 38–46.

SIPRI Yearbook 1991 (New York: Oxford University Press, 1991).

Fredric P. Smoler. "The Arming of Saddam Hussein: Cynical Politics and Profiteering." *Dissent* (Summer 1991): 346–353.

Alan R. Taylor. *The Arab Balance of Power* (Syracuse, NY: Syracuse University Press, 1982).

Charles Tripp, ed. *Regional Security in the Middle East* (New York: St. Martin's, 1984).

John Wagner. "Iraq," in Gabriel, ed., *Fighting Armies*, 63–84.

Middle East Peace Negotiations*

Diplomacy is a general term used to describe any interaction between nations (or any other international actor for that matter). Traditional diplomacy has evolved into a heavily ritualized communication system—understandable only to the initiated. In addition to traditional diplomacy, nations and agencies often become involved in a bilateral discussion as mediators. A mediator is any third party that becomes substantively involved in bilateral diplomacy, typically by providing suggestions and support. When the United States became involved in Middle East peace talks it also provided guarantees to reassure the suspicious Israelis.

HENRY KISSINGER AND THE 1973 WAR

Israel's lightning strike into Jordan, Syria, and Egypt in 1967 left Israeli troops and a growing number of settlers in power in the Golan Heights, the West Bank, the Gaza Strip, and the Sinai to the Suez Canal. None of these actions were recognized by the diplomatic community, least of which by Arab states which were determined to reverse these gains. The opportunity was seized on October 6, 1973, during the Jewish Yom Kippur feast in Israel, when Egyptian and Syrian troops launched a coordinated surprise attack on Israel.

---

*This case includes substantial portions reprinted from Linda B. Miller, "Shadow and Substance: Jimmy Carter and the Camp David Accords," #433R *Pew Case Studies in International Affairs*, © 1988 by the Pew Charitable Trusts, revised 1992 by the Institute of the Study of Diplomacy, Georgetown University.

Unlike previous Arab-Israeli wars, this battle did not produce a classic victory of West over East. To begin, Egypt had previously expelled its Soviet advisers in an ongoing effort to improve relations with the United States ("Why has Sadat done me this favor?" Kissinger asked his aides—Sheehan 1981, 49). It was thus not acting as a Soviet surrogate. More importantly, the war did not go well for Israel. By the third day it was clear that the Arab forces were well organized, well armed, and showing moderate success. The Egyptians had reclaimed the Suez and a roughly ten-mile-deep adjacent strip in the Sinai. The Syrians reclaimed as much as one-third of the Golan and its forces pushed to within five miles of the Israeli border (Dockrill 1991, 109).

Henry Kissinger took note of this rather unusual circumstance by endeavoring to "consolidate the stalemate":

> I believed that only a battlefield stalemate would provide the foundation on which fruitful negotiations might begin. Any equilibrium—if only an equilibrium of mutual exhaustion—would make it easier to reach an enforceable solution. (Kissinger 1982, 496)

During the period from October 10 to November 9, Kissinger exerted considerable pressure on Israel to accept a cease-fire and a negotiated settlement. On October 11, President Richard Nixon accepted Kissinger's recommendation to forward an airlift of military supplies, having failed to secure Egyptian acceptance of an immediate cease-fire (see Map 19.1). Shortly thereafter, Arab members of the Organization of Petroleum Exporting Countries (OPEC) imposed an embargo on the export of oil to the United States along with a unilateral quadrupling of crude prices.

The oil embargo added to Kissinger's desires for a negotiated settlement of the war. He sought the support of the Soviet Union in this effort. On October 22, UN Security Council Resolution 338, cosponsored by the two superpowers, demanded the immediate cessation of hostilities and the beginning of a peaceful settlement (along the lines of a two-state solution called for in UN Security Council Resolution 242). The resolution did not stop the fighting and Israeli armies swarmed across the Suez, effectively cutting off Egypt's Third Army on the eastern bank. The Soviet Union came close to intervening directly to support Egypt, but American warnings and a dramatic rise of its nuclear preparedness (Defense Condition or DEFCON) caused the Soviets to refrain. The United States simultaneously exerted pressure on Israel to pull back from the Egyptian front in order to allow the forces to be resupplied. Israel was reluctant to agree, given the considerable diplomatic leverage on Egypt this military posture commanded.

With each passing day, Kissinger became more and more directly involved in negotiating a peaceful settlement of the Suez dispute. On November 7, while in Cairo, he secured the support of President Anwar Sadat of Egypt for a six-point program providing for Third Army relief, prisoner exchange, and a future peace conference in Geneva. This has been considered a major turning point in Egyptian policy, since it represents the first time Sadat was willing to accept something less than full Israeli withdrawal to the

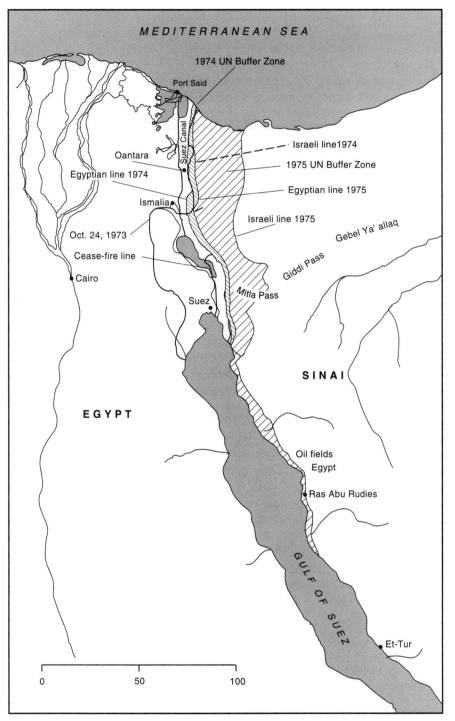

Map 19.1 1973–1975 Egyptian-Israeli troop withdrawal agreements.
Source: Lester Sobel, ed. *Peace-Making in the Middle East* (New York: Facts on File, 1980).

1967 lines (Kalb and Kalb 1974, 510). It also represented the beginning of a break in the Arab alliance, although this was more unintended than deliberate. On November 9, Israel agreed to the plan after the United States gave assurances that it would monitor the resupply effort for the Third Army. This pattern of Israeli concessions conditioned on major guarantees by the United States would repeat itself again and again during the successive talks.

Israel and Egypt were still far apart on at least two issues: "nonbelligerency" and exchange of prisoners. The Israelis sought from Egypt a firm commitment to peaceful relations, while Egypt wanted to avoid such a hazardous undertaking. Egypt was also reluctant to engage in a full-scale exchange of prisoners until it could be assured that Israeli forces were going to withdraw from Egyptian territory west of the Suez Canal.

A third issue which still divided Israel and Egypt was the central question of Palestinian rights and self-determination. Kissinger hoped to set aside this problem and move forward instead on bilateral arrangements between Israel and each of its enemies. Nonetheless, a conference was organized to study the general problem of the occupied territories as well as finalize plans for troop disengagement in both the Sinai and the Golan. In this context, Kissinger sought the participation of Syria, Jordan, and Saudi Arabia, as well as Israel and Egypt.

There was little enthusiasm for the December Geneva conference. While Israel, Egypt, and Jordan accepted invitations delivered jointly by the Soviets, Americans, and UN, Syria and Saudi Arabia declined on the grounds that Israeli withdrawal should precede any sort of a conference. Israel opposed UN participation, on which the United States insisted, so Kissinger agreed to lessen the secretary-general's role to symbolic figurehead. Israel refused to permit Palestinian representatives at the conference, which Egypt regretted but accepted. Throughout the preliminaries, all the Arab nations save Egypt seem to have assumed that the United States was able to change Israeli attitudes with the wave of a hand—in fact it seemed at times as though the reverse was more accurate. However, running throughout this process as a subtle prod to Arab attentiveness and flexibility was the implicit threat of U.S. military intervention.

The conference itself was largely symbolic, rather than substantive, and it did not lead to any larger negotiations, or even to talks between Israel and Jordan. In fact, by January what Kissinger hoped would become an ongoing negotiation process in Geneva was superseded by what became "shuttle diplomacy." On January 12, while meeting with Sadat in Cairo, Kissinger accepted the latter's invitation to act as go-between to Israeli Premier Golda Meir. The arrangement suited all the parties: not only did it give Sadat a superpower in his camp, but it calmed Israeli fears that concessions would increase Israel's vulnerability. Kissinger himself received extraordinary publicity from the process.

Most important, the process led to a rather rapid reconciliation of the conflicting demands of the major parties. By mid-January agreement was

reached on an immediate Israeli troop withdrawal and Egyptian troop rede-
ployment. On January 17, the agreement was signed and provided for a thin
line of Egyptian forces on the east bank of the Suez Canal, while Israeli
troops withdrew to a line roughly six miles to the east. Following a proposal
by Israeli Defense Minister Moshe Dayan, a UN contingent was deployed in
the narrow buffer zone between the forces, and troops near the buffer zone
were lightly armed (Sheehan 1981, 65–66). This "five-zone" approach
proved to be the recurring theme in all of the 1974–1975 disengagement
talks involving Israel.

What role did Kissinger play in these negotiations? According to Touval, he:

> was able to induce concessions without resorting to pressures. The incentives
> that the U.S. offered—economic aid to Egypt, and economic and military aid to
> Israel—do not appear to have been important causes for the parties' flexibility
> either. It was rather the pressure of circumstances in which Egypt and Israel
> found themselves that made them eager to conclude a disengagement agree-
> ment rapidly. The mediator's contribution was, however, essential in suggesting
> compromises and in arranging the indirect transaction of commitments. This
> procedure helped to reduce Sadat's vulnerability to criticism from the oppo-
> nents of the agreement, which a direct commitment to Israel might have en-
> tailed. And finally, by providing both parties with implicit and explicit guaran-
> tees, the mediator encouraged them to feel protected from some of the risks that
> they believed that their concessions entailed. (Touval 1982, 248)

Following this relatively easy success, Kissinger was drawn into two
much more contentious processes: disengagement in the Golan and a second, permanent Egyptian-Israeli disengagement in the Sinai. Because Syria
simply did not trust the United States, it was far more difficult for Kissinger
to establish warm relations, unlike the rather easy warmth that developed
between Kissinger and Sadat on the one hand and the near-infatuation between Kissinger and Meir on the other (Sheehan 1981, 72). Kissinger's first
major contribution involved conveying prisoner lists to each party in late
February and privately assuring King Faisal of Saudi Arabia that he would
quietly work for Syria's interests. Formal talks were opened on March 18,
the same day the oil embargo was finally lifted (over Syrian objections).

The key question in these talks was a rather simple one: Israel did not
want to withdraw its forces, which at the time were deep in Syrian territory—twenty-five miles from Damascus—beyond the territory it had occupied since 1967. Syria, on the other hand, insisted on gaining considerable
territory in order to prove that its war effort had been at least somewhat
fruitful. The debate focused on the eastern town of Kuneitra (El Quneitra).
which Israel firmly controlled, but which was once a regional administrative
center for Syria. Kissinger urged Israel to concede the city, or at least a sizeable portion thereof, and the Israeli's relented. When it came to determining
precisely where the Israeli troops would be deployed, the talks nearly broke
down, since Israel insisted on occupying three overlooking hills, to Syria's

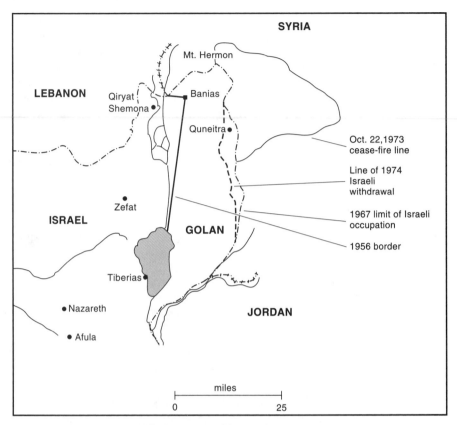

SYRIA

Mt. Hermon

LEBANON

Qiryat
Shemona •

Banias

Quneitra •

Oct. 22,1973
cease-fire line

Line of 1974
Israeli
withdrawal

1967 limit of Israeli
occupation

1956 border

• Zefat

ISRAEL

GOLAN

Tiberias •

• Nazareth

JORDAN

• Afula

miles

0   25

Map 19.2 1967–1974 Israeli-Syrian troop withdrawal agreements.
Source: Michael Dockrill, *Atlas of Twentieth Century World History* (New York: HarperPerennial, 1991), 109.

dismay. Israel insisted on allowing settlers to harvest their crops around the town, and eventually, after Kissinger repeatedly threatened to walk out, the two parties settled on slightly deeper Israeli withdrawals in exchange for harvesting rights and a fairly strong UN presence in a buffer zone around the town (see Map 19.2).

On other issues, Syria refused to inhibit clandestine PLO raids into northern Israel even though Israel refused anything less than a guarantee such attacks would cease. Kissinger intervened by pledging United States guarantees that any such attacks should be interpreted as a violation of the agreement, to which Israel could respond with all necessary means. The United States also provided considerable aid (converting a $1 billion loan to a grant and sending military hardware) as an inducement.

Perhaps most interesting in these talks is how Kissinger made himself indispensable. He made the point that Israel would have a difficult time finding a better interlocutor than a Jew from the United States. He demonstrated even-handedness with Syria to prove to Damascus that he was the best available spokesman to Tel Aviv. Thus he became indispensable. He was able to keep the talks moving forward simply by threatening to go home. On May 25, he went so far as to coauthor with President Hafez al-Assad of Syria a communique announcing the collapse of talks and laying the blame on Israel (an important threat for Tel Aviv) when, on his way out the door, Assad said to him, "What a pity. We've come so far and not succeeded. Can't anything be done. . . ?" and urged him to try once more with the Israeli leadership (Sheehan 1981, 71). On May 29, 1974, Israel and Syria signed their disengagement treaty under Henry Kissinger's watchful eye.

The second disengagement talks between Israel and Egypt stumbled from the start. The new government of Premier Itzak Rabin was adamant about a peace treaty with Egypt, while Kissinger tried to convey the political dangers this posed for Sadat vis à vis his Arab counterparts. Israel refused to abandon the strategic mountain passes of Giddi and Mitla without guarantees. It sought access to Egypt's oil, U.S. aid, and U.S. weapons. And Israel sought greater participation in the rules surrounding the UN buffer troops. The demands were so extreme and the position so obdurate that by the spring of 1975 Kissinger and other senior officials had concluded that negotiations were dead. In a highly publicized "reassessment" of U.S. policy, Kissinger and now-President Gerald Ford implicitly accused Israel of stonewalling and threatening the talks. This ambivalence precipitated a "full-court press" by the Israeli lobby in Congress, culminating in a letter signed by seventy-six congressmen urging the administration to maintain its commitment to Israeli security.

In this context, Israeli demands ultimately softened. Tel Aviv accepted the Egyptian offer of a "functional equivalent" to a peace treaty by pledging to solve all disputes by peaceful means. Egypt offered its oil to Israel at world market prices, and Israel was allowed a voice in decisions relating to the UN troops (particularly regarding their withdrawal which in 1967 had been done unilaterally by Egypt). Israel also agreed to completely withdraw from the passes and allow U.S. and UN inspection of its deployment on the ground. Egypt explicitly (and Israel implicitly) agreed to abide by this treaty for at least three years, subject to annual review, thus creating de facto the Geneva conference arrangement Kissinger had originally hoped for. On September 1, 1975, the documents and corollary agreements were formally signed and Kissinger was hailed as a miracle worker.

In exchange for these agreements, the United States made what Sheehan describes as a "marriage" in that the United States promised to protect Israeli interests on a very wide range of issues, guarantee the security of Israel, and verify compliance with the treaties. The United States also promised to refrain from contact with the Palestine Liberation Organization (PLO) so long as it did not renounce terrorism. Finally, the United States promised to veto any UN Security Council resolution which might undermine these various agreements. U.S. aid to both Israel and Egypt increased dramatically and proportionally.

CAMP DAVID

On September 5, 1978, President Anwar Sadat of Egypt and Prime Minister Menachem Begin of Israel and their delegations arrived at the U.S. presidential retreat in Maryland, Camp David, for a series of fateful meetings with President Jimmy Carter and his entourage. On March 26, 1979, the three leaders met on the front lawn of the White House to sign a peace treaty between Egypt and Israel. In the months that separated these widely publicized events, numerous obstacles to agreement arose and intensified, so that until the actual day of the signing some crucial issues remained unresolved. The entire undertaking was precarious at the time President Carter reactivated his peacemaking initiative in August 1978 and remained so even after the documents were initialed and exchanged the next year. The story of these hopeful yet frustrating months is full of twists and turns that kept participants on the edge of failure and observers on the edge of their seats.

From the perspective of more than a decade after the accords were negotiated, it is clear that one central issue dominated the talks and their aftermath. Would there be essentially a bilateral accord between Egypt and Israel, linked vaguely (if at all) to an accord on the future of the West Bank and Gaza? Or would there be a comprehensive settlement addressing all facets of the Arab-Israeli conflict, from the status of Jerusalem and the Palestinians to elaborate security arrangements and normal relations among all the players (the approach President Carter's advisers favored)? Furthermore, what and when would the United States offer to secure the allegiance of Sadat and Begin to any agreements, as the two local leaders manipulated their own domestic constituents and the American public in order to better the terms for themselves and their countries?

In November 1977, President Sadat paid his unprecedented visit to Jerusalem. His bombshell undercut the U.S. design for an international conference in Geneva. Carter was in danger of losing control over a process that had already aroused segments of the Congress and the American Jewish community, who worried that Israel would be compelled to deal with the PLO or with a Palestinian state, and others who were anxious about Syrian or Soviet meddling in the diplomatic process.

In the months of reassessment that followed Sadat's breakthrough, U.S. efforts concentrated on getting the Israelis and Egyptians to clarify their demands after bilateral talks at Ismailia stalled. Several of Carter's closest advisers "suggested moving toward a strategy of collusion with Sadat to bring pressure on Begin" (Quandt 1986, 163). While Carter and Secretary of State Cyrus Vance flirted with this idea as a way of preventing the collapse of bilateral talks in the atmosphere of ill will and hostile rhetoric, they understood that it would not produce a lasting agreement and might worsen administration relations both with Begin and with the American Jewish community. Later, when American exasperation with Begin's rigidity grew, variations on this theme of U.S.-Egyptian collaboration reappeared in ad-

ministration memos and dialogue. As 1978 proceeded, American officialdom became aware of the differing style of the two leaders: Sadat eager for
the dramatic gesture, but not the tedious detail of negotiations; Begin, insis-
tent on dotting every *i* and crossing every *t*, while lecturing his fellow politicians on Israel's security needs, its territorial claims, and the virtues of "autonomy" for the Palestinians rather than an independent Palestinian state or
some form of federation of the West Bank and Gaza with Jordan.

Thus, in the second year of his administration, President Carter, known
for his own meticulous attention to detail, faced the choice of continuing to
pursue a search for Israeli concessions on the West Bank and Gaza, perhaps
more vigorously than Sadat himself would do, or striving to arrange a bilateral Egyptian-Israeli peace treaty based on the trade of Sinai for an end to bel-
ligerency. In seeking the second course, deciding to work with Begin rather
than against him, Carter adopted a posture consonant with the national objectives of Sadat and Begin and with public opinion on Resolution 242. When
the president issued his invitations to an unusual three-way summit in September 1978, he knew that it would be necessary to promote interim arrangements for the thorniest issues—Jerusalem and the occupied territories.

Carter also knew that engaging the prestige of the presidency in such a
venture was a high-risk enterprise that could backfire both domestically and
internationally and might endanger other initiatives like the SALT II agreement with the Soviet Union or congressional approval of the Panama Canal
treaties. Stresses and strains with Egypt and Israel mounted as Sadat and
Begin pressed their respective cases with the White House, Congress, the
press, and U.S. public opinion (Spiegel 1985, chap. 8). Keeping the diplomatic game going as the administration prepared to submit a Middle East
arms package to Congress was the biggest challenge, especially as Carter
was also working on relations with China. The president's growing involvement with the minutiae of diplomacy meant that Middle East political figures would not be satisfied dealing with lesser U.S. officials. Each complicated exchange of questions and answers among Washington, Cairo, and
Jerusalem seemed to offer Washington two choices: either to confront the
parties by submitting American-drafted texts or to retreat from an active
role, with the possibility that the enterprise would bog down and Carter
personally would be blamed.

Inviting Sadat, Begin, and their closest advisers to Camp David to explore the possibilities of an accord was one thing. Keeping them there long
enough and secluded enough to develop a general formula or framework
for negotiations together with supporting details was quite another. Although President Carter believed that obtaining and retaining the trust of
the two leaders and their negotiating teams was crucial, he did not anticipate that moving beyond opening positions would take a full ten days or
more, far longer than the initial three days, or at most a week, that he had
planned to devote to the summit. One reason for the length of the negotiations was the expressed desire of both Begin and Sadat to structure agree-

ments with the United States before or, at the very least, alongside any they might conclude with each other. As Carter reports in his memoirs:

> I knew it was a good negotiation tactic by either Sadat or Begin first to reach agreement with me and then to have the two of us confront the third . . . I must admit that I capitalized on this situation with both delegations in order to get an agreement; it greatly magnified my own influence. (Carter 1982, 366)

Following ten days of successive one-on-one meetings with Begin and Sadat, Carter began to develop the essential feature of an agreement which would leave the Gaza and West Bank issues largely unresolved at Sadat's suggestion. On the eleventh day, Sadat threatened to leave—on the grounds that Israel would sign no agreements—despite the tedious days of discussion and refining of terms. Impressed as he was with the efforts of two Israelis, Moshe Dayan and Exer Weizman, to help bridge the gaps, Sadat nonetheless insisted that his advisers now counseled against signing an agreement with the United States alone, if Israel could not be brought along. According to Carter's recollections, the president approached Sadat, who was preparing to leave:

> I explained to him the extremely serious consequences of his unilaterally breaking off the negotiations: that his action would harm the relationship between Egypt and the United States, he would be violating his personal promise to me, and the onus for failure would be on him. I described the possible future progress of Egypt's friendships and alliances—from us to the moderate and then radical Arabs, thence to the Soviet Union. I told him it would damage one of my most precious possessions—his friendship and our mutual trust . . . I told Sadat that he simply had to stick with me for another day or two—after which, if circumstances did not improve, all of us simultaneously would take the action he was now planning. (Carter 1982, 392)

The experience was most likely more jarring for Sadat than Carter presents it here, for National Security Adviser Zbigniew Brzezinski remembers Carter explaining that he told Sadat his departure would mean "an end to the relationship between the United States and Egypt" (Brzezinski 1983, 272). In the end, Sadat agreed to stay, in part because Carter assured him that any tentative concession he might offer at Camp David, if not part of a treaty agreement, would not be taken as a starting point for future talks with Israel.

Significantly, neither Carter nor Brzezinski mentioned any promises of massive U.S. economic aid or military assistance to Egypt that may have been made to Sadat to induce him to stay at Camp David. The practicality of such a pledge would become clearer in the future. The president next turned to Begin and the Israelis to see if remaining differences could be resolved. As the talks neared the crucial phase on such issues as Sinai settlements, oil, and the demilitarized zones, together with the connections between Sinai and the West Bank or Gaza, Begin's stage presence, frequently overshadowed by Sadat's flair for surprise and presumed outrage, emerged.

The Likud party leader, whose ideological predilections differed from those of the Israeli Labour party leaders U.S. officials were accustomed to dealing with over the years, was careful to leave himself a loophole on the question of removing Israeli settlements from Sinai by stating he would submit the matter to the Israeli Parliament (Knesset) for a vote. In view of what would happen in later phases of interpretation and implementation, Carter was perhaps too persuaded of his own skill as a mediator at this stage: "I told him again and again that this proposal was totally unacceptable to Sadat, who insisted on a commitment to remove all Israeli settlers from his territory before any other negotiations could be conducted" (Carter 1982, 396).

Begin finally agreed to an accelerated Knesset review without the requirement of party loyalty, thus freeing up Knesset members to simply vote their conscience. This commitment was enough for Sadat, who tended to lack interest in other details of the agreement. The issues of the West Bank settlements and the status of Jerusalem were addressed with an oral agreement on Israel's part to halt the construction of new settlements until a more formal resolution could be reached. As Carter put it after the talks were through:

> After the Israelis left, Vance and I agreed that we had a settlement, at least for Camp David. There was no doubt that Sadat would accept my recommendations on the issues we had just discussed with Begin. What the Knesset might decide was uncertain, but I was convinced that the people of Israel would be in favor of the overall agreement, including the withdrawal of the settlers from the Sinai. . . . I intended to try in every way possible to shape world opinion and to get the American Jewish community to support this effort. (Carter 1982, 397)

Carter's persistence paid off. Agreement was reached, even though the final trade-offs were specific only with reference to Sinai, and they downgraded the link between the bilateral accord and the future of the occupied territories, including Jerusalem. Begin could take pride in the arrangements calling for normalization of relations with Egypt. Sadat had attained what no other Arab leader had the courage to seek—the return of occupied territory through negotiations with Israel, even though the basic formula guaranteed Egyptian national aims at the expense of wider Arab demands concerning the Palestinians. Furthermore, Sadat had succeeded in having the United States play the role of "full partner." Ironically, the price he would pay for that accomplishment would be additional demands for concessions (see Map 19.3).

The thirteen days at Camp David had produced a framework outlining transitional arrangements for the West Bank and Gaza, together with an agreement to sign an Egyptian-Israeli peace treaty within three months, plus a specific plan for the return of Sinai to Egypt with demilitarized zones and international policing of strategically sensitive areas. The issue of linkage might arise again, but, for the time being, Begin's loose formulas had prevailed.

The postconference haggling over who agreed to what, while itself predictable, threatened to heighten misunderstandings. Trust began to dissipate as the conflicting positions of Egypt and Israel on the settlements and

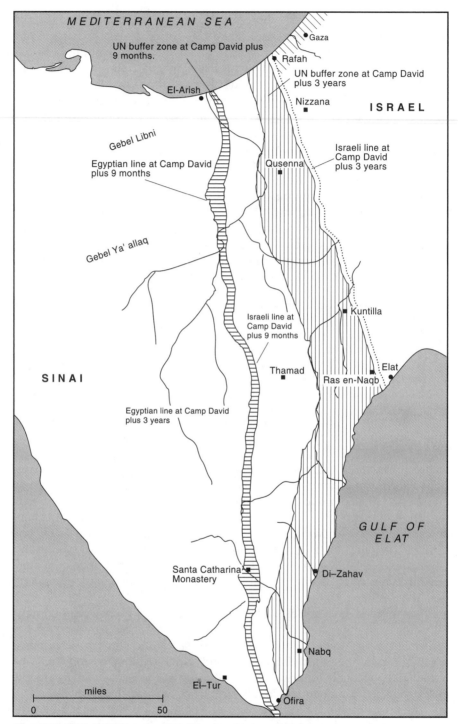

Map 19.3 1979–1982 Egyptian-Israeli troop withdrawal agreements.
Source: Lester Sobel, ed. *Peace-Making in the Middle East* (New York: Facts on File, 1980).

on linking a bilateral treaty to prospects for West Bank-Gaza hardened. The president, sensing urgency, found it difficult to comprehend the domestic political problems Sadat and Begin faced. He was well aware of his own, with the midterm elections scheduled for November 1978. He was also aware that Begin was a master at using Israeli domestic constraints as a method of dragging out the negotiations. Begin was often tougher than his advisers, while Sadat was often more accommodating. American policy-makers openly considered an overture to the PLO as a way of pressing Israel harder, but Carter demurred, citing the 1975 U.S. pledges to Israel on the subject as a test of American credibility.

Perhaps more important as the months passed after Camp David, both Begin and Sadat knew that Carter's influence had peaked in 1978 and that as the 1980 U.S. presidential election approached he would be entangled else-where. This appraisal prompted Begin to seek a deceleration of the process in order to avoid granting Palestinians any additional rights, while Sadat hoped for a measured pace toward eventual linkage with independence for the occupied territories. Cyrus Vance furthermore approached Jordan and Saudi Arabia to enlist their support for some eventual Palestinian autonomy accord, although he was also aware that this had not been made explicit in the Camp David language.

In the context of these conflicting interpretations and hidden agendas, Carter learned of Israel's intention to increase the number of settlements in the West Bank, in violation of the oral agreement at Camp David:

> It [was] obvious that the negotiations [were] going backwards . . . I told Cy [Vance] to withdraw from the negotiations at the end of this week, to let the technicians take over, and let the leadership in Israel and Egypt know that we are through devoting full time to this nonproductive effort. It [was] obvious that the Israelis [wanted] a separate treaty with Egypt; they [wanted] to keep the West Bank and Gaza permanently . . . and they [used] the settlements (on the West Bank) and East Jerusalem issues to prevent the involvement of the Jordanians and the Palestinians. (Carter 1982, 409)

By December 1978, Carter was close to throwing in the towel. The three-month deadline for an Egypt-Israeli peace treaty set at Camp David would not be met. For Carter, the confluence of U.S. domestic politics—the 1980 election—and international politics—the tumultuous Iranian revolution then unfolding—meant that an Egyptian-Israeli peace treaty must come soon, if at all. "I decided to pursue with my top advisers the possibility of my going to Egypt and then to Israel—getting together with Sadat and mak-ing my strongest appeal to the Israelis. My main purpose would be to re-mind them what they would be giving up if the treaty were lost" (Carter 1982, 415).

Prior to the trip, Carter met with Begin in Washington and managed to identify a treaty text that was "barely acceptable to the Israelis but did not quite comply with the key points on which Sadat was insisting. . . ." Upon hearing news of the treaty and Carter's impending trip to the Middle East,

Sadat "was overjoyed" (Carter 1982, 416). In advance of leaving Washington, Carter was careful to prepare Sadat, who was delighted to welcome the president to Egypt. Carter warned him that additional concessions would be needed:

> The language may not be exactly what you want, but the target date issued and the 'priority of obligations' issue are such that you can accept them and legitimately claim victory. You may or may not completely agree with me on the nuances of the exact words but, in any case, the differences are minimal when compared to the overall strategic considerations which you and I must address together. (Carter 1982, 417)

If the Camp David formula could be preserved, the details might be completed quickly while Carter was on the scene in the region. When Sadat did accept what the Israeli cabinet had approved, Carter was encouraged; yet Begin, in keeping with his previous modus operandi, told the president on his arrival in Israel that "he [Begin] could not sign or initial any agreement." As Carter wrote,

> I would have to conclude my talks with him, let him submit the proposals to the cabinet, let the Knesset have an extended debate, going into all the issues concerning the definition of autonomy, East Jerusalem, and so forth, and then only after all that would he sign the documents.

> I couldn't believe it. I stood up and asked him if it was necessary for me to stay any longer. We then spent about 45 minutes on our feet in his study. I asked him if he actually wanted a peace treaty, because my impression was that everything he could do to obstruct it, he did with apparent relish. He came right up and looked into my eyes about a foot away and said that it was obvious from the expression on his face that he wanted peace as much as anything else in the world. . . . (Carter 1982, 421)

The final breakthrough that permitted plans for the treaty signature to go forward came when Carter returned to Cairo from Israel with agreements in hand that committed the president to ask Congress for substantial aid in relocating Israeli bases from Sinai and provisions for the United States to compensate Israel for giving up Sinai oil. Also spelled out were steps to be taken if Egypt violated the treaty.

After Carter's return to Washington, amid preparations to receive Sadat and Begin in triumph, Vance, Dayan, and others strove to wrap up all the details in time for the signing. As Vance recalls, it was a close call:

> Inevitably, there were last-minute hitches. For several days prior to Begin's arrival I had discussions with Dayan on the U.S.-Israeli memorandum of agreement, as well as on the oil supply agreement and the U.S. financial and military assistance package that had seen agreed to in Jerusalem. The President also met Sadat and Begin to work out the precise details of the accelerated Israeli withdrawal from that portion of the Sinai containing the oilfields.

> The final details concerning Israeli access to Sinai oil remained an issue right down to the end. They were not finally resolved until Sadat and Begin agreed in

a meeting in the residence of Ashraf Gorbal, the distinguished and extremely able Egyptian ambassador in Washington. At that time Sadat guaranteed to the Israelis the right to bid for Egyptian oil at the world market price on a permanent basis, thus removing the last major stumbling block to the signing ceremony. We did go down to the wire on one or two minor details. . . . (Vance 1983, 252)

On March 26, 1979, then, the signatures were placed on the document and an arduous process, begun by Henry Kissinger in 1973, was completed. The implementation of the agreement, including the continuation of discussion on Palestinian autonomy, was spotty. The Israeli army left the Sinai within the prescribed deadline—a remarkable case on the part of Egypt of winning back territory through the pen rather than the sword. Autonomy talks for the Palestinians, on the other hand, were almost immediately overwhelmed by nationalist pressure in Israel and the explosion of revolution in Iran. More than a decade later, Camp David may seem to be less of an achievement than it was. If so, it is because Egyptian-Israeli peace is now taken for granted in the midst of rising political extremism in the region as a whole. That is perhaps the finest tribute to the thirty-ninth president. Other politicians come and go with less to show for their labors than Jimmy Carter.

With Carter voted out of office in November, the Middle East peace process halted. Anwar Sadat was assassinated in 1981, thus removing one of the most conciliatory Arab leaders in history. Israel invaded Lebanon in 1982, forcing Ronald Reagan to deploy peacekeeping troops in Beirut and precipitating the evacuation of the PLO headquarters and thousands of troops to places scattered across the Middle East. The PLO initiated the bloody *intifadah* in 1987—a mass uprising which continues to this day and which in turn has spurred increased Israeli repression in the West Bank and Gaza. In 1988, the PLO renounced terrorism and quietly recognized Israel's right to exist, thus allowing the United States to undertake direct talks with PLO representatives. Throughout the 1980s, however, the Israeli position hardened and the United States found itself more and more at odds with Tel Aviv over everything from Israeli police repression in East Jerusalem to increased Soviet-Jewish settlements in the West Bank.

It was not until the Gulf War in 1991 that major shifts in Middle East political alignments occurred. The war saw many Arab countries siding with the United States and therefore implicitly with Israel. Conversely, Israel broke with precedent by refraining from retaliation against Baghdad following repeated Scud missile attacks. Within a year of the war, the United States and Soviet Union, under the leadership of Secretary of State James Baker and Foreign Minister Eduard Scheverdnadze, a new multilateral Middle East peace conference was underway amid skepticism, ambivalence, and a modicum of hope. The seating at the conference of a joint Jordanian-Palestinian delegation made possible the first direct talks between Israelis and Palestinians in forty-three years. In spite of this historic breakthrough, the negotiations plodded along unsuccessfully for nearly two years. Even the election in June 1992 of Yitzhak Rabin's Labour party—traditionally more flexible on the issue of land-for-peace and Palestinian rights—had little effect. The Israeli deportation of some 400 Palestinians in December in retaliation for the Hezbollah murder of six Israeli soldiers further depressed the atmosphere at the talks.

On August 31, 1993, in the eleventh round of what seemed to be almost pointless negotiations, Israel and the PLO announced a bombshell. As a result of extended secret talks, they had concluded a deal which provided for mutual recognition and self-rule for Palestinians in parts of the West Bank and Gaza. Within two weeks Rabin and Yasir Arafat were shaking hands in front of the White House and American senators were dining with a former terrorist. President Bill Clinton was quick to take credit, if only by virtue of his intentions, even though it seems the Norwegian government had a more direct hand in facilitating the secret talks by discretely providing good offices. While the events lacked nothing for dramatic flair, problems in subsequent negotiations and continuing violence in the occupied territories demonstrate that the road to Middle East peace will yet be long and tortuous. But, even a cynic must acknowledge that all parties seem to have accepted the need to begin the process.

Questions to Consider

1. What sorts of resources did both Kissinger and Carter bring to bear to the negotiations, by virtue of their position as leaders in the United States?

2. Did Kissinger and Carter use different personal, political, or diplomatic assets in their efforts? How did this affect the outcomes of their mediation?

3. To what extent did military matters and regional power relations affect the willingness of Israel, Egypt, and others to make concessions? Was this predictable?

4. How do the experiences of the United States in the Middle East speak to Clausewitz's notion that war is merely the extension of diplomacy? Conversely, does it appear that the "the pen is mightier than the sword"?

5. What makes for a good mediator, based on these experiences?

References

Zbigniew Brzezinski. *Power and Principle* (New York: Farrar, Strauss and Giroux, 1983).

Jimmy Carter. *Keeping Faith: Memoirs of a President* (Toronto: Bantam Books, 1982).

Michael Dockrill. *Atlas of Twentieth Century World History* (New York: Harper-Collins, 1991).

Bernard Kalb and Marvin Kalb. *Kissinger* (Boston: Little, Brown, 1974).

Henry Kissinger. *Years of Upheaval* (Boston: Little, Brown, 1982).

Linda B. Miller. "Shadow and Substance: Jimmy Carter and the Camp David Accords." *#433R Pew Case Studies in International Affairs*, 1992.

William B. Quandt. *Camp David: Peacemaking and Politics* (Washington, D.C.: Brookings Institution, 1986).

Edward Sheehan. "How Kissinger Did It: Step-by-Step in the Middle East," in Jeffrey Z. Rubin, ed., *Dynamics of Third Party Intervention: Kissinger in the Middle East* (New York: Praeger, 1981), 44–93.

Lester Sobel, ed. *Peace-Making in the Middle East* (New York: Facts on File, 1980).

Steven Spiegel. *The Other Arab-Israeli Conflict* (Chicago: University of Chicago Press, 1985).

Saadia Touval. *The Peace Brokers: Mediators in the Arab-Israeli Conflict, 1948–1979* (Princeton: Princeton University Press, 1982).

Cyrus Vance. *Hard Choices: Critical Years in America's Foreign Policy* (New York: Simon & Schuster, 1983).

CASE 20

U.S. Interventionism

Carl von Clausewitz argued that the use of military instruments—coercion—was simply an extension of the give-and-take of diplomacy, not its antithesis. As more powerful nations exert pressure on smaller states, they must sometimes flex their muscle to get what they want. The more powerful a nation, the less likely it will have to resort to violence. Instead, it will blackmail, persuade, induce, cajole, bribe, tempt, and even reward nations to influence their behavior. Naked coercion is normally a last resort, but an extremely potent weapon in any nation's diplomatic arsenal. But is it diplomatic to kill people for political purposes?

As Americans consider their foreign policy choices in the post–Cold War era, a key question is whether the United States should play the role of global policeman. Should American troops be used to alter the domestic affairs of foreign nations? While on the surface the obvious answer seems to be no, in very many instances in the past, the answer has been a resounding yes. Whether justified in terms of humanitarianism, enforcement of international law, or some strategic imperative, the United States has been rather quick to deploy its troops.

To better understand this interventionist tendency, we will look carefully at three very different cases drawn from the past thirty years. Before doing so, however, it will be worthwhile to review various theories of intervention. The most obvious cause for U.S. intervention is strategic: the United States intervenes when its global interests are jeopardized (Deibel and Gaddis 1987). Given the way a great power strives for stability and preservation of the status quo, the temptation to intervene where the system is unstable can be irresistible. Some 2,500 years ago, when the small island of Melos petitioned Athens for respect of its neutrality, Athens refused, stating that it simply could not tolerate such an implicit challenge to its status as the dominant regional power. "The strong do what they can and the weak do what they must," was Athens' blunt reply.

Although not a particularly noble cause for intervention, its advocates often point to the need to preserve the balance of power and prevent enemies from encroaching on the American sphere of influence. The Monroe Doctrine of the early nineteenth century cautioned would-be imperialists in Europe from snatching colonial prizes in the Western Hemisphere. The Roosevelt Corollary to that warning carried the military teeth to back it up and coincided with American intervention in Cuba, Nicaragua, Guatemala, Panama, Mexico, and across Latin America shortly after the turn of the century. Since World War II, various senior diplomats have justified U.S. intervention in terms of simply preserving the status quo. George Ball, a former under secretary of state, has pointed out that it is up to great powers—in this case the United States—to enforce international standards of peace and stability, unilaterally if necessary (Barnet 1968, 258).

Another key factor cited by many analysts is the fear of Communist ideology and despotism generally. Although it is often difficult to distinguish fear of Soviet encroachment (a balance of power question) and fear of communism (an ideological issue), it seems many policymakers were equally concerned about both. Certainly the idealism of the Woodrow Wilson, Franklin Delano Roosevelt, and Harry Truman administrations, as well as the intense anti-Communist passions displayed by Secretary of State John Foster Dulles under Eisenhower, demonstrate that democracy, freedom, and the free market were all key preoccupations of U.S. policymakers. Woodrow Wilson drew up his "Fourteen Points" during World War I to map out a way to make the world "safe for democracy." As he put it when trying to persuade Congress to declare war on Germany in 1917:

> We have no selfish ends to serve. We desire no conquest, no dominion. We seek no indemnities for ourselves, no material compensation for the sacrifices we shall freely make. We are but one of the champions of the right of mankind. (Wilson 1990, 15)

Of course much of the justification for entry into World War II was on the basis of halting the spread of totalitarian Germany and Japan. When Harry Truman challenged Congress in 1947 to fund the incipient Cold War offensive, he declared: "I believe that it must be the policy of the United States to support free peoples who are resisting attempted subjugation by armed minorities or by outside pressures." Presidents Johnson, Reagan, and Bush have each added their own doctrines, with the result that the United States gradually expanded the scope of unilateral intervention which it considers justified. CIA Director Allen Dulles argued in the 1950s:

> [W]e cannot safely limit our response to the Communist strategy of take-over solely to those cases where we are invited in by a government still in power, or even to instances where a threatened country has first exhausted its own, possibly meager, resources in the "good fight" against Communism. We ourselves must determine when and how to act, hopefully with the support of other leading Free World countries who may be in a position to help, keeping in mind the

requirements of our own national security. (Dulles 1963, 324, cited in Barnet 1968, 258)

The fear and loathing of the Communist threat reached its height in the 1950s, during the era of Senator Joseph McCarthy's "witch-hunts" of suspected Communist sympathizers in the State Department, which were followed by John Foster Dulles' tenure as secretary of state, during which his antipathy for communism reached epic proportions (Hoopes 1973). George Kennan argued in vain against what he considered knee-jerk containment policies in the 1950s, which he felt lumped together all potential threats and gave them equal weight. He argued instead for a more case-by-case approach which would enable policymakers to more selectively identify genuine threats to U.S. interests—regardless of the ideological context (Kennan 1947). Although Kennan failed to change U.S. rhetoric, his influence on policy was more profound.

While insurrections in the Third World were not unusual during the Cold War years, only a few warranted U.S. intervention. It was those situations which combined evidence of Communist meddling with a threat to an existing U.S. alliance where intervention was most likely. A final factor that contributed to the U.S. decision to intervene was economic interest. Marxist interpretations of U.S. intervention have long stressed the role of major capitalist actors in the shaping of U.S. foreign policy. Harry Magdoff has probably gone as far as any Marxist to explain the dynamic. He argues that, although one may not find capitalists dictating policy to their political counterparts, there is an unusual harmony of interest between the two groups. American foreign investments bring large profits and extraordinary monopoly control for both business and government. American firms can control access to key raw materials, such as oil, which in turn are essential to the military—hence collusion between major capitalists and the Pentagon. These sorts of factors lead to a tendency for the state to intervene aggressively when foreign economic interests are threatened—which, as it turns out, usually involves attacking anticapitalist Third World rebels (Magdoff 1969).

Rather than attempt to assess the validity of these various perceptions of U.S. intervention, it would be better to move into the case studies mentioned earlier, and leave it to the reader to draw her or his own conclusions. The three cases of U.S. intervention are: the Dominican Republic in 1965, Chile in 1973, and Panama in 1989. Although each of these cases involved a Latin American nation, the methods, causes, and justifications of intervention were rather different. When combined with other cases of U.S. intervention discussed elsewhere in the text (Cuba, Vietnam, Iraq, Nicaragua), they should provide a fairly balanced and general view of the issue.

DOMINICAN REPUBLIC—1965

U.S. relations with the Dominican Republic epitomized for many years the imperialist impulse in U.S. foreign policy. Although independent of Spain in 1844, this island nation bordering Haiti was always vulnerable to outside interference—including a brief attempt at colonization by the United States. It had seen a succession of dictators down to the first major U.S. military intervention—an occupation force which lasted from 1916 to 1924 and which resulted in the strengthening of the army in the country and a more hospitable climate for U.S. investment (Gleijeses 1978, 18).

That armed intervention set the stage for the second major intervention by the United States into the Dominican Republic in 1965. Raphael Leonidas Trujillo overthrew the constitutional government left behind in 1930 and began a thirty-year reign of terror (Barnet 1968, 155). Trujillo's principal virtue, from the American perspective, was that he provided a stable anti-Communist bulwark in the Caribbean. Trujillo also did much to give his country the appearance of growth and prosperity, although the image concealed a deeply divided society where incomes were extremely unequal, the established wealthy class mistrusted the newcomers—"nouveau riches"—and the overzealous Trujillo family, and where the middle class was virtually nonexistent. Nonetheless, Trujillo reigned supreme until 1960, when his acts of terror against opponents at home and abroad caused even the conservative Catholic church in the Dominican Republic to repudiate him.

The United States, while supportive of conservative governments in the region, feared Trujillo would so oppress his people that he would precipitate Marxist revolution. Fulgencio Batista did just this in Cuba in 1959, and the United States was now faced with an angry Castro only ninety miles from Florida. In mid-1960, the Eisenhower administration withdrew support for the regime and endorsed economic sanctions favored by other Latin American states through the Organization of American States (OAS) (Gleijeses 1978, 21). Trujillo was assassinated on May 30, 1961, by a small group of coup plotters in the army, although their hopes of establishing a new regime were quickly dashed as Trujillo loyalists moved quickly to preserve at least the form of power if not the content.

For the new Kennedy administration, the search was underway for a moderate democratic leader, although the president acknowledged that failing that, a dictator would be better than a Communist (Barnet 1968, 158). The country went through a succession of quasi-military leaders, each receiving moderate U.S. support: the opportunistic Joaquin Balaguer, a former Trujillo cabinet member, held office with the support of Trujillo's family for a brief period following the assassination. Then the military, following the exile of Trujillo's son and brothers, took de facto control under General Pedro Echeverria (Gleijeses 1978, 57). Balaguer eventually resigned his post in favor of Rafael Bonelly, another former Trujillo official, who was even more eager to work with the United States (to the military's annoyance) (Yates 1988, 181). The United States and the OAS finally lifted the anti-Trujillo sanctions following the announcement of national elections scheduled for June 1, 1961. The Kennedy administration felt that it had finally found the path to what it sought, although there were clear disagreements on whether it could afford the risk of a Communist sympathizer winning the election.

The presidential elections saw numerous candidates from across the political spectrum, although three parties dominated the campaign: the Revolutionary Dominican Party (PRD) under Juan Bosch, the National Civic Union (UCN) which already held sway in the transitional regime, and an assortment of leftist parties dominated by the June 14 movement. Contrary to its militant name, the PRD was a moderate left-of-center party with a reformist, anti-Trujillo agenda. In contrast to the June 14 movement, which included both armed and Castroite elements, the PRD seemed a viable alternative to the parties of the right (Gleijeses 1978, 39).

The elections were honest and fair, in spite of a never-ending atmosphere of violence and unrest that gripped the country after Trujillo's death. Juan Bosch and the PRD emerged victorious with well over half of the votes cast (Bosch received 59 percent of the vote—nearly twice that of his UCN rival) (Gleijeses 1978, 86). The United States moved quickly to endorse the elections and support the Bosch administration, although U.S. ambassador John Bartlow Martin had strong reservations. He had become accustomed to the former regimes, and had even become so heavily involved in Dominican policy-making that even many conservative Dominicans had challenged his interference. Martin often criticized Bosch as a "divider" and even a "destroyer" because of his willingness to openly criticize and challenge U.S. policy in the region, including the regional aid program known as the Alliance for Progress (Barnet 1968, 166). He suspected Bosch of Marxist sympathies.

The Bosch administration was under pressure to carry out many reforms it had promised. After introducing a new constitution, restoring some sense of integrity to the government, moving squatters and landless peasants onto their own plots, and taking steps to limit profit taking by foreign corporations, the conservatives began to organize concerted opposition to the regime. An important problem, from the perspective of affluent Dominicans and the military, was Bosch's failure to deport the known Marxists in the June 14 movement and other radical parties. He argued that constitutional protection should be extended to all, regardless of their political coloration (Draper 1968, 29). This was the last straw, and in September 1963, the military took power. Bosch fled to Puerto Rico and a three-man government was set up in his place. With the resignation of one of the "triumvirate" members in December, the new military government came under the dominance of Donald Reid Cabral and secured the support of the new Johnson administration (Barnet 1968, 167). A feeble rebellion by the June 14 movement reduced the number of its armed guerrillas to less than one hundred. For the time being, the situation was stabilized and, from the perspective of ardent anti-Communists in Washington and Santo Domingo, more secure. In fact, the regime lasted little more than a year.

In spite of considerable support from the United States, the Reid regime failed from the start. Its attempts at economic development foundered amid corruption and falling sugar prices (Gleijeses 1978, 118). Its use of torture alienated the masses and spurred calls for reform and even revolution from both far left and center-left sections (including the exiled Juan Bosch). The wealthy elite grew weary of the stagnant economy and the military bristled at Reid's clumsy attempts at reform in its ranks. By early 1965, some factions of the military were organizing a revolt in combination with former Bosch as well as former Balaguer supporters, with the aim of returning constitutional government (Gleijeses 1978, 132). On April 24, the rebellion (officially termed a countercoup) erupted. On April 25, loyalists to the regime responded. The nation fell into civil war and chaos, with the heart of Santo Domingo at the epicenter.

Early on, the rebels scored impressive victories, leading to the resignation of Reid and the naming of former Bosch supporter José Rafael Molina Urena as provisional president. The victory was short-lived, however, and before the end of April Urena was forced into hiding. In the meantime, poorly organized rebels took control of the streets of the capital amid rumors of atrocities. Reports of Communists taking over leadership of the rebellion were accepted without hesitation by CIA and embassy officials and the new ambassador, W. Tapley Bennett, who requested U.S. military forces to begin evacuating American civilians trapped in the city. Once an initial wave of some 500 Marines arrived, Bennett concluded on April 28 that the situation called for still more dramatic U.S. intervention. He claimed that Americans were being shot at, and some 1,500 Communists were overrunning the capital (Barnet 1968, 171). Johnson was forced to respond on the grounds that Bennett's alarm could not be ignored, although he doubted the authenticity of the reports. The administration later chose to ignore Bennett's pleas (Yates 1988, 64).

By May 17, 1965, 24,000 troops had been deployed in and around the capital Santo Domingo. U.S. troops were originally placed around neighborhoods where Americans lived and worked to evacuate them as rapidly as possible. Once this mission was accomplished, the operation rapidly moved to containing the rebellion by virtually surrounding the inner-city area of the capital with a belt of U.S. troops (Yates 1988, 75). The move effectively eliminated any prospect for a rebel victory and assured the Loyalist military government, now under Generals Antonio Imbert Barrera and Elias Wessin y Wessin, a relatively free hand in mopping up opposition to the regime. All this, while the U.S. troops proclaimed a policy of "neutrality" in the conflict.

The constitutionalist rebels regrouped after the initial shock of the U.S. deployment and found leadership under rebel Colonel Francisco Caamano Deno. Although not a Communist himself, he allowed several Marxists a role in leading the rebellion. There is some debate over the significance of these Marxists in the rebellion (Thomas and Thomas 1967), but the consensus seems to be that, contrary to the impression of embassy, CIA, and State Department staff at the time, the anti-U.S. rhetoric that poured out of rebel headquarters during much of the war was merely posturing. In fact, the vast majority of the rebels sought merely the return of the Bosch administration rather than some Castroite revolution (Barnet 1968, 173).

Once the situation was stabilized, the United States moved to create an effective multilateral presence in the city. The OAS organized a peacekeeping force that was deployed in mid-May and that subsumed the U.S. presence. From this point, the emphasis of the operation was on finding a diplomatic solution to the crisis (Slater 1970). The U.S. troops played the role of genuine peacekeepers, not only containing the constitutionalist rebellion, but also preventing the Loyalist troops from entering their inner-city haven (Yates 1988, 145).

Ultimately, after months of effort and sporadic fighting between OAS forces and the rebels, a settlement was reached on September 3, 1965, which provided for a provisional government under the leadership of former Bosch official Hector García-Godoy. Caamano left the island on an overseas diplomatic post in January 1966, along with Urena. Marines were withdrawn from the island over the course of the year, with the last units departing on September 21 after a seventeen-month stay. The military was partially contained in the new regime, although it mounted several unsuccessful coup attempts later on. The García-Godoy regime sponsored elections on June 1, 1966, which returned Balaguer to power under a cloud of tainted voting.

CHILE—1973

Chileans elected a self-proclaimed Marxist to the presidency in 1970, much to the dismay of the White House and major U.S. firms operating in Chile at the time. The story of what they did to change the result of that election represents an example of indirect and covert intervention.

Chile, unlike the Dominican Republic, enjoyed a tradition of democratic rule that extended, at least nominally, to the pre–World War II era. When President Jorge Allessandri, leader of the conservative National Party, was defeated by Christian Democratic Party (PDC) candidate Eduardo Frei in 1964, the government moved toward the type of progressive reforms the Kennedy administration had advocated. Although a nationalist who did not want to serve as the lackey of the U.S. interests, Frei was willing to accommodate U.S. business needs. In particular, he agreed to limit government intervention in the economy to those things which had the best chance of reversing the drastic inequality of income and wealth that had developed. In his dealings with such U.S. firms as Kennecott Copper and International Telephone and Telegraph (ITT), he generally negotiated new arrangements fairly and in good faith (Kissinger 1979, 657). The principal targets of his policies were the wealthy landowners who were forced to relinquish property which was then redistributed to peasants (Sater 1990, 151). The policies of Frei were satisfactory enough to the Johnson administration that it secretly provided hundreds of millions of dollars for his party's election campaigns (Rojas Sandford 1976, 57).

Much of the support Frei received from the United States could be explained by the opposition he faced: Salvador Allende Gossens, leader of the newly formed Unidad Popular—a coalition party of leftist movements in

Chile. His party represented the greatest challenge to Christian Democrats in 1962 and 1964 elections. The radical, anti-U.S. nature of his policies were seen as inimical to U.S. interests. In the September 1970 presidential elections, however, American observers and policymakers became convinced that he would do poorly against Allessandri, and the PDC candidate Radomiro Tomic (Eduardo Frei was forbidden by the constitution to serve consecutive terms). Allende's election victory—which consisted of a 30,000 vote edge over Allessandri (out of 3 million votes cast)—came as a stunning shock in Washington (Kissinger 1979, 670). Henry Kissinger wished aloud that the United States had pumped more secret funds into the election, but he and Richard Nixon had been dissuaded by a State Department concerned about interference in domestic affairs (Kissinger 1979, 669). The ambassador, Edward Korrey, stated unequivocally that Allende's victory, while perhaps still reversible given certain provisions in the Chilean Constitution, was a serious blow.

Richard Nixon was livid over the Allende victory and was desperate to prevent his taking office in November. He told CIA Director Richard Helms to ignore the State Department and do "whatever it takes" to reverse the outcome, offering up to $10 million for immediate actions (Kissinger 1979, 673). What transpired involved two "tracks" of intervention. Track I was a fairly straightforward approach: convince conservative members of the Chilean Congress to vote against Allende's bid—an option which seemed feasible given the narrow Allende win and Allessandri's decision to contest the election. In order to accomplish this, the United States warmly endorsed Allessandri's proposal to resign as soon as the Congress elected him president, thus forcing a new election six months later. The hope was that Eduardo Frei, who could run for another nonconsecutive term, would be able to defeat Allende in a head-to-head race. Unfortunately, Frei was uninterested in the scheme (Whelan 1981, 40; Sater 1990, 162).

At the same time, Nixon engineered an economic and financial embargo of Chile through private and government channels. He wanted the Chilean economy to "scream" (Kissinger 1979, 673). With the help of Chilean conservatives in the banking sector, rumors of Marxist excesses were spread, precipitating a run on several banks and a flight of some $50 million in private savings. All of these efforts were for naught, however, and the inevitability of an Allende presidency loomed large in Washington (LaFeber 1989, 620).

Track II came into effect immediately before the late October congressional vote and involved a rather awkward attempted coup by the military with U.S. backing. Corporate executives of ITT, Pepsi-Cola, and other firms were eager to support a military takeover and lobbied the administration intensively throughout the Allende era (Sergeyev 1981, 138). At this initial stage, the coup attempt involved supporting General Roberto Viaux's attempt to kidnap the commander of the Santiago garrison, General Rene Schneider, and form a junta to replace the Congress. Weapons and funds were provided in early October, but were cut off on October 15 after Viaux failed repeatedly (Kissinger 1979, 676). Viaux continued his efforts on his own and managed to capture the general, but killed him inadvertently in a skirmish. As a result, the conservative elements in Congress and the elite within the army closed ranks around Allende and the constitution and endorsed his election victory. He was sworn in as president in November.

The Allende administration was known above all for its rhetoric, which was consistently anti-American and anticapitalist. Allende made numerous contacts with East bloc countries, receiving modest financial support from Moscow and Eastern Europe, as well as some sugar from Cuba. He moved rapidly, and often in violation of Chilean law, to nationalize not only large farms but also foreign businesses and factories (Rojas Sandford 1976, 95). Although resigned at first, the Nixon administration invoked the Gonzalez amendment and curtailed all multilateral lending to Chile pending just compensation for the seizures (LaFeber 1989, 620). Private U.S. banks dropped their lending to Chile from $219 million in 1970 to $32 million in 1971. Whereas in the 1960s Chile borrowed an average of $150 million each year from U.S. government sources, the figure slipped to $40 million in 1971 and to nothing at all in 1972 (Rojas Sandiford 1976, 148). Many state-owned firms failed for lack of spare parts and capital due to this "invisible blockade."

In spite of this aggressive anti-U.S. stand, Allende also tried to maintain a working relationship with his conservative Latin neighbors and Western financial institutions (Sater 1990, 165). After nationalizing Kennecott Copper (with the initial support of the opposition parties), Allende attempted to export copper to Europe (in contravention of international law). The executives at Kennecott tracked the shipments—allegedly with the help of the navy—and brought lawsuits against Chile in whatever country they were delivered. With the collapse of the price of copper in 1972 and the growing reticence of Europeans to deal with Allende, the sales of copper grew perilously low. This, combined with a growing international debt, forced the Allende regime into an international crisis by 1972.

Allende, unable to secure adequate support from abroad, found his domestic programs were failing. His deficit spending program to stimulate consumption and reward his proletarian supporters quickly spurred inflation, which topped the 200 percent mark by 1973. Unable to satisfy workers whose purchasing power fell, Allende was in the uncomfortable position of dealing with an increasing number of strikes by his core supporters of the past. Truckers, copper miners, physicians, and others engaged in months-long walkouts in protest over government policies, wreaking social chaos in the process. In order to preserve some semblance of stability, Allende invited military officers to his cabinet in 1972 and then again in 1973 (Whelan 1981, 6). When the generals came in the second time, they never left.

Beginning in August 1973, Allende was under pressure from an increasingly defiant military to address the civil disturbance in the country. On August 23 he accepted the resignation of his military commander, Carlos Prats Gonzales, who declared that he could no longer contain the pressure for a coup, and appointed Augusto Pinochet his successor (Rojas Sandford 1976,

179). By September Pinochet had joined with the navy in a plan to overthrow the regime. On September 11, beginning with the occupation of the port of Valparaiso, the military attacked and seized the presidential offices at la Modena. By late afternoon, Allende was dead and one of the most brutal military regimes in Latin American history was in power.

Although one can argue that the fall of Allende was made possible only by three years of American pressure, it appears that the U.S. government did not have any direct hand in the coup itself. Even critics of U.S. policy acknowledge that the CIA and the White House learned about the coup at the same time as the rest of the world (Whelan 1981, 40).

PANAMA—1989

The last of the three case studies offers an opportunity to analyze post–Cold War U.S. intervention. While the Dominican and Chilean cases were clearly influenced by anti-Communist concerns, the Panama invasion of 1989 seems to have no such ideological impetus. In fact, the strong desire on the part of the Reagan administration to preserve Panama as a listening post against the Nicaraguan Marxists (Sandinistas) led its members to overlook blatant narcotics trafficking, corruption, and despotism. When the Cold War was over and the Sandinistas were on their way out, the Panamanian government's indiscretions could no longer be tolerated (Conniff 1992, 166).

U.S. relations with Panama were as historically intimate and intrusive as its ties with the Dominican Republic. In 1908, President Theodore Roosevelt supported Panamanian independence from Colombia in order to work out a better Panama Canal treaty (Donnelly et al. 1991, 2). William Howard Taft essentially dictated presidential succession after the 1908 Panamanian elections, and under Woodrow Wilson the United States deployed troops and occupied the country after establishing a permanent military base (Conniff 1992, 76). By so doing, the Canal Zone became a sort of "micro-state"—an extension of U.S. territory abroad (Conniff 1992, 84).

Beginning in 1945, the Panamanian leadership adopted a more and more determined posture to reclaim rights to the canal, or at least profit more substantially from U.S. operations. Colonel Jose Antonio Remon pressed for a new treaty in the 1950s, and Roberto Chiari renegotiated the agreement in 1967. Anti-American demonstrations became gradually more intense over the years. Also, the democratic governments in Panama began investigating corruption in the military. In 1968, in order to solve both problems, General Omar Torrijos and the elite Guardia Nacionale overthrew the popular President Arnulfo Arias (Donnelly et al, 1991, 4).

From the emergence of Torrijos in 1968 to the capture of Noriega in 1991, the story of Panamanian leadership was one of court intrigue, populist despotism, and narcotics trafficking. In 1969 an anti-Torrijos coup succeeded for a period of time until the general returned, accompanied by loyalist Manuel Antonio Noriega, to reconquer the capital (Conniff 1992, 126). Noriega, an important CIA contact in previous years, became even more significant as the newly appointed head of Panamanian intelligence. He later had regular contact with CIA officials, including CIA Director William Casey and Vice President George Bush. This, in spite of the fact that he was identified as early as 1972 as the secret "Panama connection" in narcotics trade. Conniff has pointed out U.S. blame for military rule in Panama

> began in 1968, when Washington's professed determination to promote civilian, democratic regimes in Panama weakened in the wake of the military coup. A decade later, U.S. policy seemed to be driven by the Senate's concern over the security of the canal. At the time, a stable Panama was more critical than a democratic Panama. This meant, among other things, greater involvement by the Panamanian military in the country's domestic politics. (Conniff 1992, 153)

The Panamanian government under Torrijos scored a major victory when it signed the ill-fated Panama Canal Treaty of 1977. The promise of a new relationship with the United States was largely frustrated by the death of Torrijos and the outbreak of the anti-Sandinista operation by U.S.-led "Contras" in 1981. General Manuel Noriega moved into position to lead a military triumvirate, illegally securing the election of a loyalist, Nicolas Ardito Barletta, to the office of president (Conniff 1992, 150). The United States endorsed the outcome and established extensive intelligence-gathering operations in Panama, including direct support and training for the renamed Panamanian Defense Forces.

After weeks of growing tension between Noriega, an increasingly democratic Barletta, and Noriega's military ally, General Dias Herrera, the situation began to unravel. The decapitated body of Noriega critic Hugo Spadafora was discovered in September 1988 and investigators quickly linked Noriega to the death. He tried to shift the blame to Dias Herrera, who launched a coup attempt in retaliation. Barletta was dismissed after threatening to publicly expose Noriega's role and was replaced by Eric Arturo Delvalle. For the first time, U.S. representatives issued Noriega a stern rebuke and a warning lest he abuse his power too blatantly (Donnelly et al. 1991, 10). Senator Jesse Helms held hearings in 1986 detailing Noriega's excesses and the U.S. press began systematic attacks (Conniff 1992, 155). Noriega by now was being compared to the likes of Libya's Muammar Qaddafi and Iran's Ayatollah Khomeini as a global pariah.

In June 1987, the situation took yet another dramatic turn. Dias Herrera turned down a Noriega offer for the ambassadorship to Japan and instead exposed sordid details of Noriega's atrocities to the Panamanian press (Donnelly et al. 1991, 11). The resulting outrage, which involved not only poor Panamanians in the barrios (slums) but also middle-class professionals, precipitated a violent repression. This included Noriega's troops firing into unarmed crowds and arresting U.S. servicemen (Conniff 1992, 156).

By the time drug indictments against Noriega were issued by two U.S. courts in February 1988, the United States had already begun to develop plans for military intervention. It formally imposed economic sanctions against Panama on April 8, 1988, by freezing $56 million in Panamanian assets in the United States, cutting off most trade, and putting severe restrictions on Panama's dollar-denominated money supply (Commission 1991, 23). In retaliation, Noriega stepped up harassment of U.S. military personnel and their families. The last opportunity for a negotiated settlement of the conflict came in May 1988 when President Ronald Reagan offered to drop the drug trafficking charges in return for Noriega's retirement. The offer was rebuffed (Donnelly et al. 1991, 35).

The May 1989 presidential elections, a farce by any democratic standard, provided a new focal point for the United States following the failure of the Reagan offer. The administration spent roughly $10 million on the campaign of progressive Guillermo Endara Galimany who, according to reliable reports, received some 75 percent of the vote. Noriega, after failing to reverse the outcome through rigging, declared the election invalid and continued to govern the country. A coup attempt in October 1989 failed to dislodge Noriega in spite of participation by U.S. troops.

The question for the incoming Bush administration was how to intervene in Panama while minimizing casualties and maximizing legal justifications. Certainly the presence of some 10,000 American citizens, all of whom felt very much threatened by the growing civil violence and repression, could have been enough. Unfortunately, the argument that Noriega was a threat to international stability was hypocritical, considering the great lengths to which successive U.S. administrations had gone to build him up. Finally, on December 15 the opportunity came: Noriega declared that a "state of war" existed (and had existed for thirty months) between Panama and the United States (McConnell 1991, 281). He was then proclaimed head of state by a rump assembly of cronies which naturally endorsed the declaration by a unanimous vote. As portrayed in the U.S. press, the statements seemed very much like a formal declaration of war, although in retrospect they seem more rhetorical than substantive. When still more harassment of U.S. troops followed, culminating in the death of a marine, the Bush administration initiated "Operation Just Cause."

The operation was intended as a "decapitating" strike against a limited number of military targets. Based on Colin Powell's notion of "overwhelming force," the Bush administration deployed 24,000 troops against a Panamanian Defense Force of roughly 15,000, of which only 3,000 were combat-ready. The attacks began before dawn on December 20 and included strikes on the airport, a military academy, the prison where various political opponents to the regime were held, a naval complex, and the Noriega headquarters, known as La Comandancia. The vast majority of the troops were deployed in Panama City, where they killed several hundred Panamanian Defense Force (PDF) soldiers guarding various installations. Although the Comandancia was captured early into the fighting, Noriega slipped away, as he did on some forty other occasions before he finally sought refuge in the papal nuncio (Donnelly et al. 1991, 105).

In the midst of the fighting, Guillermo Endara and his two vice presidents were gathered into a secure location in the Canal Zone and sworn in as the legitimate leaders of the country. Washington immediately granted diplomatic recognition to the new Endara administration and offered $50 million in reconstruction aid (Conniff 1992, 164). Within a few weeks, the Bush administration renegotiated the Canal Treaty so that it provided for a significantly extended period of U.S. presence.

International reaction to the invasion was mixed. On the one hand, the OAS was clearly pleased to see Noriega gone, but it decided to "deeply regret" the U.S. intervention. For many Latins, the action seemed far more similar to the pre–Cold War policies of Teddy Roosevelt. In the United Nations, sentiments were also split in that although the United States won a slim majority for a resolution favoring the change of government, it was only because a large number of countries abstained. At home, the operation was over too quickly to precipitate any organized resistance.

U.S. troops were accused of causing large numbers of civilian deaths, although estimates vary widely (between 1,000 and 4,000). The Defense Department was clearly eager to minimize reports of "collateral damage" in the attack and reported a scant eighty-four official civilian casualties (mass graves of civilian dead were later uncovered and U.S. officials admitted to a higher figure—Commission 1991, 39). Although originally told not to shoot the many looters that were wreaking havoc in the city, on the second day the troops were given "shoot to maim" orders (McConnell 1991, 236). Attack helicopters fired numerous rounds into residential areas, causing widespread damage.

On January 3, 1990, Manuel Noriega was transported to Miami after finally being taken into custody, and by February the troops were withdrawn from the country. He was still awaiting trial as of mid-1993. Panama has yet to recover from the invasion, in spite of considerable foreign aid. Reports show that drug trafficking and government corruption are on the rise. Pressing problems in the Middle East seem to have removed Panama from the American consciousness.

CONCLUSION

There are many explanations of U.S. intervention overseas. The Cold War was a dominant preoccupation throughout the period under study—including in Panama because of its connection to Nicaragua. But the danger of Communist encroachment in the Western Hemisphere is not uniform across the cases. Clearly, in the case of Chile, the pro-Soviet connection is the most plausible—but interestingly enough this case involved the lowest degree of U.S. involvement. On the other hand, the most troops were deployed in the Panama case, where there seemed to be no Communist conspiracy whatever.

One could argue that at issue was the extent to which tangible American interests were at stake—U.S. nationals in the Dominican Republic, American corporate assets in Chile, and American government property in Panama. But here again, one finds in Chile perhaps the greatest threat to American assets but the least intervention. And is the Panama Canal such a vital interest that it deserves a massive invasion force to protect it against what was only a hypothetical threat? Only in the Dominican Republic does one find the perception of danger to both geopolitical and tangible local U.S. interests in proportion to the scale of intervention. Given the unique multilateral character of the invasion force (after OAS involvement), the Dominican Republic case challenges the notion that the U.S. always "goes it alone" in its own hemisphere.

Questions to Consider

1. Was coercion the best approach in these cases? Did the United States achieve its apparent objectives?

2. Were Johnson, Nixon, and Bush so eager to intervene because they were personally annoyed at the situation and felt a compulsion to vent their frustrations?

3. How was international law used by the United States to legitimize intervention? Is this a proper role for international law? How did international organizations enter into the picture?

References

Richard J. Barnet. *Intervention and Revolution: The United States in the Third World* (New York: New American Library, 1968).

Commission of Inquiry. *The U.S. Invasion of Panama: The Truth Behind Operation "Just Cause"* (Boston: South End Press, 1991).

Michael Conniff. *Panama and the United States: The Forced Alliance* (Athens, GA: University of Georgia Press, 1992).

Terry L. Deibel and John Lewis Gaddis, eds. *Containing the Soviet Union: A Critique of U.S. Policy* (New York: Pergamon-Brassey's, 1987).

Thomas Donnelly, Margaret Roth, and Caleb Baker. *Operation Just Cause: The Storming of Panama* (New York: Lexington Books, 1991).

Theodore Draper. *The Dominican Revolt: A Case Study in American Policy* (New York: Commentary, 1968).

Allen Dulles. *The Craft of Intelligence* (New York: Harper & Row, 1963).

Piero Gleijeses. *The Dominican Crisis: The 1965 Constitutionalist Revolt and American Intervention*, trans. by Lawrence Lipson (Baltimore, MD: The Johns Hopkins University Press, 1978).

Townsend Hoopes. *The Devil and John Foster Dulles* (Boston: Little, Brown, 1973).

George Kennan. "The Sources of Soviet Conduct." *Foreign Affairs*, 25 (July 1947): 566–582.

Henry Kissinger. *The White House Years* (Boston: Little, Brown, 1979).

Walter LaFeber. *The American Age: United States Foreign Policy at Home and Abroad Since 1750* (New York: W. W. Norton, 1989).

Harry Magdoff. *The Age of Imperialism: The Economics of U.S. Foreign Policy* (New York: Monthly Review Press, 1969).

Malcolm McConnell. *Just Cause: The Real Story of America's High-Tech Invasion of Panama* (New York: St. Martin's, 1991).

Robinson Rojas Sandford. *The Murder of Allende and the End of the Chilean Way to Socialism,* trans. by Andree Conrad (New York: Harper & Row, 1976).

William F. Sater. *Chile and the United States: Empires in Conflict* (Athens, GA: University of Georgia Press, 1990).

F. F. Sergeyev. *Chile: CIA Big Business* (Moscow: Progress Publishers, 1981).

Jerome Slater. *Intervention and Negotiaiton: The United States and the Dominican Revolution* (New York: Harper & Row, 1970).

A. J. Thomas, Jr., and Ann Van Wynen Thomas. *The Dominican Republic Crisis of 1965* (Dobbs Ferry, NY: Oceana Publications, 1967).

James R. Whelan. *Allende: Death of a Marxist Dream* (Westport, CT: Arlington House, 1981).

Woodrow Wilson. "The World Must Be Made Safe for Democracy," in John Vasquez, ed., *Classics of International Relations,* 2nd ed. (Englewood Cliffs, NJ: Prentice Hall, 1990), 12–15.

Lawrence A. Yates. *Power Pack: U.S. Intervention in the Dominican Republic, 1965–1966,* Leavenworth Papers #15 (Washington, DC: Government Printing Office, 1988).

WEALTH, POVERTY, AND THE EARTH'S FUTURE

CASE 21

OPEC

Beginning in the 1950s, Third World leaders raised a new agenda in world politics: poverty and development. What is more, they forged important diplomatic bonds in order to force this agenda on disinterested Western nations preoccupied with the Cold War in Europe and Asia. By the mid-1960s, the New International Economic Order (NIEO) was common parlance at the UN and the West was beginning to take notice of a galvanized Third World. The NIEO demanded a redress of economic wrongs by former imperialists, including increased foreign aid, support for commodity cartels, preferential trade arrangements, higher prices for their raw material exports, greater voice in international economic agencies and meetings, and recognition of special Third World economic needs. The NIEO was still rhetoric when the Organization of Petroleum Exporting Countries (OPEC) crisis catapulted it to the front burner.

Shortly after Egypt and Syria attacked Israel in October 1973, the oil-exporting states of the Middle East used access to their considerable oil resources as a political weapon for the first time. They imposed an embargo on any Western nation that refused to lessen its support for Israel in the Middle East conflict. The members of OPEC helped push up oil prices roughly fourfold in a few months.

The oil crisis of 1973–1974 epitomized the zero-sum nature of the relationship between the industrialized and developing countries. In the short run, the oil exporting nations' gains were virtually identical to the wealthy oil importers' losses. In the long run, the OPEC nations of the Middle East were among the first developing countries to pull themselves out of poverty. As late as 1970, Saudi Arabia's gross national product (GNP) per capita was a mere $616. By 1980, it had passed by the United States to reach $14,050 (Alnasrawi 1985, 118). The United Arab Emirates boasted enormous wealth—roughly twice that of the wealthiest European countries (as measured in GNP/capita figures).

This situation did not continue for long, however, and the most powerful members of OPEC soon found themselves burdened with the responsibility to control prices judiciously with a view toward the long-term consequences of their actions. Issues of stability in the economies of oil importers, aid to oil-importing developing countries, diversification of national industries in order to lessen dependence on oil, and prevention of substitution of other energy sources for oil demanded OPEC nations' attentions, all as a direct consequence of the 1973–1974 price hikes. To their surprise, OPEC nations found themselves thinking and acting more and more like rich Europeans.

In all of this, one is forced to ask whether the OPEC experience strengthened or weakened Third World solidarity in the face of Western power. Was the NIEO agenda promoted or retarded? Have the OPEC nations been co-opted by the West, and thus removed from the Third World orbit? Where will the Third World alliance go from here?

ORIGINS OF OPEC

Prior to World War II, oil exploration and extraction in the Middle East tended to be a supplement to major oil drilling in Texas, Russia, and other industrialized regions. It was not until Venezuela, foreshadowing OPEC's moves, secured a fifty-fifty split of profits from the U.S. oil companies operating there (Johany 1980, 4) that Middle East oil became attractive as a low-cost alternative (Danielson 1982, 126). During those early years, the "Seven Sisters" (marketing their oil under the famous brand names Exxon, Mobil, Chevron, Gulf, Shell, BP, and Texaco) collaborated in drilling, pumping, refining, pricing, and distributing oil, largely without regard for the various kings and sheiks governing the Middle East (Johany 1980, 8). The price of oil was largely arbitrary, since it was based on transportation costs from U.S. oil fields and served primarily as an accounting device upon which local taxes were based. Several Arab governments, including particularly Libya, frequently protested the inequity of this arrangement and pressed for either increased prices or higher taxation rates, as in Venezuela. Even the U.S. government moved to break up this very powerful cartel, although it pulled back, contenting itself with merely restricting imports of Middle East oil (Odell 1986, 220).

This reduction of oil imports to the United States precipitated a drop in overall Middle East oil sales and prompted Exxon, Shell, and BP to drop the "posted price" of their oil, resulting in lower tax revenues for Arab nations (Odell 1986, 220). This in turn led nationalist Venezuelan leader Romulo Betancourt to dispatch his oil minister Juan Perez Alfonso to the Middle East to begin organizing, along with Saudi counterpart Abdallah Tariki, an organization of oil exporting nations to counter these threats. In April 1959, the secret Maadi Pact was signed, creating a consultative committee which sought higher prices and further cooperation (Terzian 1985, 26).

A summit of five oil-exporting nations (Venezuela, Saudi Arabia, Iraq, Iran, and Kuwait) held in Baghdad in September 1960 resulted in the formation of OPEC itself, which restated some of the goals of the Maadi Pact of pressing for higher prices. OPEC's official goals included: "coordination and unification of the petroleum policies of member countries and the determination of the best means of safeguarding their interests. The organization shall devise ways and means of ensuring the stabilization of prices" (Johany 1980, 6). In addition, OPEC called for "programmation of production and solidarity between members states should concessionary companies exercise sanctions against any one of them" (Terzian 1985, 43).

There is a general misconception that OPEC functioned as a cartel, meaning a collaborative arrangement of producers to set prices, share markets, and the like. While the Seven Sisters seem to have performed this role rather effectively, OPEC rarely did, if at all. From the beginning, OPEC found itself vulnerable to internal dissent and conflicting interests. While Venezuela and other more radical members, such as Algeria and Libya who joined later, favored a confrontational approach toward the West, Saudi Arabia, Iran under the shah, and Kuwait tended to adopt a more cautious posture. OPEC's inequalities are a source of conflict—Saudi Arabia, for example, places priority on keeping oil at the center of the world economy, not reaping a windfall through militant pricing and production. Also, the difference in the approach each regime has adopted regarding the control of its own oil industry and its own relationship to the capitalist market is significant, in that more militant nations such as Libya determined in 1969 to nationalize foreign firms on a large scale, while other oil exporters were loath to antagonize foreign interests (Mikdashi 1976, 209).

As put by two analysts of OPEC:

> If one applies the defintion of export cartels used by Western countries, the OPEC organization does not pass the test. An export cartel not only must include rigid agreements on prices, but also related agreements in such key areas as production control and market sharing. The export cartel must also be responsible for monitoring the activities of its constituent members with a view to policing and penalizing violators. The OPEC member governments do not perform any of these cartel functions. (Mikdashi 1976, 207–208)

> The truth is that OPEC was never the united bloc, the cartel, it was accused of being. Not only did it fail to control production, most of the member countries were not even willing to endow themselves with the means to do so. (Terzian 1985, 106)

If one looks at the facts, it becomes clear that if there ever was any intention to build a cartel, it was doomed as early as January 1961, a mere four months after OPEC was created (Terzian 1985, 98).

This is not to say that OPEC does not have the potential of acting as a cartel. Typically, cartels fail because of the lack of a leader able and willing to act unilaterally to maintain production levels and prices for the commodity. Saudi Arabia has the capacity to increase its normal 500 million tons of oil per year to as much as 750 million, and to lower production to a mere 150 million without suffering financially (Odell 1986, 246). With reserves more than double that of the second-ranked country, Saudi Arabia can maintain this position of dominance for decades to come. Saudi Arabia also has a greater vested interest in maintaining stability in the market over the long run, and is therefore generally willing to intervene unilaterally.

What OPEC has historically lacked is internal solidarity and favorable world market conditions. Both of these began to change in the late 1960s. In terms of market forces, by the late 1960s, oil was the key ingredient in the industrial machine of the West. As put by Darmstadter and Landsberg:

> Several fairly distinct terms on the world energy scene helped create the climate in which the producer-country actions of 1973–74 could bear fruit. These trends revolve, in their physical manifestation, around the growth in overall energy consumption, the rising share of petroleum within the total, and, in turn, the steadily rising share—already high in the early nineteen-sixties—of Eastern Hemisphere (particularly Persian Gulf and North African) oil in accommodating that rise in oil consumption. (Darmstadter and Landsberg 1976, 16)

World energy consumption grew at a 5.5 percent annual rate during the 1960s. However, world oil consumption grew in the 1960s at an astonishing annual rate of 7.8 percent, while coal consumption grew only 1.8 percent per year. And of that increased oil consumption, Middle East oil represented by 1972 a much larger share of Western energy consumption than ten years previous. By 1972, 57.4 percent of Japanese and 32 percent of Western European energy consisted of Middle East oil, and Middle East oil made up roughly 76 percent of all oil imports in these countries (Darmstadter and Landsberg 1976, 21). As can be seen in Table 21.1, all Western nations, with the exception of Canada, were heavily dependent on oil imports by the beginning of the 1970s (note that Japan imported all but 0.7 percent of its oil in 1972). Even Britain, with its subsidized coal industry, consumed more oil from 1971 on (Odell 1986, 217).

Western dependence on oil has been compared to an addiction, particularly since there were no alternatives as of 1972 that could have been rapidly brought on stream at competitive prices. Even after the considerable price hikes of the 1970s, oil remained a relatively cheap energy source, particularly in relation to what consumers were willing to pay (Danielson 1982, 162). Although Russia and the United States had access to domestic oil, they were unable to quickly increase production at low cost. Gas, coal, solar energy, nuclear power, hydroelectricity, and other alternative fuels were either not cost-effective or were still experimental and unavailable for commercial use at the time. What is more, in the short-term of the 1967–1973 period, not only were alternative energy sources unavailable, but several alternative oil

Table 21.1 OIL CONSUMPTION, PRODUCTION, AND NET TRADE,
BY MAJOR WORLD REGIONS, 1972

	Consumption 1,000 barrels per day	Production 1,000 barrels per day	Net Imports 1,000 barrels per day	% of consumption	Net Exports 1000 barrels per day	% of production
United States	15,980	11,180	4,515	28.3%		
Canada	1,665	1,835			170	9.3%
Caribbean	1,195	3,650			2,450	67.1
Other Western Hemisphere	2,105	1,325	770	36.6		
Western Europe	14,205	435	13,735	96.7		
Middle East	1,145	17,975			16,830	93.6
North Africa	370	3,745			3,375	90.1
West Africa	200	2,085			1,885	90.4
East and South Africa, South Asia	975	86	880	90.3		
South East Asia	1,430	1,295	125	8.7		
Japan	4,800	143	4,765	99.3		
Oceania	635	306	300	47.2		
USSR, Eastern Europe, China	7,990	8,865			880	9.9
TOTAL	52,695	52,925				

Note: Includes natural gas liquids. Regional net imports or net exports may not precisely equal the difference between consumption and production, and worldwide consumption and production are not precisely equal, because different sources employ somewhat different definitions. Indonesia is included within "South East Asia" and Mexico within "Other Western Hemisphere."

Source: Raymond Vernon, ed., *The Oil Crisis* (New York: W W Norton, 1976).

suppliers were unable to get their product to market. In 1967, the Suez Canal was closed as a result of the Arab-Israeli War, inhibiting access to Persian Gulf oil for Europe. The Nigerian (Biafran) Civil War curtailed the flow of that nation's oil and, together with the Suez situation, increased the attractiveness of Libyan and Algerian oil over the short term (Johany 1980, 10). Finally, for a brief and rather unique period in 1973, refinery capacity was in short supply, indicating a larger demand for oil than the market could then accommodate.

The combination of these long-term and short-term situations certainly played into the hands of OPEC members. But it was a political development which created the oil crisis itself, as it has come to be known.

In 1965 and 1967, OPEC experimented with two tools it would come to rely on heavily. In 1965, OPEC attempted to fix prices unilaterally, but was forced to accept the terms of the oil companies. In 1967, OPEC undertook a short-lived oil embargo against countries which had supported Israel during the war. This also failed because, as put by OPEC official Nicolas Sarkis, "We cannot even prevent Arab oil from reaching Israel; how on earth could we enforce an embargo against Britain and the United States, the home countries of most of the 'majors'" (Terzian 1985, 107).

When in 1969 Muammar Qaddafi took power in Libya, he was determined to fight against imperialism as symbolized by foreign oil exploitation. In 1970, the oil companies operating in Libya, led by Exxon, quoted a price for Libyan oil based on an average of Gulf oil prices. Qaddafi protested and demanded a price based on that assigned to neighboring Algeria's oil (Ghanem 1986, 121). When persuasion failed, Libya moved to cut the amount of oil the companies could pump and demanded price concessions from Occidental Petroleum, a small independent company. In September, the company agreed to pay an additional $.30 per barrel in exchange for continued access to Libyan oil (Johany 1980, 9). This accord, known as the Tripoli Agreement, resulted in a 15 percent increase in the price of Libyan oil. When combined with an additional 5 percent income tax, the Tripoli Agreement represented "the strongest political action by a single oil-producing country against the oil companies to which it had granted concessions since Mexico's nationalization of its oil in 1938" (Odell 1986, 222).

What followed was a rapid series of fierce negotiations between the oil companies, Libya, Algeria, and OPEC. Following Libya's lead, OPEC undertook negotiations as a group with the Seven Sisters in late 1970, signing the Tehran Agreement in February 1971. This raised prices from $1.80 to $2.25 per barrel of Saudi Arabian light, the so-called "benchmark crude" (Ghanem 1986, 126). After the devaluation of the dollar in August, oil companies agreed to an inflation-indexing system to maintain the real price of oil (Johany 1980, 12). By early 1973, the price had risen to $2.59 per barrel and Saudi Arabia's cut had nearly doubled to $1.52 per barrel since 1970. During the ensuing months, OPEC members won concessions from oil companies on increased local ownership of facilities, higher royalty fees, and larger tax shares culminating in fifty-fifty ownership and a 55 percent tax rate for many OPEC countries. Throughout the period, the U.S. government was tacitly encouraging the oil companies to make concessions, both by waiving antitrust rules prohibiting collective bargaining, and by instructing emissaries to Middle East capitals to encourage higher prices (Ghanem 1986, 125). James Akins, for example, in a speech before the Arab Oil Congress in mid-1972, announced his view that oil could soon reach $5.00 per barrel because of wholly fabricated information on OPEC leaders' secret plans (Terzian 1985, 189). According to Odell, the United States was eager for Europeans to pay higher prices for imported oil since their energy bill was even lower than the United States. U.S. officials and oil executives also recognized that profits from higher oil prices could be considerable and would perhaps offset the drag higher energy prices could have on the U.S. economy (Odell 1986, 224–225).

THE YOM KIPPUR WAR AND THE FIRST OIL CRISIS

By October 1973, then, OPEC had already learned many valuable lessons and won many significant victories against the West: a doubling of its incomes and much higher status in international circles. When Egypt and Syria attacked Israel on October 6, OPEC ministers were gathered to discuss future negotiating strategies. Oil prices on the day-to-day "spot market," already approaching $10 per barrel and always sensitive to crises, soared to over $16 per barrel immediately (See Figure 21.1). OPEC unilaterally raised prices to $11.65 per barrel (a compromise between extreme demands by Libya, Algeria, and even Iran and Saudi Arabia's conservative proposals). OPEC appeared to be functioning as the Third World's first genuine producer cartel.

In connection with this price move, Organization of Arab Petroleum Exporting Countries (OAPEC) members met to determine which actions they would take against Israel's allies. The United States and the Netherlands were singled out as targets of an embargo. Henry Kissinger promised a more even-handed Middle East policy, to pressure Israel to withdraw from the West Bank, and hinted of possible potential military action against Arabs in order to break the embargo, which finally collapsed in March 1974 (Ghanem 1986, 147). France, Japan, Britain, Germany, and other Western powers either withdrew their open support of Israel or simply intensified their criticism of Israel's activities, and adopted a more neutral or even pro-Arab policy in the Middle East in order to avoid the embargo (Ghanem 1986, 144). Even these countries were hurt by the 25 percent drop in production.

Although oil prices stabilized over the next five years, the galvinized OPEC members worked to consolidate and expand their gains in other ways. As pointed out by Raymond Vernon,

> By almost any definition . . . it is evident that power . . . shifted in important ways since, say, the early nineteen-fifties, when Iran could be soundly chastised for its unwelcome attempts to gain control of its own oil and when Saudi Arabia could be regarded as a reliable ward of American oil interests. (Vernon 1976, 245)

OPEC nations in 1974 had at their disposal at least three sources of power relative to the West: control over a valuable resource, purchasing power resulting from oil profits of roughly $100 billion, and the political power which vast sums of money can provide, such as the ability to offer aid or build industry (Vernon 1976, 147). The capacity to apply this power selectively enabled OPEC to co-opt countries like France, which sought "special relationships," and prevent the consolidation of a consumer's cartel (the International Energy Agency formed at U.S. insistence). As put by Odell:

> . . . in 1975 and 1976 neither the American-sponsored strategy, based on undermining the OPEC cartel by means of confrontation through an alliance of consuming countries, nor the French strategy, requiring successful long-term special relationships with the existing important oil-producing and exporting countries, produced very effective results. . . . Neither pleas nor threats from the Western world could easily alter this situation for individual exporters at a time

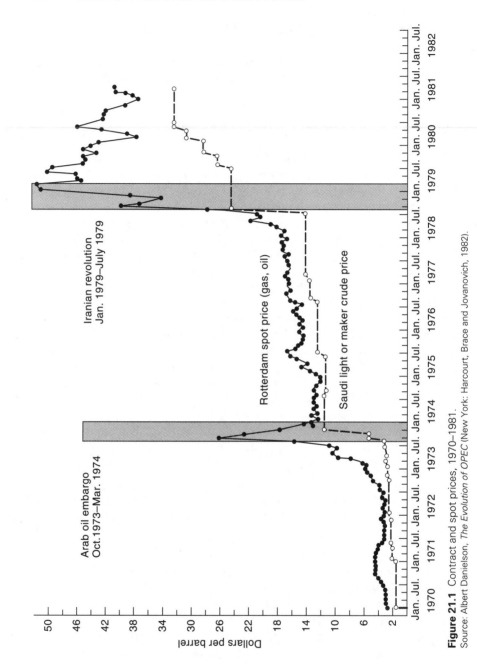

Figure 21.1 Contract and spot prices, 1970–1981.

Source: Albert Danielson, *The Evolution of OPEC* (New York: Harcourt, Brace and Jovanovich, 1982).

when the solidarity of OPEC had produced so many benefits for its members. (Odell 1986, 243)

OPEC nations became the financial and emotional foundation of the NIEO during the years immediately following the oil crisis. Algeria served as the intercessor between OPEC and the more militant Non-Aligned movement during the oil crisis. It understood well the potential of OPEC's success as a key to galvinizing the moribund Third World coalition in world politics (Alnasrawi 1985, 138). Algeria's Houari Boumedienne envisioned OPEC as the cutting edge of the NIEO strategy.

If the Third World could present a united front against the "North," with oil hanging in the balance, it just might be possible to achieve the "new economic order" that Algiers had been working towards ever since it was entrusted with the presidency of the Non-Aligned movement. . . . The time had come to redefine OPEC's role, this time in the framework of "North-South" relations (Terzian 1985, 212).

With the encouragement of Algeria, as well as Libya, OPEC members endorsed the 1973 Non-Aligned Conference declarations against Western exploitation, the declaration of the NIEO agenda in 1974 at the UN, and the 1975 Dakar declaration endorsing commodity producer cartels. Perhaps more important, the OPEC nations individually and collectively set in place considerable funding for both development purposes as well as to assist oil-importing developing nations to pay for the more expensive fuel. Thus, although many developing nations resented the higher oil prices and the tendency for OPEC nations to invest their profits in the West (Girvan 1976, 156), OPEC gave them some $3.4 billion in 1974 and $5.5 billion in 1975 (Terzian 1985, 211).

As put by Alnasrawi:

The concept of solidarity found expression also in the U.N. system, since OPEC aid represented a major departure from the traditional pattern of donor-recipient in which the donor was a developed country and the recipient a developing country. Under the emerging system of financial solidarity, both donor and recipient countries were developing countries. (Alnasrawi 1985, 131)

And further, according to Girvan:

The OPEC action was unusual and unprecedented because it was taken by a group of Third World, primary-product-exporting countries. For the first time in modern history, some non-industrialized countries had succeeded in securing market power in world trade in their export commodity, and they had used this market power to impose a substantial improvement in their terms of trade with the industrialized West. This rudely disrupted the established pattern of center-periphery power relations that had governed the economic relationship between the developed countries and the Third World. It also served as an inspiration, a lever, and a possible financial base for similar attempts by other Third World exporting countries to secure market power in other commodities. (Girvan 1976, 145–146)

OPEC nations also provided aid via international lending institutions, both in order to assist developing nations as well as to increase their voting power in these Western-dominated institutions. By the late 1970s, Saudi Arabia's presence in these organizations exceeded many Western nations (Terzian 1985, 206). Also, OPEC members supported efforts by other commodity exporters by providing seed monies to undertake producer cartels. Venezuela, for example, backed the ill-fated coffee cartel in 1974 (Vernon 1976, 250).

Another benefit to the Third World was the demand for immigrant labor in the Gulf states, particularly Kuwait and Saudi Arabia, whereby Palestinian, Jordanian, and other Arab workers found employment. In Kuwait, 61 percent of the work force was foreign by 1975. The 700,000 Egyptian workers in Kuwait sent home $1.8 billion in 1978 (representing more than 10 percent of Egypt's GNP) (Alnasrawi 1985, 133–134). This is not to say that the jobs were always seen as a boon to the workers, since in most Gulf states immigrants were denied any form of civil rights, no matter how long they stayed.

Militant members of OPEC feared Saudi Arabia and other conservative members would find themselves co-opted by the West. As Saudi investments in Europe and the United States increased (estimated at $42 billion by 1978 in the United States alone), they would become more concerned about protecting their own interests by preventing recession in the West. More radical OPEC members worried this would jeopardize the solidarity of OPEC and the Third World as a whole.

In order to prevent such an occurrence, Algeria and Libya pressed for a strong statement of Third World unity at the 1975 OPEC summit in Algiers. Algerian President Boumedienne proposed an ambitious political-economic-military alliance for the sake of Third World unity and progress. "It seemed grandiose, like other projects that Boumedienne, then at the peak of his prestige in the Third World, was launching onto the international scene. But its very scale frightened the other OPEC members, whose ambitions within the organization were apparently limited to a corporate alliance more or less tinged with Third Worldism, according to the regime in power at the time" (Terzian 1985, 214).

At this summit, a "Solemn Declaration" was adopted, reaffirming solidarity against exploitation by the North, asserting the NIEO demands, and calling for a North-South summit (which was in fact held in Paris in September, although it produced no resolution) (Alnasrawi 1985, 140). While the verbiage was impressive, subsequent events belied the authors' sincerity. According to Hunter, the militant vs. conservastive split in OPEC prevented a united pro–Third World stand after 1975. Furthermore, OPEC's interest in preserving the centrality of oil in industry (including Third World industry) and the general health of Western consuming societies ran counter to the more rational Third World strategy of sustainable development and North-South rivalry (Hunter 1984, 266–268).

OPEC AND THE SECOND OIL CRISIS

"[C]ontrary to the general impression, power did not unite OPEC. OPEC was more united when the world market situation was against it than when it was in its favor" (Ghanem 1986, 161). Although tensions had existed from OPEC's beginnings over whether to adopt a confrontational approach with the West, by 1977 the issue had nearly paralyzed the organization. Saudi Arabia was so alarmed at the trend for higher and higher prices in OPEC, that it bolted from the consensus and posted an official price some sixty cents lower than the rest of OPEC in 1977 (Ghanem 1986, 150; Odell 1986, 266). By 1978, OPEC solidarity began to evaporate. Egypt left the Arab alliance against Israel by signing the Camp David Accords (prompting a withdrawal of Arab aid). The Shah of Iran was overthrown in an Islamic Revolution led by the radical Muslim cleric Ayatollah Khomeini. In 1980, two key members of OPEC, Iraq and Iran, started a bloody and protracted war. At the same time, Saudi Arabia accepted billions in military aid from the United States, thus tacitly aligning itself with Israel's strongest supporter. The political glue that held together the Arab core of OPEC had dissolved.

The most tumultuous event of those listed above was certainly the fall of the Shah. The result was a reduction by three-fourths of Iran's oil exports, previously second only to Saudi Arabia. The immediate result was a dramatic increase in spot prices, culminating in levels well above $30 per barrel in 1980 (see Table 21.2). Although there were attempts by OPEC members to control the increase in the official price, between September 1978 and June 1980 oil exporters adopted a laissez-faire (get-it-while-you-can) policy and sought the highest prices possible on the open market (Ghanem 1986, 151). As shown in Table 21.2, wide discrepancies quickly emerged between each country's prices.

In spite of Saudi Arabia's efforts to stabilize the market through increased production (at U.S. encouragement), the general structure of the oil market became extremely unstable (Odell 1986, 248). Analysts predicted oil prices would climb to $60 per barrel by 1985 (Levy 1982, 309)!

This unpredictability in the production of oil was exacerbated by two additional developments. First was the realization in 1981 that the market was saturated due to a generally weak demand for oil in the West and excessive production by OPEC nations eager to reap a windfall from the extremely high prices.

Some of the OPEC countries could not sell their oil. Accusation and counteraccusation erupted among OPEC members. Saudi Arabia was attacked as having taken advantage of the market by keeping its oil underpriced and increasing its production without giving any consideration to the predicament of its partners in OPEC. Libya and Nigeria were the countries most affected by the market deterioration. Their sales went down so much that sometimes days would pass without them exporting a single barrel (Ghanem 1986, 167).

Table 21.2 PRICES OF CRUDE, DECEMBER 1978–JANUARY 1981

	API gravity*	December 31, 1978	January 1981
Algeria			
Zarzaitine	44	14.05	40.00
Ecuador			
Oriente	29.7	12.36	40.07
Gabon			
Gamba	31.7	13.03	36.00
Indonesia			
Walio		13.00	35.00
Iran			
Iranian Light	34	12.81	37.00
Iraq			
Basrah	34	12.58	35.96
Kuwait			
Export	31	12.27	35.50
Libya			
Brega	40	13.85	41.00
Nigeria			
Bonny	36.7	14.10	40.00
Qatar			
Dukhan	40	13.19	37.42
Saudi Arabia			
Arabian Light	34	13.33	34.00
United Arab Emirates			
Murban	39	13.26	36.56
Venezuela			
Officina	34	13.99	38.06

*API gravity: measurement of specific gravity of liquids as scaled by the American Petroleum Institute.

Source: Shukri Ghanem, OPEC: *The Rise and Fall of an Exclusive Club* (New York: KPI,1986).

Ten years of energy conservation efforts, oil exploration in Alaska and the North Sea, and experimentation with gas, solar energy, and other alternative energy sources had resulted in real reduction in Western energy consumption. By 1983, in spite of considerably higher economic activity, oil consumption in the West was down to 83 percent of 1973 levels (Odell 1986, 255). This structural shift was not recognized by OPEC leaders who sought instead to increase producer discipline and strengthen Saudi Arabia's leadership role, the transformation of which was the second new development.

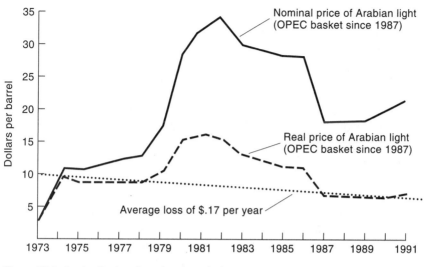

Figure 21.2 Crude oil prices in real and nominal terms—1973–1991.
Source: OPEC 1992.

Saudi Arabia decided in 1981 to abdicate its authority in OPEC and join in the rush for earnings during the period of high prices, then to undercut OPEC competitors by offering discounts and special deals (Ghanem 1986, 170). By early 1982, OPEC had lost all significance and was on the verge of collapse (Terzian 1985, 296).

In March 1982, OPEC oil ministers gathered to determine whether any potential existed for salvaging the organization and restoring order to world oil markets. Ironically, they had the enthusiastic support of many Western consuming countries yearning for some new order in oil prices (Terzian 1985, 341). Saudi Arabia decided to allow OPEC members to dictate Saudi price and production levels, a clear change of policy which transformed OPEC, however briefly, into a genuine cartel (Terzian 1985, 298). The oil ministers agreed to a relatively low production ceiling in order to bring about a price which would later be made official. This arrangement did little to alter the basic structure of the oil market, which by now OPEC simply no longer dominated. When Iraqi and Iranian oil came back on stream in 1985, oil prices dropped precipitously to $8 per barrel on the spot (Odell 1986, 285). Saudi Arabia, after letting its oil production fall to only 20 percent of normal, again resorted to undercutting OPEC prices through such creative arrangements as "net-back pricing" whereby it covered much of the production costs for oil companies. Official prices fell to pre-1978 levels, meaning that, after inflation, oil prices actually fell from 1973 to 1990 (OPEC 1992, 25—See Figure 21.2).

Overall, the volatile period of 1978–1986 left OPEC scarred but intact. Arab oil lost its role as preeminent energy source for the West and the prospects for renewal were slim. Furthermore, Third World solidarity was largely frustrated, particularly as the debt crisis divided the Third World into three distinct groups with little in common: oil-importing debtors, oil-exporting debtors, and oil-exporting creditors. More and more, each group found its future in collaboration with the West. Debtors were eager to maintain access to Western capital and markets and they one by one chose capitalist liberalization as the path out of indebtedness. OPEC countries found they were just as dependent on the West's consumers as the latter had once been on them. Few developing nations found benefits from antagonizing the West.

As far as the great OPEC aid experiment is concerned, Hunter gives this qualified indictment:

> The central thesis that emerges from this study is that the OPEC countries have failed to act vigorously and with determination to advance Third World objectives. Moreover, the OPEC countries' use of aid has generally followed the established pattern of the traditional donors, and consequently they have failed to use aid in any systematic manner to achieve Third World goals. However, the other—and equally important—thesis of this study is that OPEC's failure has not been due to its members' conscious deception in representing their goals and aspirations as being essentially the same as those of the rest of the Third World. Rather, this failure has been the almost inevitable outcome of basic contradictions relating both to intra-OPEC relations and to those between OPEC and the rest of the Third World—contradictions that came to the fore after the events of 1973. (Hunter 1984, 264)

THE FUTURE OF OPEC AND THE THIRD WORLD

To a large extent the glory days of OPEC are over. OPEC has been the victim of its own success, in that whereas there were relatively few world-class suppliers of oil in the 1970s, there are now several, with many untapped resources still available (according to some estimates, Africa is using only one-quarter of 1 percent of its potential—Odell 1986, 266). Not only have alternative suppliers come on line, but alternative energy sources are far more commonly available. While oil use has remained fairly flat since 1980, natural gas consumption has risen 40 percent. As put by Odell:

> One could argue that the major exporting countries of the Gulf have themselves created the conditions which necessarily exclude them from the future world of oil. These are the consequences of policies which have pushed the price of the commodity as to make their production decreasingly relevant in a world which, with a much lower growth rate in oil use, has alternative oil supply options open to it. (Odell 1986, 280)

In a recent article, Morse projects that the time of soft oil markets may soon end, however. Given shrinking excess capacity at refineries, rising demand, increasing imports, and smaller output from non-OPEC sources currently on line, oil prices will likely begin to rise again in the mid-1990s (Morse 1990/91, 42–45). OPEC is less able and willing to intervene to support high prices, however, because of their considerable downstream assets (in oil refining, shipping, and marketing). In general, then, oil is and will continue to be largely governed not by politics but by market forces.

Imagine that you have been asked to plot a strategy that would lead to a strengthening of OPEC's place in the world oil market. Of course, your research budget is considerable, given the keen interest of your Middle East clients. How best could OPEC return to the glory days of 1973–1974? To what extent was this a unique and ephemeral period? Can this be duplicated? Should it be duplicated?

Specifically, how should Saudi Arabia approach OPEC's role? To what extent should it cater to the West, as it did, for example, during the Persian Gulf War and since by increasing production to make up for the Iraqi oil boycott? What benefits and risks are there to an accommodationist approach? Who will benefit most within Saudi Arabia?

Would your answer indicate what factors must be in place before one can even speak of OPEC resurgence? To what extent are external factors significant, and are they beyond OPEC's control?

Questions to Consider

1. Did OPEC help or hurt the goal of Third World solidarity? Is the Third World cause more or less vibrant?

2. How did internal solidarity and leadership affect OPEC's negotiating strength? What could/can be done to change this?

3. What would it take for the Third World agenda to return to the center of global attention?

References

Abbas Alnasrawi. *OPEC in a Changing World Economy* (Baltimore: Johns Hopkins University Press, 1985).

Albert Danielson. *The Evolution of OPEC* (New York: Harcourt, Brace and Jovanovich, 1982).

Joel Darmstadter and Hans Landsberg. "The Economic Background," in Vernon, ed., *The Oil Crisis*, 15–37.

Shukri Ghanem. *OPEC: The Rise and Fall of an Exclusive Club* (New York: KPI, 1986).

Norman Girvan. "Economic Nationalism," in Vernon, ed., *The Oil Crisis*, 145–158.

Shireen Hunter. *OPEC and the Third World: The Politics of Aid* (Bloomington, IN: Indiana University Press, 1984).

Ali D. Johany. *The Myth of the OPEC Cartel: The Role of Saudi Arabia* (New York: John Wiley & Sons, 1980).

Merrie Gilbert Klapp. *The Sovereign Entrepreneur: Oil Policies in Advanced and Less Developed Capitalist Countries* (Ithaca, NY: Cornell University Press, 1987).

Walter J. Levy, ed. *Oil Strategy and Politics, 1941–1981* (Boulder, CO: Westview Press, 1982).

Zuhayr Mikdashi. "The OPEC Process," in Vernon, ed., *The Oil Crisis*, 203–216.

Edward Morse. "The Coming Oil Revolution." *Foreign Affairs* 69 #5 (Winter 1990/91): 57–73.

Peter Odell. *Oil and World Power* (New York: Penguin, 1986).

OPEC. *Facts and Figures: A Graphical Analysis of World Energy Up to 1991* (Vienna: OPEC, 1992).

Pierre Terzian. *OPEC: The Inside Story*, trans. by Michael Pallis (London: Zed Books, 1985)

Raymond Vernon, ed. *The Oil Crisis* (New York: Norton, 1976).

CASE 22

Third World Debt

While many international relations scholars look at the world as a struggle for power between nation-states, many Third World experts describe the world as a vast socioeconomic "system." To these and others, the world does not consist of nation-states so much as it is made up of global social classes, transportation networks, financial flows, and resource extraction. To the extent that we understand these fundamental global relations, we will see that international politics is as much a symptom as a cause. While inheriting some of Marx's notions of class structure, this approach goes beyond Marx to consider global relations in all their complexity, with an emphasis on fundamental economic and social relations. Patterns of international debt are representative of these pervasive and deep global structures which transcend diplomacy and war.

In August 1982, then-President of Mexico Jose´ Lopez Portillo declared that his country would be unable to meet the quarterly deadline for interest payments on over $80 billion in foreign debts. The move came as several other Latin American governments were expressing serious concerns about meeting payments on another $200 billion in debts. As the Federal Reserve Bank put it: "International bankers and policy makers faced a threat of financial disorder on a global scale not seen since the Depression" (Spero 1990, 181). For the next ten years, international bankers, world powers, international institutions, and numerous Third World actors would be riveted by the problem of preventing global financial collapse. How did these players interact? What were the global structures evidenced by their behavior? Where do we stand today, and who "won"?

To many people, the world of international finance is mystifying, if not troubling. One cannot easily imagine the flow and multiplication of the tens of trillions of dollars worth of international currency circulating through the world economy on any given day. The changes that can occur as a result of one simple deposit can be mind-boggling. To help orient the student to some of these problems, we will begin by defining some basic terms in international finance, then go over the history of the Third World debt crisis. To complete the chapter, we will look carefully at the questions raised above.

INTERNATIONAL FINANCE PRIMER*

Perhaps the most confusing aspect of international finance is understanding the role of money and currency. Originally conceived as a convenience to lighten the burden of seafaring merchants who otherwise would have been forced to carry gold bullion, paper money has since developed a life of its own. Because it has no inherent value, the worth of paper money stems from the strength of the government and society that produces it. To the extent that buyers and sellers require use of the currency or trust it as a medium of exchange, the value of a currency increases. In addition, the faster the economy grows, the lower the inflation rate, the higher the interest rate one may earn by depositing in banks from that country, the stronger a country's currency.

Over time, certain currencies have emerged as the more secure and valuable, and are called "hard currencies." These currencies are used by traders and investors even if they are not dealing directly with the country that mints it. For example, virtually all the oil in the world is bought and sold with U.S. dollars. As a result, even if Saudi Arabia sells oil to Lithuania, it can expect payment in dollars. Dollars in circulation outside of the United States are called "Eurodollars" or in the case of oil-related capital, "Petrodollars."

No Third World country can boast of a hard currency of its own. Because of this, no Third World country can buy products overseas without first obtaining one or another hard currency to consummate the transaction. Because it cannot rely on its own mint to produce hard currency, a Third World nation has four options if it wants to do business abroad: (1) export products in exchange for hard currency (hence the importance of trading with wealthy, developed countries), (2) borrow hard currency from private banks in the West, (3) obtain grants and/or loans from governments which control hard currencies, or (4) attract foreign investment. While barter trade is becoming more popular among multinational firms, and much international aid is "in kind" (in the form of a physical product rather than cash transfer), the four means of obtaining hard currency listed above are far and away the most popular beginning points for international business for a Third World nation.

Once you understand the importance of obtaining hard currency for a Third World nation, you can now understand why many solutions to the

---

*Students are referred to the excellent primer on the subject: John Charles Pool and Steve Stamos, *The ABCs of International Finance* (Lexington, MA: Lexington Books, 1987).

debt crisis were simply not feasible. Although the United States has at times increased its money supply (printed more currency) to more easily pay off foreign debts, this would be impossible for any Third World government. Some have tried to stimulate their economies through dramatically increasing the money supply, but the result has as often as not been triple-digit inflation and a weaker currency abroad.

Another set of ideas essential to understanding the debt crisis is the operation of the "multiplier effect" in banking. As you may know, banks want to keep as much of their money in circulation as possible. Simply put, your individual deposit of $1,000 does not sit in a vault until you decide to withdraw it. Depending on the regulations of the country, roughly 85 percent of all deposits are loaned out to collect interest. Banks attempt to maximize the difference between interest charged on loans and interest paid on savings accounts in order to clear a profit. An important result of this natural flow of the banking system is the geometric increase in the total amount of money in circulation. A $1,000 deposit, through this process of lending and re-lending, can generate as much as $6,000. When expanded to the global scale, where bankers typically shift their liquid (readily accessible with withdrawal) deposits from one time zone to the next in order to continue generating interest throughout the twenty-four-hour cycle and where institutional investors and money market account managers move billions for the sake of half a percentage point, one can see that the multiplier effect is one of the most significant phenomena in international finance (Strange 1986).

Finally, because it became the focal point of efforts to rectify the situation after 1982, it is important to clarify what is meant by "adjustment." In general terms, any effort on the part of a country to pay its international bills could be termed "adjustment," although this usually refers to several specific things. First, since access to foreign capital is the highest priority, governments are expected to "adjust" policies which discourage foreign currency from entering the country. This means exports must be encouraged, typically by first reducing the value of the currency relative to the hard currencies (devaluation), promoting export-oriented sectors of the economy, reducing restrictions on foreign investment to encourage businesses to invest in your nation, and generally building a favorable business climate (low taxes on profits, easy repatriation of earnings, strong infrastructure, capable and placid work force).

Second, the government must end practices which cost money above and beyond what the nation can afford. Borrowing from abroad to pay for social programs is a likely target since any deficit spending hurts the chances for balancing other accounts. Imports should be discouraged—especially imports of consumer goods which do not contribute to the health of the economy overall. In general terms, the economy should be "liberalized," meaning that private enterprise should be encouraged and state intervention minimized. In the case of many Third World nations, this involves selling off huge amounts of public-owned enterprises, much like the Eastern European nations have been doing of late. The result is supposed to be a more dynamic, if perhaps less equitable and generous, government and economy (note that adjustment is rarely sufficent, by itself, to turn an economy around—see Schwartz 1991).

ORIGINS OF THE DEBT CRISIS

There is still much debate on the causes of the debt crisis. Suffice it here to say that we will focus on the most obvious factors concerning which there is a consensus. The most obvious "cause" of the debt crisis was the willingness of private bankers to lend huge amounts of foreign currency to dynamic and successful Third World nations and charge them high levels of interest for it, followed by a reversal of fortune for the debtors. Beyond this obvious explanation, we should look at some antecedents to this dubious bargain.

In 1973, the Third World finally had its day. The members of the Organization of Oil Exporting Countries (OPEC) managed to quadruple the price of crude oil in a six-month span in conjunction with the Arab war against Israel. The immediate effect was the indirect transfer of over $80 billion from Western consumers to Arab governments (Sampson 1981, 151). While much of this was spent on Rolls Royces and in purchasing a few foreign companies, the bulk of this money sat in banks in the Middle East and across the West. Rather than simply let it rest, American and European bankers were forced to deal with this situation, which at the time seemed a crisis. The money could not be easily lent, since it was liquid (short-term deposits) and because the recession of 1974 created a very cautious atmosphere among the banks' usual corporate clients.

The decision to move the "sovereign lending" was not a once-and-for-all choice by the bankers. Citibank paved the way and others quickly followed by lending to countries like Brazil, Mexico, Argentina, and Poland, each of whom had the appearance of being safe risks—they had all undergone dramatic and seemingly successful industrialization programs, each had logged high gross national product growth during the previous period, fueled largely by record-setting commodity prices (petroleum, cereals, tropical goods, metals, meats), and they each had a generally favorable disposition toward the international market and foreign investment. What was most attractive—they each had the power to use coercive government means to repay debts if necessary (Kahler 1985, 358–360).

Third World governments were eager to borrow from private sources because this appeared to eliminate the dangers of "tied aid," whereby government lenders often attach political conditions to aid. Private bankers were far more impartial, although they charged much higher interest. As a consequence, some $100 billion was lent during the first year after the oil shock, and the total amount would rise dramatically over the next decade (See Figure 22.1).

This "recycling" of oil money was the fuel of the debt crisis. In addition, the tendency for borrowers to spend the funds on consumer goods and im-

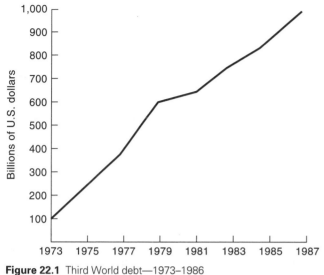

Figure 22.1 Third World debt—1973–1986
Source: John Charles Pool and Steve Stamos, *The ABCs of International Finance*
(Lexington, MA: Lexington Books, 1987)

ports, as well as large-scale infrastructure projects such as road and dam building, meant that few profitable activities were funded by foreign debt (Aliber 1985–1986). As interest charges combined with additional lending, the cost to developing countries would eventually outweigh the new money coming in. By 1983 more money was flowing back into Western banks than was flowing into Third World nations (World Bank 1988, 30).

This situation would not have been problematic had it not also been for the collapse of commodity prices, led by declines in oil prices, after 1976 (Gilpin 1987, 352). Overall, even non-oil commodities lost some 50 percent of their 1973 value during the decade that followed. Because commodity exports are a primary source of hard currency revenue for most developing countries, the decline in these prices was devastating. As early as 1974, Peru was forced to ask its creditors to reschedule (postpone payment of) its foreign debt and agree to a strict adjustment program. In the late 1970s, many African states formed a line outside the International Monetary Fund to intercede on their behalf with Western creditors. By 1979, many developing country debtors were in serious financial straits in spite of promising signs only five years before.

In 1979, two additional events triggered the beginning of the end of the financial system of the 1970s. First, the second oil shock occurred following revolutionary Iran's withdrawal from international oil trade, with the immediate result that crude oil prices rose first to $20 per barrel in 1979 and then to over $40 per barrel in 1980. This event dramatically increased the oil import bill Third World countries were forced to pay to OPEC nations. Because this had to be paid in dollars, this took away from their ability to repay foreign debts. In addition, it put pressure on bankers to lend even more money at a time when they were becoming increasingly reluctant to throw good money after bad.

Second, Paul Volcker was appointed chairman of the Federal Reserve Board (Fed). He felt his job was to eliminate the surplus money supply in the American economy by raising interest rates the Fed charges to large banks, and by increasing the reserve requirement of cash banks must keep on hand (in order to limit the size of the multiplier effect) (Isaak 1991, 206). While this policy eventually achieved its goal of reducing inflation in the United States, it did so at the cost of the worst recession since the 1930s and precipitating the Third World debt crisis. As interest rates rose to 18 percent and more in the early 1980s, Third World countries became increasingly unable to keep up interest payments on variable interest rates loans which were the bulk of the debt.

As if these factors were not enough to send any debtor into a tailspin, the recession in 1982 in the West meant fewer markets for already depressed Third World exports as well as an oil "glut" as Iran's oil came back on a saturated market. Commodity prices dipped further and even oil exporters found themselves unable to keep up debt payments. One could add to these systemic factors a variety of individual problems within certain countries, such as rampant corruption in Zaire, tax evasion in Argentina, overbureaucratization in Peru, investment in nonprofitable infrastructure projects in Turkey, and simple mismanagement and stop-and-go practices in Brazil. Because blame can be passed around liberally, it is often difficult to know which behavior precipitated the crisis of a specific nation.

DEALING WITH THE CRISIS

Mexico's stunning announcement was just the first of many. Within months, Brazil, Argentina, Peru, Poland, Turkey, Jamaica, and dozens of other Third World debtors announced their inability to pay interest payments and requested rescheduling. By now total Third World debt had swollen to roughly $700 billion and the prospect of a debtor cartel (coordinated default) loomed large on the international financial horizon. Because private bankers were unwilling to lend additional funds and the only major international finance organization—the International Monetary Fund (IMF or Fund)—was undercapitalized in relation to a problem of such vast scale, wealthy governments quickly organized themselves to postpone payment of the immediate interest due. As the "Paris Club," the United States, Britain, Germany, France, Japan, and others rescheduled $629 billion of Third World debt in 1982 (IMF 1984, 67). Private banks, at IMF prodding, eventually postponed deadlines on some $70 billion in 1982–1983. For the short term, then, the debt crisis had been resolved.

The role of the Paris Club, the IMF, and private bankers in rescheduling Third World debt was pivotal, in that they coordinated and consulted with each other throughout the process. The IMF is governed by a group of nations which have more votes depending on their wealth and financial support to the institution. As a result, the "major shareholders" (United States, United Kingdom, Germany, Japan, France, Italy, Canada) have the power to block any undesirable policies and press forward their preferred approach. As the organizers of the Paris Club, the "Group of Seven" as they are called, have also influenced the rescheduling of Third World debt by working directly with private bankers. They, in their expanded form of the Group of Ten, have also combined to create the "General Agreements to Borrow"—a pool of several billion dollars from which the IMF can lend directly to major borrowers to prevent disruption of the financial system. Finally, when considering a rescheduling, private bankers work with the IMF to determine, along with the debtor, what adjustment measures need to be taken before they will lend fresh money. Bankers are also conscripted for the good of the world economy to lend money where they otherwise would not. Where the home government of a bank is firmly committed to supporting a particular borrower, it is more likely that the bank will continue lending in spite of itself (Wellons 1985).

From the Third World perspective, IMF-monitored (coerced?) adjustment is anything but cooperative. In general terms, Third World leaders have accused the IMF of interference in what are purely domestic matters. When the IMF recommends cuts in subsidies for basic food and fuel, it takes a highly political action. In some cases, the government may be sympathetic to the move toward "austerity," but it can rarely admit this without jeopardizing its political viability. In Egypt, Jordan, Venezuela, and many other nations, IMF adjustment programs have been immediately followed by food riots and other expressions of public dissatisfaction. Jaafar Nimeiri, leader of Sudan, got into the habit of taking an extended foreign holiday after announcing each new round of budget and service cuts. His government fell during one such trip (Stiles 1991, 60)!

Governments also resent the imposition of power on the part of the international financial community, represented by the Fund. Argentina and Brazil have at various times simply refused to implement the austerity measures agreed to with the Fund on the grounds that they reserved the right to control the future of their economy. Argentina in particular, with its steadier financial situation and considerable reserves (deposits of foreign currency), has had the capacity to thumb its nose at the banking system with far more success. The high point of debtor defiance came in late 1984 with a summit of debtors at Cartagena, Colombia. There the leaders of Mexico, Argentina, and other major debtors discussed the possibility of threatening a coordinated default in order to shift the balance of power in their favor. In order to prevent such a calamity, bankers often sought out one or another major debtor and offered a very favorable rescheduling agreement in order to undermine the unity of the group. This co-optation strategy worked remarkably well, and by 1985 most debtors had resigned themselves to compliance with austerity. With few exceptions, most debtor nations were committed to austerity and liberalization.

In spite of efforts to rectify the situation by bankers and debtors alike, by 1985 it had become apparent that the situation was getting worse, not better. Total Third World debt was fast approaching $1 trillion. By now the ability of Third World countries to repay the debt had almost vanished. The "debt service" ratio of interest due relative to export earnings was over 50 percent for the highest debtors and nearly 40 percent overall. This meant that nearly half of all earnings derived from exports would have to go toward paying the foreign debt rather than rebuilding the country. Total gross national product growth was negative in many developing debtor nations and with commodity prices consistently low there was little prospect for reversal of fortunes.

In this context, U.S. Treasury Secretary James Baker called on the world community to significantly increase new lending to developing nations to the tune of $20 billion, along with greater financial discipline on the part of debtors (Spero 1990, 186). The results of the appeal were minimal, and in 1989 it was officially abandoned in favor of a more pragmatic if sobering alternative: debt forgiveness.

Debt forgiveness is the capitulation of the banking system. It means that all hope of collecting a debt is abandoned and it is taken off the books. In 1987 the "book value" of most Third World debt had declined from 70 percent of face value to below half. This meant that if a bank wanted to unload a bad debt on another lending institution, it could only recoup half of the original loan. As this reality became apparent to shareholders and depositors, bankers moved in 1987 and 1988 to increase their reserves against a possible default or forgiveness of a debt. Bank of Boston led the way, but was quickly followed by the other major institutions. While the profits for quarters in which these admissions were made were lower, this pragmatic approach seems to have strengthened the confidence of members of the community overall. This phase has been described as "debt fatigue" by Joan Spero (Spero 1990, 190).

The United States announced the Brady Plan in early 1989 with a three-pronged approach: debt forgiveness, concessional government lending (aid), and firm commitment to repayment. Each approach would target a different third of the total debt problem. The IMF under new leadership promptly responded with a significant increase in concessional lending to Sub-Saharan African countries. Much Third World debt was simply written off beginning in 1988, and in 1991 Britain called for general debt forgiveness (*New York Times,* July 18, 1991, D3). Banks became interested in so-called "debt-equity swaps" whereby a loan would be traded for a tangible asset worth a fraction of the loan's book value. Although there is a natural limit to the amount of assets which can thus be transferred, there is some hope that by finalizing the status of these debts, both participants can get a better handle on what remains. "Debt-for-nature" swaps also came into vogue for a period of time. This involved purchase of a loan by environmental groups and private firms in exchange for a guarantee to create nature preserves in the debtor nation. A recent example involved the World Wildlife Fund and the largest bank in Japan working with the government of Ecuador (*Wall Street Journal*, March 27, 1992, 9A).

Mexico has been by far the most successful debtor when it comes to co-operating with industrialized countries. Never defiant, Mexico has continually strengthened its ties with the United States, culminating in the inclusion of Mexico in a free trade zone for North America in August 1992. In 1989, Mexico was able to obtain forgiveness for enough of its foreign debt to lower its annual interest payments by $1.5 billion and secure an additional $2.5 billion in fresh loans (Spero 1990, 194). For the first time, Mexico and the Third World's overall debt began to decline after 1988, although the total remains close to $1.3 trillion (*New York Times*, December 16 1991, D2).

In general terms, the Third World debt crisis can be declared over, if only because other crises have supplanted it. The Gulf War, the multibillion dollar savings and loan bailout, the 1990–1992 recession, the collapse of the Soviet Union and the related financial needs in its new republics, and the prospect of European unification have all eclipsed the Third World debt problem as the most important issues on the American and global agenda today. Even *Fortune* magazine has as much as declared the crisis over and analyst Benjamin J. Cohen was prompted to ask what had become of it (Cohen 1991). This is therefore perhaps a good time to take stock of the situation and reflect on what it can teach us about global structures.

GLOBAL STRUCTURES AND THIRD WORLD DEBT

In our discussion of global structures, we mentioned radical interpretations of international affairs as an aspect of hierarchical international social and economic relations. A common criticism of the handling of the Third World debt situation comes from the left and focuses on collusion between the major players in international finance. As pointed out earlier, the IMF, the Group of Seven industrialized nations, and major private banking institutions cooperated with each other in setting policy and establishing precedents. But to what extent was this cooperation or reluctant crisis management? The question is important in the context of the discussion on global structures.

Bankers were no doubt the most reluctant participants in this process, being unwilling in the early stages of the crisis to reschedule any debts at all. They viewed the lending of additional money to borrowers who had already demonstrated their uncreditworthiness as the height of bad business. As put by one senior British official: "It makes the Marshall Plan look like peanuts . . . but because it's concealed as businesslike banking, it's much more acceptable. . . " (Sampson 1981, 398). Sampson pointed out that bankers were trapped in their role of lending good money after bad. What is more, the IMF routinely pressured banks to lend additional funds as part of its negotiations with debtor nations in order to extract a promise of adjustment.

On the other hand, bankers have proved tough bargainers. For example, when Argentina became defiant during 1984, bankers closed ranks and refused to extend additional credits. In spite of appeals to intercede on behalf of the government, the IMF and other international governmental organizations supported the bankers' firm position. The result was a new plan of austerity and privatization by the Argentine government (Stiles 1991, 190). Particularly where the debtor is relatively small, as in the case of Jamaica, large creditor institutions have the capacity to demand repayment of arrears without any great fear of the consequences of default. Peru, Brazil, and Argentina each experimented with refusing to pay debt as it fell due (moratorium), however as individual countries they were vulnerable to retaliatory action by the international community. In the case of Peru, the International Monetary Fund and G-7 countries refused to extend it any additional credits until it began repaying its past debts. This was tantamount to exclusion from the entire international banking system since the private banks generally followed the IMF's lead. Brazil was able to carry on its strategy for a time but came up against stiffened resistance from banks which in 1987 were better positioned to suffer earnings losses (Spero 1990, 191). The overall result is that for many developing nations, the general direction of the flow of money was negative, in that more funds were going to pay off loans than was coming into the nation through export earnings, new loans and other aid (Lever and Huhne 1985).

Although governments and bankers are motivated by very different concerns, bankers typically follow the flag when it comes to foreign lending, seeking some semblance of protection from the government in spite of the possibility that this could lead to some unwise business decisions (Wellons 1985). The few exceptions, such as private lending to Nicaragua and Vietnam at times when these governments had poor relations with the United States, stand out in stark contrast to the general trend. But in general terms, the radicals' argument that there is some form of cooperation between governments and bankers seems to hold up.

It is also clear from our historical study that governments tended to work together. The mere existence of the Group of Seven symbolizes the shared interests of these governments and their desire to work together. Particularly when the United States, the United Kingdom, and Germany were each governed by conservative, procapitalist leaders (Ronald Reagan, Margaret Thatcher, and Helmut Kohl, respectively) it was easy to reach agreement on a rather unforgiving approach. However, it should be pointed out that developed countries are not above treating each other with a certain callousness. When Great Britain's pound began to lose its value in the 1970s, rather than intervene to support it, the United States and Germany allowed it to drop and used the crisis to force Britain to undertake adjustment measures of its own. The recent trade and financial friction between Japan, Germany, and the United States illustrates the fact that one cannot assume cooperation on even matters of global welfare when unemployment and trade deficits are on the rise.

The other side of the coin is that Third World governments are assumed by radicals to be exploited by the rich players in the debt game. Although it may seem that Third World countries are hopelessly outclassed vis à vis international financiers, several points call this conclusion into question. There is much potential power in the hands of the debtors as a group and individually. As pointed out already, bankers feared the coming together of major debtors in a cartel. Short of this, the threat of coordinated action was a serious concern to the international community, since there was no direct leverage available to deal with large-scale action. This allowed particularly Latin debtors to obtain significant concessions in the mid-1980s when their cartel efforts were at their strongest and most public.

Because it is ultimately up to the government to implement the adjustment process and provide data to demonstrate its success or failure, it is often possible for individual debtors to maintain the appearance of austerity without enacting the substance of it. Perhaps the most egregious case of this duplicity was in Zaire in the early 1980s when the government had become so corrupt and adjustment such a farce that the IMF actually sent a team to take control of major economic ministries in the country. Even at that, the IMF could not overcome local resistance and eventually gave up. Throughout the process, Zaire continued to receive sporadic funding from the IMF and was able to keep the flow of private lending (Stiles 1991, 64–86). Overall, Saunders and Subrahmanyam conclude that on balance the gains from rescheduling debt under conditions of austerity have been shared by both creditors and debtors and that no clear victory for either side can be claimed (Saunders and Subrahmanyam 1991). Figure 22.2 illustrates the net movement of resources between creditors and debtors, which reaffirms this conclusion by illustrating the balance between flows.

The IMF, as an international organization, is obligated to respect the sovereignty and diplomatic rights of its members. As a result, any appearance of intrusion is quickly seized upon by opponents of the Fund as an excess of authority. In a strongly worded pamphlet issued in 1983, the IMF declared that it is not in the business of "imposing" austerity, but that all its programs are approved by the debtor nation after extensive negotiations.

Perhaps the most puzzling outcome of the debt crisis was a "nonevent": there never emerged a coherent "debtor cartel." Guillermo O'Donnell, a prominent Latin American sociologist showed that, unlike OPEC and other more successful cartels, the group of debtors in Latin America lacked a leader willing to carry the burdens of joint default. Argentina was certainly willing to confront the West, but was not able to survive in the long run without access to foreign capital. It certainly was not in the position to bankroll the debt of the other Latin American states. Saudi Arabia had the capacity to lead a debtor cartel, but it had no desire to sink its vast wealth into a losing cause. Mexico had neither the capacity nor the will, and as a result did not actively participate in forming a debtor cartel.

In addition to the unwillingness or inability of the major debtors to organize a cartel and undertake a coordinated default (or threat thereof), the private bankers went out of their way to prevent the groups from coalescing. In 1984–1985, at various points when the group seemed about to congeal, private banking consortia offered a very attractive rescheduling

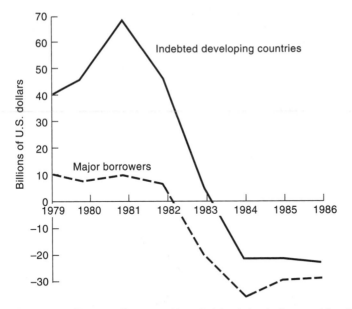

Figure 22.2 Resource flow to and from indebted developing countries, 1979–1986.
Source: John Charles Pool and Steve Stamos, *The ABCs of International Finance* (Lexington, MA: Lexington Books, 1987), 95.

arrangement to either Brazil, Argentina, or Mexico, with the result that the nation withdrew from the cartel negotiations (O'Donnell 1985).

Overall, then, the result of the debt crisis has been a greater acceptance on the part of developing nations of their need for Western capital and therefore a greater willingness to comply with Western demands, including adjustment. Is a radical interpretation a valid one, then? Perhaps. It will be important for you to also consider the degree to which debtor nations have become measurably poorer as a result of the debt crisis, and whether wealthy nations have profited proportionally. This may tell us something about whether the North has exploited the South as global structuralists would assume. Of course, other approaches may help answer this question, namely: focusing on the degree of dependence of the debtor nations on the North; focusing on inequality within the South; focusing on potential vs. actual growth following the debt crisis; etc.

The IMF has always been on the defensive with regard to its attitude toward the poor. It has generally excluded calculations of the impact of conditionality on poverty on the grounds that this issue was beyond the scope of its mandate and mission. This position has been difficult to hold, given the obvious and immediate impact of IMF conditionality on the living conditions of the poorest segments of society. Removing price subsidies on bread, for example, thereby allowing the retail price to increase as much as tenfold in certain countries, is a policy with clearly damaging consequences for the poor—yet this sort of policy is often urged by the Fund's officials. It was not

Table 22.1 ECONOMIC GROWTH OF 17 LARGEST DEBTORS

	1973–80	1980–85	'86	'87	'88	'89	'90
(annual average in %)							
GDP (Gross domestic product) Growth	5.2	0.2	3.5	1.7	1.5	1.3	−1.6
GDP/cap (Gross domestic product per capita) Growth	2.6	− 2.6	1.7	0.5	− 1.0	− 1.3	− 3.4
Growth in Exports	1.2	2.4	− 3.7	8.2	12.1	− .06	—
Growth of Debt	21.8	13.6	11.4	8.8	− 4.6	− 2.4	3.5

Source: World Bank Annual Report 1991.

Table 22.2 INCOME DISTRIBUTION—PROPORTION OF WEALTH CONTROLLED BY RICHEST 20% OF POPULATION

	1968–1975	1976–1983	1984–1988
Brazil	66.6 (72)	62.6 (83)	
Yugoslavia		38.7 (78)	42.8 (87)
Costa Rica	54.8 (71)		54.4 (86)
Peru	61.0 (72)		51.9 (86)
Philippines	54.0 (71)		52.5 (85)
Venezuela	54.0 (70)		50.6 (87)

Sources: Various World Bank annual reports.

until 1989 that the IMF began explicitly taking into account poverty in its conditionality arrangements and setting aside funds for the poorest debtors.

In fact, the jury is still out concerning the actual impact of IMF conditionality on standards of living. In an exhaustive study, Bradshaw and Wahl conclude that foreign debt and IMF conditionality seem to have had, in many cases, a positive effect on living conditions in Africa and an ambiguous impact on Latin America (Bradshaw and Wahl 1991, 207). In other words, many nations have grown wealthier in spite of high levels of external debt.

These findings may seem difficult to accept in the light of other, more general data on economic trends among the highest debtors. The World Bank has been tracking the progress of the seventeen most deeply indebted nations in the world (mostly Latin American) and has concluded that the debt crisis is far from over and that conditions are generally strained at best. As can be seen from Tables 22.1 and 22.2, overall growth rates among the deepest debtors have been sluggish at best and recently went negative. When figured on a per capita basis, given high population growth in many of these countries, the negative trend is accentuated. The only bright signals are in trade and overall indebtedness, where until 1990 trends were quite favorable.

Another way of measuring the progress of the poor in debtor nations, albeit impressionistically, is with income distribution figures. Countries are generally reluctant to publish these figures since they clearly show how few people control the bulk of the wealth—a politically sensitive question to say the least. In the case of many debtors, where cultural and historical patterns have resulted in high concentrations of wealth in the hands of a few, these numbers almost never appear. In spite of this, the World Bank has published a few indicators for a few debtors, which are reported below. As can be seen, except in the case of Yugoslavia, where market reforms have given rise to a burgeoning capitalist class, the general pattern of income distribution is toward slightly more equity and balance, in spite of chronic debt. You should note that this is merely a rough indication of a trend, not an exact measurement.

Overall, there seems to be no clear pattern with regard to the impact of debt on poverty in the Third World. Perhaps this should lead to caution with regard to the global structuralist analysis.

It is equally difficult to determine to what extent Western powers profited at the debtors' expense. We have already seen that banks suffered to a degree and were ultimately forced to sell or forgive much of the loans. In general terms, the 1980s was a prosperous period for developed nations, but has lately proven to have been yet another cyclical boom. Average annual gross national product growth for developed countries during the 1980s was a robust 3 percent, while inflation was a modest 4.3 percent. The 1990s have been difficult for most developed nations—the U.S. growth rate has been anemic at roughly 1 percent per year, and even Japan and postreunification Germany have seen the bloom come off the rose. Germany is struggling under a trillion dollar reconstruction burden, and Japan's stock market has recently collapsed. The American Savings and Loan crisis, involving some $200 billion in bank bailouts, has severely restricted lending in spite of historically low interest rates. The arrival of a huge Russian economic problem has also arrested the attention of the Western nations at a time when they are ill-prepared to provide for their own recovery.

Because so many other factors enter into the equation, it is difficult to isolate winners and losers. In general terms, it seems difficult to conclude that the wealthy countries exploited the poor and profited from their troubles. In fact, there is evidence that in the 1990s the fate of the nations of the world is more inextricably linked than ever.

Questions to Consider

1. Who were the winners and losers of the debt crisis? To what extent did those who were directly involved in making and receiving loans suffer?

2. To what extent were the debtor nations victims of international forces beyond their control? Why were the burdens so unevenly spread across countries?

3. To what extent did the debt crisis demonstrate where the world's power lies? Were there any surprises?

References

Roger Aliber. "The Debt Cycle in Latin America." *Journal of Interamerican Studies and World Affairs* 27 #4 (Winter 1985–1986).

York Bradshaw and Ana-Maria Wahl. "Foreign Debt Expansion, the International Monetary Fund, and Regional Variation in Third World Poverty." *International Studies Quarterly* 35 #3 (September 1991): 251–272.

Benjamin J. Cohen. "What Ever Happened to the LDC Debt Crisis?" *Challenge* 3 #3 (May 1991): 47–51.

Stanley Fischer and Ishrat Husain. "Managing the Debt Crisis in the 1990s." *Finance and Development* (June 1990): 24–27.

Robert Gilpin. *The Political Economy of International Relations* (Princeton: Princeton University Press, 1987).

International Monetary Fund. *Annual Report, 1984* (Washington: IMF, 1984).

Robert Isaak. *International Political Economy: Managing World Economic Change* (Englewood Cliffs: Prentice Hall, 1991).

Miles Kahler. "Politics and International Debt: Explaining the Crisis." *International Organization* 39 #3 (Summer 1985): 357–382.

Harold Lever and Christopher Huhne. *Debt and Danger: The World Financial Crisis* (New York: Atlantic Monthly Press, 1985).

New York Times, July 18, 1991, D3

New York Times, December 16, 1991, D2

Guillermo O'Donnell. "External Debt: Why Don't Our Governments Do the Obvious?" *CEPAL Review* 27 (December 1985): 27–33.

Anthony Sampson. *The Money Lenders: The People and Politics of the World Banking Crisis* (New York: Penguin, 1981).

Anthony Saunders and Marti Subrahmanyam. "LDC Debt Rescheduling: Who Wins, Who Loses," in Robert Kolb, *The International Finance Reader* (Miami: Kolb Publishing, 1991), 107–116.

Herman Schwartz "Can Orthodox Stabilization and Adjustment Work? Lessons from New Zealand, 1984–90." *International Organization* 45 #2 (Spring 1991): 221–256.

Joan Spero. *The Politics of International Economic Relations,* 4th ed. (New York: St. Martin's Press, 1990).

Kendall Stiles. *Negotiating Debt: The IMF Lending Process* (Boulder: Westview, 1991).

Susan Strange. *Casino Capitalism* (Oxford: Basil Blackwell, 1986).

Wall Street Journal, March 27, 1992, 9A

Philip Wellons. "International Debt: The Behavior of the Banks in a Politicized Environment." *International Organization* 39 #3 (Summer 1985): 441–472.

World Bank. *World Development Report, 1988* (New York: Oxford University Press, 1988).

Europe Uniting

While a global order based on respect for law and tolerance of differences seems beyond our grasp for now, many hope that such a sphere of peace can be established at the regional level. A region is whatever its members choose, but typically it involves contiguous territory, common culture, and interdependent economies and societies. While regional organizations have tended to fall flat (the Organization of African Unity is a case in point), there are indications that in Europe and perhaps elsewhere regionalism is healthy and offers a real opportunity for improving people's living conditions. Economic integration is one form of regionalism and involves reducing obstacles to trade, investment, and migration. Political integration culminates in some federal or unitary state. While the United States represents political integration well, the European Community illustrates what is meant by economic integration.

January 1, 1993, came and went in Europe with little fanfare, even though many hoped it would be the dawn of a new age. The 1986 Single European Act (SEA) was approved by the European Community and established December 31, 1992, as the deadline for complete European integration. In reality, important reforms have yet to take hold, due to hard political bargaining and hesitancy on the part of key nations to drop protective barriers. Will Europe look back on 1992 as a missed opportunity? Or will future Europeans honor the vision fathers in what could ultimately become the United States of Europe? In order to predict this, one must first gain a historical perspective on European integration as well as a deeper appreciation for the centripetal and centrifugal political forces at work on the continent.

Plans for European unity were borne of a disgust with war and carnage—not World War II but the Thirty Years' War. After the end of the devastating war in 1648, French royal adviser de Sully developed a "Grand Design" for European unity based on religious tolerance. Although stillborn, de Sully's proposal was the first of a string of concepts for European unity. Following the nearly successful attempt of Louis XIV to secure French domination over Europe in the early 1700s, William Penn and the Quakers in Britain, along with the Abbé de Saint-Pierre in France, developed complex and elaborate schemes for a form of collective security for Europe (Heater 1992, 54, 58). During the nineteenth century, while idealists continued to work on a global organization, which culminated in the League of Nations, the great powers experimented for a time with the Concert of Europe—an informal arrangement among the dominant European powers to keep minor conflicts in check through collaborative intervention.

Throughout the period of planning and scheming for Europe, there was a tension between the desire to preserve sovereignty and the goal of creating genuine supranational institutions which could coordinate state action. To a large extent, this tension has yet to be resolved.

THE EMERGENCE OF THE COMMON MARKET: 1945–1957

The Common Market had its origins in both external and internal forces. As we have seen elsewhere in this text, the post–World War II environment was one of utter devastation which required urgent and dramatic steps. In addition, the growing and clear threat of Soviet/Communist encroachment on West European democracy prompted an acceleration of reconstruction and stabilization efforts. Administrative efficiency and capital utilization required a regional rather than a national approach. Hence later American enthusiasm for the Marshall Plan and the regional cooperation this entailed.

Within Europe, the disastrous experience with fascism and German expansionism led many to adopt a "never again" attitude and plans were developed to both solidify democratic regimes, punish fascists, and intertwine German war-making capacity into a broader European network. Germans also sought a means of legitimizing their new democratic state and put Nazism behind them. This, combined with the strength of Christian-Democratic parties across Europe, along with their pro-Europe policies, paved the way for Jean Monnet and Paul-Henri Spaak to have great influence.

In 1948, European leaders organized a conference at the Hague, in the Netherlands, where the "European Movement" was founded to act as a sort of continental lobbying group to press for more integration and unity. Winston Churchill did much to promote European unity in a series of speeches in the late 1940s and by serving as president of the Hague Conference. Here again, one finds a conflict emerging between the "federalists"—mainly the French and Germans—who envisioned a powerful European federal government and the "unionists" who sought merely ad hoc agreements to deal with particular problems piecemeal (Gerbet 1987, 39).

A series of events in 1948–1950 brought the conflict between federalist and unionist conceptions of Europe to a head. The economic and social crisis in Europe was extreme following the disastrous harvest of 1948. Soviet expansion in Eastern Europe seemed relentless and foreboding, and the rise of

Communist parties in France, Italy, and other Western European states seemed to mirror the threat to the East. All of this gave the United States reason to intervene in dramatic fashion to rescue Europe from what appeared an inevitable World War III, fought this time over German industry. Jean Monnet, writing of his feelings at the time, said:

> [I recall] the anxiety that weighed on Europe five years after the war: the fear that if we did nothing we should soon face war again. Germany would not be its instigator this time, but its prize. So Germany must cease to be a potential prize, and instead become a link. At that moment, only France could take the initiative. What could be done to link France and Germany . . . ?" (Monnet 1978, 289)

The Marshall Plan (formally known as the European Recovery Program) was an essential stopgap to provide necessary capital and materials for European reconstruction, the Bretton Woods institutions (World Bank, International Monetary Fund) having proven inadequate to the task. In conjunction with the Marshall Plan, the Organization for European Economic Cooperation (OEEC) was quickly founded in 1948 to give Europeans a role in distributing the resources flowing from the United States. The OEEC did not have authority to force nations to coordinate their plans, but "thanks to the part played by the Secretariat, the member states became used to cooperating and comparing their economic policies"(Gerbet 1987, 36).

The OEEC was not the first regional organization devoted to economic coordination in Europe. In fact, the Benelux countries (Belgium, Netherlands, Luxembourg) had already gone far to create a common market and customs union among themselves. Beginning in 1922, Belgium and Luxembourg pledged to eliminate tariff barriers between each other (thus creating a common market) and coordinate their trade policies toward the rest of the world (customs union). They also promoted the free movement of labor and capital, thus increasing labor migration and foreign investment. When the Netherlands joined in 1947 the group became a genuinely multilateral arrangement, complete with regional institutional structures and governing authority. This Benelux arrangement would serve as a model for what was later to become the European Economic Community (Hurwitz 1987, 11).

It should be noted in passing that the economic cooperation being forged in the 1940s coincided with efforts at military and political cooperation, although we will see that their progress soon diverged. Northern Europe organized a peacetime military alliance shortly after the war, culminating in the Brussels Treaty Organization in 1948, to which the United States was almost immediately invited. The North Atlantic Treaty Organization (NATO), founded in 1949, pledged mutual assistance in the event of an attack against any member, and grew to include Germany, Italy, and European countries both to the north and to the south. NATO also provided significant American military support for Europe, including the placement of hundreds of thousands of U.S. troops and substantial stockpiles of nuclear weapons. Efforts to forge a truly European military pact failed in the 1950s, which may have led to greater attention to the economic sphere.

Economics and politics were never separate as far as European integration was concerned. An important illustration of this is the emergence of the European Coal and Steel Community (ECSC). By 1950, it had become clear that German industry was on the road to rapid recovery. In fact, Germany was consuming so much coal and coke from the Ruhr Valley near the Rhine that France and other Europeans were experiencing shortages. Jean Monnet, leader of France's industrial plan, saw this crisis as an opportunity to introduce plans for integration he had developed as early as 1941. As he saw it, integrating German coal and French iron ore production would solve not only France's immediate shortage problem, but a much wider problem as well:

> All successive attempts to keep Germany in check, mainly at French instigation, had come to nothing, because they had been based on the rights of conquest and temporary superiority—notions from the past which happily were no longer taken for granted. But if the problem of sovereignty were approached with no desire to dominate or take revenge—if on the contrary the victors and the vanquished agreed to exercise joint sovereignty over part of their joint resources—then, a solid link would be forged between them, the way would be wide open for further collective action, and a great example would be given to the other nations of Europe. (Monnet 1979, 293).

Thus the ECSC was as much a way to keep Germany's military capacity in check as to support French economic goals. As put by Robert Schuman, the French premier who formally proposed Monnet's concept: "The community of production, which will in this manner be created, will clearly show that any war between France and Germany becomes not only unthinkable but in actual fact impossible "(Hurwitz 1987, 20).

The ECSC was created in 1951 with the signing of the Treaty of Paris on April 18 by France, Germany, Italy, and the Benelux countries. It provided for a "High Authority," an international panel with powers to organize production levels, map out distribution, and promote equity across the member states. Article 9 of the treaty specified that "in the performance of these duties, [the High Authority] shall neither seek nor take instructions from any Government or any body.... Each member state undertakes to respect this supranational character ... " (Heater 1992, 162). One can see clearly that the federalists carried the day insofar as the ECSC is concerned. It is also interesting to note that the treaty provided for a parliament, made up of delegations from member countries based on population, a council with advisory powers where each state had one vote, and a court to review actions of states relative to the High Authority's decisions.

The ECSC quickly demonstrated its effectiveness and gave impetus for the creation of yet more regional institutions. Jean Monnet was instrumental in establishing EURATOM—a European organization to facilitate cooperative development of nuclear technology.

Efforts by France and Britain to exert influence overseas in the mid-1950s failed. This led both countries to seek refuge in a regional home where their influence could be strong. Britain thereupon emphasizsed its Atlantic ties to the United States while the French looked to Europe.

The Soviet intervention in Hungary further convinced Europeans that now was the time to create what unity they could, a decision given form at a conference in Messina, Italy, in 1955 (Kusters 1987, 81). While the French government fell solidly behind the integration plans (partly out of fear the other Europeans would proceed without it), the British distanced themselves from what they considered a continental question.

Paul-Henri Spaak was the principal author of the 1957 Treaty of Rome, the formal agreement constituting the Common Market (officially called the European Economic Community or EEC). He served as the first head of the Organization for European Economic Cooperation in 1948 and head of the Council of Europe in 1949—known as "Mr. Europe" (Heater 1992, 165). He supported the ECSC but was eager for deeper integration and became chair of the team charged at the 1955 Messina Conference with drafting a treaty for a customs union and common market. The European Economic Community was constituted with the objective of promoting:

> throughout the Community a harmonious development of economic activities, a continuous and balanced expansion, an increased stability, an accelerated raising of the standard of living and closer relations between its member states. (Article 2)

Countries joined the EEC for a variety of reasons. Germany saw this as a vehicle for international acceptance—a way to regain its sovereignty (an ironic goal, since other Europeans saw it as a way to lose theirs! See Urwin and Paterson 1990, 188). France hoped to use the EEC as a way to dominate European politics diplomatically, as well as placate the strong political pressure of their farmers. Italy hoped the EEC could provide economic as well as diplomatic rehabilitation as well as development funding for its southern half, while the Benelux countries were eager to lower continental trade barriers which they felt discriminated against their own more efficient industries. As time went on, these different motivations created interesting and often complex political alliances and antagonisms (see Map 23.1).

THE EEC STRUCTURE

The institutions of the EEC are presented in Figure 23.1. The distribution of power between the various organs was largely a compromise arrangement, and modified the strongly federal conception of the ECSC. The European Commission was given power to propose, implement, and enforce regional policies with an eye to ever-expanding integration. It is made up of seventeen commissioners, of which one serves as president and seven as vice presidents. They individually and collectively manage a number of "directorates" which are staffed by upwards of 50,000 "Eurocrats" (see Figure 23.1).

The Council of Ministers is a small body consisting of international economic policy chiefs of each member state. It has power to approve commission recommendations and develop policies unilaterally. The question of how much influence the Council would have relative to the Commission has

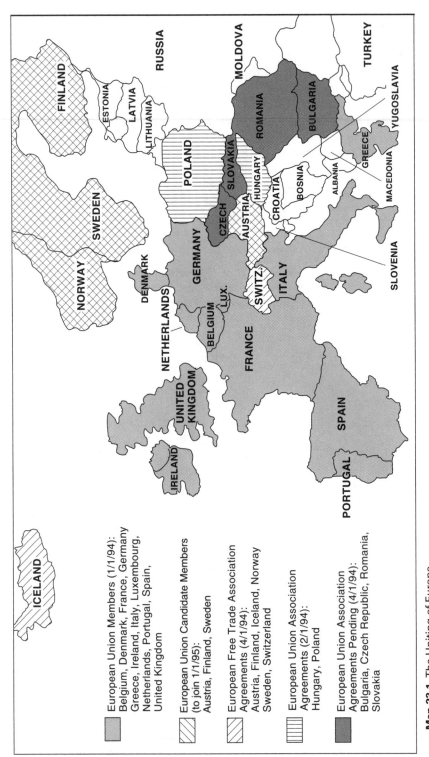

Map 23.1 The Uniting of Europe.

Sources: Adapted from *Christian Science Monitor*, December 30, 1992, and the Washington offices of the European Commission.

European Union Members (1/1/94):
Belgium, Denmark, France, Germany
Greece, Ireland, Italy, Luxembourg,
Netherlands, Portugal, Spain,
United Kingdom

European Union Candidate Members
(to join 1/1/95):
Austria, Finland, Sweden

European Free Trade Association
Agreements (4/1/94):
Austria, Finland, Iceland, Norway
Sweden, Switzerland

European Union Association
Agreements (2/1/94):
Hungary, Poland

European Union Association
Agreements Pending (4/1/94):
Bulgaria, Czech Republic, Romania,
Slovakia

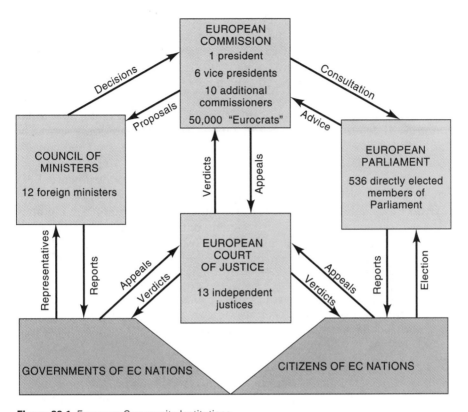

Figure 23.1 European Community Institutions.
Source: Adapted from Clive Archer and Fiona Butler, *The European Community Structure and Process* (New York: St. Martin's, 1992.

been at the cutting edge of EEC politics since its inception. Federalists hoped that the supranational authority of the commission would grow, while unionists favored expanding the political power of the council. The commission was given broad authority to recommend policies to the council, without regard for nationalism—subnational entities such as business and labor groups from individual countries often participated in the commission's decision-making process (Taylor 1983, 94). In reality, there was a steady erosion of commission power through the 1970s as the EEC was gradually reformed.

After the election of Charles de Gaulle as president of France in 1958, France adopted a more "unionist" approach to EEC institutions. While most European states were interested in expanding the authority of the commission, de Gaulle sought to enhance the powers of the council, with France in the dominant role (Wistrich 1990, 31). And on the council, France blocked efforts to institute majority voting, as called for in the Treaty of Rome, on the grounds that it would dilute French influence. De Gaulle blocked the British application for membership in 1963 because he feared a further weakening of French power as well as introducing an essentially non-European actor into the Community (Britain's trade and diplomacy were primarily oriented toward the commonwealth and the United States). France's intransigence culminated in her boycott of council meetings in late 1965 and a summit meeting to address the majority-vote issue. The Luxembourg Compromise was approved by the other five EEC members and provided for each nation to have the power to veto Community policy if it felt the proposal threatened national interest in a significant way. Since it was left to the individual countries to determine whether a threat existed, this compromise seriously undercut the notion of majority rule and led to paralysis on the council (Wistrich 1990, 33).

Other reforms tended to follow the unionist philosophy toward EEC power in the 1960s. First, a Committee of Permanent Representatives (COREPER), made up of ambassadorial-rank delegates from each member state, was created to provide more ongoing participation on the part of governments in commission activities. This substantially weakened the commission's ability to shape the council's agenda and programs. As put by Archer and Butler:

> When a draft proposed arrives from the Commission, it is not discussed directly by the particular national ministers. Instead, the Council's Committee of Permanent Representatives acts as a 'sieve'. . . . its content, general significance and national negotiating positions are sifted. (Archer and Butler 1992, 29)

After 1974, even the Council's power was undermined by the establishment of thrice-annual EEC summit meetings of heads of state or government (known as the European Council). These meetings were used for resolving the most contentious regional issues—particularly budgetary problems.

The European Parliament and the European Court of Justice were secondary institutions during the first thirty years of the EEC. The Parliament, consisting originally of delegates from each member appointed by their respective national parliaments, had very little power beyond providing suggestions to the commission. Only its votes on the budget carried any weight. The Court of Justice was charged primarily with handling disputes over implementation of EEC rules, although the most serious problems were handled by the council and summit meetings. The Court of First Appeals was later added to deal exclusively with intra-EC issues. It was not until 1979, when the European Parliament was elected directly by European citizens, and the court became involved in issuing authoritative and binding interpretations of EEC law, that the influence of these two institutions began to grow.

THE EEC AT WORK: 1957–1973

The first task of the EEC was the promotion of free trade within the Community. This goal was to be achieved through the creation of a common market in which barriers to trade are dropped, a customs union through which each country's trade toward other nations is uniform, free movement of labor and capital, and harmonization of social policy. The creation of a common market took less time than expected (Williams 1991, 51). As early as 1968, all internal tariffs on industrial products were eliminated—almost two years ahead of schedule (Wistrich 1990, 33).

The ease with which the common market was created was largely due to nondiplomatic factors. The period of the 1960s was one of extraordinary growth in Europe. Average annual growth rates for the EEC Six ranged from 4.4 percent for West Germany to 5.7 percent for France. In such circumstances, it was relatively easy for the six to lower barriers without fear of unemployment resulting from more intense competition. If a firm was uncompetitive in one sector, another opportunity soon presented itself. Not only did the economies of the six grow during this period, but trade was diverted from non-EEC to intra-EEC partners. In 1958, EEC countries imported only 29 percent of all goods from the other six, but by 1972 that figure had risen to 52 percent (Williams 1991, 33).

Another important factor that explained the ease of creating the common market was the close similarity between the economies of the original EEC members. Although Italy and France enjoyed a strong industrial base, they were still substantially agrarian societies. Germany and the Benelux countries were among the most sophisticated economies in the world. Germany, by the mid-1970s, was the world's largest industrial exporter. We will see later that with the accession of Ireland, Greece, Spain, and Portugal, regional differences became a serious problem to the EEC.

By the early 1970s, the OPEC crisis, "stagflation" (the combination of inflation and recession), currency instability, and a decline of American leadership in global trade liberalization led Europeans to become less eager to remove protective trade barriers. Once the "easy" stage of negative integration had passed, the barriers remaining before EEC members were far more controversial. Nontariff barriers, including health regulations, product specifications, and distribution networks, were not included in the initial round of trade liberalization reforms. Germany, for example, had relatively strict specifications regarding alcoholic beverage categories, which French liqueur did not meet. Unable to prevent Germans from prohibiting the product because of their de facto veto in the Council of Ministers, it took a 1978 ruling by the Court of Justice to convince Germany to dismantle the restrictions.

The other principal activity of the EEC during the 1960s was the establishment of the Common Agricultural Program (CAP). Considered a crucial element of the Treaty of Rome (Article 38) by France, the CAP provided for a common market and customs union in all foodstuffs, price guarantees, and structural reforms. In addition, the CAP aimed at ensuring "a fair standard of living for the agricultural community." Although such an approach seems excessive by today's standards, Marsh points out that in the 1950s, Europe was a net food importer and had recently imposed food rationing. Farmers were able to argue that the only way to ensure that Europe would have sufficient food would be through producing it at home. Success in agriculture was considered essential for national security (Marsh 1989, 148).

The key element in this equation was the price guarantees, which served to placate the highly politicized and powerful farm lobbies in France, Italy, and Germany. Although several options existed, the EEC Six determined in 1962 to proceed with a price support mechanism involving the purchasing Community surplus production to be stored until it could be sold without lowering the price. In order to appease German farmers, the price levels agreed upon were the high, heavily subsidized German prices. This decision resulted in the CAP becoming far and away the most significant Community expense. The Council of Minsters had hoped at the time that these high price supports would be temporary, as the common market would force inefficient producers out of business, but this was not to be the case. Instead, the price supports became a permanent element in the EEC (Taylor 1983, 237).

By 1970 nearly all agricultural products (with the exception of tropical products found in the Mediterranean EEC members) were covered by the CAP with high guaranteed floor prices. The EEC budget grew exponentially during the 1960s largely because of the cost of the CAP, which at times absorbed three-fourths of the EEC budget (Williams 1991, 43). The growth continued unchecked until the late 1980s, and by 1986 the EEC had in storage some 1.4 million metric tons of surplus butter. As pointed out by Lodge, the CAP is neither capitalist nor effective, but it has become such a vital ingredient in the political and even physical landscape of Europe that any attempt at reform risks consequences that could easily outweigh the benefits (Lodge 1990, 212). It is interesting to note that in the midst of the revisions to the Treaty of Rome in the late 1980s, there has been significant downsizing of the CAP and experimentation with alternative policies to maintain prices.

With de Gaulle out of office in 1969, the Community proceeded with the accession of Britain, Denmark, Ireland, and Norway (where the proposal was rejected in a referendum). Given Britain's heavy reliance on imports of food from New Zealand and Australia, and the relatively small size of its agricultural sector, it was inevitable that it would be disadvantaged by the EEC's emphasis on the CAP. The differences were largely left unresolved and the accession was completed in 1973. This "first enlargement" came amid optimism for the future of the EEC. A 1972 summit meeting which included the three "members in waiting" committed the Community to deeper integration including "completion of the internal market, common tariffs, a common currency, and a central bank" (Williams 1991, 50). Few anticipated the trying years which were soon to come.

THE EEC UNDER STRESS: 1973–1985

The quadrupling of the price of oil in 1973 had devastating effects on European economies, where a decade of stagflation set in and Britain's economic life was in constant jeopardy. The linchpin of stable currencies was already gone and the OPEC demand on the part of oil importers to relinquish their support to Israel went far to undermine the political unity that contributed to economic cooperation. France and Germany abandoned Israel while the Netherlands endured the oil embargo. The British pound collapsed in the mid-1970s and labor unrest in France and Italy derailed their economic growth. Germany struggled with terrorism and Ireland and Italy pleaded for additional development financing from the Community. None of the Europeans knew quite how to respond to the growing trade threat from Japan and the Far East. As put by British Prime Minister Edward Heath:

> After the oil crisis of 1973–74 the Community lost its momentum and, what was worse, lost the philosophy of Jean Monnet: that the Community exists to find common solutions to common problems. (Williams 1991, 50)

Amid this unraveling came a crisis of identity over Britain's role in the Community. As a major industrial power, Britain expected to play a leading role in the EEC, but she had been "absent at the creation" and therefore was forced to deal with a set of rules and procedures which were not of her making. The most significant issue was the budget. Britain continually found herself in conflict with the Franco-German "axis" during the 1970s (Urwin and Paterson 1990, 187).

Before going too far, we need to discuss the EEC budget. Originally, the budget was simply based on a national quota calculated loosely in terms of gross national product and renegotiated each year by the members. In 1970, this system was replaced with the "own resources" concept: the EEC would claim certain revenues on the grounds that they belonged by right to Europe as a whole. Although states initially collected these taxes, they were obligated to transfer them to the EEC. Included in these "own resources" were all taxes on imports from outside the Community. Since the tariff rates were set by the Community, and since there were limited entry points into the continent (for example, Rotterdam took in the lion's share of imports bound for other EEC nations), it was decided that cost of these revenues ought to be shared among all EEC members. A more contentious source of revenue was the 1 percent value-added tax (VAT)—a sort of indirect sales tax that was universal in Europe in the 1970s. Given differential rates of VAT taxation across Europe and the need to prevent one country being in a position to undercut another's products through low taxes, a formula was developed in 1978 to spread these EEC-bound VAT earnings equitably (Taylor 1983, 234).

While the revenue system provided a more stable and seemingly more equitable system than the rather unpredictable national quota system, one member was particularly hard hit by the arrangement. Britain suffered from a threefold vulnerability: much of Britain's food imports came from non-EEC countries, meaning that large amounts of tax revenues previously kept would now be going to Brussels. Although Britain's VAT levels were relatively low (nonexistent on food), the high degree of consumption relative to production (measured in a persistent trade deficit) led to high VAT revenues, the loss of which would hurt Britain severely. Finally, Britain received almost no EEC funds through the CAP since its agricultural sector was efficient and small. As a result, Britain in the late 1970s was consistently sending Brussels some $3 billion more than it was getting back—at the same time France was netting some $800 billion (Taylor 1983, 238).

The very real inequity of the situation was exacerbated by Britain's political ambivalence about European federalism generally. In 1979, Margaret Thatcher was elected prime minister on an anti-EEC platform. Her government exaggerated Britain's disadvantage by focusing on absolute rather than per capita revenues. Considering the EEC process seriously flawed and even illegitimate, the Thatcher government took an aggressive position that alienated the other EEC members. She told the EEC members bluntly "I want my money back."

In 1982, Britain began pressing the European Community for some form of financial relief. It demanded a 1.5 billion European Currency Units (ECU) rebate to be paid by CAP beneficiaries (France and Italy in particular). When agreement was slow in coming, Britain threatened to use its veto to block further action by the Community. Britain came close to precipitating a profound split in the Community by 1984. Helmut Kohl of Germany left a meeting in protest over British intransigence:

> When he rose from the table in anger at 6:30 p.m. on 20 March 1984 in Brussels, he revealed a carelessness about UK reactions which carried an unmistakable and ominous warning for the latter. They could, as it were "take it or leave it." Kohl's action was decisive in revealing the flaw in the British diplomatic armament—that they were prepared to make sacrifices in order to avoid being excluded from the inner sanctum—and more than any other single act it changed the direction of movement of the tide of European integration in the mid-1980s. (Taylor 1989, 7)

In essence, Germany called Britain's bluff. This is not to say that the United Kingdom failed, however. On the contrary, the European Community provided a 1 billion ECU rebate in 1984 and promised additional rebates of roughly two-thirds of the difference between Britain's VAT-generated payments to the EC and its receipts from Brussels (Urwin and Paterson 1990, 193). However, as part of this arrangement, Germany was permitted to increase substantially its share of the European Community expenses—and power.

Apart from the budgetary and philosophical tensions in the Community, a serious problem arose from the growing disparity of development between the members of the EEC. Moving from the EC Six to the EC Nine was not particularly painful, in and of itself, except for the budget question described above. However, the addition of Greece in 1981 and of Spain and Portugal in 1986 created unexpected stress.

Greece was permitted to enter the EEC prematurely, EEC officials today acknowledge. Greek industry is still not competitive with the rest of Europe. Greek agriculture is far too tropical and labor-intensive to survive full integration (for example, average Greek farm size is only one-fifth that of Luxembourg). The Greek government in power in the early 1980s proved to be one of the few pro-EEC governments the Greeks would elect. Successive Greek regimes have challenged this memebrship decision (Williams 1991, 65).

Table 23.1 SELECTED ECONOMIC PERFORMANCE STATISTICS FOR GREECE, PORTU-GAL, GERMANY, AND BRITAIN IN 1989

	Greece	Portugal	Germany	Britain
GDP/cap. (Gross Domestic Product per capita)	$5,350	$4,250	$20,440	$14,610
GDP from Agriculture	16%	9%	2%	2%
Total Exports (millions) of $)	7,353	12,798	340,628	152,403
Energy Use per Capita (kilo oil equivalent)	2,046	1,470	4,383	3,624
Monthly Minimum Wage	$350	$190	$1,300	$720

Sources: World Bank 1991 and Allen M. Williams, The European Community (Cambridge: Blackwell, (1991).

Spain and Portugal applied in 1977 and were admitted in 1986, despite serious reservations. Spain's size, combined with Portugal and Greece's poverty placed heavy burdens on the rest of Europe. Spain and Portugal felt accession would guarantee newfound democracy and preserve strong links to the EC Nine. The European Community nations feared the imbalance of prices, wages, and wealth between Spain and Portugal and the rest of the Community. Their accession was permitted only with seven- to ten-year transitional provisions in fishing, semitropical foods, external industrial tariffs, and budget obligations (Williams 1991, p. 69).

Table 23.1 shows the persistence of development gaps between regions in the EEC.

Efforts to rectify the discrepancies have come primarily through regional development programs administered by the European Regional Development Fund (ERDF). Never more than 10 percent of the total EEC budget, the funds funneled through the ERDF were aimed primarily at rural Mediterranean regions (not countries), although a new program set in place in the mid-1980s provides funds for certain depressed industrial areas (Williams 1991, 130). Regional reform is an important aspect of the Single European Act, but with the dramatic change in the status of Eastern European countries, regional disparity has taken on a much broader significance that has yet to be definitively addressed.

The last policy area which gained significance during the 1970s was monetary reform. The notion of a European Monetary System (EMS) had been discussed early on after the Treaty of Rome was signed, but it did not take shape until the collapse of the dollar-centered Bretton Woods system in 1971 forced Europeans to take more responsibility for their own monetary stability. The "Werner Report," calling for fixed exchange rates which would fluctuate in parallel, was implemented in 1971. This system proved untenable after the oil crisis. Because inflationary pressures hit different countries unequally, and because each nation decided to adopt a different monetary strategy to deal with the crisis, currency values began to separate dramatically. Maintenance of fixed exchange rates required intervention by the governments (buying up and selling currency, increasing interest rates, etc.), so in 1974 the "snake" system as it was called was abandoned in favor of the EMS, known as the "snake in the tunnel" approach (Wistrich 1990, 35).

The EMS allowed European currencies to fluctuate freely against each other within a 4.5 percent band around the deutsche mark. This meant that governments accepted the responsibility to unilaterally adopt policies that would either raise or lower the value of their currencies relative to the mark whenever they approached this range. The agreement was actually drawn up and signed by the central bankers of the EEC, and was to be implemented by them, rather than by political leaders. They agreed not only to conservative monetary principles, but also to consultation, coordination, and convergence of money policy. All of this was to be done voluntarily, however, and the EMS was never subject to the rigors of court intervention. Indeed, the EMS:

> says nothing about the adjustment of central rates. In a related resolution of the European Council, it was agreed that central rate adjustments would be 'subject to mutual agreement by a common procedure,' a vague formula consistent with essentially unilateral action in the first few realignments. (Woolley 1992, 165)

In order to support the goal of the EMS, the central bankers agreed to provide credit to weak currency nations through the European Monetary Cooperation Fund. Furthermore, the EMS called for the eventual creation of a common European currency. The European Currency Unit (ECU) quickly became a convenient unit of accounting for EEC purposes, but its practical application would have to wait.

The Exchange Rate Mechanism (ERM) was also included in the EMS system. This provided for warning to be issued to the banks of countries whose currencies fell outside a narrower 3.5 percent band around the deutsche mark, although strong currencies used heavily in the European banking system received a slightly wider range of tolerance. The effect was to impose particularly strict discipline on smaller countries (Lehment 1983, 187).

The EMS has worked surprisingly well, although the overwhelming role of the dollar in the 1980s may have accounted for much of this. The question of a common currency was a central feature of the Delors Plan of 1989 (the EMS is being replaced by the European Monetary Union or EMU) and has been a major ingredient to the SEA and the Maastricht agreement. Key elements yet to be resolved include the creation of a central bank for Europe with authority to set interest rates, impose fiscal discipline, and harmonize macroeconomic policies. Many Europeans have resisted European Community encroachment on monetary policy, including especially Margaret Thatcher, whose Conservative party dismissed her in early 1992 over her opposition to deeper integration.

The end of this period of relative turmoil came with an epiphany—a deep recognition that the EEC was at a crossroads. The Community could either continue the unionist approach advanced by Thatcher, or adopt the federal approach which was embraced by Germany, France, and the Netherlands.

RENEWAL: 1986–1992

Much of what has happened to the EEC has involved proposals which have yet to be fully implemented. Because at the time of writing the European Community is in upheaval, the remainder of the chapter will focus on the series of major proposals which have been put forward, followed by a discussion of their implications and the prospects for implementation.

Single European Act

In 1984, the European Parliament approved a draft treaty of European union which committed the region to eventually merge its foreign and defense policies. By 1985, talk began to shift to the need for genuine unification of economic policies across the European Community, and committees were formed to study the question of a single market. British official Lord Cockfield developed a plan of action with a list of 282 directives to be adopted by the end of 1992 (Goldstein 1991–1992, 130). At the December 1985 Luxembourg summit, the Single European Act (SEA) was approved and later ratified in 1986. The treaty represented a major modification of the Treaty of Rome and called for implementation of the "four freedoms": (1) Free movement of goods—this involves dismantling the many nontariff barriers not specifically listed in the Treaty of Rome and which were still impeding trade in the Community, including the establishment of a minimum sales (VAT) tax rate with numerous exclusions. (2) A free market in services—this included banking, insurance, transportation, airlines, telecommunications, etc. (3) Free movement of people—in other words, unrestricted immigration within the community. (4) A free market in capital—specifically a pledge to eliminate government intervention in currency exchange and the eventual establishment of a common currency (although it was the Delors Plan that gave this movement its impetus).

Beyond the important symbolism of the SEA, the concrete changes were substantial. By the end of 1992, virtually all government-made barriers to trade were to be eliminated, and efforts were to be set in motion to create united markets in fields where there were none. For example, as of January 1, 1993, trucks may travel across the European Community without stopping at border crossings. This, in and of itself, will cut costs and improve efficiency substantially. Banking has now been liberalized to the point that any stable European banks can establish subsidiaries anywhere in the European Community (Americans should note that this privilege is not yet available to U.S. banks!). Commercial insurance is liberalized, and plans are underway to do the same in the airline industry. By the end of 1992, some 95 percent of the SEA proposals had been implemented.

At the institutional level, although the SEA modifies the Treaty of Rome, it does so by simply changing the powers of existing bodies. The European Parliament is given greater voice on such matters as admitting new members (Lodge 1990, 216). The Commission is strengthened and its scope of operation is broadened, which increases the likelihood that Europe-wide policies will be developed. Perhaps most important, the prospects for further progress in the future have been strengthened by the adoption of majority-rule on the Council of Ministers, eliminating the debilitating use of the veto (Pinder 1986, 73).

Delors Plan

In 1988, the European Council (or summit meeting) commissioned the new president of the European Commission, Jacques Delors, to devise a plan for monetary and currency union. In 1989 the Delors Plan was accepted. It called for a three-phase process to begin with the establishment of a European System of Central Banks (ESCB) centered on a European Central Bank and each of the twelve nation's central banks—to be governed with little political interference. This network would be the vehicle through which the commission and Council of Ministers would set monetary and currency policy, including the gradual harmonization of fiscal policy (government spending and taxation), currency valuation (exchange rates), monetary policy (interest rates, money supply, etc.), and bank powers (political independence of central bank leaders). After the nations of Europe have completed this transition phase and have satisfied the requirements of prudent monetary policy (defined flexibly by the Council of Ministers and European Council), the members of the Community will abandon their own currencies and central bank controls and hand over monetary policy to a single European entity. At this point, the European monetary system will be even more centralized and disciplined than the United States' (Habermeier and Ungerer 1992, 27–29).

Maastricht

With the end of the Cold War in 1989 and the reunification of Germany in 1990, Europe faced a very different political context. As put in the *Economist*, "This is the decade the European Community was invented for" (Colchester 1992, p. S1). Amid the turmoil of this political upheaval, Germany and France pressed for the rapid and full adoption of the spirit of Monnet and Spaak: European Union. Rather than wait for a united Germany to assert its own identity, both Helmut Kohl and François Mitterand moved to incorporate it into the European Community network and subject German expansionism to European imperatives. The fall of Margaret Thatcher accelerated the process. These forces, as well as the growing threat from Japan and the questions about the future American role in Europe, were key to the pell-mell pace of the negotiation of the Maastricht agreements in December 1991.

The Maastricht agreements called for the institution of a European Union, which would revitalize the moribund Greater European Union treaty of the 1950s and emphasize its provisions for a united foreign and defense policy across Europe. France and Germany had already engaged in joint military maneuvers and the European Community acted in a fairly united fashion on the Gulf War in 1990. The war in Yugoslavia has proven to be a test of EC unity, in that Germany's enthusiasm for intervention there has been restrained by the other nations' ambivalence. The general prospects for political unity are less promising than the substantial movement forward in the economic and social sphere.

The first element of Maastricht is the strengthening of the EC-led integration itself, to be accomplished by the year 2000. This is done by broadening its authority into such areas as education, health policy, consumer protection, law enforcement, immigration, and even culture. The Council of Ministers will act on the basis of a qualified majority vote (taking into account the size of the countries in tabulating their vote while eliminating the veto altogether), but must obtain the European Parliament's approval on many questions. The commission, while somewhat weaker in relation to the council, will retain the initiative as the only organ authorized to propose new programs. The principle of "subsidiarity" will limit the EC authority to those programs where collective action is clearly preferable to national unilateralism—but the specific parameters of this concept will have to be determined in the pro-integration European Court of Justice. On the monetary front, the Delors Plan will be implemented on an accelerated schedule, culminating in a common European currency by 1997. This will mean that central banking and independent fiscal policies will no longer be national prerogatives.

On the political front, the Maastricht Treaty envisions the establishment of a European foreign ministry and defense ministry via the Western European Union (WEU) architecture. The existing European Community machinery will share power with these new bodies. Whether this will lead to a single European seat in the UN Security Council and General Assembly is unclear, but unlikely.

Ratification of Maastricht

The Maastricht agreement was finalized in relative secrecy, but with the strong support of the negotiators. Once the treaty was signed, it required the ratification of each member state before it could enter into force. In June 1992 the Danish electorate rejected the treaty by a slim margin, and in September the French approved it by an equally slim margin. Thus, the question arose whether the Maastricht agreement would ever enter into force. A modified version of Maastricht was accepted in November 1993. On January 1, 1994, the European Community was formally renamed the European Union (EU). Implementation of Maastricht still hinges on several issues:

Broadening Austria, Turkey, Norway, Sweden, Finland, and many East European nations have sought access to the EU single market. The Scandinavians have even been willing to accept membership in the European Economic Area, where nations can participate in the free market but may not have a voice in policy-making. Hungary, Poland, and the Czech Republic will be interested in pursuing an accelerated, but nonetheless gradual, admission to the Community, and their recent association agreements are the first step. On January 1, 1995, Austria, Sweden, and Finland will see their dream of European Union membership fulfilled. One can easily imagine a twenty-member EU by the year 2000—one in which the relatively informal arrangements of the EC Six will no longer be adequate and where the differences between members will make the admission of Portugal seem simple in comparison. On the other hand, the EU, especially if strengthened by Maastricht, will be a genuine—if ambivalent—superpower.

German Fiscal Troubles The reunification of Germany is expected to cost the western half of the country some $1 trillion over ten years. Although it is reasonable to expect that by the year 2000 the eastern half will be dynamic and productive, this fiscal burden has weakened Germany's enthusiasm for taking on the EU budget as a pet project. In addition, the difficulties of German reunification have brought intense opposition to the open-door immigration policy of Bonn and other countries and has led to a tightening of immigration policy. Labor unrest in eastern Germany simply exacerbates the problems. How Germany deals with these conditions will doubtless have an impact on EU behavior and policy.

EMU Troubles A series of major disruptions of currency markets in late 1992 led to the pound and several other currencies leaving the EMU for a time, as well as widespread concern about the viability of a single European currency. It is too soon to tell what will be the lasting effect of this financial turmoil, but it certainly will delay the Delors Plan's implementation schedule. These problems are compounded by a serious recession on the European horizon, which will mean less revenues to fund EU projects and more demands for EU support.

Russian Rehabilitation No one knows for sure how much money it will take to rehabilitate the Russian economy. Conservative estimates place the figure in the trillions of dollars. Obviously, the world community is disinclined to come to Russia's rescue at this point, and the result has been a gradual retreat from liberalization as Boris Yeltsin fends off attacks from conservative former Communists. Should the Russian problem reach a crisis point, however, it is entirely possible that the West will feel an obligation to intervene dramatically. Any major funding of Russian development will affect the EU objectives.

Questions to Consider

1. What key factors seem to be reviving European unity? Are these forces relatively constant, or will they wax and wane?

2. Who wants European unity? The masses? The "Eurocrats"? The politicians? What do they expect to get from European unity?

3. Why is it so difficult to move from negative integration to positive integration to political unity? Will these obsacles persist in the future?

References

Clive Archer and Fiona Butler. *The European Community Structure and Process* (New York: St. Martin's Press, 1992).

Nico Colchester. "The European Community—A Survey." *The Economist* (July 11, 1992): S1–S30.

Pierre Gerbet. "The Origins: Early Attempts and the Emergence of the Six (1945–52)," in Pryce, ed., *The Dynamics of European Union*, 35–48.

Walter Goldstein. "EC: Euro-stalling." *Foreign Policy* 85 (Winter 1991–1992): 129–147.

Karl Habermeier and Horst Ungerer. "A Single Currency for the European Community." *Finance and Development* (September 1992): 26–29.

Derek Heater. *The Idea of European Unity* (New York: St. Martin's Press, 1992).

Leon Hurwitz. *The European Community and the Management of International Cooperation* (New York: Greenwood Press, 1987).

Leon Hurwitz, ed. *The Harmonization of European Public Policy: Regional Responses to Transnational Challenges* (Westport, CT: Greenwood Press, 1983).

Hanns Jurgen Kusters. "The Treaties of Rome (1955–57)," in Pryce, ed., *The Dynamics of European Union*, 78–104.

Harmen Lehment. "The European Monetary System," in Hurwitz, ed., *The Harmonization of European Public Policy*, 183–196.

Juliet Lodge, ed. *The European Community and the Challenge of the Future* (New York: St. Martin's Press, 1989).

Juliet Lodge. "European Community Decision-Making: Toward the Single European Market," in Urwin and Paterson, *Politics in Western Europe Today*, 206–226.

Juliet Lodge, ed. *European Union: The European Community in Search of a Future* (New York: St. Martin's Press, 1986).

John Marsh. "The Common Agricultural Policy," in Lodge, ed., *The European Community*, 148–166.

Jean Monnet. *Memoirs* (New York: Doubleday, 1979).

John Pinder. "Economic Union and the Draft Treaty," in Lodge, ed., *European Union*, 70–87.

Roy Pryce, ed. *The Dynamics of European Union* (New York: Croom Helm, 1987).

Alberta Sbragia, ed. *Euro-politics: Institutions and Policymaking in the "New" European Community* (Washington, DC: Brookings Institution, 1992).

Paul Taylor. *The Limits of European Integration* (New York: Columbia University Press, 1983).

Paul Taylor. "The New Dynamics of EC Integration in the 1980s," in Lodge, ed., *The European Community*, 3–25.

Derek Urwin and William Paterson, eds. *Politics in Western Europe Today: Perpsectives, Policies and Problems Since 1980* (New York: Longman, 1990).

Allan M. Williams. *The European Community: The Contradictions of Integration* (Cambridge: Blackwell, 1991).

Ernest Wistrich. *After 1992: The United States of Europe* (New York: Routledge, 1990).

John T. Woolley. "Policy Credibility and European Monetary Institutions," in Sbragia, ed., *Euro-politics*, 157–190.

World Bank. *World Development Report* (New York: Oxford University Press, 1991).

U.S.-Japan Trade Rivalry

Over the centuries, chauvinistic politicians have proclaimed their nation's independence from the rest of the world. In the United States, isolationism—the notion that America should ignore events in Europe as inconsequential—was the dominant philosophy through the nineteenth century. In the twentieth century, such attitudes have been dispelled by the recognition that the country was far from immune to changes beyond its shores. Conversely, world leaders became impressed by the apparent interconnectedness of international events: increases in oil prices in Saudi Arabia led to layoffs and smaller cars in Detroit; Vietnamese desires for independence and national unity precipitated the fall of Lyndon Johnson; European efforts at food security led to trade wars with Japan and the United States. This mutual vulnerability and sensitivity has been called "interdependence."

We have all heard the stories of Japan's economic power. We know that whole regions of the country are reeling under pressure from Japanese imports. It is expected that by the end of the century, Japan will have more investments in the United States than the British and Canadians combined and that Japan's gross national product will surpass that of the United States. The Japanese routinely purchase more than a third of U.S. Treasury Bills and one-quarter of all traded stocks on Wall Street, and they have maintained a trade surplus with the United States hovering around $50 billion for nearly a decade. In areas such as semiconductors (the "brains" of a computer), consumer electronics, automobiles, steel, and machine tools the Japanese have enjoyed an overwhelming advantage, to the point that their American competitors are struggling for survival (Choate 1990, xvi). High-visibility acquisitions of the Seattle Mariners, the Rockefeller Plaza, and Columbia Pictures by Japanese investors have dredged up deep resentment and fear in many Americans, 46 percent of whom recently told pollsters

Japanese investment was bad for the country (Franklin 1989). Even where Japanese firms are bringing new jobs, they are often criticized for discriminating against local suppliers. Whether the Americans are buying Japanese imports, working for Japanese firms, or letting them pay for our deficit by buying Treasury Bills, it seems we resent them! What has led to this situation?

In this brief review of U.S.-Japanese trade relations, we will endeavor to be as impartial as possible, recognizing that for those who have already decided who is to blame this will not sit well. It is hoped that whether you feel corporate America, Japanese protectionism, the General Agreement on Tariffs and Trade (GATT), or something else is to blame, you will come away from this review a bit more sophisticated and tolerant, if not necessarily certain of the future.

A BRIEF HISTORY OF U.S.-JAPANESE TRADE RELATIONS

Early Contact and Japanese Ascension: 1850–1945

The first American tourist who visited Japan in 1848 was captured, caged, and put on display in Tokyo, as was the custom at the time (Lewis 1991, 17). Perhaps even more amusing than this rather curious treatment was the fact that the sailor's name was Ranald (pronounced "Ronald") MacDonald (perhaps the Japanese were better at recognizing a threat to the status quo than they are given credit).!

Commodore Matthew Perry opened the Japanese economy with a show of force and savvy diplomatic protocol in 1853, and by 1858 the conservative Tokugawa shogunate had accepted trade agreements with France, Russia, and Britain. In 1868, the Meiji dynasty came to power with a vow to modernize the nation and open it to foreign influence. By systematically suppressing domestic reactionary opposition, the new government established a modern, industrialized, increasingly cosmopolitan and relatively democratic social order in what had previously been a land forbidden to foreigners (Atlas 1987, 136).

Japan began acting as a world power in defeating Russia in 1895, annexing Korea in 1910, and entering World War I on the Allied side in 1914. During the 1920s, Japanese policy became more openly aggressive, with the occupation of China's Shantung province in spite of international protest and the subsequent occupation of all Manchuria in northern China. The Japanese government, as a result of assassination and coup d'état, lost its democratic content, culminating in the ascension of Prime Minister Hideki Tojo in 1941 and the establishment of a military dictatorship. The experience of World War II is well known and need not be reviewed here.

Post–World War II Relations: 1945–1975

The occupying American armies under General Douglas MacArthur played an active role in reorganizing the Japanese economy, society, and polity. The so-called "Peace Constitution" which prohibits the establishment of an offensive military capability and the deployment of Japanese troops overseas, was strongly encouraged by the occupying army, and has since been embraced by Japanese society as a whole. The famed "keiretsu," large family-dominated economic conglomerates (the Mitsubishi and Matsui keiretsu were the largest private firms at the turn of the century), were dismembered and the government was charged with playing an active role in shaping the new Japanese economy.

For twenty years the United States encouraged export-led economic growth and prudent monetary policy in order to more completely incorporate Japan in the global economic system, even if this meant trade disadvantages for the United States in the short term (Destler 1979, 191). The Truman and Eisenhower administrations expended considerable political capital in order to bring Japan into the General Agreement on Tariffs and Trade (GATT) and other liberal institutions. This is not to say the United States was unwilling to impose protectionist measures on Japan, as its "voluntary export restraint" (VER) agreement on textiles in the 1950s attests (Friman 1992). This mechanism allowed the United States to impose an informal quota on Japanese textile imports by obtaining their voluntary, if coerced, consent to limit exports to the United States, while preserving the appearance of free trade. This informal arrangement also permitted the Japanese to pursue an export-led growth strategy without allowing direct foreign control, since bilateral arrangements were concluded outside the multilateral GATT agreements (Rapp and Feldman 1979, 118).

Overall, even aggressive industrialization and export-led growth in Japan were not enough to overcome a substantial trade deficit with both the United States and the rest of the world until 1965—twenty years after the end of the war (Destler 1979, 194). The Japanese learned to incorporate basic technologies in electronics and steel, as well as build on their successful textiles and shipbuilding industries, by analyzing foreign technology and seeking access to international scientific communities. In all of this, the Japanese government made use of cooperative arrangements with business and labor at home to forge a genuinely Japanese economic program.

Between 1967 and 1973 several developments strained U.S.-Japanese relations. To begin, the United States escalated involvement in the Vietnam War, much to Tokyo's dismay. The strain this situation placed on U.S.-Japanese relations was severe, and the pacifist elements of the Liberal Democratic party as well as the growing Socialist party urged a reconsideration of the U.S.-Japanese security treaty. Japan also began to post a trade surplus with the United States, contributing to a severe U.S. balance of payments deficit by 1971. Finally, U.S. refusal to work with the Communist government in China grew increasingly difficult for Japan and pressures mounted to recognize Beijing in spite of U.S. objections.

These pressures were addressed in a variety of ways. In 1971, the United States went off the gold standard and placed a 10 percent tariff on all imported goods, including those from Japan. After this shock treatment, the

Table 24.1 U.S.-JAPANESE TRADE LEVELS

	U.S. Trade Deficit with Japan ($ billion)	U. S Exports to Japan as a Percentage of Imports from Japan
1969	–$ 1.4	71
1970	–$ 1.2	80
1971	–$ 3.2	56
1972	–$ 4.2	53
1973	–$ 1.3	86
1974	–$ 1.6	87
1975	–$ 1.7	85
1976	–$ 5.3	65
1977	–$ 8.0	56
1978	–$11.6	51
1979	–$ 8.7	67
1980	–$ 9.9	68
1981	–$15.8	58
1982	–$16.7	56
1983	–$19.3	53
1984	–$33.6	41
1985	–$46.2	33
1986	–$55.0	33
1987	–$56.3	33
1988	–$52.1	42
1989	–$49.0	48
1990	–$41.1	54
1991	–$43.4	52
1992*	–$43.7	52

*projected estimate

Sources: Survey of Current Business, Stephen D. Cohen, *Cowboys and Samurai* (New York: Harper Business, 1991).

United States quickly resurrected the free trade philosophy and set in motion the Tokyo Round of multilateral tariff reductions. The United States placed extraordinary pressure on Japan to restrict its textiles exports to the United States and, while it did not concede, Japan undertook a dramatic liberalization of quota restrictions on industrial products during the period. The United States ended the Vietnam War and took dramatic steps to recognize the People's Republic of China, both of which liberated Japan diplomatically. By the end of the period of upheaval, U.S.-Japanese relations became as warm as ever (Destler 1979, 194). Japan had emerged not as a secondary political ally, but as a primary economic rival (Cohen 1985, 17) (see Table 24.1.).

Economic Rivalry: 1975+

"By the mid-seventies, Japan's emergence as a bona fide international economic superpower had become a sensitive global issue" (Cohen 1985, 24). Concerned about arousing envy among its neighbors, Japan undertook reforms aimed at reducing the economic imbalance: lowering tariffs, both unilaterally and in the context of the Tokyo Round; revaluing the yen so that American and European products would be more competitive in Japan and less attractive abroad; accepting a number of rather unequal bilateral trade restricting agreements—in color televisions, for example—and refraining from retaliating against blatantly unfair unilateral trade practices—such as tough new provisions in U.S. trade law. Nonetheless, much of this effort was seen as either "too little, too late," or merely "window dressing," and fundamental structural problems persisted.

In 1977, U.S. President Jimmy Carter inflated the U.S. economy in order to pull the world out of the post-oil shock recession, but could not persuade Japan to do likewise (MacEachron 1979, 15). Later that year, a delegation of U.S. officials went to Tokyo to attempt a far-reaching bilateral agreement that would satisfy both American exporters frustrated at their inability to penetrate the Japanese market and American manufacturers worried about continued Japanese encroachment and rising U.S. market share. Although overdramatized, the meetings managed to produce more Japanese promises to liberalize and a general commitment to undertake a more consumption-oriented economic strategy (Destler 1979).

While some effort was made during the late 1970s to open access to the Japanese market, a policy of maintaining an "undervalued" yen and promoting high savings rates did much to perpetuate the imbalance. The value of a nation's currency is, in a way, a price adjuster for the entire country's goods bound for foreign markets. Just like with a "half-off" sale at a department store, a currency which is kept artificially low through national policies (low interest rates, for example) serves as an across-the-board discount to foreign buyers. Some argue that the yen undervaluation was a key factor in the trade deficit in 1982 (Turay 1991, 11), while others point out that even during the period of a strong yen in the early 1970s, the trade deficit increased (Rapp and Feldman 1979, 121).

With the recession of 1982 and growing frustration on the part of both the Japanese and Americans for what had come to be perceived as a problem largely of the other party's making, U.S.-Japanese relations hit a new low. In several areas, Japan had all but eliminated trade restrictions, but to Americans, it was the remaining restrictions which caused the most grief. In beef and citrus, a Japanese quota prevented increasing American exports (although Japanese officials were quick to point out the fact that U.S. exports were relatively high in spite of this—Tomabechi 1985). Rice imports were banned altogether. Customs and inspection procedures in Japan had long been cumbersome and seemingly arbitrary. Japanese attempts to convince

Americans of the sincerity of their attachment to free trade fell on deaf ears (Turay 1991, 11). As put by Stephen D. Cohen:

> The market opening measures announced by the government of Japan in 1980 were the first of a long series, without precedent in their volume, their tentativeness, and their failure to produce any significant change in Japanese import patterns. (Cohen 1991, 32–33)

Not until the mid-1980s was Prime Minister Yasuhiro Nakasone able to convince American President Ronald Reagan that Japan was embarking on a new course. Reagan was eager to embrace the affable Nakasone, although most midlevel officials and corporate executives were unimpressed. Much of this was due to Japanese efforts at giving the appearance of cooperativeness, without the substance. For example, the Japanese government initiated talks in 1981 on restricting the amount of automobiles headed for the United States to 1.7 million per year in order to avert what it perceived as growing hostility to successful Japanese subcompacts. The apparant goal of this action was to permit American firms some "breathing room" to develop quality subcompacts of their own. Two unanticipated consequences resulted, however: the relocation of Japanese firms to the United States (transplants) and the gradual "upscaling" of Japanese imported vehicles (note the introduction of the Acura, Lexus, and Infiniti lines) where profit margins are greater. Neither of these moves helped the U.S. corporations, and in fact have made competition fiercer (since Japanese can take advantage of low real estate and pension costs in the United States) over a wider range of products (which now includes luxury, sport, minivan, small pickup and even large pickup trucks—an American bastion).

In 1986 the overall trade deficit for the United States was approaching $150 billion while Japan was enjoying a trade surplus of roughly $100 billion. The trend was exacerbated by an overvalued dollar fueled by high interest rates, which in turn were swelled by a $2 trillion federal debt and growing annual budget deficits (Cohen 1991, 42). The United States became the world's largest debtor and Japan the largest creditor, even passing the United States in total foreign aid. The pressures from Congress to act vigorously against Japanese trade barriers became intolerable. In 1985 Congress came close to passing protectionist legislation, and Congressman Richard Gephardt pressed actively for increased pressure on Japan (Gephardt 1989). Secretary of the Treasury James Baker III moved toward a policy of devaluation of the dollar and the overall trade deficit narrowed from a high of $170 billion in 1987 to below $100 billion by 1990. In spite of this, the U.S.-Japanese deficit remained roughly the same.

Congress finally acted with the passage of the 1988 Omnibus Trade and Competitiveness Act which contained the "Super 301" provision requiring the new administration of George Bush to specifically identify countries which were guilty of a pattern of unfair trade and single out specific issues to target. The administration was in an extremely awkward position of implementing trade policy initiated by Congress, but managed to select programs which would minimize international conflict (Krauss and Reich 1992). These negotiations had the effect of liberalizing trade in supercomputers (a technology whose obsolescence is a major factor in IBM's 1992 downsizing), satellites, and wood products. Again, however, U.S. discontent was not assuaged and trade negotiations both in Tokyo and in Geneva at the GATT became increasingly hostile.

The most recent development in the relationship is the emergence of a so-called "revisionist" school of Japanese international relations. Beginning with Chalmers Johnson in the early 1980s and since joined by Stephen Krasner and a host of analysts, the revisionist school argues that Japan is an inherently different type of country—a "developmental state"—which will never be fully absorbed into the Western world (Johnson 1982; Krasner 1987). Revisionists argue that Japanese culture and social structure are unitary, in the sense that they are so tightly intertwined that they are inseparable, and efforts to negotiate with one element of the nation will lead to frustration. The implication was that the United States and others victimized by Japan, Inc., should aim at changing the entire society in order to create an environment of free and fair trade.

Japanese officials and executives, on their side, began to develop a more intransigent and openly defiant tone by the 1990s, directly accusing the West of blaming Japan for its own problems (Tomabechi 1985). In "The Japan That Can Say No," Shintaro Ishihara forcefully made the argument that Japan was strong enough to resist pressure to accommodate the West. The commemoration of the fiftieth anniversary of Pearl Harbor Day was a cause for increased acrimony rather than healing (Baker and Frost 1992). In other words, both positions seemed to be hardening, and it was only a temporary slowdown in the Japanese economy that prevented what would have amounted to a trade war in 1992. By mid-1994, however, the United States was again in a stand-off with Japan over market access.

CAUSES OF CONFLICT AND POSSIBLE SOLUTIONS

The rivalry between the United States and Japan threatens a great many people on both sides of the Pacific and carries the very real danger of escalating to the point that millions, perhaps even hundreds of millions, will see their quality of life seriously diminished as a result of trade war or economic boycotts. To explore the dangers of the present situation and their root causes, we will need to spend a bit of time on basic economics.

The clash between the United States and Japan can be understood as a conflict between two economic philosophies: laissez-faire capitalism and mercantilism. Laissez-faire is a French phrase meaning "allow it to happen" and refers to the principle of noninterference with the economy on the part of the state. Specifically, laissez-faire economics assumes that the market mechanism of supply and demand will serve as an automatic regulatory mechanism, an "invisible hand," to govern production, distribution, prices, etc., in such a way that the greatest possible social good will ultimately be achieved. Free trade is the keystone of this strategy. As each nation specializes in those products it can produce most efficiently given its "factor endowment" (relative amounts and quality of land, labor, and capital), prices will fall, demand and production will rise, leading to greater wealth and employment. Trade is the epitome of the win-win situation.

Mercantilism is based on realist assumptions about national power and security, and takes for granted that a state has an obligation to protect and defend the economic and natural resources of the nation. Mercantilists do not accept the invisible hand theory, arguing that wealth will tend to gravitate toward those nations that happen to be endowed with marketable factors, whether it be natural resources, human capital, abundance of fertile land, or whatever. The terms of trade (meaning the unit-to-unit prices of exports relative to imports) of products from tropical and less well-endowed regions will tend to deteriorate: in order to exchange their goods for a given quantity of goods from more naturally fortunate countries, they will be forced to produce ever increasing amounts. The result will not be a win-win but a zero-sum arrangement in which one nation will grow increasingly rich and secure at others' expense. In order to prevent this scenario, the state must intervene to support uncompetitive industries, especially if they are deemed essential to the national interest (products that have strategic, political, cultural, or other significance to the government in power). This can be done by limiting access to the home market or providing incentives and subsidies for local producers.

No nation can be described as a "pure" free trader or a "pure" mercantilist. The United States is far from free in areas such as steel, textiles, agriculture, or professional sports. Conversely, even Japan's economy is extremely liberal in terms of its tariff levels. But in general terms, one can find that the conflict between the two nations can be characterized in these terms. This terminology will help you recognize patterns in the following description of general problems and solutions to the trade dispute.

MACROECONOMICS AND U.S.–JAPANESE TRADE

Of perhaps greatest significance in international trade are the national policies that affect exchange rates, since this single variable automatically affects the price of all traded goods. The currency rate is controlled indirectly in the current international system of floating exchange rates, where supply and demand are the ultimate determinants. Why do some currencies attract more buyers than others? First, the amount of products the nation sells determines much of this demand: for nearly every export from the United States there must be a payment made in dollars, which in turn requires the exchanging of one currency for dollars—a purchase of dollars, as it were. The level of exports is in turn determined by the competitiveness of the products—which is affected by the exchange rate. Second, investors seeking a higher return on their more liquid funds will seek out nations that offer high interest rates in relation to their inflation rate (the real interest rate).

Comparing interest rates across countries will reveal where the return is greatest and which currency must be acquired in order to make that investment.

What determines an interest rate? Again, it is indirect and complex, but the key factors are: the prime lending rate the Federal Reserve Bank charges its best customers, the amount of debt in the nation relative to lendable funds—in particular the amount of debt incurred by the government—and the general productivity and health of the economy (bankruptcies tend to drive up interest rates as bankers attempt to recoup their losses). Economists argue that currency exchange rates should be primarily based on "purchasing power parity," a concept that describes what you can buy at home with a given country's currency. In Japan, for example, the prices of many consumer goods are inflated, such that the yen simply does not buy as much as a dollar in the United States (Japanese will fly to American cities in order to buy sophisticated Japanese-made electronics and pay for the ticket with what they save!). Finally, currency exchange rates are affected by direct government actions to produce currency (the money supply), holding onto other nations' currencies as a reserve asset, and selling or buying your own currency to or from other nations.

Fred Bergsten and William Cline have long emphasized that the key to achieving balance in U.S. trade is to cut the national debt, balance the annual federal budget, and thereby lower the interest rate and the value of the dollar (Bergsten and Cline 1987). Observers noted that with a small decline in the nominal interest rates in the United States and a relatively rapid decline of the dollar after 1986 (which had to be slowed down by the Japanese purchasing large amounts of dollars), some tightening of the trade deficit did occur, without the predicted inflationary effects in the United States (Yoshitomi 1989). In fact, the overall U.S. trade deficit shrank by roughly 30 percent in the late 1980s, although the deficit with Japan rose again to its $50 billion level. It would seem that although cutting the deficit and increasing the savings rate will be generally good for the U.S. economy and for the overall trade balance, the root of the U.S.-Japanese trade problem lies elsewhere.

AMERICAN AND JAPANESE CORPORATE TACTICS

By "corporate tactics," we are referring to a whole array of actions available to private corporations acting alone and in conjunction with other private and even public actors. Naturally, the same sorts of things that make a product more successful at home contribute to its success abroad: quality, usefulness, appropriateness, marketing strategy, distribution network, etc. These obvious factors have often escaped our corporate leaders in their debates over Japanese trade policy. It wasn't until 1992, following a disastrous trip to Tokyo by President Bush and Detroit auto executives ("to bush" has become a slang verb in Japanese meaning "to vomit"), that a U.S. auto firm seriously marketed a car with right-side drive in Japan though the Japanese have always driven on the left! American firms doing business with Japan are finally learning that the 1 percent error tolerance they were used to is un-acceptable in Japan, where products must generally have no more than 0.1 percent errors. Even at the most basic levels of communication, very few U.S. corporate executives can speak Japanese, while fluency in English is al-most universal among Japanese businessmen (although living overseas for extended periods of time can lead to a subtle ostracism for a Japanese per-son).

The modern version of the keiretsu has been an obstacle in U.S.-Japanese trade negotiations (Powell and Rich 1991). These vast conglomerates coordi-nate a wide variety of activities under unified management. Numerous senior Japanese executives enjoy membership on several corporate boards and work with the government to protect their vast interests. Networks of supply and purchasing within the conglomerates have effectively shut out foreign firms in many cases (Kreinin 1988), and there is little in the way of antitrust law to combat this. The Japanese government's policy of coordinating economic growth by targeting specific industries with subsidies and joint business-gov-ernment ventures exacerbates this system. Small and midsized American firms seem especially at a loss to understand the intricacies of Japan's market (Namiki 1988). By contrast, Japanese firms generally have little trouble inter-facing with U.S. firms as suppliers or competitors on American soil.

An important difference in American and Japanese corporate attitudes has been the urgency of getting a return on investment. Every quarter, American firms must reveal their earnings. Shareholders typically expect a profit each quarter and are quick to express frustration and even hostility against CEOs and other executives who fail (Yamamoto 1989/90). Numer-ous U.S. corporations, squeezed by heavy debt burdens carried over from the merger-mania of the 1980s, have been forced to cut work forces dramati-cally in order to quickly turn a profit, although even such draconian mea-sures have failed. Japanese firms, on the other hand, have traditionally viewed success in terms of market share, or their firm's share of the total purchases of a given product. The result of this view is a strategy of under-pricing (verging on dumping, when products are sold for less than produc-tion costs) in the initial phases of introducing a new product and lower prof-its in the early years, combined with intense two-way loyalty between firm and work force. Note U.S. executives' response to the increase in Japanese car prices following implementation of the 1981 VER: rather than keep their prices lower in the United States in order to regain market share, U.S. auto firms raised prices an average of 14 percent and saw sales decline by roughly 10 percent (Husted and Melvin 1990, 197). In early 1993, when the U.S. dollar lost 10 percent of its value against the yen, rather than taking ad-vantage of the chance to lower prices and increase market share, American exporters to Japan simply reaped a 10 percent windfall profit instead (*New York Times*, May 5, 1993, A1).

This is not to say that U.S. firms are irrevocably outclassed by Japanese corporations. The Federal Express corporation regularly receives visits from Japanese management analysts, a midsized firm in Seattle exports tons of chop sticks to Japan each year, and several service industries have forged trans-Pacific links (Sutton 1992; Lewis 1991, 13). IBM, NCR, McDonald's, and other firms have flourishing operations in Japan and have little difficulty exporting their products. The key ingredient seems to be whether existing Japanese firms have already developed a similar product (copyright rules are broadly interpreted and strictly enforced). At any rate, there does seem to be some hope for U.S. firms doing business in and with Japan.

NATIONAL TRADE POLICIES AND NEGOTIATIONS

In 1991 a California salesman placed a one-pound bag of U.S.-grown rice on a display table at a trade show in Tokyo. Within moments customs officials seized the bag and fined him for bringing an illegal substance into the country: foreign rice! While this treatment was perfectly predictable, it served to highlight a perception of Japan as a protectionist country. But is this perception valid?

There is a wide array of policies available to any state that seeks to promote exports and inhibit imports. The most obvious is a tariff on imports—a simple tax assessed at the border based on the type and value of the product. Every nation has tariff barriers, although the successive multilateral trade negotiations sponsored by the GATT have dramatically reduced them—particularly those tariffs which relate to manufactured goods. Japan, along with the rest of the world, has dropped its tariff rates to the point that on specific products they are generally lower than the United States, and other industrialized countries, and are much lower overall (see Table 24.2 and Turay 1991).

If tariffs are not the primary means of protecting markets, there are many other so-called nontariff barriers. Quotas, or a numerical cap, are a common alternative to tariffs, and are not uncommon in Japan. The ban on imported rice has been mentioned, but twenty-six other quotas on both agricultural and manufactured goods have been in place in recent times (Turay 1991, 18). Retaliatory measures have frequently been taken by France, Germany, Italy, and most recently, the United States. The introduction of VERs, discussed earlier, is aimed at removing quotas and other barriers by informally instituting retaliatory quotas on the other side. VERs in automobiles, textiles, semiconductors, and other areas have been set in place. One should understand that all tariffs, quotas, and VERs violate the spirit and often the letter of the GATT agreements, although since VERs are rarely formalized, they fall between the legal cracks (Krishna 1989, 75–76).

Other techniques employed to restrict trade include: health and safety regulations, cumbersome customs procedures, licensing fees, domestic content legislation, government procurement policies, restricted bidding arrangements, export subsidies, and subsidies for local producers. Each of these are easily found in both the United States and Japan, but they fail to tell the whole story. As put by Bergsten and Cline, "It is clear that any difference that does exist can explain, at most, a modest part of the bilateral trade imbalance or even its growth in recent years . . . [and] is not nearly

Table 24.2   TARIFF RATES FOR SELECTED COUNTRIES (1987) (NOMINAL TARIFF
WEIGHTED BY OWN-COUNTRY IMPORTS)

	Japan	U.S.	Germany	Britain
Textiles	3.3*	9.2	7.4	6.7
Clothing	13.8	22.7	13.4	13.3*
Wood Products	0.3*	1.7	2.9	3.1
Furniture	5.1	4.1*	5.6	5.6
Paper Products	2.1	0.2*	5.2	4.9
Rubber Products	1.1*	2.5	3.8	2.7
Iron and Steel	2.8*	3.6	5.9	4.7
Metal Products	5.2	4.8*	5.4	5.6
Glass Products	5.1*	6.2	7.9	7.9
Electrical Machinery	4.3*	4.4	8.3	8.1
Nonelectrical Machinery	4.4	3.3*	4.5	4.2
Manufactures (misc.)	4.6	4.2	5.6	3.0*
Overall	2.9*	4.3	6.3	5.2

*lowest tariff of the four nations on these items

Source: Steven L. Husted and Michael Melvin, *International Economics* (New York: Harper and Row, 1990).

enough to justify the shrill calls for 'reciprocity' which imply that the playing field is tilted sharply against the United States" (Bergsten and Cline 1987, 119).

Of much greater significance is the degree of general support on the part of the Japanese and American governments relative to industry. This is done through research and development incentives, infrastructure development, employee training programs, etc. These arrangements typically have long historical and deep political roots and are particularly impervious to efforts at reform. They are more properly viewed as cultural factors.

As explained by the "revisionists," the Japanese society is better understood not as a free market but as a national movement. The state plays such an active part in promoting specific industries, such as consumer electronics, that there is little in the way of market pressure on the businesses. One can compare the treatment of Japanese consumer-oriented firms to the American treatment of defense contractors. As put by Stephen Krasner:

> At the core of the developmental state are a group of interlocked private, political, and public institutions—large industrial and financial enterprises, the Liberal Democratic Party, the Ministry of Finance, and the Ministry of International Trade and Industry (MITI)—which share core values emphasizing the central importance of aggregate economic performance. . . . The survival of the community, rather than the interests of particular groups or individuals, is the fundamental objective. (Krasner 1987, 13)

But how does one fight against these various obstacles? Tariffs and quotas are perhaps the easiest to deal with, since there is legal and diplomatic precedent for removing these barriers. In fact, bilateral negotiations, which have become increasingly broad, have produced some modest results, although largely superficial. The more coercive talks stemming from the Super 301 actions in 1989 were targeted at steel, semiconductors, and certain agricultural products. Regrettably, the results of these talks, while apparently promising, have done little to end the result of trade imbalance (U.S. Congress 1988).

One could easily consider two options, which need not be mutually exclusive: American firms could abandon the goal of penetrating the Japanese market and instead focus on building up industry at home to better compete against Japanese imports, or American firms and negotiators can take a more aggressive approach to open Japanese markets while maintaining the status quo at home. The former approach has been generally supported by internationalists, many Democrats, and laissez-faire economists who fear trade wars. The national elite have generally swung in favor of what could be called an "industrial strategy" of public sector promotion of consumer-oriented manufacturing and technology. Rather than concentrating as it has on military technology, the industrial strategy would promote such innovative technologies as high-definition television, commercial aircraft, high speed railway systems, and a variety of "green" technologies such as electric cars. If in fact macroeconomics and trade negotiations are of limited value, then this approach promises substantial rewards, at the cost of rigid adherence to laissez-faire economics.

The more aggressive approach is advocated by longtime trade negotiators who are increasingly impatient and revisionists who fear Japanese ascendance and power. The Structural Impediments Initiative developed over the last four years has aimed at addressing a wide variety of nontariff and even invisible barriers to trade with Japan (U.S. Congress 1990). The results as yet have been modest, but the scope of the talks is encouraging. Unfortunately, it is just this sort of negotiation that has precipitated the anti-American sentiment described earlier. U.S. negotiators are portrayed as either whiners or bullies, generally unwilling to admit their own mistakes. Targeting specific sectors with threats of retaliation, while promising in the short run, seem to be souring the atmosphere in the long run. There is also a limit to the effectiveness of bilateral strategies, since Japan's economy is becoming increasingly diversified, both in terms of products and trading partners (Japanese trade with other Asian countries now exceeds its trade with the United States). The GATT has as yet been unable to impose penalties—its enforcement powers revolve around granting authorization to a country that has proved its injury to take unilateral retaliatory steps (in essence, the lynch mob gets permission from the judge before hanging the prisoner!). In general, the retaliatory strategy poses the greatest risk of trade war.

SOCIAL AND CULTURAL FORCES

We observed earlier that the devaluation of the dollar since 1986 has apparently had little effect on U.S.-Japanese trade. As put by Shafiquil Islam, "the failure of macroeconomics to reduce the trade imbalances is no surprise because the problem is structural and cultural: Japan keeps its markets closed through various unfair trade practices, and its economy does not respond to exchange-rate changes and usual market forces" (Islam 1989/90, 177). We have already noted the keiretsu, corporate relations with government, and other cultural factors that inhibit trade with the United States. "Only cultural factors can explain why the Japanese continue to venerate a large trade surplus long after they have achieved a strong industrial base and massive holdings of foreign reserves" (Cohen 1991, 231).

Japanese society is largely governed by the twin social obligations known as "giri" and "on" through which any favor commits the recipient to being beholden essentially forever. While a key to binding together the society, these feelings of mutual obligation to neighbors, relatives, and business associates tend to exclude outsiders. Extremely inefficient and expensive corner stores cater not only to locals, but maintain ties with grown-up children who have moved away by providing catalogues of their overpriced wares. Corporate loyalty on the part of employees is notorious, including extensive hazing ceremonies and long hours of social obligatory drinking with co-workers after work. Japanese workers spend 10 percent more time on the job than their American counterparts, primarily out of duty.

Trade-related Japanese culture is also expressed in the high savings rate and reluctance in many circles to consume. This phenomenon is in the midst of change and young professionals are increasingly afraid of dying from overwork (known as "karoshi"—Kawahito 1991). Travel and leisure are increasing significantly, and the savings rate is declining somewhat.

Contrast this with the American attitude most of us know well, of carrying large debt burdens in order to enjoy the benefits of numerous consumer goods. Although leisure time is contracting in relative terms, household expenditures and debt levels reached alarming proportions in the late 1980s, with the result that during the recession of 1990–1992 millions were forced out of their homes and saw their belongings repossessed. U.S. workers feel little loyalty to American corporations which likewise show little willingness to sacrifice on their behalf. Exorbitant CEO compensation, widespread layoffs, and general downsizing have left many demoralized and resentful.

Regarding Japanese politics, the Liberal Democratic party, which ruled Japan since the mid-1950s, is better understood as a collection of factions led by various professional politicians. Political support is based on sectoral support from key industrial and economic groups, such as the powerful rice farmers (rural areas are disproportionately represented because there has been no redistricting since the 1950s in spite of substantial rural flight). Japanese governments have fallen as a result of trade liberalization policies and bureaucratic resistance to change is great (Curran 1985). In addition, a compulsion to dominate has become apparent in Japanese trade policy, as explained by Peter Drucker who describes Japan as an "adversarial trader":

> Competitive trade aims at creating a customer. Adversarial trade aims at dominating an industry ... competitive trade is fighting a battle. Adversarial trade aims at winning the war by destroying the enemy's army and its capacity to fight. (Drucker 1988, 129–130, cited in Cohen 1991, 229)

In July, 1993, the Liberal Democratic Party lost its majority in the Diet amid scandals and popular frustration with economic stagnation. The new prime minister is a committed reformer and has pressed for democratization and opening of the country's political and economic systems. It is too soon to tell what the effect of this change will be on U.S.-Japanese trade.

When it comes to U.S. politics, it is important to understand the ambivalence the government now feels toward free trade. The executive branch has historically been devoted to free trade, although for much of the post-war era Congress has attempted to inhibit this liberal impulse. Where Democrats generally favored free trade through the 1960s, the free trade baton has been passed to the Republicans. The net result of this vacillation on trade policy across time, parties, and branches of government is a strange collection of programs and policies with conflicting purposes. The United States drafted and signed the GATT and all other international free trade programs, while preserving protectionism in agriculture, textiles, autos, steel, and many other areas. Much of this is as dependent on the positions of parties and politicians as on the effectiveness of lobbyists working on behalf of foreign interests (a situation described in great detail in Choate 1990).

Other general societal and cultural factors that have an impact on U.S.-Japanese trade include the relatively high costs of health care, insurance, and litigation in the United States in comparison to Japan, and the high cost of real estate in Japan relative to the United States. It is estimated that roughly 10 percent of the price of each U.S.-made automobile goes to cover health care costs, while rental costs of office space in Tokyo is roughly twice that of downtown Los Angeles.

In general, the argument that removal of all trade barriers and macroeconomic impediments will still not lead to balanced trade between Japan and the United States must be taken seriously. This is not to say that Japanese will refuse to shop at Toys 'R Us (as they have) or buy Levi's jeans (as they do), but that for the United States to sell as many products to Japan as America buys will require substantial changes in the basic makeup of the Japanese society. As put by Stephen D. Cohen:

> Japan's efforts at internationalization have fallen short of the mark. The country's retention of its insular, tradition-bound mentality has collided with the sheer magnitude of its export success, as well as what is arguably the most pervasive international trend of the late twentieth century: accelerated economic interdependence. (Cohen 1991a, 184)

CONCLUSION

Figure 24.1 summarizes the previous discussion. While the number of forces at work in determining a country's trade balance are bewildering, what is most troubling is sorting out which factors are most significant. Can you sell a useless product if the price is low enough? Can the exchange rate be so high that no one will buy even your best and cheapest products? Is industrial productivity (output per hour worked) more significant than marketing techniques? Perhaps even more important, can lowering Japanese trade barriers assure American exporters of greater success?

In the final analysis, it seems the prospects for a resolution of U.S.-Japanese trade rivalry are rather dim, not that one should automatically conclude that the relationship is destined to deteriorate. The truth of the matter seems to be that "the trade disequilibrium is best viewed as the tip of the iceberg, with domestic factors as the main underlying causal factors" (Cohen 1991a, 153). While certain "symptoms" of this problem can be addressed via traditional trade policy negotiations, the introduction of the Structural Impediments Initiative represents a promising departure. As tensions mount and accusations intensify, there is real danger that both sides to the dispute will provoke reactions from their rival which will cause hardship all around. To the extent that diplomacy can help bring about the very necessary structural changes within each economy, so much the better, but just as weapons rarely bring peace in and of themselves, trade negotiators must not be expected to carry the burden of the nation.

Questions to Consider

1. How does the U.S.-Japanese trade rivalry affect me? What could a resolution of the problem do to improve my own life?

2. To what extent is the United States or Japan for blame for the situation? Is the United States a closet mercantilist and Japan a closet free trader?

3. Should the United States take a more aggressive posture toward Japanese trade practices? What would be the likely consequences?

4. How can the United States become more competitive? Whose responsibility should it be?

References

Atlas of World History (New York: Rand McNally, 1987).

Howard H. Baker and Ellen L. Frost. "Rescuing the U.S.-Japan Alliance." *Foreign Affairs* 71 #2 (Spring 1992): 97–113.

William J. Barnds. *Japan and the United States: Challenges and Opportunities* (New York: New York University Press, 1979).

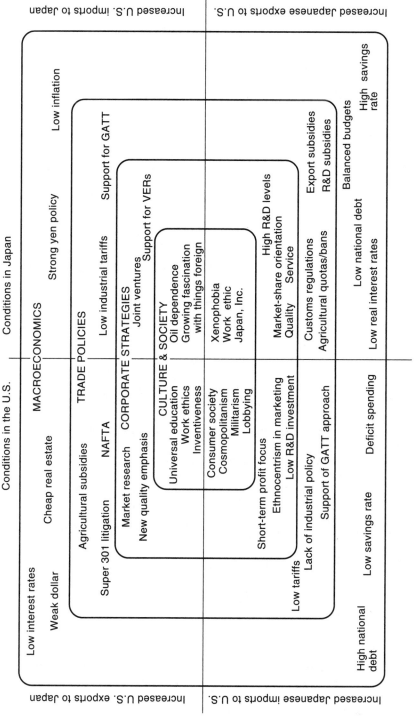

Figure 24.1 Factors affecting U.S.-Japanese trade balance.
Source: Author

C. Fred Bergsten and William R. Cline. *The United States-Japan Economic Problem* (Washington, DC: Institute for International Economics, 1987).

Pat Choate. *Agents of Influence* (New York: Alfred A. Knopf, 1990).

Stephen D. Cohen. *Cowboys and Samurai: Why the United States Is Losing the Industrial Battle and Why It Matters* (New York: HarperBusiness, 1991).

Stephen D. Cohen. *Uneasy Partnership: Competition and Conflict in U.S.-Japanese Trade Relations* (Cambridge, MA: Ballinger Pub, 1985).

Stephen D. Cohen. "United States-Japanese Trade Relations." *Current History* 90 #555 (April 1991a): 152–55, 184–187.

Timothy J. Curran. "The Politics of Trade Liberalization in Japan," in Katz and Friedman-Lichtschein, eds., *Japan's New World Role*, 105–122.

I. M. Destler. "U.S.-Japanese Relations and the American Trade Initiative of 1977: Was This 'Trip' Necessary?" in Barnds, *Japan and the United States*, 190–230.

Peter Drucker. *The New Realities: In Government and Politics / In Economics and Business/In Society and World View* (New York: Harper and Row, 1988).

William E. Franklin. "Japan and the United States: Responsibility Sharing." *Vital Speeches of the Day* 55 #21 (August 15, 1989): 647–649.

H. Richard Friman. "Dancing with Pandora: The Eisenhower Administration and the Demise of GATT" (manuscript, 1992).

Richard A. Gephardt. "U.S.-Japanese Trade Relations." *Vital Speeches of the Day* 55 #15 (May 15, 1989): 450–454.

Steven L. Husted and Michael Melvin. *International Economics* (New York: Harper and Row, 1990).

Shintaro Ishihara. *The Japan That Can Say No*, trans. by Frank Baldwin (New York: Simon and Schuster, 1991).

Shafiquil Islam. "Capitalism in Conflict." *Foreign Affairs* 69 #1 (1989/90): 172–182.

Chalmers Johnson. *MITI and the Japanese Miracle: The Growth of Industrial Policy, 1925–1975* (Stanford: Stanford University Press, 1982).

Joshua Katz and Tilly C. Friedman-Lichtschein, eds. *Japan's New World Role* (Boulder, CO: Westview Press, 1985).

Hiroshi Kawahito. "Death and the Corporate Worker." *Japan Quarterly* 38 #2 (April 1991): 149–157.

Stephen D. Krasner. *Assymetries in Japanese-American Trade: The Case for Specific Reciprocity* (Berkeley: Institute of International Studies, 1987).

Ellis S. Krauss and Simon Reich. "Ideology, Interests, and the American Executive: Toward a Theory of Foreign Competition and Manufacturing Trade Policy." *International Organization* 46 #4 (Autumn 1992): 857–898.

Mordechai E. Kreinin. "How Closed Is Japan's Market: Additional Evidence." *World Economy* 11 #4 (December 1988): 529–542.

Kala Krishna. "What Do VERs Do?" in Sato and Nelson, eds., *Beyond Trade Friction*, 75–92.

Michael Lewis. *Pacific Rift* (New York: W. W. Norton, 1991).

David MacEachron. "New Challenges to a Successful Relationship," in Barnds, *Japan and the United States*, 1–20.

T. David Mason and Abdul M. Turay, eds. *US-Japan Trade Friction* (New York: St. Martin's Press, 1991).

Nobuaki Namiki. "Japanese Trade Barriers: Perceptions of Small Business Exporters." *Advanced Management Journal* 54 #1 (Winter 1988): 37–41.

New York Times, May 5, 1993, A1.

Robert S. Ozaki and Walter Arnold. eds. *Japan's Foreign Relations: The Global Search for Economic Security* (Boulder, CO: Westview Press, 1985).

Bill Powell and Thomas Rich. "Japan: All in the Family." *Newsweek* (June 10, 1991): 38–39.

William V. Rapp and Robert A. Feldman. "Japan's Economic Strategy and Prospects," in Barnds, *Japan and the United States,* 86–154.

Ryuzo Sato and Julianne Nelson, eds. *Beyond Trade Friction: Japan-U.S. Economic Relations* (New York: Cambridge University Press, 1989).

Judy Sutton. "Japanese-U.S. Transportation: We Need Each Other." *Global Trade* 112 #3 (March 1992): 10–14.

Toshihiro Tomabechi. "The U.S.-Japan Connection in the Changing World Marketplace: A Trader's Perspective," in Katz and Friedman-Lichtschein, eds., *Japan's New World Role,* 43–48.

Abdul M. Turay. "The Economic Dimensions and Sources of US-Japan Trade Friction," in Mason and Turay, eds., *US-Japan Trade Friction,* 7–29.

U.S. Congress, House. *United States-Japan Economic Relations: Structural Impediments Initiative,* Hearings for Committee on Foreign Relations, 101st Congress 2nd session (February 20 and April 19, 1990).

U.S. Congress, House. *United States-Japan Relations: The Impact of Negotiated Market Openings,* Hearings for Committee on Foreign Affairs, 100th Congress 2nd session (September 27, 28, and October 13, 1988).

Shin'ichi Yamamoto. "Japan's Trade Lead: Blame Profit-Hungry American Firms." *Brookings Review* 8 #1 (Winter 1989/90): 14–18.

Masaru Yoshitomi. "Changing U.S.-Japan Economic Relationships and International Payments Imbalances." *Business Economics* 24 #1 (January 1989): 29–35.

United States in Decline?

"Hegemony," a Greek term meaning leadership and supremacy, is one of those malleable terms which scholars not only interpret differently, but pronounce differently as well (HEH-geh-MON-ee, heh-GEH-mon-ee, HEH-juh-MON-ee, or heh-JUH-mon-ee)! In general, it refers to a country which, while not ncessarily the center of the world, enjoys a preponderance of power in political, military, and especially economic spheres. The two candidates for the title are the United States since World War II and Britain in the nineteenth century. A hegemon has such an overwhelming presence that although it cannot dictate its wishes, it can shape the rules and institutions of international relations to its liking. In the economic sphere, it is expected that a hegemon will strive to establish a liberal, open system where its sophisticated, inexpensive products will dominate, and where lesser powers will be able to grow and ultimately flourish. Unfortunately, there has been a tendency for hegemons to grow weaker over time. Is this happening now to the United States? That is the question.

THE QUESTION

While running for president in 1980, Ronald Reagan repeatedly called on the nation to embrace his call for American "renewal" —to lift the country out of the "malaise" of the late 1970s and rediscover its own power and stature. Seven years later, historian Paul Kennedy declared that the United States was inexorably in decline, and that the only option was to "'manage' affairs so that the relative erosion of the United States' position takes place slowly and smoothly, and is not accelerated by policies which bring merely short-term advantage but longer-term disadvantage" (Kennedy 1987, 534).

Millions of Americans and billions living throughout the world have been anxious about the question of American decline. Statistics have been marshaled for both sides of the debate like so much ammunition, and each new claim precipitates a new counterclaim and accusation of distortion. While there is little prospect of resolving this debate in this chapter, it is important that the perspectives be clearly and objectively surveyed to enable the reader to come to a personal conclusion.

The central aspects of the decline debate are: (1) Is the United States in economic decline and is this going to affect American living standards? (2) Is the United States losing its role as a world leader? (3) Should Americans worry about who might replace us in world leadership? Question one depends largely on competitiveness and adjustment to new economic conditions. Question two is a matter of power conversion—how do economic forces combine with diplomatic and military capabilities to create political power. Question three involves anticipating and predicting future trends of U.S. power relative to other nations.

Some may ask, rather cynically, why does it matter that the United States is in decline? There are several answers to this. Naturally, if American living standards are declining in absolute terms—meaning that there will simply be less wealth for the nation in the future than in the past (an unlikely but not impossible scenario)—then many Americans will find themselves unable to survive. Recent statistics indicate that for the poorest segments of society, such as single mothers and black youth in the inner city, incomes are in decline when inflation is taken into account. This would be consistent with an "absolute decline" scenario. Furthermore, a condition of absolute decline would create serious problems for would-be reformers, since less resources would be available for investment, purchases of goods, and public services such as education. The possibility of a vicious downward spiral would be dangerously real, particularly in pockets of the country.

Aside from the rather extreme version of absolute economic decline, many worry that in a competitive, technology-driven world economy, losing even a razor's edge of industrial competitiveness could be disastrous. The fact that the United States has lost its edge in video and computer technologies (VCRs, semiconductors, flat-screen computer displays, high-definition television) as well as other high-tech fields (aircraft, high-speed rail, luxury automotive) has led to numerous plant closings and job losses (Bergsten 1988).

On a grander scale, many worry that without the predominant influence of the United States in world economic diplomacy the grand postwar scheme of building global cooperation and community through international institutions devoted to free trade and investment will atrophy. There is a fear that the "beggar-thy-neighbor" economic warfare that prevailed during the era of the Great Depression will reemerge as the United States will become aggressive in its efforts to stay on top (Conybeare 1984; Kindelberger 1981). This perspective has been formalized into what many call "hegemonic stability theory."

For many reasons, American decline is a cause for concern. It may lead to Americans losing their wealth and even their livelihood, Americans losing their voice in international fora, and the world itself losing its way.

A BRIEF HISTORY OF THE U.S. AND WORLD ECONOMIC ARRANGEMENTS

Beginning as early as 1934, the United States took the lead in establishing a liberal international economic order where capitalism could flourish. The United States worked to lower trade barriers, strengthen currency exchange mechanisms, and make sufficient investment capital available to promote development. These goals were institutionalized during the 1944 negotiations at Bretton Woods, New Hampshire, where the International Monetary Fund (IMF) and World Bank were born. The proposed International Trade Organization was never approved but the General Agreement on Tariffs and Trade (GATT) of 1947 went far to lower trade restrictions. Each of these organizations is pledged to promote free market forces and favorable business climates worldwide.

The IMF was intended to help Europeans build strong enough national economies to allow them to trade their currencies in the international market and use them as a means of exchange worldwide (rather than rely on the dollar). Given the devastation of World War II and the lack of IMF resources at the time, this "currency convertibility" proved far more difficult than imagined. The United States decided to step in with the Marshall Plan in 1947, whereby some $23 billion was lent or given to European economies. They finally achieved currency convertibility in 1958, at which point one could say that their economies were fully rehabilitated.

In these early days, the currencies of the world were "pegged" to the dollar, meaning that their value was calculated in relation to the U.S. dollar. The dollar was based on the "gold standard," and from 1944 to 1971, the official value of the dollar was one-thirty-fifth an ounce of gold. This gave remarkable security to the entire international financial system and eliminated many of the fears which unregulated currency fluctuations instilled in the 1930s. The world economy grew at an unprecedented rate during the 1950s.

The U.S. economy grew in parallel to the world economy during this period, but by 1965 began to show signs of weakness. Industrial productivity grew at a slower rate than the European nations and Japan. As a result, U.S. trade competitiveness began to stall in the 1960s. The U.S. trade surplus shrank gradually. At the same time, the federal government began to run a deficit to finance the Vietnam War and Great Society programs of the Johnson administration. In addition, the total amount of dollars in circulation by the 1960s far exceeded the available gold stock. By 1968, foreigners who held dollars were so fearful of this problem and so deeply resented bearing the burdens of American budget deficits that they began to sell off huge amounts of dollars for gold. This "run" on the dollar precipitated the U.S. government taking the dollar off the gold standard for most transactions.

This went far to relieve the pressures on the currency and the growing problems of an ever shrinking trade surplus. In 1971, the United States registered its first trade deficit in a generation as confidence in the dollar nearly collapsed. In response to these pressures, the Nixon administration reneged on the Bretton Woods Treaty and took the dollar off the gold standard entirely. All other currencies previously pegged to the dollar would now "float"—meaning that their values would be determined by their importance as a means of international exchange rather than by government edict. The Bretton Woods System, which had given rise both to unprecedented prosperity and deep resentment of American privileges, was over.

Since 1971, governments have tried to establish new rules to govern international trade and currency reform. In the trade area, the Kennedy and Tokyo rounds of the GATT resulted in a dramatic drop in tariffs worldwide, to the point that overall tariffs are well below 10 percent in most industrialized nations. This is not to say that trade is unrestricted—simply that nations have moved to other methods of controlling trade flows. "Nontariff barriers," such as import quotas, "voluntary" agreements to fix trade levels bilaterally, and strict (even arbitrary) health and safety codes have done much to prevent goods from flowing. In fact, in the 1980s, pressure to use more and more of these nontariff barriers has resulted in what many call "new protectionism" —with the United States taking the lead in many cases.

On the monetary side, governments have reached several agreements to control exchange rates although the two oil shocks have left many uncertainties. In general terms, major currencies have remained fairly stable. The appreciation of the dollar and the yen during the 1980s led some currencies, such as the pound and the lira, to fall into disuse. Efforts at creating a common European currency unit (ECU) have been blocked by the British and Germans at times, and have struggled under the weight of weak economies (the September 1992 pound crisis is a case in point). Overall, the floating currency market has been a fairly stable system in which international trade and investment have flourished. Global growth rates attest to a healthy international financial system overall.

In the 1980s and 1990s, the United States took a far more combative posture in international economic negotiations. Although still the largest economy by far at twice the size of the closest competitor, Japan, its ability to compete in international trade and the failure of numerous major industries (steel, textiles, autos) has been a cause for serious concern. Most Americans favor restrictions on trade with Japan, whose exports to the United States far outweigh its imports. Fears of foreigners buying up controlling interest in numerous American firms in the 1980s also gave rise to xenophobic reactions and a desire to limit foreign investment.

U.S. budget deficits, which mushroomed nearly out of control during the Reagan administration, have made borrowing by private interests more difficult and have required more involvement of foreigners. Because much of the U.S. debt is short term, there is reason to be concerned about the near future. Fortunately, Germany, Japan, and the European Community in general are less appealing to international investors during the sluggish 1990s, so U.S. investments retain their relative attractiveness.

Finally, the North American Free Trade area represents an effort by the United States to bypass the stalemated Uruguay round of trade negotiations sponsored by the GATT. It is too soon to tell whether this is indicative of a U.S. withdrawal from world leadership or merely a tactical maneuver.

U.S. ECONOMIC DECLINE?

This rough sketch of U.S. economic leadership may give a superficial impression of a failed and declining hegemon. Before reaching that conclusion, however, it is important to focus more precisely on what U.S. leadership means. Can it truly be measured in statistics, or is there a deeper significance to the concept of "leadership" ?

Because statistics have been at the heart of the debate on America's decline, it is worth noting a few numbers which are used first by the "declinists," as Samuel Huntington calls them (Huntington 1988). Compared to the late 1940s, the U.S. share of total world wealth has declined from a high of roughly 50 percent to only about 23 percent today (Nye 1988, 105). The country slipped from the position of greatest creditor nation to largest debtor in the 1980s after registering its first trade deficit (value of imports exceeded exports) in the 1970s. Japan's national wealth has increased from roughly one-fifteenth of the United States' in the 1950s to one-half in the 1980s and is still rising. Once the leader, the United States now ranks near the bottom of industrialized countries in terms of educational standards, life expectancy, personal income, and investment and savings (World Bank 1992).

Economic Vitality

While the United States is still indisputably the world's largest economy by several trillion dollars, the rate of growth has slowed, allowing other nations to begin "catching up." In 1982, for example, the United States was mired in a deep recession—the worst economic contraction since the Great Depression—and logged a negative 2.5 percent growth rate. Meanwhile, Japan's economy grew by a robust 3.1 percent. From 1980 to 1982, U.S. average growth was a negative .3 percent, while Japan grew at an average 3.7 percent (Bergsten 1988, 37). Over the course of the decade of the 1980s, the differences are less stark. Average annual U.S. gross national product growth was an impressive 3.22 percent while for Japan the figure was an even more impressive 4.1 percent! What does this tell us? Very little, when one considers the United States grew at a faster rate than France, Britain, Italy, and many other major industrialized countries.

Table 25.1   RATIO OF U.S. PERFORMANCE TO THAT OF NEXT HIGHEST POWER (IN PARENTHESES)

	Income per Capita	GNP (Size)	Share of World Trade
1860	1.1(GB)	1.4 (GB)	.36 (GB)
1880	0.8 (GB)	1.2 (GB)	.37 (GB)
1900	0.9 (GB)	1.7 (GB)	.43 (GB)
1913	1.1 (GB)	2.1 (RUS)	.83 (GB)
1928	1.5 (GB)	3.2 (USR)	1.3 (GB)
1937	1.3 (GB)	2.7 (USR)	1.1 (GB)
1950	1.8 (GB)	3.1 (USR)	1.4 (GB)
1960	2.1 (GB)	2.8 (USR)	2.1 (GB)
1972	1.3 (GERM)	2.1*(USR)	1.2 (GERM)
1980	0.7 (SWTZ)	2.1*(USR)	1.2 (GERM)
1985	1.0 (SWTZ)	2.9 (USR)	1.9 (JAP)
1989	0.7 (SWTZ)	1.8 (JAP)	1.4 (GERM)

*estimate GNP = gross national product
  GB = Great Britain
  USR = USSR
  SWTZ = Switzerland
  JAP = Japan

Sources: World Bank Tables and Stephen Krasner, "State Power and the Structure of International Trade", *World Politics* (April 1976).

Stephen Krasner has taken an interesting tack to assess U.S. economic vitality. He compares the ratio of U.S. wealth and other economic strengths to those of the nearest competitor, going back to the nineteenth century. Table 25.1, which has been updated to 1989, tells the story of a dominant economy which has stumbled only slightly. The U.S. gross national product has been consistently about twice the size of its nearest competitor and its share of world trade about half again larger. Although the chart was originally used to show U.S. decline, the more recent numbers seem to show otherwise. Especially when one considers that no single country is a serious rival in all three dimensions, U.S. preeminence, however precarious, has yet to show any pattern of collapse.

Trade Competitiveness

If trade competitiveness is a measure of a nation's overall economic vitality, one should ask what specifically is measured in this statistic. First, an export is any product which is shipped to a foreign country. This says nothing about who owned the firm that produced the product and where the profits will end up. A Honda built in Ohio and sold in Mexico is counted as a U.S.

export although most of the profit winds up in Japan. Likewise, an import is any product coming into the country. A Chrysler automobile financed, designed, marketed, and maintained by Americans in the United States would still be considered an import if it were manufactured—or even merely assembled—in Windsor, Canada, across the river from Detroit. On the other hand, if a Californian bought the Ohio Honda, it would be counted as a domestic sale, even though it is the product of Japanese engineering and the profits will leave the country. In fact, transfer of products within a single corporation with foreign subsidiaries is considered an import even if the product is in pieces (Helleiner 1977).

Susan Strange has pointed out that it is a fundamental misconception to focus on trade as an indicator of economic wealth since it is a consequence of other, more fundamental economic and political relations. Also, measuring American industrial and economic competitiveness by focusing only on national statistics ignores the vast arena of world wealth dominated and controlled by American interests, but held outside the territory of the United States (Strange 1987). When put in these terms, American economic power is still overwhelming. In 1989, roughly one-third of all imports into the United States were the products of U.S. firms operating overseas. American firms control roughly $700 billion in foreign assets as of 1991 (*Survey of Current Business* 1992, 42).

Much was made of the huge trade imbalance in the late 1980s. U.S. merchandise imports exceeded U.S. exports by some $170 billion in 1987. However, this was as much the result of faulty monetary policy as it was a sign of poor competitiveness (Huntington 1988). In the early 1980s, the Federal Reserve under Paul Volker deliberately maintained high U.S. interest rates in order to stifle inflation. This made the dollar more attractive as an investment for foreigners and the value of the dollar on international markets rose dramatically. By 1985, the dollar was worth a third more than in 1981. The result was cheaper imports for Americans, since their dollars could automatically buy a third more than five years before, and more expensive U.S. exports to foreigners. Hence the dramatic trade deficit. When combined with American habits of accumulating consumer debt and German and Japanese tendencies to save, the situation seemed out of control. However, once the policy of artificially high interest rates was reversed in the mid-1980s, the trade deficit almost immediately shrank, from a high of nearly $200 billion in the mid-1980s to a low of roughly $20 billion in the early 1990s. It is thus difficult to use these trade statistics as conclusive proof of American decline.

Finance and Investment

Many declinists have focused not so much on trade figures as on general failures on the part of American business to keep up with foreigners in specific, high-tech activities. Perhaps the most embarrassing examples are products that began as an essentially American invention—the video cassette recorder for example—and became Japanese specialities when no U.S. corporation was willing to adopt it. There are clear concerns that the same may be happening now to what is called "high-definition television" —a breakthrough in picture quality. The Japanese government's Ministry of International Trade and Industry (MITI) has provided government loans to promote research in the area, while American firms are ill-equipped to initiate the expensive programs needed to develop such a product.

American firms have found it more and more difficult to compete with foreign firms even at home. American auto manufacturers have seen their U.S. market share consistently decline. U.S. steel firms have nearly vanished because of the inability to sell below Japanese prices. Much of this difficulty in the manufacturing sector stems from the failure to invest in more productive manufacturing techniques. Robotics and computerized design, adopted long ago in Japan and Europe, were slow to enter the U.S. factory. American productivity, historically higher than European and Japanese productivity, has steadily dropped over the last 30 years as a result. The Japanese now take, on average, 30 percent less time and manpower. The sad story is told by Gilpin:

> Whereas the United States in the early post-war period produced 30 percent of world manufacturing exports, by 1986 its share had dropped to a mere 13 percent. American productivity growth, which had outpaced the rest of the world for decades, declined dramatically from a growth rate of 3 percent annually in the early postwar years to an incredible low of .8 percent in the 1970s. (Gilpin 1987, 344)

These figures are naturally troubling, particularly in areas of the country where manufacturing jobs form the basis of the local economy. Hundreds of thousands of jobs have been lost in the 1980s, and the recession of the early 1990s forced further millions to find new employment in the service sector at low pay and without benefits. Even pro-work Dave Thomas, head of the Wendy's corporation, admitted that a poor single mother would be better off on welfare than getting a job at one of his restaurants.

Foreign firms have been dramatically increasing their ownership of U.S. firms and building new plants in the United States. While the British are still the number one investor in the United States, the Japanese have come on strong to take the number two spot. When considering portfolio and direct investment, at the end of 1988 foreigners controlled some $1.8 trillion in U.S. assets. This compares with a net investment outflow of $5 billion in 1965, $3 billion in 1970, $24 billion in 1975, and $20 billion in 1980 (*Survey of Current Business* 1980). Such symbolic purchases as the Rockefeller Plaza in Manhattan reinforce the image that the United States is being "sold out."

It is perhaps too soon to declare the end of U.S. industry and too soon to become alarmed at the investment appetite of the Japanese. After all, many of these Japanese firms are attracted to the United States not just because of favorable exchange rates and real estate prices, but also because of the productivity of American workers. Productivity at Japanese "transplants" has been impressive. The persistence of significant amounts of foreign investment in the United States in spite of very low interest rates in 1992 gave a solid indication of the strength of the U.S. economy as a safe haven. Furthermore, the direct investment picture—which measures full-fledged industrial and concrete purchases in U.S. capital stock, is still a tiny fraction of the total U.S. economy, measuring less than 5 percent. And Japanese direct investment is only some 20 percent of that total. In short, the picture of U.S. competitiveness and investment is mixed, at best.

The U.S. dollar, while fluctuating through the 1980s, continues to be the currency of choice for millions of investors and traders. Whenever a global crisis erupts, the value of the dollar almost always rises. When the British pound collapsed in late 1992, the value of the dollar rose almost immediately to new highs. When Iraq invaded Kuwait, when the Berlin Wall fell, when the Soviet Union collapsed, investors were drawn to the dollar for stability and security. The dollar remains the central global currency.

The Time Frame

The overwhelming U.S. preeminence during the 1940s and 1950s was essentially an accident of war. In the early decades of the century, the United States was growing dramatically. By the end of World War I, it was already the largest economy in the world but controlled only one-quarter of the world's wealth. The devastation that World War II wracked on America's industrialized trading partners and industrial rivals was catastrophic. Nations were set back decades in their industrial development, and it naturally took decades to restore that lost wealth and industry. It was in this unusual situation that U.S. wealth swelled to half the world total. From Nye's perspective, it is not so much that the United States has "declined" since World War II, it is that the Europeans and Japanese have rebuilt. In the process of rebuilding, they have posted impressive economic figures. Based on this, U.S. economic strength has basically been steady since the 1920s (Nye 1990).

U.S. MILITARY/POLITICAL DECLINE?

If the question of U.S. economic decline is significant, it is primarily because of its implications for the ability and willingness of the United States to play a leadership role in world affairs. Hegemonic stability theory assumes that the dominant nation will be willing to sacrifice immediate gain and advantage in order to bring about a liberal international order—particularly economic. One must ask, then, has this been the case with the United States?

On the surface, there is every indication that the United States followed the pattern of the hegemonic leader during the two decades after World War II. As we have already mentioned, the United States led the way, in close consultation with the British, in establishing institutions and rules that would maximize interdependence and capitalist enterprise. When the institutions showed signs of inadequacy, the United States stepped in with considerable sums to buttress the faltering European and Japanese systems. For a period of time, the dollar was the only hard currency in the world, until the Europeans were essentially back on their feet in the late 1950s.

Through it all, the United States paid a price not only in purely financial terms, but also by sacrificing access to others' markets in exchange for opening its own. The United States tolerated the British practice of excluding outsiders from markets in the commonwealth and encouraging European integration, but to no avail. It made available huge loans—the most famous of which was the Marshall Plan—in order to shore up its neighbors. While most of these loans have been repaid, many were simply forgiven or forgotten.

Overall, the American behavior seems to match the benevolent hegemon image conjured up in the literature. In reality, it is perhaps an overstatement to say that the United States embraced this role enthusiastically and for purely altruistic reasons. The struggle that the International Monetary Fund, World Bank, and General Agreement on Tariffs and Trade (GATT) treaties precipitated when presented to the Congress for ratification was profound. Republicans in Congress argued that the Truman administration was selling out the nation. Truman made substantial concessions to Congress, such as abandoning the International Trade Organization, to avoid the appearance of disunity in the early days of the Cold War.

On the other side of the Atlantic, the British were quite stubborn about complying with U.S. requests to dismantle the system of imperial preferences which made much of Africa, Australia, and other former British colonies inaccessible to American products. The Torquay meetings of the GATT in the early 1950s were nearly abandoned because of the U.S.-British conflict on this issue (Stiles 1995).

To say that the United States was interested solely in the well-being of its European counterparts would also be an exaggeration, since U.S. support for European reconstruction did not pick up steam until the Soviet threat became imminent in 1947. With the expansion of Soviet control in Eastern Europe, American policymakers became alarmed at the vulnerability of many European democracies gripped by social upheaval and rampant poverty. It being much easier to retain an ally than regain one after losing it, the prudent decision was made to shore up the defenses before it was too late.

As the Cold War ebbed and flowed, the United States at various times lost its competitive urge. Although the fears of the Soviet Union catching up with the United States in missiles and bombers in the 1950s proved illusory, by the late 1960s, there was a general consensus that the Soviets had achieved nuclear and military parity. This impression was reinforced by the Vietnam debacle and the Soviet incursions in Angola and elsewhere across the Third World. It seemed that containment strategy had failed. American policymakers used arms control as a means to limit the growth of Soviet arsenals.

Relative U.S. decline in the military arena coincided with a retreat from leadership on the economic front. The collapse of Bretton Woods in 1971 sent international markets into a tailspin which required frequent and only partially successful attempts at rebuilding a stable and predictable order in international currency and finance. The United States was able in 1971 to force other nations to raise the values of their own currencies in order to make United States products more competitive! Successive agreements at the Smithsonian, in Jamaica, and at numerous summits of the seven leading economic powers resulted in tenuous accords at best.

In the late 1970s, spiraling inflation prompted the United States to raise interest rates at home, but this in turn prompted cries of alarm when foreign currencies began losing value as international investors converted their money to dollars to take advantage of the high yields. In the mid-1980s, the complaint came again as these interest rates persisted in spite of low inflation in the United States. However, the reversal of the policy and the free-fall of the dollar in the late 1980s led to intervention by other central banks. The United States was unable to prevent the dollar from returning to a higher value because of intervention by outsiders. The world had become fully integrated and the United States had lost its ability to lead currency markets unilaterally. It is ironic that today the principal complaint is that German interest rates are too high and U.S. rates to low to keep money flowing smoothly. The United States is barely first among equals as the 1990s unveil the new order.

In the area of international trade, the United States took the lead throughout the 1970s to expand the scope and depth of free trade arrangements negotiated at the GATT. This is not to say the U.S. market was open. Particularly in steel, textiles, and agriculture American trade was anything but free. As the 1980s rolled around, the United States became increasingly protective of its markets and far more demanding of its trading partners. The United States negotiated so-called "voluntary" export restraints with Japanese automobile manufacturers to limit the number of vehicles arriving each year. Congress passed a law requiring the administration to develop a list of "unfair traders" to be targeted for retaliation. Efforts to establish new global trade rules were all but abandoned in favor of a far more malleable system of a North American Free Trade Area where the United States could be "first without equal" (Bergsten 1988, 70–72).

In general terms, the retreat from leadership in trade and finance seem to mirror the relative military decline of the United States during this period. In fact, the military strength of the United States was a factor in its economic decline, since the investment of some $300 billion each year into military procurement was money that could not be invested elsewhere and which was borrowed against the earnings of future generations. While SALT I and SALT II accomplished the goal of leveling the playing field to a certain extent, it also permitted the Soviets to abandon less profitable procurement programs and focus instead on the most rewarding weapons (see case #8). MIRVing, submarine technology, ABM systems, and other innovations on both parts led to a perception by the late 1970s that the Soviets had cheated their way through arms control to outright superiority—a belief that propelled Ronald Reagan to the White House.

Obviously, much has changed since 1980. To speak of an arms race in the late 1980s or early 1990s is virtually nonsensical. To speak of U.S. military inferiority likewise makes little sense in light of the lack of rivals. As pointed out in a 1992 talk by Susan Strange, where can one find a nation so powerful that it can announce in advance the outbreak of war, declare the target, set the date, and announce its completion? Yet this is precisely what the United States did in the Gulf War against Iraq in 1990–1991. The fear that many developing nations now have is that there exists no force in the world community strong enough to stop a determined American military force. This sort of power, while gratifying to those who possess it, is naturally a fearsome thing to most everyone else!

THE CONCLUSIONS

The conclusion of Joseph Nye's work on American leadership is implied in the book's title, "Bound to Lead." In both the sense of obligation and of inevitability, the United States will continue to take on a leadership role in the political-military arena. President Bush's 1992 address before the UN General Assembly pointed to a more active support for peacekeeping efforts and a more activist posture vis à vis international disputes. The chance of the United States retreating into isolationism is low.

Leadership on the economic front is another matter entirely. As the European Community consolidates, however hestitantly, and Japan moves to build an economic network across Asia, the United States seems increasingly peripheral to the global economic pulse. The United States finds it difficult to lead when crises erupt, such as filling the yawning chasm of resources in the former Soviet Union and across Africa. There is little expectation that this will soon change in the context of persistent federal budget deficits and cries of taking care of business at home coming from the electorate.

But the question arises: Does the world "need" a hegemonic leader? Robert Keohane addressed the question directly and answered with a resounding "no." Given the benefits many nations derive from institutions established many years ago with U.S. leadership, and given the customs, habits, and convergence of values that have emerged in the past five decades, the nations of the world are committed enough already to principles of cooperation and laissez-faire that there is no urgent need for one country to bribe and cajole the rest (Keohane 1984).

Naturally, others disagree and lament the passing of the hegemon and the era of freedom and prosperity this engendered. Still others agree that a hegemon is needed, and that the United States can still fill that role if only it wanted to. Finally, a few wonder, rather cautiously, about the prospects for a Japanese hegemony in the near future (Inoguchi 1989). Perhaps the most interesting insight is found in the term "minilateralism" developed by the Yarbroughs (1987), which conceives the posthegemonic world as a collection of fairly cooperative networks of regional trading areas (as opposed to the fearsome "blocs" most realists imagine).

Questions to Consider

1. Does U.S. economic decline really matter to me? And is the evidence of decline convincing enough anyway?

2. Is U.S. leadership necessary for world cooperation? Has American leadership been important in the past?

3. How much should the country be willing to sacrifice in order to remain a leader? How much should I be willing to sacrifice?

References

C. Fred Bergsten. *America in the World Economy: A Strategy for the 1990s* (Washington, DC: IIE, 1988).

John C. Conybeare. "Public Goods, Prisoners' Dilemmas and the International Political Economy." *International Studies Quarterly* 28 #1 (March 1984): 5–22.

Robert Gilpin. *The Political Economy of International Relations* (Princeton: Princeton University Press, 1987).

G. K. Helleiner. "Transnational Enterprises and the New Political Economy of U.S. Trade Policy." *Oxford Economic Papers* 29 #1 (1977): 102–116.

Samuel Huntington. "The U.S.—Decline or Renewal?" *Foreign Affairs* 67 #2 (Winter 1988): 76–96.

Takashi Inoguchi. "Four Japanese Scenarios for the Future." *International Affairs* 65 #1 (Winter 1989).

Paul Kennedy. *The Rise and Fall of the Great Powers* (New York: Random House, 1987).

Robert Keohane. *After Hegemony: Cooperation and Discord in the World Political Economy* (Princeton: Princeton University Press, 1984).

Charles Kindelberger. "Dominance and Leadership in the International Economy: Exploitation, Public Goods, and Free Riders." *International Studies Quarterly* 25 #2 (June 1981): 222–254.

Stephen Krasner. "State Power and the Structure of International Trade." *World Politics* 28 #3 (April 1976).

Joseph S. Nye, Jr. *Bound to Lead: The Changing Nature of American Power* (New York: Basic Books, 1990).

Joseph S. Nye, Jr. "Understanding U.S. Strength." *Foreign Policy* 72 (Fall 1988): 105–129.

Kendall Stiles. "The Inhibited Hegemon: The United States, Congress, and the GATT, 1946–54" (forthcoming in *Review of International Political Economy*, Fall 1994).

Susan Strange. "The Persistent Myth of Lost Hegemony." *International Organization* 41 #4 (Autumn 1987): 551–574.

Survey of Current Business. June 1992; June 1980.

World Bank. *World Development Report 1992*. (New York: Oxford, 1992).

Beth Yarbrough and Robert Yarbrough. "Cooperation in the Liberalization of International Trade: After Hegemony, What?" *International Organization* 41 #1 (Winter 1987): 1–26.

Greenpeace

Traditional theories of international relations focus on diplomatic relations between nation-states. International law, warfare, and even international organization emphasize this conventional view. More recent theories of international relations, however, emphasize the growing importance of such nontraditional actors as international businesses, interest groups, terrorist groups, churches, and other nonprofit associations. These groups have in common a fluid organizational structure which cuts across national boundaries easily. While their role is as yet unclear, obviously their numbers are growing as is their impact on international affairs. Greenpeace represents only one example of such "transnational" actors.

Intercepting whale hunters off Japan, chaining yourself to a bundle of harp seal pelts in Newfoundland, sailing to a nuclear test site in the South Pacific, hanging antipollution banners from smokestacks—all these and more would you be doing if you were a member of Greenpeace. The story of Greenpeace is a model of transnational activity in the environmental arena and as such has drawn a great deal of attention: "Internationally, Greenpeace has become the most ambitious attempt to build a world-scale radical organization since Lenin's Communist International of the early twentieth century" (Ostertag 1991, 33). Conversely, a German critic stated:

> These Greenpeacers do not know what they are longing for. But they do feel the strong need to protest the perceived destruction of the earth by industrialism and capitalism. The Marxist elements are interspersed with a new kind of romanticism and anarchism. (Spencer 1991, 180)

Greenpeace is one the largest international nonprofit organizations, with an annual budget of roughly $150 million in 1992 (Spencer et al. 1991, 174; DeMont 1991, 46; Horton 1991, 112), some five times the budget of the

UN Environmental Program (although former leader David McTaggart stresses that it is puny in comparison to the corporate giants they fight against—Horton 1991, 112). It has offices in twenty-seven countries, a full-time staff of over 1,000 (Christrup 1991, 13), and a total membership of some 5 million citizens across the globe. Armed with these resources—not to mention a large dose of chutzpah—Greenpeace has played a pivotal role in halting mining in Antarctica, stopping the seal hunt in Canada, curtailing ocean dumping of pollutants, and securing a moratorium on whaling.

How did Greenpeace achieve this degree of power and prominence while many others have failed? It is to this story that we turn.

ORIGINS AND GROWING PAINS

Greenpeace emerged from a notion that nonviolent resistance, "bearing witness" in the Quaker tradition, and publicity-generating stunts laced with sarcasm could exert enough pressure on the "bad guys" to change their behavior. A small group of American and Canadian environmentalists and pacifists became increasingly frustrated at the conservativism and apolitical character of mainstream organizations like the Sierra Club. They hoped to combine their efforts to protect the earth and their fight against militarism. Marie Bohlen is credited with first proposing that the group move vigorously against American nuclear testing in the Amchitka Island area, west of Alaska along the Aleutian chain, on the grounds that this represented a threat to both world peace and to the environment. A detonation near the notoriously unstable "Ring of Fire" might trigger earthquakes, tidal waves, and volcanic eruptions. On this basis, James Bohlen, Irving Stowe, Bill Darnell, and Paul Cote officially formed the "Don't Make a Wave Committee" and set about hiring a boat to take them into the testing zone in the summer of 1971 (Hunter 1979, 116; DeMont 1991, 46). They convinced skipper John Cormack to pilot his rather sorry-looking ship named after his wife (Phyllis Cormack) some 2,000 miles from Vancouver. Along the way, the group suffered through bad weather, engine trouble, internal conflict, and a Coast Guard cutter manned by draft-dodgers before turning back. On the return trip the ship encountered even more threatening sea conditions. In the words of eyewitness Bob Hunter:

> Up in the wheelhouse we had to hang on to the wheel with both hands. So much water had splashed in through the port doorway that even with boots on we would be slipping and sliding around. . . . Nobody except Cormack could hold the wheel for much more than half an hour at a time. There was nothing languid or slow motion about the movement of the Phyllis Cormack now. We came down the sides of the waves like a one-hundred-ton surfboard. The bow was smashing the upcoming wall like a battering ram, and with each crash the whole boat shuddered. "We're starting to torpedo" Bohlen announced. Cormack himself wasn't joking any longer. We were finally in trouble. The wind was coming across the hunching shoulders of the waves in sandblast bursts up to eighty miles an hour. "Gotta watch out for the freak ones. . . . They're the ones come up

like a pyramid—like that one there—all green. . . . One of them comes up under the bow a certain way and she can flip yuh right over. . . . (Hunter 1979, 83)

They returned safely to port and almost immediately set out on another rented boat christened *Greenpeace Too* but failed to reach the test site on account of storms. The detonation occurred in early November, and the resulting five megaton blast measured 7.2 on the Richter scale and killed many animals, including some 1,000 sea otters (Hunter 1979, 93). The team discovered that although the venture was unsuccessful in halting the test, it had attracted worldwide attention. They would learn to use this media interest in their activities to the fullest in the years to come.

Shortly after the Vancouver-based Amchitka operation ended, the "Don't Make a Wave Committee" reorganized itself as Greenpeace with $9,000 in the bank. The group had at the time three competing priorities, each espoused firmly by different members: conducting antinuclear testing demonstrations, halting whaling, and stopping the hunt of baby harp seals whose snow-white pelts were highly prized by European furriers. With little sense of organization, Greenpeace moved rapidly from one "campaign" to another, sometimes allowing individual activists to work at cross-purposes (whales that were saved by one segment of the group naturally ate the seals saved by the other faction!) (Hunter 1979, 125).

A pivotal event took place in 1972 and 1973 when, after responding to an ad for a pacifist with an ocean-worthy boat, David McTaggart, a relatively successful if unscrupulous real estate developer, spearheaded what would become an ongoing struggle between Greenpeace and the French government over nuclear testing in the South Pacific. In the summer of 1972, McTaggart piloted the *Vega* into the French nuclear blast zone near Moruroa (about 800 miles east of Tahiti). The boat was rammed by a French warship and the test went on as scheduled. The next summer, McTaggart was back, joining several other protest ships. The French this time sent a commando unit which boarded his ship and attacked him and his two colleagues (one of whom managed to take a few well-publicized photographs of the event). McTaggart's right eye was "obliterated" when one of the commandoes beat him around the head and neck. The French later denied the incident, but the photos and personal accounts of McTaggart and his crew so embarrassed the French government that they halted aboveground testing and moved to underwater testing (which Greenpeace continued to oppose) (King 1986, 119; Horton 1991, 110). McTaggart moved from this experience to a drawn-out court battle in Europe where he maneuvered to set in place a number of new Greenpeace offices (Ostertag 1991, 34).

By 1975 Greenpeace was active in its three different arenas. A vessel was patrolling the North Pacific in search of Japanese and Russian whaling ships in order to disrupt and photograph the hunt. "All we would have to do was get close to a whaling ship, drop a Zodiac into the water, and then race ahead of the harpoon, positioning ourselves between the gunner and the whales, making a clear shot impossible" (Hunter 1979, 127). In essence, the action involved risking one's life in exchange for preserving the whale's. During one mission, the Greenpeacers fortuitously caught a Russian harpoon in midflight over the head of the Greenpeace boat. The resulting photograph produced what Greenpeace called a "mind-bomb" which shattered preconceptions about whaling as a heroic and courageous lifestyle (Horton 1991, 48). This began the process of adopting new limits on whaling.

On the harp seal front, Greenpeace adopted an especially militant posture in 1976 by opposing any seal hunting whatever, rather than trying to work with local Inuit and Eskimo tribes as well as local whites. As put by moderate Greenpeacer Bob Hunter:

> They were determined to run a "pure" campaign, which meant that there would be no further talk of negotiations with the Newfoundlanders. The fragile alliance we'd initiated during the first antisealing campaign with the fisherman's union and the outport landsmen, in league against the big commercial hunt, was thrown out the window. Greenpeace's official policy was now absolutely rigid: no seals were to be killed by anybody, not even Eskimo or Indians. (Hunter 1979, 368)

The result—the eventual ban on seal hunting—was economically devastating to local Eskimo tribes dependent on the seal harvest. "Probably some people went hungry," acknowledged a Greenpeacer many years later (Ostertag 1991, 34).

While these various campaigns and McTaggart's lawsuit continued, the Vancouver offices of Greenpeace slipped deeper and deeper into debt. Various offices had sprung up around the world, particularly a booming operation in San Francisco, which made use of the Greenpeace name and logo without providing any funding to the Vancouver "pioneers." Almost all of the Greenpeace founders had by 1975 left the organization, largely due to burnout (Hunter 1979, 242). A new financial officer, Bill Gannon, was hired to set the financial house of the Vancouver office in order, but found that although merchandizing (T-shirts, buttons, etc.) went far to stabilize the situation, the problem remained that there was no central coordination of Greenpeace offices and no central budgeting (Brown and May 1989, 65). As put by a Vancouver protagonist:

> It might be that we entered 1977 with an organizational situation that could only be described as a nightmare, a financial situation that was ludicrous—with Vancouver carrying the debt (some $150,000) and all the other offices exploiting the name that had been built up at such cost—but none of these factors had the effect of slowing anything down at all. Rather, the agitation and friction seemed to act upon us as though we were molecules in a pan of water being brought to the boiling point. Activity was up, not down. (Hunter 1979, 367)

The tensions became more and more public until in 1978 the Vancouver office filed a lawsuit against the San Francisco office over copyright infringement. The San Francisco office countersued for slander (Ostertag 1991, 37).

It was at this point, on the eve of the court battle, that David McTaggart, flush from victory over the French in his own court case, arrived to place a proposal before the North American Greenpeace affiliates. He joined his European offices with those in the United States and Toronto and confronted the "old-timers" in Vancouver. "The outcome was that Greenpeace Europe paid off the Canadian debts and the U.S., Canadian and European groups agreed to the formation of a new umbrella organization—Greenpeace International ... McTaggart would stay on as the chief executive officer and chairman" (Brown and May 1989, 68).

The move has been interpreted by some as Greenpeace's salvation, by others as a crass power play. At any rate, David McTaggart was firmly in command of a loose coalition of offices on two continents by the close of the 1970s. Greenpeace boasted an international headquarters in Amsterdam, a global membership of 25,000, and a growing budget fed by contributions amounting to 24 percent of each office's fund-raising (Spencer et al. 1991, 176).

GREENPEACE GALVANIZED

For the next ten years Greenpeace's activities centered on bigger and bigger "direct action" campaigns, all of which were submitted to Amsterdam for approval. The organization bought and reequipped a number of vessels, including a 145-foot ship christened the *Rainbow Warrior* (purchased in part with a grant from the World Wildlife Federation) to go after numerous environmental and pacifist targets. In the early 1980s, Greenpeace activists launched their inflatable Zephyrs against ocean polluters who were dropping one-ton barrels of toxic waste (one of which nearly killed activist Gijs Thieme when it landed in his boat) and after Russian nuclear-powered military ships (Brown and May 1989, 83). These and other previous efforts resulted in the banning of acid dumping in the North Sea in 1980, approval by the International Whaling Commission of a phased-in ban on whaling in 1982, a ban on European imports of harp seal fur and a halt on dumping of radioactive material by the London Dumping Convention in 1983, and nomination for the Nobel Peace Prize in 1986.

This period also saw a gradual shift of Greenpeace in the direction of working with, rather than exclusively against, established government agencies—particularly at the international level. Certainly persistent lobbying of the European Commission in the 1970s was a key factor in that body's decision to halt seal fur imports (albeit on a voluntary basis). More intriguing is the method employed by Greenpeace to get the International Whaling Commission to consider a ban on whaling. In 1978, Greenpeace organizers began systematically "packing" the relatively small commission—at the time dominated by the half-dozen whaling nations of the world. By paying the $20–$30,000 membership fee, Greenpeace secured a seat on the Commission for such small nations as Panama and St. Lucia. By 1982, enough Greenpeace sympathizers were being sent by these new members that they were able, with the help of some increasingly ambivalent Scandinavian members, to shift the majority in favor of a ban (Spencer 1991, 177).

Greenpeace has also been active in other international organizations, both as a player and by virtue of its observer status with the Economic and Social Council of the UN. The London Dumping Convention, for example, involves deliberation between some thirty countries on topics related to ocean dumping. In the late 1980s, Greenpeace became directly involved as an observer to the discussion and a consultant to several national delegations. The debate at the time centered on whether the dumping of a particular substance should be allowed pending scientific evidence that its presence in the environment caused harm, or whether such a substance could be banned before the scientific evidence was clear. Greenpeace sided clearly with the "preventive" approach and in opposition to the "permissive" approach espoused and advocated by the United States and Britain. While unable to vote on the question, Greenpeace participants provided crucial information of both a scientific and political nature. For example, the Greenpeacers translated scientific addresses delivered in English for the German and Scandinavian participants, presenting new scientific findings to refute the "permissive" approach, drafting language for specific clauses of the new agreements, and publicizing the events of the conference for outsiders (Stairs and Taylor 1992, 129). At one point, the conference approved a version of an antidumping clause which merely "capped" total waste dumping at given levels without eventually banning them altogether, as Greenpeace had proposed. The group thereupon took their case to legislatures in twenty countries in a campaign that cost some $30 million and secured in October 1990 a new treaty which called for an eventual ban on ocean dumping (Stairs and Taylor 1992, 128).

In 1991, Greenpeace succeeded in pushing forward the Madrid Treaty on mining in Antarctica. Greenpeace established a permanent base on Antarctica in 1986 in order to join the negotiations concerning the use of Antarctica's natural resources. Although it failed to be a full player in these talks, Greenpeace was able to set an example for other, more polluting, bases by recycling its waste and leaving the ground untouched. In addition, Greenpeace was able to publicize the behavior of the other "colonists" on a year-round basis. The operation cost Greenpeace $1 million for each of four years, but was a contributing factor to the ultimate agreement in Madrid to ban mining in Antarctica for fifty years (Cross 1991, 17). As put by McTaggart:

> Antarctica was a perfect example of quiet activism. Setting up our base down there was like a dog peeing, staking out territory. If anyone had really had a legitimate claim to Antarctica, they would have run us out, and they didn't. In the long term, saving that whole continent will be one of the major things Greenpeace did, yet I don't even know how you'd write about all the behind-the-scenes work we did. (Horton 1991, 112).

Greenpeace also became a paid consultant to a number of progressive governments eager to address the growing environmental concerns being expressed at the ballot. Sweden and Germany became regular consumers of

Greenpeace's advice and maturing scientific expertise in the latter half of the 1980s (Stairs and Taylor 1992, 113).

Perhaps the most famous event connected with Greenpeace during this period was the sinking of the *Rainbow Warrior* in 1985 in the context of a general campaign against nuclear testing in the Pacific. The *Rainbow Warrior* traveled through the American-controlled Marshall Islands, where nuclear tests in the 1950s left many inhabitants diseased and eager to leave their homes with Greenpeace's help (King 1986, 11). The ship harbored in New Zealand in preparation for leading a flotilla into Moruroa to stall French nuclear tests. While there, it became the target of French frogmen who installed two large explosives on the hull below the waterline. The ship was destroyed beyond repair and an Italian photographer, Fernando Pereira, drowned after being stunned by the second explosion (King 1986, 47). Subsequent investigations revealed the *Rainbow Warrior* crew had been the target of infiltration and espionge by the French for months. The affair precipitated a high-profile legal battle between the governments of New Zealand and France, as well as Greenpeace itself, resulting in a $5 million settlement in New Zealand's favor. Greenpeace generated such sympathy through this event that its contributions increased threefold (Spencer 1991, 178).

GREENPEACE GROWN-UP

In the last four years, Greenpeace has achieved a presence on the international scene which is almost unparalleled in its field. Its success is remarkable and its membership, in the millions, gives it genuine clout. Greenpeace is also going through a crisis of identity—as a "victim of its own success" as it were (Ostertag 1991, 85): should it continue its unorthodox and rather radical tactics and agenda or work to become a player in the mainstream mode of the Sierra Club in order to effect deeper changes on a larger scale. While Greenpeace has never skirted controversy (on the contrary!), its struggle with this question has stirred critics from both the left and the right.

Greenpeace, as a private nonprofit organization, need account for its activities to almost no one. Although Greenpeace organizers feel that their support depends on an image of activism (Horton 1991, 108), in the final analysis, the day-to-day operations and campaigns need obtain the approval only of the international organizers before going into effect. The result has been, sometimes, a rather cavalier and self-absorbed conduct. First revealed in the Greenpeace decision to fight all seal hunting, no matter the cost to local Eskimo populations, Greenpeace has been guilty of a "hit-and-run" approach to many environmental problems. In the United States, for example, where poor residents have fought toxic waste dumps in their inner-city neighborhoods in spite of weak scientific and technical background support, Greenpeacers chose not to contribute to an eight-state project to train minority ecologists but instead to set up their own program with Native Americans in the West (Ostertag 1991, 84).

Greenpeace has sometimes lashed out at critics in a rather intolerant spirit. Magnus Gudmundsson made a film in 1989, "Survival in the High North," which showed communities in Greenland where "the seal hunting business was devastated after the successful campaign by Greenpeace and animal rights groups to ban sealskin imports to Europe." Greenpeacers denounced the film and attempted to block its showing by suing the filmmaker (Spencer 1991, 178). In the late 1980s, a University of Florida researcher, Richard Lambertsen, was attacked by Greenpeace for conducting experiments on tissue from dead whales until he was ultimately dismissed. According to a recent *Forbes* article, his research in fact focused on finding cures for whale diseases (Spencer 1991, 176).

Greenpeace has been accused of taking credit for operations it either never supported or at one time opposed. The issue of banning tuna imports from countries that engaged in drift-net fishing—often the cause of needless dolphin and porpoise deaths—was extremely pressing in the late 1980s. Greenpeace determined that such a ban would have such serious economic and social costs in Latin America (see below) that it chose not to support the widespread efforts to impose a ban. Nonetheless, Greenpeace fund-raisers routinely pointed to the eventual ban as evidence of "the sort of thing" Greenpeace did. A video filmed by Sam LaBudde and sponsored by the Earth Island Institute which graphically portrayed the deaths of dolphins at the hands of industrial tuna fishermen was distributed by Greenpeace with its own logo—as if their product (Horton 1991, 48).

Greenpeace has further been accused of betraying its own ethical standards. By providing financial support for eco-terrorists such as some members of Earth First! who are famous for "spiking" trees, some argue that Greenpeace has violated its nonviolence position (Spencer 1991, 180). As put by former Earth-Firster Mike Roselle, "I don't campaign fundamentally differently here than I would have with Earth First! and I didn't have to promise [USA director] Peter Bahouth I wouldn't spike trees on my off time" (Horton 1991, 110). David McTaggart's rather abrupt departure from Greenpeace on September 2, 1991, to be replaced by "squeaky-clean" Matti Wuori, raises questions about whether McTaggart may have reverted to his past habit of swindling money from investors only to skip town before anyone could pin down charges against him. His extraordinary power as chairman of a lucrative and rather loosely organized coalition certainly gave him the opportunity, according to some cynics (Spencer 1991, 174–175).

Just as critics from the right accuse Greenpeace of being a radical, overbearing, manipulative organization that poses a threat to capitalism itself, critics on the left accuse Greenpeace of selling out to the mainstream in order to have more power and legitimacy. Even Greenpeace officials, such as Greenpeace Canada director Michael Manolson, acknowledge, "We have grown up. Our size has given us greater political influence and greater legitimacy" (DeMont 1991, 46). Although David McTaggart has criticized the size of his organization, he feels that it serves a clear purpose. According to Allan Thorton, "David's point of view is that we have a sort of Manifest Destiny to grow and organize into every part of the globe" (Horton 1991, 112).

This drive to expand internationally has been, to a certain extent, a distraction for Greenpeace. McTaggart's preoccupation with entering the Soviet Union and forging a strong relationship with Mikhail Gorbachev (in both of which he succeeded) seemed to take him away from other projects and campaigns during the late 1980s. Current efforts to organize in Latin America on a large scale have plunged Greenpeace into the North-South debate in surprising and often disconcerting ways.

Greenpeace offices have been established in Mexico, Argentina, Chile, and Brazil, with plans for many more throughout the continent. Upon arriving, Greenpeace organizers were stunned to find fierce opposition on the grounds that the organization supported the tuna ban. At the time, fishing companies from Mexico and other Latin American companies were on the verge of taking over much of the international tuna fishing industry, but had as yet not invested in the various net styles, and warning devices needed to prevent dolphins and whales from becoming entangled in the nets. When the United States banned tuna catches from these types of fishermen, it had the effect of replacing Latin American firms with more sophisticated American operations and forcing hundreds of local fishermen into unemployment. The whole operation was so successful, authorities in Mexico suspected Greenpeace was actually working for the CIA (Ostertag 1991, 84)!

As a result of such fiascoes, Greenpeace changed its strategy and some of its policies. It left the tuna ban coalition and became an advocate for global solutions to address not only the needs of the environment but also the needs of the poor. Steve Sawyer, executive director of Greenpeace International, recently explained the new perspective:

> The U.S. has been [damaging] the world for decades, telling the banana republics what's good for them. That's sanctimonious, hypocritical behavior for a nation that consumes twenty-five percent of the world's resources with only six percent of its people. The tuna [boycott] was a clear case of the U.S. trying to [strangle the economy of] Mexico or Venezuela . . . further widening the gulf with Latin and South America. Yes, life is more complicated when you look at the whole world, but that's what Greenpeace has to do now (Horton 1991, 48).

Greenpeace aspires to be one of very few channels for North-South cooperation on the environment. It aims to do so, "not on the traditional basis of 'aid' to the poor South, nor of 'solidarity' with leftist vanguards. Instead, Greenpeace is attempting to construct a disciplined, centralized, international organization against common enemies—from transnational corporate polluters to the World Bank" (Ostertag 1991, 87). Such efforts at consensus-building will naturally require a great many concessions to local culture, priorities, and aspirations. They are in fact bearing fruit, however. In 1990, Greenpeace was instrumental in bringing together North and Latin American governments at the Inter-American Tropical Tuna Commission by focusing on technology transfer rather than merely environmental preservation (Ostertag 1991, 85). Greenpeace is also finding that the traditional tactic of civil disobedience may no longer be a viable approach for its Latin American affiliates, since traditions of military rule and political intolerance create far greater dangers for would-be activists (Ostertag 1991, 86).

The new conservativism of Greenpeace in its newer fields of operation seems to have paralleled a certain tentativeness at home, according to Greenpeace critics on the left. Earth Island Institute's Dave Phillips commented: "[F]rom an operational point of view they definitely have gotten so big they have lost their edge" (Horton 1991, 48). Paul Watson left Greenpeace back in 1977 on the grounds that it was too conservative and founded the militant Sea Shepherds. Steven McAllister left in 1990 to "freelance" because he felt the organization had lost its combativeness (Horton 1991, 110–112). Greenpeace was recently downgraded from a five to a four on an "ecological combativeness" scale published by *Outside* magazine, placing it in the company of such stodgy organizations as the Sierra Club and the Natural Resource Defense Council (Horton 1991, 48).

A crucial aspect of this debate is the question posed internally: Is the organization more important than the struggle? McTaggart welcomed challenges that would risk bankrupting the organization, while some "newer people" began to focus on the survival of the organization itself (Horton 1991, 112). Such newcomers as U.S. executive director Peter Bahouth have encouraged fund-raising through mass mailings, which now absorb some 30 percent of the organization's budget. In addition to its extensive offices and membership, Greenpeace owns seven ships, a hot air balloon, two helicopters, an extensive international telecommunications network, and is even considering buying a satellite of its own (Ostertag 1991, 32). Financial considerations certainly seem to be taking on a more and more significant place in Greenpeace strategizing, and when combined with the organization's international reach and its associated political compromises, it seems Greenpeace is destined to move more and more into the mainstream.

The fact that critics on the left and the right both challenge Greenpeace's place is probably heartening to an organization eager to change the very nature of the environmental debate. It seems to indicate that Greenpeace may be on the way to finding an elusive balance between participation and defiance. As put by Tom Horton, "The bottom line is that the only real Greenpeace credo, within broad limits such as nonviolence, seems to be Whatever Works" (Horton 1991, 110). Janine Ferretti of Canada's Pollution Probe concluded, "Greenpeace's approach has changed the environmental movement forever" (DeMont 1991, 47).

Questions to Consider

1. What is the dilemma Greenpeace faces with regard to maintaining a defiant, activist image while working with governmental organizations for environmental progress?

2. What have been the key ingredients of Greenpeace's success over the years? What has slowed the organization down?

3. How is it that a private, nonprofit organization can become a major player in international diplomacy? Is Greenpeace a model of transnationalism?

4. Do you feel that the power of such organizations as Greenpeace strengthens or undermines the democratic features of international affairs?

References

Michael Brown and John May. *The Greenpeace Story* (London: Dorling Kindersley, 1989).

Judy Christrup. "Our Twentieth Anniversary." *Greenpeace* (January/February/March 1991): 13–20.

Michael Cross. "Greenpeace to Leave Antarctica Without a Trace." *New Scientist* (April 20, 1991): 17.

John DeMont. "Frontline Fighters." *MacLean's* (December 16, 1991): 46–47.

Tom Horton. "The Green Giant." *Rolling Stone* (September 5, 1991): 42–48, 108–112.

Robert Hunter. *Warriors of the Rainbow: A Chronicle of the Greenpeace Movement* (New York: Holt, Rinehart and Winston, 1979).

Michael King. *Death of the Rainbow Warrior* (London: Penguin Books, 1986).

Bob Ostertag. "Greenpeace Takes Over the World." *Mother Jones* (March/April 1991): 32–37, 84–87.

Leslie Spencer, Jan Bollwerk, and Richard Morais. "The Not So Peaceful World of Greenpeace." *Forbes* (November 11, 1991): 174–180.

Kevin Stairs and Peter Taylor. "Non-Governmental Organizations and the Legal Protection of the Oceans: A Case Study," in Andrew Hurrell and Benedict Kingsbury, eds., *The International Politics of the Environment* (Oxford: Clarendon Press, 1992), 110–141.

ACKNOWLEDGMENTS

INDEX